Fodor's

THE COMPLETE GUIDE TO
AFRICAN SAFARIS

WELCOME TO YOUR AFRICAN SAFARI

African safaris produce unforgettable moments, whether a lion's powerful roar shakes your core, a hyena's maniacal laugh tingles your spine, or a mountain gorilla's piercing gaze freezes you in your tracks. These singular events hold you in thrall and profoundly connect you to your environment. And what environments they are: the golden plains of the Serengeti, the pristine waterways of the Okavango Delta, the star-shaped sand dunes of the Namibian desert. Africa's varied landscapes stage nature's most spectacular wonders, and a safari is your front-row seat.

TOP REASONS TO GO

★ **Accommodations:** Supremely comfortable lodges and camps surrounded by wilderness.

★ **Parks and Reserves:** Africa's protected areas are home to the most animals on earth.

★ **Village Visits:** Fascinating tours of Himba, Maasai, Zulu, and other local communities.

★ **Beaches:** Coastal towns such as Zanzibar, Durban, and Mombasa have beautiful shores.

★ **Epic Landscapes:** Mt. Kilimanjaro, Victoria Falls, the Bwindi rain forest, and more.

★ **Adventure:** Walking safaris, balloon flights, and camel treks are thrilling journeys.

Fodor's THE COMPLETE GUIDE TO AFRICAN SAFARIS

Publisher: Amanda D'Acierno, *Senior Vice President*

Editorial: Arabella Bowen, *Editor in Chief*; Linda Cabasin, *Editorial Director*

Design: Tina Malaney, *Associate Art Director*; Chie Ushio, *Senior Designer*; Ann McBride, *Production Designer*

Photography: Jennifer Arnow, *Senior Photo Editor*; Mary Robnett, *Photo Researcher*

Production: Linda Schmidt, *Managing Editor*; Evangelos Vasilakis, *Associate Managing Editor*; Angela L. McLean, *Senior Production Manager*

Maps: Rebecca Baer, *Senior Map Editor*; David Lindroth; Mark Stroud, Moon Street Cartography, *Cartographers*

Sales: Jacqueline Lebow, *Sales Director*

Marketing & Publicity: Heather Dalton, *Marketing Director*; Katherine Punia, *Publicity Director*

Business & Operations: Susan Livingston, *Vice President, Strategic Business Planning*; Sue Daulton, *Vice President, Operations*

Fodors.com: Megan Bell, *Executive Director, Revenue & Business Development*; Yasmin Marinaro, *Senior Director, Marketing & Partnerships*

Writers: Claire Baranowski, Angus Begg, Colleen Blaine, Christopher Clark, Mark Eveleigh, Lauren Everitt, Narina Exelby, James Gifford, Linda Markovina, Christine Marot, Lee Middleton, Karena du Plessis, Kate Turkington, Tara Turkington, Anne-Marie Weeden, Andrea Weiss

Editor: Eric Wechter

Production Editor: Carrie Parker

4th Edition

ISBN 978–1–101–87818–7

ISSN 1941–0336

All details in this book are based on information supplied to us at press time. Always confirm information when it matters, especially if you're making a detour to visit a specific place. Fodor's expressly disclaims any liability, loss, or risk, personal or otherwise, that is incurred as a consequence of the use of any of the contents of this book.

SPECIAL SALES

This book is available at special discounts for bulk purchases for sales promotions or premiums. For more information, e-mail specialmarkets@penguinrandomhouse.com

PRINTED IN THE UNITED STATES OF AMERICA

10 9 8 7 6 5 4 3 2 1

CONTENTS

ABOUT THIS GUIDE

Fodor's Recommendations

Everything in this guide is worth doing—we don't cover what isn't—but exceptional sights, hotels, and restaurants are recognized with additional accolades. **Fodor's Choice★** indicates our top recommendations; and **Best Bets** call attention to notable hotels and restaurants in various categories. Care to nominate a new place? Visit Fodors.com/contact-us.

Trip Costs

We list prices wherever possible to help you budget well. Hotel and restaurant price categories from $ to $$$$ are noted alongside each recommendation. For hotels, we include the lowest cost of a standard double room in high season. For restaurants, we cite the average price of a main course at dinner or, if dinner isn't served, at lunch. For attractions, we always list adult admission fees; discounts are usually available for children, students, and senior citizens.

Hotels

Our local writers vet every hotel to recommend the best overnights in each price category, from budget to expensive. Unless otherwise specified, you can expect private bath, phone, and TV in your room. For expanded hotel reviews, facilities, and deals visit Fodors.com.

Top Picks	Hotels &
★ **Fodor's**Choice	**Restaurants**
	⌂ Hotel
Listings	↩ Number of
✉ Address	rooms
✉ Branch address	⏣ Meal plans
☎ Telephone	✕ Restaurant
🖷 Fax	⌲ Reservations
⊕ Website	⌂ Dress code
✍ E-mail	⊟ No credit cards
🎫 Admission fee	$ Price
⊙ Open/closed times	**Other**
Ⓜ Subway	⇨ See also
⊹ Directions or Map coordinates	☞ Take note
	🏌 Golf facilities

Restaurants

Unless we state otherwise, restaurants are open for lunch and dinner daily. We mention dress code only when there's a specific requirement and reservations only when they're essential or not accepted. To make restaurant reservations, visit Fodors.com.

Credit Cards

The hotels and restaurants in this guide typically accept credit cards. If not, we'll say so.

EUGENE FODOR

Hungarian-born Eugene Fodor (1905–91) began his travel career as an interpreter on a French cruise ship. The experience inspired him to write *On the Continent* (1936), the first guidebook to receive annual updates and discuss a country's way of life as well as its sights. Fodor later joined the U.S. Army and worked for the OSS in World War II. After the war, he kept up his intelligence work while expanding his guidebook series. During the Cold War, many guides were written by fellow agents who understood the value of insider information. Today's guides continue Fodor's legacy by providing travelers with timely coverage, insider tips, and cultural context.

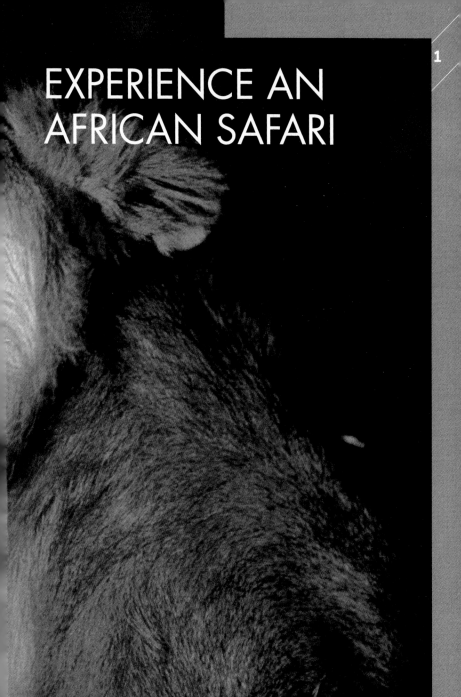

EXPERIENCE AN AFRICAN SAFARI

1

WHAT'S WHERE

The following numbers refer to chapters.

4 Kenya. Expect golden lions, red-robed warriors, snowcapped mountains, pristine white beaches, orange sunsets, and coral-pink dawns. You'll also experience some of the world's most famous safari destinations—Masai Mara, the Rift Valley—and world-class beach destinations like Diani Beach and the tiny town of Lamu.

5 Tanzania. Also part of East Africa, Tanzania attracts far fewer tourists than Kenya and South Africa, even though it boasts some of Africa's greatest tourist attractions—the Serengeti, the Great Migration, Olduvai Gorge, Ngorongoro Crater, Selous Game Reserve, and Lake Victoria.

6 South Africa. Africa's most developed country, at the very tip of the continent, is many worlds in one: modern bustling cities, ancient rock art, gorgeous beaches, fabulous game lodges, well-run national parks, mountain ranges, desert, and wine lands. It's home to Kruger National Park and the KwaZulu-Natal Parks.

7 Rwanda and Uganda. Trekking mountain gorillas in these countries of undulating hills, terraced farmlands, volcanic mountain chains, and dense rain forests is an experience unlike any other.

8 Botswana. The country itself is a natural wonder with terrain that varies from vast salt pans to the pristine waterways of the Okavango Delta. Expect lots of game, few tourists, and stars brighter than you'll ever see—the Kalahari Bushmen say that you can hear them sing.

9 Namibia. From the Namib Desert—the earth's oldest—to the fog-enshrouded Skeleton Coast. The great game park of Etosha, Damaraland's stark beauty, desert elephants, small cities with a fascinating mix of colonial and modern: you've never been anywhere like Namibia.

10 Victoria Falls. Shared by Zambia and Zimbabwe, Vic Falls is one of the greatest natural wonders of the world. It's the adventure center of Africa where adventurers can try everything from bungee jumping and white-water rafting to canoeing, rappelling, and Jet Skiing.

11 Seychelles. In the Indian Ocean 932 miles off Africa's eastern coast, this archipelago of 115 islands lies just northeast of Madagascar and has some of the world's best-preserved natural habitats and pristine beaches.

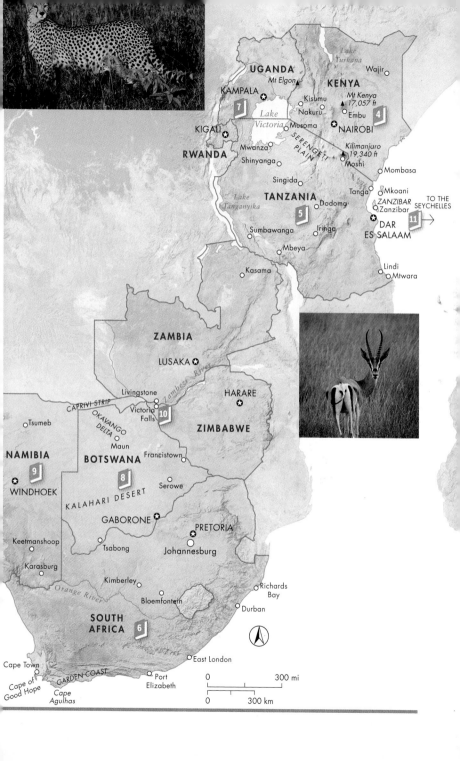

UGANDA

KAMPALA

Mt Elgon

Lake Turkana

Wajir

KENYA

Kisumu

Nakuru

Mt Kenya
17,057 ft

Embu

KIGALI

Lake Victoria

Musoma

NAIROBI

4

RWANDA

Mwanza

Shinyanga

SERENGETI PLAIN

Kilimanjaro
19,340 ft

Moshi

Mombasa

7

Singida

Tanga

Mkoani

ZANZIBAR

Zanzibar

TO THE SEYCHELLES

TANZANIA

Dodoma

Lake Tanganyika

5

Sumbawanga

Iringa

DAR ES SALAAM

11

Mbeya

Lindi

Mtwara

Kasama

ZAMBIA

LUSAKA

Livingstone

Zambezi River

HARARE

CAPRIVI STRIP

Victoria Falls

10

Tsumeb

OKAVANGO DELTA

ZIMBABWE

NAMIBIA

Maun

9

BOTSWANA

Francistown

WINDHOEK

Serowe

8

KALAHARI DESERT

GABORONE

PRETORIA

Keetmanshoop

Tsabong

Johannesburg

Karasburg

Kimberley

Orange River

Bloemfontein

Richards Bay

Durban

SOUTH AFRICA

6

East London

Cape Town

GARDEN COAST

Port Elizabeth

0   300 mi

Cape of Good Hope

Cape Agulhas

0   300 km

IF YOU LIKE

The Out of Africa Experience

Turn back the clock to the great, glorious days of the early safaris, when Ernest Hemingway and Teddy Roosevelt stalked the golden grass of the plains with the Big Five in their rifle sights. Forget the rifles, but shoot as much as you like—with cameras. We have the perfect spots.

Cottars 1920s Safari Camp, Kenya. For an original safari replay it doesn't get much better than this—claw-foot tubs, antique rugs, wrought-iron candlesticks, old gramophones, polished butlers' trays— all under white safari tents.

Finch Hattons, Kenya. Live your every African dream at this classy camp where you'll dine at a table sparkling with silver and crystal as strains of Mozart softly fill the African night.

Il Moran, Kenya. Situated where Kenya's first colonial governors used to twirl their handlebar moustaches and sip their G&Ts while on safari, you'll enjoy the exclusive location, teeming game, and bygone elegance.

King's Pool, Botswana. From the ancient tree dominating the main deck to the lush accommodations, everything is on a regal scale—a tribute to the European royalty who used to hunt in this area.

Sabi Sabi Selati Camp, South Africa. Formerly a private hunting lodge, the early-1900s ambience stems from genuine train memorabilia. Old leather suitcases, antique wooden chairs, and signals recall the days of an 1870s train line.

To See the Great Migration

No matter where you stay during the Great Migration, you'll be assured of unforgettable sights. But we've highlighted a few camps where sightings may be even more spectacular. Remember that world weather cycles are changing— there's no guarantee that at that particular place and time your game-viewing will live up to the National Geographic TV Channel.

Grumeti River Camp, Tanzania. Watch out for galloping wildebeest at this exclusive camp on the banks of the famed Grumeti River, where you'll be perfectly positioned to witness one of the greatest shows on earth.

Little Governors' Camp, Kenya. A ferry ride across the Mara River and a short walk escorted by armed guides takes you to this lovely camp sited directly in the path of the wildebeest migration.

Mara Serena Safari Lodge, Kenya. If you get tired of looking at the endless grasslands where the migration takes place in front of your eyes, then spot game at the lodge's own busy water hole.

Naibor Camp, Kenya. Situated in a particularly game-rich area 20 minutes away from one of the legendary migration river crossings, this is the perfect base for watching the migration.

Sayari Camp, Tanzania. This camp is perfectly poised for watching the Mara River crossing, when hundreds of thousands of wildebeest plunge into the crocodile-infested water on their journey north.

Serengeti Under Canvas, Tanzania. This luxury mobile camp follows the migration, staying put for a couple of months and then moving north with the herds. Not cheap but worth every penny.

Drop-Dead Luxury

So you want the whole game experience but don't want to rough it? No problem. Our favorites will tempt you to defect from the real world and live like kings and queens.

Banyan Tree, Seychelles. One of Seychelles' most romantic resorts, the Banyan Tree's white Victorian-style buildings and truly impeccable service lend this gem a colonial feel.

Great Fish River Lodge, Kwandwe, South Africa. Colonial luxury with genuine antiques combine with stunning river views in this malaria-free Big Five reserve

MalaMala Game Reserve, Mpumalanga, South Africa. One of the oldest and most distinguished of all Southern African bush lodges, this is the haunt of royalty, celebs, and the jet set.

Mombo Camp, Botswana. The spacious, graciously decorated en suite rooms of this legendary camp may have a tented feel, but they're ultraluxurious with great game-viewing.

Ngorongoro Crater Lodge, Tanzania. The theme here is Great Zimbabwe ruins meets SS *Titanic* baroque, and your abode will be palatial and the game-viewing equally fabulous.

North Island, Seychelles. This private island of granite cliffs and powder-white beaches hosts 11 villas that are each as large as most people's homes, kitted out in a Robinson-Crusoe-envisioned-by-Galliano dream.

Singita Sabi Sand, Kruger, South Africa. Hide yourself away at these multiaward-winning bush getaways, with superb game and service to match.

Thanda Main Lodge, KwaZulu-Natal, South Africa. This exquisite lodge has beehive-shape dwellings that blend elements of royal Zulu with an eclectic pan-African feel. Shaka never had it this good.

Vlei Lodge, Phinda, South Africa. Six sumptuous secluded suites with private plunge pools look out over an open wetland stretching to the horizon. Expect game galore, magnificent birdlife, and superb service.

Animal Encounters

Addo Elephant-Back Safaris, South Africa. Be introduced to a small group of trained African elephants. Take a short elephant ride, go for a scenic walk through the bush with them, touch them, feed them, and watch them bathe.

Clouds Mountain Gorilla Lodge, Uganda. Profits from this luxury lodge fund local community conservation projects, helping support the future of this critically endangered ape.

Cousine Island, Seychelles. Tiny Cousine's rehabilitation has resulted in the return of thousands of nesting seabirds. A stay in one of the four luxurious villas is a birder's delight.

Desert Rhino Camp, Namibia. If it's rhinos you're after, especially the rare black rhino, then this remote tented camp in the heart of the private Palmwag Reserve is a must.

Greystoke Mahale, Tanzania. About 60 of the area's 1,000 or so wild chimpanzees live in the forest near this gorgeous lodge on a deserted beach, so you have an excellent chance of spotting them.

Londolozi, South Africa. This is the place to see leopards. The most beautiful and successful of all feline predators, watching a leopard move through the bush is a truly awesome sight.

Ol Kanjau Camp, Kenya. The focus is on elephants, which have been studied here for nearly 40 years. You'll never forget the thrill of your nose-to-trunk introduction to one of the 52 great matriarchal herds.

IF YOU LIKE

To Get Away from the Crowds

If you choose any of the following camps and lodges you'll be assured privacy and exclusivity.

Duba Plains, Botswana. Deep in the Okavango Delta, this tiny camp on an isolated island has superb game-viewing. Only two 4x4 open game vehicles operate in the whole reserve.

Jack's Camp, Botswana. If you're bold-spirited, reasonably fit, and enjoy a rugged pioneer experience, then Jack's is for you. Try quad-biking, sleeping out under the stars, or walking with the bushmen.

Mnemba Island Lodge, Tanzania. For the ultimate beach escape where time stands still and where sand, sea, and horizon melt into each other, this exclusive lodge with only 20 guests is hard to beat.

Nduara Loliondo, Tanzania. A true old-style private safari experience away from the big lodges and busy safari routes with excellent guides, cooks, waiters, and camp attendants.

Ruzizi Tented Lodge, Rwanda. Far from the gorilla-trek hordes, the grunt of baboons and the splash of bathing elephants are all you'll hear at this secluded ecolodge in Akagera National Park.

Sand Rivers Selous, Tanzania. Above a wide bend of the Rufiji River—hundreds of miles away from touristy Africa—this lodge is just about as isolated and exclusive as you can get.

Sarara Tented Camp, Kenya. At this small remote tented camp below the Mathews Mountains in the 75,000-acre Namunyuk Wildlife Conservation Trust, the only strangers in the night you'll see are the wildlife residents.

!Xaus Lodge, South Africa. In one of South Africa's most remote parks, !Xaus (pronounced "Kaus") provides great hospitality, game drives, desert walks, and introductions to local bushmen.

To Interact with the Locals

Many of the cultural and village visits aren't entirely authentic given the need for tourist dollars, but we've identified a few genuine experiences.

Deception Valley Lodge, Botswana. At this lodge in the Central Kalahari Game Reserve you'll meet the desert-dwelling Naru people, who built it entirely by hand. Expect pure magic during a three-hour walk with the bushmen themselves.

Forest Lodge, Phinda, South Africa. Learn about the fascinating customs, traditions, and beliefs of the legendary Zulu nation on a village tour. The local *sangoma* (traditional healer) will even foretell your future.

Il'Ngwesi Lodge, Kenya. Learn about hunting, gathering honey, animal trapping with indigenous poisons, and fashioning beadwork at the nearby Maasai village.

Lake Manyara Serena Lodge, Tanzania. Take a guided walk to Mto wa Mbu, a small town that's home to more than 100 different tribes. Here you'll visit homes, a school, a church, the market, and a banana-leaf bar.

Ol Seki Hemingway's Mara, Kenya. At this eco-friendly camp you'll visit authentic, nontouristy Maasai villages, where you might be lucky enough to witness a genuine betrothal or post-initiation ceremony.

Serra Cafema, Namibia. Only the nomadic Himba people share this awesome remote area, and a visit to a local village will be a life-changing experience.

To Go to the Beach

Going on safari is also about where you're going to go before or after your game-viewing, and there are plenty of beach resort options to choose from.

Four Seasons Resort, Seychelles. Located on one of Mahé Island's most beautiful bays, this gorgeous resort helps visitors enjoy its perfect slice of white sand with fantastic beach service, plenty of ship-shape equipment from snorkeling gear to kayaks, and one of the island's best snorkeling areas.

Kiwayu Safari Village, Kenya. Northeast of Lamu, this village is one of the most romantic spots in all of Kenya. The area is known for its deep-sea fishing, and the hotel is close to the Kiunga Marine National Reserve, a great place for snorkeling. Book far in advance.

Mnemba Lodge Tanzania. For the ultimate beach escape head to this tiny island off the tip of Zanzibar. You can dive and snorkel off a pristine coral reef, and you might just rub elbows with the rich and famous.

Oyster Box, South Africa. A South African icon for more than half a century, this gorgeous hotel, which seamlessly blends old colonial décor with contemporary African art, sits on a golden beach guarded by a lighthouse.

Ras Nungwi, Tanzania. You'll find this resort on the northern tip of Zanzibar overlooking the Indian Ocean's turquoise waters. The balmy breezes and numerous lounge areas beg you to just sit down and relax; if you can't, there are water sports, a spa, and local tours to Stone Town, spice plantations, and Jozani Forest.

Rocktail Beach Camp South Africa. If you're in the mood for pristine beaches, surf fishing, amazing scuba diving, and snorkeling, then coming to this lodge nestled in the Maputaland Coastal Reserve will be the perfect beach getaway after your safari.

Natural Wonders

Sub-Saharan Africa is home to some awe-inspiring natural wonders.

Explosion Crater Drive. This stunning three-hour drive traverses the Katwe crater field in Uganda. It's littered with steep-sided volcanic craters, each containing its own micro-habitat from ancient rainforest to a sulfurous lake.

The Great Migration. This annual journey of more than 2 million animals through Kenya and Tanzania is a safari seeker's Holy Grail; some consider it to be one of the world's greatest natural wonders.

Mt. Kilimanjaro. Kili, as it's fondly called, is the continent's highest peak and the tallest free-standing mountain in the world. It's one of the easier mountains to climb; about 12,000 people each year set out for the summit.

The Namibia Dunes. In Namib Naukluft Park, the largest game park in Africa, lie the mythical Namibia sand dunes. Said to be the highest dunes in the world, this is an adventure seeker's dream.

The Ngorongoro Crater. Nearly 3 million years old, this UNESCO World Heritage Site in northern Tanzania is a haven for wild game. Though it does get busy during high season, your experiences far outweigh the annoyances.

Okavango Delta. At its peak, the world's largest inland delta covers some 16,000 square km (6,177 square miles) of northwest Botswana.

Victoria Falls. More than 91 meters (300 feet) high and visible from 50 km (31 miles) away, the Falls are one of the world's seven natural wonders.

TOP EXPERIENCES

Seeing a Lion

Lions. Are. Awesome. You probably already knew that. However, when it comes to seeing a lion on safari, forget all you know. The sight of these big cats in their natural habitat is an event every time. We've repeatedly seen veteran safari guides visibly humbled by lion encounters. When you get close to a lion in the wild it's an irreducible moment. You're held in thrall, suspended in a world that consists of just you and one special animal, and this dimension simply does not exist in a zoo. The animal may be the same, but there's an incomparable gravitas to seeing it in the environment in which it must struggle to survive. View a lion on safari, and on an unconscious level you'll process not only its marvelous appearance, but also its dramatic relationship to its surroundings. You may happen on a pride sleeping under the shade of an acacia tree and be overcome by how endearing the scene is. But you also understand that you're witnessing more than a lazy afternoon nap. On an unspoken level you just *know* that the slumbering cats are storing their energy for an epic hunt. Or, as you watch a group of lionesses intently stalking through tall grass, you might even *feel* the urgency of their primal hunger. And don't even get us started on leopards.

Not Seeing a Lion

As breathtaking as it is to see a lion on safari, spotting them shouldn't be a single-minded pursuit. If you're preoccupied with seeing a big cat, or other Big Five animals, every time you set out on a game drive, you may unintentionally miscalculate the success rate of your journey. When asked about their drives, people often say, "It was great! We saw four lions and two cheetahs!" Or, "It was good, but we didn't see any rhinos or leopards." This kind of scorekeeping fails to account for the numerous sightings that can be equally wondrous. Often when lions are found, your driver will cut the engine so that you can silently behold their splendor. We highly recommend that you direct this kind of undivided attention to other, more "common" sights throughout your drive as well. Ask your driver to cut the engine at random intervals. Then sit stock still and observe the open plain. Feel it teeming with life. Listen to it. You've never quite "heard" silence like the quiet of the savanna. The landscape is playful—watch the "Kenya Express," an affectionate term for the famously skittish warthogs throughout Kenya, who comically dash with their tails up like antennas at the slightest disturbance. The landscape can be poignant—witness the heart-wrenching vulnerability of a baby giraffe that has strayed too far from its mother. The landscape can be stoic; see shaggy waterbuck, relatively fearless because lions rarely prey on them, blithely lounging in the grass, staring at you with practiced indifference. But most of all, the landscape is a wonderland with the subtle interplay of wildlife happening everywhere. Receive all it has to offer and you'll be well rewarded.

Getting the Perfect Shot

Three graceful giraffes, dwarfed by towering Mt. Kilimanjaro, bathed by the orange glow of the setting sun, are surveying the plains. Suddenly, all three at once turn to look straight at you, practically mugging for the camera, and *click*. You got it: an image you'll cherish, a picture worth a thousand words and 8,000 miles of travel. Sure, there are tons of professional images of African wildlife that put your lucky shot to shame. But this is your

special moment; you own it, and there's a particular pride that comes with every image you capture. Your pictures document your trip through a highly personal lens. Perhaps this is why the exact same scene captured with superior contrast ratio and composition doesn't inspire nearly as strong a reaction. When you get your "perfect" shot, there's a personal poetry to it that can't be duplicated by anybody else's camera. Your pictures tell *your* story.

Not Getting the Perfect Shot

The problem with the perfect shot is the amount of time you can spend viewing your surroundings through a tiny LCD screen to get it. Although you may never have another chance to photograph the gaping maw of a giant hippo as he suddenly rises from the river, you may also never get another chance to *experience* that moment. Too often folks on safari witness spectacles unfold not before their very eyes (or even through binoculars), but through a tiny screen—waiting for fauna to fall into place, waiting to capture the best action shot. It's somewhat disorienting to consider that you can be in Africa (Africa!), alternating your gaze between the digital image you're trying to capture and the one that you just took. The splendid rise of a hot-air balloon over the sand dunes of Namibia or the impressive leaps of Maasai warriors are singularly unique events that shouldn't be witnessed solely through a single-lens reflex. Before you know it, your firsthand experiences will seem nebulous and your memories prematurely dim, leaving you with a succession of moments that can only be recalled through photos and video. Set up your shots, take lots of pictures; they're precious. But more precious is the primary, full-sensory, romantic experience that can only be achieved by unencumbered engagement with your surroundings.

Going on a Sundowner

A lot of the recommendations above are variations on "be in the moment"—based on the notion that because safaris are exhilarating adventures with a raft of stimuli, it sometimes takes a concentrated effort to drink in the here-and-now. Well, quite literally, there's nothing like a sundowner to help you drink it all in. The recipe is simple: take one particularly scenic spot, often with vistas that span country borders and stretch to distant mountains, add your choice of cocktails, and watch the sun drench what seems like half of Africa in various hues of orange and pink. Most luxury and semi-luxury camps offer this supernal show, and it shouldn't be missed. They often set you up with director's chairs, which is appropriate, because it's here, in the fading light, as tranquillity envelopes the land, that you feel in charge—fully recharged. Raise a glass and toast your glorious day—"*kwahafya njema!*"—as the African sun makes its graceful exit.

Not Going on a Sundowner

Just kidding. You should go.

FINDING THE BIG 5

The fauna that can be found on an African safari is as varied and vast as the continent's landscape. Africa has more large animals than anywhere else in the world and is the only place on earth where vast herds still roam the plains.

		African Buffalo	Elephant	Leopard	Lion	Rhino
BOTSWANA	The Okavango Delta	●	●	●	●	●
	Moremi Wildlife Reserve	●	●	●	●	●
	Chobe Nat'l Park	●	●	●	●	●
	Kwando Game Reserve	●	●	●	●	○
KENYA	Masai Mara	●	●	●	●	●
	Amboseli Nat'l Park	●	●	●	●	●
	Tsavo Nat'l Park	●	●	●	●	●
	Laikipia Plateau	●	●	●	●	●
NAMIBIA	Namib Naukluft Park*	○	○	◑	◑	○
	Damaraland	○	●	○	○	●
	Etosha Nat'l Park	●	●	●	●	●
SOUTH AFRICA	Kruger Nat'l Park	●	●	●	●	●
	Sabi Sands Game Reserve	●	●	●	●	●
	KwaZulu-Natal Parks	●	●	●	●	●
	Kgalagadi Transfrontier Park	○	○	●	●	○
TANZANIA	Serengeti Nat'l Park	●	●	●	●	●
	Ngorongoro Crater	●	●	●	●	●
	Lake Manyara Nat'l Park	●	●	●	●	○
	Selous Game Reserve	●	●	●	●	●
	Gombe Stream and Mahale Mountains Nat'l Parks**	○	○	○	○	○

*This park is noted for its stunning scenic beauty - not game
**These parks are primarily for primate viewing - chimpanzees and monkeys
KEY: ● = yes ◑ = Rarely ○ = No

There's nothing quite like the feeling of first setting eyes on one of the Big Five—buffalo, elephant, leopard, lion, and rhino—in the African bush. Being just a few feet from these majestic creatures is both terrifying and exhilarating, even for the most seasoned safari-goer.

THE BIG 5

updated by
Kate Turkington

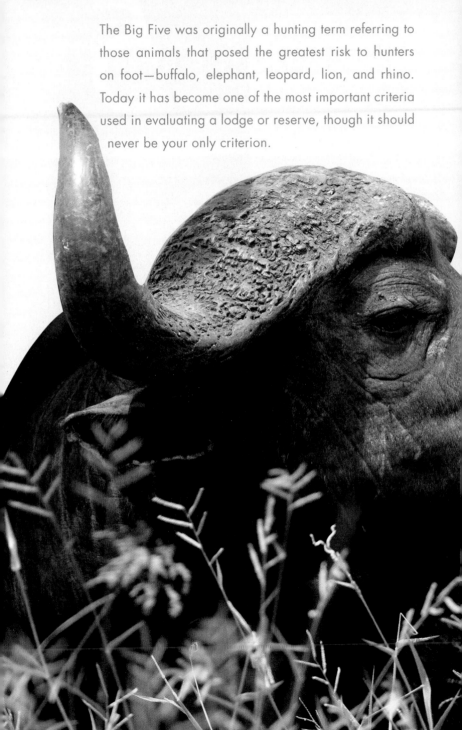

The Big Five was originally a hunting term referring to those animals that posed the greatest risk to hunters on foot—buffalo, elephant, leopard, lion, and rhino. Today it has become one of the most important criteria used in evaluating a lodge or reserve, though it should never be your only criterion.

THE AFRICAN BUFFALO

Often referred to as the Cape buffalo, this is considered by many to be the most dangerous of the Big Five because of its unpredictability and speed. Do not confuse it with the docile Asian water buffalo as the Cape buffalo is a more powerful and untameable beast with a massive build and short strong legs. They have few predators other than human hunters and lions. It generally takes an entire lion pride to bring down an adult buffalo, although calves or weak and sick adults can be taken by wild dog and spotted hyena. Lions risk being mobbed by the herd when they do attack, and are sometimes trampled and gored.

Cape buffalo can reach up to 1,900 pounds and in the wild can live up to 15 or so years, much longer if they are in captivity. Never found very far from water, they are grazers and widespread throughout sub-Saharan Africa, especially in Kenya, Tanzania, Botswana, Zambia, Zimbabwe, and South Africa. Large, mixed herds can number up to a few hundred, and in the Serengeti, during the rains, in their thousands. You shouldn't fear a herd, but beware lone old males, which have mostly been thrown out of the herd and are now bad-tempered and volatile. Known as "Dagha Boys"—dagha is the clay mixture used for building traditional huts—they spend much of their days in mud wallows and are usually thickly coated in the stuff. While seemingly lethargic these old boys can turn on a dime and charge like lightning. If you are charged, run for cover or climb the nearest tree.

THE ELEPHANT

The largest of the land animals, it once roamed the continent by the millions. Today, according to the World Wildlife Fund (WWF), the population, mainly found in Southern and Eastern Africa, is between 470,000 and 690,000. The continent's forest elephants (of central and West Africa) are still under severe threat.

African elephants are divided into two species. Savannah elephants are the largest, at 13 feet and 7 tons, and can be found by lakes, marshes, or grasslands. Forest elephants have an average height of 10 feet and weight of 10,000 pounds. They're usually found in central and West African rainforests.

An elephant's gestation period is 22 months—the longest of any land animal. The aver-

age calf is 265 pounds. When calves are born, they are raised and protected by the entire herd—a group of about 10 females led by the oldest and largest. Males leave the herd after 15 years, often living with other males or alone.

When an elephant trumpets in a showy manner, head up and ears spread, it's a mock charge—frightening but not physically dangerous. If an elephant stomps the ground, holds its ears back and head forward, and issues a loud, high-pitched screech, this means real trouble. A charging elephant is extremely fast and surprisingly agile. If you're on foot make for the nearest big tree or embankment; elephants seldom negotiate these obstacles. If you're in a vehicle, hit the gas.

THE RHINO

There are two species of these massive primeval-looking animals in Africa: the black, or hook-lipped rhino, and the white, or square-lipped rhino. Both species have poor eyesight but excellent hearing, and because of their erratic tempers, they may sometimes charge without apparent reason. These animals are surprisingly agile for their size. The white rhino is slighter taller (up to 60 inches at the shoulder) and heavier at over two tons, the black rhino is shorter and stockier by a few inches and can weigh up to one and a half tons. Although they share habitats, the white rhino is a grazer eating only grasses, the black, a browser, eating leaves and shrubs. The black rhino which is more aggressive than the white, prefers thick thornveld and dense vegetation, while the white sticks more to open grassland and the plains. Both love to wallow in mud. They mark their territory by means of defecating in individual middens, or dung heaps, which they make along rhino paths and territorial boundaries, regularly patrolling these 'signposts' on the look out for intruders.

The black rhino tends to be more solitary unless it is a very small mother/father/calf group; the white rhino stays together in small groups called crashes. Calves of both species stay with their mothers until they are four or five, when they leave to find a new territory.

Sadly, the survival of this incredible mammal is under serious threat from poaching. Today, many are protected in sanctuaries or reserves, but poaching is a constant threat—in South Africa in 2011 alone, 448 rhino were slaughtered for their horns by mid-year. By July 2012, another 281 had been killed. These are traded on the black market as aphrodisiacs (an empty claim) and as potential dagger handles in the Middle East to symbolize wealth and power.

However, major efforts by conservationists are in hand to try to stem the problem.

THE LION

Known as the king of beasts—the Swahili word for lion, "simba," also means "king," "strong," and "aggressive"—this proud animal was once found throughout the world. Today, the majority of the estimated 23,000 lions are found in sub-Saharan Africa—a small population is also found in India—in grasslands, savannah, and dense bush.

Watching a lion stalk its prey can be one of the most exciting safari encounters. Females do most of the hunting, typically setting up a plan of attack, which is then carried out by the pride. Lionesses take turns hunting and this collective labor allows them to conserve their energy and survive longer in the bush. They are most active from dusk to dawn. A pride consists of between four and six adults but occasionally may go up to 20 or even 30. Botswana's Savute region is known for its large prides. The males, identified by their gorgeous golden-red or black manes, are often brothers who behave territorially; their main task is to protect the females and the cubs. Typically, the females in the pride will give birth at approximately the same time, and the cubs will be raised together. Litters usually consist of two to three cubs that weigh about three pounds each. Sometimes, males that take over a pride will kill existing cubs so that they can sire their own with the lioness.

Lions can sleep for up to 18 hours a day. Lounging about in the grass, lions will often lick each other, rub heads, and play. But don't be fooled by their charms. When a lion moves, it can do so with awesome speed and power—a charging lion can cover 330 feet in four seconds. If you come face to face with a lion, never, ever turn your back and try to run—that is your death warrant. Your best bet is to stand as still as possible and try to outface the lion.

THE LEOPARD

Secretive, stealthy and shrewd, the leopard is the most successful predator of all Africa's big cats. They are often difficult to spot on safari, primarily because they are nocturnal, but if you go on a night game drive your chances will increase tremendously. South Africa's Sabi Sands area has the highest density of leopards in the world and you would be very unlucky not to see one there.

Leopard can vary in appearance, their coat ranging from a light tawny hue in dry areas to darker shades in the forest. Their spots, called rosettes, are round in East Africa, but square in Southern Africa. Leopard can also be found in India, China, Siberia, and Korea. The female leopard, whose litter usually ranges from about one to three cubs, will keep her young hidden for about two months after birth, then feed and nurse them for an additional three months or so until her cubs are strong enough to roam with her. What about dad? Male leopards play no part in rearing the cubs. In fact, the male is usually long gone by the time the female gives birth. He leaves her after they mate, although he has been known to return to kill the cubs, hence the reasoning behind keeping them hidden for the first few months of their lives.

Leopard use a combination of teeth and razor-sharp claws to kill their prey; it's not uncommon for a leopard's lunch to be taken away by lion or hyena. In order to avoid this, the leopard will often drag their larger kills up a tree where they can dine amongst the leaves in relative peace and quiet.

THE LITTLE 5

We've all heard of the Big Five, but keep a look out for the Little Five, a term given to the animals with names that include the Big Five: antlion, buffalo weaver, elephant shrew, leopard tortoise, and rhinoceros beetle.

RHINOCEROS BEETLE

The rhinoceros beetle grows up to two inches long. It has large spikes—similar in appearance to a rhino's horns—which are used in battle with other rhino beetles, or for digging, climbing, and mating.

LEOPARD TORTOISE

The largest tortoise in sub-Saharan Africa, the leopard tortoise can grow up to two feet long and weigh up to 100 pounds. It lives in the grasslands of East and Southern Africa and doesn't mate until it's at least 10 years old. Its name stems from its black and yellow-spotted shell, which resembles a leopard's coat.

ELEPHANT SHREW

These ground-dwelling mammals range in size from that of a mouse to a large rabbit. They live in lowland forests, woodlands, rocky outcrops, and deserts and eat small fruits and plants. They get their name from their long nose, which resembles a miniature elephant's trunk.

ANTLION

Also known as a "doodlebug" because of the winding patterns it leaves in the sand when building traps, the antlion makes its home on dry, sandy slopes sheltered from the wind. Essentially larva, it eventually grows into an insect akin to a dragonfly.

RED-BILLED BUFFALO WEAVERS

These black birds with red bills and legs make big sturdy communal nests out of sticks which are defended by the dominant male and nearly always face westward. Inside, the nests are separate chambers with individual tunnels leading to the outside. Their mating is unique amongst birds as it lasts up to two minutes instead of seconds as in most birds.

FAUNA

OTHER ANIMALS

You'll be amazed by how many visitors ignore a gorgeous animal that doesn't "rank" in the Big Five or lose interest in a species once they've checked it off their list. After you've spent a few days in the bush, you'll hopefully understand the idiocy of racing about in search of five animals when there are 150 equally fascinating species all around you. Here are a few to look out for.

Baboons

(A) These are the most adaptable of the ground-dwelling primates and can live in all manner of habitats as long as they have water and a safe place to sleep. Baboons travel in groups of up to 40, sleeping, eating, and socializing together. Although they're hugely entertaining to watch, always keep your vehicle windows rolled up. Like other animals, they can be vicious when they feel threatened, and they have huge canine teeth. They eat mainly plants, but will also consume small quantities of meat.

Cheetah

(B) Reaching speeds of 70 mph, cheetahs are the world's fastest land animals—they have slender, muscular legs and special pads on their feet for traction. With its characteristic dark spots, the cheetah also has a distinctive black "tear" line running from the inside corner of its eye to the mouth. A solitary, timid creature, cheetahs are found mainly in open savanna. Males and females can sometimes be seen together after mating, but usually one or two males—often brothers—are alone and females are with the cubs. Cheetahs generally prey on gazelles and impalas. Sadly, this stunning cat is one of the most endangered animals, due to shrinking habitat, loss of prey, and disease.

Giraffe

(C) The biggest ruminant and tallest living animal, giraffes are social creatures that live in loose herds that can spread out over half a mile. Although there are no leaders, the males fight over females using a "necking" technique, winding their necks around each other, pushing and shoving. Giraffes either walk or gallop and are ubiquitous in most national parks. It's easy to tell the difference between males and females. The tops of the male's horns are bare and shiny from fighting; the females have bushy tips like paintbrushes.

Hippo

(D) Though they may be comical looking, these are actually one of Africa's most dangerous animals. The most common threat display is the yawn, which is telling you to back off. Most guides will give them a wide berth. Never get between a hippo and its water, as this will appear to them that you're trying to corner them and may result in an attack. The comical nighttime sounds of hippos snorting and chortling will be one of your safari's most memorable experiences.

Impala

(E) One of the most populous animals in the African bush, impalas can be found in grasslands and wooded areas, usually near water. Similar in appearance to a deer, these one-of-a-kind antelopes are reddish-brown with white and black markings. A typical herd has one dominant male ruling over his harem, although bachelor herds are usually in the vicinity, with hopeful individuals awaiting their turn to oust the ruling male. It's a hugely successful animal, because it's both a grazer and a browser.

FAUNA

African Wild Dogs

(F) Also called the "painted dog" or "painted wolf" because of each uniquely spotted coat, the wild dog is headed toward extinction with numbers of approximately 3,000 to 5,000 and shrinking. This highly social animal with bat-like ears and a furry tail lives in small packs of about 15; only the alpha male and female are allowed to breed. Intelligent and quick, wild dogs hunt as a coordinated pack running down their prey, which varies from antelopes to zebras, until exhausted. They have an amazingly successful catch rate of 85%. They breed in underground dens, often those abandoned by warthogs.

Bush Baby

(G) These small nocturnal primates, which make cries similar to that of a human baby, range in size from 2 ounces to 3 pounds. During the day, they stay in tree hollows and nests, but at night you'll see them leaping and bouncing from tree to tree in pursuit of night-flying insects. Their main predators are some of the larger carnivores, genets, and snakes.

Hyena

(H) Hyenas live in groups called clans and make their homes in dens. They mark their territory with gland secretions or droppings. Cubs are nursed for about 18 months, at which point they head out on hunting and scavenging sprees with their mothers. Both strategic hunters and opportunists, hyenas will feed on their own kill as well as that of others. Aggressive and dangerous, African folklore links the hyena with witchcraft and legends.

Nile Crocodile

(I) Averaging about 16 feet and 700 pounds, this croc can be found in sub-Saharan Africa, the Nile River, and Madagascar. They eat mainly fish but will eat almost anything, including a baby hippo or a human. Although fearsome looking

and lightning quick in their attack, they're unusually sensitive with their young, carefully guarding their nests until their babies hatch. Their numbers have been slashed by poachers, who seek their skins for shoemakers.

Springbok

(J) This cinnamon-color antelope has a dark brown stripe on its flanks, a white underside, and short, slender horns. It often engages in a mysterious activity known as "pronking," a seemingly sudden spurt of high jumps into the air with its back bowed. Breeding takes place twice a year, and the young will stay with their mothers for about four months. These herbivores travel in herds that usually include a few territorial males.

Wildebeest

(K) This ubiquitous herbivore is an odd-looking creature: large head and front end, curved horns, and slender body and rear. Often called "the clowns of the veld" they toss their heads as they run and kick up their back legs. Mothers give birth to their young in the middle of the herd, and calves can stand and run within three minutes and keep up with the herd after two days.

Zebra

(L) Africa has three species: the Burchell's (or common) zebra, East Africa's Grevy's zebra (named after former French president Jules Grevy), and the mountain zebra of Southern and Southwestern Africa. All have striped coats and strong teeth for chewing grass and often travel in large herds. A mother keeps its foal close for the first few hours after birth so it can remember her stripes and not get lost. Bold and courageous, a male zebra can break an attacking lion's jaw with one powerful kick.

FAUNA

BIRDS

Many people come to Africa solely for the birds. There are thousands of winged beauties to "ooh" and "aah" over; we mention a few to look out for.

Bateleur Eagle

(A) This spectacular bird, which looks as if it's "balancing" in the air, is found throughout sub-Saharan Africa and is probably one of the best known birds in Africa. Mainly black with a red back, legs, and beak and white underneath its wings, the Bateleur eagle can fly up to 322 km (200 miles) at a time in search of prey, which includes antelope, mice, other birds, snakes, and carrion. They mate for life, often using the same nest for several years.

Lappet-Faced Vulture

(B) The largest and most dominant of the vultures, this scavenger feeds mainly on carrion and carcasses that have been killed by other animals. The most aggressive of the African vultures, it will also, on occasion, kill other weaker birds or attack the nests of young birds as prey. The Lappet-faced vulture has a bald head and is pink in color with a wingspan of up to 8½ feet.

Lilacbreasted Roller

(C) This stunning-looking bird with a blue-and-lilac-color breast is found in the open woodland and savanna throughout sub-Saharan Africa. It's usually solo or in pairs sitting in bushes or trees. Both parents nurture the nest and are extremely territorial and aggressive when it comes to defending it. During mating, the male flies up high and then rolls over and over as it descends, making screeching cries.

Kori Bustard

(D) One of the world's heaviest flying birds is found all over Southern and East Africa. Reaching almost 30 pounds and about 3½ feet in length, the male is much

larger than the female but both are gray in color, have crests, and gray-and-white necks. Although it does fly, the majority of its time is spent on land where it can find insects, lizards, snakes, and seeds. One male mates with several females, which then raise the young on their own.

Pel's Fishing Owl

(E) A large, monogamous, ginger-brown owl with no ears, bare legs, and dark eyes, it lives along the banks of rivers in Kruger Park, South Africa's Kwa-Zulu Natal province, Botswana's Okavango Delta, and Zimbabwe. One of only three fishing owls in the world, it hunts at night with its sharp talons and dozes in tall trees during the day. The owls communicate with each other through synchronized hooting at night as they guard their stretch of riverbank.

Wattled Crane

(F) The rarest African crane is found in Ethiopia, Zambia, Botswana, Mozambique, and South Africa. A gray-and-white bird, it can reach up to 5 feet tall and, while mating, will nest in pairs along the shallow wetlands of large rivers. They're omnivorous and sometimes wander onto farmlands where they're vulnerable to poisoning by farmers. They occur in pairs or sometimes in large flocks, especially in the Okavango Delta. The crane is on South Africa's critically endangered list.

FLORA

Although the mammals and birds of Africa are spectacular, we'd be remiss if we didn't mention the amazing plant life of this varied landscape. The floral wealth of the African continent is astounding, with unique, endemic species growing in all parts—the South African Cape has one of the richest of the world's six floral kingdoms. There are also several species of non-native plants and trees in Africa that have become the subject of lively environmental debates due to their effect on the environment.

TREES

African Mahogany

(A) Originally from West Africa, you'll find this majestic tree in warm humid climates like riverine forests; you'll also find them in the Florida everglades. A member of the Khaya genus, the mahogany requires significant rainfall in order to thrive and can reach up to 140 feet with a 6-foot trunk diameter. Its much-prized, strong, richly colored wood is sought after for furniture making and boat building.

Baobab

(B) A huge, quirky-looking deciduous tree that grows throughout mainland Africa, the baobab has a round, hollow trunk with spiny-looking branches growing out at the top in all directions—it almost looks like it's upside down with the roots sprouting out at the top. Known for storing water in its trunk, the baobab is found in dry regions and can live up to 400 years; some have lived for more than 1,000 years. The hollow trunks have been home to a prison and a post office.

Fever

(C) The fabled fever tree, which thrives in damp, swampy habitats throughout sub-Saharan Africa, has a luminous, yellow-green bark that's smooth and flaky, and its branches have white thorns and clusters of yellow flowers. It's so named because

before mosquitoes were known to carry malaria, travelers often contracted the disease where fever trees grew and thus they were wrongly thought to transmit malaria. Bees are attracted by the sweet smell of the flowers, and birds often nest in its branches as the thorns offer extra protection against predators.

Fig

(D) There are as many as 50 species of fig trees in Southern and East Africa, where they may reach almost gigantic proportions, growing wherever water is nearby. Although figs provide nourishment for a variety of birds, bats, and other animals, they're most noted for their symbiotic relationship with wasps, which pollinate the fig flowers while reproducing. The fig seed is dispersed throughout the bush in the droppings of animals who feed on the rich, juicy fruit.

Jackalberry

(E) The large, graceful jackalberry, also known as the African ebony, is a riverine tree found all over sub-Saharan Africa. It can grow up to 80 feet tall and 16 feet wide. It bears fragrant white flowers and a fleshy yellow fruit that jackals, monkeys, baboons, and fruit-eating birds love. Its bark and leaves are used in traditional medicine with proven pharmacological benefits.

Sausage

(F) This unique tree, found in Southern Africa, bears sausagelike fruit that hangs from ropelike stalks. The tree grows to be about 40 feet with fragrant red flowers that bloom at night and are pollinated by bats, insects, and the occasional bird. The fresh fruit, which can grow up to 2 feet long and weigh as much as 15 pounds, is poisonous but can be made into various medicines and an alcohol similar to beer.

FLORA

PLANTS

Magic Guarri

This round shrub grows along floodplains and rivers. It has dark green leaves and white or cream-color flowers, and its fruit is fleshy and purple with a seed in its center. The fruit can be fermented to produce an alcoholic beverage, and the bark is used as a dye in basket making. The twigs have been used as toothbrushes, while the root can be used as mouthwash. The wood, sometimes used to make furniture, is said to have magical or supernatural powers and is never burned as firewood.

Strelitzia Flower

(G) Also known as Bird of Paradise or the crane flower, the strelitzia is indigenous to South Africa. It grows up to 6½ feet tall with a beautiful fan-shape crown with bright orange and bluish-purple petals

that grow perpendicular to the stem, giving it the appearance of a graceful bird.

Welwitschia mirabilis

(H) With its long, wide leathery leaves creeping over the ground, this somewhat surreal-looking plant is also one of the world's oldest plants; it's estimated that welwitschia live to about 1,500 years, though botanists believe some can live to be 2,000 years old. It's found in the Namib Desert and consists solely of two leaves, a stem base, and roots. The plant's two permanent leaves lie on the ground getting tattered and torn, but grow longer and longer each summer.

Wild Thyme

(I) Also called creeping thyme, wild thyme grows mainly in rocky soil and outcrops. Its fragrant flowers are purple or white, and its leaves are used to make herbal tea. Honeybees use the plant as an important source of nectar. There's also a species of

butterfly whose diet consists solely of wild thyme.

Cape Fynbos

(J) There are six plant kingdoms—an area with a relatively uniform plant population—in the world. The smallest, known as the Cape Floral Kingdom or Capensis, is found in South Africa's southwestern and southern Cape; it's roughly the size of Portugal or Indiana and is made up of eight different protected areas. In 2004 it became the sixth South African site to be added to the UNESCO World Heritage list.

Fynbos, a term given to the collection of plants found in the Cape, accounts for four-fifths of the Cape Floral Kingdom; the term has been around since the Dutch first settled here in the 1600s. It includes no less than 8,600 plant species including shrubs, proteas, bulbous plants like gladiolus and lachenalia (in the hydrangea family), aloe, and grasslike flowering plants. Table Mountain alone hosts approximately 1,500 species of plants and 69 protea species—there are 112 protea species worldwide.

From a distance, fynbos may just look like random clusters of sharp growth that cover the mountainous regions of the Cape, but up close you'll see the beauty and diversity of this colorful growth. Many of the bright blooms in gardens in the United States and Europe, such as daisies, gladioli, lilies, and irises, come from indigenous Cape plants.

PLANNING A SAFARI

Updated by Claire Baranowski

A safari is one of the biggest travel adventures you can have. Planning well is crucial to ensure you get the most out of it. Even a basic question like "What should I wear?" is extremely important. In this safari section, we'll cover all the special considerations and lingo you'll need, with plenty of insider tips along the way.

Most people start planning a safari six to nine months in advance, but it's never too soon to start planning your trip. In fact, planning your trip 12 months in advance isn't unreasonable, especially if you want to travel during peak season—November through February in South Africa, July through October elsewhere—and have your heart set on a particular lodge.

If you're keen to see big game, particularly the Big Five (⇨ *Special feature in Chapter 1)*, then your best bets for success will be in East Africa and South Africa. The Serengeti National Park (⇨ *Chapter 5)* in Tanzania is known for its plentiful game and is the stomping ground for approximately 1.5 million wildebeest, 200,000 zebra, and 350,000 antelope that race more than 1,931 km (1,200 miles) every July to find enough water and grass to survive during the Great Migration. The Masai Mara National Reserve (⇨ *Chapter 4)* in neighboring Kenya is probably best known for its large population of big cats, as well as hippos and the rare black rhino and spotted hyena. In South Africa, Kruger National Park and the private Sabi Sand game reserve just outside of Kruger (⇨ *Chapter 7)* are ideal places to observe the Big Five as well as leopards and hundreds of other species. In Kruger alone, there are an estimated 1,200 species of flora and fauna. You'll see the African elephant everywhere in the park, with lions more abundant in the central and eastern regions; rhinos and buffalo make their home in the woods of southwest Kruger.

Deciding where you want to go and choosing the right safari operator (⇨ *Chapter 3)* are the most important things you need to do. Start planning for your safari the way you would any trip. Read travel books about the areas that most interest you. Talk to people who have been on a similar trip; word-of-mouth advice can be invaluable. Surf the 'net. Get inspired. Line up your priorities. And find someone you trust to help plan your trip.

GETTING STARTED

AIR TRAVEL

Traveling by plane is the best and most viable means of transportation to most safari destinations. If you're visiting a game lodge deep in the bush, you'll be arriving by light plane—and you really will be restricted in what you can bring. Excess luggage can usually be stored with the operator until your return. Don't just gloss over this: charter operators take weight very seriously, and some will charge you for an extra ticket if you insist on bringing excess baggage. ⇨ *For airline contact information and specific information for each country, see Air Travel, in the Getting Here and Around section of each chapter.*

AIR PASS

If you're planning to fly between a few of the countries mentioned in this book, consider the Star Alliance African Airpass, which can be purchased only by international passengers arriving in Africa on a Star Alliance carrier (Continental, United, US Airways, Air Canada, South African Airways, etc.); it's good for 3 to 10 flights on Ethiopian Airways, South African Airways, Brussels Airlines, and EgyptAir. The flights are sold in segments, priced by the distance between cities. These are a bargain for the longer routes, such as from Nairobi to Johannesburg. If your itinerary includes more than 2 of the 23 cities served in Africa, this may be a good choice.

If you're flying on American Airlines or British Airways, another option is the Visit Africa Pass by Oneworld Alliance (there are 15 airlines in the alliance), which uses a zone system between cities in South Africa, Namibia, and Zimbabwe. The minimum purchase is two segments and the maximum is 20. It's a great value when compared to regular fares.

Air Pass Information Oneworld Alliance ⊕ www.oneworld.com. **Star Alliance** ⊕ www.staralliance.com.

CHARTER FLIGHTS

Charter flights are a common mode of transportation when getting to safari lodges and remote destinations throughout Southern and East Africa. These aircraft are well maintained and are almost always booked by your lodge or travel agent.

On-demand flights, those made at times other than those scheduled, are very expensive for independent travelers, as they require minimum passenger loads. If it's just two passengers, you'll be charged for the vacant seats. Keep in mind that you probably won't get to choose the charter company you fly with. The aircraft you get depends on the number of passengers flying and can vary from very small (you'll sit in the co-pilot's seat) to a much more comfortable commuter plane. Those with a severe fear of small planes might consider road travel instead.

Luggage limits: Due to the limited space and size of the aircraft, charter carriers observe strict luggage regulations: luggage must be soft sided, preferably with no wheels, and weigh no more than 15 kg (33 lbs). Weight allowances may vary by company, so be sure to ask what the limits are before packing.

⇨ *For information regarding charter companies in each country, see the Air Travel section in each country chapter.*

CUSTOMS AND DUTIES

Visitors traveling to South Africa or other Southern Africa Customs Union (SACU) countries (Botswana, Lesotho, Namibia, and Swaziland) may bring in new or used gifts and souvenirs up to a total value of R3,000 (in South African rand, US$280 at this writing; ⇨ *See individual chapters for currency values*) duty-free. For additional goods (new or used) up to a value of R12,000, a fee of 25% is levied. In addition, each person may bring up to 200 cigarettes, 20 cigars, 250 grams of tobacco, two liters of wine, one liter of spirits, 50 ml of perfume, and 250 ml of eau de toilette. The tobacco and alcohol allowance applies only to people 18 and over. If you enter a SACU country from or through another in the union, you aren't liable for any duties. You will, however, need to complete a form listing items imported.

The United States is a signatory to CITES, a wildlife protection treaty, and therefore doesn't allow the importation of living or dead endangered animals, or their body parts, such as rhino horns or ivory. If you purchase an antique that's made partly or wholly of ivory, you must obtain a CITES preconvention certificate that clearly states the item is at least 100 years old. The import of zebra skin or other tourist products also requires a CITES permit.

U.S. Information U.S. Customs and Border Protection ⊕ *www.cbp.gov.* **U.S. Fish and Wildlife Service** ⊕ *www.fws.gov.*

INTERNATIONAL DRIVER'S LICENSE

If you're taking a self-driving safari or renting a car in countries other than South Africa and Namibia, you'll need an international driver's license. These licenses are valid for one year and are issued at any American Automobile Association (AAA) office in the United States; you must have a current U.S. driver's license. You need to bring two passport-type photographs with you for the license. A valid U.S. driver's license is acceptable in South Africa and Namibia.

MONEY MATTERS

Most safaris are paid in advance, so you need money only to cover personal purchases and gratuities. (The cash you take should include small denominations, like US$1, US$5, and US$10, for tips.) If you're self-driving, note that many places prefer to be paid in the local currency, so make sure you change money where you can. Local currency information is discussed in individual chapters. MasterCard and Visa

Rondavels at Taita Hill Lodge, Kenya

are accepted almost everywhere; American Express is often refused in Botswana. Neither Diners Club nor Discover is recognized in most African countries. ■TIP➔ It's a good idea to notify your credit-card company that you'll be traveling to Africa so that unusual-looking transactions aren't denied.

Reporting Lost Cards **American Express** ☎ 800/528–4800 in the U.S. ⊕ www.americanexpress.com. **MasterCard** ☎ 800/627–8372 in the U.S., 636/722–7111 collect from abroad ⊕ www.mastercard.com. **Visa** ☎ 800/847–2911 in the U.S., 303/967–1096 collect from abroad ⊕ www.visa.com.

FIGURING YOUR BUDGET

Consider three things: your flight, the actual safari costs, and extras. You can have a low-budget self-catering trip in a national park or spend a great deal for a small, exclusive camp. Almost every market has high-priced options as well as some economical ones.

Besides airfare and safari costs, make sure you budget for visas, tips, medications, and other sundries such as souvenirs. You'll likely stay at a hotel in your arrival/departure city on your first and last nights in Africa. Rates range from US$50 for basic accommodations to US$750 a night in the most luxurious hotels. If you do splurge on your safari, but want to keep costs down elsewhere, look for special offers—sometimes South African lodges will throw in a free night's accommodation in Cape Town, for example.

Plan to spend US$15–US$25 a day per traveler on gratuities (⇨ *see Tipping below*). In South Africa tips are on the higher end of this range and usually are paid in rand; you may also use U.S. dollars for tips, however. Elsewhere in Southern Africa, U.S. currency is preferred.

LUXURY SAFARIS

The most popular option is to book with a tour operator and stay in private lodges, which are owned and run by an individual or company rather than a country's government (⇨ *See Chapter 3, Choosing an Outfitter*). Prices at these lodges include all meals and, in some cases, alcoholic beverages, as well as two three- to five-hour-long game-viewing expeditions a day. Occasionally high-end lodges offer extra services such as spa treatments, boat trips, or special-occasion meals served alfresco in the bush. Prices range approximately from US$500 to US$1,800 per person per night sharing a double room. If you travel alone, expect to pay a single supplement because all safari-lodge rooms are doubles.

SAFARIS ON A SHOESTRING BUDGET

Don't let a tight budget deter you. There are many opportunities for great big-game experiences without going over the top. And, you won't have to completely abandon the idea of comfort and style either. Here are some money-saving tips that every budget can appreciate.

Drive yourself and/or self-cater. The least expensive option is to choose a public game park—Kruger National Park in South Africa, for example—where you drive yourself and self-cater (shop for and prepare all meals yourself). Most South Africans travel this way. The price of this type of trip is approximately a tenth of that for private, fully inclusive lodges.

Rates for national park camps, called rest camps, start at about US$80 a day for a two-bed *rondavel* (a round hut modeled after traditional African dwellings) and go up to $175 for a four-bed bungalow. The South African National Parks website (⊕ *www.sanparks.org*) has photos and prices for all their different accommodations around the country. Budget about $6 for breakfast, $8 for lunch, and $12 for dinner per person for each day on the trip (less if you're self-catering). You'll need to factor in park entry fees, however, and these can add quite considerably to the cost of your trip.

Driving yourself can be enjoyable, but keep in mind that you'll have to identify all the animals yourself, and you can't go off-road. Hire a guide from the main office of the park or opt for a game drive in a national park vehicle if you're in South Africa; it's inexpensive and will add a great deal to your experience. South Africa, Botswana, and Namibia are the best places to self-drive, as road conditions are good. Elsewhere, you may need a 4x4 vehicle. Cars are difficult to rent in Zimbabwe, and the roads are very poor in Kenya. Keep in mind that car rentals can be expensive. (⇨ *For more information, see Self-Drive Safaris below.*)

Stay in accommodations outside the park or in a nearby town. This cuts down on the "mark-ups" that you may experience for the convenience of staying inside a park, and you can come into the park on day trips, so you won't miss anything.

Stick to one park or visit a lesser-known one, and keep your trip short. The high-end safari-goer may visit up to four different parks in different terrains and areas of the country, but the budget traveler would do well to stick to just one. Lesser-known parks can be just as good as famous ones, and sometimes being far from the madding crowds is a luxury in itself. Many travelers tack a two- or three-day safari onto the end of a beach holiday; this is enough time to see the Big Five and get a good understanding of the animals you'll encounter.

Consider mobile-camping safaris. Travel is by 4x4 (often something that looks like a bus), and you sleep in tents at public or private campsites. There are different levels of comfort and service, and the price varies accordingly: at the lower end, you'll pitch your own tent and help with cooking; but with a full-service mobile-camping safari, your driver/ guide and a cook will do all the setup. The cost will also vary according to the number of people on the tour. You'll really feel at one with nature and the wildlife if you take this option, but you'll need to be able to put up with a certain level of roughing it. A full-service safari costs in the region of US$200–US$500 a day, depending on the comfort level.

Book a private lodge in the off-season. Many lodges—South Africa's Sabi Sands area, for example—cost about US$800 per person per night during the high season but can drop to about US$500 a night during the slower months of July and August; on average savings can be 30%– 40%. In the rainy season, however, roads may be impassable in some areas and the wildlife hard to spot, so do your research beforehand. Sometimes, the high season merely correlates with the European long vacation. In South Africa, the low season is from May to September, mostly because Cape Town is cold and wet during this time. Regions north of the country, such as Kruger, are excellent for game-viewing during this time, as the winter is the dry season and grasses are short. Early morning and nighttime can get cold, but the daytime is usually dry and sunny. You'll also have the benefit of fewer crowds, although if you're very social, you may find the off-season too quiet. If you're a honeymooner, it's perfect.

Cheap flights are out there, but you'll have to work for them. Aggregators such as Skyscanner.net and ebookers.com can help you search for the best fares that meet your requirements. American travelers can sometimes save money by flying through Europe. Book a flight to a regional hub like Nairobi or Johannesburg, and then catch a connecting flight to your destination. Many of Kenya's budget airlines fly from Nairobi to destinations in Tanzania, and South Africa's budget airline Kulula Airlines (⊕ *www.kulula.com*) flies from South Africa to Kenya, Namibia, Zambia, and Zimbabwe. For flights to South Africa, look into flying via Dubai or Doha. You'll add extra time to your flight, but you could save big. Always book at least two months in advance, especially during the high season.

Budget for all aspects of your trip and watch out for hidden extras. Most safaris are all-inclusive, so you don't think about the cost of your sundowner drink, snacks on your game drive, or cocktails at mealtime. However, some lodges charge extra for drinks and excursions (e.g., a visit to a Maasai village in Kenya). You can keep your costs down by going to a place where things are à la carte and pay only for the things you deem important. ■TIP→ Local beer is usually cheap, but wines are often imported (outside of South Africa) and are quite expensive.

When you book your trip, be clear as to whether extras such as airport transfers, use of equipment (including sleeping bags on some mobile-camping safaris), and entry fees are included in the price.

Book your trip locally, or at the last minute. Last-minute deals can offer massive discounts, as long as you're prepared to be flexible about everything to do with your trip. Alternatively, book a trip locally once you're at your destination. This is popular in Kenya and Tanzania. You can also gather a group of people at your lodging and do a group booking. This way you'll have the benefit of a guide, too, with the cost shared among a number of people. You can also save money by booking with a tour operator that is based in the country you are visiting, as you will be cutting out the commission charged by an American agent. Make sure that you thoroughly research your prospective tour operator first, however, to ensure they have a consistently good reputation. (⇨ *A good place to start is the Choosing an Outfitter chapter in this book.)*

TIPPING

Ranger/Guide: About US$20 per person, per day.

General staff: Roughly $15 a day (per couple) into the general tip box, and $15 each to your tracker and butler (if applicable), and $15 per trip for a vehicle transfer. (Note that some safari operators, such as Micato, include tips in their price, so you don't have to worry about carrying around the correct denominations.)

It's also nice if you bring thank-you cards from home to include with the tip as a personal touch. Fodor's Forum member atravelynn adds, "Put bills in an envelope for your guide and in a separate envelope with your name on it for the camp staff. Sometimes the camps have envelopes, but bringing some from home is also a good idea."

PASSPORTS AND VISAS

A valid passport is a must for travel to any African country. ⚠ Certain countries, such as South Africa, won't let you enter with a soon-to-expire passport; also, you need two blank pages in your passport to enter South Africa. If you don't have a passport, apply immediately, because the process takes approximately five to six weeks. For a greatly increased fee, the application process can be shortened to as little as one week, but leaving this detail to the last minute can be stressful. If you have a passport, check the expiration date. If it's due to expire within six months of your return date, you need to renew it at once.

■TIP→ If you're planning a honeymoon safari, make sure the bride's airline ticket, passport, and visas all use the same last name. Any discrepancies, especially between a passport and an airline ticket, will result in your trip being grounded before you even take off. Brides may want to consider waiting to change their last name until after the honeymoon. Do be sure to let the lodge know in advance that you're on your honeymoon. You'll get lots of special goodies and extra-special pampering thrown in. ⇨ *For country-specific information regarding*

DOCUMENT CHECKLIST

- Passport
- Visas, if necessary
- Airline tickets
- Proof of yellow-fever inoculation, if necessary
- Accommodation and transfer vouchers
- Car-rental reservation forms
- International driver's license
- Copy of information page of your passport

- Copy of airline tickets
- Copy of medical prescriptions
- List of credit-card numbers and international contact information for each card issuer
- Copy of travel insurance and medical-emergency evacuation policies
- Travel agent's contact numbers
- Notarized letter of consent from one parent if the other parent is traveling alone with their children

passports and visas, see the Passports and Visas section, under Planning, in each country chapter.

U.S. Passport Information **U.S. Department of State** ☎ 877/487–2778 ⊕ *www.travel.state.gov.*

U.S. Passport and Visa Expediters **A. Briggs Passport & Visa Expediters** ☎ *800/806–0581, 202/338–0111* ⊕ *www.abriggs.com.* **American Passport Express** ☎ *800/455–5166* ⊕ *www.americanpassport.com.* **Passport Express** ☎ *800/362–8196* ⊕ *www.uspassportexpressinc.com.* **Travel Document Systems** ☎ *800/874–5100, 202/638–3800* ⊕ *www.traveldocs.com.* **Travel the World Visas** ☎ *866/886–8472, 202/223–8822* ⊕ *www.world-visa.com.*

SAFETY AND PRECAUTIONS

Although most countries in Southern and East Africa are stable and safe, it's a good idea to do your homework and be fully aware of the areas you'll be traveling to before planning that once-in-a-lifetime trip.

The CIA's online World Factbook has maps and facts on the people, government, economy, and more for countries from Afghanistan to Zimbabwe. It's the fastest way to get a snapshot of a nation. It's also updated regularly and, obviously, well researched.

There's nothing like the local paper for putting your finger on the pulse. World-Newspapers.com has links to English-language newspapers, magazines, and websites in countries the world over.

The U.S. State Department's advice on the safety of a given country is probably the most conservative you'll encounter. That said, the information is updated regularly, and nearly every nation is covered. Just try to parse the language carefully. For example, a warning to "avoid all travel" carries more weight than "avoid nonessential travel," and both are much stronger than a plea to "exercise caution." A travel warning is more permanent (though not necessarily more serious) than a so-called public announcement, which carries an expiration date.

SAFARI PLANNING TIMELINE

SIX MONTHS AHEAD
- Research destinations and options and make a list of sights you want to see.
- Start a safari file to keep track of information.
- Set a budget.
- Search the Internet. Post questions on bulletin boards and narrow your choices. Watch out for fake trip reviews posted by unscrupulous travel agents.
- Choose your destination and make your reservations.
- Apply for a passport, or renew yours if it's due to expire within six months of travel time. Many countries now require at least two empty pages in your passport.
- Buy travel insurance.

THREE TO SIX MONTHS AHEAD
- Find out which travel documents you need.
- Confirm whether your destination requires visas and certified health documents.
- Arrange vaccinations or medical clearances.
- Research malaria precautions.
- Book excursions, tours, and side trips.

ONE TO THREE MONTHS AHEAD
- Create a packing checklist. ⇨ See Packing.
- Fill prescriptions for antimalarial and regular medications. Buy mosquito repellent.
- Shop for safari clothing and equipment.
- Arrange for a house and pet sitter.

ONE MONTH AHEAD
- Get copies of any prescriptions and make sure you have enough of any needed medicine to last you a few days longer than your trip.
- Confirm international flights, transfers, and lodging reservations directly with your travel agent.
- Using your packing list, start buying articles you don't have. Update the list as you go.

ONE WEEK AHEAD
- Suspend newspaper and mail delivery.
- Collect small denominations of U.S. currency ($1 and $5) for tips.
- Check antimalarial prescriptions to see whether you need to start taking medication now.
- Arrange transportation to the airport.
- Make two copies of your passport's data page. Leave one copy, and a copy of your itinerary, with someone at home; pack the other separately from your passport. Make a PDF of these pages and email them to yourself for access.

Travel Warnings Central Intelligence Agency (*CIA*). ⊕ *www.cia.gov.* **U.S. State Department** ⊕ *www.travel.state.gov.* **World-Newspapers.com** ⊕ *www. world-newspapers.com.*

TRAVEL INSURANCE

You may want to consider a comprehensive travel-insurance policy in addition to any primary insurance you already have. Travel insurance incorporates trip cancellation; trip interruption or travel delay; loss or theft of, or damage to, baggage; baggage delay; medical expenses; emergency medical transportation; and collision damage waiver if renting a car. These policies are offered by most travel-insurance companies in one comprehensive policy and vary in price based on both your total trip cost and your age.

It's important to note that travel insurance doesn't always include coverage for threats of a terrorist incident or for any war-related activity. It's important that you speak with your operator before you book to find out how they would handle such occurrences. For example, would you be fully refunded if your trip was canceled because of war or a threat of a terrorist incident? Would your trip be postponed at no additional cost to you?

■ TIP➔ Purchase travel insurance within seven days of paying your initial trip deposit. For most policies this will not only ensure your trip deposit, but also cover you for any preexisting medical conditions.

Many travel agents and tour operators stipulate that travel insurance is mandatory if you book your trip through them. This coverage isn't only for your financial protection in the event of a cancellation but also for coverage of medical emergencies and medical evacuations due to injury or illness, which often involve use of jet aircraft with hospital equipment and doctors on board and can amount to many thousands of dollars.

Consider signing up with a medical-evacuation assistance company. A membership in one of these companies gets you doctor referrals, emergency evacuation or repatriation, 24-hour hotlines for medical consultation, and other assistance. International SOS and AirMed International provide evacuation services and medical referrals. MedjetAssist offers medical evacuation.

Insurance Allianz Travel Insurance ⊕ *www.allianztravelinsurance.com.* **HTH Worldwide** ⊕ *www.hthworldwide.com.* **International Medical Group** ⊕ *www. imglobal.com.* **Travel Guard** ⊕ *www.travelguard.com.* **Wallach & Company** ⊕ *www.wallach.com.*

Medical-Assistance Companies Air Med ⊕ *www.airmed.com.* **International SOS** ⊕ *www.internationalsos.com.* **MedJet Assistance** ⊕ *www.medjetassist. com.*

VACCINATIONS

Traveling overseas is daunting enough without having to worry about all the scary illnesses you could contract. But if you do your research and plan accordingly, there will be no reason to worry.

	Yellow Fever	Malaria	Hepatitis A	Hepatitis B	Typhoid	Rabies	Polio	Other
Kenya	●	●	●	●	●	●	●	Meningitis
Tanzania	●	●	●	●	●	●	●	
South Africa	◑	●	●	●	●	●	●	
Botswana	◑	●	●	●	●	●	●	
Namibia	◑	●	●	●	●	●	●	
Zambia	◑	●	●	●	●	●	●	
Zimbabwe	◑	●	●	●	●	●	●	

KEY: ● = Necessary
● = Recommended
◑ = The government requires travelers arriving from countries where yellow fever is present to have proof that they got the vaccination

The Centers for Disease Control, or CDC, has an extremely helpful and informative website where you can find out country by country what you'll need. Remember that the CDC is going to be extremely conservative, so it's a good idea to meet with a trusted health-care professional to decide what you'll really need, which will be determined by your itinerary. We've also included the basic information on the countries we cover in the preceding chart.

Keep in mind that there's a time frame for vaccines. You should see your health provider four to six weeks before you leave for your trip. Also keep in mind that vaccines and prescriptions could run you anywhere from $1,000 to $2,000. It's important to factor this into your budget when planning, especially if your plans include a large group.

You must be up-to-date with all of your routine shots such as the measles/mumps/rubella (MMR) vaccine, and diphtheria/pertussis/tetanus (DPT) vaccine. If you're not up-to-date, usually a simple booster shot will bring you up to par. If you're traveling to northern Kenya December through June, don't be surprised if your doctor advises you to get inoculated against meningitis, as this part of the continent tends to see an outbreak during this time.

We can't stress enough the importance of taking malaria prophylactics. But be warned that all malaria medications aren't equal. Chloroquine is *not* an effective antimalarial drug. And halofantrine (marketed as Halfan), which is widely used overseas to treat malaria, has serious heart-related side effects, including death. The CDC recommend that you do *not* use halofantrine. Their website has a comprehensive list of the different malaria medications available, and which are recommended for each country. ⇨ *For more information on malaria, or other health issues while on safari, see Health below.*

Health Warnings Centers for Disease Control (*CDC*). ☎ *800/232–4636 for international travelers' health line* ⊕ *wwwnc.cdc.gov/travel.*

HEPATITIS A AND B AND OTHER BOOSTERS

Hepatitis A can be transmitted via contaminated seafood, water, or fruits and vegetables. According to the CDC, hepatitis A is the most common vaccine-preventable disease in travelers. Immunization consists of a series of two shots received six months apart. You only need to have received the first one before you travel. This should be given at least four weeks before your trip.

The CDC recommends vaccination for hepatitis B only if you might be exposed to blood (if you're a health-care worker, for example), have sexual contact with the local population, stay longer than six months, or risk exposure during medical treatment. As needed, you should receive booster shots for tetanus-diphtheria (every 10 years), measles (you're usually immunized as a child), and polio (you're usually immunized as a child).

YELLOW FEVER

Yellow fever isn't inherent in any of the countries discussed in this book. Some countries, however, such as Kenya, will require you to present a valid yellow-fever inoculation certificate if prior to arrival you traveled to a region infected with yellow fever.

PACKING

You'll be allowed one duffel-type bag, approximately 36 inches by 18 inches and a maximum of 26 kilos (57 pounds)—less on some airlines, so it's essential you check ahead—so that it can be easily packed into the baggage pods of a small plane. A personal-effects bag can go on your lap. Keep all your documents and money in this personal bag.

■TIP➔ At O.R. Tambo International Airport in Johannesburg and Cape Town International Airport you can store your bags at Bagport (⊕ www.bagport.co.za). The cost is approximately US$8 per bag per day, and the facility is open 24 hours a day, 7 days a week. Many travelers also pay to have their luggage wrapped in shrinkwrap, but locking your suitcase should be sufficient.

BINOCULARS

Binoculars are essential and come in many types and sizes. You get what you pay for, so avoid buying a cheap pair—the optics will be poor and the lenses usually don't stay aligned for long, especially if they get bumped, which they will on safari. Whatever strength you choose, pick the most lightweight pair, otherwise you'll be in for neck and shoulder strain. Take them with you on a night drive; you'll get great visuals of nocturnal animals and birds by the light of the tracker's spotlight. Many people find that when they start using binoculars and stop documenting each trip detail on film, they have a much better safari experience.

CLOTHING

You should need only three changes of clothing for an entire trip; almost all safaris include laundry as part of the package. If you're self-driving you can carry more, but washing is still easy, especially if you use drip-dry fabrics that need no ironing. On mobile safaris you can wear tops and bottoms more than once, and either bring enough underwear to last a week between lodges, or wash as you go in the bathroom sink. Unless there's continual rain (unlikely), clothes dry overnight in the hot, dry African air.

■ TIP→ In certain countries—Botswana and Tanzania, for example—the staff won't wash undergarments because it's against cultural custom.

For game walks, pack sturdy but light walking shoes or boots—in most cases durable sneakers suffice for this option. For a walking-based safari, you need sturdy, lightweight boots. Buy them well in advance of your trip so you can break them in. If possible, isolate the clothes used on your walk from the remainder of the clean garments in your bag. Bring a couple of large white plastic garbage bags for dirty laundry.

ELECTRICITY

Most of Southern Africa is on 220/240-volt alternating current (AC). The plug points are round. However, there are both large 15-amp three-prong sockets (with a ground connection) and smaller 5-amp two-prong sockets. Most lodges have adapter plugs, especially for recharging camera batteries; check before you go, or purchase a universal plug adapter before you leave home.

Safari hotels in the Serengeti, the private reserve areas outside Kruger National Park, and the less rustic private lodges in South Africa are likely to provide you with plug points and plugs, and some offer hair dryers and electric-razor sockets as well (check this before you go). Lodges on limited generator and solar power are usually able to charge cameras, as long as you have the right plug.

TOILETRIES AND SUNDRIES

Most hotels and game lodges provide toiletries such as soap, shampoo, and insect repellent, so you don't need to overpack these items. In the larger lodges in South Africa's national parks and private game reserves, stores and gift shops are fairly well stocked with clothing and guidebooks; in self-drive and self-catering areas, shops also carry food and drink. Many lodges have small shops with a selection of books, clothing, and curios.

Continued on page 58

SAFARI
STYLE

A frequently asked question on the Fodor's Forums is, "What do I wear on safari?" Your first thoughts might be of Meryl Streep in *Out of Africa* or Grace Kelly (seen here). But Hollywood didn't exactly get it right. Don't worry though, because we're here to help you figure out exactly what is and is not appropriate safari wear. Remember, khaki is the safari black.

WHAT TO WEAR

SUNGLASSES: The sun is bright here, and good UV protection is a must. Glasses also keep flying debris (like sand) out of your eyes. Plus you never know when you might see a spitting cobra—they aim for the eyes.

INSECT REPELLENT: Make sure yours has at least 20% DEET and is sweat resistant. We suggest OFF! Active. It has 25% DEET and comes in a 3-ounce pump spray bottle—perfect for those Transportation Security Administration (TSA) restrictions.

HAT: This is a must to keep off the sun and keep you in the shade. Make sure it has a brim all the way around and is packable and breathable. The Tilley hat (www.tilley.com) has been highly recommended in the Fodor's Forums.

CLOTHES: Make sure your clothes are cotton (read: breathable). Also we suggest you wear long pants in light earth colors—khaki and brown are best. Pants keep the bugs off, help prevent sunburn, and protect your legs from thorny bushes. Another thing to keep in mind: If you don't want to lug a bag, cargo pants are great for storage.

WALKING SHOES: The key words here are "sturdy," "support," and "traction." Though you probably won't be walking miles, you will be in and out of your vehicle and might be able to go on a walking safari. Hi-Tec (www.hi-tec.com) is an excellent brand with styles for all occasions.

HOT...

■ Usually your guide will have water for you, but if you're traveling alone it's very important that you bring water. It's imperative that you keep yourself hydrated when you're in the sun and heat.

■ Bring layers. It can be very cold in the early mornings and late evenings.

■ A photographer's vest is not a bad idea if you plan to carry a lot of film or memory cards.

■ Most lodges have pools, so make sure you pack a swim suit and a sarong. The latter is important to use as a cover-up.

WHAT NOT TO WEAR

LOTS OF MAKEUP:
Your daily regime should consist of slathering on sunscreen and spraying insect repellent, not applying blush or foundation.

DESIGNER OUTFITS:
We think this goes without saying, but one never knows. Leave the fancy threads at home. They're bound to get ruined if you bring them.

CAMOUFLAGE: This is a big no-no. Warring factions in Africa wear camouflage, and you don't want to be confused with the military or appear to be making fun of the situation.

LEAVE THE BLING AT HOME: A safari is not a fashion show, and though you may get "dressed up" for dinner, there's no need for gold bracelets or diamonds. The shininess, not to mention the clinking of jewelry, will alert the animals to your presence. And when you're in the major cities, why invite trouble? You can live without your bling for a few days.

ANYTHING WITH HEELS: Prada or Gucci? Try L.L. Bean or EMS. You need sturdy, practical footwear. Again, a safari is not a fashion show. It's all about being comfortable and enjoying the experience.

...OR NOT

■ Don't wear clothes in any variation of blue or black, especially if you're traveling to tsetse-fly areas. These colors attract the pesky sleeping-sickness transmitters.

■ Don't wear perfume. Animals have an incredible sense of smell and will sense your arrival immediately and be gone before you can say "Greater Kudu."

■ Don't wear white. It reflects sunlight and startles animals.

■ Don't overpack. Most of the small airplanes you'll be taking to your camps have luggage-weight limits.

PACKING CHECKLIST

Light, khaki, or neutral-color clothes are universally worn on safari and were first used in Africa as camouflage by the South African Boers, and then by the British Army that fought them during the South African War. Light colors also help to deflect the harsh sun and are less likely than dark colors to attract mosquitoes. Don't wear camouflage gear. Do wear layers of clothing that you can strip off as the sun gets hotter and put back on as the sun goes down.

⚠ The African sun is harsh, and if you're even remotely suscep-tible to burning, especially coming from a northern winter, don't skimp on sunscreens and moisturizers.

■ Three cotton T-shirts

■ Two long-sleeve cotton shirts

■ Two pairs shorts or two skirts in summer

■ Two pairs long pants (three pairs in winter)

■ Optional: sweatshirt and sweatpants, which can double as sleepwear

■ One smart-casual dinner outfit

■ Underwear and socks

■ Walking shoes or sneakers

■ Sandals

■ Bathing suit

■ Warm thigh-length padded jacket and sweater in winter

■ Windbreaker or rain poncho

■ Camera equipment, extra batteries or charger, and memory cards

■ Contact lenses, including extras

■ Eyeglasses

■ Binoculars

■ Small flashlight

■ Personal toiletries

■ Malaria tablets

■ Sunscreen and lip balm with SPF 30 or higher, moisturizer, and hair conditioner

■ Antihistamine cream

■ Insect repellent

■ Basic first-aid kit (aspirin, bandages, antidiarrheal, antiseptic cream, etc.)

■ Tissues and/or premoistened wipes

■ Warm hat, scarf, and gloves in winter

■ Sun hat and sunglasses (Polaroid and UV-protected ones)

■ Documents and money (cash, credit cards, etc.).

■ A notebook and pens

■ Travel and field guides

■ A couple of large white plastic garbage bags

■ Ziplock bags to keep documents dry and protect electronics from dust

■ U.S. dollars in small denomina-tions ($1, $5, $10) for tipping

ON SAFARI

Your safari will be one of the most memorable trips you'll ever take, and it's essential that your African experience matches the one you've always imagined. Nothing should be left to chance, and that includes where you'll stay and how you'll get around.

The whos, whats, and hows still need to come into focus. If you have questions like, "Where's the best place to sit in a game-drive vehicle? Can you get near a honey badger? Where do you go to the bathroom in the bush?," then read on.

By the way, "bush" is a term used to describe the natural setting of your safari—be it in forests, plains, or on riverbanks. The expression "going to the bush" means going away from urban areas and into the wilderness.

ACCOMMODATIONS

The days are long gone when legendary 19th-century explorer Dr. David Livingstone pitched his travel-stained tent under a tree and ate his sparse rations. But whether you go simple in a basic safari tent with an adjacent bucket shower and long-drop toilet, choose ultracomfort in a megatent or canvas-and-thatch chalet, or go totally over the top in a glass-walled aerie-cum-penthouse with a state-of-the-art designer interior, you'll still feel very much part of the bush.

LUXURY LODGES

Some would say that using the word "luxury" with "safari lodge" is redundant, as all such lodges fall into this category. But there's luxurious, and then there's *luxurious*. Options in the latter category range from *Out of Africa*–type accommodations with antique furniture, crystal, and wrought-iron chandeliers to thatch-roofed stone chalets, Tuscan villas, and suites that wouldn't seem out of place in midtown Manhattan. In nearly all, you can expect to find air-conditioning; in many there will be a small library, a spa, a gift shop, and Internet service—often in a "business center" (a computer in the main lodge) or Wi-Fi. You may even have your own plunge pool.

PERMANENT TENTED CAMPS

Think luxurious, oh-so-comfortable, and spacious . . . in a tent. This is no ordinary tent, though. Each has its own bathroom, usually with an outdoor shower; a wooden deck with table and chairs that overlooks the bush; carpet or wooden floors; big "windows"; and an inviting four-poster (usually) bed with puffy pillows and fluffy blankets (for those cold winter months). The public space will comprise a bar, a lounge, dining areas, viewing decks, usually a pool, and a curio shop. Some will have Wi-Fi, air-conditioning, and private plunge pools.

MOBILE TENTED CAMPS

This option varies enormously. You could have the original, roomy walk-in dome tent (complete with canvas bedrolls, crisp cotton bedding on G.I. stretchers, open-air flush toilets, and bucket showers) that's ready and waiting for you at day's end. Or you could have luxury tents

Safari Photo Tips

All the safaris included in this book are photographic (game-viewing) safaris. That said, if you spend your entire safari with one eye closed and the other peering through a camera lens, you may miss all the other sensual elements that contribute to the great show that is the African bush. And more than likely, your pictures won't look like the photos you see in books about African safaris. A professional photographer can spend a full year in the field to produce a book, so you're time might be better spent taking snaps of your trip and buying a book to take home.

■TIP→ No matter what kind of camera you bring, be sure to keep it tightly sealed in plastic bags while you're traveling to protect it from dust. (Dust is especially troublesome in Namibia.) Tuck your equipment away when the wind kicks up. You should have one or more cloth covers while you're working, and clean your equipment every day if you can.

Learning some basics about the wildlife that you expect to see on your safari will help you capture some terrific shots of the animals. If you know something about their behavior patterns ahead of time, you'll be primed to capture action, like when the hippos start to roar. Learning from your guide and carefully observing the wildlife once you're there will also help you gauge just when to click your shutter.

The trick to taking great pictures has three components: first is always good light. An hour after sunrise and before sunset are the magical times, because the light is softer and textures pop. For the few hours of harsh light each

side of midday, you might as well put your camera away. The second component is framing. Framing a scene so that the composition is simple gives an image potency; with close-ups, fill the frame for maximum impact. Using objects of known size in the foreground or middle ground will help establish scale. The third component is capturing sharp images: use a tripod or a beanbag to rest the camera on while in a vehicle. When using a long lens (upward of 200mm), you can't hand-hold a steady shot; you must have some support if you want your photos to be clear.

DIGITAL CAMERAS AND SMART-PHONES

Cameras with eight megapixels of resolution can print high-quality, smooth A4 or letter-size prints; images with five-megapixel resolution are fine as well. Recent-generation smart-phones (e.g., iPhone, Samsung Galaxy, Motorola Droid) work pretty well, too. You might consider investing in a telephoto lens to shoot wildlife, as you are often too far away from the animals to capture details with the zoom lenses generally built into most smart-phones and point-and-shoot cameras. This may mean upgrading to a more robust camera. A tripod or beanbag is also helpful; it'll stabilize your camera, especially when a zoom lens is extended.

Buy or borrow as many memory cards as you can—you'll use them. You may want to use multiple smaller memory cards to minimize the risk of losing an entire card's worth of images. And, as always, remember to bring extra batteries or your battery charger.

(with crystal chandeliers, antique rugs, and shining silver) that stay in one place for a few months during peak seasons. They're all fully serviced (the staff travels with the tents), and you'll dine under the stars or sip coffee as the sun rises.

NATIONAL PARK ACCOMMODATIONS

What you'll get in this category depends on which park you're in and what type of lodgings you're looking for. Accommodations can vary from campsites to simple one-room rondavels, or round huts, with en suite bathrooms; safari tents to two- to four-bed cottages; or possibly a top-of-the-range guesthouse that sleeps eight people. With the exception of some camping sites, and some places in South Africa, all national-park accommodations are fully serviced with staff to look after you.

CHILDREN ON SAFARI

Most safari operators and private game reserves don't accept children under a certain age, usually under 8, but sometimes the age limit is as high as 12. This age limit is largely for safety reasons. Animals often respond, not in a positive manner, to something that is younger, slower, or smaller than they are. And even though you might think your six- or seven-year-old adores all sorts of animals and bugs, you'd be surprised how overwhelmed kids can become, out of the comfort of their home and backyard, by the size and multitude of African insects and wildlife.

Take into account, also, that when you're following a strange schedule (with jet lag) and getting in and out of small planes, safari vehicles, boats, and the like with other people whom you probably won't know, there often is no time to deal with recalcitrant children—and fussing will, you can be guaranteed, annoy the other people in your plane or lodge, who have spent a great deal of money for what may be a once-in-a-lifetime safari trip.

One option, if you can afford it, is to book a private safari where no other people are involved and you dictate the schedule. Many private lodges will rent you the entire property for the length of your stay; this is often the only way these camps allow children under age eight on safari. At the very least, a camp will require that you pay for a private safari vehicle and guide if you have children under 12. Be advised that, even if you're renting the whole camp, babies and toddlers still aren't allowed out on game-viewing trips.

Another great family option is to stay with &Beyond, a safari operator with children's programs at several of its upscale camps throughout Southern and East Africa. While you follow your own program, your kids pursue their own wilderness activities; and you all meet up later for meals and other activities.

KID-FRIENDLY CAMPS

Basecamp Masai Mara, Kenya. Located just outside the Masai Mara game reserve, this relaxed camp makes children feel very welcome. There's an activity club for kids aged 6-plus, and kids 15-plus can go on walking safaris. On top of this, the camp has impressive eco-tourism credentials.
Berg-en-Dal, Kruger Park, South Africa. Kids can explore in safety at this

CONSIDERATIONS FOR CHILDREN

Consider the following if you're thinking about bringing children to a private safari lodge:

■ **Are they afraid of the dark?** A safari camp that runs on generator-powered batteries will have minimal lights at night.

■ **Are they startled easily?** Large animals may come quite close to rooms or tents or near safari vehicles.

■ **Are they comfortable with strangers?** Most meals at safari lodges are at communal tables, and shared six-seat planes are the basic form of transportation between remote safari camps.

■ **Are they troubled by bugs?** The African bush can be filled with moths as big as small birds as well as a host of other flying and crawling insects.

■ **Are they picky eaters?** Meals are usually buffet-style and food for camps is often ordered at least a month in advance, so your child's favorite food may not be available.

attractive, fenced camp, which has a great pool and curio shop. Get them to walk around the camp's perimeter and spot game.

Kwandwe Ecca Lodge, South Africa. The Eastern Cape is malaria-free, and this lodge is exceedingly child-friendly, with flexible dining, free child care, and a play area and special activities for kids, such as going on a frog safari or on game drives to see nondangerous wildlife.

Ngorongoro Serena Safari Lodge, Tanzania. Apart from game drives, there are guided walks to the crater's rim or along the nature trail around the lodge, and culturally interactive trips to local schools or villages.

Okaukuejo, Etosha, Namibia. The 24-hour floodlighted water hole—regarded as one of the finest in Africa—will keep kids entranced for hours. They can sit, stand, or run (quietly) around.

Seba Camp, Botswana. Children of all ages are welcome here, which is unusual for Botswana, but families with young kids will need to hire private vehicles for game drives. Facilities include family rooms with private plunge pools, toy boxes, and sandpits, and there's a special kids' menu.

A much cheaper alternative is also one of the most enjoyable for a safari as a family: a self-driving trip where you stay at national parks. No destination is better in this regard than Kruger National Park in South Africa, where there are comfortable accommodations and lots of other families around. You'll be able to set your own schedule, rent a cottage large enough for the entire family, and buy and prepare food you know your children will eat.

It's best not to visit malarial areas with children under age 10. Young kidneys are especially vulnerable to both the effects of malaria and the side effects of malaria prophylactics. You might opt to practice stringent nonchemical preventive measures, but know the risks: malaria's effects on young children are much worse than they are on older people.

2

Babies aren't allowed in safari vehicles. Some lodges, such as those at MalaMala, provide babysitting services for infants. The sound of an infant crying puts most predators on alert—dangerous to other passengers as well as the child. Keep in mind also that the bush is often a hot and dusty place with little in the way of baby-friendly amenities. You'd have to bring all your own supplies, and if something were to go wrong there would be no way to get immediate help until a flight could be arranged.

COMMUNICATIONS

You will notice that pretty much everyone in Africa has a cell phone, and areas with 3G reception are increasing rapidly and can include remote areas. Don't count on it, though. This is Africa, and networks can be down. If you urgently need to get in touch with home, most camps have a radio or satellite phone.

INTERNET

Most lodges will have a computer with Internet access, but remember that there's often one computer for all the guests to use, and service is probably coming via satellite so availability may be limited. Many have Wi-Fi, too, although the service can be erratic and slow.

PHONES

> ### TELEPHONE COUNTRY CODES
>
> ■ United States: 1
> ■ Botswana: 267
> ■ Kenya: 254
> ■ Namibia: 264
> ■ South Africa: 27
> ■ Tanzania: 255
> ■ Zambia: 260
> ■ Zimbabwe: 263
>
> Note: When dialing from abroad, drop the initial 0 from local area codes.

If you really want to save on international phone calls, the best advice is to provide a detailed itinerary back home and agree on a schedule for calls. Internet calling like Skype may work well from the United States, but it's not always functional in Africa, unless you're on a reliable high-speed Wi-Fi or 3G connection. However, if you have a South African "free" cell phone (meaning you can receive calls for free; all phones using a South Africa SIM card do this), someone in the United States can call you from their Skype account, for reasonable per-minute charges, and you won't be charged. You can also buy a cheap local SIM card, but remember that any phone that you take abroad must be unlocked by your company in order for it to accept a different SIM card.

Cell phones can be rented by the day, week, or longer from the airport on your arrival, but this is an expensive option. If you plan on bringing a U.S. cell phone while you're traveling, know that plans change frequently, so try to gather as many details before leaving to figure out which plan is right for you. Some allow free calls to your number, but charge rates close to landline calls if you call the United States. If you don't text message at home, you'll learn to in Africa, where a simple text message costs a fraction of the cost of making an actual call. This is a handy option for meeting up with friends, but for making hotel reservations, it's best to make the call. You can use Skype to make calls to local landlines or mobile numbers, if there is a decent 3G connection—it's cheaper than a straight call and reception is often better.

The least complicated way to make and receive phone calls is to obtain international roaming service from your cell-phone service provider before you leave home, but this can be expensive and often has to be activated before you leave home. Make sure your phone's roaming capabilities are turned off, though, if you're just using it to receive calls and texts. ■ TIP➡ At this writing most Verizon customers can't use their phones in Africa, so call first to find out your coverage.

⇨ *For country-specific information on phones, see the Communication section, under Planning, in each country chapter.*

GAME DRIVES

In most regions the best time to find game is in the early morning and early evening, when the animals are most active, although old Africa hands will tell you that you can come across good game at any time of day. Stick to the philosophy "you never know what's around the next corner," and keep your eyes and ears wide open all the time. If your rest camp offers guided night drives on open vehicles with spotlights—go for it. You'll rarely be disappointed, seeing not only big game but also a lot of fascinating little critters that surface only at night. Book your night drive in advance or as soon as you get to camp.

Arm yourself with specialized books on mammals and birds rather than a more general one that tries to cover too much. Airports, lodges, and camp shops stock a good range, but try to bring one with you and do a bit of boning up in advance. Any bird guide by Ken Newman (Struik Publishers) and the *Sasol Guide to Birds* are recommended.

Many national parks have reception areas with charts that show the most recent sightings of wildlife in the area. To be sure you see everything you want to, stop at the nearest reception and ask about a spotting chart, or just chat with the other drivers, rangers, and tourists you may encounter there, who can tell you what they've seen and where.

BATHROOM BREAKS
On your game drive you'll very likely be pointed to a nearby bush (which the ranger checks out before you use it). Tissues and toilet paper are usually available in the vehicle (but you may want to make sure). Sometimes there might be a toilet—well, actually, it'll very likely be a hole in the ground below a toilet seat—called drop toilets. Bury any paper you use. If you have an emergency, ask your ranger to stop the vehicle and he or she will scout a suitable spot.

GAME RANGERS AND TRACKERS
Game rangers (sometimes referred to as guides) tend to be of two types: those who've come to conservation by way of hunting and those who are professional conservationists. In both cases they have vast experience with and knowledge of the bush and the animals that inhabit it. Rangers often work in conjunction with trackers, who spot animals,

Making friends with giraffes in South Africa

and advise the rangers where to go. Often a tracker will be busy searching out animal tracks, spoor, and other clues to nearby wildlife while the ranger drives and discusses the animals and their environment. Rangers often communicate with each other via radio when there's been a good sighting.

The quality of your bush experience depends heavily on your guide or game ranger and tracker. A ranger wears many hats while on safari: he's there to entertain you, protect you, and put you as close to the wilderness as possible while serving as bush mechanic, first-aid specialist, and host. He'll often eat meals with you, will explain animal habits and behavior while out in the bush, and, if you're on foot, will keep you alive in the presence of an excitable elephant, buffalo, hippo, or lion. This is no small feat, and each ranger has his particular strengths. Because of the intensity of the safari experience, with its exposure to potentially dangerous animals and tricky situations, your relationship with your guide or ranger is one of trust, friendliness, and respect. Misunderstandings may sometimes occur, but you're one step closer to ensuring that all goes well if you know the protocols and expectations.

INTERACTING WITH YOUR RANGER
Acknowledge that your guide is a professional and an expert in the field, and defer to his knowledge. Instead of trying to show how much you know, follow the example of the hunter, which is to walk quietly and take notice of all the little signs around you. Save social chatter with the guide for when you're back at camp, not out on a game drive. Rangers appreciate questions, which give them an idea of your range of knowledge and of how much detail to include in their animal

descriptions. However, if you like to ask a lot of questions, save some for later, especially as several other people are likely to be in the safari vehicle with you. Carry a pocket notebook on game drives and jot down questions as they occur; you can then bring them up at dinner or around the campfire, when your ranger has more time to talk and everyone can participate in the discussion.

Don't let your ranger "guide by the numbers"—providing only a list of an animal's attributes. Politely ask questions and show you'd like to know more. Even the best guides may experience "bush burnout" by the end of a busy safari season with demanding clients, but any guide worthy of the title always goes out of his way to give you the best possible experience. If you suspect yours has a case of burnout, or just laziness, you have a right to ask for certain things. There's never any harm in asking, and you can't expect your guide to read your mind about what you like. If, for example, you have a preference for birds, insects, or whatever, ask your guide to spend time on these subjects. You may be surprised by how happy he is to oblige.

BUSH WALKS

Guided bush walks vary, but usually a maximum of eight guests walk in single file with the armed ranger up front and the tracker at the back. A bush walk is a more intimate experience than a drive. You're up close with the bush and with your fellow walkers and guides. Your guide will brief you thoroughly about where and how to walk, emergency procedures, and the like. If you're in a national park, you'll most likely have to pay an additional fee to have an armed park ranger escort you on your walk.

VEHICLES ON GAME DRIVES

Your safari transportation is determined by your destination and could range from custom-made game-viewing vehicles (full-service safari) to a combi or minivan (basic safari or self-drive). There shouldn't be more than six people per vehicle. To make sure you experience every view, suggest to your ranger that visitors rotate seats for each drive. Be warned if you're going it alone: roads in Africa range from superb to bone crunching. Plan your route carefully, arm yourself with reliable maps, and get up-to-date road conditions before you go.

In closed vehicles, which are used by private touring companies operating in Kruger National Park, sit as close to the driver-guide as possible so you can get in and out of the vehicle more easily and get the best views.

OPEN-SIDED LAND ROVERS

This is the most common game-viewing vehicle, especially in **South Africa, Tanzania,** and **Botswana,** and is usually a Land Rover or a Land Cruiser. Each vehicle seats six to eight people. Vehicles that have raised, stepped seating—meaning the seats in back are higher than the ones in front—are used for game drives. There are usually three rows of seats after the driver's row; the norm at a luxury lodge is to have two people per row. The more expensive the camp, the fewer people in the vehicle. Sit beside the ranger/driver if you're a bit unsteady, because you won't have to climb up into the rear. In the front row you'll have the clearest conversations with the ranger, but farther back you'll have a clearer, elevated view over the front of the car. The back seats tend to be bumpy, but you get great views.

POP TOPS

Used mainly in **Kenya,** because of dirt, dust, and rain (and cheetahs, who like to jump on the roof or hood of the vehicle!), these hard-topped minivans pop up so you can stand up, get a better view, and take photos in every direction. If you're claustrophobic or very tall, this might not be the vehicle for you, but there are outfitters that have larger vehicles that can "stretch." If it gets really hot outside, you'll be happy to close up and turn on the air-conditioning. Make sure water and sodas are available.

MINIVANS

It's unlikely that you'll use one of these unless you're on a very cheap safari or a self-drive—they are, however, perfect for the **Namibia Desert.** The advantage is that they sit high off the ground and provide much better views; some outfitters offer vehicles that can expand. If you're self-driving, make sure you get a van with air-conditioning and power steering. The farther north you go, check out your prospective vehicle's year and make sure it's as recent as possible.

SMALL PLANES

As many camps and lodges are inaccessible by land, or are in very remote places, you'll often fly in a 6- to 10-seat plane. Always take a bottle of water with you (small planes can get very hot), and make sure you have medication ready if you're prone to motion sickness. Keep in mind the strictly enforced luggage restriction: usually 12 kg (26 lbs) of luggage in a soft bag that can squeeze into the plane's small hold, but check in advance. Flights can be bumpy, and landing strips are often just baked earth. Also keep in mind there are no bathrooms on these planes, which, if you're practicing good hydration, can be problematic for flights that are more than an hour!

WATERCRAFT

If your lodge is on or near a river, expect to go out in a boat. Options range from the big sunset safari boats with bars and bathrooms on the **Zambezi** and **Chobe rivers** to a six- or eight-seater along the **Okavango** and smaller rivers, where your amenities include a cool box of drinks and snacks but no toilet. One of the highlights of your stay in the Okavango Delta will be gliding in a *mokoro* (a canoe) poled by an expert local waterman through papyrus-fringed channels where hippos and crocs lurk.

HEALTH

Of all the horror stories and fantastic nightmares about meeting your end in the bush, the problem you're most likely to encounter will be of your own doing: dehydration. Also be wary of malaria, motion sickness, and intestinal problems. By taking commonsense precautions, your safari will be uneventful from a health perspective but memorable in every other way.

The Travel Health Online website is a good source to check out before you travel because it compiles primarily health and some safety information from a variety of official sources, and was created by a medical publishing company. The CDC has information on health risks associated with almost every country on the planet, as well as what precautions to take. The World Health Organization (WHO) is the health arm of the United Nations and has information by topic and by country. Its clear, well-written publication *International Travel and Health,* which you can download from the website, covers everything you need to know about staying healthy abroad.

Health Warnings Centers for Disease Control (*CDC*). ☎ *800/232–4636 for international travelers' health line* ⊕ *wwwnc.cdc.gov/travel.* **Netcare Travel Clinic** ☎ *011/898–6520* ⊕ *www.travelclinic.co.za.* **Travel Health Online** ⊕ *www.tripprep.com.* **World Health Organization** (*WHO*). ⊕ *www.who.int.*

DEHYDRATION AND OVERHEATING

The African sun is hot and the air is dry, and sweat evaporates quickly in these conditions. You might not realize how much bodily fluid you're losing as a result. Wear a hat, lightweight clothing, and sunscreen—all of which will help your body cope with high temperatures. If you're prone to low blood sugar or have a sensitive stomach, consider bringing along rehydration salts, available at camping stores, to balance your body's fluids and keep you going when you feel listless.

Drink at least two to three quarts of water a day, and in extreme heat conditions as much as three to four quarts of water or juice. Drink more if you're exerting yourself physically. Alcohol is dehydrating, so try to limit consumption on hot or long travel days. If you do overdo it at dinner with wine or spirits, or even caffeine, you need to drink even more water to recover the fluid lost as your body processes the alcohol. Antimalarial medications are also very dehydrating, so it's important to drink water while you're taking this medicine.

Don't rely on thirst to tell you when to drink; people often don't feel thirsty until they're a little dehydrated. At the first sign of dry mouth, exhaustion, or headache, drink water, because dehydration is the likely culprit. ■TIP➔ **To test for dehydration, pinch the skin on the back of your hand and see if it stays in a peak; if it does, you're dehydrated.** Drink a solution of ½ teaspoon salt and 4 tablespoons sugar dissolved in a quart of water to replace electrolytes.

Heat cramps stem from a low salt level due to excessive sweating. These muscle pains usually occur in the abdomen, arms, or legs. When a child says he can't take another step, ask if he has cramps. When cramps occur, stop all activity and sit quietly in a cool spot and drink water. Don't do anything strenuous for a few hours after the cramps subside. If heat cramps persist for more than an hour, seek medical assistance.

INSECTS

In summer ticks may be a problem, even in open areas close to cities. If you intend to walk or hike anywhere, use a suitable insect repellent. After your walk, examine your body and clothes for ticks, looking carefully for pepper ticks, which are tiny but may cause tick-bite fever. If

Long-sleeve clothing will make your evenings comfortable and reduce insect bites.

you're bitten, keep an eye on the bite. Most people suffer no more than an itchy bump, so don't panic. If the tick was infected, however, the bite will swell, itch, and develop a black necrotic center. This is a sure sign that you'll develop tick-bite fever, which usually hits after about 8 to 12 days. Symptoms may be mild or severe, depending on the patient. This disease isn't usually life-threatening in healthy adults, but it's horribly unpleasant. ■TIP➜ Check your boots for spiders and other crawlies and shake your clothes out before getting dressed.

Always keep a lookout for mosquitoes. Even in nonmalarial areas they're extremely irritating. When walking anywhere in the bush, watch out for snakes. If you see one, give it a wide berth and you should be fine. Snakes really bite only when they're taken by surprise, so you don't want to step on a napping mamba.

INTESTINAL UPSET

Micro-fauna and -flora differ in every region of Africa, so if you drink unfiltered water, add ice to your soda, or eat fruit from a roadside stand, you might get traveler's diarrhea. All reputable hotels and lodges have filtered, clean tap water or provide sterilized drinking water, and nearly all camps and lodges have supplies of bottled water. If you're traveling outside organized safari camps in rural Africa or are unsure of local water, carry plenty of bottled water and follow the CDC's advice for fruits and vegetables: boil it, cook it, peel it, or forget it. If you're going on a mobile safari, ask about drinking water.

MALARIA

The most serious health problem facing travelers is malaria. The risk is medium at the height of the summer and very low in winter. All travelers heading into malaria-endemic regions should consult a health-care professional at least one month before departure for advice. Unfortunately, the malarial agent *Plasmodium* seems to be able to develop a hardy resistance to new prophylactic drugs quickly, so the best prevention is to avoid being bitten by mosquitoes in the first place.

After sunset, wear light-color (mosquitoes and tsetse flies are attracted to dark surfaces), loose, long-sleeve shirts, long pants, and shoes and socks, and apply mosquito repellent (containing DEET) generously. Always sleep in a mosquito-proof room or tent, and if possible, keep a fan going in your room. If you're pregnant or trying to conceive, some malaria medicines are safe to use but in general it's best to avoid malaria areas entirely.

Generally speaking, the risk is much lower in the dry season (May–October) and peaks immediately after the first rains, which should be in November, but El Niño has made that a lot less predictable.

If you've been bitten by an infected mosquito, you can expect to feel the effects anywhere from 7 to 90 days afterward. Typically you'll feel like you have the flu, with worsening high fever, chills and sweats, headache, and muscle aches. In some cases this is accompanied by abdominal pain, diarrhea, and a cough. If it's not treated you could die. It's possible to treat malaria after you've contracted it, but this shouldn't be your long-term strategy for dealing with the disease. ⚠ **If you feel ill even several months after you return home, tell your doctor that you've been in a malaria-infected area.**

MEDICAL CARE AND MEDICINE

As a foreigner, you'll be expected to pay in full for any medical services, so check your existing health plan to see whether you're covered while abroad, and supplement it if necessary. South African doctors are generally excellent. The equipment and training in private clinics rival the best in the world, but public hospitals tend to suffer from overcrowding and underfunding and are best avoided.

OVER-THE-COUNTER REMEDIES

You can buy over-the-counter medication in pharmacies and supermarkets. For expediency, however, you should bring your own supply for your trip and rely on pharmacies just for emergency medication.

MOTION SICKNESS

If you're prone to motion sickness, be sure to examine your safari itinerary closely. Though most landing strips for chartered planes aren't paved but rather grass, earth, or gravel, landings are smooth most of the time. If you're going on safari to northern Botswana (the Okavango Delta, specifically), know that small planes and unpaved airstrips are the main means of transportation between camps; these trips can be very bumpy, hot, and a little dizzying even if you're not prone to motion sickness. If you're not sure how you'll react, take motion-sickness pills just in case. Most of the air transfers take an average of only 30 minutes and the rewards will be infinitely greater than the pains.

2

■TIP➜ When you fly in small planes, take a sun hat and a pair of sunglasses. If you sit in the front seat next to the pilot, or on the side of the sun, you'll experience harsh glare that could give you a severe headache and exacerbate motion sickness.

SWIMMING

⚠ Don't swim in lakes or streams. Many lakes and streams, particularly east of the watershed divide (i.e., in rivers flowing toward the Indian Ocean), are infected with *bilharzia* (schistosomiasis), a parasite carried by a small freshwater snail. The microscopic fluke enters through the skin of swimmers or waders, attaches itself to the intestines or bladder, and lays eggs. Avoid wading in still waters or in areas close to reeds. If you've been wading or swimming in dubious water, dry yourself off vigorously with a towel immediately upon exiting the water, as this may help to dislodge any flukes before they can burrow into your skin. Fast-moving water is considered safe. If you've been exposed, pop into a pharmacy and purchase a course of treatment and take it to be safe. If your trip is ending shortly after your exposure, take the medicine home and have a check-up once you get home. Bilharzia is easily diagnosed, and it's also easily treated in the early stages.

PEOPLE WITH DISABILITIES

Having a disability doesn't mean you can't go on safari. It's important, however, to plan carefully to ensure that your needs can be adequately met. South African lodges, especially the high-end private ones, are the easiest to navigate and have the fewest steps. Keep in mind that all-terrain 4x4 vehicles don't have seat belts, so you need enough muscle control to keep yourself upright while the vehicle bumps along the unpaved roads. Getting in and out of these elevated vehicles can also be challenging. MalaMala Game Reserve in South Africa is completely accessible and even has specially equipped four-wheel-drive safari vehicles with harness seat belts. Many of Kruger's camps have special accommodations.

SEASONS

The seasons in sub-Saharan Africa are opposite of those in North America. Summer is December through March, autumn is April and May, winter is June through September, and spring is October and November. The Seychelles follows a similar pattern, with the notable addition that stormier seas make winter unsuitable for keen divers.

HIGH SEASON/DRY SEASON

High season, also called dry season, refers to the winter months in East and Southern Africa when there's little to no rain at all. Days are sunny and bright, but the nights are cool. In the desert, temperatures can plummet to below freezing, but you'll be snug and warm in your tent wherever you stay. The landscape will be barren and dry (read: not very attractive), but vegetation is low and surface water is scarce, making it easier to spot game. This is the busiest tourist time.

The exception is South Africa and Seychelles, where high season is linked with the summer vacation schedules of South Africans (December–mid-January), and both the European summer vacations (July and August) and Christmas holidays (December and January) in the Seychelles.

LOW SEASON/RAINY SEASON

When we say "low season," we're saying that this is the rainy season. Although the rains are intermittent—often occurring in late afternoon—the bush and vegetation are high and it's more difficult to spot game. It can also get very hot and humid during this time. However, the upside is that there are far fewer tourists, lodge rates are much cheaper (often half price), and the bush is beautifully lush and green. Plus there are lots of baby animals, and if you're a birder all the migrant species are back from their winter habitats. Seychelles' low season occurs during the cusp times of February through April, October, and November, which can be the nicest times to visit in terms of both weather (especially April and November) and better prices.

SHOULDER SEASON

The shoulder season occurs between summer and winter; it's fall in the United States. The rains are just beginning, tourist numbers are decreasing, and the vegetation is starting to die off. Lodges will offer cheaper rates.

To find out exactly what the weather will be for your destination, **African Weather Forecasts** (⊕ *www.africanweather.net*) lists weather information for the entire continent.

TYPES OF SAFARIS

FLY-IN SAFARIS

The mode of transportation for fly-in safaris is as central to the experience as the accommodations. In places such as northern Botswana, where few roads are paved, or northern Namibia, where distances make road transfers impractical, small bush planes take you from lodge to lodge. These planes are usually six-seat Cessna 206 craft flown by bush pilots. The planes have no air-conditioning and in summer can be very hot, especially in the afternoon. Bring a bottle of water with you. And go to the bathroom before flying; there are no restrooms on these planes. Most flights are short—approximately 30 minutes or so—but some can be up to an hour.

Flying from destination to destination is a special experience. The planes stay at low altitudes, allowing you to spot game along the way: you might see elephant and buffalo herds lined up drinking along the edges of remote water holes, or large numbers of zebras walking across the plains. Fly-in safaris also allow you to cover more territory than other types of safaris. In Botswana, for example, the trip between the diverse game destinations of the Moremi Wildlife Reserve in the Okavango Delta and northern Chobe National Park is 40 minutes by plane; it would take six hours by vehicle, if a road between these locations existed.

		Summer				Fall		Winter				Spring	
		Dec	Jan	Feb	Mar	Apr	May	Jun	Jul	Aug	Sep	Oct	Nov
BOTSWANA	The Okavango Delta	●	●	●	●	●	●	●	●	●	●	●	●
	Moremi Wildlife Reserve	●	●	●	●	●	●	●	●	●	●	●	●
	Chobe Nat'l Park	●	●	●	●	●	●	●	●	●	●	●	●
	Kwando Game Reserve	●	●	●	●	●	●	●	●	●	●	●	●
KENYA	Masai Mara	●	●	●	●	●	●	●	●	●	●	●	●
	Amboseli Nat'l Park	●	●	●	●	●	●	●	●	●	●	●	●
	Tsavo Nat'l Park	●	●	●	●	●	●	●	●	●	●	●	●
	Laikipia Plateau	●	●	●	●	●	●	●	●	●	●	●	●
NAMIBIA	Namib Naukluft Park	●	●	●	●	●	●	●	●	●	●	●	●
	Damaraland	●	●	●	●	●	●	●	●	●	●	●	●
	Etosha Nat'l Park	●	●	●	●	●	●	●	●	●	●	●	●
SOUTH AFRICA	Kruger Nat'l Park	●	●	●	●	●	●	●	●	●	●	●	●
	Sabi Sands Game Reserve	●	●	●	●	●	●	●	●	●	●	●	●
	KwaZulu-Natal Parks	●	●	●	●	●	●	●	●	●	●	●	●
	Kgalagadi Transfrontier Park	●	●	●	●	●	●	●	●	●	●	●	●
TANZANIA	Serengeti Nat'l Park	●	●	●	●	●	●	●	●	●	●	●	●
	Ngorongoro Crater	●	●	●	●	○	○	●	●	●	●	●	●
	Lake Manyara Nat'l Park	●	●	●	●	●	●	●	●	●	●	●	●
	Selous Game Reserve	●	●	●	○	○	○	●	●	●	●	●	●
	Gombe Stream and Mahale Mountains Nat'l Parks	●	●	●	●	●	●	●	●	●	●	●	●

KEY: ● = Low Season, Park Open   ● = Shoulder Season Park Open   ● = High Season Park Open
○ = Low Season, Park Closed   ○ = Shoulder Season Park Closed   ○ = High Season Park Closed

Watercraft safaris such as those offered in Chobe National Park, Botswana, provide special wildlife encounters.

Hopping from place to place by plane is so easy and fast that many travelers make the mistake of cramming their itineraries with too many lodges. Plan your trip this way and you'll spend more time at airstrips, in planes, and shuttling to and from the airfields than tracking animals or enjoying the bush. You'll glimpse animals as you travel back and forth—sometimes you'll even see them on the airstrips—but you won't have time to stop and really take in the sights. Try to spend at least two nights at any one lodge; three nights is better.

The best way to set up a fly-in safari is to book an all-inclusive package that includes airfare. (It's impractical to try to do it yourself.) A tour operator makes all the arrangements, and many offer standard trips that visit several of its lodges.

■ TIP→ If your bag is over the weight limit, or if you weigh more than 220 pounds, you'll be required to purchase an additional plane seat (usually about US$100).

LUXURY LODGE–BASED SAFARIS

The majority of safari-goers base their trips at luxury lodges, which pack the double punch of outstanding game-viewing and stylish, atmospheric accommodations. A lodge may be made up of stone chalets, thatch-roof huts, rondavels, or large suitelike tents. Mosquito nets, leather furnishings, and mounted trophies add to the ambience. Dinners are served inside or in an open-air boma. All have hot-and-cold running water, flush toilets, toiletries, laundry service, electricity, and, in most cases, swimming pools. Some lodges also have air-conditioning, telephones, hair dryers, and minibars. The most lavish places also have private plunge pools.

Make no mistake: you pay for all this pampering. Expect to spend anywhere from US$400 to US$1,500 per person per night, depending on the season. All meals, beverages, house wines, game drives, and walks are included. A three-night stay is ideal, but two nights are usually sufficient to see the big game.

The time you spend at a private lodge is tightly structured. With some exceptions, the lodges offer almost identical programs of events. There are usually two three- to four-hour game drives a day, one in the early morning and another in the evening. You spend a lot of time sitting and eating, and in the afternoon you can nap and relax. However, you can always opt for an after-breakfast bush walk, and many lodges now have spas and gyms. If you're tired after your night drive, ask for something to be sent to your room, but don't miss the bush *braai* (barbecue) and at least one night in the boma.

On game drives at bigger camps, rangers stay in contact with one another via radio. If one finds a rhino, for example, he relays its location to the others so they can bring their guests. The more vehicles you have in the field, the more wildlife everyone is likely to see. But don't worry, most lodges are well disciplined with their vehicles, and there are rarely more than three or four at a sighting. As your vehicle arrives, one already there will drive away. In choosing a game lodge, remember to check how much land a lodge can traverse and how many vehicles it uses. Try to go on a bush walk with an armed ranger—an unforgettable experience, as the ranger can point out fascinating details along the way.

All lodges arrange transfers from nearby airports, train stations, or drop-off points. In more remote areas most have their own private airstrips carved out of the bush and fly guests in on chartered aircraft at extra cost. If you're driving yourself, the lodge will send you detailed instructions because many of the roads don't appear on maps and lack names.

MOBILE AND OVERLAND SAFARIS

Most mobile-safari operations are expertly run but are aimed at budget-conscious travelers. They're mostly self-sufficient camping affairs with overnights at either public or private campgrounds, depending on the safari's itinerary and price. Sometimes you stay at basic lodges along the way. Travel is often by something that looks like a 4x4 bus.

For young, hardy people, or the young at heart, mobile safaris are a great way to see the land from ground level. You taste the dust, smell the bacon cooking, stop where and when you want (within reason), and get to see some of the best places in the region. Trips usually run 14 to 21 days, although you can find shorter ones that cover fewer destinations. Prices start at US$750 and climb to US$2,500 for all-inclusive trips. Not sure whether all-inclusive is right for you? Consider combining a mobile safari with a lodge-based one, which gives you the best of both worlds. A minimum of 10 nights is recommended for such an itinerary.

SELF-DRIVE SAFARIS

A self-drive safari, where you drive yourself in your own rental vehicle, is a great option for budget travelers and for those who feel comfortable seeing the bush without a ranger at hand to search out game or explain what you're seeing. Some popular and easy-to-navigate options are South Africa's Kruger National Park, Pilanesburg National Park, Hluhluwe-Imfolozi Game Reserve, and Kgalagadi Transfrontier Park, and Namibia's Etosha National Park. These parks have paved, well-marked roads and a wide range of accommodations that include family-size chalets, small huts, tents, and camping sites. You may buy your own groceries and cook for yourself at all of these areas; some options, especially in Kruger, have restaurants and stores on site.

> ### STARSTRUCK
>
> You'll be awed by the brilliance of the night skies on safari, especially if you live in a city. To add romance and interest to your stargazing, study up on the southern skies and bring a star guide. Also most guides are knowledgeable about the stars, so ask questions.

If possible, rent a van or a 4x4, because the higher off the ground you are the better your chances of spotting game (although a two-wheel-drive car is fine); remember that you have to stick to marked roads. In addition to patience, you'll need drinks, snacks, and a ready camera. Keep your eyes and ears open and you may come across game at any time, in any place.

■ TIP→ Purchase a good park map that shows roads, watering holes, different eco-zones, and the types of animals you can expect to find in each. You can buy these maps when you enter a park or at rest-camp shops, and it would be foolish to pass them up.

Plan your game-drive routes around as many water holes and rivers as possible. Except during the height of the summer rains, most game come to permanent water sources to drink. In winter, when the land is parched, a tour of water holes is bound to reap great rewards. Even better, take a picnic lunch and park at the same watering hole for an hour or two, especially in winter, when the car interior doesn't become too hot. Not only will you see plenty of animals, but you'll find yourself slipping into the drama of the bush.

DRIVING TIPS AND SAFETY

Although most animals in popular parks are accustomed to vehicles with humans in them and will carry on unperturbed in many cases, a vehicle should still approach any animal carefully and quietly, and the driver should "feel" the response. This is for your own and the animals' safety. A delicate approach also gives you a better chance of getting as close as possible without alarming the animal. Be conservative and err on the side of caution, stopping as soon as circumstances suggest.

Human presence among wild animals never goes unnoticed. Don't get out of the vehicle, even if the animals appear friendly, and especially don't feed the creatures. Animals don't associate people in a vehicle with the potential food source or possible threat that they do when people are out of the vehicle. But for this ruse to work you must be quiet and still. The smell of the exhaust fumes and noise of a vehicle mask the presence of the human cargo, so when the engine is off you need to exercise extra caution. This is especially true when closely viewing lions and

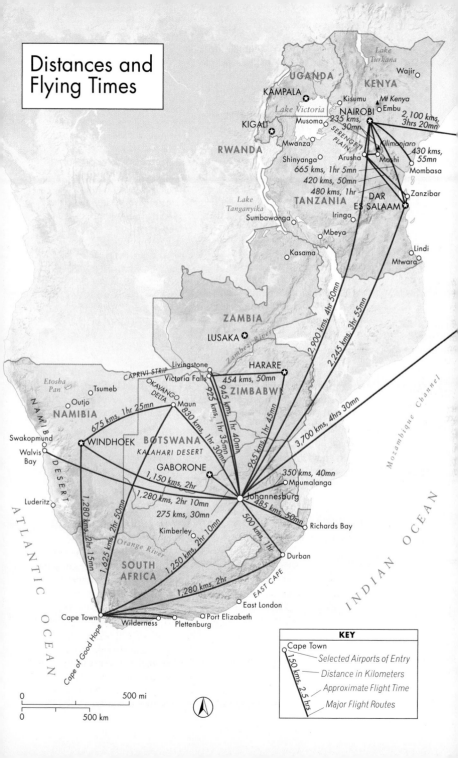

Distances and Flying Times

UGANDA

KAMPALA

Lake Victoria

KIGALI

RWANDA

Lake Tanganyika

Musoma

Mwanza

Shinyanga

Sumbawanga

KENYA

Wajir

Lake Turkana

Kisumu

Mt Kenya

NAIROBI

235 kms, 30mn

Embu

2,100 kms, 3hrs 20mn

SERENGETI PLAIN

Kilimanjaro

Arusha

Moshi

430 kms, 55mn

665 kms, 1hr 5mn

420 kms, 50mn

480 kms, 1hr

Mombasa

Zanzibar

DAR ES SALAAM

TANZANIA

Iringa

Mbeya

Kasama

Lindi

Mtwara

ZAMBIA

LUSAKA

Zambezi River

2,000 kms, 4hr 50mn

2,245 kms, 3hr 55mn

Mozambique Channel

Livingstone

CAPRIVI STRIP

Victoria Falls

HARARE

454 kms, 50mn

925 kms, 1hr 35mn

945 kms, 1hr 40mn

965 kms, 1hr 45mn

ZIMBABWE

3,700 kms, 4hrs 30mn

Etosha Pan

Tsumeb

Outjo

NAMIBIA

OKAVANGO DELTA

Maun

830 kms, 1hr 30mn

675 kms, 1hr 25mn

Swakopmund

WINDHOEK

Walvis Bay

BOTSWANA

KALAHARI DESERT

GABORONE

1,150 kms, 2hr

Luderitz

1,280 kms, 2hr 10mn

275 kms, 30mn

350 kms, 40mn

Mpumalanga

Johannesburg

185 kms, 50mn

Richards Bay

1,280 kms, 2hr 15mn

1,625 kms, 2hr 50mn

Kimberley

2hr 10mn

500 kms, 1hr

Durban

Orange River

SOUTH AFRICA

1,250 kms, 2hr 20mn

1,280 kms, 2hr

EAST CAPE

East London

Cape Town

Wilderness

Plettenburg

Port Elizabeth

Cape of Good Hope

ATLANTIC OCEAN

INDIAN OCEAN

NAMIB DESERT

0 — 500 mi

0 — 500 km

KEY

Cape Town — Selected Airports of Entry

— Distance in Kilometers

150 kms, 2.5 hrs — Approximate Flight Time

— Major Flight Routes

elephants—the two animals most likely to attack a vehicle or people in a vehicle. When approaching lions or elephants, never leap out of your seat or talk loudly; you want to be able to get as close as possible without scaring them off, and you want to avoid provoking an attack.

SPOTTING GAME

It does take time to develop your ability to find motionless game in thick bush. All those fancy stripes and tawny colors really do work. Slowly, though, you learn to recognize the small clues that give away an animal in the bush: the flick of a tail, the toss of a horn, even fresh dung. To see any of this, you have to drive *slowly*, 15 to 25 kph (10 to 15 mph). Fight the urge to pin back your ears and tear around a park at 50 kph (30 mph) hoping to find something big. The only way to spot game at that speed is if it's standing in the road or if you come upon a number of cars already at a sighting. But remember that being the 10th car at a game sighting is less exciting than finding the animal yourself. Not only do the other cars detract from the experience, but you feel like a scavenger—a sort of voyeuristic vulture.

A VOYAGE OF DISCOVERY

As you embark on your safari, consider how lucky you are to be witnessing these rare species in their natural habitat. To this day, researchers in Africa continue to unearth new species. In the summer of 2007, for example, a group of scientists in the Democratic Republic of the Congo discovered six new species (a bat, a rodent, two shrews, and two frogs) in a remote forest that had been off-limits to scientists for almost 50 years, and in 2013 an international team of scientists discovered five new species of bat in West Africa. One can't help but wonder what else is out there or who will find it and when.

WALKING SAFARIS

Many lodges offer walks as an optional way to view game. On a walking safari, however, you spend most, if not all, of your time in the bush on foot, accompanied by an armed guide. Because you're trekking through big-game country, there's an element of danger. But it's the proximity to wilderness that makes this type of trip so enchanting—and exciting. Of course, you can't stop every step of the way or you'd never get very far, but you'll stop frequently to be shown something—from a native flower to spoor to animals—or to discuss some aspect of animal behavior or of tracking.

Walking treks take place on what are known as wilderness trails, which are natural tracks made by animals and are traversed only on foot, never by vehicle, to maintain their pristine condition. These trails usually lead into remote areas that you would never see on a typical safari. In some cases porters carry the supplies and bags. Accommodation is usually in remote camps or occasionally in tents.

■TIP→ Consider your physical condition for walking safaris. You should be in good health and be able to walk between 6.4 and 16 km (4 and 10 miles) a day, depending on the scope of the trip. Some trips don't allow hikers under age 12 or over age 60 (but Kruger Park makes

Safari Do's and Don'ts

Do observe animals silently. Talking loudly frightens animals and disturbs their activities.

Don't attempt to attract an animal's attention. Don't imitate sounds, clap hands, pound the vehicle, or throw objects.

Do respect your driver and guide's judgment. They have more knowledge and experience than you. If they say no, there's a good reason.

Don't leave your vehicle. On self-drives, drive slowly, and keep ample distance between you and the wildlife.

Do dress in neutral tones. If everyone is wearing earth tones, the animal sees one large vegetation-color mass.

Don't litter. Any tossed item can choke or poison animals.

Don't attempt to feed or approach animals. This is especially important at lodges and campgrounds where animals are accustomed to humans.

Don't smoke. The bush ignites easily.

---

exceptions for those over 60 if you produce a doctor's certificate). Also, you shouldn't scare easily. No guide has time for people who freeze up at the sight of a beetle, spider, or something more menacing; guides need to keep their attention on the wilds around them and on the group as a whole. Guides are armed, and they take great caution to keep you away from trouble. To stay safe, always listen to your guide and follow instructions.

WILDLIFE SAFETY AND RESPECT

Nature is neither kind nor sentimental. Don't be tempted to interfere with natural processes. The animals are going about the business of survival in a harsh environment, and you can unwittingly make this business more difficult. Don't get too close to the animals and don't try to help them cross some perceived obstacle; you have no idea what it's really trying to do or where it wants to go. If you're intrusive, you could drive animals away from feeding and, even worse, from drinking at water holes, where they're very skittish and vulnerable to predators. That time at the water hole may be their only opportunity to drink that day.

Never feed any wild creature. Not a cute monkey, not an inquisitive baboon, not a baby tree squirrel, or a young bird out of its nest. In some camps and lodges, however, animals have gotten used to being fed or steal food. The most common animals in this category are baboons and monkeys; in some places they sneak into huts, tents, and even occupied vehicles to snatch food. If you see primates around, keep all food out of sight, and keep your windows rolled up. (If a baboon manages to get into your vehicle, he will trash the interior as he searches for food and use the vehicle as a toilet.)

Never try to get an animal to pose with you. This is probably the biggest cause of death and injury on safaris, when visitors don't listen to or believe the warnings from their rangers or posted notices in public parks. Regardless of how cute or harmless they may look, these animals aren't tame. An herbivore hippo, giraffe, or ostrich can kill you just as easily as a lion, elephant, or buffalo can.

Immersion in the African safari lands is a privilege. In order to preserve this privilege for later generations, it's important that you view wildlife with minimal disturbance and avoid upsetting the delicate balance of nature at all costs. You're the visitor, so act like you would in someone else's home: respect their space. Caution is your most trusted safety measure. Keep your distance, keep quiet, and keep your hands to yourself, and you should be fine.

NIGHTTIME SAFETY

Never sleep out in the open in any area with wildlife. If you're sleeping in a tent, make sure it's fully closed as in zipped or snapped shut; if it's a small tent, place something between you and the side of the wall to prevent an opportunistic bite from the outside. Also, if you're menstruating, be sure to dispose of your toiletries somewhere other than in or near your tent. All in all, if you're in your tent and not exposed, you should be quite safe. Few people lose their lives to lions or hyenas. Malaria is a much more potent danger, so keep your tent zipped up tight at night to keep out mosquitoes.

Never walk alone. Most camps and lodges insist that an armed ranger accompany you to and from your accommodation at night, and rightly so.

VOCABULARY

Mastering the basics of just two foreign languages, Zulu and Swahili, should make you well equipped for travel through much of the region. Zulu is the most common of the Southern African Nguni family of languages (Zulu, Shangaan, Ndebele, Swazi, Xhosa) and is understood in South Africa and Zimbabwe. Swahili is a mixture of Arabic and Bantu and is used across East Africa. In Namibia, Botswana, and Zambia your best bet initially is to stick with English.

SAFARI SPEAK

Ablution blocks: public bathrooms

Banda: bungalow or hut

Big Five: buffalo, elephants, leopards, lions, and rhinoceroses, collectively

Boma: a fenced-in, open-air eating area, usually circular

Braai: barbecue

Bushveld: general safari area in South Africa, usually with scattered shrubs and trees and lots of game; also referred to as the bush or the veld

Camp: used interchangeably with lodge

Campground: a place used for camping that encompasses several campsites and often includes some shared facilities

Campsite: may or may not be part of a campground

Concession: game-area lease that's granted to a safari company and gives it exclusive access to the land

Game guide: used interchangeably with ranger; usually a man

Hides: small, partially camouflaged shelters from which to view game and birds; blinds

Kopje/Koppies: hills or rocky outcrops

Kraal: traditional rural settlement of huts and houses

Lodge: accommodation in rustic yet stylish tents, rondavels, or lavish suites; prices at lodges usually include all meals and game-viewing

Marula: tree from which *amarula* (the liquor) gets its name

Mobile or overland safari: usually a self-sufficient camping affair set up at a different location (public or private campgrounds) each night

Mokoro: dugout canoe; plural *mekoro*

Ranger: safari guide with vast experience with and knowledge of the bush and the animals that inhabit it; used interchangeably with game guide

Rest camp: camp in a national park

Rondavel/rondawel: a traditional round dwelling with a conical roof

Sala: outdoor covered deck

Self-catering: with some kind of kitchen facilities, so you can store food and prepare meals yourself

Self-drive safari: budget safari option in which you drive, and guide, yourself in a rented vehicle

Sundowner: cocktails at sunset

Tracker: works in conjunction with a ranger, spotting animals from a special seat on the front of the 4x4 game-viewing vehicle

Veld: a grassland; see *bushveld*

Vlei: wetland or marsh

SOUTH AFRICAN WORDS AND PHRASES

BASICS

Abseil: rappel

Bakkie: pickup truck (pronounced "bucky")

Berg: mountain

Boot: trunk (of a car)

Bottle store: liquor store

Bra/bru/my bra: brother (term of affection or familiarity)

Buck: antelope

Chommie: mate, chum

Dagga: marijuana, sometimes called *zol*

Djembes: drums

Dorp: village

Fanagalo: a mix of Zulu, English, Afrikaans, Sotho, and Xhosa

Highveld: the country's high interior plateau, including Johannesburg

Howzit?: literally, "How are you?" but used as a general greeting

Indaba: literally, a meeting, but also a problem, as in "That's your indaba."

Ja: yes

Jol: a party or night on the town

Kloof: river gorge

Kokerbooms: quiver trees

Lekker: nice

Lowveld: land at lower elevation, including Kruger National Park

Mopane: nutrient-poor land

More-ish: so good you'll want more, mouthwatering

Muthi: traditional (non-Western) medicine (pronounced "mooti")

Petrol: gasoline

Plaas: farm

Robot: traffic light

Sangoma: traditional healer or mystic

Shebeen: a place to drink, often used for taverns in townships

Sis: gross, disgusting

Sisi or usisi: sister (term of affection or respect)

Spar: name of grocery market chain in Africa

Spaza shop: an informal shop, usually from a truck or container

Stoep: veranda

Takkie: sneaker (pronounced "tacky")

FOOD AND DRINK

Biltong: spiced air-dried (not smoked) meat, made of everything from beef to kudu

Bobotie: spiced, minced beef or lamb topped with savory custard, a Cape Malay dish

Boerewors: Afrikaner term for a spicy farmer's sausage, often used for a braai (pronounced "boo-*rah-vorse*")

Bredie: a casserole or stew, usually lamb with tomatoes

Bunny chow: not a fancy name for salad—it's a half loaf of bread hollowed out and filled with meat or vegetable curry

Chakalaka: a spicy relish

Gatsby: a loaf of bread cut lengthwise and filled with fish or meat, salad, and fries

Kabeljou: one of the varieties of line fish

Kingklip: a native fish

Koeksister: a deep-fried, braided, sugared dough

Malva: sponge cake dessert, usually including apricot jam and served with custard or ice-cream

Melktert: a sweet custard tart

Mogodu: beef or ox tripe

Moroho: mopane worms

Pap: also called *mielie pap,* a maize-based porridge

Peppadew: a patented vegetable, so you may see it under different names, usually with the word *dew* in them; it's a sort of a cross between a sweet pepper and a chili and is usually pickled.

Peri-peri: a spicy chili marinade, Portuguese in origin, based on the searing hot *piri-piri* chili; some recipes are tomato-based, others use garlic, olive oil, and brandy

Potjie: pronounced "poy-*key*" and also called *potjiekos,* a traditional stew cooked in a three-legged pot

Rocket: arugula

Rooibos: an indigenous, earthy-tasting red-leaf tea

Samp: corn porridge

Snoek: a barracudalike fish, often smoked, sometimes *smoorsnoek* (braised)

Sosaties: local version of a kebab, with spiced, grilled chunks of meat

Waterblommetjie: water lilies, sometimes used in stews

Witblitz: moonshine

SWAHILI ESSENTIALS

ANIMALS
Buffalo: nyati

Cheetah: duma

Crocodile: mamba

Elephant: tembo

Giraffe: twiga

Hippo: kiboko

Impala: swala

Leopard: chui

Lion: simba

Rhino: kifalu

BASICS
Yes: ndio

No: hapana

Please: tafadhali

Excuse me: samahani

Thank you (very much): asante (sana)

Welcome: karibu

Hello: jambo

Beautiful: nzuri

Good-bye: kwaheri

Cheers: kwahafya njema

FOOD AND DRINK

Food: chakula

Water: maji

Bread: mkate

Fruit(s): (ma)tunda

Vegetable: mboga

Salt: chumvi

Sugar: sukari

Coffee: kahawa

Tea: chai

Beer: pombe

USEFUL PHRASES

What's your name?: Jina lako nani?

My name is . . . : Jina langu ni . . .

How are you?: Habari?

Where are you from?: Unatoka wapi?

I come from . . . : Mimi ninatoka . . .

Do you speak English?: Una sema Kiingereza?

I don't speak Swahili.: Sisemi Kiswahili.

I don't understand.: Sifahamu.

How do you say this in Swahili?: Unasemaje kwa Kiswahili?

How much is it?: Ngapi shillings?

May I take your picture?: Mikupige picha?

Where is the bathroom?: Choo kiko wapi?

I need . . . : Mimi natafuta . . .

I want to buy . . . : Mimi nataka kununua . . .

No problem.: Hakuna matata.

ZULU ESSENTIALS

BASICS

Yes: yebo

No: cha

Please/Excuse me: uxolo

Thank you: ngiyabonga

You're welcome. nami ngiyabonga

Good morning/hello: sawubona

Good-bye: sala kahle

2

FOOD AND DRINK

Food: ukudla

Water: amanzi

Bread: isinkwa

Fruit: isthelo

Vegetable: uhlaza

Salt: usawoti

Sugar: ushekela

Coffee: ikhofi

Tea: itiye

Beer: utshwala

USEFUL PHRASES

What's your name?: Ubani igama lakho?

My name is . . . : Igama lami ngingu . . .

Do you speak English?: Uya khuluma isingisi?

I don't understand.: Angizwa ukuthi uthini.

How much is it?: Kuyimalini lokhu?

May I take your picture?: Mikupige picha?

Where is the bathroom?: Likuphi itholethe?

I would like . . . : Ngidinga . . .

I want to buy . . . : Ngicela . . .

CHOOSING AN
OUTFITTER

3

WHY GO WITH AN OPERATOR?

Booking a vacation yourself online is now very much the norm, and there's a widespread perception that you'll get a more authentic and reasonably priced experience if you do it all yourself.

This approach often works for American or European city visits, but not as frequently for a safari in Africa. You may save money, but you could end up with hassles that outweigh the savings.

An exception is an overland safari, or a self-drive safari in South Africa (⇨ *See Planning Your Safari for more about the various types of safaris*). One of the main reasons to book yourself is to choose what you want to do and when, but all of the outfitters we feature offer customized trips.

THINGS TO CONSIDER

Do you have only 12 days or less? Africa is huge and infrastructure isn't well developed outside South Africa. Flights from the United States and Europe are long and seldom direct, and if one leg is delayed you can miss your connection and derail your whole itinerary. Just getting to a lodge from an airstrip can be a time-consuming journey, too. A tour operator will know the ins and outs of local travel so you're aware of traveling times in advance, and they'll sort things out if they don't go as planned. They also know the best ways to contact lodges and airlines, which can be challenging due to time differences between countries on the continent and the United States, as well as unreliable phone and Internet.

Safety and surprises. Although the countries you're likely to visit are largely stable and safe, first-time travelers in particular can be anxious about their virgin journey into unknown terrain. Political climates can change quickly, and news can be slow to filter out through traditional news channels. Your operator has contacts on the ground who keep them up-to-date with relevant information. Natural disasters, or even heavier-than-expected rainfall, can make roads dangerous or impassable, and a tour operator can adjust your itinerary accordingly. And they will be accountable if anything goes wrong or if you don't receive the service you paid for.

Specific requests or interests. When you plan a safari, you're presented with multiple countries and infinite options, depending on your budget, the time of year, whether you want to see animals and landscape in a vehicle, on foot, on horseback, or on a boat, and whether you want to stay in a canvas tent or a hotel. You may have dietary or health issues, or want an eco-holiday rather than a butler and private plunge pool. You might want to see three countries in 10 days or just one in a week. A good tour operator will discuss your preferences and tailor an experience that delivers exactly what you want and how you want it, saving you weeks of research. Tour operators also have the kind of overview of an area and its various options that you can't pick up from reading individual reviews of places online.

Details, big and small. Weight allowance on planes, yellow-fever certificates, visas, tipping—these are just some of the easily overlooked details that a good outfitter will tend to. You'll also receive valuable information about local culture and customs.

Choices and prices. Hotels and lodges have two sets of prices—rack rates, which are what the public pays, and a cheaper rate for tour operators. The operator will add their own markup, but you often still pay less, and you'll be aware of all the costs involved upfront, which allows you to budget better. Tour operators will also buffer you against currency fluctuations—the price you'll pay months in advance of a trip will be guaranteed. Also, many lodges don't take bookings directly from the public because they also prefer their clients to go through an operator, so you'll automatically lose out on a lot of good choices.

TYPES OF SAFARI OPERATORS

African tour operator. Usually based in the United States, this type of company specializes in tours and safaris to Africa and works with a safari operator that provides support on the ground. Start dates and itineraries are set for some trips, but customized vacations can almost always be arranged. Travelers can find out the details of these trips through retail travel agents but can also deal directly with the company, usually by talking with them about their preferences on the phone and then receiving a personalized itinerary and quote via email.

African safari operator/ground operator. This type of outfitter is a company in Africa that provides logistical support to a U.S.-based tour operator by seeing to the details of your safari. An operator might charter flights, pick you up at the airport, and take you on game-viewing trips. Some operators own or manage safari lodges. In addition, a safari operator communicates changing trends and developments in the region to tour operators and serves as your on-site contact in cases of illness, injury, or other unexpected situations. For example, Cheli & Peacock is an African tour operator that uses a ground operator to handle logistics and accommodations. Micato and Roar Africa, on the other hand, handle every stage of your trip themselves.

Retail travel agent. In general, a travel agent sells trip packages directly to consumers. In most cases an agent doesn't have a geographical specialty. When called on to arrange a trip to Africa, the travel agent turns to an African tour operator for details.

Before you entrust your trip to tour operators or travel agents, do your best to determine the extent of their knowledge as well as the level of enthusiasm they have for the destination. There are as many travel companies claiming to specialize in Africa as there are hippos in the Zambezi, so it's especially important to determine which operators and agents are up to the challenge. We've featured some of the best further on in this chapter.

After choosing a tour operator or travel agent, it's a good idea to discuss with him or her the logistics and details of the itinerary so you know what to expect each day. Ask questions about lodging, even if you're traveling on a group tour. A lodge that's completely open to the elements may be a highlight for some travelers and terrifying for others, particularly at night when a lion roars nearby. Also ask about the amount of time you'll spend with other travelers. If you're planning a safari honeymoon, find out if you can dine alone when you want to, and ask about honeymoon packages.

QUESTIONS TO ASK A SAFARI SPECIALIST

We recommend you withhold your deposit until you've considered your operator's answers to most of the following questions. Once you pay the deposit, you're liable for a penalty if you decide to cancel the arrangements for any reason.

■ How many years have you been selling tours in Africa?

■ Where do you have offices—do you have any in the destination itself?

■ To which professional organizations do you belong? For example, the American Society of Travel Agents (ASTA) or the United States Tour Operators Association (USTOA)? International Airlines Travel Agent Network (IATAN) members must have annual sales exceeding US$250,000 and carry a US$1 million liability insurance policy, which eliminates fly-by-night operators.

■ Do you have bonding insurance? (This protects you if the company goes under and your agent defaults before your trip.)

■ Can you handle arrangements from start to finish, including flights?

■ Do you have your own guides and vehicles? What certification and/ or training is required for your guides?

■ Do you charge a fee? (Agents and operators usually make their money through commissions.)

■ What's included in the cost? Are all tips included, for instance?

■ What's your cancellation policy?

■ Is the trip guaranteed to operate regardless of the number of travelers?

■ What level of fitness is required for this trip?

■ What other companies and charities does your company associate with? Can I get involved with your philanthropic efforts or learn about volunteering efforts?

■ Do you have any affiliation to a particular lodge chain, or will you refer me to lodges or camps you own yourself only? (An operator can keep costs down by doing this, but you'll benefit the most from impartial advice.)

Consider how responsive the agent is to your queries. If they take a long time to get back to you, aren't easy to get hold of on the phone, don't read your emails properly, or make mistakes with details in the beginning stages, it's not a good sign. The level of service you receive when gathering information and booking the trip is a strong indicator of the company's professionalism.

GOING GREEN

How do you ensure that your operator is committed to sustainability, works with the local community, and leaves as light an impact on the landscape as possible? It can be tricky because many companies "greenwash"—they apply an eco tag to their trips or services without any real follow-through. Until an official ratings system is in place, you'll have to do the research yourself—though Kenya has a reliable website with ratings (⇨ *See box in Chapter 4*). Helpful watchdog agencies include: Tourism Concern (⊕ *www.tourismconcern.org.uk*) and Green Globe (⊕ *www.greenglobe.com*). Conservation organizations such as World Wildlife Fund (⊕ *www.worldwildlife.org*) or the African Wildlife Foundation (⊕ *www.awf.org*) also promote green tourism standards.

In addition, you can ask your operator the following questions to find out where they stand on the 4 C's: Commerce, Conservation, Community, and Culture.

■ Are the lodges on the itineraries solar-powered?

■ What are the recycling, water conservation, and waste management practices?

■ Does the lodge's dining menu use local ingredients? Or, even better, are ingredients sourced on site?

■ Do the safari guides, rangers, and trackers belong to tribes from the region in which you're traveling?

■ Do the chefs and porters hail from the surrounding area?

■ Does the company, or the lodges it uses, provide economic opportunities for local communities?

■ Does the company have any philanthropic or "voluntourism" projects?

Many reputable outfitters have established foundations that make donations to local peoples or wildlife, and some will arrange trips to nearby schools, orphanages, or neighborhoods. We've highlighted the

Cottars 1920s Safari Camp

philanthropic endeavors of a number of top operators in our Tour
Operators list below.

GREEN LODGINGS

Here's a short list of camps that are big on luxury and small on eco-
footprint; these spots look after the environment, local communities,
and wildlife so you can feel good while you're having fun.

Campi ya Kanzi, Kenya. This was the first camp in Kenya to be gold rated
by Ecotourism Kenya for its efforts in sustainable tourism and is one of
the most environmentally friendly camps in East Africa.

Damaraland Camp, Namibia. A joint community venture with the local
riemvasmakers (thong makers), this eco-friendly isolated camp has won
numerous awards for its successful integration of local communities,
the environment, and wildlife.

Delta Camp, Botswana. A major conservation plus for this enchanting
camp set deep in the Okavango is that motorboats aren't used; the
emphasis is on preserving the purity of the environment.

Porini Amboseli Camp, Kenya. A silver eco-award winner, this camp is
co-owned with the local Maasai community. You'll see very few visitors (numbers are limited to 12 per day), but lots of game, including
predators and elephants.

Sabi Sands Safari Lodge, South Africa. In addition to extensive community programs, this lodge uses low-voltage lightbulbs, leftover food
cuttings for local pig food, rain water for gardens, and recycles tins,
plastic and glass.

Saruni Mara, Kenya. This exclusive eco-friendly lodge just outside the Masai Mara boasts the Masai Wellbeing Space, which uses local plants for its treatments and is considered one of the best spas in Kenya.

TOUR OPERATORS

Our list of tour operators hardly exhausts the number of reputable companies, but the following operators, sorted alphabetically, are well-established firms that offer a good selection of itineraries ranging from overland safaris, walking and fly-in safaris, under-canvas safaris, to safari lodges. They all offer fully customizable trips, too. *(⇨ See Planning Your Safari for more about the various types of safaris.)*

TOP 10 OUTFITTERS

&Beyond. This luxury tour operator offers ready-made trips and tours to all parts of Southern or East Africa, or can tailor a safari to your needs. They offer some of the best destinations and accommodations in Africa (and manage 33 of its own highly regarded properties) from the Okovango Delta to remote Indian Ocean islands. Unique trips for the discerning traveler can be planned around learning, conservation, and sustainability, or "luxury in the bush," which includes more holistic activities, such as yoga safaris. They also offer active adventures such as rhino darting for conservation, walking safaris, and turtle-hatching expeditions.

Destinations: Botswana, Kenya, Madagascar, Malawi, Mauritius, Mozambique, Namibia, Rwanda, Seychelles, South Africa, Tanzania, Uganda, Zambia, Zimbabwe. **Popular packages:** Treasures of Tanzania, 8 nights, from $6,685; Grand Botswana, 10 nights, from $9,967. **Philanthropy:** They have raised and committed R100 million (US$11.5 million) to implement and operate projects in six African countries. **What they do best:** Luxury in the bush; impeccable attention to detail; honeymoons. ✉ *Pinmill Farm, 164 Katherine St., Sandton, South Africa* ☎ *27/11809–4300 in South Africa, 888/882–3742 in U.S.* ⊕ *www.andbeyond.com.*

Abercrombie & Kent. In business since 1962, this company is considered one of the best in the business and is consistently given high marks by former clients. From your first decision to go on safari to its successful conclusion, A&K offer seamless service. Their tailor-made safaris hearken back to days past when intrepid adventurers such as Teddy Roosevelt and Ernest Hemingway relied on private guides to create a safari program and escort them through the bush from start to finish. The company has a professional network of local A&K offices in all its destination countries, staffed by full-time A&K experts, and maintains its own fleet of four-wheel-drive safari vehicles and trains its own drivers. The head office in the U.S. is in Illinois.

Destinations: Botswana, Kenya, Namibia, South Africa, Tanzania, Uganda, Zambia, Zimbabwe. **Popular packages:** Kenya & Tanzania, 12 days, from $5,995. **Philanthropy:** Extensive projects benefit ecosystems and wildlife, communities and cultures, and health and education.

Outfitter	Location	Tel. no.	Website	Countries Covered
&Beyond	South Africa	27/11809-4300 888/882-3742	www.andbeyond.com	All
Abercrombie & Kent	USA	888/611–4711	www.abercrombiekent.com	All
Africa Adventure Company	USA	800/882–9453	www.africa-adventure.com	All
Africa Serendipity	USA	212/288-1714	www.africanserendipity.com	Kenya, Tanzania
Africa Travel Resource	UK	0845/450-1520	www.africantravelresource.com	All
African Portfolio	USA	800/700-3677	www.onsafari.com	All
Big Five	USA	800/244–3483	www.bigfive.com	All
Cheli & Peacock	Kenya	254/20/60–4053	www.chelipeacock.com	Kenya
Deeper Africa	USA	888/658-7102	www.deeperafrica.com	Kenya, Tanzania
Eyes on Africa	USA	888/450-9247	www.eyesonafrica.net	All
Gamewatchers Safaris	Kenya	877/710-3014	www.porini.com	Kenya, Tanzania, South Africa, Botswana, Zambia
Journey Beyond	South Africa	27-11/781-9210	www.journey-beyond.com	All
Ker & Downey	USA	800/423–4236	www.kerdowneysafaris.com	All
Micato Safaris	USA	212/545-7111	www.micatosafaris.com	All
Natural Habitat Adventures	USA	800/543-8917	www.nathab.com	All
Nomad Tanzania	Tanzania	255/784-734490	www.nomad-tanzania.com	Tanzania
Premier Tours	USA	800/545–1910	www.premiertours.com	All
Pulse Africa	South Africa	2711/325-2290	www.pulseafrica.com	All
ROAR Africa	USA	855/666-7627	www.roarafrica.com	All
Skyview of Africa	Kenya	254-20/252–8721	www.skyviewofafrica.com	All
Wilderness Safaris	South Africa	27-11/807–1800	www.wilderness-safaris.com	South Africa, Botswana, Namibia, Zambia, Zimbabwe
Tauck	USA	203/899–6814	www.tauck.com	Kenya, Tanzania, South Africa
The Wild Source	USA	720/497-1250	www.thewildsource.com	Tanzania, Botswana

Guests can meet local people making a difference in their communities. Many guests build their safari around several of these projects. **What They Do Best:** Destination knowledge—they have some of the most experienced guides on the continent. ⊠ *1411 Opus Pl., Downer's Grove, Illinois* ☎ *888/611–4711* ⊕ *www.abercrombiekent.com.*

Africa Serendipity. This New York–based company has excellent Africa-based operators and specializes in Kenya and Tanzania exclusively. Although they offer suggested itineraries, the trip is ultimately custom-designed for the client and dependent on the time of the year and budget. Clients often combine Kenya and Tanzania into one trip. Africa Serendipity is flexible, as they offer prospective clients what they wish and at a price that meets their budget.

Destinations: Kenya and Tanzania and their coastal islands. **Popular packages:** Serengeti and/or Masai Migration, 12–14 days, from $6,100. A beach escape can be added to the end of any safari. **Philanthropy:** They have no direct involvement with any charities, but the ground outfitters they use only employ local residents and are involved in community schemes. **What They Do Best:** Kenya and Tanzania. Their focus on these two countries truly makes them experts. ⊠ *1670 York Ave., New York, New York* ☎ *212/288–1714* ⊕ *www.africaserendipity.com.*

African Portfolio. African Portfolio's team members visit each in-country operator annually and are on a first-name basis with the managers of the properties they use. They pride themselves on discovering the best places, whether they're hidden gems, up-and-coming properties, or well-established classics. With each client, they're committed to providing a safari reminiscent of what captivates them about Africa. Their mission is to provide unique and memorable experiences through nature-based travel that educate, entertain, inspire, and provide participants with opportunities to directly contribute to conservation.

Destinations: Botswana, Kenya, Malawi, Mauritius, Mozambique, Namibia, Rwanda, Seychelles, South Africa, Tanzania, Uganda, Zambia, Zimbabwe. **Popular packages:** Great Rift Valley Safari, Tanzania, 10 days, from $6,000. **Philanthropy:** African Portfolio was started in Zimbabwe and their philanthropic efforts are directed there; this includes support for orphanages and a wildlife sanctuary. **What they do best:** Assisting travelers with "off the beaten path" trips. ⊠ *146 Sound Beach Ave., Greenwich, Connecticut* ☎ *800/700–3677* ⊕ *www. onsafari.com.*

Gamewatchers Safaris. This Nairobi-based company specializes in delivering luxury tailor-made safaris to small camps and lodges in the top game-viewing areas of East Africa. Every traveler is guaranteed a personal, authentic safari and the opportunity to experience the magic of the African bush while helping protect Africa's wildlife, ecosystems, and cultures. Gamewatchers run their own ground operations, ensuring guests are well looked after from the start of their trip to the finish. Guests often add beach trips to the end of their safaris.

Destinations: Botswana, Kenya, Mauritius, Rwanda, Seychelles, South Africa, Tanzania, Zambia. **Popular packages:** African Splendours Safari, 12 nights, from $5,895; Gamewatchers Adventure Camping Safari, 6 nights, from $1,995. **Philanthropy:** They support a school in Kibera, Nairobi, and more than 1,000 Maasai families are directly benefiting as a result of their conservancies. They have also set up outreach programs to assist with water provision, education, and predator protection. **What they do best:** A personal, authentic experience, as far from mass-market tourism as it's possible to get. ☎ 877/710–3014 ⊕ *www.porini.com.*

Micato Safaris. Family-owned and -operated, this New York–based operator offers ultraluxurious trips driven by a sustainable ethos. Safari lodges enchant with such unadulterated luxuries as private plunge pools and personal butlers. Cultured safari guides educate, instruct, and amuse, while itineraries offer an irresistible array of experiences from the sophisticated pleasures of Cape Town to the celebrated savannas of the Serengeti and the near-spiritual beauty of the Kalahari. Micato has long been praised for its ability to deliver seamless personalized "un-group-like" service and over-the-top luxury without sacrificing true immersion in the "real Africa." Stand-out inclusions on Micato programs include time-saving bush flights between lodges and an "all tips included" policy.

Destinations: Botswana, Kenya, Mozambique, Namibia, Rwanda, South Africa, Tanzania, Uganda, Zambia, Zimbabwe. **Popular packages:** The Hemingway Wing Safari, Kenya, 14 days, from $13,175 per person. **Philanthropy:** Their charitable endeavours are impressive, with visits to the Micato-AmericaShare Harambee Community Center a highlight for many clients. In addition, every safari sold puts one Kenyan child in school through Micato-AmericaShare's One for One program. **What They Do Best:** Impeccable service from start to finish alongside excellent community projects. ✉ *15 W. 26th St., New York, New York* ☎ *212/545-7111* ⊕ *www.micatosafaris.com.*

Natural Habitat Adventures. Nicknamed "The Nature People," this operator is known for its focus on wildlife and conservation. Nat Hab's headquarters are in Colorado, and although they organize trips to destinations around the world they have a good reputation for arranging incredible safari itineraries. They always choose the best destinations for viewing wildlife in its natural habitat and focus on small groups and intimate lodges in secluded, off-the-beaten-track settings. Their online safari-building tool, iSafari.com, is a useful starting point for getting an idea of what's possible before speaking to one of the experts in their team. They can also arrange photo expeditions and family safaris.

Destinations: Botswana, Congo-Brazzaville, Kenya, Madagascar, Namibia, Rwanda, South Africa, Tanzania, Zambia, Zimbabwe, Uganda. **Popular packages:** Secluded Botswana (includes Victoria Falls on the Zambia side), 13 days, from $10,995. **Philanthropy:** The Natural Habitat Foundation focuses on conservation, and arranges volun-tourism programs. They're the first carbon-neutral travel company and the travel partner for the World Wildlife Fund (WWF). **What they do best:** Sustainable ecotourism for small groups with a focus on wildlife and conservation. ✉ *833 W. South Boulder Rd., Boulder, Colorado* ☎ *800/543–8917* ⊕ *www.nathab.com.*

Wolwedans Private Camp

Nomad Tanzania. Nomad Tanzania owns and operates their own collection of unique camps and privately guided safaris across the most geographically diverse areas in Tanzania. They also offer an efficient ground-handling and safari-planning service throughout Tanzania and Zanzibar and use their experience and approach to recommend other camps that they feel meet their exacting standards. They have a reputation for employing excellent guides and for always going the extra mile for their guests. All of their team members have a deep love for the African bush and a desire to share their passion with others. Their website has some sample itineraries for inspiration, but each trip is fully customized.

Destinations: Tanzania. **Popular packages:** Serengeti Safari, 8 nights, from $5,000. **Philanthropy:** A microfinance scheme allows guides to purchase their own safari vehicles, which Nomad then rents from them. They have also introduced steel water bottles for all guests so as to reduce the use of plastic. The Nomad Trust raises charitable donations for a range of community projects. **What they do best:** Excellent guides, camps, comprehensive itineraries and service in a specialized region. ☎ *255/784–734490* ⊕ *www.nomad-tanzania.com.*

Roy Safaris. Based in Arusha in Tanzania, and going strong for more than 25 years, Roy Safaris maintains a midsize operation with a clear focus on adding value at every stage of your trip. They are dependable and responsive, offering both tailor-made and small group tours, and more than 70% of their business comes from repeat customers or referrals. They can also arrange photographic safaris with specially customized vehicles. The company owns a hotel, the African Tulip in Arusha, and they are about to open their second, although they do not influence clients to stay at their properties.

Destinations: Kenya and Tanzania. **Popular packages:** Majestic Tanzania, 11 days, from $4,500; Tanzania Migration Safari, 12 days, from $4,900. **Philanthropy:** Their Sasha Foundation has an annual budget of about $40,000 and picks one project to see through per year. This includes education grants, building classrooms, and clean water development. Unused marketing funds from both the company and hotel are allocated to the foundation, as well as parts of the proceeds of safari and room sales. **What they do best:** Excellent, personalized service, and good value. ⊠ *2 Serengeti Rd., Arusha, Tanzania* ☎ *255/272–502–115* ⊕ *www.roysafaris.com.*

Wilderness Safaris. One of Africa's most respected and innovative tour operators, Wilderness Safaris assures you impeccable service, pristine wilderness destinations, spacious safari camps and wildlife galore. The company operates a wide array of safari camps and lodges, from "seven star" premier accommodation to mobile safaris known as Explorations, to tailor-made itineraries and honeymoon packages. Wilderness has more than 70 lodges and camps, all with different styles, so there is something for everyone. They have a regional office in each country in which they operate, as well as a head office in Gaborone, Botswana, ensuring that their ground operations run very smoothly.

Destinations: Botswana, Congo, Malawi, Namibia, Seychelles, South Africa, Zambia, Zimbabwe. **Popular packages:** The Great Wilderness Journey, Botswana, 11 days, from $9,773; Desert Dune Safari, 10 days, from $5,000. **Philanthropy:** In addition to a 4C's sustainability program (Conservation, Community, Culture and Commerce), Wilderness has also created two nonprofit programs to further its aims of helping children in Africa: Children in the Wilderness and the Wilderness Wildlife Trust. **What they do best:** Incredible destinations, authentic experiences and seamless service from start to finish. ⊠ *373 Rivonia Blvd., Rivonia, South Africa* ☎ *27–11/807–1800* ⊕ *www.wilderness-safaris.com.*

HIGHLY RECOMMENDED OUTFITTERS

Access2Tanzania. After living in Tanzania for two years as a Peace Corps volunteer, owner Brian Singer set up Access2Tanzania in 2004 with his wife Karen and Tanzanian partner Michael Musa. Brian and Karen handle all pre-safari planning, and Michael takes care of ground logistics. They are one of few companies in Tanzania that do not subcontract their guides; each one is a full-time employee and they all consistently receive rave reviews. They own and maintain their own air-conditioned vehicles, which have unlimited mileage and pop-up roofs to allow 360-degree views. ⊠ *253 Duke St., St. Paul, Minnesota* ☎ *718/715–1353* ⊕ *www.access2tanzania.com.*

Africa Adventure Company. Based in Florida, the Africa Adventure Company is renowned for arranging low-impact and personalized travel. Their experienced staff listen closely to what kind of experience their clients are after and match it with a suitable itinerary. Owner Mark Nolting has spent more than 25 years exploring and researching Africa and has written several guidebooks. His partner Alison managed safari camps for many years and now works on developing new safari programs for both repeat and new clients as well organizing community and volunteer programs. They promote camps that are symbiotic with nature and the community, and offer exquisite game viewing with top-notch guides. They also offer add-on tours, such as beach escapes and honeymoon packages. ✉ *2601 E. Oakland Blvd., Suite 600, Fort Lauderdale, Florida* ☎ *800/882–9453* ⊕ *www.africa-adventure.com.*

Big Five. Offering more than 100 tours to Africa, this Florida-based operator promises its clients a trip of a lifetime—if you're not happy with the choices given, Big Five will custom create one for you. You can be assured that whatever trip you choose, your knowledgeable agent will be able to draw on personal experience to assist you. Since its inception in 1973, the company has been committed to responsible travel that fosters the preservation of natural and cultural heritage and, equally importantly, the well-being of local communities. ✉ *1551 S.E. Palm Ct., Stuart, Florida* ☎ *800/244–3483* ⊕ *www.bigfive.com.*

Cheli & Peacock. Born out of a passion to conserve Kenya's wildlife and wilderness areas, this upmarket company is owner-managed and has offices in Nairobi, Nanyuka, and Arusha, Tanzania. It has developed over the years to become one of Kenya's leading destination-management companies and inbound tour operators, specializing in East Africa. The variety of locations covers a broad selection of ecosystems, game, and conservation, and features small luxury camps and lodges in top national parks and reserves. Their trips are very creative; for example, helicopter rides across the Great Rift Valley, or walking with camels across the Laikipia plateau. They manage all ground arrangements themselves. Beach escapes can be added to safari trips. ✉ *Lengai House, Wilson Airport, Nairobi, Kenya* ☎ *254–20/600–3090* ⊕ *www.chelipeacock.com.*

Deeper Africa. This small, hands-on company, based in Colorado, specializes in East Africa, Botswana and Namibia. If you want to catch the Serengeti wildebeest migration, explore the Okavango Delta, trek mountain gorillas, or scout for desert-adapted animals in the Namib Desert, they have very detailed knowledge of these areas and can get you privileged access to places you'd never find on your own. Their guide-to-guest ratio is high: one guide for every four or five guests. Ethical tourism is a cornerstone of their approach and they aim to educate as well as to entertain and indulge their guests. They can deliver a fully customized itinerary within an hour of conversation. ✉ *5353 Manhattan Circle, Suite 202, Boulder, Colorado* ☎ *303/415–2574* ⊕ *www.deeperafrica.com.*

Eyes on Africa. Whether you're a honeymooner, wildlife enthusiast, or photographer, Chicago-based Eyes on Africa will find a trip to match your budget. A wide range of interests and preferences can be catered to, and they have a long list of budget options, too. Along with safaris, they also cover mountainous destinations and beaches. They are becoming well known for their occasional group photography trips, and are planning to expand out of Africa in order to service requests from their existing customer base. ✉ *1743 W. Fletcher St., Chicago, Illinois* ☎ *888/450–9247* ⊕ *www.eyesonafrica.net.*

Good Earth Tours. Established in 1995 in Arusha, Tanzania, Good Earth Tours is a small company with a sales and bookings office in the United States (and Canada) that combines an intimate knowledge of Africa with a hands-on approach. They have plenty of experience with U.S. clients and are familiar with all their requirements. The staff are deeply committed to Africa, and their mission is to connect people from all over the world to this beautiful continent. You're assured of outstanding adventures at a good value, whether you are embarking on a safari with luxury accommodation or a comfortable camping experience followed by an Indian Ocean escape. ✉ *13017 Wisteria Dr., Suite 223, Maryland* ☎ *813/856–4773* ⊕ *www.goodearthtours.com.*

Ker & Downey. One of the oldest and most respected safari companies in Africa (it's been operating since 1946), Ker & Downey also has an office in Texas. The company utilizes its exclusive camps to provide luxury safari experiences and offers in-house expertise for all destinations as well as excellent on-the-ground service. They work hard to get to know all clients to match them with the ultimate itineraries. They pioneered the concept of the photographic safari and often organize trips for film crews as well as corporations and private clients. ✉ *6703 Highway Blvd., Katy, Texas* ☎ *800/423–4236* ⊕ *www.kerdowney.com.*

Premier Tours. Although based in Philadelphia, Premier Tours is owned and managed by people born and raised in Africa who have organized all kinds of safaris, from basic camping trips to celebrity vacations. CEO Julian Harrison specializes in the development of ecotourism on the continent and is the founding member (and first USA tour operator) of the UN's Environment Program's Initiative on Sustainable Tourism Development. Other team members lead tour groups as naturalist guides, and participate in research projects in various African countries. Beach escapes can be added to safaris. ✉ *21 S. 12th St., Philadelphia, Pennsylvania* ☎ *800/545–1910* ⊕ *www.premiertours.com.*

Pulse Africa. More than 75% of Pulse Africa's clients are repeats or have been recommended by others. The company is based in South Africa, so it has up-to-date information on travel in Southern Africa, East Africa, and the Indian Ocean Islands. Every member of the team has personally visited each place that they recommend. "Pulse Packages" are trips primarily to one destination (either beach or safari); as a result they're more affordable than a tailor-made trip. ✉ *2nd fl., Hyde Square, Jan Smuts Ave., Johannesburg, South Africa* ☎ *2711/325–2290* ⊕ *www.pulseafrica.com.*

ROAR Africa. ROAR Africa offers a one-of-a-kind travel service for personalized, custom tours. The founder's family dates back to 1688, ensuring a wealth of information and a well-established network that can only come from years of actually living in Africa. Clients have had memorable and life-changing adventures, such as meeting with artists and tribesmen, sleeping under the stars in the Kalahari, dinner with a CEO from their industry, participation in rhino conservation efforts, the opportunity to meet wildlife documentary producers Dereck and

Beverly Joubert, VIP wine tours by helicopter, and visiting township schools. ROAR is headquartered in New York but also has offices in South Africa. They run their own ground operation, which enables concierge-level service and support during both the planning phase and travel. They also meet clients at the door of the airplane upon arrival, whisk them through customs, and can offer their own plane for private flights. ✉ *1111 Lexington Ave., New York, New York* ☎ *855/666–7627* ⊕ *www.roarafrica.com.*

Safari Infinity. You can be sure of high-quality guides and excellent customer service with a personal touch from this young and growing tour operator based in Tanzania. All of their safari, mountain, and Zanzibar packages are completely customizable. From the moment you send your first inquiry to the end of your journey, staff are attentive and professional, ensuring a well-planned trip that is exactly how you imagined. ✉ *Box 14345, Arusha, Tanzania* ☎ *255/688–285–354* ⊕ *www.safari-infinity.com.*

Skyview of Africa. This Kenyan-owned and -operated company offers a wide range of memorable safaris throughout the year to international clients. Destinations include the Ngorongoro Crater, the Serengeti, Masai Mara, Amboseli, and even a Mt. Kenya climb. All the itineraries featured on their website can be customized. They only offer private safaris, so guests don't have to share vehicles with other guests. This affords greater flexibility with dates and itineraries. ☎ *254–20/252–8721* ⊕ *www.skyviewofafrica.com.*

Tauck. Tauck operates its African safaris in cooperation with the award-winning documentary filmmakers BBC Earth, and clients have the opportunity to use the same equipment as the filmmakers, such as infrared cameras, night-vision goggles, and long-distance microphones to immerse themselves in their surroundings in new and exciting ways. Premium-quality trips are virtually all-inclusive, with all excursions, most meals and gratuities, airport transfers, luggage handling, and other expenses built into the price. ✉ *10 Norden Pl., Norwalk, Connecticut* ☎ *203/899–6814* ⊕ *www.tauck.com.*

The Wild Source. Wildlife biologist Bill Given started taking small groups of people on private trips to Botswana, and essentially became a one-man safari operator. He formed the Wild Source and now employs a number of staff members, all of whom are wildlife biologists or naturalists with guiding experience. Their Tanzanian guide team in particular receive rave reviews for providing "hard core" game-viewing, with all-day game drives and no mileage limits. At this writing the company is slated to open a new camp in Kenya in June 2015 called Enaidura Mobile Camp, the only one of its kind. It has been created and designed to support top local guides—some of them legendary—who wish to set up on their own but struggle to market themselves to new clients. In this way, some of the profits of the safari industry can go directly to local entrepreneurs. ✉ *Golden, Colorado* ☎ *720/497–1250* ⊕ *www. thewildsource.com.*

KENYA

WELCOME TO KENYA

TOP REASONS TO GO

★ **The Great Migration.** Millions of plains game move in an endless cycle of birth and death from Tanzania's Serengeti to Kenya's Masai Mara.

★ **Eyeball Big Game.** Visiting Kenya's legendary national parks and game reserves almost guarantees that you'll see the Big Five as well as huge herds of plains animals and hundreds of colorful birds.

★ **Africa's Fabled Tribe.** The tall and dignified red-robed Maasai have held explorers, adventurers, and writers in thrall for centuries.

★ **Beach Escapes.** Miles of white sandy beaches lined by an azure ocean and water sports galore. From diving and snorkeling to windsurfing, there's something for everyone.

★ **Turn Back the Clock.** Check out ancient history along the coast where Arab traders and Vasco da Gama once sailed. In the tiny UNESCO World Heritage town of Lamu you'll find an Arabic way of life unchanged for centuries.

1 Masai Mara. Located in Southern Kenya, in the area known as the Great Rift Valley, the park covers 1,510 km (938 miles) at altitudes of 1,500 meters to 2,170 meters above sea level. It's considered by many to be the world's greatest game park because of the abundance of animals here. During July and August when the Great Migration reaches here, you can see hundreds of thousands of wildebeests, zebras, and gazelles feeding on the new grass, followed by dozens of predators.

2 Amboseli National Reserve. The snow-capped peak of Kilimanjaro, huge herds of elephants, and quintessential Kenyan landscape (open plains, acacia woodland, grasslands, bush, and marshland) greet you along the Tanzania border.

3 Tsavo National Park. Once known for its legendary man-eating lions, Tsavo, which is made up of two parks, Tsavo East and Tsavo West, is now home to peaceful prides and loads of other game. The park's proximity to the coast makes it a great choice for those who want to combine beach and beasts.

4 Laikipia Plateau. Fast becoming Kenya's hottest game destination, this area is home to the Samburu National Reserve, which boasts more game per square mile than anywhere else in the country, and some of its classiest camps and lodges.

GETTING ORIENTED

Kenya lies on Africa's east coast. It's bordered by Uganda to the west, Tanzania to the south, Sudan and Ethiopia to the north, Somalia to the northeast, and the Indian Ocean to the southeast. It's a land of amazing diversity with extraordinary tourist attractions: great game reserves including Masai Mara and Samburu, the Great Rift Valley, fertile highlands, parched deserts, long pristine beaches and coral reefs, marine parks, mountains such as Mt. Kenya and Mt. Meru, and rivers and lakes, including Lake Turkana—Kenya's largest lake. Its two major cities couldn't be more different. Nairobi, the capital, is a bustling city where colonial buildings rub shoulders with modern skyscrapers. Steamy Mombasa on the coast retains its strong Arabic influence and history as it continues to be Kenya's largest and busiest port. Kenya is also home to the Maasai people, who've roamed the plains for centuries.

Updated by Narina Fxelby and Mark Eveleigh

Kenya is where "going on safari" started. A hundred years or so ago, visitors from all over the world, including Teddy Roosevelt, started traveling to Africa, lured by stories of multitudes of wild animals; there were more than 3 million large mammals roving East Africa's plains at the time. Today visitors continue to flock to this East African nation each year. Although humans have made their mark, Kenya still holds onto its pristine wilderness.

But Kenya's tourism industry, the main source of foreign revenue, is very susceptible to perceptions of tourist safety. Tourism declined in the late 1990s following a series of attacks on tourists and the terrorist bombing of the U.S. Embassies in Nairobi and Dar es Salaam in 1998, but visitor numbers were on the rise again before the crisis in 2007–08. Widely televised at the time, the ethnic violence that arose after disputed election results still tarnishes Kenya's reputation, even though no tourists were in any danger. The crisis was, however, a large contributing factor to a new constitution signed into law in 2010, which is aimed at limiting presidential powers and keeping corruption in check. It'll take years to implement, but there's a new optimism among Kenyans and, more than ever, there seems to be little reason to consider Kenya unsafe as a tourist destination.

Kenya's human history dates back at least 6 million years. In 2001 the controversial Millennium Man was discovered near Lake Baringo in the northwest. This find and Richard and Mary Leakey's discovery of *Homo habilis* in the '60s fuel ongoing excavations.

Today there are more than 70 ethnic groups in Kenya that range from the Maasai, Samburu, Kikuyu, and Turkana tribes to the Arabs and Indians that settled on the coast and the descendants of the first white settlers in and around Nairobi and the Kenya highlands. In Nairobi, about 40% of the population is Kikuyu—a Bantu people numbering more than 6 million. Islam arrived along the coast in the 8th century, followed in the 15th century by Portuguese explorers and sailors who

FAST FACTS

Size 582,645 square km (224,960 square miles).

Capital Nairobi.

Number of National Parks 49, including the Masai Mara National Reserve, Amboseli National Park, and Tsavo National Park.

Number of Private Reserves Too many to count, but includes Laikipia Plateau and Lewa Wildlife Conservancy.

Population Approximately 43 million. www.tradingeconomics.com/kenya/population-total-wb-data.html

Big Five You'll find them all here.

Language Kiswahili is the official language, but most people speak English.

Time Kenya is on EAT (East Africa Time), which is three hours ahead of Greenwich Mean Time and eight hours ahead of North America's Eastern Standard Time.

came looking for the sea route to India. During the rule of Seyyid Said of Oman in the 1830s, German, British, and American merchants established themselves on the coast, and the notorious slave routes were created.

The British created what was then known as British East Africa in the late 1800s. After a much publicized and often sensationalized struggle by native Kenyans against British rule in the 1950s, known as the Mau Mau era, Kenya finally won independence in 1963.

The perennial African life-and-death drama plays out among vast populations of prey and predators in what's widely called one of the world's greatest wildlife destinations. This is what most tourists flock to the country for—but don't be put off by people who say that there are far too many tourists, which sometimes makes you feel like you're in a big zoo. With massive conservancy areas opening up around the edge of many of Kenya's reserves, wildlife viewing these days effectively knows no bounds.

Kenya isn't just about big game. It has a gorgeous tropical coastline with white sandy beaches, coral gardens, superb fishing, and snorkeling, diving, and vibey beach resorts. Traditional triangular-sailed *dhows* still ply their trade providing unforgettable seafood to the surrounding restaurants. You'll discover unique islands with ancient stone Arab buildings, where a donkey is the main means of transport, and where time really does seem to stand still.

PLANNING

WHEN TO GO

Generally speaking, Kenya, which straddles the equator, has one of the best climates in the world with sunny, dry days; daytime temperatures average between 20°C (68°F) and 25°C (77°F). The coast can get hot and humid, though sea breezes cool things down, and the mountainous regions can get very cold—remember there's snow all year round on the highest peaks. Try to avoid the long rains of March and April or the short rains of October, November, and December because park roads can become impassable and mosquitoes are at their busiest and deadliest. Game-viewing is at its best during the driest seasons (May–September, January, and February) because the lack of surface water forces game to congregate at water holes. Safari high season runs July through November when the annual wildebeest migration is in full swing, but it's much cheaper to go in the low season (April and May) when rates drop dramatically. High season at the coast is September through January (the hottest time is December and January), but avoid Christmas and New Year periods as holiday resorts are packed. If you're a birder, aim to visit between October and April when the migrant species have arrived.

GETTING HERE AND AROUND

AIR TRAVEL

When booking flights, check the routing carefully as some involve stop-overs or require you to change airlines. Several flight options from the United States require long layovers in Europe before connecting to Nairobi or Mombasa. This is especially true for the cheaper flight options.

Airports Jomo Kenyatta International Airport (JKIA) (NBO). ⊠ Nairobi ☎ 020/661-1000 ⊕ www.kaa.go.ke. **Moi International Airport** (MBA). ⊠ Airport Rd., Mombasa ☎ 020/357-7508, 020/357-7052 ⊕ www.kaa.go.ke. **Wilson Airport** (WIL). ⊠ Langatta Rd., Nairobi ☎ 072/425-5343.

Air Travel Resources in Kenya Kenya Airports Authority ☎ 020/661-1000 ⊕ www.kaa.co.ke.

CHARTER FLIGHTS

The major charter companies—African Sky Charters, East African Air Charter, Phoenix Aviation, and Safarilink—run daily shuttles from Wilson Airport to numerous destinations in East Africa including safari spots, Mombasa, and Nairobi. Safarilink also flies to Mt. Kilimanjaro. All flights should be booked directly through the charter service.

Charter Companies African Sky Charters ☎ 020/600-1467 ⊕ www.asc.linkcafe.org. **East African Air Charters** ☎ 073/588-0011 ⊕ www.eaaircharters.co.ke. **Phoenix Aviation** ☎ 0733/632-769 ⊕ www.phoenixaviation.co.ke. **Safarilink** ☎ 020/600-0777 ⊕ www.flysafarilink.com.

FLIGHTS

Most major European and African airlines fly into Jomo Kenyatta International Airport (JKIA), Kenya's major airport. There are no direct flights from the United States to Kenya; indirect flights leave from most major cities, that is, New York, Chicago, Atlanta. Flying via London, Amsterdam, or Dubai is a popular option. There are plenty of cheap and efficient domestic flights available, including daily flights on Air Kenya between Nairobi and Mombasa, Malindi and Lamu. Air Kenya also flies daily to Amboseli, Diani Beach, Kiwayu, the Masai Mara, and Samburu. Fly540, an airline covering East Africa, has services between Nairobi, Lamu, Malindi, Mombasa, Kisumu, and Kitale. Safarilink has the widest network of flights, with daily services between Nairobi, Amboseli, Naivasha, Tsavo West, Nanyuki, Loisaba, Samburu, Lewa Downs, Lamu, Diani, and Kilimanjaro, and from Mara to Migori, which links travelers from Mara to the Serengeti. There are also numerous charter flights available from Nairobi to the major tourist destinations and individual lodges and camps. When you book your safari, it's a good idea to ask your accommodation destination to book your internal flights for you as part of your package. Another option is to get an operator like Twiga Tours (⊕ *www.twiga-tours.com*), who can take care of all overland travel arrangements and flights, to arrange this for you.

Kenya Airways and Thomsonfly fly from London to Mombasa, and Condor flies to Frankfurt from Mombasa. Emirates offers flights to JKIA via Dubai, and Qatar Airways via Doha. British Airways offers direct flights to Nairobi. KLM flies to Nairobi via Amsterdam. Connections to Mombasa from Nairobi can be made several times a day using Air Kenya, Kenya Airways, or Fly540.

Airport departure tax is included in your scheduled flight tickets.

Domestic Airlines Air Kenya ☎ *020/391-6000* ⊕ *www.airkenya.com.* **Fly540** ☎ *071/0-540-540* ⊕ *www.fly540.com.* **Kenya Airways** ☎ *020/327-4747* ⊕ *www.kenya-airways.com.* **Safarilink** ☎ *020/600-0777* ⊕ *www.flysafarilink. com.*

International Airlines British Airways ☎ *0844/493-0787 in U.K.* ⊕ *www. britishairways.com.* **Condor** ☎ *0180/676-7767 in Germany* ⊕ *www.condor. com.* **Emirates** ☎ *0344/800-2777 in U.K., 0800/777-3999 in U.S.* ⊕ *www. emirates.com.* **KLM** ☎ *0207/660-0293 in U.K.* ⊕ *www.klm.com.* **Thomsonfly** ☎ *0203/451-2688 in U.K.* ⊕ *www.thomsonfly.com.*

CAR TRAVEL

If time is not too much of an issue, consider going on a self-drive safari. There is very little that can beat the thrill of setting off on your own adventure. ■TIP→ Poor road conditions in many places means there's often a big difference between distance on a map and driving time (for example, it takes about six hours to drive from Nairobi to the Mara, a 150-mile [240km] journey). However, don't let this discourage your sense of adventure; driving between parks is a fantastic way to see the country. There are a number of companies that specialize in hiring 4x4s as well as camping equipment, and most will also offer the services of a driver-cum-mechanic (at an extra fee). Expect to pay from $135 a day to hire a 4x4, about $35 a day for camping equipment and $20 a day for a driver.

Self-drive safari companies Erikson Rover Safaris ✉ *Nakuru* ☎ *072/464-7982* ⊕ *www.roversafari.com.* **Roving Rovers** ✉ *Nakuru* ☎ *072/355-4557* ⊕ *www.rovingrovers.com.*

ESSENTIALS

COMMUNICATIONS
PHONES
Calling Within Kenya: Local landline calls are quite cheap, but hotels add hefty surcharges to phone calls. Prepaid cards for public telephones can be purchased at cafés, newsstands, convenience stores, and telephone company offices. City codes are (020) for Nairobi, (041) for Mombasa, (042) for Malindi, (040) for Diani Beach, and (012) for Lamu; include the first 0 when you dial within the country. When making a phone call in Kenya, always use the full 10-digit number, including the area code, even if you're in the same area.

Contacts Airtel directory enquiries ☎ *232 from an Airtel number, 073/3100–100 from another number.* **Orange directory enquiries** ☎ *100 from an Orange number, 020/222–1000 from another number.* **Safaricom directory enquiries** ☎ *200 from a Safaricom number, 072/200–2200 from another number* ⊕ *www.safaricom.co.ke.*

Calling Outside Kenya: When dialing out from Kenya, dial 000 before the international code. So, for example, you would dial 000 (0001) for the United States. Other country codes are 00044 for the United Kingdom, 00027 for South Africa, and 00033 for France.

Access Codes MCI WorldPhone ☎ *0800/220–111 from Kenya* ⊕ *www.mci.com.*

MOBILE PHONES
The biggest mobile-phone service providers in Kenya are Airtel, Safaricom, and Orange. You can buy a Kenyan pay-as-you-go SIM card for your mobile phone (from one of the service-provider stores—there's no shortage of them) and top up the airtime as you need it.

Contacts Airtel ☎ *073/3100–100* ⊕ *www.africa.airtel.com.* **Orange** ☎ *100 from an Orange number, 020/222–1000 from another number* ⊕ *www.orange.co.ke.* **Safaricom** ☎ *200 from Safaricom number, 072/200–2200 from another number* ⊕ *www.safaricom.co.ke.*

CUSTOMS AND DUTIES
Each person may bring 200 cigarettes (or 50 cigars or 250 g of tobacco), one bottle of spirits or wine, and up to 568 ml of perfume. The tobacco and alcohol allowance applies only to people 18 and over.

Contact Kenya Customs Service Department ⊕ *kenya.visahq.com.*

HEALTH AND SAFETY
Kenya is a relatively poor country, and crime is a reality for residents and tourists alike; follow these basic precautions for a safe trip.

Mugging, purse snatching, and pickpocketing are rife in big towns. Leave good jewelry and watches at home, and unless you're on safari, keep cameras, camcorders, and binoculars out of sight. Always lock valuables in the hotel or lodge safe. If you must carry valuables, use a money belt under your clothes, keep some cash handy so you don't reveal your money belt in public. Bring copies of all your important documents and stash them away from the originals. Carry extra passport photos in case you need new documents fast. Don't venture out on foot at night. Never take food or drinks from strangers—it could be drugged.

Be on the lookout for street scams like hard-luck stories or appeals to finance a scholarship. Don't be fooled if a taxi driver says on arrival that the fee you negotiated was per person or that he doesn't have change for large bills (bring small bills to avoid this). Be polite but firm if you're stopped by police officers charging you with an "instant fine" for a minor infraction. If you ask to go to the police station, the charges are often dismissed.

You'll need full medical travel insurance, and if you're planning to dive, trek, or climb, make sure your insurance covers active pursuits. Check with your health-care provider to see what vaccinations might be necessary for your destination(s). Very important: Kenya is a yellow-fever zone, and you will need to produce your yellow fever vaccination card when you leave Kenya. Always use sunscreen and bug repellent with DEET. HIV/AIDS is rampant, and malaria is an issue in certain areas (not in Nairobi but definitely on the coast and game reserves).

The Flying Doctors Service offered by AMREF provides air evacuation services for medical emergencies in Kenya, Tanzania, and Uganda, or anywhere within a 1,000 km (621 miles) radius of Nairobi. The planes fly out of Nairobi's Wilson Airport 24 hours a day, 365 days a year. They also provide transportation between medical facilities, fly you back to Europe, Asia, or North America, or provide you with an escort if you're flying on a commercial carrier.

Embassies U.S. Embassy ⊠ *United Nations Ave., Gigiri, Nairobi* ☎ *020/363–6000* ⊕ *nairobi.usembassy.gov.* **British High Commission** ⊠ *Upper Hill Rd., Nairobi* ☎ *020/284-000* ⊕ *www.gov.uk.*

Emergencies Kenya Police ☎ *999* ⊕ *www.kenyapolice.go.ke.*

Medical-Assistance Companies AMREF Flying Doctors ☎ *020/699–2299 for emergencies, 020/600–0090 for customer service* ⊕ *www.flydoc.org.*

MONEY MATTERS

The official currency is the Kenya shilling (Ksh). Available notes are 50, 100, 200, 500, and 1,000 shillings. Available coins are 50 cents, and 1, 5, 10, 20, and 40 shillings.

At this writing, the shilling exchange is about Ksh88 to US$1. Kenya is still relatively inexpensive given the quality of lodgings, which cost probably two-thirds the price of comparable facilities in the United States, although some hotels in the cities have been known to charge expensive rates for tourists.

To avoid administrative hassles, keep all foreign-exchange receipts until you leave the region, as you may need them as proof when changing any unspent local currency back into your own currency.

As the shilling is a relatively weak currency, hotels tend to quote in U.S. dollars. However, for small amounts, such as restaurants, shopping, and tips, it's easiest to withdraw shillings from an ATM once you're in the country. If you pay with dollars, you may find the exchange rate used is lower than the official one.

ATMS AND BANKS

Banks open at 9 on weekdays and close at 3; on Saturday they open at 9 and close at 11. Banks are closed on Sunday. Most ATMs are open 24 hours. Many banks can perform foreign-exchange services or international electronic transfers. Try to avoid banks at their busiest times—at 9 and from noon to 2 on Friday, and at month's end—unless you're willing to arrive early and line up with the locals. Major banks in Kenya are Barclays, Kenya Commercial Bank, National Bank of Kenya, and Commercial Bank of Africa.

Major credit cards such as Visa and MasterCard are accepted at Kenyan banks and by ATMs. Most ATMs accept Cirrus, Plus, Maestro, Visa Electron, and Visa and MasterCard; the best place to withdraw cash is at an indoor ATM, preferably one guarded by a security officer. If you're unsure where to find a safe ATM, ask a merchant.

Contacts Central Bank of Kenya ⊠ *Haile Selassie Ave., Nairobi* ☎ *020/286–0000* ⊕ *www.centralbank.go.ke.*

TIPPING

Tipping isn't mandatory, but porters do expect something, and 10% is customary in restaurants. Some hotels and most permanent tented camps have a gratuity box for you to put a tip for all of the staff at the end of your stay. Tip your safari driver and guide approximately US$10–US$15 per person, per day.

PASSPORTS AND VISAS

Your passport must be valid up to six months after you leave Kenya. Single-entry visas (US$50), valid for three months, are available at Nairobi's Jomo Kenyatta International Airport (you can use US$, euros, or UK pounds sterling) and can be used to move freely between Kenya and Tanzania.

Contacts Kenya Embassy ☎ *202/387–6101 for embassy (Washington, D.C.), 212/421–4741 for consulate (NYC)* ⊕ *www.kenyaembassy.com.*

TAXES

In Kenya the value-added tax (V.A.T.), currently 16%, is included in the price of most goods and services, including accommodations and food. To get a V.A.T. refund, foreign visitors must present receipts at the airport and carry purchased items with them or in their luggage. Fill out Form V.A.T. 4, available at the airport V.A.T. refund office. Make sure that your receipts are original tax invoices, containing the vendor's name and address, V.A.T. registration number, and the words "tax invoice." Refunds are paid by check, which can be cashed immediately at an airport bank or refunded to your credit card with a small transaction fee. Visit the V.A.T. refund desk in the departures hall before you go through check-in, and organize receipts as you travel. Officials will go through your receipts and randomly ask to view purchases.

Airport taxes and fees are included in the price of your ticket.

Contacts Kenya Revenue Authority ☎ *020/499–9999* ⊕ *www.kra.go.ke.*

ABOUT THE RESTAURANTS

Kenya prides itself on game meat and seafood, organically grown vegetables, and tropical fruits (such as passion fruit, papaya, and mangoes) are excellent. Sample traditional Indian and Arab food when you're near the coast, and look for Kenya-grown tea and coffee and Tusker beer, a local brew. "Swahili tea" is very similar to chai in India. You'll find most cuisines, from Chinese to French to Ethiopian, in restaurants in Nairobi.

⇨ *For information on what you can expect at the restaurants and hotels on the Kenyan coast, see the Beach Escapes section below.*

KEEP IT GREEN

Before booking a hotel, lodge, or camp in Kenya, check to see if the property has been rated by Ecotourism Kenya (⊕ *www. ecotourismkenya.org*). Ratings are given based on the properties' efforts to promote environmental, social, and economic values. Participation is voluntary on the part of the hotel, lodge, or camp, but ratings are determined by a preset list of criteria.

ABOUT THE HOTELS AND LODGES

There are more than 2,000 licensed hotels, camps, and lodges in Kenya. There are modern hotels in Nairobi, but some older establishments offer comparable service and comfort plus colonial ambience. Price categories in this chapter treat all-inclusive lodges differently from other lodgings. Lodging, meals, and activities are included at private lodges; find out in advance if park fees (US$40 to US$100 per day) are included. There are rarely elevators in lodging facilities outside hotels in big cities, but most everything is at ground level. Children aren't always welcome at lodges. Some camps, lodges, and coastal hotels are closed during rainy months; ask in advance.

Hotel prices usually include dinner and a full English breakfast. Many lodges and hotels offer special midweek or winter low-season rates. Campsites have few or no facilities and aren't really an option for a visitor with time restrictions or for first-timers. There are all kinds of luxurious beach accommodations available, but these resorts can get crowded during holiday season, so it's essential to book in advance.

WHAT IT COSTS IN U.S. DOLLARS				
	$	$$	$$$	$$$$
Hotels	under $250	$250–$450	$451–$600	over $600
Dining	under $12	$12–$20	$21–$30	over $30

Restaurant prices are the average cost of a main course at dinner or, if dinner is not served, at lunch. Hotel prices are the lowest cost of a standard double room in high season.

ABOUT THE PARKS

Unfortunately, you probably won't be able to see all of Kenya in one trip. So our listings are broken down into **Must-See Parks** (Masai Mara National Reserve, Amboseli National Park, Tsavo National Park, and Laikipia Plateau) and **If You Have Time Parks** (Nairobi National Park, Meru National Park, and Lakes Nakuru and Naivasha) to help you better organize your time. It's suggested, though, that you research *all* of them before you make your decision.

VISITOR INFORMATION

There's no official tourist office in Nairobi and the one in Mombasa isn't very good. Your best option is to consult the Kenya Tourist Board website before you leave home. The website for Kenya Wildlife Services is a good source if you're going to a national park.

Visitor Information Kenya Tourism Federation ☎ *020/600–4767 for tourist helpline* ⊕ *www.kenyatourism.or.ke.* **Kenya Tourist Board** ☎ *020/271–1262* ⊕ *www.magicalkenya.com.* **Kenya Wildlife Service** ☎ *0800/597–000* ⊕ *www. kws.org.*

MASAI MARA

4

Game
★★★★★
Park Accessibility
★★★★★
Getting Around
★★★★★
Accommodations
★★★★★
Scenic Beauty
★★★★

The legendary Masai Mara Game Reserve ranks right up there with Tanzania's Serengeti National Park and South Africa's Kruger National Park in terms of the world's finest wildlife sanctuaries.

Established in 1961, some 275 km (171 miles) southwest of Nairobi, the Mara covers an area of 1,800 square km (702 square miles) and includes part of the Serengeti ecosystem that extends from northern Tanzania into southern Kenya. This ecosystem of well-watered plains supports one of the largest populations of numerous animal groups on earth. There are more than 1 million wildebeests; 250,000 Thomson's gazelles; 250,000 zebras; 70,000 impalas; 30,000 Grant's gazelles; and a huge number of predators including lions, leopards, cheetahs, jackals, and hyenas. There are also more than 450 species of bird, including 57 species of raptor. Every January the wildebeests start to move in a time-honored clockwise movement around the Serengeti toward the new, fresh grazing in the Masai Mara. It's an unforgettable experience.

Local communities, not Kenya Wildlife Services, manage this reserve giving the Maasai, who are pastoralists, the rights to graze their stock on the perimeters of the reserve. Although stock is lost to wild animals, the Maasai manage to coexist peacefully with the game, and rely only on their own cattle for subsistence; in Maasai communities wealth is measured by the number of cattle owned. You'll see the Maasai's *manyattas*—beehive huts made of mud and cow dung—at the entrance to the reserve. The striking appearance of the Maasai, with their red robes and ochre-dyed and braided hair, is one of the abiding images of Kenya. Many lodges offer visits to traditional Maasai villages and homes, and although inevitably these visits have become touristy, they're still well worth doing. Witnessing the dramatic *ipid,* a dance in which the *moran* (warriors) take turns leaping high into the air, will keep your camera clicking nonstop. The Maasai people named the reserve *mara,* which means "spotted," but whether mara applies to the landscape, which is spotted with vegetation, or the hundreds of thousands of wildebeest and

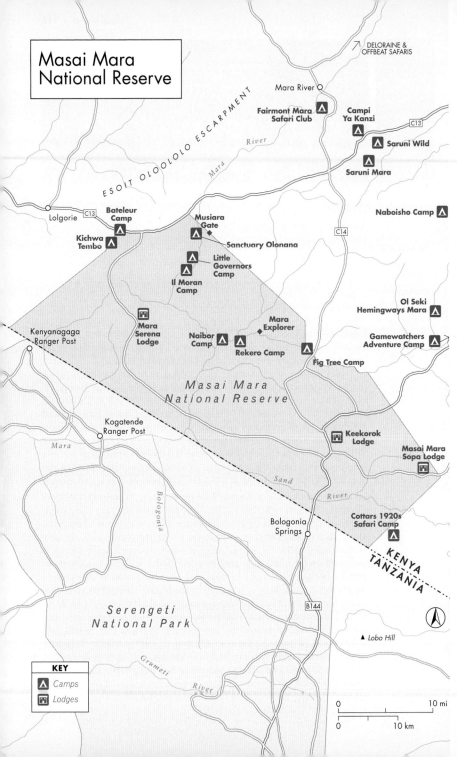

other game that spot the landscape, is anybody's guess.

WHEN TO GO

There's no real best time to visit the Mara, but most people come in the July–October dry season, when the Great Migration is taking place and there are plenty of wildebeest and zebras for the lions, leopards, and cheetahs to prey on. There's no guarantee of seeing any epic river crossings, however. The rainy season is April and May and November, and many roads become inaccessible.

> **DID YOU KNOW?**
>
> National Parks are wildlife and botanical sanctuaries. National Reserves can be used for things other than nature conservation, such as agriculture or pastoralism.

GETTING HERE AND AROUND

Most people fly to the Mara from Nairobi Wilson airport, and scheduled daily air services (45-minute flight) land at eight airstrips in the area. The cost is approximately $185 each way (some lodges include this flight and transfer in their rates). If you're a nervous flyer, note that you'll usually travel in small turbo prop aircraft; however, many tour operators do offer a driving option. The Mara is 270 km (168 miles) from Nairobi and takes approximately six hours to drive. You'll need a four-wheel-drive vehicle. Don't attempt to drive in the rainy season. Once in the park, there are few signposts, so make sure you know exactly where you're going before you depart. The park fee is $80 per person per day, which is often included in package tours.

WHERE TO STAY

All prices have been quoted at high-season rates, as most people will want to come during the migration. However, in low- and mid-season, rates can be considerably cheaper. Check for special offers before you book.

LUXURY LODGES

$$$$ 🏨 **Keekorok Lodge.** The first lodge built in the Masai Mara, Keekorok is an unpretentious lodge with comfortable accommodations. Its superb location—directly in the path of the wildebeest migration—means you won't have to leave camp to see animals galore. You'll stay in a stone chalet or an A-frame wood-and-stone bungalow, both tastefully furnished with comfortable beds, mosquito nets, and an en-suite, old-fashioned white-tile bathroom with bath and overhead shower, and private balcony. Outside there's a small stone veranda with a rustic table and camping chairs. There's a 300-meter (984 feet) raised wooden walkway that leads to a viewing deck with great views of the plains and a hippo pool. The camp is unfenced, so you'll often see elephants and buffalos around its perimeter. Activities include lectures on the Maasai culture, wildlife video viewings, hot-air-balloon rides, tanning by the pool or indulging in the spa. **Pros:** seeing animals outside your room; beds are comfortable. **Cons:** dining is buffet-style; Internet access is expensive. [$] *Rooms from: $650* ✉ *Masai Mara Reserve* ☎ *077/413–6519* 🌐 *www.africanmeccasafaris.com* 🛏 *101 rooms, 10 chalets, 2 suites* 🍴 *All meals.*

$$$$ ⌂ **Mara Serena Safari Lodge.** Perched high on a hill deep inside the reserve, attractive domed huts echo the style and shape of the traditional Maasai *manyattas*. Each hut has rooms that echo the ethnic theme of the exteriors with soft, honey-color furnishings and a personal balcony that overlooks the plains and the distant Esoit Oloololo escarpment—the views are spectacular. Though it's highly unlikely, if you do get tired of gazing out at the endless rolling grasslands where the migration takes place each year, then keep watch at the busy water hole below the restaurant for a continuous wildlife show. Activities include ballooning (expensive but the trip of a lifetime), guided walks, bush barbecues, and game drives. After bouncing around in an open-sided game vehicle, it's great to enjoy a relaxing massage at the Maisha Spa. The Maasai dancing is also spectacular. **Pros:** amazing views from the bedrooms; the breakfasts at the hippo pool. **Cons:** the décor is a bit dated; rooms lack tea- and coffee-making facilities. $ *Rooms from: $610* ✉ *Masai Mara Reserve* ☎ *020/284–2333* ⊕ *www.serenahotels. com* ⌐ *74 rooms* ❑ *All meals.*

$$$$ ⌂ **Saruni Mara.** This exclusive eco-friendly lodge lies just outside the
FAMILY   Masai Mara National Reserve, inside Mara North Conservancy in a remote valley of olive and cedar trees. Each of the six cottages has polished wooden floors and is furnished with hand-carved cedar wood beds, Persian rugs, African art, colonial antiques, and comfortable chairs. You'll dine at a long table at Kuro House, the main lodge, which combines an eclectic mix of old-style Africa and modern design. The Italian cuisine here is superb, but there's also a wide international menu available that uses fresh, locally grown, organic produce. You can also participate in a bush barbecue or dine alone by candlelight on your veranda. The library has a superb collection of Africana—it's definitely worth a visit. Children of all ages are welcome. The tucked-away Masai Wellbeing Space, which uses local plants for its treatments, is run by one of Italy's most famous spas, Centro Benessere Stresa, and is considered one of the best spas in Kenya. All the guides are members of the Kenya Professional Safari Guides Association, and Saruni supports the innovative Koyiaki Guiding School, which trains young Kenyans. Make sure you factor in the $116 per-person, per-day park fee into your expenses as this is not included with the lodge's fees. **Pros:** specialized guiding, such as bird-watching, is available; there's a forest view; because of the altitude, there are no mosquitoes. **Cons:** the camp is a fair distance to the Masai Mara National Reserve, where you can see migrating wildebeest. $ *Rooms from: $1560* ✉ *Mara North Conservancy* ☎ *073/595– 0903* ⊕ *www.sarunicamp.com* ⌐ *6 cottages* ❑ *All meals.*

PERMANENT TENTED CAMPS

$$$$ ⌂ **&Beyond Bateleur Camp.** If you're among the many who saw *Out of Africa* and began fantasizing about your own African experience, then you'll be happy to know that this totally private and very romantic world-class camp is just below the famous hill from the unforgettable final scene. The spacious tents are pitched under an A-frame wood structure with polished wooden floors and a wooden deck with steps leading down to the bush and encircling trees below. A massive four-poster bed dominates the tent's interior—a handy, long, padded stool,

great for sitting on while putting on and taking off your boots after a game drive or bush walk, sits at the foot of the bed. The public areas—also made of wood and canvas—are decorated with old leather armchairs, antique Persian rugs, and a small but well-stocked library. The game-viewing will keep you busy day and night, but do try to include a picnic on the edge of the Great Rift Valley—it will induce dreams of those who once hunted and gathered here millennia ago. **Pros:** the service is excellent; there are unexpected surprise touches along the way. **Cons:** there's no telephone or Internet access at the camp (although guests can access Wi-Fi a four-minute walk away); no baths (showers only). [$] *Rooms from: $2470* ✉ *Masai Mara Reserve* ☎ *27/11–809–4300* 🌐 *www.andbeyond.com* 🛏 *18 tents* 🍴 *All-inclusive.*

4

$$$$ FAMILY Fodor's Choice ★ **&Beyond Kichwa Tembo Tented Camp.** Kichwa Tembo, which means head of the elephant in Kiswahili, is one of Kenya's most sought-after camps. Perched on the edge of a riverine forest below the Oloololo Escarpment, the camp lies directly in the path of the migration. The en-suite tents are spacious and have seemingly neverending views of the plains from the verandas. You'll be surrounded by the unforgettable sounds of the African night as you drift off to sleep. During the day you can take a dip in the shady pool between activities or just relax on your veranda while you fill out your bird and mammal lists. Don't forget to keep an eye out for passing animals: there'll be predators galore, as well as blue- and red-tailed monkeys, the mischievous banded mongoose, and, if you're really lucky, the endangered black rhino. The candlelit dinner on the banks of the Sabaringo River is a must-do for anyone. The staff here are attentive and charming. **Pros:** there's an excellent curio shop; Internet access. **Cons:** no bathtubs; hair dryers in luxury tents only. [$] *Rooms from: $1190* ✉ *Masai Mara Reserve* ☎ *27/11–809–4300* 🌐 *www.andbeyond.com.* 🛏 *40 tents* 🍴 *All-inclusive.*

$$$$ FAMILY Fodor's Choice ★ **Cottars 1920s Safari Camp.** If you want to turn back the clock and immerse yourself in the kind of original safari ambience that Ernest Hemingway enjoyed, this is the place to do it. From the superb and gracious service to the touches of antique luxury—claw-foot tubs, faded antique rugs, wrought-iron candlesticks, old gramophones, polished butlers' trays—the Cottar family's 80 years of experience certainly shows. Sit outside your own spacious, authentic white tent on a wooden rocking chair and watch the hills and valleys below, or relax in the deep red armchairs of the main tented lounge and admire the old photos and prints. At night as you sip a brandy snifter under the soft glow of oil lamps by a log fire, you'll forget all about the 21st century. The tents, with separate lounge and bedroom areas and floor-level canvas decks, are in a huge, 250,000-acre exclusive concession between the Masai Mara, Serengeti, and Loliondo reserves. Because it's a private concession, you won't see the masses of other tourists that you can hardly help bumping into elsewhere in the Masai Mara itself. Because they operate just outside the reserve, Cottars' game vehicles are also allowed off-road, which means more freedom to follow game. (Try a bone-jolting ride in an ox wagon for a genuine early pioneer experience.) The legendary fourth-generation Kenyan Calvin Cottar could be your guide (at extra cost), but his experienced colleagues won't let you down either.

Enjoy a quiet moment in the tented reading room, or rest in a hammock by the natural rock pool. The owners pay the local Maasai community for land use and have helped finance the local school and nearby clinics so that the camp and its activities are seen as a part of the surrounding land and its people. **Pros:** complimentary massages; you will seldom see another game vehicle. **Cons:** hair dryers can be used only in the office; rate does not include air transfers. [$] *Rooms from: $1974* ✉ *Olderkesi Conservancy, Masai Mara Reserve* ☎ *073/377–3377* 🌐 *www.cottars.com* 🛏 *6 en-suite tents, 4 family tents* 🍴 *All-inclusive.*

$$ 🏨 **Fairmont Mara Safari Club.** Although the Fairmont's camp area has manicured lawns and flowers, it is surrounded on three sides by the croc- and hippo-filled Mara River, so you are always close to the wildlife. Within each spacious tent, the bedspread of the four-poster mosquito-netted beds are made of the iconic red cloth used for Maasai warrior robes, while brightly colored handwoven rugs, comfortable chairs, and big windows ensure après-safari comfort. The main lodge is themed old-style safari with deep padded-leather-and-fabric armchairs, beaded lamps, an open fireplace, and an inviting wood-panel bar. Keep family and friends informed of your big-game adventures with Internet access in the library, or write in your journal on the spacious outside deck that leads to a pool, complete with bar and private massage tents. Forgo one morning game drive in favor of a hot-air-balloon safari over the Mara plains followed by a bush champagne breakfast—you'll thank us—or stroll in the footprints of the hippo-trodden path, escorted by a Maasai warrior (four people minimum). **Pros:** rooms have hair dryers; the views of the river from the rooms are excellent. **Cons:** it's not in the park itself or near any migration routes; sundowners and bush walks cost extra. [$] *Rooms from: $315* ✉ *Masai Mara Reserve* ☎ *020/226–5555* 🌐 *www.fairmont.com/masai-mara-safari* 🛏 *51 tents* 🍴 *All meals.*

$$$ 🏨 **Fig Tree Camp.** This budget option on the banks of the Talek River overlooks the plains and its location on the northeastern boundary of the reserve gives it easy access to all the game areas. You'll stay in a safari tent or stone-and-thatch chalet, both furnished in African ethnic themes, but you should try for a tent with a river view; be sure to have taken your malaria *muti* (the generic African word for medicine). Both tents and chalets are en suite and have small verandas or balconies. There are two bars, an indoor and outdoor eating area, and a treehouse coffee deck where you can watch the passing animal show. Don't expect the ultimate in luxury, but you'll get good value for your money and also get to meet lots of international visitors. There's electricity only from 4 to 9 am, noon to 3 pm, and 6 pm to midnight. If you want more luxury and exclusivity, go for one of the Ngaboli tents, where you'll sleep in a four-poster bed and have lots more room. Bonuses for camp guests include lectures, a resident nurse, and an in-house medical clinic. Activities are extra: night safaris, bush walks, champagne breakfasts, and bush dinners range in price from US$55 to US$100. **Pros:** there is a lovely pool area; there's evening entertainment with Maasai dancers or music. **Cons:** hot showers are available only at certain times; tents are located close to each other so can be noisy. [$] *Rooms from:*

"Early in the morning in the Masai Mara, we came across these . . . cubs, walking along a dirt road in the midst of a sea of long golden grass. . . ." —Nick Gordan, Fodors.com member

$485 ⊠ *Masai Mara Reserve* ☎ *020/250–0273* ⊕ *www.madahotels.com* 🛏 *38 tents, 32 chalets, 10 Ngaboli tents* ⍾⊙⍾ *All meals.*

$$$$ 🏕 **Gamewatchers Adventure Camp, Ol Kinyei.** Gamewatchers Adventure Camp offers the same exclusivity as luxurious camps, but with more basic accommodation in large Coleman camping tents. In the Ol Kinyei conservancy, in a picturesque valley among soaring fever and tortilis trees, the camp is visited by game of all sorts. You sleep on mattresses on the floor of your tent and have your own private shower and washroom. Drinks are served around the "bush telly" (fire pit) and communal meals are served at a long table in the mess tent. Game drives are excellent and active big cat sightings are common. You have to book a minimum of three nights at this camp; the rate includes conservancy fees and park fees. **Pros:** the conservancy is very exclusive; the guides are fantastic. **Cons:** the fence surrounding the tents entirely blocks the view; walks are often undertaken without the security of an armed ranger. ⑊ *Rooms from: $840* ⊠ *Ol Kinyei Conservancy, Masai Mara Reserve* ☎ *077/413–6523* ⊕ *www.porini.com* 🛏 *9 rooms* ⊟ *No credit cards* ☉ *Closed Apr.–June, Nov., and Dec.* ⍾⊙⍾ *All meals.*

$$$$ 🏕 **Il Moran.** One of the famous Governors' Camps, Il Moran is where Kenya's first colonial governors used to twirl their handlebar moustaches and sip their gin and tonics while on safari—as you can imagine, it boasts an exclusive location that's teeming with game. *Il Moran,* which means warrior in Maasai, sits on the edge of the plains, nestled in a private forest on the banks of the Mara River. Once upon a time there were 20 tents here, but the owner decided to reduce the number of visitors so as to give you an even more exclusive experience. Today

Ol Seki

Mara Explorer

Datolour

there are just 10 tents, imaginatively furnished with original furniture hand-carved from ancient olive trees, the antique Persian rugs that seem obligatory in so many safari accommodations, battered old leather suitcases, and glowing oil lamps. You'll feel like a pampered Victorian gentleman or lady as you soak in your claw-foot tub—the Victorian gentry would certainly approve of the bidet as well. There are once-in-a-lifetime game drives and guided bush walks, but treat yourself to the hot-air-balloon ride (an extra cost) with a champagne breakfast in the bush to follow. **Pros:** the beds are very comfortable; there's a maximum of four guests per game vehicle. **Cons:** they no longer offer fishing or night drives. [$] *Rooms from: $1590* ✉ *Masai Mara Reserve* ☎ *020/273–4000* 🌐 *www.governorscamp.com* 🛏 *10 tents* 🍴 *All meals.*

$$$$ 🏨 **Little Governors' Camp.** Getting to this camp is a mini adventure in itself. First you take a small boat that ferries you across the Mara River followed by a short, escorted walk with armed guides (so you don't become lion food) before arriving at this gorgeous little camp. You can be assured of superb service and comfortable accommodations. Each tent has an en-suite bathroom with constant hot and cold running water and flush toilet. Lighting, as at many of the traditional Masai Mara camps, is by gas, kerosene lantern, and candlelight. If you're lucky enough to be here during a full moon, you can watch the game come and go at the large water hole in front of the camp. You'll eat superb home-cooked meals under a blue sky or at night in a candlelit dining tent. If you need to stretch your legs after a muscle-clenching, nerve-wracking game drive, go on a guided walking safari or visit a nearby Maasai village and join in the *ipid* jumping dance with the warriors. **Pros:** the camp sits directly in the path of the wildebeest migration; the tents are situated around a busy waterhole. **Cons:** the tents are close together, and there is no privacy on the verandas. [$] *Rooms from: $1400* ✉ *Masai Mara Reserve* ☎ *020/273–4000* 🌐 *www.governorscamp.com* 🛏 *17 tents* 🍴 *All meals.*

$$$$ 🏨 **Mara Explorer.** At this intimate little camp tucked in a riverine forest on a bend on the Talek River, you'll be able to watch elephants wading, hippos snorting, and all other sorts of game from your outdoor claw-foot bathtub that overlooks the river. Of course, a cocktail of choice makes the scene so much more appealing. Legendary explorer Dr. Livingstone never knew what he was missing. A handcrafted wooden bed dominates the en-suite tent, but there's still room for the bedside tables fashioned from logs, old chests, and weather-beaten tin trunks that serve as tables, and an old-fashioned rocking chair where you can sit and tick off your mammal and bird lists. Move a little farther outside and you can laze on your wooden deck, savoring every tranquil moment. You'll be awed by the number of predators you see—lion, leopard, cheetah, hyena—preying on the plains herbivores. All the Masai Mara activities are available, and you'll particularly enjoy the breakfast picnics where the lions can watch *you* feeding. You'll eat delicious meals in an open-air dining area, which looks out over the river, and there are a cozy lounge and small library for those moments when you want to sit still. **Pros:** the camp is a short drive from the Mara River, where thousands of wildebeest make their perilous crossing every year between July and

September; meals are taken overlooking the Talek River. **Cons:** hot water is available only at fixed times. $ *Rooms from: $1580* ⊠ *Masai Mara Reserve* ☎ *020/444–6651* ⊕ *www.heritage-eastafrica.com* ⇗ *10 tents* ⦿*All meals.*

$$$$
Fodor's Choice
★

Naboisho Camp. Quite possibly the best camp in all of the Mara area, Naboisho Camp is in the 50,000-acre Naboisho Conservancy, which was established only a few years ago. According to the camp's manager, the density of wildlife increases every year. While you take your breakfast under the shade of an acacia tree, you're likely to see herds of antelope grazing the plains, a handful of giraffes nibbling at the trees, and numerous zebras mingling between wildebeest, impala, and buffaloes. Along with all the big game, the Naboisho Conservancy has also become home to a large pride of lions, as well as the rare painted dog. Naboisho Camp is exceptionally well designed, and each of the eight spacious tents are set well apart from one another, giving you that beautiful sense of having the bush entirely to yourself. Tents are tastefully decorated and all have en-suite bathrooms with indoor and outdoor bucket showers. The comfortable dining and lounge areas extend out onto a wooden deck, where you can while away your time in comfortable couches, G&T in hand, viewing game close by. The couple who manage the camp have two young daughters and have introduced many special features that make this a wonderful family destination. All activities, from game walks and drives to learning to shoot with a bow and arrow, are included in the price. **Pros:** the guides at this camp are excellent; the area is very exclusive; there are two family tents. **Cons:** no Wi-Fi. $ *Rooms from: $1930* ⊠ *Naboisho Conservancy, Masai Mara Reserve* ☎ *020/232–4904* ⊕ *naboisho.asiliaafrica.com* ⇗ *8 tents* ⦿*All-inclusive.*

$$$$
FAMILY

Naibor Camp. Only 20 minutes away from one of the legendary migration river crossings, this stylish accommodation doesn't exclusively follow traditional safari camp feel, rather it aims for a fusion of old and new with pale khaki and white mesh tents, minimalist hand-carved wooden furniture, roof-to-ceiling earth-color drapes, and plain couches and chairs highlighted with ethnic-patterned cushions. The whole camp lives up to its name—*naibor* means purity and whiteness in Maa, the language of the Maasai people—but you'll never lose that essential sense of being on an African safari. The spacious tents on the banks of the Talek River are furnished with handwoven straw mats, a hand-carved figwood bed, and simple bedside tables. Soft white bed linen is complemented with brightly colored cushions and throws. There's a big private veranda from where you can catch the elephants going down to drink, or listen to and watch the myriad birds. The game here is exceptionally good. **Pros:** it's sociable, with drinks around the fire; excellent bird walks; there's room service for drinks and snacks. **Cons:** there's no pool; bucket showers only (although they are hot). $ *Rooms from: $794* ⊠ *Masai Mara Reserve* ☎ *072/940–6582* ⊕ *www.naibor.com* ⇗ *9 tents* ⦿*All meals.*

$$$$

Ol Seki Hemingways Mara. This eco-friendly camp is named after the *olseki* or sandpaper tree, which is a Maasai symbol of peace, harmony, and wealth. Set on round wooden platforms on a rocky outcrop surrounded by bird-filled trees, the 12-sided tents look as if they are sailing through the bush. Inside, it's all space and light, with simple, stylish furnishings: a double and single bed, cream and earth-tone soft furnishings, straw mats, carefully planned lighting, and en-suite toilet and shower. The lean, clean effect is carried through to the attractive dining tent and library, which has a fireplace. The tents have been refurbished, and two new suites (with two bedrooms each) have private living and dining areas, as well as their own kitchens, ensuring the ultimate in privacy. There's a full range of activities, including morning and night drives with lots of game—you might get one of Kenya's few women guides—bush picnics, star-gazer walks, botanical walks, and visits to authentic, nontouristy Maasai villages, where you might be lucky enough to witness a genuine betrothal or post-initiation ceremony. **Pros:** flights from Nairobi are included, and there's a private airstrip 10 minutes away from the camp; there's power supply 24 hours a day and Internet and telephone on request. **Cons:** it's located outside the reserve, so you'll need to enter the reserve to see the migration; game might not be as dense (but you won't encounter other vehicles). [$] *Rooms from: $1320* ✉ *Naboisho Conservancy, Masai Mara Reserve* ☎ *072/220–4251* 🌐 *www.olseki.com* 🛏 *8 tents* 🕒 *Closed Apr.* 🍴 *All meals.*

$$$$ Fodor's Choice ★ 🏨 **Rekero Camp.** Rekero is tucked away in a grove of trees more than 40 km (25 miles) from the main tourist throng farther east. It's beautifully situated on a river bank near the confluence of the Talek and Mara rivers. You'll sleep in one of only nine tents (which include two family tents), each hidden from the other and all with great views of the plains and the river. There's an ancient wildebeest crossing practically on your doorstep, so you won't have to bounce around for hours in an open-sided game vehicle to find the game. Tents are bright and comfortably furnished with double beds, handwoven rugs, and en-suite bathrooms with flush toilets and canvas bucket showers. As the camp is unfenced, expect all kinds of game to wander past your tent, but you'll be safe within your canvas walls, and a Maasai warrior will escort you to and from the main areas. **Pros:** each tent is tucked into the bush along the river, so you have great views and absolute privacy; good location next to a river crossing point. **Cons:** the access road is particularly rough; meals are taken around a large communal dining table. [$] *Rooms from: $1690* ✉ *Masai Mara Reserve* 🌐 *www.rekerocamp.com* 🛏 *9 tents* 🕒 *Closed Apr. and May* 🍴 *All-inclusive.*

$$$$ FAMILY 🏨 **Sanctuary Olonana.** Named after an honored Maasai chief, this attractive eco-friendly camp in game-rich country rests just outside the northwestern border of the reserve, overlooking the Mara River and the Oloololo Escarpment. Feeling really lazy? Hibernate in your huge wood-floor tent—it's more like a minipavilion—prop yourself up on pillows in your queen-size bed, and watch the river below. There are floor-to-ceiling mosquito-proof "windows" and stone-wall en-suite bathrooms with his and her basins and stools, and a roomy shower. Feeling energetic? Take a guided bush walk or hike up the escarpment. Don't let the lodge's manyatta-style entrance fool you. Once inside the main lodge you'll find the understated luxury of hand-carved wooden

"We watched in awe as the cheetah chose his prey and set out on the chase." —The Swain Family, Fodors.com members

furniture; cream, russet, and brown linens; handwoven African rugs; and indigenous art and artifacts. The reed-roofed main viewing deck overlooks a hippo pool with daylong entertainment from these overgrown clowns. The food is superb, and you have the option to dine with your fellow guests or on your own veranda. There is an inviting pool, a small but good library, and excellent opportunities to observe the everyday lives of the Maasai in the adjacent village. **Pros:** the honeymoon tents are beautiful; you can watch hippos from your tent. **Cons:** rate excludes park fees. $ *Rooms from: $1378* ⊠ *Masai Mara Reserve* ☎ *020/695–0002* ⊕ *www.sanctuaryretreats.com* ⤳ *14 tents* ○ *All-inclusive.*

$$$$ **Saruni Wild.** You certainly won't come across another vehicle at this
FAMILY exclusively sited camp in the northern section of the Masai Mara ecosystem. It has three comfortable Bedouin-looking tents with en-suite bathrooms with hot and cold running water and flush toilets. One of the tents is suitable for families, with two bedrooms and bathrooms. You can track elephants on foot or take action-packed night drives when you have more than a good chance of spotting a leopard, as well as other nocturnal animals such as bush babies and genets. **Pros:** because the camp is in a conservancy, you'll hardly see another vehicle; there's a high chance of seeing rare nocturnal species. **Cons:** it's far from the more popular migration routes during migration time. $ *Rooms from: $1560* ⊠ *Mara North Conservancy* ☎ *020/269–4338* ⊕ *www.saruniwild.com* ⤳ *3 tents* ○ *All-inclusive.*

MOBILE TENTED CAMPS
HORSEBACK SAFARI

$$$$ 🏕 **Offbeat Safaris.** A truly wonderful and unique way to see game and experience Kenya close up is to go on a horse safari; you should do this only if you're an experienced rider—you want to be able to gallop if you meet a hungry predator—and if you're fit enough to ride four to six hours a day. Your safari begins at Deloraine, the beautiful old colonial mansion owned by Tristan and Lucinda Voorspuy, who keep more than 80 horses on the estate. Tristan served in the British Household Cavalry, so he really knows his oats. The estate, which has welcomed British royalty, is on the western edge of the Great Rift Valley on the lower slopes of Mt. Londiani. When you choose the Mara safari, you'll stay at small rustic but comfortable tented camps along the way, sometimes spending two or three nights at the same camp, depending on which route you choose. But even if you get a bit saddle-sore, riding alongside hundreds of thousands of plains game is a once-in-a-lifetime experience. Offbeat also has riding safaris in Amboseli and Laikipia. **Pros:** an adventurous and original way of viewing game; a bit of a hidden secret. **Cons:** must be an experienced horseback rider; it's tricky getting photos when you are on horseback. $ *Rooms from: $7400* ⌧ *Masai Mara Reserve* ☎ *070/490–9355* ⊕ *www.offbeatsafaris.com* ❙❙ *All-inclusive* ⌔ *Rate is per person for a 7-night horseback safari, all-inclusive.*

BUDGET LODGING

$$
FAMILY 🏕 **Masai Mara Sopa Lodge.** On a hillside near the Oloolaimutia Gate, this budget lodge (*sopa* means "welcome" in the Maasai language) is one of the most popular in the reserve. Even though they're always busy, the delightfully friendly and experienced staff will make you feel special. You'll sleep in a *rondavel* (small, round, thatch-roof hut) that has a tiny veranda and is simply but pleasantly furnished in traditional African style with lots of earth-color soft furnishings. The brightly decorated public areas are nestled among flowering plants and trees; notices telling you about mealtimes, balloon booking times, how to book a picnic, and other information are pasted throughout the main area. Don't expect all the bells and whistles of the luxury lodges—hot water is available mornings and evenings only—but the setting and the feeling of Africa on your doorstep more than compensate. Plus, there's a great pool to cool off in after a hot dusty game drive, where events such as Maasai dancing or African food are held. There's also a quaintly named "Wild Animals Viewing Deck" in camp. Because you're more than 6,000 feet above sea level, you'll be cool in summer and will definitely need a jacket or sweater in winter. **Pros:** it's very near the entrance to the reserve; you can see hyenas and bush babies feeding. **Cons:** hot water is available only at limited times; rondavels are located close to each other. $ *Rooms from: $347* ⌧ *Masai Mara Reserve* ☎ *020/375–0183, 020/375–0235* ⊕ *www.sopalodges.com* ⤵ *77 rondavels, 12 suites, 1 presidential suite* ❙❙ *All meals.*

AMBOSELI NATIONAL RESERVE

Game
★★★★
Park Accessibility
★★★★★
Getting Around
★★★★★
Accommodations
★★★★★
Scenic Beauty
★★★★★

Amboseli National Reserve, immediately northwest of Mt. Kilimanjaro and 240 km (150 miles) southeast of Nairobi on the Tanzanian border, is certainly one of the most picturesque places in the whole of Africa to watch game. Where else could you watch a great herd of elephants on a wide empty plain dominated by Africa's highest mountain, Kilimanjaro?

At dawn, as the cloud cover breaks and the first rays of sun illuminate the snow-capped 5,895-meter (19,340-foot) peak, the sky, colored by rosy pinks and soft reds, provides the perfect backdrop for the plains below. It gets even better at dusk, when the mountain stands out in stark relief against the fiery sun.

Amboseli has a checkered history. First established as a natural reserve in 1948, it was returned to Maasai ownership and management in 1961 but soon became environmentally degraded with too many cattle and too many tourists. Some 10 years later, 392 square km (151 square miles) were designated a national park, and cattle-grazing was forbidden. This angered the pastoral Maasai, who took their revenge by killing a majority of the rhino population. Eventually peace was restored with some expedient land swapping, and today there's a responsible environmental program that controls the well-being of the game, puts limits on tourist numbers, and enforces a strict policy on off-road driving.

There are five different habitats in Amboseli: open plains, acacia woodland, thornscrub, swamps, and marshlands. To the west is the Ol Donyo Orok massif and Lake Amboseli, which is usually dry. But when the heavy rains return, so do the flamingos, and the surrounding area becomes green and lush again. Expect some impassable roads at these times, as well as when the lake is completely dry because the fine alkaline dust that blows up from the lake bed is hell for tires.

Amboseli is filled with great game: zebra, warthog, giraffe, buffalo, impala, wildebeest, the long-necked mini giraffe-like *gerenuks,* and baboons galore. But your chances of seeing predators are not as good as in the Masai Mara. Maasai hunters almost killed off Amboseli's lions because they preyed on their herds of cattle. Those that survived are still skittish and often not comfortable with vehicles. Interestingly, the hunting methods of cheetahs within the park have changed dramatically because of tourist pressure. Accustomed to hunting at dawn and dusk, they've now resorted to hunting at midday—tourist siesta time—with poorer success rates, thus their numbers are decreasing. But if it's elephants you're after, then Amboseli is the place. Perhaps the oldest and most studied elephant population in sub-Saharan Africa lives here. There are more than 1,500 of these great pachyderms today, and because they're accustomed to visitors and vehicles you'll experience eyeball-to-knee-high close encounters.

Game-viewing is best around the main swamps of Enkongo Narok, which means "black and benevolent," and the Amboseli landmark, Observation Hill. Enkongo Narok, in the middle of the park, is where you can see water seeping up from the lava rocks. Observation Hill provides a surefire opportunity to spot game, especially elephants, as it looks out over the plains.

Bird life is also prolific, with more than 420 recorded species. There are dozens of birds of prey including more than 10 different kinds of eagles. In the swamp areas, which are fed by the melting snow of Kilimanjaro, seasonal flamingo and more than 12 species of heron are among the profusion of water birds.

WHEN TO GO

January and February, and June through September are the best times to come here. During April and May, the rainy season, roads might become rough—you'll need a 4x4—but it is a favorite time for photographers and birders to be here, when everything is green. There might also be rain in November and December.

GETTING HERE AND AROUND

Amboseli is 260 km (160 miles) from Nairobi. Scheduled flights from Nairobi's Wilson Airport and Mombasa land at three airstrips. Note that you'll be flying in a small aircraft. The journey by road takes about four hours. The last 16 km (10 miles) are full of potholes, so you'll need a 4x4. There's no public transport within the park. Park fees are $80 per person per day. This fee is included in package tours and most lodge accommodations.

WHERE TO STAY

LUXURY LODGES

$$ **Amboseli Serena Safari Lodge.** Situated beside a natural flowing spring, this lodge enjoys spectacular views of Mt. Kilimanjaro. Ochre-color guest rooms line paved walkways that weave through landscaped gardens. The food, cooked with homegrown herbs and vegetables, is excellent, particularly the homemade pasta. Because the lodge is near the

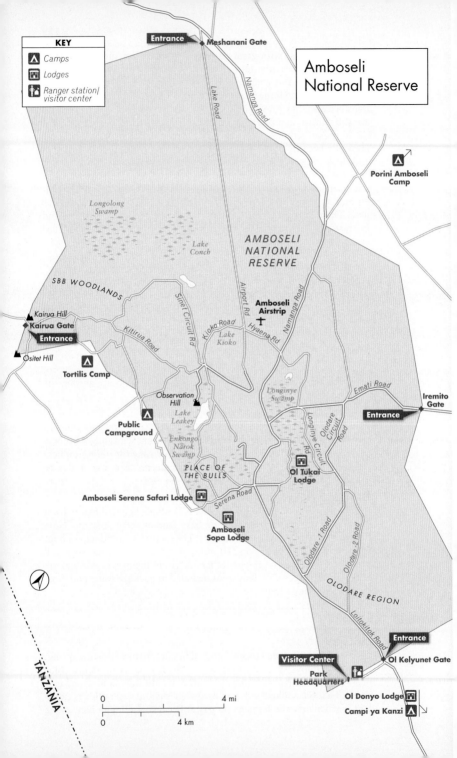

Amboseli National Reserve

KEY
- Camps
- Lodges
- Ranger station/ visitor center

Entrance — Meshanani Gate

Lake Road

Namanga Road

Porini Amboseli Camp

Longolong Swamp

Lake Conch

AMBOSELI NATIONAL RESERVE

SBB WOODLANDS

Sinet Circuit Rd

Kioko Road

Airport Rd

Amboseli Airstrip

Hyaena Rd

Kairua Hill

Kairua Gate
Entrance

Ositet Hill

Kitirua Road

Lake Kioko

Tortilis Camp

Observation Hill

Lake Leakey

Longinye Swamp

Emati Road

Iremito Gate

Entrance

Public Campground

Enkongo Narok Swamp

PLACE OF THE BULLS

Longinye Circuit

Olodare Circuit Road

Ol Tukai Lodge

Amboseli Serena Safari Lodge

Serena Road

Olodare-1 Road

Olodare-2 Road

Amboseli Sopa Lodge

OLODARE REGION

Loitokitok Road

Entrance

Visitor Center

Ol Kelyunet Gate

Park Headquarters

Ol Donyo Lodge

Campi ya Kanzi

TANZANIA

0   4 mi

0   4 km

"Amboseli Park was dry, and the plain was hazy at dusk. The cheetahs were stalking under the watchful eyes of the wildebeest." —Liz1940, Fodors.com member

Enkongo Narok Swamp, there's always plenty of game around. Take a game drive, go walking with a Maasai guide, enjoy a bush breakfast, and always remember to keep your doors and windows closed to keep out marauding vervet monkeys, which look cute but can make off with your belongings. The rooms are small, and fairly basic, with an en-suite bathroom. There is one suite, which has its own private garden and rooftop balcony, and which has direct views to Mt. Kilimanjaro. What the lodge lacks in luxury is more than made up by the friendly and helpful staff. **Pros:** good value for money; the lodge balcony has views out onto the plains; the water hole in front of the dining area is floodlit at night. **Cons:** game drives are not included in the price; not all the rooms have views. $ *Rooms from: $400* ⊠ *Amboseli National Reserve* ☎ *020/284–2000* ⊕ *www.serenahotels.com* ⇗ *92 rooms, 1 suite* ⊚ *All meals.*

$$
FAMILY
🏠 **Amboseli Sopa Lodge.** When Ernest Hemingway wrote *The Snows of Kilimanjaro*, he stayed near the area that this attractive lodge was eventually built. It's in lush established gardens in the foothills of Mt. Kilimanjaro near the Tanzanian border. You'll stay in roomy mud-and-thatch en-suite hut, gaily decorated with wood, animal motifs, and brightly colored soft furnishings. Enjoy a hearty breakfast and lunch buffet inside in the big Africa-theme dining room, or eat out beside the pool, where there's also a pleasant poolside bar. In the evening sit down to a four-course meal where you can choose between European, African, or Asian dishes. There is a stunning lounge area and great viewing deck. It's also a great place for kids—there's plenty of room for them to run around, a lovely pool, and babysitters are always available if you want to be child-free for an evening. The lodge offers lots of activities, which

are an additional cost, including game drives, guided walks, and trips to Maasai villages. If you want to have a go at climbing Mt. Kilimanjaro, the lodge can arrange that, too. **Pros:** the backdrop of Mt. Kilimanjaro; the hotel arranges night feeding of the animals. **Cons:** the lodge is half an hour's drive from Amboseli itself; hot water can be erratic. $ *Rooms from: $337* ✉ *Amboseli National Reserve* ☎ *020/375–0235* ⊕ *www. sopalodges.com* ⇴ *83 rooms* ⦿ *Some meals.*

PERMANENT TENTED CAMPS

$$$$ **Porini Amboseli Camp.** This exclusive, back-to-nature tented camp is in the remote and game-abundant Selenkay Conservancy, a few miles north of Amboseli National Park. A gold eco-award winner, the camp is co-owned with the local Maasai community. Because the area is relatively new to tourism, you'll see few visitors, but lots of game including lion, leopard, cheetah, and the ubiquitous Amboseli elephants. Birdlife is prolific, with lots of raptors. Big, comfortably furnished tents are solar-powered and have en-suite bathrooms with a basin, shower, and flush toilet. You'll eat hearty, home-cooked meals outside the mess tent while being serenaded by birdcalls by day and nocturnal animals by night. Game drives are taken in an open-sided safari vehicle—yours will be the only one for miles (there are only six gamedrive vehicles in the 15,000-acre conservancy). You'll visit an authentic Maasai village, take an informative walk in a dry riverbed, enjoy a picnic lunch in Amboseli itself, and at night you'll return to your own little private spot in the African wilderness. The all-inclusive price covers round-trip road transfers, Amboseli park fees, conservancy fees, all game drives, sundowners, walks with Maasai warriors, Maasai village visits, full board, and free house wine, beer, and soft drinks. The gift shop is superb—do all of your souvenir shopping here (plus it benefits the local community). **Pros:** the camp benefits the local community and is eco-friendly; there are few visitors but lots of game. **Cons:** as with most camps, you'll struggle to get a phone signal. $ *Rooms from: $1220* ✉ *Selenkay Conservancy, Amboseli National Reserve* ☎ *077/413–6523* ⊕ *www.porini.com* ⇴ *9 tents* ⦿ *All meals.*

$$$$ **Tortilis Camp.** This multi-award-winning rustic bush camp, refur-
FAMILY   bished in 2011, is named after the flat-topped *Acacia tortilis* trees that surround the camp. The main thatch-roof open bar, lounge, and dining room overlook a water hole and have superb views of Mt. Kilimanjaro and Mt. Meru in neighboring Tanzania. Your large tent sits under a huge thatch canopy and is raised up on a small platform with wooden floors, a king-size bed, and an en-suite bathroom with hot showers and flush toilets. If you want to catch up on your journal or bird and mammal lists, then relax on the comfortable furniture on your personal sitting area, or laze by the pool in between activities (such as game drives or guided bush walks, which the lodge provides at an extra cost). There's also a family house with one double and one twin-bed room if you don't fancy splitting up between two tents. The mainly northern-Italian food is delicious and is whipped up from the manager's original family recipes. The food is made even tastier by homegrown herbs and vegetables. There's a two-night minimum-stay requirement. While Tortilis borders Amboseli, it sits within its own private conservancy,

Amboseli Serena Safari Lodge bedroom interior

Camp ya Kanzi

Ol Donyo

which means that game walks and night drives are possible. The price includes the conservancy but not park fees. **Pros:** stunning views of Mt. Kilimanjaro; excellent library; lots of elephants and great birdlife. **Cons:** many of the tents are accessed by steep steps. $ *Rooms from: $1210* ⊠ *Amboseli National Reserve* ☎ *073/012–7000* ⊕ *www.tortilis.com* ⤴ *16 tents, 1 family tent, 1 private house* ¶⊘ *All-inclusive.*

BUDGET LODGING

$
FAMILY

☷ **Ol Tukai Lodge.** Within the boundaries of Amboseli National Park but on private land, this is an ideal location to spot game such as the famously studied Amboseli elephants. In fact, Ol Tukai claims that this is the best place in the world to watch elephants. Apart from the plains game and its attendant predators, there are more than 400 species of birds to be identified, and Ol Tukai offers specially designed bird walks through its grounds for beginners and experts alike; it's a wonderful opportunity to introduce yourself or the kids to the world of birds. This resort manages to be both modern and traditional—its facilities are world class, but its feel and ambience are unmistakably African. The resort is set amid acres of well-kept lawns dotted with the familiar symbol of the plains—*Acacia tortilis* trees—and has a superb view of Mt. Kilimanjaro. En-suite chalets, built of local stone and slate, are furnished with handcrafted wooden furniture and decorated with faux animal-skin fabrics, rugs, and throws; each has a personal veranda. Public areas are open and spacious; everywhere you go you'll have a different view. For that special group celebration, choose the three-bedroom stone and wood Kibo Villa, tucked away in its own private 5 acres where you can self-cater or eat at the main lodge. Babysitters are available. **Pros:** rooms are very spacious; the views of Kilimanjaro are fantastic; the large, fenced-in property is great for kids. **Cons:** game drives and other activities are not included in the price. $ *Rooms from: $220* ⊠ *Amboseli National Reserve* ☎ *073/535–0005* ⊕ *www.oltukailodge.com* ⤴ *80 chalets, 1 villa* ¶⊘ *All meals.*

NEAR AMBOSELI AND TSAVO EAST AND WEST
LUXURY LODGES

$$$$
FAMILY

☷ **Ol Donyo Lodge.** This camp is perched on a hillside, so every suite has great views of the plains, Mt. Kilimanjaro, and the water holes. No two of the ten large suites in six stand-alone villas are the same. They all have rooftop "star beds," which are accessed from the veranda by a winding stone staircase. They allow you the option of sleeping under the stars but with all the comforts of your suite just below. All but two of the suites have private pools, too. Some villas have four beds each and private sitting rooms and are ideal for families or small groups of friends. Excellent food and friendly, attentive service are the norm. Meals are taken in the centrally positioned dining room with a big open fireplace for those chilly nights. **Pros:** the horizon pool has stunning views of Mt. Kilimanjaro; suites have indoor and outdoor showers as well as bathtubs; the "star beds" are an indescribable experience. **Cons:** there's less concentrated game than in the main areas, but no other people. $ *Rooms from: $2060* ⊠ *Chyulu Hills* ☎ *020/600–5108*

🌐 *www.greatplainsconservation.com* ⇆ *10 suites* ⏲ *Closed Apr.* 🍴 *All-inclusive.*

PERMANENT TENTED CAMPS

$$$$ FAMILY Fodor's Choice ★ **Campi ya Kanzi.** One of the most environmentally friendly camps in East Africa, this lovely camp, whose name means "Camp of the Hidden Treasure" in Swahili, is in the Kuku Group Ranch, the natural corridor between Amboseli and Tsavo National Parks. It was the first camp in Kenya to be gold rated by Ecotourism Kenya for its efforts in sustainable tourism, and has won other prestigious international ecotourism awards. It's also co-owned by the Maasai from the ranch area and Luca Belpietro and his wife, Antonella Bonomi. The ranch itself stretches 1,115 square km (400 square miles) from the foothills of Mt. Kilimanjaro to the the Chyulu Hills in the east, and because of the different altitudes you'll find all sorts of habitats, from wide plains and riverine bush to high mountain forests. You'll also find plenty of game—more than 60 mammals and 400 bird species—but few tourists. To see all this, choose between game drives (where the game is really wild and not used to vehicles), guided game walks, botanical walks, bird-watching, and cultural visits. Take your kids to the Maasai school and open their eyes to a completely different way of life. The main lounge and dining areas are in Tembo (Elephant) House, which has superb views of Mt. Kilimanjaro, the Taita Hills, and Chyulu Hills. All the tents have great views, as well as wooden floors, a veranda, and an en-suite bathroom with bidet, flush toilet, and hot and cold running water. The Hemingway and Simba tented suites boast king-size beds, a dressing room, en-suite bathroom with his-and-her washbasins, and verandas overlooking Mt. Kilimanjaro. Note that there is an additional US$100 per-person, per-day conservation fee, which entirely benefits the local Maasai community. **Pros:** the cottages are very private; staff are from the local Maasai community. **Cons:** no pool. [$] *Rooms from: $1500* ✉ *Chyulu Hills* ☎ *072/046–1300* 🌐 *www.maasai.com* ⇆ *6 tents, 2 suites* 🍴 *All-inclusive.*

TSAVO NATIONAL PARK

Game
★★★

Park Accessibility
★★★★

Getting Around
★★★★

Accommodations
★★★★

Scenic Beauty
★★★★

At almost 21,000 square km (8,108 square miles), Tsavo National Park is Kenya's largest park. It includes the areas of Tsavo West and Tsavo East. Both stretch for about 130 km (80 miles) along either side of Nairobi/Mombasa Highway, the main road from Nairobi to Mombasa. It's amazing that just a few miles away from the constant thunder of motor traffic on Kenya's busiest road is some of Kenya's best wildlife viewing.

TSAVO WEST

Tsavo West covers 7,065 square km (2,728 square miles), which is a little less than a third of the total area comprising all of Kenya's national parks. With its diverse habitats of riverine forest, palm thickets, rocky outcrops and ridges, mountains and plains, it's more attractive and certainly more accessible than Tsavo East. In the north, heavily wooded hills dominate; in the south there are wonderful views over the Serengeti Plains. Take a boat ride or go birding on Lake Jipe, one of the most important wetlands in Kenya. If you like birds, you'll be keen to get a glimpse of the whitebacked night heron, African skimmers, and palm-nut vultures. The lake, which lies in the park's southwest corner on the Kenya/Tanzania border, is fed from the snows of Kilimanjaro and the North Pare mountains. There's evidence of volcanic activity everywhere in the park, especially where recent lava flows absorb the rainfall. In one spectacular spot, this rainfall, having traveled underground for 40 km (25 miles) or so, gushes up in a pair of pools at Mzima Springs, in the north of the park. There's a submerged hippo blind here, but the hippos have gotten wise to tourists and often move to the far side of the pools. Because of the fertile volcanic soil and abundance of water, the park is brimming with animal, bird, and plant life. You'll see lion and cheetah—especially in the dry season when the grass is low—spotted hyena, buffalo, the beautiful Masai giraffe, and all kinds of antelope, including Thomson's and Grant's gazelle—the prettiest of the antelope.

WHEN TO GO

You'll have a good experience whenever you go, but bear in mind that the long rains are from March to May, and the short rains are October to December. January to March can be very hot.

GETTING HERE AND AROUND

Tsavo West is approximately 100 km (62 miles) from Mombasa, making it a good option if you're staying by the coast or plan to visit the coast after your safari. There's no public transport to the park, so you'll have to self-drive or fly from Mombasa or Wilson airport. If you drive yourself, be aware that signage in the park is unclear and you'll need a GPS. Park fees are $75 per person per day.

WHERE TO STAY

LUXURY LODGES

$$ 🏨 **Kilaguni Lodge.** This lovely old lodge was Kenya's first lodge in a national park. Timber, stone, and thatch buildings complement the natural wilderness surroundings and when it's not wreathed in clouds, there's a good view of Mt. Kilimanjaro. You can watch game and birds from any one of several viewing decks, or enjoy a drink in the bar carved out of rocks. En-suite rooms are decorated in the ubiquitous African-theme fabrics, but are comfortable and spacious. Buffet meals with plenty of variety are way above the average. You can book all sorts of activities at the lodge, including morning and afternoon game drives, bush breakfasts and dinners, and guided walks. **Pros:** there's an on-site medic; there's a busy watering hole that can be viewed from the hotel. **Cons:** not all rooms have great views; room decor is a bit dated. [$] *Rooms from: $320* ✉ *Tsavo West* ☎ *020/284–2000* 🌐 *www.serenahotels.com* 🛏 *56 rooms* 🍴 *Some meals.*

PERMANENT TENTED CAMPS

$$$$ 🏨 **Finch Hattons.** If you saw the movie *Out of Africa,* then you'll have some idea, even if it's rather over-romanticized, of who Denys Finch Hatton was. At the turn of the 20th century he left his native England and fell in love not only with Karen Blixen but also with Kenya. A big-game hunter and host extraordinaire, he soon cultivated a reputation for leading classy, exclusive safaris for American tycoons and British royalty, among others. His legend lives on in this superb camp—frequently voted "Best Tented Camp in Africa" by top writers and travelers—where your every whim is catered to, your every dream of Africa comes true, and where you'll dine at a table sparkling with silver and crystal as strains of Mozart (Denys's favorite composer) softly fill the African night. The camp is in groves of old acacia trees around a natural spring that is home to numerous hippos, crocodiles, and different species of birds near the Kenya/Tanzania border. The tents are luxuriously furnished with antique furniture, wooden chests, and even a daybed on your personal veranda; all tents have outside showers, free-standing copper bath tubs and viewing decks facing the hippo pools. A recent addition to the camp is a spa and wellness center, which includes a hammam, gym, yoga studio and two infinity pools. It's expensive, but this

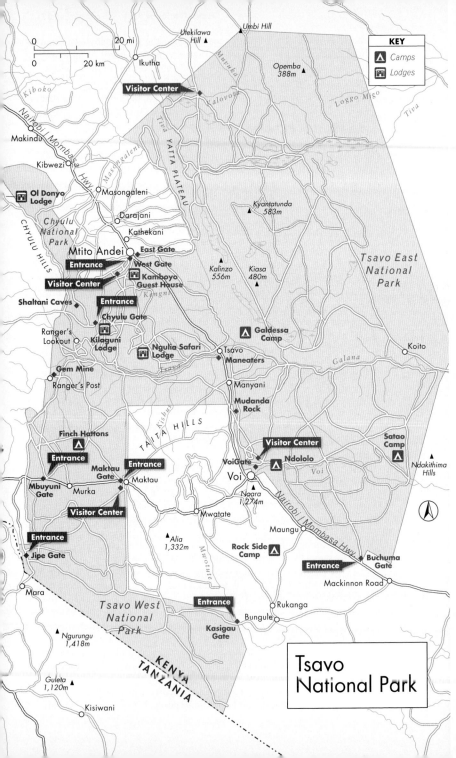

Tsavo National Park

KEY

⛺ Camps
🏠 Lodges

0 ——— 20 mi
0 ——— 20 km

Umbi Hill
Utekilawa Hill ▲
Ikutha
Opemba 388m ▲
Visitor Center
Kiboko
Kalovoto
Mnzuka
Loggo Migo
Tiva
Makindu
Nairobi / Mombasa Hwy
Tiva
Kibwezi
Masongaleni
Masongaleni
🏠 Ol Donyo Lodge
Chyulu National Park
Tiva YATTA PLATEAU
Darajani
Kyantatunda 583m ▲
Kathekani
Mtito Andei
East Gate
Chyulu Hills
Entrance
West Gate
Kalinzo 556m ▲
Kiasa 480m ▲
Tsavo East National Park
Visitor Center
🏠 Kamboyo Guest House
Entrance
Kenya
Shaltani Caves ▲
Chyulu Gate
Ranger's Lookout
🏠 Kilaguni Lodge
⛺ Galdessa Camp
Koito
Gem Mine
🏠 Ngulia Safari Lodge
Tsavo Maneaters
Galana
Ranger's Post
Tsavo
Manyani
Finch Hattons
⛺
Mudanda Rock
Entrance
TAITA HILLS
Visitor Center
⛺ Ndololo
Satao Camp ⛺
Maktau Gate
Entrance
VoiGate
Voi
Voi
Ndakithima Hills ▲
Mbuyuni Gate
Murka
Maktau
Visitor Center
Noara 1,274m
Entrance
Mwatate
Maungu
Nairobi / Mombasa Hwy
Alia 1,332m ▲
Rock Side Camp ⛺
Buchuma Gate
Entrance
Jipe Gate
Mara
Entrance
Mwotate
Entrance
Rukanga
Mackinnon Road
Tsavo West National Park
Kasigau Gate
Bungule
Ngurungu 1,418m ▲
KENYA
TANZANIA
Guleta 1,120m ▲
Kisiwani

lodge is worth it. **Pros:** you'll see an extraordinary array of wildlife right in the camp; food and service are outstanding. **Cons:** game drives and park fees are extra; the generator is switched off at 11:30 pm. [$] *Rooms from: $1040* ✉ *Tsavo West* ☎ *020/357–7500* 🌐 *www.finchhattons.com* 🛏 *34 tents* 🍴 *All meals.*

THE LEGEND OF THE BAOBAB

Legend has it that when the gods were planting the earth, the baobab refused many locations. In anger, the gods threw them out of heaven and they landed upside down. Take a good look. When not in leaf, they look exactly as if their roots are sticking up into the air.

BUDGET LODGING

$$ FAMILY 🏨 **Ngulia Safari Lodge.** High on the edge of the Ndawe escarpment with panoramic views of the plains below, this unassuming, basic lodge offers all the generic game park activities (not included) plus spacious en-suite rooms all overlooking the wide savanna. Thatch and wood *bandas* (thatch and canvas bungalows) raised just above ground level, each with its own veranda, blend in aesthetically with the bush environment. Inside they have tiled floors and brightly colored soft furnishings. There's a pool surrounded by flowering shrubs and trees, two bars, and a restaurant with good home-cooked food. Because the lodge is in the park, you don't have to travel far to see lots of big game: lions, cheetahs, a leopard if you're lucky, elephants, buffalos, and hundreds of pretty little gazelles. **Pros:** lodge overlooks a watering hole; you have a good chance of seeing a leopard. **Cons:** bathrooms are dated; pool area is not shady. [$] *Rooms from: $425* ✉ *Tsavo West* ☎ *866/527–4281 in the U.S. for reservations (toll-free)* 🌐 *www.africanmeccasafaris.com* 🛏 *52 rooms* 🍴 *All meals.*

NATIONAL PARKS ACCOMMODATIONS

There are very basic camping facilities in Tsavo East and Tsavo West, but at $15 per person per night, camping is a very affordable option. You'll need your own vehicle (4x4 only) and be well equipped with camping gear.

$ 🏨 **Kamboyo Guest House.** This reasonably priced, self-catering government guesthouse is 8 km (5 miles) from the Mtito Andei Gate, an easy 240-km (149-mile) drive from Nairobi. Built of red brick and red tiles, it has four clean, sparsely furnished bedrooms. Linens, soap, towels, and basic kitchen implements are provided; bring drinking water and firewood. You are allowed up to 10 guests; it's a bit of a squash, but worth it for the proximity to attractions such as Mzima Springs. **Pros:** there's a fireplace and outside shower. **Cons:** electricity from 6 to 10 pm only; there are only two bathrooms, one en suite. [$] *Rooms from: $240* ✉ *Tsavo West* ☎ *020/600–0800* 🌐 *www.kws.org* 🛏 *1 guesthouse* 🍴 *No meals.*

TSAVO EAST

Tsavo East—11,747 square km (4,535 square miles)—is a fairly harsh landscape of scrubland dotted with huge baobab trees, and photographers will revel in the great natural light and the vast plains stretching

Galdessa

Galdessa

to the horizon. There's lots of greenery along the banks of the Voi and Galana rivers, and the big Aruba Dam, built across the Voi, attracts game and bird life galore. You'll see herds of elephants and buffalo, waterbuck, and all kinds of animals coming to drink at the dam. The Lugard Falls, on the Galana River, is more a series of rapids than actual waterfalls; walk along the riverbank to catch a glimpse of the water-sculpted rocks. Another fascinating feature in the park is the 290-km-long (180-mile-long) Yatta Plateau, one of the world's longest lava flows. It runs parallel to the Nairobi/Mombasa Highway and is 5 to 10 km (3 to 6 miles) wide and 305 meters (1,000 feet) high. Mudanda Rock, a 1.5-km (2-mile) outcropping, is a water catchment area. You'll see plenty of wildlife coming to drink at the dam below. There's a lot of game in this park, including zebras, kongoni antelope, impalas, lions, cheetahs, and giraffes, and rarer animals such as the oryx, lesser kudu, and the small klipspringer antelope, which can jump nimbly from rock to rock because of the sticky suction pads under their feet. And yes, it's true: those fat and hairy marmotlike creatures you see sunning themselves on the rocks—the hyraxes—are first cousins to elephants.

The park became infamous in the late 1890s because of the "Man Eaters of Tsavo," a pride of lions that preyed on the Indian migrant laborers who were building the railway. More than 130 workers were killed; the incident was retold in the 1996 thriller, *The Ghost and the Darkness,* starring Val Kilmer. In the 1970s and '80s Tsavo became notorious once again for the widespread poaching that decimated the elephant population and nearly wiped out rhinos altogether. Today, thanks to responsible management, enlightened environmental vision, and proper funding, both elephant and rhino populations are on the rise.

WHEN TO GO

Tsavo East is accessible year-round, so the peak season is actually based on demand months such as migration time in Kenya (July–October) and also vacationers getting away during the winter months—especially Europeans. That being said, March through May is the rainy season, and there are short rains in October and December. Humidity is high from December to April.

GETTING HERE AND AROUND

Tsavo East is 233 km (148 miles) south of Nairobi and 250 km (155 miles) north of Mombasa. There are nine airstrips. There's no public transport within the park. Park entry fees are $75 per person per day, which is usually included in a package tour.

WHERE TO STAY

LUXURY LODGES

$$ **Galdessa Camp.** This beautiful, remote camp is on the south bank of the Galana River. Overlooking the Yatta Plateau upstream from the Lugard Falls, it's actually two camps; the main lodge has 12 spacious bandas, including one honeymoon banda; the other, private camp (exclusive use only) has three bandas, also including a honeymoon one. Each lodge has its own lounge, dining area, and bar overlooking the river. The elegant and imaginatively decorated thatch-roof bandas are built on wooden platforms with an A frame and a private veranda

that has breathtaking river views. The furnishings are Africa-themed with huge hand-carved beds, wooden chests, deep-cushioned armchairs, handwoven rugs, and wall hangings. There's an en-suite bathroom with flush toilet and bucket shower. If you want total privacy, then opt for the honeymoon bandas, which have separate verandas on stilts—perfect for canoodling to your heart's content under the stars. Don't be surprised if you see a herd of elephant strolling along the riverbank or crocodiles and hippos right in front of your banda, as during the dry season many animals come to the river to drink. **Pros:** bush walks are excellent; the quality and standard of the food is superb. **Cons:** credit cards are not accepted; dinners are off a set menu. $ *Rooms from: $540* ⊠ *Tsavo East* ☎ *040/320–2271, 040/260–8458* ⊕ *www.galdessa.com* ⤴ *15 bandas* ▤ *No credit cards* ⦿ *All meals.*

PERMANENT TENTED CAMPS

$$ **Satao Camp.** This small and friendly camp lies on a traditional migra-
FAMILY tion route, so it's not short of game. It's not short on comfort either. You'll stay in one of 20 tents placed in a semicircle looking out onto a water hole, each with its own veranda. All are built under individual thatch canopies and shaded by ancient tamarind trees. There's a handmade bed inside your green canvas tent, with lots of attractive African-patterned soft furnishings. The food is wholesome and fresh, and it's great to sit under the 200-year-old tamarind tree and watch the elephants at the water hole. There's a thatch viewing deck on stilts where you can sit and read, or just watch, wait, and see what walks up. There's an attractive dining area under thatch, but lunch is usually taken alfresco under the trees. Kids under 2 stay free, and those 2 to 12 pay 50% of the adult rate. **Pros:** excellent views of a watering hole from the observation tower; it's fully equipped for people with disabilities. **Cons:** parts of the camp looks onto unsightly power lines. $ *Rooms from: $436* ⊠ *Tsavo East* ☎ *020/243–4600* ⊕ *www.sataocamp.com* ⤴ *15 tents, 5 suites* ⦿ *All meals.*

BUDGET LODGINGS

$ **Rock Side Camp.** Between Tsavo East and West, this former hunting camp (formerly Westermann's Safari Camp) is a great base to explore both parks. The Tozers, who live here permanently, have transformed this delightful getaway into a luxury destination that's simply but tastefully decorated with en-suite facilities. Accommodations are at the foot of a rocky *kopje* (small hill) that look out toward plains in the foreground and mountains in the background. It's all about personal service and individual attention here. The slate, stone, and thatch bar and restaurant with rustic wooden furniture is surrounded by flowering plants and trees—you can't help but feel immediately at home here. Food is homemade, often homegrown, and delicious. The camp doesn't offer game drives, but you can go for a walk in the bush, climb up the kopje, or just sit with the tipple of your choice and watch the spectacular sunsets. **Pros:** Rock Side is inexpensive because it's not in the park; it's been upgraded. **Cons:** activities are not offered; they don't take credit cards. $ *Rooms from: $165* ⊠ *Tsavo East* ☎ *020/204–1443* ⊕ *www.rocksidecamp.com* ⤴ *16 bandas, 7 bungalows* ▢ *No credit cards* ⦿ *All meals.*

LAIKIPIA PLATEAU

4

Game
★★★★
Park Accessibility
★★★★
Getting Around
★★★
Accommodations
★★★
Scenic Beauty
★★★★

Stretching across the western flank of Mt. Kenya, Laikipia Plateau, gateway to Kenya's little-visited northern territory, isn't in itself a national park or reserve, but it's become one of Kenya's most recent conservation successes. It's still free from the hordes of game vehicles and flashing cameras that are found in more well-known regions.

Amid spectacular scenery, traditional ways of pastoral life continue side by side with an abundance of free-roaming game. This is high country, with altitudes from 1,700 meters (5,577 feet) to 2,600 meters (8,530 feet), so bring those sweaters and jackets. Habitats range from arid semidesert, scrubland, and sprawling open plains in the north and south, to the thick forests of cedar and olive trees in the east. The area around the Laikipia Plateau has one of the biggest and most diverse mammal populations in Kenya—only the Masai Mara can boast more game. The Big Five are all present, plus the wide-ranging painted dogs; there's even a chance of seeing the rare aquatic sitatunga antelope. Grevy's zebra, which is more narrowly striped than its southern cousin, was once hunted almost to extinction for its fine desirable skin, but is reestablishing itself well in the area.

GETTING HERE AND AROUND

Laikipia is about a six-hour drive from Nairobi, but few travelers attempt these far northern areas (the fringe of the old Northern Frontier District) on their own. There are many superb private lodges in the area, and they will look after your transport arrangements from Nairobi.

WHERE TO STAY

LUXURY LODGES

$$$$
FAMILY
Fodor's Choice
★

Borana. The traditional Borana cattle ranch—a part of Kenyan highland history—was given a whole new lease on life with eight luxuriously spacious and well-appointed cottages. Private verandas offer views of large numbers of resident game that come to drink at the lake in front of the lodge in a landscape that has attracted countless artists and photographers. Visitors are given an added opportunity to sample ranch life with some of Africa's most spectacular horseback safaris. Aerial tours (in small planes or helicopters—a part of daily life in these remote areas) at neighboring Lewa Downs are a regular part of any visit to beautiful Borana. The rate includes conservation fees. **Pros:** unique views up to the peak of Mt. Kenya; a chance to meet the Dyer family, one of Kenya's founding farming dynasties. **Cons:** people are often surprised at how chilly it can be at night at this altitude, but hot-water bottles and romantic open fireplaces in all cottages add to the cozy atmosphere. $ *Rooms from: $1490* ⊠ *Borana Ranch, Laikipia Plateau* ☎ *020/211–5453* ⊕ *www.borana.co.ke* ⇋ *8 cottages* ⦿ *All-inclusive.*

$$$$ 🗉 **Il'Ngwesi Eco Lodge.** Situated on a rocky outcrop in the north of the Lewa Wildlife Conservancy, this intimate and environmental award-winning lodge prides itself on its successful efforts to integrate community development and sustainable environmental management. The comfortably furnished open-walled bandas with open-air showers are made of local materials and built on a slope—their fronts rest on wooden stilts—thus giving uninterrupted views of the surrounding wilderness. Make sure you take the opportunity to sit out at the main lodge and watch the water hole below or cool off in the horizon pool, which gently flows down into the bush below; water is gravity-piped from a nearby natural spring. You'll see plenty of game including lion, leopard, cheetah, hyena, the elusive wild dog, and large herds of elephants and buffalo, plus the plains game. Learn about hunting, gathering honey, animal trapping with indigenous poisons, or fashioning beadwork with the local Maasai at the nearby Masai Cultural Manyatta. You won't want to miss the dancing of the warriors and maidens—it's the genuine article. Il Ngwesi Camp is a shining example of how a safari lodge can reduce poverty and strengthen partnerships between the tourist trade and local communities. Built only with local materials, the camp is completely solar-powered, and its water comes from a nearby spring and is gravity-fed to the lodge. The local Maasai community helped build and continues to run the camp through a communal group. **Pros:** good children's facilities; you can sleep under the stars; excellent community outreach and sustainability. **Cons:** open-air showers only; no a/c. $ *Rooms from: $782* ⊠ *Laikipia Plateau* ☎ *020/203–3122* ⊕ *www. ilngwesi.com* ⇋ *6 bandas* ⦿ *All-inclusive.*

$$$$ 🗉 **Lewa Wilderness Trails.** Lewa Downs, at the foot of Mt. Kenya, is
FAMILY another one of Laikipia's conservation successes. The Craig family emigrated from England in 1924 and still lives on the same 65,000-acre property, but instead of raising cattle, with the cooperation of the local communities they have returned the area to a wildlife haven. Descendants of the original family will lead you on all sorts of activities and claim that you'll see as much game here as almost anywhere else in Africa. Game drives are thrilling and action packed, but try game-spotting from a different angle—on top of a camel or from the back of a horse, or on your own two feet. (If you've got a dodgy back forget about the camel riding.) Look out for Grevy's zebra, the more elegant cousin of the regular plains zebra, and the rare aquatic sitatunga antelope.

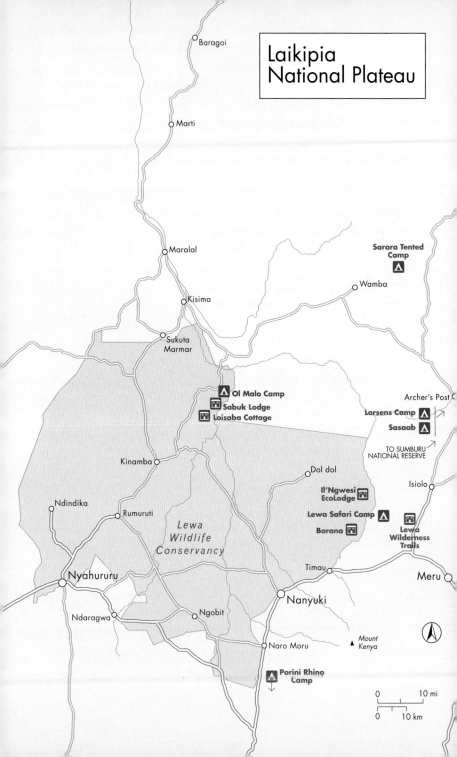

Laikipia
National Plateau

Baragoi

Marti

Maralal

Kisima

Sukuta
Marmar

Sarara Tented
Camp

Wamba

Ol Malo Camp

Sabuk Lodge

Loisaba Cottage

Archer's Post

Larsens Camp

Sasaab

TO SUMBURU
NATIONAL RESERVE

Kinamba

Dol dol

Il'Ngwesi
EcoLodge

Isiolo

Ndindika

Rumuruti

*Lewa
Wildlife
Conservancy*

Lewa Safari Camp

Borana

Lewa
Wilderness
Trails

Nyahururu

Timau

Meru

Ndaragwa

Ngobit

Nanyuki

Naro Moru

▲ Mount
Kenya

Porini Rhino
Camp

0   10 mi

0   10 km

The 10 cottages are attractively furnished with a big wooden bed, hand-carved chests, comfy chairs, and en-suite bathroom. Hot water and electricity are available morning and evening; if you need to cool off, take a dip in the lovely pool. The food is wholesome and hearty with lots of organically grown herbs, vegetables, and fruit. **Pros:** it's ideal for families; there's a huge range of activities available. **Cons:** you need to book in advance. [$] *Rooms from: $1800* ✉ *Lewa Wildlife Conservancy, Laikipia Plateau* ☎ *020/600–0457, 073/333–0007* 🌐 *www.lewawilderness.com* 🛏 *10 cottages* 🍴 *All-inclusive.*

DID YOU KNOW?

More than three quarters of all Kenya's game is found on private land, not in the national parks and reserves.

$$$$ FAMILY 🏨 **Loisaba Cottage.** Loisaba Cottage sits plumb in the middle of game-rich Laikipia, on a 300-meter (984-foot) plateau that looks south to Mt. Kenya with stunning views across the Laikipia plains. Built of cedar, stone, and wood, this lovely lodge is nestled among gardens of aloes, succulents, and flowering trees. If you fancy something even more special, opt for one of the star beds (closed in November), which have been created with the local community. Don't expect a meager stretcher under the stars. You'll stay in an en-suite "platform" with half-covered thatch roof, handcrafted furniture, and wooden floors set among big rocks. The Kiboko star beds overlook a water hole, whereas the Koija star beds overlook the Ewaso Nyiro river. Every evening your friendly and attentive Laikipia Maasai attendants will wheel out your double bed under the star-studded clear night sky, where, carefully shrouded under a mosquito net, you can watch the world turn. If you're looking for something even more different, go for a quad bike ride. **Pros:** other activities include game drives, tennis, horseback riding, and camel trekking; laundry service is included. **Cons:** no a/c; Internet connection is slow. [$] *Rooms from: $990* ✉ *Laikipia Plateau* ☎ *020/600–3090* 🌐 *www.loisaba.com* 🛏 *7 rooms, 8 star beds* 🍴 *All-inclusive.*

$$$$ FAMILY 🏨 **Sabuk Lodge.** This lodge organically created out of local thatch, stone, and wood clings to a hillside on the northwest of the Laikipia Plateau. Overlooking the ever-flowing Ewaso Nyiro River, the lodge offers spectacular views and great hospitality. In between activities, lie on your uniquely designed handcrafted big bed in your charming open-front room and gaze out at the river below. If you can't tear yourself away from the view, then just move into the bathroom, slip in the deep stone bath, flip water over the edge to the rocks below and keep gazing. The comfortable main open-side lodge ensures you're never far away from those memorable views. On chilly nights a roaring log fire keeps you cozy and warm. Food is plentiful, fresh, and delicious with superb breakfasts on the viewing deck. Spend a night out under the stars at a fly camp after a day's camel safari, go walking, birding, or fishing, or try tubing down the river. Game is plentiful, and you should see elephants, lions, leopards, giraffes, Grevy's and plains zebras, and much, much more. Because there are no fences, the game can wander at will. **Pros:** the food is excellent; camel safaris highly recommended. **Cons:** rooms

don't have safes; no à la carte menus. $ *Rooms from: $1450* ⊠ *Ewaso Nyiro River, Crocodile Jaws, Laikipia Plateau* ☎ *071/813–9359, 020/359–8871* ⊕ *www.sabuklodge.com* 🛏 *5 cottages* 🍽 *All-inclusive.*

PERMANENT TENTED CAMPS

$$$$

FAMILY

Larsens Camp. The best tent camps provide peaceful refuge from the bush without sacrificing outdoor magnificence, and few can match the exquisite relief you'll find at Larsens. The arid Samburu environs give way to a cool, shady retreat under the thick forest that envelops this Small Luxury Hotels camp along the Ewaso Nyiro River. A young Maasai stands with slingshot at the ready, so that you can enjoy a gourmet riverside meal undisturbed by the vervet monkeys who wander the grounds. (They are unharmed; he merely disperses them.) Come out of the shade to swim in the pool with gorgeous views of the Samburu hills to the east. Or head up to Larsens' tree platform overlooking the hills to the west for a spectacular sundowner. Your tent with private porch is just a short stroll away. Inside you'll find a generous king-size bed (some with an additional twin) and spacious bathrooms with large rainshowers and thoughtful touches such as Molton Brown toiletries. **Pros:** game viewing right from your porch; dense trees provide a sanctuary feel; large, comfortable common areas. **Cons:** monkeys can be a nuisance; no in-room safe. $ *Rooms from: $998* ⊠ *Laikipia Plateau* ☎ *077/413–6523* ⊕ *www.porini.com* 🛏 *20 tents* 🍽 *All meals.*

$$$$

FAMILY

Lewa Safari Camp. If it's rhinos you're after, then this delightful but small tented camp in the 65,000-acre Lewa Wildlife Conservancy, right where the old Rhino Sanctuary headquarters used to stand, is for you. There's a comfortable main building for eating and relaxing, and wide verandas outside each tent for soaking up the beautiful environs. But if it's game-viewing you're after, then one of the camp's expert team of professional guides will take you on an exhilarating drive. Spacious tents protected by a sturdy thatch roof have comfortable beds, desks for keeping up on those precious journal notes, and spacious en-suite bathrooms. The food is homegrown and tasty. Bird-watching is spectacular in this area, but it's likely that while you're watching out for feathered friends, you're likely to spot big game as well, including lions. Burn up some calories and have a unique experience at the same time by going on a guided game walk. **Pros:** tents are private; very few other vehicles. **Cons:** no a/c. $ *Rooms from: $1228* ⊠ *Lewa Wildlife Conservancy* ☎ *073/012–7000* ⊕ *www.lewasafaricamp.com* 🛏 *12 tents, 3 rooms* 🍽 *All-inclusive.*

$$$$

FAMILY

Ol Malo. Choose a luxurious thatch cottage perched on a cliff edge at this lovely camp to the west of Samburu overlooking Mt. Kenya. You'll find yourself under the personal supervision of the owners, Rocky and Colin Francombe. The stone-and-thatch cottages, some built on two levels, have king-size beds and baths that you can lie in and look out at the passing wildlife. The main lodge, also built of natural rock and olive wood, is cozy and comfortable. There's a huge pool, which clings to the rock edge, spilling its waters to the rocks below. Drives are extremely rewarding with game galore, but for something a little different try a camel ride (not for bad backs), a nature walk, an overnight stay in the Look Out Hut—a little wooden hut in the bush—or

Sabuk

Sabuk

Il'Ngwesi Lodge

go camping under the stars. Horse-back riding is a fascinating way to spot game: there are also safe and friendly ponies for kids, and children's gift packs on arrival, plus other kids' activities. There's also the opportunity to meet and mix with the local Samburu people and to take part in some of their activities. **Pros:** it's very child-friendly; the afternoon tea is excellent. **Cons:** no a/c; no TV in rooms. $ *Rooms from: $1800* ✉ *Laikipia Plateau* ☎ *020/600–0457* ⊕ *www.olmalo. com* ⟿ *4 cottages* ⦿ *All-inclusive.*

$$$$ 🛏 **Porini Rhino Camp.** This delightful eco-friendly tented camp is nestled among Kenya's ubiquitous *Acacia tortilis* trees in a secluded valley in the Ol Pejeta Conservancy. This 90,000-acre stretch of game-rich wilderness lies between the snow-capped Mt. Kenya and the foothills of the Aberdares. This location treats guests to a double whammy—abundant game including the Big Five, the African wild dog, and the endangered black rhino, as well as superb views across the open plains. Each beautifully placed tent has stunning views from its personal veranda, and inside there's an en-suite bathroom with flush toilet and bucket shower with hot water heated by solar power. Sip sundowners from a carefully chosen vantage point, and then take a spectacular night drive. By day stretch your legs on a guided bush walk with a Maasai guide or have your heartstrings tugged at the nearby Sweetwaters Chimpanzee Sanctuary. If you're feeling extra energetic and really want to walk on the wild side, then the camp also offers walking safaris. ■TIP➜ **The all-inclusive price includes round-trip transfers by air from Nairobi, Ol Pejeta conservancy fees, all game drives, sundowners, walks with Maasai warriors, full board, and free house wines, beer, and soft drinks.** Porini Rhino Camp is located in the largest black rhino sanctuary in East Africa. The camp has no permanent structures and is strategically constructed around trees and shrubs to minimize the human footprint on the natural landscape. The camp uses solar power for electricity, and water is heated with eco-friendly, sustainable charcoal briquettes; there is no generator. The camp has a silver eco-rating for its low eco-footprint. **Pros:** the camp benefits the local community and is eco-friendly; single supplements are reasonable; the price includes conservancy fees and a visit to a chimpanzee sanctuary; the water hole in front of the camp attracts a lot of wildlife. **Cons:** it can be cooler than reserves south of the country; there is only solar power, no electricity. $ *Rooms from: $1100* ✉ *Ol Pejeta Conservancy, Laikipia Plateau* ☎ *877/710–3014, 072/250–9200* ⊕ *www.porini.com* ⟿ *6 tents* ⦿ *All-inclusive.*

$$$$ 🛏 **Sarara Tented Camp.** This small, tented camp lies below the peaks of the Mathews Mountains in the 850,000-acre Namunyak Wildlife Conservation Trust, a community project between landowners and the

BRINGING UP THE CHIMPS

Established in 1993, Sweetwaters Chimpanzee Sanctuary (⊕ *www. olpejetaconservancy.org*) provides lifelong refuge to chimpanzees. Today, the sanctuary, located in the Ol Pejeta Conservancy, has more than 40 chimps in its protection. Visitors to the conservancy have free access to the sanctuary, which is open daily, but anyone can make a donation.

local Samburu people. Accommodation is in six spacious tents, sited under pole-supported thatch roofs with flush toilets and open-air showers. There is also a two-bedroom house with a shared sitting/dining area. The main sitting room and dining area sits on stilts in front of the water hole and natural rock pool—yes, you swim here overlooking the water hole and you are quite safe—with stunning views of the Mathews Mountains. Game is plentiful with resident lion and leopard, and there's an excellent chance of seeing wild dog as there are two packs in the area. Look out for the attractive colobus monkeys when you go for a guided hike in the forest. Go donkey trekking in the mountains, or take a camel safari with an overnight stop at a fly camp. **Pros:** there's a wide range of activities available; staff are from the local community. **Cons:** it's off the beaten track; no power points in tents; Wi-Fi is available only during the day. ⓢ *Rooms from: $1800* ⊠ *Namunyak Conservancy, Laikipia Plateau* ☎ *020/600–0457* ⊕ *www.sararacamp.com* ⤳ *6 tents* ☺ *Closed Apr. 15–May and Nov.* ⦿*All-inclusive.*

$$$$ 🛏 **Sasaab.** It's not just where Sasaab is located but how it's situated
FAMILY   that makes it a wonderful place to stay in Samburu. Because it's in
Fodor's Choice   a conservancy rather than a game reserve, you can explore the sur-
★   roundings without a vehicle; and because it spreads across a hillside high above the Ewaso Nyiro River, there are spectacular views from every vantage. You can go on a morning bird walk, take an afternoon hike over *koppies* (hills) to a spectacular sundowner, or ride a camel through a dry riverbed. There's also the opportunity to go walking and fly-camping in the further reaches of the conservancy. Sasaab balances opulence, characterized by oversize rooms and fine Moroccan architecture, with environmental consciousness, exhibited by solar-powered electricity and community outreach. They actively support local villages and collaborate with Ewaso Lions, a lion conservation-study program. Every room is a palatial, split-level affair with four-poster beds, personal plunge pools, and grand sitting rooms that quite possibly have the longest couches you've ever seen. **Pros:** sumptuous, spacious rooms; guided walking safaris; beautifully designed common areas. **Cons:** some rooms are far from the dining lodge; long, bumpy drive to and from local airstrip. ⓢ *Rooms from: $870* ⊠ *Samburu Game Reserve, Laikipia Plateau* ☎ *020/502–0888* ⊕ *www.sasaab.com* ⤳ *9 tents* ⦿*All meals.*

IF YOU HAVE TIME

Although the reviews go into great detail about the must-see parks in Kenya, there are many others to explore if you have time. Here, a few good ones are mentioned.

NAIROBI NATIONAL PARK

The most striking thing about Nairobi National Park, Kenya's oldest national park, isn't a mountain or a lake but the very fact that it exists at all. This sliver of unspoiled Africa survives on the edge of a city of more than 3 million people. Where else can you get a photo of animals in their natural habitat with skyscrapers in the background? As you travel into the city from Jomo Kenyatta International Airport, you're likely to see hartebeests grazing near the highway.

The park is tiny compared with Kenya's other game parks and reserves; it covers only 117 square km (44 square miles). It's characterized by open plains that slope gently from west to east and rocky ridges that are covered with rich vegetation. Seasonal streams run southeast into the Mbagathi Athi River, which is lined with yellow-color fever and acacia trees. In the west the river runs through a deep gorge where rocky outcrops are the favored habitat of leopards.

Fences separate the park from the nearby communities of Langata and Karen, but they don't always prevent the occasional leopard or lion from snacking on a dog or horse. This is because of an open corridor to the south that allows wildebeests and other animals to move to other areas in search of food; researchers believe the annual migration in this area was once as spectacular as that in the Serengeti.

Despite the urban pressures, the park contains a good variety of wildlife, especially during the dry season. Animals migrate here from other areas knowing that there's always a source of permanent water. You can see the Big Five, minus elephants as the area isn't big enough to support them. ■TIP➜ If you want to see baby elephants, visit the David Sheldrick Elephant Orphanage close to the main entrance of the park. Zebras, elands, impalas, and Grant's and Thomson's gazelles are well represented. Warthogs and ostriches are common on the open plains. Larger game includes Masai giraffes, which browse in the woodland, and a breeding population of about 40 black rhinos, sometimes found in the light bush around the forest area. Black rhinos have been particularly successful here because it's been easier to keep track of and control poachers. In the extreme western border of the park, a low ridge covered by a stand of hardwood trees is home to herds of bushbucks and impalas as well as some of the park's olive baboons. Impala Point, at the edge of the ridge, makes a good vantage point to scan the plains with binoculars for concentrations of game.

Predators include a healthy population of lions, and you have an excellent chance of seeing a lion kill. Rangers keep a careful note of the movements of the larger animals, so it's worth asking at the gate where to look for lions or rhinos.

Continued on page 158

Blue wildebeest in Tanzania's Serengeti National Park

THE GREAT MIGRATION

by Kate
Turkington

Nothing will prepare you for the spectacle that is the Great Migration. This annual journey of more than 2 million animals is a safari-seeker's Holy Grail, the ultimate in wildlife experiences. Some say it's one of the world's greatest natural wonders.

The greater Serengeti ecosystem, which includes Kenya's Masai Mara (north) and Tanzania's Serengeti (south), is the main arena for this awesome sight. At the end of each year during the short rains—November to early December—the herds disperse into the southeast plains of Tanzania's Seronera. After calving early in the new year (wildebeests drop up to 8,000 babies a day), huge numbers of animals start the 800-km (497-mile) trek from these now bare southeast plains to lush northern pastures. On the way they will face terrible, unavoidable danger. In June and July braying columns—40 km (25 miles) long—have to cross the crocodile-infested Grumeti River. Half of the great herds which successfully survive the crossing will stay in northern Tanzania, the other half will cross over into Kenya's Masai Mara. In early October the animals begin their return journey back to Seronera and come full circle, only to begin their relentless trek once again early the following year.

WHO'S MIGRATING

What will you see during the migration?

More than **2 million** wildebeest
250,000 Thompson's gazelle
200,000 zebra
70,000 impala
30,000 Grant's gazelle

In addition, huge numbers of predators follow the herds. You're likely to see lion, leopard, cheetah, jackal, hyena, and numerous smaller predators.

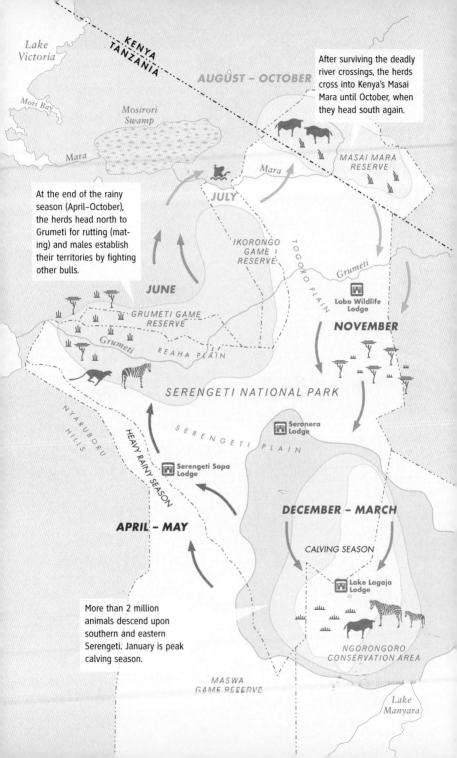

Lake
Victoria

Mori Bay

KENYA
TANZANIA

AUGUST – OCTOBER

After surviving the deadly
river crossings, the herds
cross into Kenya's Masai
Mara until October, when
they head south again.

Mosirori
Swamp

Mara

Mara

*MASAI MARA
RESERVE*

JULY

At the end of the rainy
season (April–October),
the herds head north to
Grumeti for rutting (mat-
ing) and males establish
their territories by fighting
other bulls.

*IKORONGO
GAME
RESERVE*

Grumeti

JUNE

*GRUMETI GAME
RESERVE*

Grumeti

REAHA PLAIN

Lobo Wildlife
Lodge

TOGORO PLAIN

NOVEMBER

SERENGETI NATIONAL PARK

N
Y
A
R
U
B
O
R
U

H
I
L
L
S

HEAVY RAINY SEASON

S E R E N G E T I   P L A I N

Seronera
Lodge

Serengeti Sopa
Lodge

APRIL – MAY

DECEMBER – MARCH

CALVING SEASON

Lake Lagaja
Lodge

More than 2 million
animals descend upon
southern and eastern
Serengeti. January is peak
calving season.

*NGORONGORO
CONSERVATION AREA*

*MASWA
GAME RESERVE*

Lake
Manyara

DRIVEN BY DINNER

WHERE THE MAGIC HAPPENS

The Serengeti more then lives up to its awesome reputation as an amazing spot to see wildlife and it's here that the Great Migration begins and ends. The park's ecosystem supports some of the most abundant mammal populations left anywhere on earth and it covers almost 15,000 square km (9,320 square miles) of seemingly endless plains, riverine bush, forest and scrubland roughly the size of Northern Ireland or Connecticut. It stretches between the Ngorongoro highlands, Lake Victoria, and Tanzania's northern border with Kenya. It was named a UNESCO World Heritage Site in 1978 and an International Biosphere Reserve (a UNESCO international conservation area) in 1981.

WHEN TO GO

Because rainfall patterns are unpredictable, it's difficult to anticipate timings for the migration. But usually, by the beginning of each year, the grazing on the southeast plains of Serengeti's Seronera is exhausted and the herds start to move northwest into Tanza-

STAGGERING NUMBERS

The Great Migration, as we know it, is a fairly young phenomenon, having only started in the 1960s when wildebeest numbers exploded. However, an estimated 250,000 wildebeests don't survive the annual migration.

nia's Western Corridor. The actual crossing of the Grumeti River, usually between June and July, when an unrivalled bloody spectacle of terrified frantic wildebeest and huge lashing crocodiles unfolds, is a gruesome, unforgettable spectacle. You'll see hundreds of thousands of animals between March and November, including predators. Seronera in March, April, and May is an ideal time for a safari because there are huge concentrations of predators preying on all the baby animals. Safaris are much cheaper between April and June, and although you may not witness the actual river crossings, you'll still be privy to prime game-viewing experiences. Plus there will be far fewer vehicles.

More than 500 species of permanent and migratory birds have been spotted in the park. Around the dams used to create marshes you'll find Egyptian geese, crowned cranes, yellow and saddle-billed storks, herons, African spoonbills, sacred ibis, hammerkops, Kittlitz's sand plovers, and marabou storks. In the plains look for secretary birds, vultures, helmeted guinea fowls, bustards, yellow-throated sand grouse, larks, pipits, and Jackson's widow birds, which display their long tails and attractive plumage during the long rains in May and June. The forests hold cuckoo shrikes, sunbirds, waxbills, flycatchers, and warblers.

GETTING HERE AND AROUND

A 20-minute drive from downtown Nairobi (7 km [4 miles]), the park's network of paved and all-weather dirt roads can be negotiated by cars and vans, and junctions are generally signposted and clearly marked on the official park map, which you can pick up at the gate or any bookstore or tourist office. Don't leave your vehicle except where permitted, as unsuspecting tourists have been mauled by lions and attacked by rhinos.

BOOKING AND VISITOR INFORMATION

Most safari operators will arrange a trip, usually four to five hours long, to the park. Otherwise, you can take a taxi. The park is very busy on weekends, when locals visit.

Contact Kenya Wildlife Service ☎ *072/661–0533 for reservations, 020/258–7435 for Nairobi National Park* 🌐 *www.kws.org* 🎫 *$50* 🕒 *Daily 6 am–7 pm.*

WHERE TO STAY

Until recently, there were no accommodations available in the park. Now, there's a luxury lodge and a luxury tented camp. Both are a good way to kick-start your safari. Stay here and you could be viewing lions and rhinos within an hour of stepping off your plane.

$$$$ 🏨 **The Emakoko.** A half-hour drive from Nairobi's international airport is a luxurious paradise bush lodge in a seemingly remote and hidden valley. In earshot of the roars of the Nairobi lions, the Emakoko offers spacious, beautifully designed rooms with huge verandas overlooking a jungle valley. Game drives are included in the room price. The owners are experts on Kenya and its wildlife and could be the best advisors you encounter on any of your travels. The lodge bar and communal dining (optional) frequently offer further opportunities to pick up safari tips and anecdotes. **Pros:** very close to Nairobi's airport, but in a remote area; dinner by the pool is a starlit experience; log fires in the rooms turn potentially icy highland nights into sheer romance. **Cons:** the beautiful freestanding baths are positioned immediately in front of large panorama windows. [$] *Rooms from: $960* ✉ *Nairobi National Park* ☎ *077/123–8218* 🌐 *www.emakoko.com* 🛏 *10 rooms* 🍴 *All-inclusive.*

$$ 🏨 **Nairobi Tented Camp.** Insulated by a hidden glade—home to leopards, lions, and hyenas—Nairobi Tented Camp is in a secluded part of Nairobi National Park, providing an authentic bush experience within a few miles of the city center. Tents are luxuriously equipped with large en suite bathrooms (with traditional canvas hot water bucket showers). The lounge tent is sumptuously furnished with all the comforts of home (and then some), but this is a carefully prepared eco-camp that could

potentially be removed within 48 hours, leaving zero imprint on the natural habitat. Hot water bottles tame Nairobi's cool high altitude nights but the bush around is as wild as anywhere in Africa; you might have a giraffe or rhino wandering around the camp. **Pros:** in the bush in the city—best of both worlds!; night drives aren't allowed in the park, but if your plane lands after dark you'll be treated to a night drive en route to the camp. **Cons:** the dining area feels rather formal for such an atmospheric bush camp. $ *Rooms from: $260* ⊠ *Nairobi National Park* ☎ *020/260–3337* ⊕ *www.nairobitentedcamp.com* ⇨ *9 tents* ⦿*Breakfast.*

MERU NATIONAL PARK

4

Situated 370 km (230 miles) northeast of Nairobi and west of Mt. Kenya, this little-visited park (1,810 square km [699 square miles]) offers some of Kenya's wildest country, but was taken off the mainstream safari circuit because of the lawless poachers who wiped out the white rhino population in the 1980s. Although the Kenyan government has gotten a grip on the security situation, the park still finds it difficult to shake off its negative image. But rest assured that all is now well and the park is a safe and fulfilling destination—after all, this is the place where wildlife champions Joy and George Adamson hand-reared Elsa the lioness made famous by the 1966 film *Born Free.*

A successful rehabilitation program reintroduced elephants and rhinos to the park in 2001; both populations are doing well. There's a lot of other game here, including buffalo, lions, leopards, cheetahs, hippos, lesser kudu, hartebeests (grassland antelope), Grevy's and Burchell's zebras, the gerenuk, the reticulated or Somali giraffe, waterbuck, oryx, and Grant's gazelles. The park is part of an ecosystem that includes Kora National Park and Mwingi, Rahole, and Bisanadi reserves. It straddles the equator and is home to a great variety of habitats, including scrubland dotted with baobab trees, lush green grasslands, and riverine forests. Tana, Kenya's longest river, is fed by 13 rivers that create a superb habitat for bird life, including the Somali ostrich and raptors such as the red-necked falcon and the palm-nut vulture. You may also see that megascore on a serious birder's "life list," the Pel's fishing owl, which hides in the huge ancient trees along the rivers.

GETTING HERE AND AROUND

There's a daily flight between Meru National Park and Nairobi Wilson Airport with Airkenya, which takes 1¾ hours. You can drive from Nairobi; the road isn't particularly bad but it takes five to six hours. If you're already at a property in the area, it can make sense to drive. Visitors would need a 4x4 vehicle for driving within the park.

Contact **Kenya Wildlife Service** ☎ *061/230–3094 for Meru National Park* ⊕ *www.kws.org* ⊠ *$75 per day* ☉ *Daily 6–6.*

WHERE TO STAY

$$$$ ⊡ **Elsa's Kopje.** This multi-award-winning lodge is set above George
FAMILY Adamson's original campsite, where he and his wife, author Joy Adamson, released their lioness Elsa (after which the lodge is named) back

The Kikuyu people account for almost 25% of Kenya's population, and most live around Mt. Kenya.

into the wild. It's a strikingly attractive lodge both for its elevated position and for its imaginatively designed thatch cottages. Each cottage is unique, with boulders for walls, trees growing through the roof, and spacious interiors furnished with handcrafted furniture, handwoven rugs, and earth-tone cushions, throws, and bedspreads. All the cottages have complete privacy, but if you would like your family to stay together and have your own private infinity pool, go for Elsa's Private House, which sleeps four (extra beds can be added for kids) and has a small garden. Watch the plains game ambling through the grasslands from your veranda or view predators or rhinos in open-sided game vehicles before sundowners at the palm-fringed hippo pools. The home-cooked, homegrown food is principally northern Italian, but if you're not a pasta person, there's plenty more to choose from. **Pros:** delicious homegrown vegetables; free laundry service. **Cons:** not all rooms have tubs; no a/c. $ *Rooms from: $1394* ⌂ *Meru National Park* ☎ *073/012–7000* ⊕ *www.elsaskopje.com* ⤴ *10 cottages, 1 private house* ⍾ *All meals.*

$$$$ 🏨 **Leopard Rock Lodge.** Antique furniture, Persian rugs, and understated elegance characterize this exclusive lodge, which sprawls out along the banks of the Murera River. You'll stay in one of the thatch and wood bandas, with his-and-her en-suite bathrooms; or a family cottage or suite, all with stunning views. The food is superb even by high Kenyan standards, and there's a great wine list and open-air kitchen. The lodge offers a pottery workshop and an unforgettable pool that allows you to come safely nose to nose—there's a glass panel between the river and the pool—with crocs in the river. **Pros:** other activities on offer include fishing and bird-watching; there's a pool bar and Jacuzzi. **Cons:** dinner requires formal dress. $ *Rooms from: $690* ⌂ *Meru National Park*

CLOSE UP

Kenya's Tribes

KIKUYU

The Kikuyu account for almost 25% of the country's total population. Most Kikuyu live around Mt. Kenya, and because of the fertility of the land there, they have become largely a pastoral people, farming the rich fields around the mountain and up in the Kenyan highlands. The Mau Mau Rebellion (1952–58) was a sad time in Kikuyu—and Kenyan—history, with frustrations among Kenyan tribes toward the colonizing British resulting in guerilla warfare. During this time, many Kikuyu were killed and detained in British camps. This difficult era spurred the move toward independence, and in 1964 Jomo Kenyatta, a Kikuyu, became Kenya's first president. Kenya's third president, Mwai Kibaki, is also Kikuyu, as is Nobel Peace Prize–winner and Greenbelt Movement founder Wangari Maathai.

LUO

Mainly in Western Kenya, the Luo tribe is one of the country's largest, accounting for about 15% of the population. Most members make their living through fishing and farming. The culture is rich in musical traditions, and the sounds and melodies common in their music are said to be the basis for Kenya's modern pop music. Raila Odinga, the top opposition-party leader who ran against Mwai Kibaki in the much-disputed 2007 presidential election, is Luo. Odinga and Kibaki entered into a power-sharing government in early 2008. Barack Obama's father was from the Luo tribe.

MAASAI

Known to be great warriors, the Maasai are also largely associated with Kenya. This red-clad tribe is mainly found in southern Kenya and Tanzania.

4

☎ *020/600–0031* ⊕ *www.leopardmico.com* ⇲ *15 cottages, 5 family cottages, 10 suites* ⦿ *All meals.*

THE LAKES OF KENYA

In addition to its great game parks, Kenya is home to huge, beautiful lakes that are often covered with uncountable flocks of flamingos. Here's just a snapshot of four of them.

LAKE NAIVASHA

One of the Rift Valley's few freshwater lakes, Lake Naivasha is a popular spot for day trips and weekends away from Nairobi. The pleasant forested surroundings, which are a far cry from the congestion and noise of Nairobi, are another big draw. Keep an eye out for the fever trees, and the abundant populations of birds, monkeys, and hippos. Such an attractive location lured a group of British settlers to build their homes on its shores. Known collectively as "White Mischief," these settlers were internationally infamous for their decadent, hedonistic lifestyle. A 1987 movie of the same name, starring Greta Scacchi, was based on a notorious society murder set during this time in this location.

GETTING HERE AND AROUND

Lake Naivasha is a one- to two-hour drive from Nairobi. There are two routes—a shorter but badly potholed route along the escarpment, or a longer but better maintained road, the A104 Uplands, which leads to Naivasha town. Hotels and lodges in the area will arrange pickups from Nairobi, and taxis can transport you around the area.

EXPLORING

Crescent Island Game Park. Cross over by boat to Crescent Island Game Park, where you can see (and walk with) giraffes, zebras, and other plains herbivores; there are no predators. ✉ *Naivasha* ☎ *050/202–1030* 🌐 *www.crescentisland.co* 🎫 *$30.*

WHERE TO STAY

$ 🏨 **Camp Carnelly's.** Camp Carnelly's offers simple budget rooms and nicely designed banda chalets, but the real pleasure of a visit here lies in camping in this idyllic fever-tree forest on the southern shore of Lake Naivasha. Vervets and colobus monkeys flit through the canopy, hippos graze on the shoreline at night, and the area is a bird-watcher's dream. Come prepared to self-cater and your evenings around a Naivasha campfire could become a highlight of your trip to Kenya. **Pros:** a low electric fence offers security from feisty hippos at night; the wood-fired pizzas are the best in Kenya. **Cons:** the restaurant could be considered unnecessarily expensive; the open air showers (with wonderful supplies of hot water) don't have changing areas or anywhere to leave clothes. [$] *Rooms from: $40* ✉ *South Lake Road, Naivasha* ☎ *072/226–0749* 🌐 *www.campcarnelleys.com* 🛏 *16 rooms* 🍴 *No meals.*

$ 🏨 **Crater Lake Tented Camp.** About a half-hour drive from the town of Naivasha, Crater Lake Tented Camp is situated in the cauldron of a crater, on the edge of a lovely saltwater lake. The views here are exquisite: pale fever trees flank the water, and more than 200 species of birds are found here. The honeymoon suite and permanent tented rooms all look across the lake, and the brick-built standard rooms are set back a little. The décor is underwhelming, but the views more than make up for it. This is a good spot to relax for a few days. **Pros:** the views are lovely; there is a swimming pool; there are no other hotels or camps on this lake. **Cons:** steep steps to access tents—not suitable for people with disabilities. [$] *Rooms from: $208* ✉ *Naivasha* 🌐 *www.craterlakecamp.com* 🛏 *11 rooms* 🍴 *No meals.*

$ 🏨 **Naivasha Simba Lodge.** Naivasha Simba Lodge, though primarily a conference center, has lovely grounds, big rooms, and loads of facilities. It's set back from the lake so you won't have water views, but you will look out onto the resident herd of waterbuck that graze beneath the fever trees. There's a heated swimming pool, a well-designed restaurant area, a pub open on weekends, a gym, and basic spa facilities. The rooms are comfortable and well appointed, and have a sunken lounge. **Pros:** play area for children; the birding here is excellent. **Cons:** can get crowded on weekends. [$] *Rooms from: $360* ✉ *Moi South Lake Rd., Naivasha* ☎ *072/278–8830* 🌐 *www.marasimba.com* 🛏 *70 rooms* 🍴 *All meals.*

LAKE TURKANA

The tip of Lake Turkana, in Kenya's northwest, runs into the Ethiopian highlands, but the rest of Kenya's biggest lake stretches 250 km (155 miles) south. Sometimes called the Jade Lake because of its vivid green color, it's a shallow alkaline lake in the Great Rift Valley that's been drying up alarmingly over the past decade. Surprisingly, it's still home to the legendary giant Nile perch, huge herds of hippos, and more Nile crocodiles than anywhere else in the world—more than 20,000 reside here. There's abundant bird life with many European migrants wintering around its shores.

GETTING HERE AND AROUND

The roads to Lake Turkana are in bad condition, so it's better to fly. Fly540 flies daily from Nairobi JKIA to Lodwar, via Kitale.

4

Contact **Kenya Tourism Board** ☎ *020/271–1262* ⊕ *www.magicalkenya.com.*

LAKE VICTORIA

Kenya shares Africa's biggest freshwater lake with its neighbors, Uganda and Tanzania. Tanzania has the lion's share: 49%; Uganda has 45%; Kenya only 6%. The lake is so huge (68,000 square km [26,000 square miles]) that it has its own weather system with unpredictable storms, squalls, and high waters just like the ocean. The dhow was first introduced to Lake Victoria by Arab slave traders, and the local Luo shipbuilders quickly adopted the shape and lateen sail. You'll see fishing fleets of white-sailed dhows all over the lake, fishing mainly for the delicious Nile perch. These fish, which can reach the size of a fully grown shark, now account for about 80% of the fish in the lake. Their presence still arouses controversy. On the one hand, they're the basis for a multimillion-dollar processing and export industry; on the other, scientists say they're destroying the lake's ecosystem.

GETTING HERE AND AROUND

Kenya Airways and Fly540 fly from Nairobi to Kisumu, a town on Lake Victoria. The flight takes approximately 45 minutes. The airport is 4 km (2½ miles) out of the center of town (a 10-minute drive). Driving from Nairobi will take about 5½ hours. When you're in Kisumu, bicycle taxis are a quick and cheap way of getting around.

EXPLORING

Kisumu. Situated on Lake Victoria's shore, Kisumu is the main town of western Kenya, and Kenya's third largest, although it lacks the post-independence prosperity and development of Mombasa and Nairobi. It's got a bit of a run-down feel reminiscent of some of the small towns on the Indian Ocean coast.

WHERE TO STAY

Rusinga Island Lodge (⊕ *www.rusinga.com*) and **Mfangano Island Camp** (⊕ *www.governorscamp.com*) are top-of-the-range luxury lodges.

NAIROBI

As Nairobi is Kenya's capital city and the main hub for visitors, it's very likely that you'll be spending an overnight here between flights. The following information will help you plan those hours productively and safely.

The starting point for safaris since the days of Teddy Roosevelt and Ernest Hemingway, Nairobi is still the first stop for many travelers headed to the wildlife parks of East Africa. Just over a century ago Nairobi was little more than a water depot for the notorious "Lunatic Express." Every railhead presented a new nightmare for its British builders. Work was halted by hungry lions (a saga portrayed in the film *The Ghost and the Darkness*) as well as by masses of caterpillars that crawled on the tracks, spoiling traction and spinning wheels. Nearsighted rhinos charged the noisy engines. Africans fashioned jewelry from the copper telegraph wires, leading to a head-on collision between two engines after the communication wires were cut.

Nairobi, which means "cool water" in the language of the Maasai, wouldn't remain a backwater for long. In her 1942 memoir, *West with the Night,* aviatrix Beryl Markham wrote that less than three decades after it was founded, the city "had sprung from a collection of corrugated iron shacks serving the spindly Uganda Railway to a sprawling welter of British, Boers, Indians, Somalis, Abyssinians, natives from all over Africa and a dozen other places." Its grand hotels and imposing public buildings, she wrote, were "imposing evidence that modern times and methods have at last caught up with East Africa."

Today Nairobi's skyline surprises first-time visitors, whose visions of the country are often shaped by wildlife documentaries on the Discovery Channel or news reports on CNN. Since it was founded little more than a century ago, Nairobi has grown into one of the continent's largest capitals. Some early architecture survives here and there, but this city of around 3 million people is dominated by modern office towers. This isn't to say the city has lost all its charm—the venerable Norfolk and Stanley hotels recall the elegance of an age long since past.

Sometimes you can even describe the city as beautiful. After a good rain the city seems to have more green than New York or London. Brilliant bougainvillea line the highway from the airport, flame trees shout with color, and, in October, the horizon turns lavender with the blossoms of jacaranda.

But Nairobi has more than its share of problems. This city that grew too fast has paralyzing traffic jams, with many unsafe or overloaded vehicles on the road, and no hint of emissions control. Crime is on the rise, and stories about muggings and carjackings have led to the capital's moniker "Nairobbery." In addition, there's a growing disparity between rich and poor. Private estates on the edge of Nairobi resemble those in Beverly Hills or Boca Raton, with elaborate wrought-iron fences surrounding opulent mansions with stables, tennis courts, and swimming pools. The upper crust is known as the *wabenzi,* with *wa* a generic prefix for a people or tribe and *benzi* referring to the ubiquitous Mercedes-Benz cars lining the driveways. Not far away you can glimpse vast mazes of tin shacks, many with no electricity or running water.

These problems have pushed many travelers to the sanctuary of the suburbs. The Ngong Hills, mark the southwestern boundaries of Nairobi, embracing the suburbs of Langata and Karen. The latter is named after Baroness Karen Blixen, who wrote under the pen name Isak Dinesen about her life on a coffee farm here. Purple at dusk, the Ngong Hills are a restful symbol of *salaam,* Swahili for "peace."

Exclusive guest homes, such as the Giraffe Manor, Ngong House, and the House of Waine, provide a sense of peace in the suburban bush. Some of the better boutiques selling everything from antiques to art are found in Karen and Langata. The suburb of Langata lies on the edge of the Nairobi National Park, a great introduction to the magnificent wildlife of Kenya. No wonder many visitors return here year after year. They discover how Blixen felt when she wrote in one of her letters, "Wherever I may be in future, I will always wonder whether there's rain on the Ngongs."

GETTING HERE AND AROUND

Nairobi National Park is to the south of the city, with Jomo Kenyatta International Airport and Wilson Airport on the park periphery. Karen and Langata, suburbs of Nairobi, are southwest of the city center, and the Ngong Hills, on the edge the Great Rift Valley, are beyond them. Muthaiga, Gigiri, and Limuru are to the north.

Most major European airlines fly into Jomo Kenyatta International Airport (JKIA), Kenya's major airport, which is 15 km (9 miles) from the city. The airport has several ATM-equipped banks and Bureaux de Change. Barclays Bank, National Bank of Kenya, and Transnational Bank have branches and 24-hour money changing daily. You can also use the ATMs, although some accept only Visa. It usually takes about 40 minutes to drive from the airport to the city center by taxi (about US$20; always negotiate first) or regular shuttle bus, although protracted road works mean that it can take about two hours in rush hour. Many hotels have shuttle services; be sure to organize this when you book your room.

Wilson Airport, 6 km (4 miles) south of the city on the Langata Road, is Nairobi's second airport. It's used for domestic, charter, and some international flights. A taxi into the center of town is about $15.

There are plenty of cheap and efficient domestic flights available, including daily flights on Air Kenya between Nairobi and Mombasa, Malindi, and Lamu. Air Kenya also flies daily to Amboseli, Kiwayu, Lamu, Malindi, Masai Mara, and Meru. Fly540 flies from Nairobi JKIA to Lamu, Malindi, Masai Mara, and Mombasa, and Safarilink flies from Nairobi Wilson to Diani Beach, Lamu, Amboseli, Samburu, Tsavo, and Masai Mara. When you book a local flight, make sure to note which airport it departs from.

You're probably only in Nairobi overnight or for a few hours, so you definitely won't need a car. Take a taxi. There's an 80 km (50 miles) per hour speed limit, and it's compulsory to buckle up. Always negotiate the price before setting out. Locals travel around on *matatus* (passenger minivans carrying up to 15 passengers), but the drivers are notoriously reckless and the vehicles not always roadworthy.

Airports Jomo Kenyatta International Airport (*NBO*). ☎ *020/661–1000* ⊕ *www.kaa.go.ke.* **Wilson Airport** (*WIL*). ⊠ *Langata Rd.* ☎ *072/425–5343* ⊕ *www.kaa.go.ke.*

EMERGENCIES

Police in general are friendly and helpful to tourists. There are two private hospitals (avoid the government hospitals) with excellent staff and facilities, which have 24-hour pharmacies. There are plenty of pharmacies all over downtown Nairobi. Consult your concierge or host.

Emergency Contacts Aga Khan University Hospital ⊠ *3rd Parklands Ave., Parklands* ☎ *020/366–2000* ⊕ *hospitals.aku.edu/nairobi/Pages/home.aspx.* **Central Police Station** ⊠ *University Way* ☎ *999 from a landline, 112 from a mobile* ⊕ *www.kenyapolice.go.ke.* **Nairobi Hospital** ⊠ *Argwings Kodhek Rd.* ☎ *020/284–6000* ⊕ *www.nairobihospital.org.*

EXPLORING

TOP ATTRACTIONS

FAMILY **David Sheldrick Orphanage for Rhinos and Elephants.** Take a morning excursion, which you can book through your tour guide or hotel concierge, to this amazing rescue center that was set up by Dame Daphne Sheldrick after the death of her husband, David, who was famous for his anti-poaching activities in Tsavo National Park. You'll be able to watch baby elephants at play or having a bath, knowing that one day when they're old enough they will be successfully reintroduced into the wild. It's an absolutely unmissable and heartwarming experience. Make a donation, however small, or go for gold and adopt your own baby elephant. ⊠ *Magadi Rd., entrance at maintenance gate* ☎ *020/230–1396* ⊕ *www.sheldrickwildlifetrust.org* ⊠ *Ksh500* ⊗ *Daily 11 am–12 pm.*

Karen Blixen Museum. *Out of Africa* author Karen Blixen lived in this estate from 1913 to 1931. This is where she threw a grand dinner party for the Prince of Wales and where she carried on a torrid relationship

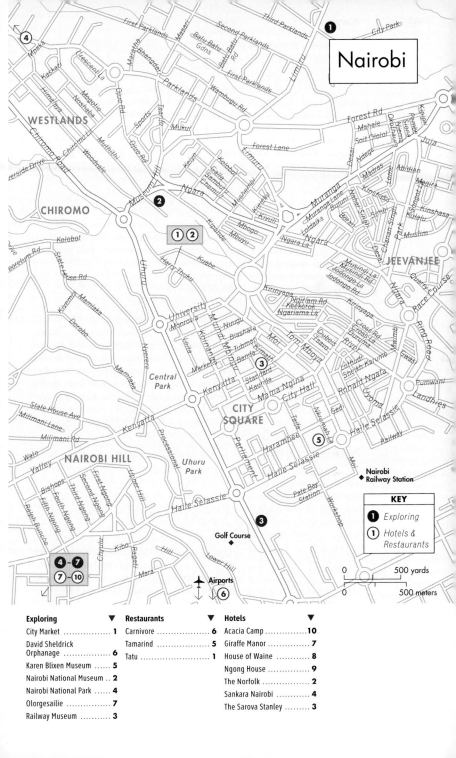

Nairobi

KEY
- ❶ Exploring
- ① Hotels & Restaurants

0   500 yards
0   500 meters

with aviator Denys Finch Hatton. The museum contains a few of her belongings and some of the farm machinery she used to cultivate the land for coffee and tea. There's also some of her furniture, but most of it is found in the McMillan Library in Nairobi. There is a magnificent view of the surrounding hills from her lawn, which is dominated by euphorbia, the many-armed plant widely known as the candelabra cactus. On the way to the museum you may notice a signpost reading "ndege." On this road, whose Swahili name means "bird," Finch Hatton once landed his plane for his visits with Blixen. After his plane crashed in Voi, he was buried nearby in the Ngong Hills. Guides will take you on a tour of the garden and the house, but there is little reference to the literary works by Blixen, who wrote under the pen name Isak Dinesen. ⊠ *Karen Rd., Karen* ☎ *020/800–2139* ⊕ *www.museums. or.ke* ⊠ *Ksh1200* ⊗ *Daily 9–6.*

Nairobi National Museum. On Museum Hill off Chiromo Road, this interesting museum has good reproduction rock art displays and excellent prehistory exhibits of the archaeological discoveries of Richard and Mary Leakey. When working near Lake Turkana in the 1960s, the Leakeys discovered the skull and bones of *Homo habilis,* believed to be the ancestor of early humankind. Their findings established the Rift Valley as the possible Cradle of Humankind, although both South Africa's Sterkfontein Caves and Ethiopia's Hadar region claim the same distinction. There are also excellent paintings by Joy Adamson, better known as the author of *Born Free,* and a good collection of Kenya's birds and butterflies. The Kenya Museum Society takes guided bird walks every Wednesday morning at 8:45. There are some good craft shops and a museum shop, and it's worthwhile popping in to the Kuona Trust, the part of the museum that showcases young Kenyan artists. ⊠ *Museum Hill, off Chiromo St.* ☎ *020/374–2161, 020/374–2131* ⊕ *www. museums.or.ke* ⊠ *Ksh1200* ⊗ *Daily 8:30–5:30.*

Nairobi National Park. ⇨ *See If You Have Time, above, for more information about this park.*

WORTH NOTING

City Market. Designed in 1930 as an aircraft hangar, this vast space is a jumble of color, noise, and activity. Head to the balcony to view the curio stands on the main level. Outside the market entrance is Biashara Street, where you'll find even more curios, as well as flower sellers and butchers. Look for *kikois* and *kangas,* traditional fabrics worn by Kenyan women. They make for colorful sarongs that are good for wearing over a bathing suit or throwing over a picnic table. They're half the price here than in the hotel shops. ⊠ *Muindi Mbingu St.* ⊠ *Free* ⊗ *Mon.–Sat. 8–4.*

FAMILY **Railway Museum.** Established to preserve relics and records of East African railways and harbors, this museum is enormous fun for rail enthusiasts and children of all ages. You can see the rhino catcher that Teddy Roosevelt rode during his 1908 safari and climb into the carriage where Charles Ryall, a British railroad builder, was dragged out a window by a hungry lion. There are great photos and posters, plus silver service from the more elegant days of the overnight train to Mombasa. Rides on steam trains take place on the second Saturday of each month. ✉ *Off Haile Sellasie Ave.* ☎ *020/222–1211* 🌐 *www.krc.co.ke* 🎟 *Ksh400* 🕒 *Daily 8–5.*

OFF THE BEATEN PATH

Olorgesailie. Set in the eastern branch of the Great Rift Valley, Olorgesailie is one of Kenya's best-known archaeological sites. Discovered in 1919 by geologist J. W. Gregory, the area was excavated by Louis and Mary Leakey in the 1940s. They discovered tools thought to have been made by residents of the region more than a half million years ago. A small museum shows some of the axes and other tools found nearby. The journey here is unforgettable. As you drive south on Magadi Road, you'll find that past the town of Kiserian the route climbs over the southern end of the Ngong Hills, affording fine views of the entire valley. Volcanic hills rise out of the plains as the road drops into dry country where the Maasai people graze their herds. ✉ *65 km (40 miles) south of Nairobi* 🌐 *www.museums.or.ke* 🎟 *Ksh500* 🕒 *Daily 8–6.*

4

WHERE TO EAT

	WHAT IT COSTS IN U.S. DOLLARS			
	$	$$	$$$	$$$$
Dining	under $12	$12–$20	$21–$30	over $30

Restaurant prices are the average cost of a main course at dinner or, if dinner is not served, at lunch.

$$$$ BARBECUE

🍴 **Carnivore.** A firm fixture on the tourist trail, Carnivore became famous for serving wild game. Although this is no longer the case, you can still get crocodile, camel, and ostrich as well as beef and lamb. The emphasis, as ever, is firmly on meat—and lots of it. Waiters carry the sizzling meat to your table on long skewers and carve whatever you wish onto the cast-iron platters that serve as plates. Only when you offer a little white flag of surrender do they stop carving. As strange as it may seem, there are also many excellent choices for vegetarians. There's an à la carte option if you feel your appetite may not be equal to the set menu. [$] *Average main: $40* ✉ *Carnivore Rd., off Langata Rd.* ☎ *073/31–1608* 🌐 *www.tamarind.co.ke* ✍ *Reservations essential.*

$$$$ SEAFOOD

🍴 **Tamarind.** Hands down the finest seafood restaurant in town, Tamarind is famous for its deep-fried crab claws, ginger crab, and *piri piri* (spicy, buttery prawns grilled over charcoal). Everything is flown up daily from the coast, including the Malindi sole and the Kilifi oysters, tiny but very flavorful and served either raw or as classic oysters Rockefeller. Try the delicious *kokonda,* based on a famous dish from Fiji: raw fish and shrimp are marinated in lime juice, coconut cream, fennel, mustard seed, and local chili peppers. The restaurant has moved from Nairobi's CBD to the lovely Karen Blixen Coffee Garden. [$] *Average main: $60* ✉ *Karen Rd.* ☎ *071/934–6349* 🌐 *www.tamarind.co.ke* ✍ *Reservations essential.*

$$$ INTERNATIONAL

🍴 **Tatu.** The interior of the Norfolk Hotel's fine-dining restaurant is minimalist and modern, with large black-and-white prints of tribespeople on the walls, an open-plan kitchen, leather tablecloths, and soft lighting in muted shades of orange, yellow, and green. The menu specializes in steaks, with some interesting sides, such as truffled Parmesan fries and mac 'n' cheese. There's a fantastic selection of seafood, too, including Mombasa spiny lobster, giant tiger prawns, Nile perch, and classic comfort dishes such as chicken potpie. The wine list features New World labels with a good selection by the glass. Waitresses in beautiful kanga-print dresses round off what is altogether a very elegant dining experience. $ *Average main: $30* ⊠ *Norfolk Hotel, Harry Thuku Rd.* ☎ *020/226–5000* ⊕ *www.fairmont.com.*

WHERE TO STAY

The two landmark lodgings in the capital, the Norfolk Hotel and the Sarova Stanley, have opened their doors to visitors for more than a century. Both have been renovated in recent years and now have everything from health clubs to business centers. Newer luxury hotels, such as Sankara Nairobi, are giving them a run for their money.

Although corporate travelers may need to stay in Nairobi, those wishing to get away from the hustle and bustle can head to the distilled air of the Ngong Hills, which prompted Karen Blixen to write, "Here I am, where I ought to be." Many visitors feel the same affinity with this landscape where several country establishments offer more peaceful surroundings.

Another option, perfect to kick-start your safari, is to stay in Nairobi National Park. There are two properties—the Emakoko, a luxury lodge, and Nairobi Tented Camp, which is tucked into a forest in the park. Both offer fantastic, comfortable accommodations within an hour of Nairobi's airports. ⇨ *See the section on Nairobi National Park for details.*

WHAT IT COSTS IN U.S. DOLLARS			
$	$$	$$$	$$$$
Hotels	under $150	$150–$250	$251–$350	over $350

Hotel prices are the lowest cost of a standard double room in high season.

Hotel reviews have been shortened. For full information, visit Fodors. com.

$ 🖾 **Acacia Camp Nairobi.** Acacia Camp was set up for overland truck **B&B/INN** groups and self-drive safari desperados in Land Rovers, but it offers a range of accommodation for backpackers, from dorms with shared showers to simple en-suite rooms. **Pros:** staff can assist you in arranging all ongoing travel logistics; there is a simple, hospitable bar and restaurant. **Cons:** because this is a popular starting point for overland truck tours, it can be noisy (or fun, depending on your outlook). $ *Rooms from: $45* ⊠ *Magadi Rd.* ☎ *020/245–9083* 🛏 *18 rooms* ⊟ *No credit cards* ⦿ *No meals.*

$$$$ 🖾 **Giraffe Manor.** Yes, giraffes really do pop their heads through the windows and bat their eyelashes at you at this stately old look-alike gabled **RESORT** **FAMILY** Scottish hunting lodge. **Pros:** the rate is all-inclusive, with no hidden extras; nonguests can book a table for lunch, subject to availability.

Cons: you need to book ahead as it's often full; no pool. $ *Rooms from: $1152* ✉ *Koitobos Rd., Karen* ☎ *020/502–0888* ⊕ *www.giraffemanor. com* ⇲ *10 rooms* ⊙ *All meals.*

$$$$
HOTEL
FAMILY
🏠 **House of Waine.** You'll find nostalgia, history, and romantic surround-ings at this family-owned boutique hotel. **Pros:** you can choose to take your meal in your room, next to the pool, or in the dining room; the swimming pool is heated. **Cons:** the dining room feels too formal; the wooden floors can be noisy. $ *Rooms from: $550* ✉ *Masai La., off Bogani Rd., Karen* ☎ *020/260–1455* ⊕ *www.houseofwaine.com* ⇲ *11 suites* ⊙ *Breakfast.*

$$$$
ALL-INCLUSIVE
🏠 **Ngong House.** A contrast to the rather grand, colonial-era hotels such as the Norfolk and Stanley, Ngong House is a fabulous boutique hotel located in the quiet suburb of Karen. **Pros:** the design of the treehouses is wonderfully quirky; guests are invited to gather by the bonfire for pre-dinner drinks. **Cons:** small pool; the nocturnal tree hyraxes are fascinat-ing, but can be extremely noisy. $ *Rooms from: $980* ✉ *Ngong Rd., Karen* ☎ *072/243–4965* ⊕ *www.ngonghouse.com* ⇲ *9 rooms* ⊟ *No credit cards* ⊙ *All-inclusive.*

$$$
HOTEL
🏠 **The Norfolk Hotel.** This grand old colonial lady will take you back to the heady early days when settlers, adventurers, colonial officers, and their ladies arrived in the capital to make their names and their fortunes. **Pros:** the breakfast buffet is the best in town; the terrace is a great place to watch the world go by. **Cons:** Internet use is not free. $ *Rooms from: $259* ✉ *Harry Thuku Rd.* ☎ *020/226–5555* ⊕ *www. fairmont.com* ⇲ *129 rooms, 18 suites, 6 luxury cottages* ⊙ *No meals.*

$$$
HOTEL
🏠 **Sankara Nairobi.** This stylish city hotel is conveniently located in West-lands, close to a number of restaurants and shopping centers, although you will find all you need for a relaxing stay in the hotel itself. **Pros:** varied dining options; the hotel has been beautifully designed. **Cons:** the pool is small; spa treatments are expensive. $ *Rooms from: $320* ✉ *5 Woodvale Grove, Westlands* ☎ *020/420–8000* ⊕ *www.sankara. com* ⇲ *156 rooms* ⊙ *No meals.*

$$
HOTEL
🏠 **The Sarova Stanley.** Also one of Nairobi's oldest hotels, the Stanley was named after the journalist Henry Morton Stanley who immortalized himself by discovering a long-lost Scots explorer with one of the best sound bites in history: "Dr. Livingstone, I presume?" **Pros:** security is good; the pool is heated. **Cons:** standard rooms are small. $ *Rooms from: $173* ✉ *Corner Kenyatta Ave. and Kimati St.* ☎ *020/275–7000* ⊕ *www.sarovahotels.com/stanley* ⇲ *217 rooms* ⊙ *No meals.*

BEACH ESCAPES

Intricately carved doorways studded with brass and white walls draped with bougainvillea distinguish the towns that dot Kenya's coastline. Arab traders who landed on these shores in the 9th century brought their own culture, creating a different style of dress and architecture from what you see in other parts of Kenya.

Men stroll the streets wearing traditional caps called *kofias* and billowing caftans known as *khanzus,* while women cover their faces with black veils called *bui-buis* that reveal only their eyes. The creation of the Swahili language, a combination of Arabic and African Bantu, came about when Arab traders married African women. The term "Swahili" comes from the Arabic words *sahil,* meaning "coast," and *i,* meaning "of the." As seductive as the rhythm of the sea, Swahili is one of the most melodic tongues on earth. The coastal communities of Lamu, Malindi, and Mombasa are strongholds of this language and culture that once dominated communities from Somalia to Mozambique.

Mombasa, the country's second-largest city, was once the gateway to East. Mombasa's harbor still attracts a few large cruise ships, but nothing like the hundreds that sailed here before World War I. In Lamu, a Swahili proverb prevails: *Haraka haraka haina baraka* (Haste, haste, brings no blessing). The best-preserved Swahili town in Kenya, Lamu has streets hardly wide enough for a donkey cart. Winding alleyways are lined with houses set tight against one another. It's said that the beautifully carved doors found here are built first, then the house constructed around them. By the same token, a mosque is built first, and the town follows.

Azure waters from Lamu to Wasini are protected by the 240-km (150-mile) coral reef that runs parallel to the coast. The beaches have calm and clear surf that hovers around 27°C (80°F). As Ernest Hemingway put it, "The endless sand, the reefs, the lot, are completely unmatched in the world."

PLANNING

GETTING HERE AND AROUND

Getting to the towns along the Kenya Coast is easier than ever. Mombasa has an international airport, but you can also fly directly to Malindi, Diani Beach, or Lamu. Traveling by car around Mombasa is fairly safe.

ABOUT THE RESTAURANTS

The excellent cuisine reflects the region's rich history. Thanks to Italians, basil is everywhere, along with olive oil, garlic, and fresh lettuce. The Portuguese introduced tomatoes, corn, and cashews. Everything is combined with pungent spices such as coriander and ginger and the rich coconut milk often used as a cooking broth.

The Indian Ocean delivers some of the world's best fishing, so marlin, sailfish, swordfish, kingfish, and many other types of fish are on every menu. Not surprisingly, sashimi made from yellowtail tuna is favored by connoisseurs (and was listed on menus here as "fish tartare" before the rest of the world discovered Japanese cuisine). Prawns can be gargantuan, and wild oysters are small and sweet. Diving for your own lobster is an adventure, but you'll easily find boys who are happy to deliver fresh seafood to your door. You can even place your order for the next day.

ABOUT THE HOTELS

Accommodations along the Kenya Coast range from sprawling resorts with several restaurants to small beach houses with kitchens where you can prepare your own meals. Most accommodations along the coast can arrange snorkeling, windsurfing, waterskiing, and deep-sea fishing.

For an alternative to a hotel stay, there's a large variety of cottages and houses for rent along the beach. Most come with a cook and housekeeper. You provide your own food—which is easy to do as there are nearby stores and supermarkets. Check out the following websites to start your search: ⊕ *www.kenyaholidayvillas.com,* ⊕ *www.dianibeach. com,* and ⊕ *www.lamu.org.*

WHAT IT COSTS IN U.S. DOLLARS			
	$	$$	$$$	$$$$
Hotels	under $150	$150–$250	$251–$350	over $350
Dining	under $12	$12–$20	$21–$30	over $30

Restaurant prices are the average cost of a main course at dinner or, if dinner is not served, at lunch. Hotel prices are the lowest cost of a standard double room in high season.

Our hotel reviews have been shortened. For full information, visit Fodors.com.

MOMBASA

You may well find yourself in Mombasa for a few hours or an overnight stop. The city (actually an island linked to the mainland by a ferry) is the second oldest trade center with Arabia and the Far East. Today it still plays an important role as the main port for Kenya. Although it lacks the beautiful beaches of the north and south, it has a rich, fascinating history. Visit the Old Town with its narrow streets lined with tiny shops and *souks* (markets). The Old Harbour, frequented by numerous dhows, is an ideal place to arrange a short cruise on one of these local boats that have plied the oceans for centuries. Fort Jesus, designed by an Italian and built by the Portuguese in the late 16th century, is a major visitor draw and well worth a visit. In summer there's an impressive sound-and-light show.

THE BEACH BOYS

Hawkers and hustlers known as "beach boys" prowl Kenya's coastline, although their numbers have reportedly dwindled. They sell everything from boat rides and souvenirs to drugs and sex, and their incessant pestering can ruin a beach walk (hotels employ guards to keep them off hotel grounds). A strategy may be to go on a boat trip or purchase something from one of them, and in theory, the rest should leave you alone. Otherwise, be firm and don't engage.

GETTING HERE AND AROUND

Kenya Airways and Fly540 have daily flights between Nairobi and Mombasa, and from Mombasa you can fly to Malindi and Lamu. Safaris to Tsavo East or Tsavo West can also depart from here. The airport is located 10 km (6 miles) from the city center, on the mainland. Several taxi companies operate from the airport and have fixed rates to either the center of town or the beach resorts. You can also arrange for your hotel to pick you up. Taxis in Mombasa are inexpensive. The drivers are friendly and helpful and will wait or return to collect you if you ask. Tired of flying? There's an overnight train that runs four times a week from Nairobi to Mombasa. It departs Nairobi at 7 pm and arrives in Mombasa around 10 am the following morning. First class is very basic, but clean, and dinner and breakfast are included in the price ($75 one-way). You can buy tickets at the station but it's best to book in advance. It saves you a battle with Nairobi traffic (it really is a nightmare). Karen-based operator Twiga Tours (⊕ *www.twiga-tours. com*) can reserve and purchase the ticket for you.

MONEY MATTERS

Most major banks have ATMs in Mombasa. If you want to change money, Forex Bureau has exchange shops on Digo Road near the Municipal Market and near the entrance of Fort Jesus.

SAFETY

The best way to see Mombasa is on foot, but you shouldn't walk around at night. If you take a taxi at night, make sure it delivers you all the way to the door of your destination. Purse snatchers are all too common. Beware of people who might approach you on Mombasa's Moi Avenue offering to become your guide. Tell them, "*Hapana, asante sana*" ("No, thank you"), and move on.

ESSENTIALS

Emergencies Emergency Hotline ☎ *999.* **Mombasa Central Police Station** ☎ *041/225–501.*

Hospitals Aga Khan Hospital ⊠ *Vanga Rd., Kizingo* ☎ *041/222–7710* ⊕ *www. agakhanhospitals.org/mombasa.* **Pandya Memorial Hospital** ⊠ *Dedan Kimathi Ave.* ☎ *041/231–3577, 072/220–6424* ⊕ *www.pandya.kbo.co.ke.*

Taxis Kenatco Taxis Ltd ☎ *078/850–2237* ⊕ *www.kenatco.co.ke.*

Visitor Information Kenya Coast ⊕ *www.kenya-coast.com.*

EXPLORING
WORTH NOTING

Anglican Cathedral. Built in the early part of the last century, the cathedral is a memorial to Archbishop James Hannington, a missionary who was executed in 1885. The influence of Middle Eastern Islamic architecture is clear in the frieze, the dome, and the tall, narrow windows. The paneling behind the high altar is reminiscent of the cathedral in Stone Town. ⊠ *Nkrumah Rd. and Cathedral Rd.* ☎ *041/223–0502* ⊕ *www. ackmombasacathedral.com.*

Biashara Street. To get a good insight into the daily life of downtown Mombasa, head to narrow, cluttered Biashara (Swahili for "business") Street, which is just off Mombasa Road. Here, you'll find all sorts of small shops that have been around for generations—selling everything from leather to textiles, live chickens, and food. People are friendly and hospitable but, as in most poor backstreet areas, watch your belongings. While you're here, take a wander through the vegetable and spice market, near where Biashara Street meets Mombasa Road. ⊠ *Off Moi Ave.*

Fort Jesus. This massive edifice was built in the late 16th century by the Portuguese, who were keen to control trade in the region. When the Omanis captured the fort at the end of the 17th century, they made some adjustments. The walls were raised to account for the improved trajectory of cannons mounted aboard attacking ships. By the end of the 18th century, turrets were erected. For water, the garrison relied on a pit cistern, which was used for bathing when the fort was a prison, between 1895 and 1958. The captain's house retains some traces of the Portuguese—note the outline of the old colonnade. The exhibits at the museum include an important display on ceramics of the coast and the remains of a Portuguese gunner, *San Antonio de Tanna*, which sank outside the fort at the end of the 17th century. Objects from the ship—shoes, glass bottles, a powder shovel, and cannon with its muzzle blown away—bring the period to life. There are also exhibits of finds from archaeological excavations at Gedi, Manda, Ungwana, and other sites. ⊠ *End of Nkrumah Rd.* ☎ *041/222–0058* 🖅 *Ksh 1200* ⊙ *Daily 8–6.*

New Burhani Bohra Mosque. The elaborate facade and soaring minaret of this mosque overlook the Old Harbor. Built in 1902, it's the third mosque to occupy this site. ⊠ *Off Ndia Kuu Rd.*

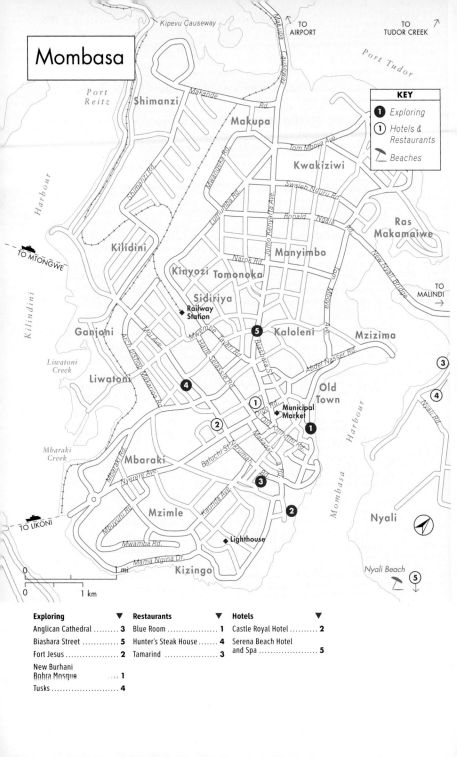

Mombasa

KEY

- **1** Exploring
- **(1)** Hotels & Restaurants
- Beaches

Tusks. Dominating Moi Avenue are the famous elephant tusks that cross above the roadway. They were erected to commemorate the 1952 visit of Britain's Princess Elizabeth, now Queen Elizabeth II. Up close, they can be somewhat disappointing, as they are made of aluminum. ✉ *Moi Ave. at Uhuru Gardens.*

WHERE TO EAT

$ | × **Blue Room.** Serving the best samosas in Mombasa, this family-owned Indian restaurant has been in business for more than 50 years. It seats 140 people, making it one of the largest restaurants in the city. The menu features more than 65 items of both Western and Indian origin, and its bright clean interior with tiled floors and plenty of chairs and tables keeps people coming. The curries and Indian vegetarian dishes are especially good, as are the tasty snacks. Try the samosas, kebabs, or even fish 'n' chips. There's also an ice cream parlor. You'll find a cybercafé inside, where you can send an e-mail back home. You'll need a Ksh5 coin to use the bathroom. Ⓢ *Average main: $8* ✉ *Intersection of Haile Selassie Rd. and Digo Rd.* ☎ *072/178–6868* ⊕ *www.blueroomonline.com.*

INDIAN

$$$ | × **Hunter's Steak House.** This small, intimate international restaurant is one of Mombasa's best, very popular with foreign visitors and Mombasa's expatriates. With trophy animals mounted on the walls, the place resembles a hunting lodge. Although it serves a wide range of dishes including excellent seafood and venison, Hunter's is best known for its mouthwatering steaks and homemade desserts like apple pie. It's also a good place to stop for a cold beer. Ⓢ *Average main: $22* ✉ *Mkomani Rd., Nyali* ☎ *041/474–759* ▭ *No credit cards* ☼ *Closed Tues.*

STEAKHOUSE

$$$$ | × **Tamarind.** What the Carnivore restaurant does for meat in Nairobi, this fine restaurant does for seafood in Mombasa. A 15-minute drive from downtown and a welcome house cocktail—a *dawa* made of lime, vodka, honey, and crushed ice—will introduce you to a memorable meal and an unforgettable experience. Overlooking a creek flowing into the sea, the restaurant is designed like an old Moorish palace with high arches, and tiled floors. If you love seafood, you'll be in heaven. You can also take a lunch- or dinner-dhow cruise ($80 for a set menu) around Tudor Creek and soak up some sun and sea air by day, or watch the moon rise over Mombasa Old Town by night, as soft Swahili music makes the food and wine go down even better. The restaurant's Clifftop Terrace is a stylish sushi and cocktail bar, which is fantastic for pre-Tamarind dinner drinks, or a casual evening of sushi, ceviche, and cocktails. Ⓢ *Average main: $60* ✉ *Cement Silos Rd., Nyali* ☎ *041/447–4600* ⊕ *www.tamarind.co.ke.*

SEAFOOD

ARCHITECTURE

The region's architecture is characterized by arcaded balconies and red-tile roofs. One of the great concepts of coastal interiors is the *baraza*, an open sitting area with cushions perfect for parties or intimate conversations. Lamu furniture, with its deep brown color, provides a compelling contrast to the white walls. Local decorations can include fish traps made of palm rib or bamboo, and items made of old dhow wood.

4

WHERE TO STAY

$ 🏠 **Castle Royal Hotel.** Originally built in 1919, this white old colonial
HOTEL   building is in Mombasa's town center only a short distance away from
the old town and Fort Jesus. **Pros:** the central location is unbeatable;
rooms have fridges. **Cons:** some of the rooms are very noisy; hot water
only available in the mornings and evenings. $ *Rooms from: $135*
✉ *Moi St., Central Mombasa* ☎ *041/222–8780* ⊕ *www.sentrim-hotels.*
com ⤴ *68 rooms* �‖○‖ *Multiple meal plans.*

$$ 🏠 **The Serena Beach Hotel and Spa.** This gorgeous resort at Shanzu Beach
RESORT   was built to resemble a 13th-century Arab town. **Pros:** there's a free
daily shuttle to Mombasa town; the spa is good. **Cons:** the resort has
a serious monkey problem; Internet is not free. $ *Rooms from: $185*
✉ *Shanzu Beach* ☎ *020/284–2333* ⊕ *www.serenahotels.com* ⤴ *164*
rooms �‖○‖ *Some meals.*

SOUTHERN BEACHES OF MOMBASA

Kenya's coast south of Mombasa has some of the country's most beauti-
ful beaches. The highway from Mombasa runs all the way to the Tan-
zania border, providing easy access to a string of resorts.

GETTING HERE AND AROUND

Most people fly into Mombasa's Moi International Airport and make
their way down the coast by taxi, rental car, or hotel shuttle. There's an
airstrip at Ukunda for charter flights. You must take the Likoni Ferry
to travel south of Mombasa. Two ferries run simultaneously, departing
about 20 minutes apart, with fewer departures late in the day and in
the evening. Vehicles are charged by length, usually about Ksh90 per
car. Pedestrians ride free.

SAFETY

If you take a taxi at night, make sure it delivers you all the way to your
destination. Tourist Police officers patrol beaches, but don't tempt fate
by bringing jewelry, cameras, or cash. Women shouldn't walk alone
on the beach.

If you're walking from Tiwi to Diani, consult the tidal chart before-
hand. A creek that you must swim across at high tide is known as
"Panga Point."

Drink plenty of bottled water and wear sunscreen. It's a good idea to
wear a thick T-shirt to protect your back from sunburn when snorkeling.

EXPLORING
TOP ATTRACTIONS

Kaya Kinondo Sacred Forest. If you're in the Diani Beach area, be sure
to spend an hour or two exploring the Kaya Kinondo forest. This
UNESCO World Heritage Site has been sacred territory for the Digo
people for centuries. You'll need to walk with a guide, who will tell you
about the beliefs and ceremonies held here, as well as the medicinal and
culinary uses of the plants growing in the forest which, although only
75 acres, is said to boast 187 species of tree. You'll also see colobus
and Sykes monkeys, as well as baboons. A walk here is highly recom-
mended. If you have time, ask your guide to show you around the

local Digo village, or even to introduce you to the spiritual healer. ✉ *4 km south from the end of the tarmac at Diani Beach* ☎ *072/244–6916* 🌐 *www.kaya-kinondo-kenya.com* 🎫 *Ksh1000.*

BEACHES

Diani Beach. Once a true tropical Eden with gorgeous weather and equally gorgeous scenery this 20-km (12-mile) stretch of sand, 30 km (19 miles) south of Mombasa, is the most developed along the southern coast. One reason that it's so popular is that the reef filters out the seaweed, so the sandy shores are truly pristine. If you stay in one of the private cottages, local fishermen will take your order and deliver lobsters and other delicacies of the deep to your door. **Best for:** snorkelling, sunrise, walking, windsurfing. **Amenities:** food and drink, water sports.

Shimoni. Just 60 km (37 miles) south of Diani, on the tip of a peninsula known for its excellent deep-sea fishing you'll find the village of Shimoni, which means "place of the holes." Ocean currents dug out a maze of coral caves, one of them 11 km (7 miles) long. This catacomb was used as an underground tunnel for loading slaves onto dhows. You can see iron shackles that still remain on the cave walls. There is no beach here, but you can take a dhow from here to the Kisite-Mpunguti Marine National Park. **Best for:** fishing. **Amenities:** none.

4

WHERE TO EAT

$ AFRICAN

🍴 **African Pot.** This relaxed beachfront restaurant, made of thatch and wood, is in front of the Coral Beach cottages, 300 meters (984 feet) north of Ukunda junction, Diani Beach. It serves excellent Swahili food, including greens, gumbo, and the traditional *ugali,* which some say is the inspiration for grits. Live African music is occasionally featured here. [$] *Average main: $8* ✉ *Near entrance to Coral Beach Cottages, Diani* ☎ *072/234–6155* ✉ *africanpotrestaurants@yahoo.com* 💳 *No credit cards.*

$$$$ SEAFOOD

🍴 **Ali Barbour's Cave.** You can dine in a naturally formed cave deep underground at this popular seafood restaurant, where the experience and location outweigh the meal. You can't go wrong with the crab salad marinated with lemon and chilies. You can also dine on French food. There is a shuttle bus that will pick up people staying in the Diani Beach area. No children under 6. [$] *Average main: $50* ✉ *Ali Barbour's Rd., Diani Beach* ☎ *071/445–6131* 🌐 *www.alibarbours.co* ✍ *Reservations essential.*

WHERE TO STAY

Most of the hotels and resorts are on one or two roads running parallel to the beach. Often the properties aren't numbered, so landmarks are used to guide people instead. Everyone knows where all the places are, so you don't need to instruct a taxi driver with specific details.

$$$ RESORT

🏨 **Diani Reef Beach Resort and Spa.** This luxurious resort will make sure you get the best out of your beach break. **Pros:** the staff are extremely friendly; organized activities are good. **Cons:** wine and Internet use are expensive; resident monkeys can be annoying. [$] *Rooms from: $280* ✉ *Diani Beach Rd.* ☎ *040/320–2723, 073/320–2723* 🌐 *www.dianireef.com* 🛏 *143 rooms* 🍴 *Some meals.*

$$$$ ALL-INCLUSIVE FAMILY Fodor's Choice ★

🏨 **Kinondo Kwetu.** One of Kenya's finest boutique resorts, Kinondo Kwetu Beach Resort was built in an idyllic beachfront location in a section of sacred forest. **Pros:** dinner can be served in a variety of romantically secluded locations, so you need never eat in the same place twice; there are a variety of activities, including yoga and horseback riding on the beach. **Cons:** the beach is only swimmable at high tide. [$] *Rooms from: $660* ✉ *Diani Beach Rd., Kinondo, Diani Beach* ☎ *071/089–8030* 🌐 *www.kinondo-kwetu.com* 🛏 *7 suites, 4 cottages, and 1 villa* 🍴 *All-inclusive.*

MALINDI

Malindi, the country's second-largest coastal town, is 120 km (75 miles) north of Mombasa and has been an important port for hundreds of years. In ancient Chinese documents, "Ma Lin De" is referred to as a stop on the trade route. The town battled with Mombasa for control of the coast, which explains why Portuguese explorer Vasco da Gama received such a warm welcome when he landed here in 1498 but was given the cold shoulder in Mombasa. The Vasco da Gama Cross, made from Portuguese stone, sits on a promontory on the southern tip of the bay. Malindi has become very much an Italian holiday destination, and although it's laid-back, it has a somewhat seedy atmosphere, and sex tourism is rife. That being said, the beaches are picture-postcard-perfect, with white sand and coconut palms, and there are some good restaurants in the town and some excellent resort hotels. Old Town is a great place to hunt for colorful fabrics, antiques, and sandals, and the beach is clean and attractive, although it does get a bit seaweedy in spring. Malindi has two nearby parks, Malindi Marine National Park and Watamu Marine National Reserve. These are marine parks, where you can watch fish and coral from a glass-bottom boat or snorkel, but the collection or destruction of shells is strictly forbidden. It also offers deep-sea fishing and other water sports. It's an easy place to get around because there are lots of *tuk tuks* (auto rickshaw) and *boda bodas* (bicycle taxis), which are everywhere day and night.

GETTING HERE AND AROUND

Kenya Airways and Fly540 fly to Malindi frequently.

Taxis are inexpensive. The drivers are friendly and helpful and will wait or return to collect you if you ask. There are lots of tuk tuks, and although the journey can be bumpy, they're an easy and inexpensive way to get around town.

SAFETY

The best way to see Malindi is on foot, but you shouldn't walk around at night. If you take a taxi at night, make sure it delivers you all the way to the door of your destination. Purse snatchers are all too common.

EXPLORING

WORTH NOTING

Jamaa Mosque. The 14th-century tombs beside this mosque are among the oldest in Malindi. It was here in the 1800s that slaves were auctioned weekly until 1873. ✉ *Off Silversand Rd.*

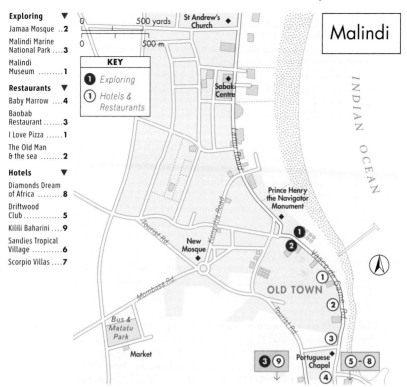

Malindi Marine National Park. Home to an impressive variety of color-ful coral, you'll find two main reefs here that are separated by a deep sandy-bottom channel. There's very little commercial fishing in the area, which means the kingfish found here are trophy size. The water ranges from 25°C (77°F) to 29°C (84°F), making this a particularly pleasant place to snorkel or scuba dive. If you want to stay dry, try one of the glass-bottom boats, although visibility is not very good from January to March. ⊠ *Offshore from Malindi* ⊕ *www.kws.org* ✉ *US$20 entry fee* ☽ *Dawn–dusk.*

Malindi Museum. Delve into some of Malindi's fascinating history at this museum, which was once the home of a 19th-century trader. You'll find it on the seafront near the Malindi jetty and the fish market. It has temporary exhibitions and also serves as a visitor information center. ⊠ *Vasco da Gama Rd.* ☎ *042/31479* ⊕ *www.museums.or.ke* ✉ *Ksh 500* ☽ *Daily 8–6.*

WHERE TO EAT

$$$
ITALIAN

✕ **Baby Marrow.** Malindi's fine-dining option is, naturally, Italian owned, so you'll be able to sample prosciutto e melone, pizzas, and a variety of pastas (including "baby marrow" [zucchini] ravioli) alongside such sea-food dishes as ginger and black-pepper crab, jumbo prawns, and lobster. Seating is under an attractive thatch roof, and it's rather romantic at night. $ *Average main: $27* ⊠ *Silversand Rd.* ☎ *072/758–1682* ▭ *No credit cards.*

$ ✕ **The Baobab Restaurant.** Eat breakfast, lunch, or dinner or just have
CAFÉ   a beer or juice at this friendly, cheerful restaurant. There's a choice of soup, burgers, pasta, steak, and seafood. The fish curry is particularly tasty, and there is a good selection of African dishes. $ *Average main: $7* ⊠ *Vasco da Gama Rd.* ☎ *072/282–9867* ▭ *No credit cards.*

$ ✕ **I Love Pizza.** Overlooking the bay, this place is famous for its, you
PIZZA   guessed it, pizza, although there is a good selection of sophisticated seafood dishes, such as kingfish carpaccio with horseradish, and risotto with clams, prawns, and squid. The calamari salad is excellent. $ *Average main: $7* ⊠ *Vasco da Gama Rd.* ☎ *042/20672* ▭ *No credit cards.*

$ ✕ **The Old Man and the Sea.** Near the fishing jetty, this stylish former Arab
AFRICAN   house is known as one of the best places in town for its fresh seafood. Try the marinated prawns wrapped in smoked sailfish, a Malindi specialty, or the red snapper with a champagne sauce. $ *Average main: $8* ⊠ *Silversand Rd.* ☎ *042/213–1106.*

WHERE TO STAY

Rates can be very high in season—June through October—but prices drop dramatically off-season. It's best to stick to lodging near the beach as downtown gets noisy, isn't always safe, and accommodations can be squalid.

$$$$ 🏨 **Diamonds Dream of Africa.** There are four Planhotels stretched out in
RESORT   a row down this part of the coast, and their five-star resort, Diamonds Dream of Africa, is the jewel in the crown—the perfect place for a honeymoon or some après-safari pampering. **Pros:** there are only 35 rooms; all alcohol except premium brands included. **Cons:** the beds are a little hard; rooms do not look out onto the ocean. $ *Rooms from: $365* ⊠ *Casuarina Rd.* ☎ *020/268–2229* ⊕ *www.planhotel.com* ⇆ *35 rooms* ❙⊙❙ *All meals.*

$$ 🏨 **Driftwood Club.** In an attractive garden, these Swahili-style individual
B&B/INN   bandas, each with a thatch roof and small veranda, are seconds away
FAMILY   from the pool and beach. **Pros:** right on the beach; rooms have good a/c. **Cons:** rooms are a bit basic for a hotel in this price range; use of the in-room safe is extra; some bandas look out onto the walkway so are not very private. $ *Rooms from: $200* ⊠ *Silversands Rd.* ☎ *020/261–7300* ⊕ *www.driftwoodclub.com* ⇆ *37 rooms* ❙⊙❙ *Breakfast.*

$$ 🏨 **Kilili Baharini Resort and Spa.** This elegant resort, much favored by Ital-
RESORT   ians, is on a large estate amid a profusion of tropical flowering plants 4 km (2½ miles) from Malindi. **Pros:** rooms have a/c; there are five pools. **Cons:** lunch is buffet only; airport transfers not included. $ *Rooms from: $180* ⊠ *Casuarina Rd.* ☎ *077/020–6500* ⊕ *www.kililibaharini. com* ⇆ *29 rooms, 6 suites* ⊘ *Closed May–July* ❙⊙❙ *All meals.*

$$ 🏨 **Sandies Tropical Village.** This extensive seafront resort, three kilometers
ALL-INCLUSIVE   from Malindi, has spacious thatched or beamed rooms and suites, all of which have sizeable verandas opening onto lush gardens. **Pros:** each room has a minibar fridge; if you're in a suite, there's a free laundry service and room service for breakfast. **Cons:** no sea-facing rooms; pool area can be noisy; public beach is overserviced by beach vendors.

Kenya's beautiful beaches are a great place to relax after a safari.

$ *Rooms from: $240* ✉ *Casuarina Rd.* ☎ *072/060–7075, 073/595–5666* ⊕ *www.sandies-resorts.com* ⌁ *109 rooms* ⦾ *All-inclusive.*

$

HOTEL

⌨ **Scorpio Villas.** The thatch-roof rooms of this hotel are filled with hand-crafted furniture such as huge Zanzibar beds and day couches are scattered around the exotic gardens of this resort near the Vasco da Gama Cross. **Pros:** the half-board option allows you to choose lunch or dinner; rooms have fridges. **Cons:** use of the safe is extra; payment by cash only. $ *Rooms from: $130* ✉ *Mnarani Rd.* ☎ *042/212–0194* ⊕ *www.scorpio-villas.com* ⌁ *45 villas* ▭ *No credit cards* ⦾ *Some meals.*

LAMU

Designated a UNESCO World Heritage Site in December 2001, Lamu Old Town is the oldest and best-preserved Swahili settlement in East Africa. Some 260 km (162 miles) north of Mombasa—and just two degrees below the Equator—Lamu is separated from the mainland by a narrow channel that's fringed with thick mangroves protected from the sea by coral reefs and huge sand dunes. Winding narrow alleyways lead past the ornate carved doorways and coral walls of magnificent merchant houses to the bustling waterfront. Life goes on much as it did when Lamu was a thriving port town in the 8th century; there are no cars (all transport and heavy lifting is by donkey), and more than 1,000 years of East African, Omani, Yemeni, Indian, and Portuguese influences have resulted in a unique mix of cultures, reflected in the faces of its inhabitants as well as in its architecture and cuisine. A stronghold of Islam for many centuries, you'll see men in *kofias* (traditional caps that Muslims wear) and *khanzus* (white caftanlike robes) and women in *bui-buis* (black veils). Some merchant houses have been converted into gorgeous boutique hotels, and rooftop restaurants offer abundant, fresh seafood for very little.

The island is roughly divided into two parts: Lamu Town, in the south, and Shela, a smaller, quieter village in the north and next to the beach. Some visitors split their holiday between staying on both sides of the island, or you could opt to stay on Manda Island or in farther flung hotels on the far northern or southern edges. You can walk between Lamu Town and Shela in about 45 minutes; a popular option is to walk one way and take a boat back. The beach offers 13 km (8 miles) of unspoiled coastline.

It's very easy to relax into the *pole-pole* ("slowly" in Swahili) pace of life in Lamu, spending hours on the beach or on your hotel terrace reading a book and sipping a delicious fresh fruit juice. There's also plenty for the energetic to do here—windsurfing, kayaking, fishing, and snorkeling. You can also take a dhow cruise to visit ruins on Pate and Manda islands.

Tourism hasn't made much of an impact on Lamu, and that's what makes it so special.

GETTING HERE AND AROUND
Flights land on Manda Island, and a speedboat takes about 10 minutes to get to Lamu (your hotel will pick you up). Lamu is an easy town to get around because it's so small. The cobbled streets are laid out in a grid fashion with the main street—known simply as Main Street—running parallel to the harbor.

Kenya Airways has daily flights from Nairobi. AirKenya has frequent flights to Lamu and Kiwayu from Nairobi, Mombasa, and Malindi. It also offers hops from Lamu to Kiwayu. Fly540 flies here from Nairobi and Malindi.

Most hotels can arrange for a trip by dhow between Lamu and Shela. Find out the going price from your accommodation and confirm with the captain before setting out.

FESTIVALS AND SEASONAL EVENTS
The Maulidi festival, marking the birth of Muhammad, has been celebrated on Lamu for more than a century. Dhow races, poetry readings, and other events take place around the town's main mosques. Maulidi, which takes place in the spring, attracts pilgrims from all over Kenya. The three-day Lamu Cultural Festival takes place each November and offers a unique insight into island life. The event showcases traditional dance, handicraft displays, and music and theater performances from both local and visiting artists.

EXPLORING
Ask at your lodging for a local guide to take you around the city. Agree on a price before you head out, and then let him introduce you to the history of this remarkable little town.

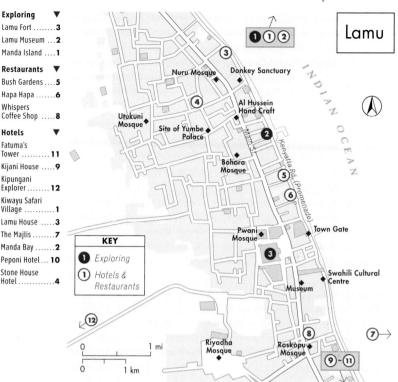

TOP ATTRACTIONS

Lamu Fort. This imposing edifice, completed in 1821, is set one street away from the seafront. It was used as a prison from 1910 to 1984, when it became part of the country's museum system. Today, it is a central part of the town as it hosts conferences, exhibits, and theater productions. If you have a few moments, climb up to the battlements for some great views of Lamu, and pop into the vegetable and meat markets, which are just to the left of the fort. If you see a man pressing sugarcane, limes and ginger to make juice, buy a glass—it's delicious. The entrance fee is a package and includes entry to Takwa, Pate, and Siyu Ruins, as well as Lamu Museum, Swahili House and German post office. ⊠ *Main St.* ⊕ *www.museums.or.ke* 🕮 *Ksh 3000* ☉ *Daily 8–6.*

Lamu Museum. You enter the museum through a brass-studded door that was imported from Zanzibar. Inside there are archaeological displays showing the Takwa Ruins excavations, some wonderful photos of Lamu taken by a French photographer from 1846 to 1849 (you'll be amazed at how little has changed in Lamu), some intricately carved Lamu headboards and throne chairs, and a library. In the Balcony Room upstairs is a fascinating display of musical instruments including the famed Lamu *siwa* horn, which is made of brass and resembles an elephant tusk; the Pate siwa horn, made of ivory, is now in the Nairobi Museum. Dating from the 17th-century, they're reputed to be the oldest surviving musical instruments in sub-Saharan Africa. ✉ *Seafront* 🌐 *www.museums.or.ke* 🎫 *Ksh 500* 🕒 *Daily 8–6.*

Manda Island. Just across the channel from Shela, the mostly uninhabited Manda Island once held one of the area's largest cities. The once-thriving community of Takwa was abandoned in the 17th century, and archaeologists have yet to discover why. Reached by taking a dhow up a baobab treelined creek, the ruins are a popular day trip from Lamu and Shela. ✉ *10 mins by boat from Lamu.*

WHERE TO EAT

Most of the restaurants and hotels in Lamu town are along the seafront or the road parallel to it, called Main Street.

$ SEAFOOD 🍴 **Bush Gardens.** Service isn't the fastest in the world at this lively waterfront eatery, but it's worth waiting for the delicious seafood and fresh fish—definitely try the tuna, barracuda, or snapper. Entrées are served with coconut rice or french fries. If you stop by for breakfast, make sure to sample the fresh fruit juices. [$] *Average main: $7* ✉ *Seafront, south of the main jetty* ☎ *071/493–4804* 💳 *No credit cards* 🕒 *Daily 7 am–10 pm.*

$ SEAFOOD 🍴 **Hapa Hapa.** With a name that is Swahili for "Here, Here," Hapa Hapa is known for its outstanding seafood. Make sure to try the barracuda. This restaurant is on the waterfront, making it a great spot to watch the fishing boats heading out into the Indian Ocean. [$] *Average main: $8* ✉ *Seafront* ☎ *071/252–6215* 💳 *No credit cards.*

$ CAFÉ 🍴 **Whispers Coffee Shop.** Located in the same building as the Baraka Gallery (which has a wonderful collection of African art, jewelry, and souvenirs for sale), this upscale café has a pretty, quiet courtyard where you can relax over a cappuccino. There are also lunch and dinner menus, focusing on salads, pastas, and deli items, or you can order a packed lunch to take away. The homemade ice creams are good. [$] *Average main: $8* ✉ *Main St.* ☎ *042/463–2024* 💳 *No credit cards* 🕒 *Closed May and June.*

WHERE TO STAY

$ HOTEL 🏨 **Fatuma's Tower.** Set against the dunes in little Shela village, Fatuma's Tower is a beautiful, cool, calm escape from the narrow alleys of the village. **Pros:** there's a cook who can do your food shopping and preparation of all meals; it's extremely peaceful and there's total serenity beyond the sound of motorboat engines. **Cons:** mosquitoes can occasionally be a nuisance (there's no malaria in the area). [$] *Rooms from: $125* ✉ *Shela* ☎ *072/227–7138* 🌐 *www.fatumastower.com* 🛏 *10 rooms* 🍽 *Some meals.*

$$ HOTEL 🏨 **Kijani Hotel.** Located right on the waterfront in Shela, Kijani Hotel is a mix of art deco and antique Swahili furniture. **Pros:** rooms look out onto the waterfront; the hotel is five minutes' walk from the beach. **Cons:** can get hot at night. [$] *Rooms from: $235* ✉ *Shela* ☎ *073/354–5264* 🌐 *www.kijani-lamu.com* 🛏 *11 rooms* 🕒 *Closed May and June* 🍽 *Breakfast.*

$$$$ HOTEL 🏨 **Kipungani Explorer.** On the southwestern tip of Lamu Island, this lodge is for anyone who's looking for a truly secluded getaway. **Pros:** the

hotel's engagement with the local community; the sunsets from the swimming pool; plenty of water sports. **Cons:** electricity on 8–noon and 6–midnight only; full-board option only. $ *Rooms from: $450* ✉ *Kipungani* ☎ *020/444–6651* ⊕ *www.heritage-eastafrica.com* ⤴ *12 cottages* ¡◎¡ *All meals.*

$$$$
ALL-INCLUSIVE

▦ **Kiwayu Safari Village.** Fifty kilometers (31 miles) northeast of Lamu you'll find one of the most romantic destinations in Kenya. **Pros:** the bandas are beautifully furnished; there are great water-sport activities on offer. **Cons:** no swimming pool; trips to Lamu are extra. $ *Rooms from: $1200* ✉ *Kiwayu Island* ☎ *020/600–9414, 020/600–891* ⊕ *www.kiwayu.com* ⤴ *18 cottages* ⊘ *Closed end Apr.–mid-July* ¡◎¡ *All-inclusive.*

$$
HOTEL

▦ **Lamu House Hotel & Beach Club.** The rooms in this boutique hotel, located next to the Donkey Sanctuary on Lamu's waterfront, are all different, but each one is superbly decorated in traditional Swahili style and has a separate dressing room and a terrace looking out either onto the water or the town. **Pros:** each room has a fridge; there are free boats to shuttle you to Shela Beach; breakfast is available all day. **Cons:** it can be noisy as it's in the center of town; if narrow, steep staircases are a problem for you, request a ground-level room. $ *Rooms from: $170* ✉ *Seafront* ☎ *070/804–3164, 070/827–9905* ⊕ *www.lamuhouse.com* ⤴ *10 rooms* ¡◎¡ *Breakfast.*

4

$$$$
RESORT
FAMILY

▦ **The Majlis.** The rooms in this spectacular hotel are in three villas, and as each has a sitting room with white couches, antique Swahili furniture, and African paintings and sculptures, you'll feel as though you're staying in an ultrastylish private beach house. **Pros:** unforgettable dhow sunset cruises; an excellent beach; rooms have a/c. **Cons:** trips to Lamu aren't included; alcohol isn't included in the full-board option. $ *Rooms from: $420* ✉ *Manda Island* ☎ *020/712–3301, 070/807–3126* ⊕ *www.themajlisresorts.com* ⤴ *25 rooms* ¡◎¡ *All meals.*

$$$$
RESORT

▦ **Manda Bay.** At high tide, you can dive right off your veranda into the ocean; at low tide, a lovely strand of beach appears in front of your room. **Pros:** truly a private island getaway; boutique-hotel amenities with laid-back feel; fantastic for both honeymooners and families. **Cons:** music from the bar can be heard in cottages near the main area. $ *Rooms from: $515* ✉ *Manda Island* ☎ *020/211–5453* ⊕ *www. mandabay.com* ⤴ *16 cottages* ¡◎¡ *All meals.*

$$$
HOTEL

▦ **Peponi Hotel.** Peponi is well known for its beachfront location in Shela, lovely accommodations, and superb food. **Pros:** only hotel guests get seating on the outside balcony at dinner; you can sleep with the sea-facing windows and doors open (guards are on duty all night). **Cons:** drinks are not included in the full-board option. $ *Rooms from: $285* ✉ *Shela Seafront* ☎ *072/220–3082* ⊕ *www.peponi-lamu.com* ⤴ *29 rooms* ⊘ *Closed May and June* ¡◎¡ *Breakfast.*

$
HOTEL

▦ **Stone House Hotel.** This lovely 18th-century house is in the heart of Old Lamu. **Pros:** staff are very friendly; in the heart of Lamu Town. **Cons:** slightly overpriced for what, in reality, are relatively basic rooms. $ *Rooms from: $60* ✉ *Off Main St.* ☎ *042/633–544, 042/463–3544* ⊕ *www.stonehousehotellamu.com* ⤴ *10 rooms (4 share bathroom)* ▬ *No credit cards.*

TANZANIA

WELCOME TO TANZANIA

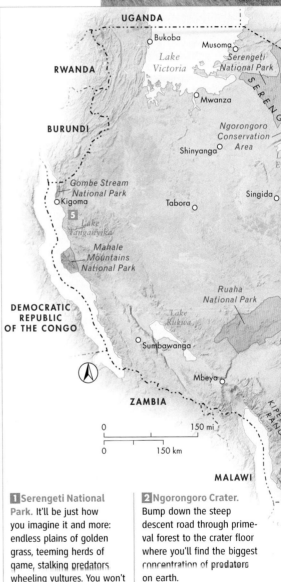

TOP REASONS TO GO

★ **The Great Migration.** This annual movement is one of the great natural wonders of the world.

★ **Big Game Adventures.** You'll be amazed at how close up and familiar you get not only with the Big Five, but with thousands of other animals as well.

★ **Sea, Sand, and Sun.** Tanzania's sun-spoiled but deserted beaches are lapped by the turquoise blue waters of the Indian Ocean. Swim, snorkel, scuba dive, sail, fish, or just chill on soft white sands under waving palm trees.

★ **Ancient Cultures.** From the traditional red-robed, bead-bedecked nomadic Maasai in the north to the exotic heady mix of Arab and African influences in Zanzibar, you'll encounter unique peoples and cultures just about everywhere you go.

★ **Bird-Watching.** Stay glued to your binoculars in one of the finest bird-watching destinations in the world. You'll be able to watch hundreds of species in a variety of habitats.

1 Serengeti National Park. It'll be just how you imagine it and more: endless plains of golden grass, teeming herds of game, stalking predators wheeling vultures. You won't be disappointed.

2 Ngorongoro Crater. Bump down the steep descent road through primeval forest to the crater floor where you'll find the biggest concentration of predators on earth.

3 Lake Manyara National Park. Tree-climbing lions, huge troops of baboons, elegant giraffes, harrumphing hippos, myriad birds, ancient forest, lakeside plains, and towering cliffs characterize this enchanting, little-visited park.

4 Selous Game Reserve. Escape the tourist crowds in the world's second-largest conservation area where you can view game on foot, by boat, or from your vehicle.

5 Gombe Stream and Mahale Mountains National Parks. Follow in the footsteps of world-famous primatologist Jane Goodall and come face-to-face with wild chimpanzees. It's an unforgettable wildlife encounter.

GETTING ORIENTED

Covering an area of 886,037 square km (342,100 square miles), which includes the islands of Mafia, Pemba, and Zanzibar, Tanzania is about twice the size of the state of California. It's bordered by the Indian Ocean in the east, Kenya to the north, and Mozambique to the south. The country is home to some of the most coveted tourist destinations in the world: Serengeti, Ngorongoro Crater, Zanzibar, Lakes Victoria, Tanganyika and Malawi, and Mt. Kilimanjaro, Africa's highest freestanding mountain. Tourism doesn't come cheap, but you'll be rewarded with spectacular views, legions of game, and unique marine experiences. It also boasts more than 1,130 bird species. Traveling distances are vast, so be prepared for lots of trips in different-size planes, or bite the bullet and face the notoriously bad potholes and seriously bumpy surfaces of dirt roads.

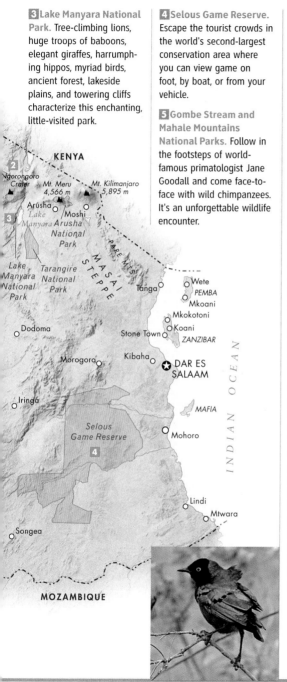

KENYA

Ngorongoro Crater
Mt. Meru 4,566 m
Mt. Kilimanjaro 5,895 m
Arusha
Moshi
Lake Manyara
Arusha National Park

Lake Manyara National Park
Tarangire National Park

MASAI STEPPE

PARE MTS

Dodoma

Tanga
Wete
PEMBA
Mkoani
Mkokotoni
Koani
ZANZIBAR
Stone Town

Morogoro
Kibaha
DAR ES SALAAM

Iringa

MAFIA

Selous Game Reserve
Mohoro

INDIAN OCEAN

Lindi
Mtwara

Songea

MOZAMBIQUE

Updated by Linda Markovina

Tanzania is the quintessential, definitive Africa of your dreams. And who wouldn't want to visit a place where the names of its legendary travel destinations roll off the tongue like an incantation: Zanzibar, Serengeti, Mt. Kilimanjaro, Lake Tanganyika, Lake Victoria, the Rift Valley, the Ngorongoro Crater, and Olduvai Gorge, "the Cradle of Humankind."

Great plains abound with legions of game, snow-capped mountains soar above dusty valleys, rain forests teem with monkeys and birds, beaches are covered in sand as soft and white as talcum powder, and coral reefs host myriads of jewel-like tropical fish. Although Tanzania's economy—one of the poorest in the world—depends heavily on agriculture, which accounts for almost half of its GDP, it has more land (more than 25%) devoted to national parks and game reserves than any other wildlife destination in the world. Everything from pristine coral reefs to the Crater highlands, remote game reserves, and the famous national parks are protected by government law and placed in trust for future generations.

There are two circuits you can follow in Tanzania: the conventional northern tourist circuit, which includes the Serengeti and Ngorongoro Crater, or the lesser traveled southern tourist circuit of Selous Game Reserve and Ruaha, Mahale, and Gombe national parks among others. You'll be amply rewarded for the often lengthy traveling to these southern locations by having the places much more to yourself and usually at cheaper rates.

Serengeti *is* all it's cracked up to be with endless plains of golden grass (Serengeti means "endless plain" in the Maasai language), teeming game, abundant bird life, and an awe-inspiring sense of space and timelessness. Ngorongoro Crater justly deserves its reputation as one of the natural wonders of the world. The ride down onto the crater floor is memorable enough as you pass through misty primeval forest with wild orchids, swinging vines, and chattering monkeys, but once

FAST FACTS

Size 945,203 square km (364,898 square miles).

Capital Dar es Salaam, though legislative offices have been transferred to Dodoma, which is planned as the new national capital.

Number of National Parks 15, including the Serengeti, Tarangire, Lake Manyara, Gombe Stream, Ruaha, Selous, Katavi, and Mt. Kilimanjaro.

Number of Private Reserves Too many to count, but includes the Singita Grumeti Reserves.

Population Approximately 43 million.

Big Five All the Big Five, including black and white rhinos.

Language Official languages are Kiswahili and English.

Time Tanzania is on EAT (East Africa Time), which is three hours ahead of Greenwich Mean Time and eight hours ahead of Eastern Standard Time.

on the floor you could well be in the middle of a National Geographic TV program. You can follow in the footsteps of legendary hunters and explorers when you visit Selous Game Reserve in the south. Although it's the second-largest conservation area in the world after Greenland National Park, only 5% of the northern part is open to tourists; but don't worry, you'll see all the game and birds you could wish for with the advantage of seeing it by boat and on foot. If it's chimpanzees you're after, then Gombe Stream and Mahale Mountains national parks are the places to head for. A lot of traveling (much of it by boat) is required, but the experience is well worth the effort, and you'll join only a small community of other privileged visitors who have had the unique experience of coming face-to-face with wild chimpanzees.

The animals aren't the only wonders Tanzania has to offer. There are the islands of Zanzibar, Pemba, and Mafia, as well as Mt. Kilimanjaro, Mt. Meru, and the three great lakes of Victoria, Tanganyika, and Malawi. Wherever you go, you're guaranteed travel experiences that you'll remember for the rest of your life.

PLANNING

WHEN TO GO

There are two rainy seasons: the short rains (*mvuli*) October through December and the long rains (*masika*) from late February to early May. Given the influence of global warming, these rains aren't as regular or as intense as they once were. It's best to avoid the two rainy seasons because many roads become impassable. Ngorongoro Crater is open all year, but the roads become extremely muddy and difficult to navigate during the wet seasons. High season is January through the end of September, but prices are much higher during this time. Make sure you find out in advance when the lodge or destination of your choice is closed as many are open only during the dry season. The coast is always pretty hot and humid, particularly during the rains, but is cooler and more pleasant the rest of the year. The hottest time is December just before the long rains. In high-altitude areas such as Ngorongoro Highlands and Mt. Kilimanjaro, temperatures can fall below freezing.

GETTING HERE AND AROUND

AIR TRAVEL

Most travelers arrive in Tanzania through Dar es Salaam airport. Many airlines fly directly to Dar es Salaam from Europe, but there are no direct flights from the United States.

KLM offers a daily flight to Dar es Salaam from Amsterdam's Schiphol airport as well as Emirates daily flights from Dubai. Other airlines that fly here frequently are Air Tanzania, Emirates, Ethiopian Airlines, Kenya Airways, Fast Jet, South African Airways, and Swiss Air. Turkish Airlines flies from Istanbul to Dar es Salaam and Kilimanjaro. Oman Air flies to Dar es Salaam via Muscat and then on to Zanzibar. Qatar Airways flies to Dar es Salaam and Zanzibar via Doha. British Airways flies to Dar es Salaam via Doha. Air Tanzania has daily flights to Dar es Salaam from destinations within East Africa.

Airlines Air Tanzania ☎ 255/222–11–7500 ⊕ www.airtanzania.co.tz. **British Airways** ☎ 022/211–3820 ⊕ www.britishairways.com. **Emirates** ☎ 255/222–116–100–3 ⊕ www.emirates.com. **Ethiopian Airlines** ☎ 022/211–7063 ⊕ www.ethiopianairlines.com. **Fast Jet** ✉ Samora Ave., Dar es Salaam ☎ 022/788–540–540 ⊕ www.fastjet.com. **Kenya Airways** ☎ 254/20–327–4747 ⊕ www.kenya-airways.com. **KLM** ☎ 022/216–3914 ⊕ www.klm.com. **Oman Air** ☎ 968/2453–1111 ⊕ www.omanair.com. **Qatar Airways** ☎ 022/219–8301 ⊕ www.qatarairways.com/tz. **South Africa Airways** ☎ 022/211–7045 ⊕ www.flysaa.com. **Swiss Air** ☎ 022/211–8871 ⊕ www.swiss.com. **Turkish Airlines** ☎ 022/284–4371 ⊕ www.turkishairlines.com.

AIRPORTS AND TRANSFERS

Julius Nyerere International Airport is about 13 km (8 miles) from the city center. Plenty of white-color taxis are available at the airport and will cost you about Tsh 30,000 (US$18) to the city center. There is a board detailing the standard rates, but this will be more expensive if you have not organized your own taxi. Most hotels will send drivers to meet your plane, if arranged in advance, although this will cost more. Taxis to Msasani Peninsula, a bay to the north of the city where many of the hotels listed in this guide are located, cost about Tsh 40,000 (US$24). Prices can usually be negotiated. Traffic into the city is notorious, especially during rush hours.

Airport Contacts Arusha Airport ✉ A 104, Arusha ☎ 027/250–5920 ⊕ www.taa.go.tz. **Julius Nyerere International Airport** ✉ Julius Nyerere Rd., Dar es Salaam ☎ 022/284–4371 ⊕ www.taa.go.tz. **Kilimanjaro International Airport** ✉ Kilimanjaro Airport Rd. ☎ 027/255–4252 ⊕ www.kilimanjaroairport.co.tz **Zanzibar Airport** ✉ Nyerere Rd., Zanzibar Town, Zanzibar ☎ 024/223–3979 ⊕ www.zanzibar-airport.com.

CHARTER FLIGHTS

The major charter companies run daily shuttles from Dar es Salaam to popular tourism destinations, such as Serengeti. Keep in mind that you probably won't get to choose the charter company you fly with. The aircraft you get depends on the number of passengers flying and can vary from very small (you'll sit in the co-pilot's seat) to a much more comfortable commuter plane. ■ TIP➔ Those with a severe fear of small planes might consider road travel instead, although distances are far and the roads are very bumpy.

Due to the limited space and size of the aircraft, charter carriers observe strict luggage regulations: luggage must be soft-sided and weigh between 15 and 20 kg (33 to 44 pounds) depending on the plane

Contacts Coastal Air ⊠ *Slipway, Dar es Salaam* ☎ *255/222–842–700* ⊕ *www. coastal.cc.* **Flightlink** ⊠ *IT Plaza, 3rd fl., Ohio/Garden Ave., Dar es Salaam* ☎ *782/354–448* ⊕ *www.flightlinkaircharters.com.* **Precision Air** ⊠ *NIC Building, Samora & Pamba Rd., Dar es Salaam* ☎ *022/216–8000* ⊕ *www.precisionairtz. com.* **Tanzanair** ⊠ *Dar es Salaam* ☎ *022/284–3131, 022/211–3151* ⊕ *www. tanzanair.com.* **ZanAir** ⊠ *Dar es Salaam* ☎ *022/33–670* ⊕ *www.zanair.com.*

> ### SERENGETI HIGHWAY
>
> In 2014, the East African Court of Justice ruled against a paved and commercial highway through the Serengeti national Park. It was contended that the highway would cause irreparable damage to the Serengeti itself and increase wildlife poaching. As of this writing the court has prevented the creation of an asphalt road; the existing dirt road will potentially be upgraded. A highway of some sorts might be inevitable.

5

ESSENTIALS

COMMUNICATIONS

PHONES

If you run across a number with only five digits, it's a remnant of the old system that was changed in 1999. Because telephone communications are difficult, many people in the travel business have mobile phones.

Calling within Tanzania: The "0" in the regional code is used only for calls placed from other areas within the country.

Calling Tanzania from abroad: To call from abroad, dial the international access number 00, then the country code 255, then the area code, (e.g., 22 for Dar es Salaam), and then the telephone number, which should have six or seven digits.

Mobile Phones: Vodacom, Airtel Tanzania, and Zantel are the main service providers in Tanzania. The best option is to bring your own phone (if it's not locked to a particular network) or rent a phone and buy a SIM card on arrival. The starter packs for pay-as-you-go cell phones are very reasonable. You'll have to buy credit for your phone, but this is easily done at shops or roadside vendors.

Contacts Airtel Tanzania ⊕ *www.africa.airtel.com.* **Tigo** ⊕ *www.tigo.co.tz.* **Vodacom** ☎ *082/111* ⊕ *www.vodacom.co.za.* **Zantel** ⊕ *www.zantel.co.tz.*

CUSTOMS AND DUTIES

You can bring in a liter of spirits or wine and 200 cigarettes duty-fee. The import of zebra skin or other tourist products requires a CITES (Convention of International Trade in Endangered Species of Wild Fauna and Flora) permit. Although you can buy curios made from animal products in Tanzania, your home country may confiscate them on arrival. Don't buy shells. It is illegal to export elephant ivory, wildlife skins, and sea turtle products without permits

HEALTH AND SAFETY

Malaria is the biggest health threat in Tanzania, so be vigilant about taking antimalarials and applying bug spray. Consult with your doctor or travel clinic before leaving home for up-to-date antimalarial medication. At time of writing HIV/AIDS is less a risk than in some other African countries, but the golden rule is *never* to have sex with a stranger. It's imperative to use strong sunscreen: remember you're just below the equator, where the sun is at its hottest. Stick to bottled water and ensure that the bottle seal is unbroken. Put your personal medications in your carry-on and bring copies of prescriptions.

The Flying Doctors Service offered by AMREF provides air evacuation services for medical emergencies in Kenya, Tanzania, and Uganda or anywhere within a 1,000-km (621-mile) radius of Nairobi. The planes fly out of Nairobi's Wilson Airport 24 hours a day, 365 days a year. They also provide transportation between medical facilities, fly you back to Europe, Asia, or North America, or provide you with an escort if you're flying on a commercial carrier.

SHOTS AND MEDICATIONS

Be up-to-date on yellow fever, polio, tetanus, typhoid, meningococcus, rabies, and Hepatitis A. It's not necessary to have a cholera jab, but if you're visiting Zanzibar it's sensible to get a cholera exception form from your GP or travel clinic. Visit a travel clinic 8 to 10 weeks before you travel to find out your requirements. If you're coming to Tanzania for a safari, chances are you're heading to a malarial game reserve. Millions of travelers take oral prophylactic drugs before, during, and after their safaris. It's up to you to weigh the risks and benefits of the type of antimalarial drug you choose to take. If you're pregnant or traveling with small children, consider a nonmalarial region for your safari.

Embassies U.S. Embassy ✉ *686 Old Bagamoyo Rd., Msasani, Dar es Salaam* ☎ *022/229–4000* ⊕ *tanzania.usembassy.gov.* **German Embassy** ✉ *Umoja House, Garden Ave. and Mirambo St., Msasani, Dar es Salaam* ☎ *022/211–2944* ⊕ *www.daressalam.diplo.de.* **Italian Embassy** ✉ *316 Lugalo Rd., Upanga, Msasani, Dar es Salaam* ☎ *022/211–5938* ⊕ *www.ambdaressalaam.esteri. it.* **United Kingdom Embassy** ✉ *Umoja House, Garden Ave., Msasani, Dar es Salaam* ☎ *022/229–0000* ⊕ *www.gov.uk/government/world/tanzania.*

Emergencies Police Hotline ☎ *112.*

Medical-Assistance Companies The Flying Doctors Service ☎ *022/211–6610 in Dar es Saalam, 022/212–7187 in Arusha* ⊕ *www.flydoc.org.*

MONEY MATTERS

The regulated currency is the Tanzanian shilling (Tsh). Notes are 500, 1,000, 2,000, 5,000, and 10,000. At this writing, the exchange rate was about Tsh 1,700 to US$1.

To avoid administrative hassles, keep all foreign-exchange receipts until you leave the region, as you may need them as proof when changing any unspent local currency back into your own currency at the airport when you leave. Don't leave yourself with any shillings—you won't be able to change them outside of Tanzania.

Bargaining, especially at marketplaces, is part of the shopping experience. But always be aware of the exchange rate and pay appropriately—you don't want to underpay, but you also don't want to be charged exorbitant "tourist" prices.

Most large hotels accept U.S. dollars and Tanzanian shillings and take all major credit cards; all budget hotels will accept Tanzanian shillings.

ATMS AND BANKS

There are banks and ATMs in all major cities; you can draw cash directly from an ATM in Dar es Salaam, Arusha, Mwanza, and Stone Town in Zanzibar. Most ATMs accept Cirrus, Plus, Maestro, Visa Electron, Visa, and MasterCard. The best place to withdraw cash is at an indoor ATM, preferably one guarded by a security officer. Most machines won't let you withdraw more than the equivalent of about $200 at a time. Don't leave withdrawing money to the last minute or late on Friday when everyone gets paid their salaries.

TIPPING

For a two- or three-night stay at a lodge or hotel, tip a couple of dollars for small services and US$2–US$5 per day for room steward and waiter. A good guide should get a tip of US$15–US$20 per day per person; if he's gone out of his way for you, then you may wish to give him more. It's a good idea to carry a number of small-denomination bills. U.S. dollars are acceptable almost everywhere, but if you're planning to go to more remote places, then shillings are preferred.

PASSPORTS AND VISAS

Most visitors require a visa to enter Tanzania. You can buy one on arrival—at the time of writing it is $50, and two passport pictures (though you might not need them). However, if possible, get your visa ahead of time to avoid long lines and headaches. Visas are valid for three months and allow multiple entries. Passports must be valid for six months after your planned departure date from Tanzania. You will need a valid yellow fever certificate to enter and exit Tanzania.

ABOUT THE HOTELS AND LODGES

You'll find the ultimate in luxury at many of the safari camps, lodges, and coastal resorts and hotels. It's highly recommended that you opt for a private camp or lodge if possible, because everything is usually included—lodging, transport to and from the lodge, meals, beverages (including excellent house wines), game drives, and other activities. Check in advance whether park fees are included in your rate, as these can get very expensive if you have to pay them daily. The southern safari circuit is cheaper in general, but you'll need to factor in the cost of transport. Many lodges and hotels offer low-season rates. If you're opting for a private game lodge, find out whether they accept children (many specify only kids over 12), and stay a minimum of two nights, three if you can. If you're traveling to the more remote parks, allow for more time. ■TIP→ Most lodges offer a laundry service to their guests and will launder everything except underwear because it's against African culture. So remember to pack plenty of pairs or make sure those you do bring are quick dry so you can wash as you go. Most lodges will provide laundry detergent in your tent for this very purpose.

National park accommodations are few and very basic. Unless you're a hardcore camper, it's advised that you stick with another type of accommodation. It's essential to note that more often than not, there won't be an elevator in your lodge—which are usually one story—and because of the rustic locations, accommodations aren't wheelchair-friendly. You'll encounter lots of steps, rocky paths, dim lighting, and uneven ground.

⇨ *For information on plugging in while on safari, see Electricity, in the Planning Your Safari chapter.*

ABOUT THE RESTAURANTS AND FOOD

Food in the lodges is plentiful and tasty, and if you head to the coast, you'll dine on superb seafood and fish with lots of fresh fruit and vegetables. All places now have at least one vegetarian course on the menu.

WHAT IT COSTS IN U.S. DOLLARS				
	$	$$	$$$	$$$$
Hotels	under $250	$250–$450	$451–$600	over $600
Dining	under $12	$12–$20	$21–$30	over $30

Hotel prices are for a standard double room in high season. All prices refer to an all-inclusive per-person, per-night rate including 12.5% tax. Restaurant prices are per person for a main course at dinner, a main course equivalent, or a prix-fixe meal.

VISITOR INFORMATION

The Tanzanian Tourist Board (TTB) has offices in Dar es Salaam and Arusha. The tourist board's website is a great online source for pre-trip planning.

Contacts Tanzania National Parks ☎ 255/272-503-471 ⊕ www.tanzaniaparks.com. **Tanzanian Tourist Board** ✉ IPS Building, 3rd fl., Samora Machel Ave., Dar es Salaam ☎ 022/211-1244 ⊕ www.tanzaniatouristboard.com.

"It's a battle of wills. . . . The lion's jaw and claws clench the wildebeest's face until it reaches a point of suffocation." —normalind, Fodors.com member.

MUST-SEE PARKS

Unfortunately, you probably won't be able to see all of Tanzania in one trip. So we've broken it down by **Must-See Parks** (Serengeti National Park, Ngorongoro Conservation Area, Mt. Kilimanjaro, Lake Manyara National Park, Selous Game Reserve, and Gombe Stream and Mahale Mountains national parks) and **If You Have Time** parks (Arusha National Park and Tarangire National Park) to help you better organize your time. We suggest, though, that you read about all of them and then choose for yourself.

SERENGETI NATIONAL PARK

Game
★★★★★

Park Accessibility
★★★★★

Getting Around
★★★★★

Accommodations
★★★★★

Scenic Beauty
★★★★

The very name Serengeti is guaranteed to bring a glint to even the most jaded traveler's eye. It's up there in that wish list of legendary destinations alongside Machu Picchu, Angkor Wat, Kakadu, Killarney, and the Great Pyramid of Giza. But what distinguishes Serengeti from all its competitors is its sheer natural beauty.

It's 15,000 square km (5,791 square miles) of pristine wilderness and that's it. Its Maasai name *Serenget* means "Endless Plain." A primeval Eden par excellence, named a UNESCO World Heritage Site in 1978 and an International Biosphere Reserve in 1981, Serengeti is all it's cracked up to be. You won't be disappointed.

This ecosystem supports some of the most plentiful mammal populations left anywhere on earth, and the animals here seem bigger, stockier, stronger, and sturdier than elsewhere in Africa. Even the scrub hares are bigger than their southern neighbors, loping rather than scampering over the tussocks and grassy mounds. Hyenas are everywhere and raptors are in perpetual motion—tawny eagles, kestrels, harriers, kites, buzzards, and vultures. Expect to see at least one baby wildebeest that has fallen by the wayside lying alone encircled by patient, voracious vultures or prowling hyenas.

But let's put you right in the picture. You'll probably land at a busy landing strip, maybe near Ntuti, where a dozen open-sided vehicles wait to pick up the new arrivals. Don't worry about lots of vehicles. In your few days driving around the Serengeti you'll certainly see others, but not too many. As you leave the airstrip, your vehicle will weave its way through herds of zebra and gazelle. Rufous-tailed weavers, endemic to northern Tanzania, flutter up from the sandy road. The plains stretch endlessly with misty mountains faint in the distance. At first the plains are ringed by trees, but then only an occasional and solitary tree punctuates the golden grass. Wherever you stay, you'll be looked after royally, with comfortable accommodation, good food, a dawn chorus of bubbling birdsong, and an evening serenade of whooping hyenas with a backing group of softly calling lions.

What will you remember about the Serengeti? The unending horizons and limitless plains. The sheer space. The wildebeest. The oh-so-beautiful Thomson's and Grant's gazelles. The bat-eared foxes playing in the early morning sun. Lions galore, and in particular, the one that may wander past your tent one night and roar under the blazing stars. The hosts of water birds by the streams, lakes, and rivers. The flat-top acacia trees, ancient guardians of this windswept wilderness. The quiet. The Big Country. Knowing how small is your place in the interconnectedness of all things. And how privileged you are to be able to experience the wonder of it all.

WHEN TO GO

If you want to see the wildebeest migration, visit July through December; if you want to see predators, June through October.

GETTING HERE AND AROUND

The drive from Arusha to Serengeti is about eight hours or 325 km (202 miles). Although there are places to refuel, breakdown facilities are virtually nonexistent. The roads outside of the cities are mostly dirt, and you'll have a lot of potholes to contend with on many of them; a 4x4 vehicle would be best if you're renting a car. Although you can drive to the Serengeti from Arusha, Lake Manyara, Tarangire, or Ngorongoro Crater, we suggest flying in, as it's quick, less of a headache, and gives you the sense of the scale of the landscape. There are scheduled and charter flights to the Serengeti from Arusha, Lake Manyara, and Mwanza. The flights are daily. A flight from Arusha to Serengeti South is an hour long, the flight from Dar es Salaam to Arusha is two hours. Most tour operators will arrange the flights for you, and lodges will be sure to have someone pick you up at the airstrip.

TIMING

The route and timing of the wildebeest migration is unpredictable. With that said, you should allow at least three days to be assured of seeing the migration on your visit, longer if you'd like to see more interactions with predators.

WHERE TO STAY

LUXURY LODGES

$$$$
FAMILY

Four Seasons Safari Lodge Serengeti. This 77-room property is not your traditional tented safari experience. You'll find five-star amenities uncommon in the bush, such as white-glove service, multiple gourmet dining options, fitness center, flat-screen TVs, rain showers, Internet, and air-conditioning. However, a sense of place is retained. The décor stays true to a colonial style with accents of local artwork and textiles, and the cuisine highlights African ingredients and cooking techniques. Of course, there are also the sweeping views of Serengeti National Park and the on-site infinity pool overlooking a nearby water hole, a

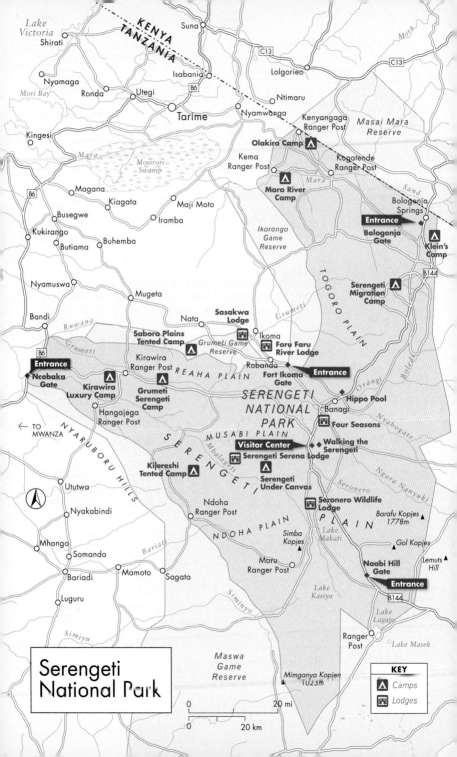

gathering spot for local wildlife. In addition to standard game drives (not included in standard room rates), the resort offers experiences like hot-air ballooning, photography classes, and bush picnics. There's also an indigenous-themed spa, a conservation and research-focused Discovery Center highlighting local culture and history and—surely a first for the bush—a business center. **Pros:** breathtaking setting; good option for families and large groups **Cons:** not the traditional Serengeti safari experience; views vary depending on room; game drives and airstrip transfers not included in all room rates. [$] *Rooms from: $1210* ✉ *Serengeti National Park* ☎ *255/888–888* 🌐 *www.fourseasons.com/serengeti* 🛏 *60 rooms, 12 suites, 5 villas* 🍴 *All meals.*

$$$$ 🏨 **Sasakwa Lodge.** This is one of four camps (plus a private villa) in the Grumeti Reserve, a 350,000-acre concession in Serengeti's Western Corridor. If you're at all familiar with the Singita name, you'll know it is associated with some of the most luxurious and elegant lodges in the Sabi Sands Private Reserve in South Africa. This superlative lodge, built in the style of a 1920s East African ranch house, adds more luster to the Singita name. You'll stay in one of the honey-color stone cottages, each elegantly furnished with hand-carved furniture, cream and white throws, cushions, and lamps, and copies of antique animal prints lining the high walls. Need some downtime? Sit out on your patio or lawn and watch for game, luxuriate in your own heated pool, or laze in your lounge and listen to the state-of-the-art sound system. There are game drives here—the game is as good as it gets—but there is also horseback riding and mountain biking, all with an armed guard in attendance. Enjoy a massage before a fine dinner served with crystal and silver. **Pros:** wonderful views of the vast Serengeti plains; it's part of the migration route; there is a wide range of exciting activities offered. **Cons:** the lodge is quite formal, but many may think that is a pro. [$] *Rooms from: $1850* ✉ *Grumeti Reserves, Serengeti National Park* ☎ *021/683–3424* 🌐 *www.singita.com* 🛏 *9 cottages, 1 villa* 🍴 *All-inclusive.*

5

PERMANENT TENTED CAMPS

$$$$ 🏨 **Faru Faru River Lodge.** The third camp in the Grumeti concession in Serengeti's Western Corridor—it joins Sabora Plains Tented Camp and Sasakwa Lodge—is sprawling but intimate and is built in a contemporary style, with lots of stone, wood and sand emphasizing the natural surroundings. It's located under sycamore trees on a hill that overlooks a gorgeous pool, river, water hole and the bush beyond. Suites, all with outdoor showers, are made out of stone and thatch, and are glass-fronted, allowing for expansive views of the water hole or river below. Buffalo, elephants, topi (an East African antelope), and giraffes all come to drink, as do predators, while black-and-white colobus monkeys scream and swing in the trees along the river. The Great Migration moves through the reserve between June and August, although there's plenty of game all year round. Bird life is prolific with more than 400 species including lots of raptors. Viewing decks and public areas jut out over the rock pool and overlook the Grumeti River, making imaginative use of local stone and wooden poles; although the effect is rustic, there is nothing rustic about the elegantly furnished tents and

"It was January, and all of the babies were being born. I loved watching the interactions of the moms with their babies, and of course watching out for the predators." —Nicki Geigert, Fodors.com member.

superb service. Dine alone with your personal waiter in attendance, or mingle with the other guests and swap fireside stories after a day's game-viewing. **Pros:** the service and personal attention are outstanding; horseback riding is excellent **Cons:** sleeping under a tent, albeit a luxury tent, might not suit all tastes. [$] *Rooms from: $1300* ✉ *Serengeti National Park* ☎ *021/683–3424* 🌐 *www.singita.com* 🛏 *9 tented suites* 🍴 *All-inclusive.*

$$$$ 🏨 **Grumeti Serengeti Tented Camp.** Situated on the banks of a Grumeti River tributary, in the western corridor of the Serengeti Grumeti, is a hospitable, delightful camp that seamlessly mixes rustic safari tents with easy sophistication. The tents combine hues of wildebeest gray with natural stone and bone, as well as bleached cypress, creating a camp that is toned down and intimate but still retains a quirky flavor. They have an extended veranda for pleasurable dining under the stars. The service is flawless with a butler station at the back of each tent. There's an abundance of birdlife and game especially from May to June when the migration passes through. As you settle in for the evening you'll hear the resident hippos munching outside the tents and grunting to one another. **Pros:** service is &Beyond at their best; great for hippo-viewing as the lodge overlooks the banks of the river. **Cons:** outdoor showers can be a bit chilly in the early mornings; river rooms will be close to the hippos and can be noisy during the night and early mornings. [$] *Rooms from: $1245* ✉ *Serengeti National Park* ☎ *27–11/809–4300* 🌐 *www.andbeyond.com* 🛏 *10 tents* 🍴 *All inclusive.*

$$$$ 🏨 **Klein's Camp.** Built on the crest of the Kuka Hills with 360-degree panoramic views over the Grumeti River valley this lovely intimate

camp prides itself on good service and quality game viewing along the river. As it lies just outside the national park on a 25,000-acre private conservancy leased from the local Ololosokwan community, you can go on unrestricted game drives and three-hour bush walks—night drives are particularly thrilling. A visit with your Maasai guide to his village will be another highlight. Stone and thatch cottages have en-suite bathrooms and a private veranda with great views. The separate dining and lounge area and very comfortable large bar have stunning views. **Pros:** great service and attention to detail; off-road game driving is allowed at this camp—not great for the environment but good to get up close to the animals. **Cons:** the concession is a one-hour drive from the Serengeti so time your stay accordingly to make the most of the migration. $ *Rooms from: $1245* ⊠ *Serengeti National Park* ☎ *27–11/809–4300* ⊕ *www.andbeyond.com/kleins-camp* ↘ *10 cottages* ⦿ *All-inclusive.*

$$$$
Fodor's Choice ★ 📷 **Mara River Camp.** Considered one of the top properties in the Northern Serengeti, the luxurious Mara River Camp has spectacular views over its namesake river and a funky, bohemian, and oh-so-chic style. Situated in the Lamai triangle—the 98,000 hectares between the Serengeti Park, the Maasai Mara, and the Mara River—the camp is within an area of one of the highest concentrations of year-round wildlife. Solar-powered, natural ventilation and attentive staff create an unfussy, gentle environment in your private tent. Art pieces by young African designers slot neatly with simple, natural fabrics. Time it right for the migration and you are in for one amazing experience. **Pros:** modern, African-inspired natural beauty of the camp; exquisite views; great food. **Cons:** very pricey; when the migration is in full swing there can be quite a smell emanating from the river due to the massive amounts of wildebeest in the area. $ *Rooms from: $1550* ⊠ *Singita Lami, Serengeti National Park* ☎ *27/21–683* ⊕ *www.singita.com* ↘ *6 tents* ⊙ *Closed Mar. and Apr.* ⦿ *All-inclusive.*

$$$$
FAMILY 📷 **Sabora Plains Tented Camp.** It's not often that you'll stay in a marquee-shaped tent elegantly furnished with silk curtains, antique furniture, stylish African artifacts, and air-conditioning, but that's what you'll get at this ultraluxurious camp set among green lawns adjacent to the Great Migration route. The game-abundant terrain ranges from open plains and rocky outcrops to riverine forest and woodlands in this 350,000-acre Grumeti concession in Serengeti's western corridor. At night, glowing gas lamps transform the tents raised on polished wooden platforms into a bush fairyland, although the only winged creatures you see will be the night birds and the fluttering moths. For a soothing experience, have a spa treatment on your veranda as you gaze out at the neverending plains. At night, enjoy the brilliance of the night sky before or after a superlative meal. **Pros:** wide, open spaces; archery, stargazing safaris, mountain biking, tennis court and a mini rangers course for the kids are all available. **Cons:** this might not be the kind of camp for those looking to step away from technology, as there is a/c in each tent and a television in the main lodge. $ *Rooms from: $1300* ⊠ *Grumeti Game Reserve, Serengeti National Park* ☎ *021/683–3424* ⊕ *www.singita.com* ↘ *9 tents* ⦿ *All-inclusive.*

5

$$$$ 🏨 **Serengeti Migration Camp.** Because this lovely camp is sited in northeast Serengeti among the rocky Ndasiata Hills, you won't see as many vehicles as you would nearer Seronera in the center of the park, but the game is all here. It's hard to believe that the accommodation is actually tented because it looks so luxurious. Spacious tents with hand-carved wooden furniture, big windowlike screens, en-suite bathroom, and a veranda facing the Grumeti River give you a ringside seat of the migration. The main areas with their deep leather chairs, sofas, handsome rugs, and elegant fittings seem more like a gentlemen's club you'd find in London or Washington, D.C., than a tent. Game is good all year round, but when the migration passes through it is awesome. Take a guided game walk from the camp, laze at the pool, or catch up on your reading in the small library. Too fast-paced for you? May we suggest sitting on your veranda to watch what's happening gamewise in the surrounding wilderness. **Pros:** 360-degree wooden deck veranda; complimentary laundry service. **Cons:** camp is about a three-hour trip from Central Serengeti; lots of steps may be a problem for people with mobility issues. Ⓢ *Rooms from: $745* ✉ *Serengeti National Park* ☎ *027/254–0630* ⊕ *www.elewanacollection.com* ↝ *20 tents* ℗ *All meals.*

MOBILE TENTED CAMPS

$$$$ 🏨 **Nduara Loliondo.** If you want to do your own thing away from the big lodges and busy safari routes, then this small, intimate camp is for you. Put yourself in the expert hands of your guide, cooks, waiters, and camp attendants to experience a true old-style safari. Accommodation is in one of six comfortable yurts with a hot bucket shower and an eco-flush toilet that uses environmentally friendly bio-digesters. There's a lounge yurt, furnished with funky leather and hide furniture, colorful textiles and deep sheepskin rugs, where you'll get together at the end of a hot dusty day, and a separate dining yurt. Your own vehicle and knowledgeable driver-guide stays with you for the length of your safari, and you can choose to do what you want, where you want. Nomad operates several mobile camps in Tanzania, but they do not take direct bookings or publish their rates, so you'll need to contact your own safari operator for more information. **Pros:** as this camp is not located in the Serengeti park but on the outskirts there is the freedom for game drives at night and bush walks; opportunity for authentic Masaai interaction. **Cons:** the migration will sometimes pass through but is not guaranteed in the Loliondo area; there are no credit-card facilities so bring cash to tip the staff. Ⓢ *Rooms from: $775* ✉ *Serengeti National Park* ⊕ *www.nomad-tanzania.com* ↝ *6 tents* ▭ *No credit cards* ℗ *All meals.*

$$$$

Fodor's Choice

★

🏨 **Olakira.** Light, delicate linens, fantastic dining, and touches of romantic Africa scattered all around the campsite make Olakira one of the finest mobile camps in the Serengeti. The location in the North (July–November) sits atop a hill right on one of the popular wildebeest crossings where you can watch the crossings from the comfort of the lounge areas or your luxury tent. When in the South (December–March) it faces the grassy Ndutu plains. Each tent has a king-size bed, large shower area, and canvas chaise lounge on a private veranda. The camp has a

Grumeti River Camp, Serengeti National Park

Grumeti Serengeti Camp

Klein's Camp

Klein's Camp, Serengeti National Park

light Arabian motif. You will be immersed in the African plains without sacrificing any comforts. ■TIP→ Check ahead when booking. If the camp is full they may place you at Olakira Kimondo—lovely, and run by the same company, but does not have the stunning location like Olakira. **Pros:** open-sided vehicles with exceptional guides; fantastic locations, including one looking over the river. **Cons:** situated right on a river crossing so there might be an odor when the migration crossing is at its peak. $ *Rooms from: $735* ⊠ *Serengeti National Park* ☎ *255/736–500–515* ⊕ *olakira.asiliaafrica.com* ⤴ *8 tents* ⟦◯⟧ *All-inclusive.*

$$$$ ⬛ **Serengeti Under Canvas.** This mobile camp follows the migration (usually in March) from Serengeti's south near Lake Ntutu on a small bluff with splendid acacia trees overlooking a small river. The camp stays put for a couple of months at a time and then moves northward with the herds. Comfortable walk-in tents (Tanzania's largest mobile tents) with chandeliers that tinkle in the breeze (yes, there's even electricity) have en-suite bucket showers, copper washbasins, a flush toilet, deep, comfortable beds with crisp linen and fluffy mohair blankets, Indian rugs, a dawn chorus of joyous birdsong, and an evening serenade of whooping hyenas with back vocals by softly calling lions. It's certainly not cheap but it's a delightful way to experience the migrations and the wonders of the Serengeti. **Pros:** an authentic safari experience; largest mobile walk-in tents in Tanzania; friendly, attentive guides and staff. **Cons:** costly; "mobile" means no guarantee being in the thick of the migration; your travel distances might change if the camp and the migration have changed locations. $ *Rooms from: $1090* ⊠ *Serengeti National Park* ☎ *27 11/809–4300* ⊕ *www.andbeyond.com* ⤴ *9 tents* ⟦◯⟧ *All-inclusive.*

BUDGET ACCOMMODATIONS

$ ⬛ **Kijereshi Tented Camp.** This small budget camp, popular with independent travelers as well as those traveling in groups, lies on the western border of Serengeti and often used as a simple stopover camp. Furnished en-suite tents and bungalows are basic but comfortable, and there's a good restaurant, bar, lounge, and pool. There's also a campsite 1 km (½ mile) from the lodge with running hot water and Western toilets. **Pros:** affordable and comfortable; great if you are driving your own vehicle and want to camp. **Cons:** popular base for overlanders; just outside the park boundaries. $ *Rooms from: $200* ⊠ *Serengeti National Park* ⊕ *www.kijereshi.co.tz* ⤴ *3 suites, 5 tents, 11 bungalows, 4 family units* ▭ *No credit cards* ⟦◯⟧ *All meals.*

$$ ⬛ **Serengeti Serena Safari Lodge.** Situated high on a hill with superb views over the central Serengeti, the two-story thatch cottages are shaped like Masai huts and are set amongst indigenous trees. Each is individually decorated with handcrafted African furniture and colorful Africa-theme soft furnishings with upper level rooms having balconies for you to spend evenings gazing over the plains. If you're in a sociable mood, head to the huge bar and dining area, also rondavel-shape, which is supported by tall pillars embellished with traditional Makonde (traditional Tanzanian) carvings. There's a gorgeous horizon pool with another great view. All the Serengeti activities are an added cost, but it's worth spending those extra pennies on an exclusive balloon safari

and champagne breakfast. **Pros:** there are great views of the Serengeti from the lodge; the expanse of open plains makes it ideal for hot air ballooning. **Cons:** with 66 rooms it's larger than most safari lodges, giving it an impersonal feel; all food is buffet style so when the hotel is full you may have to wait in line; beware of tsetse flies [$] *Rooms from: $410* ✉ *Serengeti National Park* ☎ *028/262–1507* 🌐 *www.serenahotels.com* 🛏 *66 rooms* 🍴 *All meals.*

NGORONGORO CRATER

Game
★★★★★

Park Accessibility
★★★★★

Getting Around
★★★★

Accommodations
★★★★★

Scenic Beauty
★★★★★

Ngorongoro Crater ranks right up there among Africa's must-visit wildlife destinations: Serengeti, Masai Mara, Etosha, Kruger Park, and the Okavango Delta. One of only three UNESCO World Heritage sites in Tanzania (together with the Serengeti and the Selous Game Reserve), the Crater is often called the Eighth Wonder of the World.

It lies in the Biosphere Reserve of the Ngorongoro Conservation Area, which covers 8,300 square km (3,204 square miles) in northern Tanzania. This reserve was specifically planned to accommodate both the traditional Maasai communities and tourists. You'll see Maasai villagers grazing their sheep and cattle all over.

The Ngorongoro Crater lies in a cluster of other volcanoes (sometimes seen rather ominously smoking) that borders the Serengeti National Park to the north and west. It's actually a collapsed volcano or caldera. The original volcano, which may have been higher than Kilimanjaro, collapsed in on itself over time and now forms a perfect basin. Once inside you'll feel like you're at the bottom of a deep soup bowl with very steep sides. The basin, measuring 18 km (11 miles) in diameter, lies 500 meters (1,640 feet) below the rim, which towers above it at about 2,200 meters (7,217 feet) above sea level.

Believed to have formed some 2 million years ago, the Crater harbors an astonishing variety of landscapes—forests, peaks, craters, valleys, rivers, lakes, and plains—including the world-famous Olduvai Gorge, where some of our earliest human ancestors once hunted and gathered. ⇨ *See the Cradle of Humankind box, below.*

The very steep and bumpy drive into the crater begins high up in the forest. The only downside you might face is the sheer number of safari vehicles that all clamber into the crater at opening hours, creating often dusty drives through the crater itself. But once you have left the masses behind, the charm of this site slowly leaves you in awe. Although this lush highland forest looks exactly like a rain forest, it's not. It's a *mist* forest, which depends on a regular and abundant amount of mist and drizzle. If you look closely enough, you'll see particles of mist swirling like raindrops among the ancient trees. The aptly named pillarwood trees stand sentinel over the stran-

gler figs, the croton trees, the highland *bersama* (a local evergreen), and purple wild tobacco flowers. The tree trunks and branches are home to thousands of epiphytes—specialized plants such as arboreal orchids and ferns—which cling to their hosts and absorb moisture with their own aerial roots. Look for the orchids among the curtains of Old Man's Beard, or hanging tree moss.

Monkeys, bushbuck, bush pigs, and elephants frequent the forest, although it's unlikely you'll see them. What you'll see if you're staying in one of the Crater lodges are well-mown lawns, which aren't the result of hardworking gardeners but that of zebras and buffaloes, which after dark seek sanctuary from predators here. It's not dogs you hear barking after sundown but the warning calls of vigilant zebras and baboons. The Crater floor, dominated by a huge flamingo-filled alkaline lake, holds the highest concentration of predators in the world—lions, hyenas, jackals, and leopards. Cheetahs can occasionally be seen but fall prey to lions and hyenas, which the nervous and fragile cheetah is no match for. Big herds of plains game such as Thomson's and Grant's gazelles, impalas, giraffes, zebras, and wildebeests are easy meat for the thoroughly spoiled predators that need to expend very little energy to score a megameal. You'll probably see at least one pride of bloated lions lying on their backs, paws in air, stuffed and totally damaging their noble image as the King of Beasts. Make sure to ask your guide to point out a black or white rhino if he spots one. This is also a great place to take a boat safari down one of the hippo-dense rivers.

Bird life is also spectacular with some endemic species: the Rufous-tailed weaver, Schalow's wheatear, and large flocks of the incredibly beautiful crowned cranes. Because this is a continuous killing ground, you'll quickly become a vulture expert. If you're a birder, ask for a guide who knows his birds well, because not all the guides do.

WHEN TO GO
Avoid April and May as these months are particularly wet in the Crater. Because there's no restriction on the number of vehicles, there can be far more than a hundred at one time in the high season (January to the end of September). It's amazing to have a close-up encounter with some of Africa's finest game, but not if you're surrounded by other vehicles and often very noisy, boisterous tourists. It's best to go down as early as possible (the gates open at 6 am) to avoid the later traffic jams. But the Crater is a once-in-a-lifetime experience so grit your teeth, ignore all the other tourists, and enjoy one of the world's most spectacular destinations.

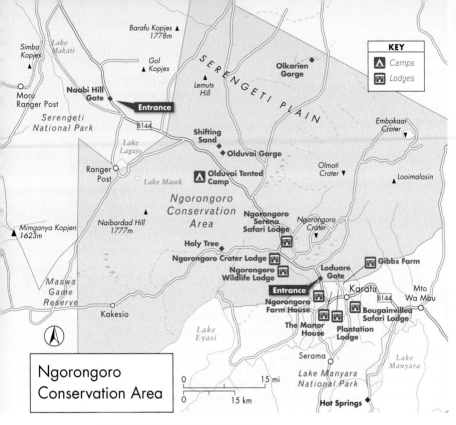

Ngorongoro Conservation Area

KEY
- ▲ Camps
- 🏠 Lodges

GETTING HERE AND AROUND

Ngorongoro is about 180 km (112 miles) from Arusha by road. You can also fly into the crater rim airstrip or Ndutu Lodge airstrip. Tour operators can arrange your transfer in advance.

ESSENTIALS

Entrance fees increase all the time, but in 2012 it cost US$50 per person to enter the Ngorongoro Conservation area, and US$200 for a car. ▪ **TIP→** You can pay in both USD and Tsh, but USD is preferred, as it's a more stable currency. Sometimes, paying in dollars can actually be cheaper by a dollar or two as well.

Packing Be prepared for thick early-morning mist all year round, which makes it quite chilly. Be sure to pack warm clothes.

WHERE TO STAY ON THE CRATER RIM

LUXURY LODGES

$$$$
Fodor's Choice
★

🏠 **Ngorongoro Crater Lodge.** Imagine walking into a Hollywood film where the spectacular setting is literally "Great Zimbabwe ruins meets SS *Titanic* baroque." Clusters of stilted rooms with woven conical banana-leaf domes and fancifully carved stone chimneys cling to the Crater's rim and somehow blend in with the natural surroundings. Your palatial abode has polished wooden floors, leather armchairs, and a dramatic mix of furniture and styles, including crystal chandeliers and hand-wrought local lamps. Ceiling-high swaths of silk taffeta drapes frame a small veranda with some of the world's most awesome views. Hand-carved doors lead to a massive bathroom with fresh-cut roses, a freestanding tub, and a tessellated tile shower straight out of a Roman villa. The main dining room has a 1920s ocean liner stateroom feel, but the adjacent lounge comes straight from an old English country house. It's a daring glamorous mix of competing styles and themes that somehow works. **Pros:** spectacular views over the Crater; unique rooms with views in every direction; expensive, but service is exceptional. **Cons:** Crater can be crowded with vehicles in peak season; high altitude means uphills are not easy to walk, and it can get very cold at night. $ *Rooms from: $1670* ✉ *Ngorongoro Crater* ☎ *27–11/809–4300 in Johannesburg* ⊕ *www.andbeyond.com* ➾ *30 rooms* ⓘ *All-inclusive.*

$$
FAMILY
Ngorongoro Serena Safari Lodge. Emerging from the natural surroundings and indigenous vines of the western rim of the Ngorongoro Crater, the Serena Safari Lodge is home to one of the most famous views this side of the Mara River. The large lodge, built from local river stone, spreads out to maximize your ability to sit back and gaze over mountain-ringed caldera. Walk to your room through tunnels of stones and enter a large space with wooden flooring, a small desk adorned with a hurricane lantern, and a large bathroom where recently renovated touches include a glass door instead of a hanging shower curtain. Because of the lodge's size and the fact that it caters to large groups, you might find it difficult to find a quiet resting place outside your bedroom. But when it comes to the views over the forest and the beautiful expanse of the Crater, you'd be hard-pressed to find better without breaking the bank. **Pros:** amazing views of the Crater from each room; close to Crater entrance; free Wi-fi. **Cons:** common areas can get crowded when the lodge is full; rooms are dated but some are being upgraded; there are a lot of stairs across the lodge. $ *Rooms from: $248* ✉ *Ngorongoro Crater* ☎ *027/254–5555, 027/253–7053* ⊕ *www.serenahotels.com* ➾ *75 rooms* ⓘ *All meals.*

$$$
Ngorongoro Wildlife Lodge. The first lodge to be built in the Ngorongoro Crater, it still retains a rather 1970s government feel with its natural stone and wood buildings and sparsely furnished motel-like rooms. En-suite bathrooms may have old-fashioned fittings but all the rooms have huge floor-to-ceiling windows with views over the fever-tree forest and crater floor that more than compensate for the Spartan interiors. The public areas also retain the 1970s ambience, but you're not going to be sitting around for long, so who needs luxury? The food is unmemorable but palatable, and the staff can organize your game-viewing excursions to the Crater floor (not included in quoted price). If you're into archaeology and the evolution of humankind, then a day visit to the Olduvai Gorge is a must, plus to nearby Laetoli, where hominid footprints are preserved in volcanic rock 3.6 million years old. **Pros:** spectacular views of the crater from the lodge and your room. **Cons:** large lodge can feel a bit impersonal; it's quite a drive from the crater floor; electricity is not on all day; packed safari lunches are

The Cradle of Humankind

If you have a great interest in evolution and human origins, Olduvai Gorge, a UNESCO World Heritage Site, is a definite must. It's about a 90-minute drive from the Ngorongoro Crater and is accessible only via a badly maintained road. The gorge, about 48 km (30 miles) long, is part of the Great Rift Valley, which stretches along East Africa. It has played a key role in palaeoanthropologists' understanding of the history of humanity by providing clues dating from about 2.5 million years ago. There's a small museum at the Gorge, but it doesn't really do justice to the magnitude of fossil discoveries made here.

Locals actually call Olduvai "Oldupai," which is the Maasai name for a sisal plant, *Sansevieria ehrenbergii*, which grows all over in the area. The view overlooking the gorge is spectacular, but be aware that visitors aren't allowed to visit the gorge itself. If you're short on time, it may not be worth your while. It's all a rather makeshift affair, and the guides aren't all fluent in English, so you may struggle to understand explanations

inevitably filled with the Latin names of fossils.

Archaeological rock stars like the Leakey family have made some of these important discoveries:

■ *Paranthropus boisei* dating back 2.5 million years. These hominids had massive jaws and large, thickly enameled molars suitable for crushing tough vegetation. Their bite was several times more powerful than that of modern humans.

■ The first specimens of *Homo habilis*, which lived about 2 million to 1.6 million years ago. This is the earliest known named species of the Homo genus. Scientists believe that *Homo habilis* was one of the first hominid species that could make and use stone tools, enhancing our ancestors' adaptability and chances of long-term survival.

■ The world's oldest stone tools date about 2 million years old, which are very primitive—basically just crude tools fashioned from pebbles.

—Tara Turkington

lackluster; Wi-fi is not free. 💲 *Rooms from: $480* ✉ *Ngorongoro Crater* ☎ *027/254–4595, 027/254–4807* ⊕ *www.hotelsandlodges-tanzania.com* ⇴ *80 rooms* ⦿ *All meals.*

WHERE TO STAY IN THE NGORONGORO CONSERVATION AREA

LUXURY LODGING

$$ ⛺ **Gibbs Farm.** If it weren't for the profusion of flowering plants and trees and sunny weather, you could believe yourself in an English country house at this working organic coffee farm midway between Lake Manyara and the Ngorongoro Crater. The 1929 farmhouse has managed to retain its old-fashioned genteel nature with a wide veranda, intimate lounges, inviting reading nooks, and a bar and dining room that look much as they must have done almost 100 years ago. Intimate, luxurious guest cottages with en-suite bathrooms are scattered

"Flying in unison over the Ngorongoro Crater, the large wingspan and bold colors of the crowned cranes provide a stark contrast to the natural browns and greens of the crater floor." —jechaft, Fodors.com member

throughout the gardens and provide a perfect base to explore the Crater and Lake Manyara National Park, as well as a perfect respite from exhilarating game drives. Expect delicious home-cooked food served with organic veggies and fruit from the farm's own gardens by friendly management dedicated to sustaining the land and supporting the nearby communities. The coffee is superb. Take advantage of the Masai health and beauty treatments developed by a third-generation Maasai healer or the six-to-seven hour hike into the crater **Pros:** locally produced food served up daily from their gardens; rooms are spacious and uniquely decorated; some of the prettiest outdoor showers around. **Cons:** a rather bumpy hour-long ride out to the Crater. [$] *Rooms from: $450* ✉ *Ngorongoro Crater* ☎ *027/253–4397* 🌐 *www.gibbsfarm.com* 🛏 *20 cottages* 🍴 *All meals.*

$$$$ FAMILY Fodor's Choice ★ 🏨 **The Manor House.** A charming mix of Afro-European Architecture from a bygone era greets you after a bumpy, dusty drive from the crater. Shake off your weary bones as staff pamper you and cater to your every need. Your personal butler will escort you to your private cottage with sun deck, luxurious Victorian baths, fireplace, his-and-hers basins and a rainfall shower. Separated from the main manor house is the stable room, a two-story family paradise perfect for those in groups or wanting to have a "holiday with a difference" for the kids—there is even a toddlers bathroom. You may never want to leave your room, but do try, because the main lodge is set around rolling hills and a working coffee plantation and has sophisticated and comfortable nooks to rest in and swap travel stories with your nearest and dearest. Make the time to relax around the gardens, get a massage from the spa, lounge by the pool or soak up the sun in any one of the beautiful vistas while enjoying some fine dining. ■ **TIP→ As it is up on a hill it can be chilly during the evenings so bring an item of warm clothing.** **Pros:** beautiful grounds and cottages; billiard room and mini movie theater in main lodge; plenty of outdoor activities like horseback riding, hikes; the drawn baths after a long day of safari will make your day. **Cons:** 90-minute drive from the Crater on winding, bumpy roads. [$] *Rooms from: $680* ✉ *Ngorongoro Crater* ☎ *255/687–068–233* 🌐 *www.elewanacollection.com* 🛏 *19 cottages, 1 family unit* 🍴 *All meals.*

$$ 🏨 **Ngorongoro Farm House.** Scattered through the winding pathways of a 750-acre coffee plantation that was once owned by a 19th-century German settler are a series of thatched cottages nestled around a generous main farmhouse. After a dusty day of game-viewing take time out to sit by the pools, take a garden tour, or enjoy the views over the valley facing the Oldeani volcano. Only 5 km (3 miles) from the Ngorongoro Lolduare gate, the lodge has rooms that are tastefully decorated, spacious, and include log fires and verandas to while away the evenings. Food is sourced from the beautiful gardens surrounding the working farm and served as either a buffet or a set menu. ■ **TIP→ Ask for a valley-facing room; it is some distance from the main lodge but the views are worth it.** **Pros:** working farm with walking tours and coffee-making experience; garden-fresh produce used in the cooking. **Cons:** rooms can be very dim and dark with some rooms taking a while to reach from the main lodge; slightly large and impersonal dining and lounge areas. [$] *Rooms from: $359* ✉ *Ngorongoro Crater* ☎ *255/73–297–5347* 🌐 *www.tanganyikawildernesscamps.com* 🛏 *49 standard, 3 suites* 🍴 *All meals.*

$$ 🏨 **Plantation Lodge.** Open spaces are at every turn here, from the hidden swimming pool to the stylish cottages with soft, earth-tone linens, accents of rich African wood, and large en-suite bathrooms. The food, albeit not traditionally Tanzanian, is very good, including the freshly baked cookies and cakes scattered around the main lodge area, which are a real treat after a day's safari. Dining is in a large public area, on your room veranda, or tucked away in a corner for an intimate experience. The bar area has outdoor seating overlooking the gardens, and make time to visit the extensive wine cellar. The lodge can arrange your daily activities, which are not included in the quoted price. **Pros:** this is a small lodge, so you will have a bit of peace and quiet; fireplace in each room. **Cons:** a bumpy drive from the Crater; Wi-Fi in main area only; two of the rooms' bathrooms are slightly old-fashioned, so be sure to request the newer ones or book in advance. [$] *Rooms from: $370* ✉ *Ngorongoro Crater* ☎ *027/253–4405* 🌐 *www.plantation-lodge.com* 🛏 *5 suites, 20 cottages* 🍴 *All meals.*

PERMANENT TENTED CAMPS

$$ 🏨 **Olduvai Tented Camp.** You'll have the opportunity to go walking on the plains of the south Serengeti with genuine Maasai warriors at this midpriced camp. Built around a large *kopje* (rocky outcrop) just south of the Serengeti border in the Ngorongoro Conservation Area, the camp is operated in partnership with the local Maasai. It's the only camp in the Olduvai Gorge and is only a 10 minute drive from the Ngorongoro Crater. The game is particularly abundant December through May,

Gibb's Farm

Gibb's Farm

Ngorongoro Serena Safari Lodge

and guests have been kept awake all night during the migration by the snuffling and snorting of thousands of wildebeest. Tents have concrete floors and thatch roofs with fully functioning bathrooms. Two thatch rondavels serve as lounge and restaurant, and there's an open fire pit where you'll can spend quality time with the authentic Maasai guides or reminisce after the day's activities, which can include a variety of superb walking safaris, game drives, or a trip to the Olduvai museum. Don't forget a flashlight for the evenings. All activities are included. **Pros:** closest camp to the Olduvai Gorge; benefits the local community. **Cons:** no Internet; camera batteries can't be charged in the rooms. [$] *Rooms from: $270* ✉ *Ngorongoro Crater* ☎ *255/784–228–883* 🌐 *www.olduvai-camp.com* 🛏 *17 tents* 💳 *No credit cards* 🍴 *All-inclusive.*

BUDGET LODGING

$ 🏨 **Bougainvillea Safari Lodge.** As a budget-friendly option either at the start or end of your safari, the Bougainvillea, halfway between Ngorongoro Crater and Lake Manyana, is a great option. There are not many frills and some of the décor is a touch on the odd side, but each cottage comes with mosquito nets, a twin or king bed, and a charming stone fireplace or veranda looking inward to the lodge and gardens. The leafy grounds are kept tidy, and the delightful staff make the lodge a welcoming place. **Pros:** fantastic budget option; big swimming pool; food is decent and plentiful. **Cons:** in Karatu Town with not much in the way of views; Wi-Fi is spotty. [$] *Rooms from: $120* ✉ *Karatu Town, Ngorongoro Conservation* ☎ *225/27–253–4083* 🌐 *www.bougainvillealodge.net* 🛏 *32 cottages.*

LAKE MANYARA NATIONAL PARK

Game
★★★
Park Accessibility
★★★★★
Getting Around
★★★
Accommodations
★★★
Scenic Beauty
★★★★

In the Great Rift Valley south of Serengeti and the Ngorong-oro Crater lies the Cinderella of Tanzania's parks—the often overlooked and underrated Lake Manyara National Park. When Ernest Hemingway faced the rust-red rocks of the almost 2,000-foot-high rift valley escarpment that domi-nates the park, he called it "the loveliest place I have seen in Africa."

Lake Manyara National Park is small, stretching only some 330 square km (127 square miles) along the base of the escarpment with two-thirds of its surface taken up by shallow, alkaline Lake Manyara. This serene lake is one of the so-called Rift Lakes, which stretch like jewels along the floor of the Rift Valley.

The park may be small, but what it lacks in size it makes up for in diversity. Its range of ecosystems at different elevations makes for dra-matic differences in scenery. At one moment you're traveling through a fairy-tale forest of tumbling, crystal-clear streams, waterfalls, rivers, and ancient trees; the next you're bumping over flat, grassy plains that edge the usually unruffled lake, pink with hundreds of flamingos.

In the deep forest where old tuskers still roam, blue monkeys swing among huge fig and tamarind trees, giant baobabs, and mahoganies, using their long tail as an extra limb. They've got orange eyes, roman noses, and wistful expressions. In the evenings as motes of dusty sun-light dance in the setting sun, there's an excellent chance of spotting troops of more than 300 olive baboons (better looking and furrier than their chacma cousins) sitting in the road, grooming each other, chatting, and dozing, while dozens of naughty babies play around them and old granddaddies look on with knowing eyes.

The thick, tangled evergreen forest eventually gives way to woodlands with tall, flat-top acacias and fever trees, and finally to open plains where hundreds of elephants, buffalo, and antelope roam, accompanied by Masai giraffes so dark they look as if they've been dipped in chocolate. This is a great place to see hippos at close hand as they lie on the banks of the lake, or as they begin to forage as dusk approaches. The park is known for its tree-climbing lions, which aren't common to see, but you can be sure if one vehicle glimpses them then the "bush telegraph" (ranger walkie-talkie chatter) will quickly reach your truck, too. No one really knows why they climb and roost in trees, but it's been suggested by one former warden of the park that this unusual behavior probably started during a fly epidemic when the cats climbed high to escape the swarms of biting flies on the ground. He suggests that the present ongoing behavior is now part of their collective memory.

If you're a birder then put this park on your must-visit list. Because of the great variety of habitats, there's a great variety of birds; more than 400 species have been recorded. As you drive through the forest you'll hear the Silvery-cheeked hornbills long before you see them flapping noisily in small groups among the massive trees, braying loudly as they fly. The edges of the lake as well as its placid surface attract all manner of water birds large and small. Along the reed-fringed lakeshore you'll see huge pink clouds drifting to and fro. These "clouds" are flocks of flamingos. White-backed pelicans paddle through the water as the ubiquitous African fish eagles soar overhead. Other water birds of all kinds congregate—waders, ducks, geese, storks, spoonbills, egrets, and herons. In the thickets at the base of the red escarpment overlooking the lake, which angles up dramatically at 90 degrees, watch out for Nubian woodpeckers, the very pretty and aptly named silver birds (flycatchers), superb, ashy, and Hildebrand's starlings, yellow wagtails, trilling cisticolas, red-cheeked cordon bleus, Peter's twinspots, bluenecked mousebirds, and every cuckoo imaginable. The Red-and-yellow barbet is known as the "bed-and-breakfast bird" for its habit of living where it eats—in termite mounds. The park is also a raptor's paradise, where you can spot up to 51 daytime species, including dozens of augur buzzards, small hawks, and harriers. Deep in the forest you might be lucky enough to see Africa's most powerful eagle, the crowned eagle, which is strong enough to carry off young antelope, unwary baboons, and monkeys. At night listen for up to six different kinds of owls, including the giant eagle owl and the diminutive but very vocal African Scops owl.

WHEN TO GO
During the dry season (May–October), it's easier to see the larger mammals and track their movements because there's less foliage. The wet season (November–April) is a great time for bird-watching, glimpsing amazing waterfalls, and canoeing.

GETTING HERE AND AROUND
You can get here by road, charter, or scheduled flights from Arusha, or en route to Serengeti and Ngorongoro Crater. The entrance gate to Lake Manyara National Park lies 1½ hours or 126 km (80 miles) west of Arusha along a newly surfaced road. There are daily flights that are 20 minutes from Arusha. Your safari operator or lodge can help you organize your transfers.

"All of a sudden . . . a downpour [began]. The wildebeests pulled in tighter to one another and just huddled together to stay protected. I thought that it created . . . an ethereal look." —Nicki Geigert, Fodors.com member.

ENTRY FEES

Entry fees for Lake Manyara National Park are US$45 per person. You can get a good map and a bird checklist at the park's headquarters at the gate as you drive in from Mto wa Mbu. **■ TIP→ You can pay in both USD and Tsh, but USD is preferred, as it's a more stable currency.**

WHERE TO STAY

LUXURY LODGES

$$ **Lake Manyara Serena Lodge.** On the edge of an escarpment this lodge presents a cluster of clean, furnished, en-suite, double-story rondavels with breathtaking views over the lake. The décor might be slightly on the garish side and the showers tiny, but what it lacks in aesthetics it makes up for in a program of varied activities. You can take Swahili lessons, amble along a gentle nature walk, or jog around the demarcated track of the lodge. There's also hiking nearby where you can explore thickly forested hillsides. A special outing is a village walk to the nearby town of Mto wa Mbu, which is home to more than 100 different tribes and one of the richest linguistic mixes in Africa. **Pros:** lovely infinity pool with views over the lake; two rooms are wheelchair-friendly; close to the air strip; free Wi-Fi in main lodge. **Cons:** the lodge is large and can feel impersonal; not all rooms have been upgraded nor do they all have views and a request will not necessarily mean you will get a room with a view; mass dining. [$] *Rooms from: $326* ✉ *Lake Manyara National Park* ☎ *027/253–9162, 027/254–5555* 🌐 *www.serenahotels.com* 🛏 *67 rooms* 🍴 *All meals.*

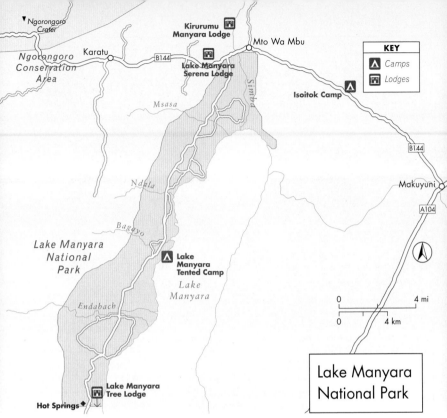

Lake Manyara National Park

KEY
▲ Camps
🏠 Lodges

$$$$ 🏠 **Lake Manyara Tree Lodge.** The 10 treehouses of this unique camp are cradled in the boughs of giant mahogany trees. It's a Swiss Family Robinson setting without the DIY aspect. You'll be greeted at forest-floor-level entrance by an array of upturned wooden canoes before climbing up to the main areas built under ancient branches heavy with foliage, fruit, and flowers. Your huge wooden thatch bedroom decorated with looped ropes of palm fronds has its own lounge area and en-suite bathroom where you can relax in a bubble bath as birds flit past the big window. Take time to sit on your wooden deck suspended above the forest floor as old elephants browse beneath you and tumultuous birdsong fills the air. There's fine dining by soft gas lamps as owls call. Bush picnics, game drives, and bird-watching trips are all part of the memorable experience at this enchanting camp. **Pros:** stay in a treehouse; there's a chance of seeing the famous Manyara tree-climbing lions when out on a game drive (not in your treehouse, though!); the long ride to the lodge from the air strip is treated as a game drive so you could see some amazing animals on the way. **Cons:** located 22 miles into the park, which requires a drive on very bumpy and dusty roads; rooms do not have views over the lake. ⑤ *Rooms from: $1245* ⊠ *Lake Manyara National Park* ☎ *27-11/809–4300 in Johannesburg* ⊕ *www. andbeyond.com* ➹ *10 rooms* ⦿ *All-inclusive.*

Lake Manyara Tree Lodge

Lake Manyara Tree Lodge

PERMANENT TENTED CAMPS

$ FAMILY Fodor's Choice ★ **Isoitok Camp.** In the morning when the Maasai head out of their bomas along the Losimingorti mountain range, you'll hear the gentle clanking of their cattle's bells from your accommodations at this very authentic camp. After a day's safari, your nights are spent around a fire with the sounds of the Esilalei community around you. Then you retire to your breezy, well-appointed tent in supreme comfort. A good base to explore Lake Manyara, Tarangire, and the Ngorongoro Crater, Isoitok has a special partnership with the local community and when you're here you feel like you're a part of it. You are able to visit one of the local bomas and dive a little deeper into the lifestyle of the Maasai without the literal song and dance (hint: you have to get up very early to fit into the local Maasai lifestyle). **TIP→ Hike up one of the hills at the back of the camp, especially at sunset to watch the Maasai heard their cattle home over the steppe.** **Pros:** staff are wonderful and food is plentiful and of an excellent standard; well-positioned camp with beautiful views towards the Rift Valley; great community and ecologically sensitive camp policy. **Cons:** two older tents are positioned at the back of the camp with partial views; no credit card facilities on site. [$] *Rooms from: $180* ✉ *Lake Manyara National Park* ☎ *027/250–3700* 🌐 *www.isoitok.com* 🛏 *8 tents* 💳 *No credit cards* 🍴 *All-inclusive.*

$$ **Kirurumu Manyara Lodge.** The 30 secluded double tents of this intimate camp are set among indigenous bush high on the escarpment and will make you feel much closer to Africa than some of the bigger lodges. Spacious thatch-roof tents, each with its own veranda, are built on wooden platforms with great views overlooking Lake Manyara. Gaily decorated with animal-motif furnishings, woven straw mats, and carved bedside lamps, all tents have an en-suite bathroom with flush toilet and ceramic hand basins. Larger family tents are also available. The camp is an ideal base for game drives in the park, mountain biking, hiking, and bird-watching and a highlight is their hike down to the waterfalls below the ridge, but you need to be quite fit for this. After an action-packed day sip your sundowner in the attractive open-sided bar with stunning views over the Rift Valley floor. **Pros:** plenty of room for families; lovely view over the Rift Valley and Lake Manyara; coffee-making facilities in the rooms. **Cons:** can get incredibly hot in the tents and around the camp in summer; bad roads leading to the camp; drinks are expensive [$] *Rooms from: $320* ✉ *Lake Manyara National Park, Lake Manyara National Park* ☎ *027/250–7011, 027/250–7541* 🌐 *www.kirurumu.net* 🛏 *30 tents* 🍴 *All meals.*

MOUNT KILIMANJARO

Game
★

Park Accessibility
★★★★

Getting Around
★★★★

Accommodations
★★

Scenic Beauty
★★★★★

Kilimanjaro, a dormant volcano on the roof of Africa, is one of the closest points in the world to the sun (Chimborazo in the Andes is the closest). It's also the highest peak on the continent and the tallest free-standing mountain in the world. So great is her global attraction that approximately 12,000 people from around the world attempt to reach her mighty summit each year.

By Debra
Bouwer

Rising to an incredible height of 5,895 meters (19,336 feet) above sea level, Mt. Kilimanjaro is a continental icon. She towers over the surrounding Amboseli plains and covers an area of about 750 square km (290 square miles). On a clear day, she can be seen from 150 km (93 miles) away. Thousands attempt to reach Kilimanjaro's highest peak, but only about 64% will officially make the summit, known as Uhuru Peak. Many reach the lower Stella Point at 5,745 meters (18,848 feet) or Gilmans' Point, at 5,681 meters (18,638 feet), which earns them a certificate from the Kilimanjaro Parks Authority.

The origin of the name Kilimanjaro has varying interpretations. Some say it means "Mountain of Greatness," while others believe it to mean "Mountain of Caravans." There's a word in Swahili, *kilima,* which means "top of the hill." An additional claim is that it comes from the word *kilemakyaro,* which, in the Chagga language, means "impossible journey." Whatever the meaning, the visual image of Kilimanjaro is of a majestic peak.

WHEN TO GO
The warmest, clearest trekking days run mid-December through February or September and October. June, July, and August are superb trekking months, too, but evening temperatures tend to be colder. The wettest months are November, early December, April, and the start of May, which brings some snow. Daytime temperatures range from 28°C (85°F) to 38°C (100°F) in the forest, but plummet to a frigid –2°C

KILIMANJARO TIPS

Choose an operator that's registered, has registered guides, has porters' interests at heart, and an environmental policy.

Communicate any health problems to your tour operator when you book.

Choose your route according to what you want: scenery, challenge, type of accommodation, and size of group.

For a quiet climb on a well-traveled route, avoid the full moon, as this is when the summit is busiest.

Train about two months before you leave—this also helps to "train your brain" that you're heading off for a challenge. Squats, lunges, and lots of hill walking with a pack are essential.

Read up on altitude sickness and symptoms and take the necessary medication with you. Add a day to get acclimated if possible or consider climbing Mt. Meru first.

Drink 3–5 liters of water a day. The rule is 1 liter per 1,000 meters (3,280 feet) ascent.

Take only photos; leave only footprints.

(28°F) to −16°C (3°F) at the summit. Generally, with every 200 meters ascended, the temperature drops one degree.

GETTING HERE
KLM has 17 direct flights a week to Kilimanjaro Airport (JRO) from Amsterdam; Kenya Airways has a number of daily flights from Nairobi; and Precision Air also has daily flights from Dar es Salaam. You can also fly direct to Zanzibar from here. Kilimanjaro Airport is located 45 km (28 miles) from Moshi and 50 km (31 miles) from Arusha, and it may be cheaper to fly to Arusha instead, so check before you book. Traveling overland is even cheaper but involves long journeys: a shuttle bus from Nairobi takes five or six hours, and from Dar es Salaam to Arusha or Moshi is seven to eight hours.

TREKKING KILI

Kilimanjaro is one of the few high peaks in the world that can be climbed without any technical gear. Most climbers head up her flanks with the aid of trekking poles, while others abandon their poles for a camera and a zoom lens. However, don't be fooled by the absence of technical gear. Oxygen levels near the summit decrease to about 60% of levels at the coast. The simple act of rolling up a sleeping bag can wear you out. Walking and ascending slowly will help your body adapt to these diminished oxygen levels. About 12,000 thrillseekers arrive on the mountain each year, each accompanied by an entourage of four to six people that include porters, guides, and a cook.

WHERE TO START
Most treks head out from Moshi, a bustling town at the mountain's base whose streets are lined with tourist stalls, tailors, banks, and restaurants. Here you'll find registered guides and accredited trekking

A giraffe roams the plains below Mt. Kilimanjaro.

companies that will arrange your climb. We like Nomadic Adventure (⊕ *www.nomadicadventures.co.za*) because they offer great personal service, have climbed the mountain many times themselves, and get involved in the big Kilimanjaro Cleanup, a project that hauls thousands of pounds of waste off the mountain each year.

THE ROUTES

There are eight common routes to the summit: Marangu, Rongai, Shira, Lemosho, Machame, Umbwe, Mweka, and the Northern Circuit—all have long-drop toilets.

Marangu is the shortest (it takes a minimum of five days) and thus the most popular route, with accommodations in huts equipped with bunk beds, public dining areas, and flush toilets. Some even have solar-heated showers. The other routes, which take at least six days to trek, require camping.

Rongai (or Loitokitok) is the quietest as it heads out close to the Kenyan border, a fair distance from Moshi. Along with Marangu, Rongai is classified as an easier route.

Shira, Lemosho, and Machame are steep and difficult, but also more scenic as they head through the distinct geographical zones: forest, shrub land, alpine desert, and snowfields.

Umbwe is the steepest, but also the most direct ascent to the summit. Mweka can only be used as a descending route from the western side.

The Northern Circuit takes eight or nine days through wilderness and there's little foot traffic. It's also the only route to cross the Northern face.

GEOLOGY AND TERRAIN

Mount Kilimanjaro has five different types of terrain that you'll encounter while trying to reach the summit.

Cultivated Farmlands: Around the outskirts of Moshi near the base of the mountain are endless subsistence plantations of maize and bananas. Small villages line the routes up to the various starting points on Kilimanjaro, and small children play in the fields.

Forests: The forest zone spreads around the base of the mountain; it's hot, humid, and generally wet. Starting at about 1,798 meters (5,900 feet)—there's cultivated farmland below this—the forest reaches up to 2,800 meters (9,186 feet) and is home to a myriad of small creatures and primates, including the black-and-white colobus monkey. Tall trees reach for the sunlight, their feet firmly anchored into a maze of roots on which cling mosses and brightly colored flowers including the rare and exotic *impatiens kilimanjari* flower, unique to this mountain. Lichens hang in sheets and small birds dart to and fro.

Shrubland or Heath Zone: At the edge of the forest zone, the vegetation suddenly changes to shrubland that's full of flowers, shrubs like the 6-meter-high (20-feet-high) *Erica arborea,* and daisy bushes that grow as big as pompoms. This zone extends up to about 3,800 meters (12,467 feet) where the landscape turns into alpine desert.

Alpine Desert: As the shrubs of the heath zone diminish in size, one enters the alpine desert, full of gnarled volcanic lava rock. Small burrows shelter the hyrax and field mice that eke out a living in this desert moonscape. Large white-naped ravens scavenge among the sand and stone.

Glaciers and Summit: As the desert rises to 5,000 meters (16,404 feet), the summit of the mountain looms above, her flanks covered in ashen scree. Massive age-old glaciers, hanging as though suspended in time, are slowly receding as the planet warms. Here among these towering blocks of ice at 5,895 meters (19,340 feet), is Uhuru Peak, the summit of Kilimanjaro.

SELOUS GAME RESERVE

Game
★★★
Park Accessibility
★★★★
Getting Around
★★★★
Accommodations
★★★
Scenic Beauty
★★★★

Most visitors come away from Selous (sel-oo) Game Reserve acknowledging that this is Africa as it is—not as tourism has made it. The reserve is one of seven UNESCO World Heritage Sites in Tanzania. A true untamed wilderness, the reserve covers 50,000 square km (19,305 square miles) and comprises 5% of Tanzania. Selous Game Reserve is the largest national park in Africa and the second largest in the world.

Only Greenland National Park at 972,000 square km (375,398 square miles), which is larger than England and France combined, beats Selous. This is still arguably the biggest area of protected pristine wilderness left in Africa, but keep in mind that most of it is off-limits to tourists. The reserve is bisected from west to east by Tanzania's biggest river, the Rufiji, and only the area north of the river is open to visitors. So although it's teeming with game, it forms only about 5% of the total park.

The other 95% is mainly leased to hunting concessions. Hunting is still a very contentious issue, and although both sides passionately argue a plausible case, it's hard for many people to accept that shooting some of Africa's most beautiful and precious animals just for fun is ethically acceptable. However, hunting is under strict government control, and half of each substantial hunting fee is put back into the management and conservation of the reserve. It's possible that without this money the Selous would not exist, and rampant poaching would take over.

The visitor area of Selous north of the Rufiji River stretches for about 1,000 square km (386 square miles) and has great game-viewing and bird-watching opportunities. The fact that there are very few lodges adds to the area's exclusivity. These are along and beside the Rufiji River, which rises in Tanzania's highlands, then flows 250 km (155 miles) to the Indian Ocean. The Rufiji boasts the highest water-catchment area in East Africa. A string of five small lakes—Tagalala, Manze, Nzerekea, Siwando, and Mzizimia—interlinked by meandering waterways, gives the area the feel of Botswana's Okavango Delta. The bird life—more than 400 recorded species—is prolific, as are the huge crocodiles and lumbering hippos.

There are major advantages to visiting this park. First, although tourist numbers are now creeping up, there's little chance that you'll be game-viewing in the middle of a bunch of noisy vehicles.

Another major draw is that much of your game-viewing and bird-watching will be done from the water. Because Selous is a game

SELOUS'S NAMESAKE

Captain Frederick Courtenay Selous was a famous English explorer and Great White Hunter who roamed the area in the late 1800s. Considered by many to be the greatest hunter of all time, he recounted his adventures in best-selling books of the day, and his safari clients included none other than Teddy Roosevelt. He was killed by a German sniper at Beho Beho in 1917 while scouting for the British against the German *Schutztruppe* (a mixed force of German troops and local Africans) during World War I. His grave lies where he fell.

reserve, not a national park, a larger range of activities is permitted, so you can walk, camp, and go on a boat safari. There's nothing quite like watching a herd of elephants showering, playing, and generally having fun as you sit in a boat in the middle of a lake or river. As you watch, lots of other game including buffalo and giraffes will also amble down to the banks to quench their thirst. If giraffes are your favorite animals, Selous will delight you because it's one of the few places in Africa where you can see big herds of up to 50.

Recently Selous has been listed on UNESCO'S list of World Heritage Sites under threat. Rampant poaching has decimated the elephant and rhino populations with numbers dropping by as much as 90% since 1982. Because of the increased demand for ivory, particularly from countries in the Far East, only some 13,000 elephants remain. Conservation efforts in Selous are desperately trying to stem the tide of poaching. There are also ongoing projects to try to protect and bolster the rhino population inside the park, which sits below 100, perhaps even as low as 30 individuals at the time of this writing. You will have a good chance of spotting the endangered African wild dog from June to August when they're denning and stay put for a few months north of the Rufiji. Selous has up to 1,300 individuals in several wide-ranging packs: double that of any other African reserve. Selous is a birder's mecca with more than 400 species. Along the river with its attendant baobab trees and borassus palms, expect to see different species of herons from the aptly named greenback heron to the Malagasy squacco heron, which winters here. Storks, skimmers, and little waders of all kinds dig in the mud and shallow water, while at dusk you may get a glimpse of the rare orange-color Pel's fishing owl, which screeches like a soul in torment. In summer, flocks of hundreds of brightly colored Carmine bee-eaters flash crimson along the banks where they nest in holes, and kingfishers of all kinds dart to and fro.

WHEN TO GO

June to October is the best time to visit, as it's the driest. During the long rains from February to May most of the camps aren't accessible, and many roads are impassable.

GETTING HERE AND AROUND

The best way to get to Selous is by charter or scheduled flight from Dar es Salaam or Arusha. Arusha to Selous is a three-hour flight, Dar es Salaam to Arusha is a two-hour flight. There's also the option of getting there by road from Dar es Salaam, which will take eight hours. However, it's recommended that you fly, especially between February and April, when the road conditions can become very bad because of the rainy season. Your operator or lodge should be able to help you arrange your transportation.

If you're brave enough to go it alone in the park, you'll need a 4x4 and very good driving skills. Permits cost US$50 per person per day, although this price fluctuates. If you're camping, you'll be required to hire an armed guard. You can also hire a guide for about US$20 per day. ■ **TIP→ You can pay in both USD and Tsh, but USD is preferred, as it's a more stable currency.**

WHERE TO STAY

LUXURY LODGES

$$$ Fodor's Choice ★ 🏨 **Beho Beho.** Many safari aficionados consider Beho Beho to be one of the best accommodations in East Africa the ultraluxurious lodge has superb views over the floodplains, fine dining, and impeccable service. Eight stone-and-thatch chalets with private en-suite bathrooms, a dressing room, and two verandas overlooking the wide floodplains are beautifully decorated with travel-worn leather trunks and suitcases, African artifacts, old maps and prints, writing desks, hand-carved wooden furniture, and comfortable Zanzibari daybeds. Although not on the river, a pool in front of the camp lets you gaze over the wilderness to spot buffalo, hippo, and other game. At the hot sulfur springs of Maji Moto, you can swim in deep natural pools. If you stay more than four nights, seize the opportunity to stay in the wonderful treehouse perched in the branches of an ancient leadwood tree, with a star bed and bathroom. After first walking through a remote part of the Selous with an armed guide for an hour to reach the treehouse, you'll be impressed by some serious bush chic for your overnight stay. ■ **TIP→ Bookings are made through the U.K.'s Africa Reps and there is an added reserve fee of $75 not included in price.** **Pros:** you don't have to leave the camp to see lots of wildlife; elegant accommodations and fantastic service. **Cons:** no night drives are allowed in the park; vehicles have to be back in the camp at dusk. [$] *Rooms from: $920* ✉ *Selous Game Reserve* ☎ *44/193226–0618 in U.K.* 🌐 *www.behobeho.com* 🛏 *8 chalets, 1 tree house* 🕒 *Closed mid-Mar.–early June* 🍴 *All-inclusive.*

$$$ 🏨 **Mivumo River Lodge.** Set high on a bluff above Tanzania's biggest river, the mighty Rufiji, Mivumo lodge hosts a beautiful location with

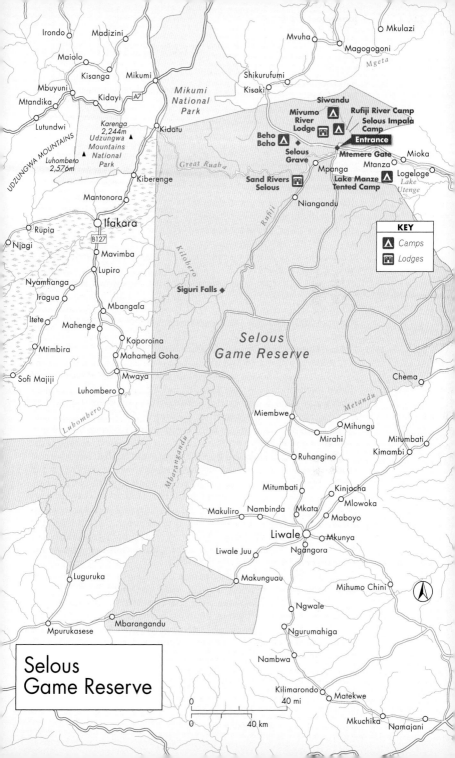

Selous
Game Reserve

relaxing river views. There are 12 large thatch-roof suites with wall-to-ceiling windows, a big en-suite bathroom with chandelier, his-and-her marble basins, a claw-foot bath, and a hand carved wooden screen and mirrors. You even have a private plunge pool (and rain shower) from where you can watch hippos snooze or crocodiles sunbathe. Spread over three levels, there is a pool deck, a viewing deck, and thatch-sheltered sitting and dining area overlooking the river. Daylong drives into the middle of the reserve where giraffe and lion abound are

> ### SELOUS RHINO TRUST
>
> In partnership with the Tanzania Division of Wildlife, the owners of **Sand River Selous** and a few dedicated partners have identified 16 black rhinos in the region—tragic, considering this part of the world supported at least 3,000 of these great beasts in the past. The Rhino Trust is steadily working to change this with constant monitoring and conservation support at Sand Rivers Selous.

spectacular. A boat trip up the Stiegler Gorge (named after a famous early 1900s elephant hunter) is a must. **Pros:** fantastic amenities combined with authentic bush experience; boat trips down Rufiji River. **Cons:** lots of steps in lodge; very rough bumpy roads; abundant game but it does require quite a drive. $ *Rooms from: $595* ✉ *Selous Game Reserve* ☎ *027/254–5555* ⊕ *www.serenahotels.com* ↩ *12 rooms* ⦿ *All meals.*

$$$$ ⛺ **Sand Rivers Selous.** Deep in the southwest corner of Selous, this lodge is just about as isolated and exclusive as you can get. Situated in the Sand River area above a wide bend of the Rufiji River, the stone and thatch lodge and chalets are literally and metaphorically hundreds of miles away from tourist Africa with its ubiquitous curio shops and gawking tourists. Your open-front, en-suite chalet has a king-size bed, elegant wooden furniture, elegant cream and white soft furnishings, carefully chosen African artifacts, and great river views. In front of the main lodge, which is shaded by a 1,500-year-old baobab tree, there's a stone walkway that curves along the riverbank, where you can sit and watch cavorting hippos and dozing crocs. Apart from its game drives, the lodge prides itself on its walking safaris; you don't have to be super fit, but a ramble through the surrounding wilderness with some of Tanzania's best guides is something you'll never forget. Watch birds and game from a gently chugging boat, or spend a night fly-camping beside Lake Tagalala to a soundtrack of roaring lions, chortling hippos, and splashing crocs. The boat trip through Stiegler's Gorge (named after a Swiss explorer who got taken out here by an elephant in 1907) is your best chance of seeing a leopard. The lodge does not take direct bookings. **Pros:** beautiful location; river cruises available; fly camping is a must here. **Cons:** mischievous monkeys have been known to raid the rooms, so put your belongings safely away; no mobile phone reception. $ *Rooms from: $925* ✉ *Selous Game Reserve* ☎ *022/286–5156* ⊕ *www.nomad-tanzania.com* ↩ *8 chalets* ⦿ *All meals.*

PERMANENT TENTED CAMPS

$$$$ 🏕 **Lake Manze Tented Camp.** Manze camp is found in the far eastern section of the reserve in a bountiful game-viewing area—just follow the well-worn elephant trail from the river to a large thatch roof spreading out over the sand floor. Meru-style walk-in tents perched between shady palms come with private verandas, flush toilets, and an outdoor shower. It's all basic but authentic and beautiful. Game drives are customized to your specifications and walking or boating safaris to view crocs, African wild dogs, hippos, lions, elephants, zebras, and hundreds of bird species are offered. It might be slightly more expensive than the cheapest camp in Selous, but the value and the attention to detail of the staff of Lake Manze is well worth the extra money. **Pros:** great value; food is plentiful; hospitality is above and beyond. **Cons:** not a luxury camp, but that is part of its unpretentious charm. $ *Rooms from: $670* ⊠ *Selous Game Reserve* ⊕ *www.lakemanze.com* ⟿ *12 tents* ⦵ *All meals.*

$$$ 🏕 **Rufiji River Camp.** This camp—the oldest in the reserve—has a great location on a wide bend on the Rufiji at the end of the eastern sector of the reserve. You'll stay in comfortable en-suite tents spread out along the river, all with private verandas and sitting rooms, some with private plunge pools. Depending on the length of your stay you can choose any or all of the activities on offer including game drives, walking safaris, boat safaris, and overnight fly-camping. **Pros:** game-viewing can be done on foot, by boat, or by vehicle; variety of game-viewing options gives you a different perspective of the wildlife and allows you to see a wide variety of animals, large and small. **Cons:** monkeys can be a problem in camp as they try to steal food from tables—don't feed them; no Wi-Fi; food is a bit basic according to traveler reviews; there is some distance to travel to view game. $ *Rooms from: $470* ⊠ *Selous Game Reserve* ☎ *078/423–7422* ⊕ *www.rufijirivercamp.com* ⟿ *11 tents, 3 suites* ⊗ *Closed April 1–June 1* ⦵ *All-inclusive.*

$$$$ 🏕 **Selous Impala Camp.** This attractive small camp on Lake Mzizimia's shores nestles among borassus palms and riverine bush with great views over the Rufiji. Tents on wooden platforms raised on stilts, each with its own en-suite bathroom and private veranda, have comfortable Africa-theme soft furnishings and rustic handmade wooden furniture. Join other guests in the main thatch lounge, which is also raised on a platform with views of the river, for meals and sundowners. If you're here in the dry season between June and October, you'll see plains game galore as the animals come to drink at the perennial river. As well as elephants, buffalo, hippos, antelopes of all kinds, and the always lying-in-wait crocodiles, there's a good chance of spotting lions and African wild dogs. Go for a guided game walk with an armed ranger, a game drive, or a boat safari; visit Stiegler's Gorge or the Maja Moto hot springs; or just chill out at this comfortable and unpretentious camp. ■ TIP➔ **There are some very good deals available if you fly in with Coastal Aviation, which operates the camp. Pros:** you rarely see any other vehicles on game drives; the staff are very knowledgeable; overall a fantastic camp. **Cons:** as there are fewer game vehicles in the area, animal sightings are not as prolific as in the north; there may be a "late departure" extra day's park or reserve entry fees charged $50 per person if you arrive in

5

Sand Rivers Selous

Beho Beho Safari Lodge

Siwandu

the morning and depart in the afternoon. $ *Rooms from: $625* ⊠ *Selous Game Reserve* ⊕ *www.adventurecampstz.com* ⊅ *8 tents* ⊟ No *credit cards* †○┤ *All meals.*

$$$$
Fodor's Choice
★

☒ **Siwandu.** In the middle of the riverine bush on the banks of Lake Nzerakera, this luxuriously appointed camp has become a real stand-out in the Selous reserve. With a stellar location, renowned guides, and beautiful tents evenly divided over two camps, this is authentic African safari at its most delightful. Built on wooden platforms, the open-sided spacious tents blend in graciously with the surrounding wilderness. King-size beds are tastefully decorated in creams, browns, and whites, and en-suite bathrooms with his-and-her brass hand basins and open-air hot-water showers overlook the bush. The camp is unfenced, so be prepared for all sorts of game to wander past your tent or the main viewing deck. At night the camp takes on a fairy-tale atmosphere when it's lit by dozens of softly glowing gas lanterns. Activities include game drives and guided walks, fly camping, boating, bird-watching, or just relaxing on the veranda or by the swimming pool. **Pros:** you rarely see any other vehicles on game drives; exceptional food and service; lovely view over the lake; brilliant boating safari; attention to detail. **Cons:** the boat trip up the Rufiji River is not available all year round, although lake trips will be available. $ *Rooms from: $850* ⊠ *Selous Game Reserve* ☎ *022/213–4802* ⊕ *www.selous.com* ⊅ *13 tents* †○┤ *All meals.*

5

GOMBE STREAM AND MAHALE MOUNTAINS NATIONAL PARKS

Game
★★

Park Accessibility
★★

Getting Around
★

Accommodations
★★

Scenic Beauty
★★★★★

If your heart is set on tracking our nearest animal relatives — the intriguing, beguiling, and oh-so-human chimpanzees — then take the time and effort to get to one or both of these rarely visited but dramatically beautiful parks. You'll meet very few other visitors, and very few other people on earth will share your experience.

The best time to see chimps is the last two months of the dry season, September and October, when they come out of the forest and move lower down the slopes—sometimes even to the beach.

Don't go trekking if you have a cold, flu, or any other infectious diseases. Chimps are highly susceptible to human diseases, and you certainly wouldn't wish to reduce the chimp population even further.

GOMBE STREAM NATIONAL PARK

Bordering Burundi to the west, Tanzania's smallest national park—only 52 square km (20 square miles)—is easily one of the country's loveliest. It's tucked away on the shores of Africa's longest and deepest lake, Lake Tanganyika, 676 km (420 miles) long and 48 km (30 miles) wide. The lake is a veritable inland sea, the second deepest lake in the world after Russia's Lake Baikal. This small gem of a park 3.5 km (2 miles) wide and only 15 km (9½ miles) long stretches from the white sandy beaches of the blue lake up into the thick forest and the mountains of the rift escarpment behind.

Though the area is famous for its primates, don't expect Tarzan-like rain forest because the area is mainly covered with thick Brachystegia woodland. There are also strips of riverine bush alongside the many streams that gouge out steep valleys as they make their way from the highlands to flow down into the lake.

You've got to be determined to get here because Gombe is accessible only by boat. But you'll be amply rewarded with one of the most excitingly close animal encounters still possible on our planet. You'll hear the chimps long before you see them. A series of hoots and shrieks rising to a crescendo of piercing whoops sounds like a major primate battle is about to begin. But it's only the members of the clan identifying one another, recognizing one another, and finally greeting one another.

Gombe became famous when Jane Goodall came to the area in 1960 to study the chimpanzee population. At the time she wasn't known or recognized as the world-renowned primatologist she would later become. Sponsored by the legendary paleontologist Louis Leakey of Olduvai Gorge, Goodall came to Gombe as an eager but unqualified student of chimpanzees. At first many of her amazing unique studies of chimp behavior were discounted because she was a young, unknown scientist. How could a chimpanzee be a hunter and meat-eater? How could a chimpanzee possibly use grass stalks and sticks as tools? Whoever had heard of inter-troop warfare? Today her groundbreaking work is universally acknowledged. Read more about her and her experiences at Gombe in her best-selling book *In the Shadow of Man*. You'll also be able to meet descendants of those chimpanzees she studied and made famous. Fifi, who was only three when Goodall arrived at Gombe in 1960, survived until 2004. Her youngest surviving son, Ferdinand, was alpha male in 2010.

But be warned—to follow in Jane or Fifi's footsteps you need to be fairly fit. Keeping up with a group of feeding and moving chimpanzees as they climb hills and forage in deep valleys can be very strenuous work. But the effort will be worth it—there's nothing on earth quite like coming face-to-face with a chimpanzee or accompanying a group as they make their way through the forest.

WHEN TO GO
The chimps don't roam very far during the wet season: February–May and November–mid-December. It'll be easier to find them, and you'll have better opportunities to photograph them, during the dry months of June–October and late December.

GETTING HERE AND AROUND
Kigoma is connected to Dar es Salaam and Arusha by scheduled flights, and to Mwanza, Dar es Salaam, and Mbeya by rough dirt roads. Kigoma to Dar es Salaam is a three-hour flight; from Kigoma to Arusha is roughly a two-hour flight. The drive from Kigoma to Mwanza is roughly 575 km (357 miles), and the roads are bad. If you go by bus it'll take two days. The lodge can arrange your travel to and from your destination; talk to your safari operator about getting to and from the camps.

TIMING
Strict rules are in place to safeguard you and the chimps. Allow at least two days to see them—they're in a wild state, so there are no guarantees where they'll be each day.

ESSENTIALS

Entry fees for Gombe are US$100 per person, the highest of any park in Tanzania; the Mahale entry fee is US$80. Your guide will cost US$25 per day. ■TIP➜ **You can pay in both USD and TSH, but USD is preferred, as it's a more stable currency.** Kids under seven aren't permitted to enter either park. Because of the traveling time you'll need to spend at least two nights in either or both of the parks.

WHERE TO STAY

BUDGET ACCOMMODATIONS

$ ☷ **Coastal View Hotel.** About 2 km (1 mile) outside of the main street in Kigoma, on top of a hill with views over the lake is Costal View, a tidy budget option. You can expect a neat and clean room with amenities such as a television, air-conditioner, a small desk and mini-refrigerator. The rooms don't have views over the lake, but the restaurant gazebo is perched high to take advantage of the breeze and the sights. **Pros:** free Wi-Fi; neat rooms; good service albeit a bit slow; good food. **Cons:** a bit of a hike to get to if you are planning to walk, take a boda transport; showers are open in the bathrooms. $⌗ *Rooms from: $50* ✉ *Kigoma* ☎ *028/280–3434* ⊕ *www.coastviewhotel.co.tz* ⤴ *30 rooms* ❍⦙ *All meals.*

$ ☷ **Kigoma Hilltop Hotel.** On a hill overlooking the lake about 2 km (1 miles) from Kigoma's town center, this hotel makes an ideal base for your chimpanzee trekking. You'll stay in a comfortable no-frills cottage with air-conditioning, a mini-refrigerator, satellite TV, and an en-suite bathroom. What puts the hotel above any other in the area is that it arranges your excursions for you, and also has all kinds of water-sports equipment for hire. Go snorkeling, fishing, swimming, or just chill out on the private beach. There are business services and a large pool. ■TIP➜ **No alcohol is sold on site, but you can buy your own in town and store it in the in-room mini-refrigerator. Pros:** lovely view of Lake Tanganyika from your balcony. **Cons:** limited menu; popular with conferencing groups; boat hire to Gombe Island will be more expensive here than if you go to the Tanap office directly; Wi-Fi is spotty. $⌗ *Rooms from: $90* ✉ *Kigoma* ☎ *028/280–4437, 0766/634–684* ⊕ *www.mbalimbali. com* ⤴ *30 cottages* ❍⦙ *All meals.*

$ ☷ **Lake Tanganyika Hotel.** One of the largest accommodations atop Kigoma and a popular spot for businesspeople and conferences, this tidy hotel boasts some of the best views in the area. The rolling manicured lawns stretch all around the grounds of the hotel down to the shores of Lake Tangangika with chalet rooms dotted around either side of the main restaurant and pool areas. You can expect all of the in-room amenities you would find in a larger resort—television, air-conditioning, large comfortable beds, desk, and mini-refrigerator. Spend a little extra for rooms with verandas facing the lake. For a spectacular sundowner head down to the bedouin-style tent closest to the shores. Service can be slow, and food is fair, but all-in-all this is a good option for Kigoma. **Pros:** large swimming pool and wonderful view over the lake. **Cons:** service is lackluster; food can be hit-or-miss. $⌗ *Rooms from: $85* ✉ *Stanley Rd., Kigoma* ☎ *028/280–3052* ⊕ *www.laketanganyikahotel.com* ⤴ *30 rooms* ❍⦙ *All meals.*

MAHALE MOUNTAINS NATIONAL PARK

Just south of Gombe on the shores of Lake Tanganyika lies Tanzania's most remote national park. Thirty times bigger than Gombe, Mahale is a stunningly beautiful park with crystal-clear streams, soaring forested mountains, and deserted, white sandy beaches. Mt. Nkungwe at 2,460 meters (8,070 feet) dominates the landscape. More than 700 chimpanzees live in the area and are more accessible and more regularly seen than at Gombe.

In 1965 the University of Kyoto in Japan established a permanent chimpanzee research station in Mahale at Kisoge, about a kilometer from the beach. It's still going strong and remains highly respected.

There are no roads in Gombe or Mahale: all your game-viewing and chimpanzee tracking is done on foot. If you're a couch potato, stick with the National Geographic TV channel. What will you see other than chimpanzees? You'll almost certainly see olive baboons, vervet monkeys, red- and blue-tailed colobus monkeys, and some exciting birds. More than 230 bird species have been recorded here, so look out for crowned eagles, the noisy trumpeter hornbills, and the "rasta" birds (the crested guinea fowls with their black punk hairdos). Don't expect to see big game; although there are roan antelope, elephants, giraffes, buffalo, lions, and African wild dogs in the eastern savanna and woodland, these areas are largely inaccessible. But you're not here for big game. You're here to meet your match.

WHEN TO GO

The dry season, May through October, is best for forest walks, although there's no problem in the light rains of October and November.

GETTING HERE AND AROUND

Arrange a charter flight from Arusha, Dar es Salaam, or Kigoma. The flight to Greystoke Mahale is around three to four hours from Arusha. The flight from Dar es Salaam to Arusha is two hours. There's also the National Park motorboat from Kigoma, which will take three to four hours.

WHERE TO STAY

LUXURY LODGES

$$$$ **Greystoke Mahale.** If you were a castaway, this would be heaven. It's
Fodor's Choice difficult to imagine almost anywhere on earth that's as wildly beauti-
★ ful and remote as this exotic camp on the eastern shore of Lake Tanganyika. Six wood and thatch bandas nestle on the forest rim. Behind them thickly wooded mountains rise almost 2,500 meters (8,200 feet); in front of them white sands stretch to the peaceful azure waters of the lake. Your banda has furniture of bleached dhow wood, a rustic toilet and shower, and a lower and upper wooden deck with views over the lake. The main building is loosely based in the style of a Tongwe chief's hut, although many of your meals will be taken on the beach, at night by glowing lanterns. It's not easy to get here: a four-hour flight from Arusha is followed by a two-hour boat ride. But once here you won't ever want to leave. About 60 of Mahale's 1,000 or so wild chimpanzees live in the forest near Greystoke, so you have an excellent chance

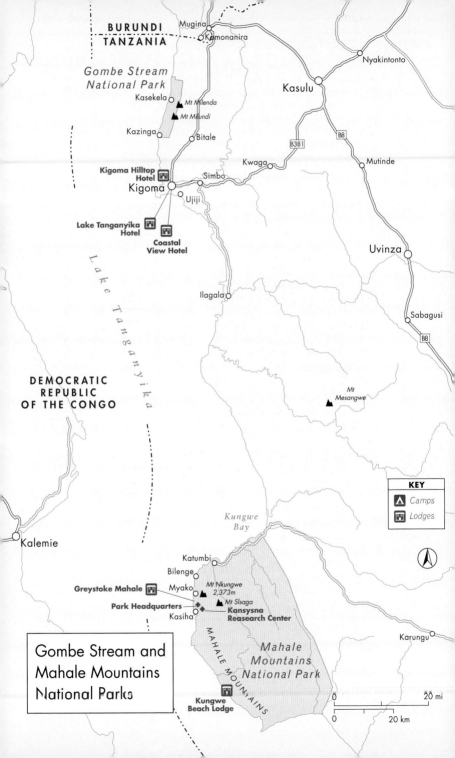

BURUNDI
TANZANIA

Mugina

Kamonanira

Nyakintonto

Gombe Stream
National Park

Kasulu

Kasekela
▲ Mt Milenda
▲ Mt Mkundi

Kazinga
Bitale

Kwaga

B381   B8

Mutinde

Kigoma Hilltop
Hotel 🏨

Simbo

Kigoma

Ujiji

Lake Tanganyika
Hotel 🏨

Coastal
View Hotel 🏨

Uvinza

Ilagala

L
a
k
e

T
a
n
g
a
n
y
i
k
a

Sabagusi

B8

DEMOCRATIC
REPUBLIC
OF THE
CONGO

▲ Mt
Mesangwe

KEY

🏕 Camps

🏨 Lodges

Kungwe
Bay

Kalemie

Katumbi

Bilenge

Greystoke Mahale 🏨

Myako

▲ Mt Nkungwe
2,373m

▲ Mt Sisaga

Park Headquarters ◆

Kasiha

◆ Kansysna
Reasearch Center

Karungu

MAHALE MOUNTAINS

Mahale
Mountains
National Park

Gombe Stream and
Mahale Mountains
National Parks

🏨 Kungwe
Beach Lodge

0   20 mi

0   20 km

of spotting them. Bookings are made only through reputable tour operators and there is a $80 park fee. ■ **TIP→ There are no roads within 100 km (62 miles) of camp, and access is only by light aircraft using the shared charter flights that operate on Monday and Thursday from Arusha only.** Flights leave early in the morning and return to Arusha early evening that same day. The flight to Greystoke Mahale is around 3–4 hours, and upon arrival at the airstrip there is an approximately 90-minute dhow trip down the lake to reach the camp. **Pros:** very secluded in the Mahale mountains; the camp gives you the opportunity to watch wild chimpanzees up close and personal. **Cons:** trekking up after the chimps is hard work; long flight to get there; with the reported increase of crocodiles in the river swimming in front of the lodge is no longer allowed. [$] *Rooms from: $1175* ✉ *Mahale Mountains National Park* 🌐 *www.nomad-tanzania.com* 🛏 *6 bandas* 💳 *No credit cards* 🍴 *All meals.*

DID YOU KNOW?

Illegal trafficking is the greatest threat to Tanzania's endangered chimpanzee population. Highly coveted for medical research, zoos, and as pets, baby chimps are taken by force resulting in the death of many protective adults.

5

$$$$ 🏨 **Kungwe Beach Lodge.** On the same stretch of the lakeshore as Greystoke, Kungwe is the only other alternative for chimp trekking in Mahale Park. Although it might not be exactly on par with its neighbors, you'll enjoy the same sunset and lake views, just with different degrees of luxury and service. Raised up off the ground on wooden decks with beautiful hardwood floors, Kungwe's tents have four-poster beds layered with mosquito nets and soft linens. A writing desk and African-inspired furnishings complete the overall tented safari look. The outside verandas are perfect for a lazy restful day after the long journey getting to one of the more remote parks in Tanzania. **Pros:** cheaper prices with fantastic lake views. **Cons:** similar long travel distances to its neighbor Greystoke; nonalcoholic drinks can be limited. [$] *Rooms from: $715* ✉ *Mahale Mountains National Park* 🌐 *www.mbalimbali.com* 🛏 *10 tents* 💳 *No credit cards* 🍴 *All-inclusive.*

IF YOU HAVE TIME

If you still have time after you've explored our picks for Must-See Parks, put the following national parks on your list, too: Arusha, Tarangire, and Ruaha.

ARUSHA NATIONAL PARK

Don't overlook the tiny Arusha National Park. Though it covers only 137 square km (58 square miles), it has more to see than many much larger reserves. You'll find three distinct areas within the park: the forests that surround the Ngurdoto Crater, the brightly colored pools of the Momella Lakes, and the soaring peaks of Mt. Meru. And with the city of Arusha only a 32-km (20-mile) drive to the northeast, it's easy to see the park in a day.

Established in 1960, the park was originally called Ngurdoto Crater National Park, but after the mountain was annexed in 1967 it became known as Mt. Meru National Park. Today it's named for the Warusha people who once lived in this area. The Maasai also lived here, which is why many of the names for sights within the park are Swahili.

WHEN TO GO

To climb Mt. Meru, the best time is between June and February, although it may rain in November. The best views of Kilimanjaro are December through February.

GETTING HERE AND AROUND

Arusha National Park/Mt. Meru/Ngurdoto Crater is a 40-minute drive from Kilimanjaro International Airport. The lakes, forest, and Ngurdoto Crater can all be visited in the course of a half-day visit.

EXPLORING

Momella Lakes. From Ngurdoto Crater drive northeast to the Momella Lakes. Reedbuck and waterbuck are common sights near the dirt road. There are numerous observation points along the way for getting a closer look at the more than 400 species of birds that have been spotted in the area. You can also arrange through your safari comapny to go on a canoe around the smaller portion of the lake. The lakes were created by lava flow from nearby Mt. Meru; each is a distinct color because of the varying mineral content in the water. Each lake, therefore, attracts different types of birds. Keep an eye out for the thousands of flamingos that feed on the algae that cover the lake in a pinky hue at certain times of the year.

Mt. Meru. From the Momella Lakes the road toward Mt. Meru leads into a forest with a profusion of wildflowers. Here you'll encounter dik-diks and red forest duikers. Rangers can accompany you on walks to the rim of Meru Crater, where you'll have a breathtaking view of the sheer cliffs rising to the summit. Keep an eye out for a diminutive antelope called the klipspringer.

Because it is not as well known, the slopes of Mt. Meru are blissfully uncrowded. ⚠ Although Meru looks diminutive alongside Kilimanjaro, do not underestimate what it takes to climb to the top. You must be in good shape, and you need to allow time to acclimatize. Climbing Mt. Meru itself takes at least three days when it is dry; during the wet season the tracks can be very slippery and it can take more than four days. The route begins at the Momella Gate, on the eastern side of the mountain. Huts along the way sleep 24 to 48 people, but inquire beforehand whether beds are available; if not, you should bring a tent. You can arrange for no-frills journeys up the mountain through the park service, or book a luxury package through a travel company that includes porters to carry all your supplies. Either way you'll be accompanied by an armed guard to protect you from unfriendly encounters with elephant or buffalo.

Ngurdoto Forest and Crater. After entering the park through the Ngurdoto Gate, you'll pass through the fig, olive, and wild mango trees of the Ngurdoto Forest. Farther along is the Ngurdoto Crater, which is actually a caldera, or collapsed crater. Unlike the nearby Ngorongoro Crater, this caldera appears to have had two cones. There are no roads into the crater itself, so the buffalo and other animals that make their homes in the swampy habitat remain protected. You can drive around the rim, where you'll find a misty landscape covered with date palms, orchids, and lichens. The grasslands to the west are known as Serengeti Ndogo ("Little Serengeti") and boast a herd of Burchell's zebras, thriving because there are no lions nearby.

Many baboons and other monkeys are found in the Ngurdoto Forest. Elegant black-and-white colobus monkeys spend most of the morning basking in the sun in the highest parts of the forest canopy, then later move lower in the branches to feed on the tender vegetation. Colobus monkeys do not drink water but get all their moisture from their food. They are endangered because their lovely fur was prized by humans.

WHERE TO EAT

Arusha might just be a stopover city for some, but there is a lot of great food on offer in the town that goes beyond packed safari lunchboxes. If you are looking for some fine dining, **Machewo** and **Arusha Coffee House** have two of the top restaurants in town. Fancy a decent drink and some good hearty food? **Blues and Chutney** has a wonderful restaurant and bar area serving up great home-cooked meals. **Abyssinia** is a favorite if you like Ethiopian food. **Damascus** (off Perfect Printers Road) has some of the best homemade tapas around. A good quick bites option is **Alpha Choice** on Sokine Road. If you have 24 hours before your safari you will not go wrong if you phone up Damascus and ask for their homemade safari tapas lunchboxes (☎ 255–76–587–8453) to take on your trip. While other safari goers are munching on sandwiches and peanuts, you'll have the option of dining on chicken satay, pita bread with coriander tomato and onion mix, meat falafels, and some divine dips to go with your cold wine and sweet puddings.

TARANGIRE NATIONAL PARK

Although this lovely 2,600-square-km (1,004-square-mile) park is an easy drive from Arusha—just 118 km (71 miles) southwest—and adjacent to Lake Manyara, it's continued to be something of a well-kept secret. This relative secrecy is odd because during the dry season it's part of the migratory movement and is second only to Ngorongoro Crater in concentration of wildlife. The best time to visit is July through September, when thousands of parched animals flock to the watering holes and thousands more make their long way to the permanent water of the Tarangire River.

WHEN TO GO
You can visit year-round, but the dry season (May–September) is the best for its sheer numbers of animals.

GETTING HERE AND AROUND
It's an easy drive from Arusha or Lake Manyara following a surfaced road to within 7 km (4 miles) of the main entrance gate. Charter flights from Arusha and the Serengeti are also possible. The flight from Arusha to southern Serengeti is roughly 1½ hours; the drive is 335 km (208 miles), which will take around eight hours.

GAME-VIEWING
During the dry season, huge herds of elephant, eland, oryx, zebra, buffalo, wildebeest, giraffe, and impala roam the park. Hippos are plentiful and pythons can sometimes be seen in trees near the swamps. If you want to spot waterbuck or the gerenuk, head for the Mkungero Pools. Tarangire is much more densely wooded than Serengeti with acacia, mixed woodland, and the ubiquitous baobab trees, although you'll find grasslands on the southern plains where cheetahs hunt.

There are more than 500 species of birds in Tarangire National Park, including martial and bateleur eagles. Especially good bird-watching can be done along the wetlands of the Silale Swamp and around the Tarangire River. Yellow-collared lovebirds, hammerkops, helmeted guinea fowl, long-toed lapwings, brown parrots, white-bellied go-away birds, and a variety of kingfishers, weavers, owls, plovers, and sandpipers make their homes here. A shallow alkaline lake attracts flamingos and pelicans in the rainy season. Raptors are plentiful, including the palm-nut vulture and lots of eagles. You may hear a cry that sounds quite similar to the American bald eagle but is in fact its look-alike cousin, the African fish eagle.

EXPLORING
Kondoa Rock Paintings. Kolo, just south of Tarangire, is where you'll find some of the most accessible Kondoa rock paintings. From the last stage of the Stone Age, these illustrations on cave walls depict hunting scenes using stylized human and animal figures. These fragile documents of an era long past were studied by Mary Leakey, who wrote a book about them called *Africa's Vanishing Art*. At a nearby site, Leakey discovered "pencils" in which ocher and other pigments had been ground and mixed with grease. Later excavations revealed that some were 29,000 years old. ⊠ *Tarangire National Park* ☎ *027/250–1930* ✉ *US$35* ☉ *Daily 6:30–6:30.*

RUAHA NATIONAL PARK

Remote and rarely visited, Ruaha is Tanzania's second-largest park— 10,300 square km (3,980 square miles). Oddly enough, it attracts only a fraction of the visitors that go to Serengeti, which could be because it's less well-known and difficult to access. But East Africa safari aficionados claim it to be the country's best-kept secret. There are huge concentrations of buffalos, elephants, antelope, and more than 400 bird species.

POACHING

Poaching continues throughout the Ruaha-Rungwa ecosytem. However, because of the devastating poaching in Selous, Ruaha now holds some of the largest elephant populations on record in East Africa. This population is also under threat as reports of increased elephant poaching in the park surface each day.

Classified as a national park in 1964, it was once part of the Sabia River Game Reserve, which the German colonial government established in 1911. Ruaha is derived from the word "great" in the Hehe language and refers to the mighty Ruaha River, which flows around the park's borders, and it's only around the river that the park is developed for tourism with a 400-km (249-mile) road circuit. The main portion of the park sits on top of a 1,800-meter (5,900-foot) plateau with spectacular views of valleys, hills, and plains—a wonderful backdrop for game-viewing. Habitats include riverine forest, savanna, swamps, and acacia woodland.

WHEN TO GO

The best time to visit is May through December because, although even in the wet season the all-weather roads are passable, it's incredibly difficult to spot game at that time because of the lush, tall vegetation. If you're into bird-watching, lush scenery, and wildflowers, you'll like the wet season (January–April).

GETTING HERE AND AROUND

Most visitors arrive by charter flight from Dar es Salaam, Selous, the Serengeti, or Arusha. The flight is 2½ hours to Ruaha from Arusha or Dar es Salaam, and one hour from Selous. It's possible to drive to Ruaha but it takes longer. Visitors often drive from Dar es Salaam, but not many drive from Arusha. The drive to Ruaha from Dar es Salaam is roughly 10 hours through Iringa. The roads do get a bit bumpy as you near the park. Safari companies will arrange road transfers if you so wish. If time is of the essence, fly; if it's interaction and experience (atmosphere) of the various places en route to Ruaha you'd like, drive.

ESSENTIALS

There's an entrance fee of US$20 per person, per 24-hour visit, and it must be paid in cash. ■ TIP➔ You can pay in both USD and Tsh, but USD is preferred, as it's a more stable currency. Ask at your lodge for a copy of the Ruaha booklet, which has maps, checklists, and hints on where to look for particular species.

TIMING

Four nights will give you the chance to fully experience the varied areas of the park.

GAME-VIEWING

DID YOU KNOW?

Tanzania is one of the world's largest producers of cashews, exporting more than 80,000 tons of raw nuts each year.

There are elephants, buffalo, lion, spotted hyena, gazelle, zebra, greater and lesser kudu, and giraffe roaming this park. If you're lucky, you might even see roan and sable antelope or witness a cheetah hunt on the open plains in the Lundu area. Lion are well habituated to vehicles, so you'd be very unlucky not to spot at least one pride, and if you've set your heart on seeing wild dogs, then try to come in June or July when they're denning; this makes them easier to spot than at other times because they stay in one place for a couple of months. There are also lots of crocs and hippos in the river areas. Bird "specials" include the lovely little Eleonaora's falcon (December through January is the best time to spot one), Pel's fishing owl, and the pale-billed hornbill.

WHERE TO STAY

LUXURY LODGES

$$$$ 🏨 **Jongomero Tented Camp.** This is the only camp in the southwest corner of Ruaha National Park. If you've come to see animals, but no other trucks or people, then this is your place. The tents, which have furniture that was made from the wood of old dhows, are perched along the banks of the (sometimes dry) Jongomero River—when you're at the lodge's bar, check out the bowl filled with handmade nails that were collected as the boats were disassembled. Take your morning or afternoon tea out on your veranda—you might catch a glimpse of a few passing animals. The food is excellent, and there is always something packed away for you when you're out on your drives. The pool is a great place to relax and ponder all that you've seen during your day, and the view of the setting sun is incredible. If you're interested, game walks with your own personal armed national parks guard, can be arranged. **Pros:** enthusiastic staff; spacious tents with enormous beds and showers; great food; there's a sense of luxury everywhere without losing its bush quality. **Cons:** tsetse flies are in the area and around the camp. [$] *Rooms from: $880* ✉ *Ruaha National Park* ☎ *022/213–4802* 🌐 *www.selous.com* 🛏 *8 tents* 🍴 *All-inclusive.*

$$$$ 🏨 **Kigelia Camp.** Set in a forest of baobabs and sausage trees along the Ifaguru sand river, Kigelia has a prime location in Ruaha. This camp has a peaceful, relaxed atmosphere. The tents are spacious, cool, and inviting. Every tent is furnished with unique, locally crafted furniture and has en-suite bathrooms with flush toilets and outdoor safari-style bucket showers under the stars. This is a perfect place to sit in the tranquility and shade of a sausage tree and relax, quietly watching the passing wildlife. A very friendly staff and good service are the mark of this welcoming camp. The game in this area during the dry months is exceptional. Bush picnic breakfast or brunch and bush sundowners can be arranged. It costs $350 to bring in a private car, and the park fee is $30 per person. **Pros:** classic tented safari camp feel with a few modern twists; there is a living room with reading material, and fire pit. **Cons:** the camp is an hour's drive from the airstrip; no Wi-Fi. [$] *Rooms from:*

$695 ⊠ Ruaha National Park ☎ 255/76–920–4159 ⊕ www.nomad-tanzania.com ⇌ 6 tents ⊙ April–May ⦙⊙⦙ All meals.

$$$ ⛺ **Mwagusi Safari Camp.** This well-established camp is situated on the shady banks of the Mwagusi River, giving it a prime position in Ruaha for game-viewing. The large, cool, comfortable bandas, crafted from local and organic materials, are tucked into the sandy banks, giving each a secluded view. Wake up to fresh brewed coffee delivered by friendly staff and take in stunning views along the river on your private veranda. It's not unusual to encounter wildlife on your doorstep. Elephants are regular visitors to the camp, as well as large prides of lion. Mwagusi is run by an owner whose passion for Ruaha and African wildlife is sincere and infectious. **Pros:** delicious food; excellent guides; friendly service. **Cons:** bandas are rustic looking from the outside; charging cameras and batteries is difficult in this remote location. Ⓢ *Rooms from: $595 ⊠ Ruaha National Park ☎ 44/0–7525170940 in U.K. ⊕ www.mwagusicamp.com ⇌ 13 tents ⊟ No credit cards ⊙ Late Mar.–late May ⦙⊙⦙ All meals.*

$ ⛺ **Tandala Camp.** Because Tandala is in a private conservancy 5 km (3 miles) outside the entrance gate, guests can take early morning game walks and game drives, engage in bird viewing or experience authentic cultural visits to the Maasai bomas, local village and market. There are no frills here, but it's very comfortable, and you stay in an en-suite tent that's built on a wooden platform that overlooks a seasonal river. There's an attractive restaurant and bar area beside the swimming pool. A nearby water hole attracts game at all times, particularly during the dry season, although elephants are hanging around most of the time. A visit to **Pros:** great views from your tent's raised deck over a water hole frequented by game; children's rates available; they can organize last-minute safaris on request. **Cons:** very bumpy road to the Ruaha park entrance (10 minutes). Ⓢ *Rooms from: $205 ⊠ Ruaha National Park ☎ 255/75–568–0220 ⌸ www.tandalatentedcamp.com ⇌ 11 tents ⊟ No credit cards ⦙⊙⦙ All-inclusive.*

GATEWAY CITIES

Many visitors to Tanzania will find themselves with a layover in Dar es Salaam or Arusha before or after their safari. Many people dismiss Dar es Salaam as a mere stopover, but it's well worth a visit for a few days. For some ideas and suggestions to help determine where you should stay, eat, and, if you have time, sightsee, read on.

DAR ES SALAAM

Graceful triangular-sail dhows share the harbor with mammoth tankers, as the once sleepy village of Dar es Salaam, which means "haven of peace" in Arabic, has been transformed into one of East Africa's busiest ports, second only to Kenya's Mombasa. The country's major commercial center, Dar es Salaam has also become its largest city, home to more than 3.5 million inhabitants. The city also serves as the seat of government during the very slow move to Dodoma, which was named the official capital in 1973. The legislature resides in Dodoma, but most government offices are still found in Dar es Salaam.

In the early 1860s, Sultan Seyyid Majid of Zanzibar visited what was then the isolated fishing village of Mzizima on the Tanzanian coast. Eager to have a protected port on the mainland, Majid began constructing a palace here in 1865. The city, poised to compete with neighboring ports such as Bagamoyo and Kilwa, suffered a setback after the sultan died in 1870. His successor, his half-brother Seyyid Barghash, had little interest in the city, and its royal buildings fell into ruins. Only the Old Boma, which once housed royal guests, still survives.

The city remained a small port until Germany moved its colonial capital here in 1891 and began constructing roads, offices, and many of the public buildings still in use today. The Treaty of Versailles granted Great Britain control of the region in 1916, but that country added comparatively little to the city's infrastructure during its 45-year rule.

Tanzania gained its independence in 1961. During the years that followed, President Julius Nyerere, who focused on issues such as education and health care, allowed the capital city to fall into a decline that lasted into the 1980s. When Benjamin William Mkapa took office in 1985, his market-oriented reforms helped to revitalize the city. The city continues to evolve—those who visited only a few years ago will be startled by the changes—as new hotels and restaurants have appeared almost overnight. There are a few sights to detain visitors, but the only one really worth a visit is the National Museum, which contains the famous fossil discoveries by Richard and Mary Leakey, including the 1.7-million-year-old hominid skull discovered by Mary Leakey in the Olduvai Gorge in 1959. What Dar es Salaam has in blossoming abundance are exciting restaurants, beautiful hotels, and some of the best nightlife around.

GETTING HERE AND AROUND

To find your way around central Dar es Salaam, use the Askari Monument, at the intersection of Samora Avenue and Azikiwe Street, as a compass. Most sights are within walking distance. Four blocks northeast on Samora Avenue you'll find the National Museum and Botanical Gardens; about seven blocks southwest stands the Clock Tower, another good landmark. One block southeast is Sokoine Drive, which empties into Kivukoni Front as it follows the harbor. Farther along, Kivukoni Front becomes Ocean Road.

Along Samora Avenue and Sokoine Drive you'll find banks, pharmacies, grocery stores, and shops selling everything from clothing to curios. Northwest of Samora Avenue, around India, Jamhuri, and Libya streets, is the busy Swahili neighborhood where merchants sell all kinds of items, including Tanzania's best *kangas* (sarongs or wraps). Farther west you'll find the large Kariakoo Market.

■ TIP➔ **Don't buy tickets for transport, especially on ferries, trains, or buses, from anyone other than an accredited ticket seller.**

Julius Nyerere International Airport, formerly Dar es Salaam International Airport, is about 13 km (8 miles) from the city center. Plenty of white-color taxis are available at the airport and cost about Tsh 20,000 ($13) to the city center. This can usually be negotiated. Most hotels will send drivers to meet your plane if arranged in advance, although this will cost more.

Ferries operated by Sea Ferries Express to Zanzibar depart daily at 9 and 11:30 am from the Zanzibar Ferry Terminal. The two-hour journey costs about Tsh 63,000 ($40). Although thousands of locals and tourists use the service every year, two ferries capsized in 2011 and 2012 due to overcrowding, so you may wish to fly to Zanzibar instead; flights are, on average, $50 with Precision Air. ■ TIP➔ **Tourists aren't thought to be at risk from pirates from Somalia.** The Kigamboni ferry to the southern beaches runs continuously throughout the day and departs from the southern tip of the city center, where Kivukoni Front meets Ocean Road. The five-minute ride costs about Tsh 200 ($2) one-way, but you can end up waiting half an hour. You buy your ticket as you walk in. By far, Azam is the safest and best ferry operator to Zanaibar.

Dar es Salaam

Exploring

Askari Monument	1
Kivukoni Fish Market	3
Tanzania National Museum and House of Culture	2

Restaurants

305 Karafuu	4
Addis in Dar	3
Angithi	12
George and the Dragon	7
Karambezi Cafe	6
Mamboz Corner BBQ	15
Sitare Rooftop Bar	14
Thai Kani	8

Hotels

Courtyard Hotel	9
Dar Es Salaam Serena Hotel	13
Hotel Slipway	10
The Oyster Bay	5
Sea Cliff Hotel	2
The Souk	1
Triniti Guesthouse	11

Tickets can be bought online, at the terminal, or in larger hotels.

Taxis are the most efficient way to get around town. During the day they're easy to find outside hotels and at major intersections, but at night they're often scarce. Ask someone to call one for you. Taxis don't have meters, so agree on the fare before getting in. Fares run about Tsh 2,000 within the city.

MONEY MATTERS

You can pay in both USD and Tsh, but USD is preferred, as it's a more stable currency. Sometimes, paying in dollars can actually be cheaper by a dollar or two as well.

SAFETY

Dar es Salaam is fine to wander around by yourself during the day, but after dark it's best to take a taxi. The area with the most street crime is along the harbor, especially Kivukoni Front and Ocean Road.

> ### IF YOU HAVE TIME
>
> Travel 70 km (43 miles) north from Dar es Salaam to the historically fascinating town of Bagamoyo, where old buildings such as the Catholic Museum, on the grounds of the Holy Ghost Mission, and the Old Fort are well worth visiting. At the Old Fort, once an Arab trader's slave prison, you can see the underground tunnel along which slaves were herded to waiting dhows. The damp walls bore witness to the most terrible human suffering. It was in Bagamoyo that Henry Morton Stanley arrived after his three-year journey across Africa.

Foreign women tend to feel safe in Dar es Salaam. But remember, women in Dar es Salaam never wear clothing that exposes their shoulders or legs. You should do the same. You'll feel more comfortable in modest dress.

VISITOR INFORMATION

The Tanzania Tourist Board's head office is in Dar es Salaam. It has maps and information on travel to dozens of points of interest around Tanzania and is very helpful. The staff will discuss hotel options with you and assist you in making reservations. ⇨ *See Health and Safety in the chapter's Planning section for information on the U.S. Embassy.*

ESSENTIALS

Ferries Azam Marine ⊠ *Dar es Salaam* ⊕ *www.azammarine.com.* **Kigamboni Ferry** ⊠ *Mainland port at Magogoni near the main fish market, past the Hyatt Regency Dar Es Salaam* ☎ *022/286–2796.* **Sea Express** ⊠ *Sokoine Dr.* ☎ *022/213-7049.* **Zanzibar Ferry Terminal** ⊠ *Sokoine Dr..*

Visitor Information Tanzania Tourist Board (*TTB*). ⊠ *IPS Building, corner of Azikiwe St. and Samora Ave., 3rd fl.* ☎ *022/211–1244 for general info, 022/212–8472 for tourism services* ⊕ *www.tanzaniatouristboard.com* ⊘ *Weekdays 9–5, Sat. 9–noon.*

EXPLORING

Askari Monument. This bronze statue was erected by the British in 1927 in memory of African troops who died during World War I. (The word *askari* means "soldier" in Swahili.) It stands on the site of a monument erected by Germany to celebrate its victory here in 1888. That monument stood only five years before being demolished in 1916. ✉ *Samora Ave. and Azikiwe St.*.

Botanical Gardens. If you are heading to the National Museum it's well worth a quiet stroll through the indigenous plants in the botanical gardens. It provides respite from the city underneath purple bougainvilleas and blue jacarandas.

Kivukoni Fish Market. If you are feeling brave and interested in experiencing Dar's fish market at its nosiest and fishiest then wake up early and head down to Kivukoni. There is no charge to walk around. Be prepared for quite a smell, but the sight of hundreds of weathered fishermen hauling in their catch and the thrumming sounds of commence—bargaining and haggling, prepping the seafood—is a fun experience. Please don't purchase any of the seashells or turtle products on sale.

> **A REAL GEM**
>
> Looking for that one-of-a-kind gift or keepsake? How about jewelry with tanzanite in it? Given by Maasai fathers to mothers upon the birth of their child, this deep-blue stone, discovered in 1967, is unique to Tanzania. And though you can purchase the gems just about anywhere these days, you can't beat the prices or the bargaining you'll find in the shops of Arusha and Dar es Salaam— you'll be able to purchase loose stones, existing pieces, or custom-ize your own design. ⚠ Don't buy any tanzanite from street vendors. Nine times out of 10 it'll be a fake stone.

5

Tanzania National Museum and House of Culture. Apart from the Leakey fossil discoveries, which are some of the most important in the world, there are also good displays of colonial exploration and German occupation. This is also a spot to learn about Tanzania's tribal heritage and the impact of the slave trade. ✉ *Between Samora Ave. and Sokoine Dr., near Botanical Gardens* ☎ *022/211–7508* 🖆 *US$4* ⊙ *Daily 9:30–6.*

BEACHES

Although the beaches north and south of Dar es Salaam may seem irresistible to those seeking the calm, cool waters of the Indian Ocean, no one goes to these beaches. Even Oyster Bay, the upmarket residential neighborhood just north of Dar es Salaam where many luxury hotels are located, isn't 100% safe. Pickpockets are everywhere. ■TIP➔ As you'll probably only be in town for a night at most, save your beach time for Zanzibar, Pemba, or Mafia Island.

WHERE TO EAT

There's no need to spend much on dining in Dar es Salaam if you stick to *hotelis* (cafés), which offer heaping plates of African or Indian fare for less than Tsh 5,000 ($5). Typical *chakula* (food) for an East African meal includes *wali* (rice) or *ugali* (a damp mound of breadlike ground corn) served with a meat, fish, or vegetable stew. A common side dish is *kachumbari*, a mixture of chopped tomatoes, onions, and cucumbers. Even less expensive are roadside stalls, such as those that line the harbor, offering snacks like chicken and beef kebabs, roast corn on the cob, and samosas. If you're in the mood for something sweet, try a doughnutlike *mandazi.* Wash it all down with a local beer—Kilimanjaro, Tusker, or Safari—or with chai.

Most tourists frequent the more upscale restaurants, which are relatively expensive; entrées can set you back $10 to $15. Even at the toniest of restaurants, reservations are rarely required. Restaurants in hotels generally are open until at least 10:30 pm, even on Sunday, although hours of local restaurants vary.

$$ CONTEMPORARY
🍴 **305 Karafuu Restaurant.** Tucked away in a small neighborhood this is a favorite with people who have been coming to Dar es Salaam for a while. Unpretentious, family-run and with some exceptionally tasty food, 305 Karafuu is all local atmosphere and good times. They specialize in meat and seafood dishes that are plentiful and delicious. Make reservations if you are a large group. [$] *Average main: $12* ✉ *Karafuu St., Kinondoni* ☎ *255/754–277–188* 🕒 *Closed Mon.*

$$ ETHIOPIAN Fodor's Choice ★
🍴 **Addis in Dar.** Located only ten minutes west of central Dar es Salaam, and near the U.S. Embassy, this popular Ethiopian restaurant has been a long standing go-to in the city. Seating is around a small table with low chairs on an outside terrace overlooking a tranquil leafy garden (bring insect repellent) amidst traditional umbrellas. Food is eaten communally and with the hands—traditional Ethiopian style—and you'll scoop delicious stews and sauces from the plate with the traditional *injera* bread. There are good options for vegetarians, too. Make sure to try the honey wine or the traditional coffee **■ TIP→ This place fills up; book in advance.** [$] *Average main: $15* ✉ *35 Ursino St.* ☎ *255/754–416–167* 🌐 *www.addisindar.com* 🕒 *Closed Sun.*

$ INDIAN
🍴 **Angithi.** It may not look like much from the busy main street corner, but this is some of the best Indian food hidden away in Dar es Salaam. Their curries are plentiful and delicious and it will not break the bank if you order from their decent wine selection. A firm favorite. [$] *Average main: $10* ✉ *Ali Hassan Rd.* ☎ *255/22–2701–866.*

$ AMERICAN
🍴 **George and the Dragon.** What do you do when you are in Africa and you need a quick fix of your local sports and a burger and chips? You head to the good old English pub known locally as "The George." Burgers are their signature dish, but there's plenty of good pub fare like fish 'n' chips and pizza on the menu. In the back of this homey establishment, you'll find beautiful gardens and big outdoor barbeques. On Friday and Saturday evening is the very popular scene called #chillaxfriday (follow the hashtag for updates) with a dance floor and festive, relaxed vibe. [$] *Average main: $10* ✉ *Haile Selassie Rd., Kinondoni* ☎ *255/717–800–002* 🕒 *Closed Mon.*

$$$ CONTEMPORARY
🍴 **Karambezi Cafe.** This popular open-air restaurant in the Sea Cliff Hotel is right next to the sea, providing the best views in town. The menu has something to suit everyone and service is prompt and efficient even if the price does not necessarily reflect the quality of the food. Lighter meals include salads, but there are also pastas, pizzas, and meatier options such as burgers, steaks, and ribs. The roast chicken is fantastic, as is the fish 'n' chips. [$] *Average main: $30* ✉ *Sea Cliff Hotel, Toure Dr., Msasani* ☎ *022/260–0380* 🌐 *www.hotelseacliff.com.*

$ INDIAN
🍴 **Mamboz Corner BBQ.** Nearly every major African city has a local joint where you can mingle, chat, eat hearty street food, and absorb the city

life as the day cools down. Mamboz, and its sister restaurant Mamboz SizGrill, are just this kind of place for Dar es Salaam. You name it, they can grill it and add in some flavorful Indian influenced sauces. Their menu is hearty, well-priced, and as local as it comes. Its only drawback is that no alcohol is sold on site, and thanks to some city council rules the barbecues are no longer allowed on the street itself, but SizGrill (Magore Street, Upanga) is still worth the visit. Cash only. $ *Average main: $10* ⊠ *Kinondoni* ▭ *No credit cards.*

$ ✕ **Sitare Rooftop Bar.** See Dar es Salaam city from a new perspective at the very top of the Hotel Sapphire. Their Sitar Rooftop sheesha bar boasts some wonderful big-screen TVs for sports and large, comfortable chairs where you lounge back with a sheesha pipe and mingle with the young and beautiful in Dar es Salaam city. The menu is primarily chicken, lamb, and vegetarian dishes, and the pizzas are good, but the star attraction here is the view over the city. Sit back on one of the open balconies and take in the pulse of a dynamic, vibrant downtown area—a perfect sundowner spot. $ *Average main: $10* ⊠ *Hotel Sapphire, Mtendeni St., City Center* ⊕ *www.hotelsapphiretz.com.*

CONTEMPORARY

$$$ ✕ **Thai Kani.** Currently the best Thai cuisine in Dar es Salaam is at Thai Kani. Don't be to put off by the prices because the portion sizes are massive and well worth it. Found down a bumpy little road just past the butcher shop (taxi drivers might find it easier if you mention this), this popular restaurant offers spicy Thai and traditional Japanese sushi. $ *Average main: $20* ⊠ *Off Kahama Rd.* ☎ *0757/165–514* ⌂ *Reservations essential* ⊗ *Closed Mon.*

ASIAN

WHERE TO STAY
Hotel reviews have been shortened. For full information, visit Fodors. com

$ ⬚ **Courtyard Hotel.** With traditional Arabic wooden balconies and stained-glass windows, and a lush courtyard, this hotel feels a lot like a welcoming riad. **Pros:** beautiful architecture and more intimate than the larger chain hotels; fantastic facilities; luggage storage available; general manager who is attentive to your every need; free Wi-Fi. **Cons:** traffic outside of the hotel is often at a standstill in peak hours. $ *Rooms from: $230* ⊠ *Seaview Ocean Rd., Oyster Bay* ☎ *022/213–0130* ⊕ *www. proteahotels.com* ⤳ *41 rooms* ⦿ *Breakfast.*

HOTEL
FAMILY
Fodor's Choice
★

$$ ⬚ **Dar Es Salaam Serena Hotel.** The Serena is a staple in Dar es Salaam as the biggest and best luxury hotel chain on the block, and it definitely fits the bill as it looms large and bright over the downtown city skyline. **Pros:** surrounded by pleasant gardens; the pool is a decent size; central location. **Cons:** very large and caters to large conferences; security to get into the hotel is laborious and time-consuming and often chaotic when the hotel is busy. $ *Rooms from: $276* ⊠ *Uhuru St.* ☎ *022/211–2416* ⊕ *www.serenahotels.com* ⤳ *230 rooms* ⦿ *Breakfast.*

HOTEL

$ ⬚ **Hotel Slipway.** Located in the eponymous shopping and leisure complex in a converted boatyard, the Slipway is a great place for an overnight or home base in Dar. **Pros:** convenient for restaurants and shopping; hotel arranges island trips. **Cons:** located in a large, busy shopping center that is undergoing massive construction; night noise from restaurants can be intrusive. $ *Rooms from: $120* ⊠ *The Slipway,*

HOTEL

5

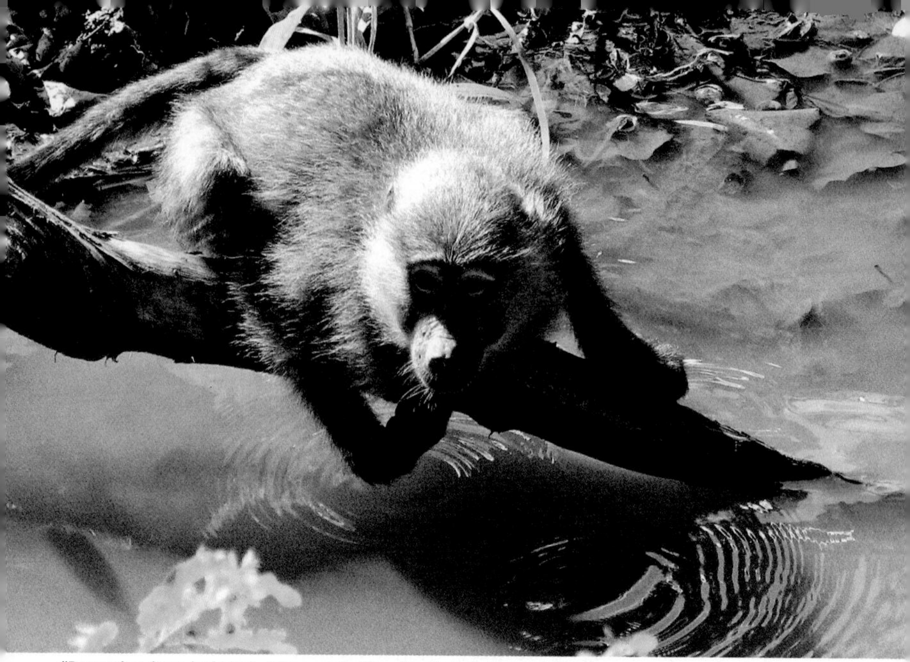

"Remember, keep hydrated while on safari!" —alfredlind, Fodors.com member.

Chole Rd., Masani Bay ☎ *022/260–0893* 🌐 *www.slipway.net* 🛏 *9 souks, 20 standard rooms* 🍴 *Breakfast.*

$$ ALL-INCLUSIVE Fodor's Choice ★ 🏨 **The Oyster Bay.** This stylish, contemporary boutique hotel has been created as a tranquil haven for guests to recuperate in before or after a flight or safari, and it certainly more than fits the bill. **Pros:** all the rooms have sea views; free Wi-Fi; there are no hidden payments when you leave—everything is included. **Cons:** it's expensive, especially if you only stay one night; there's no elevator. [$] *Rooms from: $425* ✉ *Toure Dr., Oyster Bay* ☎ *44/1932–260618* 🌐 *www.theoysterbayhotel.com* 🛏 *6 rooms* 🍴 *All-inclusive.*

$$ HOTEL 🏨 **Sea Cliff Hotel.** Only 15 minutes from downtown on the edge of the Msasani Peninsula, this classy hotel has good-size, comfortable rooms (but insist on one with a sea view), two restaurants, a casino, a pool, and a gym. **Pros:** free Wi-Fi; on-site ATM and good facilities. **Cons:** airport transfers are expensive, take a taxi instead; gym is basic; food is expensive. [$] *Rooms from: $320* ✉ *Toure Dr., Msasani Peninsula* ☎ *764/700–600* 🌐 *www.hotelseacliff.com* 🛏 *93 rooms* 🍴 *Breakfast.*

$ B&B/INN 🏨 **Triniti Guest House.** Many people will tell you that Dar es Salaam is not made for budget travel, but after spending a night at Triniti guesthouse you will change your mind. **Pros:** best budget accommodation in Dar; safe for solo travelers; food is fantastic—basic dining that is reasonably priced. **Cons:** on Friday night there is a disco on site at the main bar, it's incredibly loud and full of dancing patrons—you will either join in or get no sleep; bring mosquito repellent. [$] *Rooms from: $60* ✉ *8 Msasani Rd., Msasani* ☎ *255/0755 963–686* 🌐 *www.triniti.co.tz* 🛏 *12 rooms* 🍴 *Breakfast.*

SHOPPING

Fabric Shopping. You might want to pick up some amazing Tanzania fabric, especially the colorful kangas, kitenge and batik material. Vendors in Mnazi Mmoja on Uhuru Street or inside the Kariakoo cloth market (Congo Street) are some of your best spots to find material and cloth. Sometimes the prices are set; sometimes it's possible to haggle. ⊠ *Uhuru St.*

Mwenge Craft Market. If you are looking to take home hand-crafted items like bowls, Tinga Tinga, wooden carvings, jewelry, and antique masks then the market opposite the Village Museum is the place to find treasures of varying shapes and sizes. ⊠ *New Bagamoyo Rd..*

ARUSHA

Arusha may be the gateway to all of the Serengeti Safari but on a clear day, you can see Mt. Meru, Africa's fifth highest mountain at 4,556 meters (14,947 feet), looming in the distance. There are some wonderful accommodation options on the outskirts of Arusha that are well worth a day or two pre- or postsafari, just to recharge, relax, and be pampered while experiencing some Northern Tanzanian hospitality.

The town is bisected by the Nauru River. The more modern part is to the east of the river where most of the hotels, safari companies, and banks are located; west of the river are the bus station and main market. Most people spend an overnight here either coming or going.

GETTING HERE AND AROUND

There are no direct flights from the United States to Arusha. Generally you need to connect through a city on the mainland, the easiest being Dar es Salaam.

You'll be approached immediately after you land by taxi drivers. Be sure to agree on a price before getting in, as taxis don't have meters. The fare to downtown Arusha is approximately US$30.

SAFETY

It's unlikely that you'd want to explore Arusha at night, but if you do, take a taxi. As in any East African city, muggings and purse-snatching are common.

VISITOR INFORMATION

The Tanzanian Tourist Board (TTB) has an Arusha office where you can pick up maps and brochures for the area, as well as book cultural excursions. Tanzania National Parks also has an office here that can help you book accommodations or answer any of your safari questions.

CONTACTS

Airports Arusha Airport (*ARK*). ⊠ *A 104* ☎ *027/741–530, 027/744–317* ⊕ *www.taa.go.tz.*

Hospitals AICC Hospital ⊠ *Old Moshi Rd.* ☎ *027/250–1815* ⊕ *www.aicc.co.tz.*

Visitor Information Tanzania Tourist Board (*TTB*). ⊠ *E 47 Building, Boma Rd., Arusha* ☎ *255/27–254–8628* ⊕ *www.tanzaniatouristboard.com.*

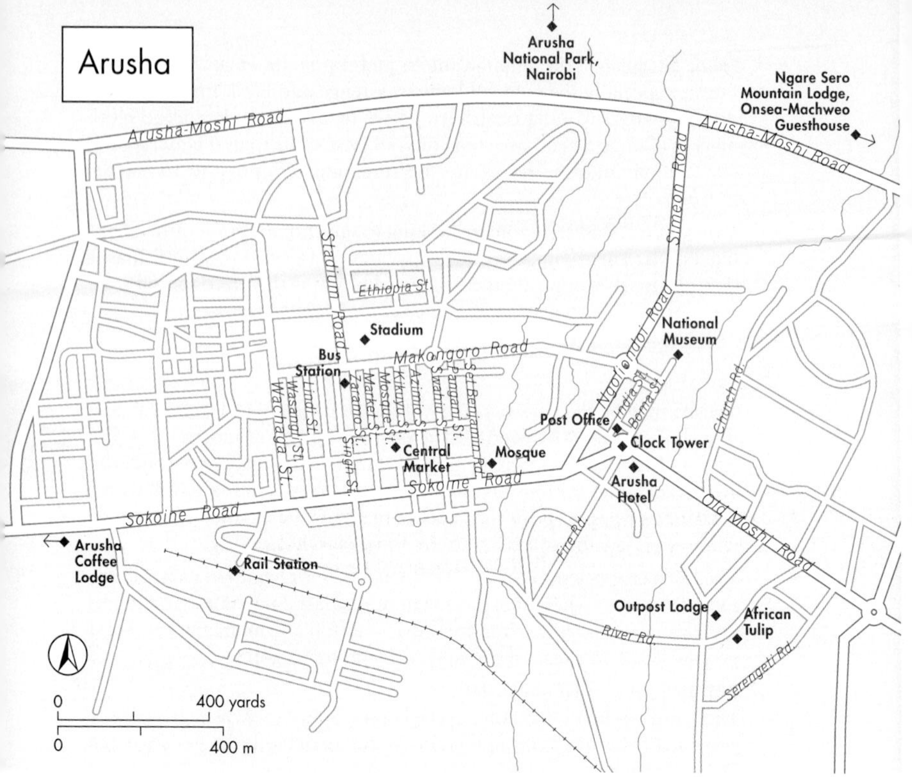

Arusha
Arusha National Park, Nairobi
Ngare Sero Mountain Lodge, Onsea-Machweo Guesthouse
Arusha-Moshi Road
Simeon Road
Stadium Road
Ethiopia St.
Stadium
Bus Station
Makongoro Road
National Museum
India St.
Boma St.
Church Rd.
Post Office
Clock Tower
Lindi St.
Wachaga St.
Zaramo St.
Market St.
Mosque St.
Kikuyu St.
Azimio St.
Swahili St.
Pangani St.
Singh St.
Central Market
Mosque
Sokoine Road
Arusha Hotel
Old Moshi Road
Fire Rd.
Arusha Coffee Lodge
Rail Station
Outpost Lodge
African Tulip
River Rd.
Serengeti Rd.
0
400 yards
0
400 m

WHERE TO STAY

$ HOTEL **The African Tulip.** If you are in need of a short stay with some modern hotel amenities before heading off for a safari, the safari-themed Tulip is a good option outside the bustle of Arusha. **Pros:** smaller hotel outside of the main city; can arrange to leave behind extra luggage if necessary. **Cons:** $10 a day for Wi-Fi; pool bar lacks atmosphere and the outside area is small; not all rooms have balconies. [$] *Rooms from: $190* ✉ *44 Serengeti Rd.* ☎ *255/27–254–3004* 🌐 *www.theafricantulip.com* 🛏 *29 rooms* 🍴 *Breakfast.*

$$ HOTEL FAMILY **Arusha Coffee Lodge.** Being 5 km (3 miles) from town and five minutes from Arusha Airport makes this a great option for pre- or post-safari layovers. **Pros:** beautiful setting; easy access to the airport; large comfortable rooms. **Cons:** near the highway so you can hear traffic. [$] *Rooms from: $350* ✉ *Serengeti Rd., Airport vicinity* ☎ *027/254–0630* 🌐 *www.elewana.com* 🛏 *18 cottages, 12 suites* 🍴 *Breakfast.*

$ HOTEL **The Arusha Hotel.** Bang in the middle of town, opposite the clock tower, this recently refurbished hotel built in 1894 retains a colonial feel, with elegantly decorated rooms and lovely gardens running down to the Themi River. **Pros:** walking distance from banks and shops; spacious rooms; you can store luggage. **Cons:** food is average; a/c and Wi-Fi are erratic; large conference hotel which can get very crowded with business meetings and socializing; location means traffic can take a while to get to airport. [$] *Rooms from: $221* ✉ *Main Rd.* ☎ *027/250–7777* 🌐 *www.thearushahotel.com* 🛏 *64 rooms, 22 executive suites* 🍴 *Breakfast.*

$ B&B/INN FAMILY Fodor's Choice ★ 🏨 **Ngare Sero Mountain Lodge.** Hidden in an old farmhouse on the outskirts of a forest area, you'll find this mountain lodge where you can really get away from it all. **Pros:** spectacular scenery with an exquisite lake and multiple activities; a quiet retreat and great place to unwind after a safari. **Cons:** rooms don't receive much natural light in them; far from town but for some that is a worthwhile aspect. [$] *Rooms from: $170* ✉ *Off A23, east of Arusha* ☎ *255/73–297–8931* 🌐 *www.ngare-sero-lodge.com* 🛏 *13 rooms* 🍴 *All meals.*

$ B&B/INN Fodor's Choice ★ 🏨 **Onsea-Machweo Guest house.** On a small, winding dirt road just off the main highway heading toward Moshi sits conjoined properties with some of the most spectacular views in the area, overlooking Arusha and Mt. Merua. **Pros:** spectacular location; beautiful outdoor deck and pool; excellent food. **Cons:** you can encounter traffic between the house and the airport; you are amidst village life so you might be woken early by chickens and cattle; many stairs so not ideal for people with mobility issues. [$] *Rooms from: $230* ✉ *Onsea Moivaro Rd.* 🌐 *www.machweo.com* 🛏 *11 chalets* 🍴 *Breakfast.*

SHOPPING

Cultural Heritage Centre. If you haven't yet picked up your gifts and curios, then stop by Arusha's Cultural Heritage Centre. It's one of the best curio shops in Tanzania and is only 3 km (2 miles) out of town. You can buy carvings, jewelry (including the gemstone tanzanite), colorful African clothing, local music, and much more. It's a bit pricey so take advantage of the museum that is part of the complex to get your money's worth. The king and queen of Norway and Bill Clinton and daughter Chelsea have all stopped to pick up last-minute gifts and souvenirs. ✉ *A 104* 🌐 *www.culturalheritage.co.tz.*

5

BEACH ESCAPES

Looking for a little R&R after your safari? Tanzania has 1,424 km (883 miles) of beautiful pristine coastline to explore. Looking for an island getaway? Tanzania has those, too. Zanzibar is the larger, louder, and more party-oriented island, unless you opt for more secluded resorts and hotels, while Mafia is home to some of the best diving in Tanzania and Pemba sits quietly in the Northern corners with its picture-perfect beaches and limited number of tourists.

ZANZIBAR

This ancient isle once ruled by sultans and slave traders served as the stepping stone into the African continent for missionaries and explorers. Today it attracts visitors intent on discovering sandy beaches, pristine rain forests, or colorful coral reefs. Once known as the Spice Island for its export of cloves, Zanzibar has become one of the most exotic flavors in travel, better than Bali or Mali when it comes to beauty that'll make your jaw drop.

Separated from the mainland by a channel only 35 km (22 miles) wide, and only 6 degrees south of the equator, this tiny archipelago—the name Zanzibar also includes the islands of Unguja (the main island) and Pemba—in the Indian Ocean was the launching base for a romantic era of expeditions into Africa. Sir Richard Burton and John Hanning Speke used it as their base when searching for the source of the Nile. It was in Zanzibar where journalist Henry Morton Stanley, perched in an upstairs room overlooking the Stone Town harbor, began his search for David Livingstone.

The first ships to enter the archipelago's harbors are believed to have sailed in around 600 BC. Since then, every great navy in the Eastern Hemisphere has dropped anchor here at one time or another. But it was

Arab traders who left an indelible mark. Minarets punctuate the skyline of Stone Town, where more than 90% of the residents are Muslim. In the harbor you'll see dhows, the Arabian boats with triangular sails. Islamic women covered by black boubou veils scurry down alleyways so narrow their outstretched arms could touch buildings on both sides. Stone Town received its odd name because most of its buildings were made of limestone and coral, which means exposure to salty air has eroded many foundations.

The first Europeans who arrived here were the Portuguese in the 15th century, and thus began a reign of exploitation. As far inland as Lake Tanganyika, slave traders captured the residents or bartered for them from their own chiefs, then forced the newly enslaved to march toward the Indian Ocean carrying loads of ivory tusks. Once at the shore they were shackled together while waiting for dhows to collect them at Baga- moyo, a place whose name means, "here I leave my heart." Although it's estimated that 50,000 slaves passed through the Zanzibar slave market each year during the 19th century, many more died en route.

Tanganyika and Zanzibar merged in 1964 to create Tanzania, but the honeymoon was brief. Zanzibar's relationship with the mainland remains uncertain as calls for independence continue. "Bismillah, will you let him go," a lyric from Queen's "Bohemian Rhapsody," has become a rebel chant for Zanzibar to break from Tanzania.

Zanzibar Island, locally known as Unguja, has amazing beaches and resorts, decent dive spots, acres of spice plantations, the Jozani Forest Reserve, and Stone Town. Plus, it takes little more than an hour to fly there. It's a popular spot to head post-safari.

Stone Town, the archipelago's major metropolis, is a maze of narrow streets lined with houses featuring magnificently carved doors studded with brass. There are 51 mosques, 6 Hindu temples, and 2 Christian churches. And though it can rightly be called a city, much of the western part of the larger island is a slumbering paradise where cloves, as well as rice and coconuts, still grow.

Although the main island of Unguja feels untouched by the rest of the world, the nearby islands of Pemba and Mnemba offer retreats that are even more remote. For many years Arabs referred to Pemba as Al Khudra, or the Green Island, and indeed it still is, with forests of king palms, mangos, and banana trees. The 65-km-long (40-mile-long) island is less famous than Unguja except among scuba divers, who enjoy the coral gardens with colorful sponges and huge fans. Archaeology buffs are also discovering Pemba, where sites from the 9th to the 15th century have been unearthed. At Mtambwe Mkuu coins bearing the heads of sultans were discovered. Ruins along the coast include ancient mosques and tombs. In the 1930s Pemba was famous for its sorcerers, attracting disciples of the black arts from as far away as Haiti. Witchcraft is still practiced, and, oddly, so is bullfighting. Introduced by the Portuguese in the 17th century, the sport has been improved by locals, who rewrote the ending. After enduring the ritual teasing by the matador's cape, the bull is draped with flowers and paraded around the village.

Beyond Pemba, smaller islands in the Zanzibar Archipelago range from mere sandbanks to Changu, once a prison island and now home to the

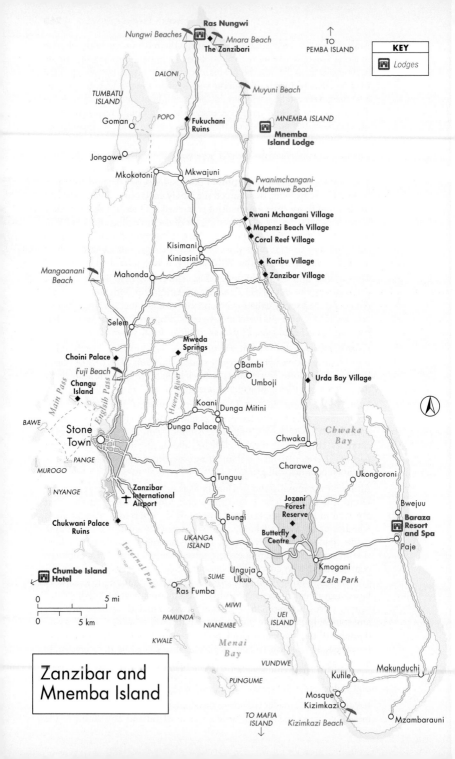

Ras Nungwi

Nungwi Beaches 🏖 ▲ *Mnara Beach*
The Zanzibari

↑
TO
PEMBA ISLAND

KEY
🏨 *Lodges*

DALONI

🏖 *Muyuni Beach*

*TUMBATU
ISLAND*

POPO

MNEMBA ISLAND

Goman ○

🏨
**Mnemba
Island Lodge**

Jongowe ○

♦ **Fukuchani
Ruins**

Mkokotoni ○

○ Mkwajuni

🏖 *Pwanimchangani-
Matemwe Beach*

♦ **Rwani Mchangani Village**
♦ **Mapenzi Beach Village**
♦ **Coral Reef Village**

Kisimani ○
Kiniasini

♦ **Karibu Village**
♦ **Zanzibar Village**

*Mangaanani
Beach* 🏖

Mahonda ○

Selem ○

♦ **Mweda
Springs**

♦ **Choini Palace**

○ Bambi

○ Umboji

♦ **Urda Bay Village**

Fuji Beach 🏖

**Changu
Island** ♦

Main Pass

Heera River

○ Koani
Dunga Mitini

♦ Dunga Palace

English Pass

**Stone
Town**

BAWE

PANGE

Chwaka ○

*Chwaka
Bay*

MUROGO

NYANGE

Charawe ○

○ Ukongoroni

○ Tunguu

○ Bwejuu

✈ **Zanzibar
International
Airport**

○ Bungi

**Jozani
Forest
Reserve**

🏨
**Baraza
Resort
and Spa**

♦ **Chukwani Palace
Ruins**

*UKANGA
ISLAND*

**Butterfly
Centre** ♦

○ Paje

🏨 **Chumbe Island
Hotel**

↙

Internal Pass

Unguja
Ukuu ○

○ Kmogani

Zala Park

0 —— 5 mi
0 —— 5 km

SUME

○ Ras Fumba

MIWI

PAMUNDA

NIANEMBE

*UEI
ISLAND*

KWALE

*Menai
Bay*

VUNDWE

Kutile ○

○ Makunduchi

Zanzibar and
Mnemba Island

PUNGUME

Mosque ○
Kizimkazi

↓
TO MAFIA
ISLAND

Kizimkazi Beach 🏖

○ Mzambarauni

giant Aldabra tortoise, Chumbe Island, and Mnemba, a private retreat for guests who pay hundreds of dollars per day to get away from it all.

WHEN TO GO

June through October is the best time to visit Zanzibar because the temperature averages 26°C (79°F). Spice tours are best during harvest time, July and October, when cloves (unopened flower buds) are picked and laid out to dry. Zanzibar experiences a short rainy season in November, but heavy rains can fall from March until the end of May. Temperatures soar during this period, often reaching over 30°C (90°F). Most travelers come between June and August and from mid-November to early January. During these periods many hotels add a surcharge.

Zanzibar observes Ramadan for a month every year. During this period Muslims are forbidden to eat, drink, or smoke between sunrise and sunset. Although hotels catering to tourists aren't affected, many small shops and restaurants are closed during the day. If you plan to arrive during Ramadan, aim for the end, when a huge feast called the Eid al-Fitr (which means "end of the fast") brings everyone out to the streets.

GETTING HERE AND AROUND

There are no direct flights from the United States. Generally you need to connect through a city on the mainland, the easiest being Dar es Saalam. From Dar es Saalam to Stone Town, there are regular flights in small twin-engine aircraft operated by Precision Air and Coastal Aviation The flight takes around 20 minutes. From Nairobi and Mombasa, you can fly to Stone Town on Kenya Airways. At this writing the airport is undergoing some major renovations so you may have to be bused around across the runways or have to wait under shaded tarpaulins before flights arrive and depart.

Visitors from the United States and Europe require visas to enter Tanzania. Zanzibar is a semiautonomous state within Tanzania, so you don't need a separate visa to visit, but you do need to show your passport and fill in an arrival form

Bikes can be rented from shops near Darajani Market. Mopeds and motorcycles are another great way to get about the island, although nothing is signposted so you could get lost frequently.

Several hydrofoil ferries travel between Dar es Salaam and Stone Town. The fastest trips, lasting about 75 minutes, are on hydrofoils operated by Sea Express and Azam Marine. Sea Express has daily departures from Dar es Salaam at 9 and 11:30 am, with returns at 7 am and 3 pm. Azam Marine departs from Dar es Salaam at 7, 9:30, 12:30, and 3:45, returning at 7 am, 9:30 pm, 12:30 pm, and 3:30 pm. Tickets can be purchased on the spot or in advance from the row of offices next to the port in Dar es Saalam. Timetables and prices are displayed on boards outside each office. Tickets for nonresidents range from $40 (Tsh 68,000) for first class to $35 (Tsh 59,500) for second class. The harbor is quite busy so keep an eye on your possessions. And if you don't want help from a porter, be firm. Note that two ferries sank in 2011 and 2012, thought to be due to overcrowding but they were the local goods and transport ferrys, which may be the cheapest way to get to Zanzibar, but by far not the safest. Whether you arrive by plane or ferry, you'll be approached by taxi drivers. Be sure to agree on a price before getting in, as taxis don't have meters. The fare to Stone Town should be around Tsh 40,000 (around $15–$20). Your driver may let you out several blocks before you reach your hotel because the streets are too narrow. Ask the driver to walk you to the hotel. Be sure to tip him if he carries your luggage.

DAY TOURS

Spice tours are a popular way to see Zanzibar. Guides take you to farms in Kizimbani or Kindichi and teach you to identify plants that produce cinnamon, turmeric, nutmeg, and vanilla. A curry luncheon will undoubtedly use some of the local spices. Any tour company can arrange a spice tour, with the average price for a spice tour ranging from $25 to $50, depending on the number of people, including lunch. Most depart around 9 am from Stone Town.

Various tour operators and most hotels offer tour options that include visits to Prison Island, Jozani Forest, and the Zanzibar Butterfly Centre. One Ocean is able to take you diving from their offices opposite the NBC bank outside of the tunnel. Unwind at Mrembo Spa with some of their signature Swahili Frangipanni massages or take a tour with a difference tailored by Different tours or Amo Zanzibar—both have good reputations on the island for offering more than just your standard spice and island tour.

HEALTH AND SAFETY

Visitors to Zanzibar are required to have a yellow-fever vaccination certificate; some websites also recommend polio, hepatitis A, and typhoid vaccinations. You should also talk with your doctor about a malaria prophylactic. The best way to avoid malaria is to avoid being bitten by mosquitoes, so make sure your arms and legs are covered and that you wear plenty of mosquito repellent, especially after dusk. Antihistamine cream is also quite useful to stop the itch of mosquito bites. Always sleep under a mosquito net; most hotels and guesthouses provide them. The sun can be very strong here, so make sure to slather yourself with sunscreen as well. Drink bottled water, and plenty of it—it'll help you avoid dehydration. Avoid raw fruits and vegetables that may have been washed in untreated water.

Although the best way to experience Stone Town is to wander around its labyrinthine streets, you should always be on your guard. Don't wear jewelry or watches that might attract attention, and keep a firm grasp on purses and camera bags. Leave valuables in the safe at your hotel.

Muggings have been reported at Nungwi and other coastal resorts, so never carry valuables onto the beach. Nungwi is known as the party side of Zanzibar; if you are want a quiet retreat free from beach boys and loud beach parties then head elsewhere.

As Zanzibar is a largely conservative, Muslim state, it's advisable for women to dress modestly. This means a long dress or skirt. Uncovered shoulders and heads are fine, but never cleavage or torsos. Many tourists

often ignore this advice, and although locals are too polite to say anything, it's not appreciated and it does not put tourists in good standing among locals. It does not take much effort to cover up, and if it is not your home country, it is respectful to adhere to basic social customs, even if you might not feel like it. Holding hands is fine, but overly intimate displays of affection should be avoided. With that being said, homosexuality is frowned on in Zanzibar, and displays of public affection can be prosecutable.

■ TIP→ Always ask permission before taking photographs, and be prepared to pay a small tip in return, particularly from the Maasai.

MONEY MATTERS

There are handy currency exchange booths in Stone Town that offer good rates. The best rates are at Forex Bureau around the corner from Mazson's Hotel on Kenyatta Road, and the Malindi Exchange across from Cine Afrique. Mtoni Marine Center, also in Stone Town, will give a cash advance on your Visa or MasterCard. It charges a commission as well as a processing fee. Most people will except U.S. dollars, but be aware of the exchange rate and make sure you're not being overcharged. ■ TIP→ Be very careful when using ATMs. Make sure you use one at a reputable bank, and check to make sure the bank is open—cards get swallowed all the time.

TELEPHONES

The regional code for Zanzibar is 024. ■ TIP→ Telephone numbers seem to lack consistency, so they're listed as they appear in promotional materials.

VISITOR INFORMATION

The free tourist magazine, *Swahili Coast,* found in hotels and shops, lists cultural events, as well as tide tables that are very useful for divers. There's a tourist information center north of Stone Town. Although not very useful for information about the city, it does book rooms at inns in other parts of the island.

CONTACTS

Airlines Coastal Aviation ⊕ www.coastal.cc. **Fly540** ⊕ www.fly540.com. **Kenya Airways** ⊠ Airport North Rd., Embakasi, Nairobi, Kenya ☎ 020/327-4747 ⊕ www.kenya-airways.com. **Mango Airlines** ⊠ South Africa ⊕ www.flymango. com. **Precision Air** ⊕ www.precisionairtz.com. **Zan Air** ⊕ www.zanair.com.

Airports Zanzibar Airport ⊕ www.zanzibar-airport.com.

Day Tours Amo Zanzibar Tours ⊠ Mkunazini St., Stone Town ☎ 255/744-590-020 ⊕ amozanzibartours.hpage.com. **Eco & Culture Tours** ⊠ 272 Hurumizi St., Stone Town ☎ 255/242-233-731 ⊕ www.ecoculture-zanzibar.org. **Mrembo Spa** ⊠ Cathedral St., Stone Town ☎ 255/777-430-117. **Neno Tours** ☎ 255/767-708-026 ⊕ www.nenotoursntravels.co.tz. **One Ocean Diving and Water Sports** ⊠ Kenyatta Rd., Stone Town ☎ 024/223-8374 ⊕ www.zanzibaroneocean. com. **The Original Dhow Safaris** ⊠ Stone Town ☎ 772/277-799 ⊕ www. dhowsafaris.net. **Zanzibar Different Tours** ⊠ Soko Muhogo St., Stone Town ☎ 255/777-430-117 ⊕ www.zanzibardifferent.com.

Ferries Azam Marine ☎ 022/213-3321 in Dar es Salaam, 024/223-1655 in Zanzibar ⊕ www.azammarine.com. **Sea Express** ⊠ Sokoine Dr., Zanzibar ☎ 022/213-7049 in Dar es Salaam, 024/223-4690 in Zanzibar ⊕ www. fastferriestz.com.

Visitor Information Zanzibar Tourist Corporation ☎ 024/223–3485 ⊕ www. zanzibartourism.net.

EXPLORING

The sights in Stone Town are all minutes from one another so you'll see them all as you walk. However, the old part of town is very compact and mazelike and can be a bit disconcerting, especially if you're a female traveler. Hiring a guide is a great way to see the city without stress, and a guide can provide information about the sights you'll see. Many tour operators offer a guided walking tour for approximately US$20–US$25. Ask your hotel for guide suggestions, or see Day Tours *above* for tour guide recommendations. That said, getting lost is part of the experience of Stone Town; it is a small, compact area and you can easily ask a vendor to point you in the general direction of the Fort, an easy landmark. Take your time around the streets, don't panic if you don't know exactly where you are—the joy of traveling is chatting to people and discovering quiet corners, intimate exchanges of daily life and, yes, the shopping. Stone Town is regarded as a mini fashion mecca for East Africa. Don't miss visiting the famous Doreen Mashinka or the delightful Upendo Means Love and Mago for unique fashion items.

TOP ATTRACTIONS

Beit el-Ajaib. Known as the "House of Wonders" because it was the first building in Zanzibar to use electric lights, this four-story palace is still one of the largest buildings in the city. Built in the late 1800s for Sultan Barghash, it was bombarded by the British in 1886, forcing the sultan to abdicate his throne. Today you'll find cannons guarding the beautifully carved doors at the entrance. Check out the marble-floored rooms, where you'll find exhibits that detail the country's battle for independence. ⊠ *North of Old Fort* 🎟 *Tsh 4000* ⊗ *Daily 9–6.*

Changu Island (*Prison Island*). This tiny island, just a 20-minute boat ride from Stone Town, was once a prison and a quarantine location. Now it's a tropical paradise that's home to the giant Aldabra tortoise (you can visit the tortoises for a small fee), the duiker antelope, and a variety of birds and butterflies. There's also decent swimming and snorkeling, and a hotel and restaurant. Note that 70% of the island is private property and thus inaccessible. ■ TIP➔ **You can visit Changu Island on a tour, or arrange transport with a fisherman on the beach outside Archipelago's for a much cheaper price. There's no entry fee for the island itself.** ⊠ *5.6 km (3½ miles) northwest of the main island* 🎟 *US$4 for tortoise visit.*

Forodhani Gardens. This pleasant waterfront park is a favorite spot for an evening stroll both for locals and tourists. Dozens of venders sell grilled fish under the light of gas lanterns—not all the food is great, but the atmosphere is fantastic for a visit. Always try to smell the seafood before you eat it as some of it can be old. There's also a children's playground. ⊠ *Mizingani St..*

Old Fort. Built by the Portuguese in 1560, this bastioned fortress is the oldest structure in Stone Town. It withstood an attack from Arabs in 1754. It was later used as a jail, and prisoners who were sentenced to death met their ends here. It has undergone extensive renovation and today is headquarters for many cultural organizations, including the Zanzibar International Film Festival and the Jahazi Literary and Jazz Festival. Performances of traditional dance and music are staged here during the week. Check the office for details ⊠ *Creek Rd. and Malawi Rd.* ☜ *Free* ⊙ *Daily 7 am–10 pm.*

WORTH NOTING

Darajani Market. This gable-roofed structure built in 1904 and also know as Estella Market, houses a sprawling fruit, fish, meat, and vegetable market. Goods of all sorts—colorful fabrics, wooden chests, and all types of jewelry—are sold in the shops that line the surrounding streets. To the east of the main building you'll find spices laid out in colorful displays of beige, yellow, and red. On Wednesday and Saturday there's an antiques fair. The market is most active in the morning between 9 and 11. ⊠ *Creek Rd., north of New Mkunazini St.* ☜ *Free* ⊙ *Daily 8–6.*

BEYOND STONE TOWN

Chumbe Island. Between the Tanzanian coast and the islands of Zanzibar, Chumbe Island is the country's first marine national park. It's home to 400 species of coral and 200 species of fish. There's scuba diving, snorkeling, island hikes, and outrigger boat rides. ■TIP➔ **The island can only be visited on an organized day trip.** ☎ *024/223–1040* ⊕ *www. chumbeisland.com.*

Jozani Forest Reserve. Jozani Chakwa Bay National Park, Zanzibar's only national park, is home to this reserve where you'll find the rare Kirk's red colobus monkey, which is named after Sir John Kirk, the British consul in Zanzibar from 1866 to 1887. The species is known for its white whiskers and rusty coat. Many of the other animals that call this reserve home—including the blue duiker, a diminutive antelope whose coat is a dusty bluish-gray—are endangered because 95% of the original forests of the archipelago have been destroyed. There's also more than 50 species of butterfly and 40 bird species. The entry fee includes entrance to the forest and a circular boardwalk walk through mangrove swamps, plus the services of a guide (tip him if he's good). ■TIP➔ **Early morning and evening are the best time to visit.** ⊠ *38 km (27 miles) southeast of Stone Town* ☜ *US$8* ⊙ *Daily 7:30–5.*

Zanzibar Butterfly Centre. This center is well worth a half-hour visit. It's a community development project, and your entry fee pays for local farmers to bring in cocoons (most of which are sent to museums overseas) and helps preserve the forest. Guided tours end in a visit to an enclosure filled with hundreds of colorful butterflies. ⊠ *1 km from Jozani Forest* ⊕ *www.zanzibarbutterflies.com* ☜ *UD$5* ⊙ *9–5.*

WHERE TO EAT

Zanzibar was the legendary Spice Island, so it's no surprise the cuisine here is flavored with lemongrass, cumin, and garlic. Cinnamon enlivens tea and coffee, while ginger flavors a refreshing soft drink called Tangawizi. Zanzibar grows more than 20 types of mangos, and combining them with bananas, papayas, pineapples, and passion fruit makes for tasty juices. When it comes to dinner, seafood reigns supreme. Stone Town's fish market sells skewers of kingfish and tuna. Stop by in the early evening, when the catch of the day is hauled in and cleaned. Try the prawn kebabs, roasted peanuts, and corn on the cob at the outdoor market at Forodhani Gardens (but not if you have a sensitive tummy). Try the vegetarian Zanzibar pizza for breakfast; it's more like an omelet.

Gratuities are often included in the bill, so ask the staff before adding the usual 10% tip. Credit cards aren't widely accepted, so make sure you have enough cash. Lunch hours are generally 12:30 to 2:30, dinner 7 to 10:30. Dress is casual for all but upscale restaurants, where you should avoid T-shirts, shorts, and trainers.

$$ × **6 Degrees South Grill and Wine Bar.** If you are looking for a sunset cock-
CONTEMPORARY tail in white loungers overlooking the Zanzibar ocean, then head on over to 6 Degrees on Shangani street. Fresh, modern Afro-continental cuisine with relaxed, breezy ambiance Try the fresh Madafu-coconut water with a kick, on a hot day it is a small life-saver. $ *Average main: $12* ✉ *Shangani St..*

$$$ × **Emerson Spice Rooftop Restaurant.** Be sure to book ahead at this charm-
AFRICAN ing but small rooftop restaurant, because there's just one seating for
Fodor's Choice dinner at 7. Arrive early to enjoy a cocktail and the sunset and then
★ enjoy a degustation menu of exquisite Swahili-inspired cuisine. Each of the five courses has three small portions that have distinct and interest-ing flavors, such as passion fruit–fish ceviche, calamari-stuffed tomato, grilled mango with cardamom, or coconut-chili fish baked in banana leaf. The menu changes daily and is only posted on a board outside around lunchtime, ensuring that fresh and seasonal ingredients are used. While Emerson himself is no longer in attendance, his spirit lives on. ⚠ **You'll climb lots of steep stairs to get to the top.** $ *Average main: $25* ✉ *Tharia St., Kiponda, Stone Town* ☎ *024/223–2776, 0775/046–395 (mobile)* ⊕ *www.emersonspice.com* ⚴ *Reservations essential.*

$$ × **House of Spices.** As usual, you'll have to climb a few steep flights of
MEDITERRANEAN stairs before arriving at this breezy, open-air terrace restaurant, but the effort is worth it. The décor is simple yet stylish, with walls painted in relaxing shades of blue and green, colorful woven place mats, dark wooden tables and chairs, and friendly waiters in blue shirts and prayer hats. If you're craving Western food, the pizzas and homemade pastas are good, and there are plenty of red meat options; otherwise there are enticing seafood dishes such as crab claws, prawns, calamari, and grilled fish with a choice of interesting sauces. ■ **TIP→ At the back of the house is a traditional tea room which is a great, intimate escape from shopping in the streets.** $ *Average main: $12* ✉ *Kiponda St.* ⊕ *www. houseofspiceszanzibar.com* ☾ *Closed Sun.*

$$$ × **Mashariki Palace.** Nothing beats a sunset dinner overlooking Stone
CONTEMPORARY Town, and it's even more special on the rooftop of a 200-year-old restored sultans palace. Mashariki Palace presents fine dining, great service, and some memorable food. It has more space in the dining area than other rooftop terraces and easy access off Forodhani square. Order the day before if you would like a seafood platter, and if it's to your taste, try the octopus carpaccio—it's out of this world. $ *Average main: $30* ✉ *Nyumba Ya Moto St.* ⚴ *Reservations essential.*

$$ × **The Post.** Sit on the terrace overlooking the colorful and lively streets and
ASIAN FUSION enjoy great views, good wine, and very decent tapas. At the Post you'll find Continental, Thai (Lemongrass) and Asian Fusion (Cafe Miwa) restau-rants, all of which have their own unique flavors mixing Zanzibar spices

5

with delicious oriental dishes like satay chicken skewers, seafood curries and out-of-this-world juice smoothies. The deli offers up fantastic breads and hams. [$] *Average main: $15* ✉ *Shangani Post Office, Stone Town.*

$$ CAFÉ 🍴 **Zanzibar Coffee House.** This little spot is a coffee lover's paradise. Head along the shopping streets amid the houses toward the Old Fort and you will start to find little wooden signs pinned onto the corners of alleyways with the Coffee House logo on it. It's inside a traditional Arab house in the midst of the town; the food is standard for a café, but what you come here for is the rich, aromatic, home-roasted coffee. [$] *Average main: $12* ✉ *Mkunazini St., Stone Town.*

WHERE TO STAY

BEACH RESORTS

$$$$ ALL-INCLUSIVE FAMILY 🏨 **Baraza Resort & Spa.** While there's nothing authentic about the Arabian décor at this award-winning hotel, there's a "wow" factor that extends from the opulent reception and lounging areas, complete with carved wooden furnishings, copper urns, and billowing drapes, to the beautifully appointed individual villas. **Pros:** a good range of tours are available; excellent service; gorgeous beach when the tide is right. **Cons:** no Wi-Fi in the rooms; the pool area gets a bit crowded. [$] *Rooms from: $853* ✉ *Bwejuu, Zanzibar* ☎ *254/720–538–148, 254/733–777–172* 🌐 *www.baraza-zanzibar.com* 🛏 *30 villas* 🍽 *All-inclusive.*

$$ ALL-INCLUSIVE FAMILY Fodor's Choice ★ 🏨 **Chumbe Island.** The island's ecotourism concept was the brainstorm of a German conservationist who, since the early 1990s, has succeeded in developing it as one of the world's foremost marine sanctuaries. **Pros:** excellent food and involved staff; excellent snorkeling this side of Zanzibar. **Cons:** the boat trip from Stone Town takes 45 minutes, and there's only one departure a day (later departures cost extra); expensive for this level of rustic but some will like it. [$] *Rooms from: $280* ✉ *Chumbe Island, Coral Park* 🌐 *www.chumbeisland.com* 🛏 *7 bungalows* 🍽 *All-inclusive.*

$$$$ RESORT 🏨 **Kilindi.** Kilindi whisks you away to a private, luxury resort on the northern-most part of the island with a combination of barefoot luxury and excellent service. **Pros:** wonderful on-site spa; your own butler to cater to your needs; remote and private location. **Cons:** location might be too remote for some. [$] *Rooms from: $650* ✉ *Kendwa* ☎ *255/272–50–0630* 🌐 *www.elewanacollection.com* 🛏 *15 rooms* 🍽 *All meals.*

$$$$ ALL-INCLUSIVE Fodor's Choice ★ 🏨 **Mnemba Island Lodge.** For the ultimate beach escape where time stands still, where sand, sea, and horizon melt into each other, where there's exclusivity, total relaxation, and impeccable food and service, it would be hard to find anywhere in the world as alluring as Mnemba Island Lodge on &Beyond's privately owned Mnemba Island. **Pros:** there's a snorkeling reef just off the shore that you can swim out to; plenty of privacy. **Cons:** you need to book in advance, as it's a sought-after destination; if you don't dive you're not taking advantage of the on-site master and being able to go out whenever you like; the doves can be noisy as can the hoards of other divers and tourists who arrive twice a day even though they are not allowed on the island (there is a hefty fine). [$] *Rooms from: $1600* ✉ *Mnemba Island* ☎ *27–11/809–4300 in Johannesburg* 🌐 *www.mnemba-island.com* 🛏 *10 bungalows* 🍽 *All-inclusive.*

$ HOTEL 🏨 **Ras Nungwi.** An hour-plus drive from the airport through local towns and over bumpy roads will be worth it because once you arrive at Ras

Nungwi, you'll feel as if you've stepped into another world. **Pros:** gorgeous beach; away from the madding crowds. **Cons:** an hour's drive from Stone Town; excursions are expensive and dining options are limited if you are not on full board. $ *Rooms from: $160* ✉ *Nungwi Peninsula, Nungwi* ☎ *024/223–3767* ⊕ *www.rasnungwi.com* ⥂ *32 rooms* ☾ *Closed Apr. and May* ❮❍❯ *Breakfast.*

$ ⬚ **The Zanzibari.** Although the standard rooms are somewhat plain
RESORT   and located in a two-story block, they all have balconies overlooking the beautiful gardens and, on the upper level, the turquoise sea beyond. **Pros:** quite and out of the way little hotel; tours and snorkeling can be arranged. **Cons:** basic rooms; swimming depends on the tides. $ *Rooms from: $196* ✉ *Nungwi Peninsula, Nungwi* ☎ *255/772–222–919* ⊕ *www.thezanzibari.com* ⥂ *8 rooms, 3 suites* ❮❍❯ *Some meals.*

IN STONE TOWN

$ ⬚ **Beyt al Chai.** This former tea house recalls days gone by, a small hotel
B&B/INN   with a whole lot of character and great service. **Pros:** authentic property; excellent location. **Cons:** basic; breakfast is decent but not incredible. $ *Rooms from: $115* ✉ *Kilele Sq., Stone Town* ☎ *0774/444–111* ⊕ *www.stonetowninn.com* ⥂ *5 rooms* ❮❍❯ *Breakfast.*

$$ ⬚ **Emerson Spice Hotel.** Two gorgeous historic buildings right in the center
B&B/INN   of the maze of alleyways that make up Stone Town have been converted into a hotel with whimsically wonderful rooms, each with a different theme. **Pros:** each room has a mobile phone for usage during your stay; enormous rooms; authentic ambience. **Cons:** lots of stairs; no mod-cons such as Wi-Fi, TV, or fridge; rooms can be gloomy. $ *Rooms from: $250* ✉ *Tharia St., Kiponda, Stone Town* ☎ *0775/046–395* ⊕ *www.emersonspice.com* ⥂ *11 rooms* ❮❍❯ *Breakfast.*

$ ⬚ **Kisiwa House.** This stylish boutique hotel, housed in a beautifully
HOTEL   restored 19th-century Zanzibari townhouse, manages to combine old-
Fodor's Choice   fashioned authenticity—steep wooden staircases, high ceilings, an inner
★   courtyard, and pretty rooftop restaurant—with modern touches, such as the contemporary art on the walls, flat-screen TVs, and large, modern, luxurious bathrooms that have bathtubs as well as showers. **Pros:** rates are very reasonable considering the amenities; great location; free Wi-Fi. **Cons:** lots of steep stairs; no views from the rooms. $ *Rooms from: $210* ✉ *572 Baghani St., Stone Town* ☎ *024/223–5654* ⊕ *www.kisiwahouse.com* ⥂ *11 rooms* ❮❍❯ *Breakfast.*

$$$ ⬚ **Mashariki Palace Hotel.** The street entrance might seem dilapidated at
HOTEL   first but as you round the corner you are greeted by giant white columns
Fodor's Choice   extending far into the ceilings—a grand entrance recalling the centuries
★   of sultans, traders, and adventurers that have graced Zanzibar's shores. **Pros:** beautiful rooms in an historical setting; excellent service; close to attractions. **Cons:** there are a lot of stairs; there is a school and temple next door that can be noisy at certain times of the day (but it does not last long). $ *Rooms from: $475* ✉ *Nyumba Ya Moto St., Stone Town* ☎ *255/776–775–774* ⊕ *www.masharikipalacehotel.com* ⥂ *18 rooms* ❮❍❯ *Breakfast.*

$$ ⬚ **Zanizibar Palace Hotel.** Within easy walking distance from Stone Town's
B&B/INN   main attractions this little boutique hotel is a trip back in time with antique furniture and traditional materials conveying Zanzibar's varied and rich history. **Pros:** romantic and authentic experience without

breaking the bank; service is wonderful; on-site spa. **Cons:** not much in the way of views. $ *Rooms from: $267* ⊠ *Kiponda St., Stone Town* ☎ *255/24–22322–30* ⊕ *www.zanzibarpalacehotel.com* ⇨ *9 rooms* ⦿ *Breakfast.*

$$
HOTEL
☖ **The Zanzibar Serena Inn.** On one side of Shangani Square, on the fringe of Stone Town, this beautiful hotel is the result of the restoration of two of Zanzibar's historic buildings: the old Telekoms building, an original colonial-era building, and the Chinese doctors' residence, where several local Chinese doctors practiced their traditional medicine. **Pros:** gorgeous location and swimming pool with views. **Cons:** lots of stairs; often fully booked; on-site beach not great; large hotel which can get loud and busy and service is slow at best; rooms around the bar area can be noisy. $ *Rooms from: $345* ⊠ *Shangani St., Stone Town* ☎ *024/223–3051* ⊕ *www.serenahotels.com* ⇨ *51 rooms* ⦿ *Breakfast.*

MAFIA ISLAND

Just 160 km (99 miles) south of Zanzibar is an archipelago of inland bays and lagoons, towering palm groves dotted with ancient 8th-century ruins, and one of the most interesting marine ecosystems and coral reefs in Tanzania. With a population of only 50,000 people, what was once a safe haven for ships searching for supplies now offers up a far more intimate island escape with a bounty of wildlife above and below the waters with only a few accommodation options and few tourists. The Marine Park was one of the first established in Tanzania, spanning 821 km (510 miles) and bordered by a barrier reef teeming with marine life. Whale sharks normally frequent the waters around Mafia from October to March. Walk through the ancient ruins at Kisimani Mafia, Kanga, Kua on Juani Island and Chole Island, visit some of the most famous boat builders in East Africa, or join a sunset cruise to spot the giant flying fox (pteropus)

GETTING HERE AND AROUND

There are daily flights from Dar es Salaam and Zanzibar to Mafia Island via Coastal Air and Zanair. Generally there are taxis at the airport, but it is best to arrange transport with your accommodation. If you are feeling brave you can take a Bajaj, which will cost around 10,000 Tsh. Roads are under construction across Mafia so be prepared for a bumpy ride. All snorkeling and diving activities inside Chole Bay are tide-dependent. It's better to book your diving as you arrive on the island and not through tour operators, unless you are an experienced diver. Take advantage of any good offers, but do so through the dive centers directly. The entry fee into the marine park is US$20 per day, to be paid in cash at the offices on the way into the park. There is no international ATM on the island but you can change foreign currency at the bank in Kilondoni.

WHERE TO STAY

Options for budget accommodation on Mafia Island are limited, and most of them will be either outside of the Marine Park, buried deep in the villages and in varying degrees of maintenance.

$
RESORT
☖ **Big Blue Dive Center.** If you are in Mafia to dive but also are watching the wallet then Big Blue has a selection of affordable tents and bungalows. **Pros:** budget friendly and right on the beach. **Cons:** rather spartan

accommodation; tents can be hot during peak summer. $ *Rooms from: $45* ✉ *Utende Beach* ☎ *255/787–474–108* ⊕ *www.bigblumafia.com* ⬦ *3 Bungalows, 6 tents* ⦿ *No meals.*

$$
ALL-INCLUSIVE

⬚ **Butiama Beach.** Situated to the southwest of the island Butiama Beach is one of the best accommodations outside of the marine park with well-appointed, colorful bungalows and inviting hammocks. **Pros:** best place for fishing or water sports and whale sightings; large, open dining and relaxation spaces with a swimming pool; close to the airport. **Cons:** outside of the Marine Park so you travel some distance on a bumpy road to get to dive sites; next to main port area so beach is not always private; room bookings are on a first-come, first-served basis and some have limited sea views. $ *Rooms from: $250* ✉ *Butiama Beach* ☎ *255/787–474084* ⊕ *www.butiamabeach.com* ⬦ *15 rooms* ⦿ *All-inclusive.*

$$
ALL-INCLUSIVE
Fodor's Choice
★

⬚ **Chole Mjini.** Climbing up the winding steps rotating around the trunk of a baobab tree, the tree houses of Chole Mjini will fulfill anyone with an island castaway fantasy. **Pros:** sleeping in a unique setting; dinner by candlelight in an ancient ruin; wonderful village atmosphere. **Cons:** no toilets in the tree house, you have to walk down stairs to get to the bathroom at night; no swimming beach; most activities are not included in the price; outhouse-style toilets. $ *Rooms from: $250* ✉ *Chole Island* ☎ *078/771–2427* ⊕ *www.cholemjini.com* ⬦ *6 treehouses, 1 ground house* ⦿ *All-inclusive.*

$
ALL-INCLUSIVE

⬚ **Kinasi Lodge.** Nestled on a hillside between an old cashew and coconut plantation, Kinasi has some of the most beautiful views of all the lodges on Mafia Island. **Pros:** gorgeous views; plenty of water sports or lounging; rooms are spread out enough to offer privacy. **Cons:** beach disappears at high tide; Wi-Fi in main dining area only; keep your rooms closed in the evenings to avoid mosquitoes; very hilly to get to lower lodges; people with mobility issues may struggle. $ *Rooms from: $160* ✉ *Mafia Island* ☎ *255/777–42–4588* ⊕ *www.kinasilodge.com* ⬦ *7 sea front, 7 garden* ⦿ *All-inclusive.*

$
ALL-INCLUSIVE

⬚ **Mafia Island Lodge.** Mafia Island Lodge suits large dive groups with one of the only beaches that is not consumed by the tide, and it's spacious and neat—perfect if you're spending most of your time outside and in the water. **Pros:** direct access to friendly and helpful dive center; spacious beachfront property great for families; the renovated superior rooms are the best. **Cons:** rooms are basic but can be a bit pricey for the standard; food can be hit or miss; tiny showers. $ *Rooms from: $130* ✉ *Utende* ☎ *255/786–3030–42* ⊕ *www.mafialodge.com* ⬦ *14 superior, 16 standard, 2 family rooms* ⊘ *Closed Apr.–June* ⦿ *All-inclusive.*

$$
ALL-INCLUSIVE

⬚ **Pole Pole.** In Swahili Pole Pole means to go slowly, and at this intimate little resort this is very much encouraged. **Pros:** privacy; lovely new swimming pool; on-site yoga instructor. **Cons:** strong winds can feel like your rooms are being buffeted; can only walk to dive shop at low tide. $ *Rooms from: $250* ✉ *Utende* ☎ *0755/3030–44* ⊕ *www. polepole.com* ⬦ *7 bungalows* ⦿ *All-inclusive.*

5

SOUTH AFRICA

6

WELCOME TO SOUTH AFRICA

TOP REASONS TO GO

★ **Big Game.** You're guaranteed to see big game—including the Big Five—both in national parks and at many private lodges.

★ **Escape the Crowds.** South Africa's game parks are rarely crowded. You'll see more game with fewer other visitors than almost anywhere else in Africa.

★ **Luxury Escapes.** Few other sub-Saharan countries can offer South Africa's high standards of accommodation, service, and food amid gorgeous surroundings of bush, beach, mountains, and desert.

★ **Take the Family.** All the national parks accept children (choose a malaria-free one if your kids are small), and many private lodges have fantastic children's programs.

★ **Beyond the Parks.** Visit Cape Town, one of the most beautiful and stylish cities in the world; the nearby stunning Winelands; the inspiring scenery of the Garden Route; the vibrant port city of Durban; and glorious, soft white-sand beaches.

BOTSWANA

4 Kgalagadi Transfrontier Park

Tswalu Kalahari Reserve

Bokspits

NAMIBIA

Kimberley

Vioolsdrif

Orange River

NAMAQUALAND

GREAT KAROO

Laaiplek

Addo Elephant Park

Wellington

CAPE FOLDED MOUNTAINS

Cape Town

GARDEN ROUTE

Wilderness

Plettenberg

Port Elizabe

Mossel Bay

Cape of Good Hope

Cape Agulhas

ATLANTIC OCEAN

1 **Kruger National Park.** A visit to Kruger, one of the world's great game parks, may rank among the best experiences of your life. With its amazing diversity of scenery, trees, amphibians, reptiles, birds, and mammals, Kruger is a place to safari at your own pace and where you can choose between upscale private camps or simple campsites.

2 **Sabi Sand Game Reserve.** The most famous and exclusive of South Africa's private reserves, this 153,000-acre park is home to dozens of private lodges, including the world-famous MalaMala and Londolozi. With perhaps the highest game and leopard density of any private reserve in Southern Africa, Sabi Sand fully deserves its exalted reputation.

ZIMBABWE

Messina

Kruger National Park **1**

Pietersburg

MPUMALANGA

MOZAMBIQUE

Pilanesberg National Park

Sabi Sand Game Reserve **2**

Madikwe Game Reserve

Nelspruit

PRETORIA

Soweto   Johannesburg

Mkuze Game Reserve

SWAZILAND

Phinda Private Reserve

Itala Game Reserve

Thanda Game Reserve

Ulundi **3**

Hluhluwe-Umfolozi Game Reserve

Drakensberg Park

Bloemfontein

Richards Bay

LESOTHO

Pietermaritzburg

DRAKENSBERG MOUNTAINS

Durban

Margate

EASTERN CAPE

Umtata

INDIAN OCEAN

East London

Grahamstown

Shamwari Game Reserve

0   200 mi

0   200 km

GETTING ORIENTED

South Africa lies at the very foot of the continent, where the Atlantic and Indian oceans meet. Not only geographically and sceni-cally diverse, it's a nation of more than 47 million people of varied origins, cultures, languages, and beliefs. Its cities and much of its infrastructure are thoroughly modern—Johannesburg could pass for any large American city. It's only when you venture into the rural areas or see the huge satellite squatter camps outside the cities or come face-to-face with the Big Five that you see an entirely different South Africa.

6

3 KwaZulu-Natal Parks. Zululand's Hluhluwe-Imfolozi is tiny—less than 6% of Kruger's size—but delivers the Big Five plus all the plains game. It has about 1,250 species of plants and trees—more than you'll find in entire countries. Mkuze and Itala are even smaller, but worth a visit, and if you're looking for the ultimate in luxury, stay at Phinda or Thanda private reserves.

4 Kgalagadi Transfron-tier Park. Together with its neighbor, Botswana's Gemsbok National Park, this park covers more than 38,000 square km (14,670 square miles)—one of very few conservation areas of this magnitude left in the world. Its stark, desolate beauty shelters huge black-mane Kalahari lions among other predators and provides brilliant birding, especially birds of prey.

Claire Baranowski, Angus Begg, Christopher Clark, Karena du Plessis, Christine Marot, Lee Middleton, Kate Turkington, Andrea Weiss

Since 1994, when Nelson Mandela spearheaded its peaceful transition to democracy, South Africa has been one of the greatest tourist destinations in the world. And it's not difficult to see why. The country is stable and affordable, with an excellent infrastructure; friendly, interesting, amazingly diverse people; and enough stunning sights, sounds, scenery, and attractions to make even the most jaded traveler sit up and take notice. And nearly everybody speaks English—a huge bonus for international visitors.

South Africa has always teemed with game. That's what drew the early European explorers, who aimed to bring something exotic home with them. After all, as Pliny the Elder, one of Africa's earliest explorers, wrote almost 2,000 years ago, "*ex Africa semper aliquid novi*" (translated, "Out of Africa always comes something new"). Sometimes it was a giraffe, a rhinoceros, a strange bird, or an unheard-of plant.

In the latter half of the 19th century, Dr. Livingstone, Scotland's most famous Christian missionary, opened up much of the interior on his evangelizing expeditions, as did the piratical Englishman Cecil John Rhodes, who famously made his fortune on the Kimberley diamond mines and planned an unsuccessful Cape-to-Cairo railway line. About the same time, lured by the rumors of gold and instant fortunes, hundreds of hunters came to the lowveld to lay their hands on much-sought-after skins, horns, and ivory. Trophy hunters followed, vying with one another to see how many animals they could shoot in one day—often more than 100 each.

Paul Kruger, president of the Transvaal Republic (a 19th-century Boer country that occupied a portion of present-day South Africa), took the unprecedented visionary step of establishing a protected area for the wildlife in the lowveld region; in 1898 Kruger National Park was born.

South Africa has 22 national parks covering deserts, wetland and marine areas, forests, mountains, scrub, and savanna. Hunting safaris

FAST FACTS

Size 1,221,037 square km (471,442 square miles).

Capital Pretoria (administrative capital); Cape Town (legislative capital); Bloemfontein (judicial capital).

Number of National Parks 22: Addo Elephant, Agulhas, Augrabies Falls, Bontebok, Camdeboo, Golden Gate Highlands, Karoo, Kruger, Mapungubwe, Marakele, Mokala, Mountain Zebra, Namaqua, Table Mountain, Tankwa Karoo, Tsitsikamma, West Coast, and Wilderness National Parks; Ais/Richtersveld and Kgalagadi Transfrontier Parks; Knysna National Lake Area; uKhahlamba/Drakensberg Park.

Number of Private Reserves Hundreds, including Sabi Sands and KwaZulu-Natal's Phinda and Thanda.

Population Approximately 48 million.

Big Five The gang's all here.

Language South Africa has 11 official languages: Afrikaans, English, Ndebele, North and South Sotho, Swati, Tsonga, Tswana, Venda, Xhosa, and Zulu. English is widely spoken.

Time SAST (South African Standard Time), seven hours ahead of North American Eastern Standard Time.

6

are still popular but are strictly controlled by the government, and licenses are compulsory. Although hunting is a controversial issue, the revenue is substantial and can be ploughed into sustainable conservation, and the impact on the environment is minimal. Increasingly, wildlife conservation is linked with community development; many conservation areas have integrated local communities, the wildlife, and the environment, with benefits for all. Londolozi, MalaMala, Phinda, and Pafuri Camp are internationally acclaimed role models for linking tourism with community-development projects.

Although the "**Big Five**" was originally a hunting term for those animals that posed the greatest risk to hunters on foot—buffalo, elephants, leopards, lions, and rhinos—it's used today as the most important criterion for evaluating a lodge or reserve. But let the lure of the Big Five turn your safari into a treasure hunt and you'll miss the overall wilderness experience. Don't overlook the bush's other treasures, from desert meerkats and forest bush babies to antelopes, the handsome caracal, and spotted genets. Add to these hundreds of birds, innumerable insects, trees, flowers, shrubs, and grasses. Don't forget to search for the "**Little Five**": the buffalo weaver, elephant shrew, leopard tortoise, lion ant, and rhinoceros beetle. A guided bush walk may let you see these little critters and more.

PLANNING

WHEN TO GO

In the north, summers are sunny and hot (never humid), with short afternoon thunderstorms. Winter days are bright and sunny, but nights can be frosty. Although November through January is Cape Town's most popular time, with glorious sunshine and long, light evenings, the best weather is in February and March. Cape winters (May–August) are unpredictable with cold, windy, rainy days interspersed with glorious sun. The coastal areas of KwaZulu-Natal are warm year-round, but summers are steamy and hot. The ocean water is warmest in February, but it seldom dips below 17°C (65°F).

GETTING HERE AND AROUND

Countless cities, towns, streets, parks, and more have gotten or will get new monikers, both to rid the country of names that recall the apartheid era and to honor the previously unsung. The names in this book were accurate at time of writing but may still change.

AIR TRAVEL

At this writing, only South African Airways and Delta provide direct service from the United States to South Africa, but flights routed through Europe may be preferable since they allow you a stop en route.

In peak season (midsummer, which is from December to the end of February, and South African school vacations), give yourself at least a half hour extra at the airport for domestic flights, as the check-in lines can be endless—particularly on flights to the coast at the start of vacations and back to Johannesburg's O. R. Tambo International Airport at the end.

If you are visiting a game lodge deep in the bush, you will be arriving by light plane—and you will be restricted in what you can bring. Excess luggage can usually be stored with the operator until your return. Don't just gloss over this: charter operators take weight very seriously, and some will charge you for an extra ticket if you insist on bringing excess baggage

AIRPORTS

Most international flights arrive at and depart from Johannesburg's O. R. Tambo International Airport, 19 km (12 miles) from the city. The country's other major airports are in Cape Town and Durban, but international flights departing from Cape Town often stop in Johannesburg. O. R. Tambo has a tourist information desk, a V.A.T. refund office, several ATMs, and a computerized accommodations service. If you're leaving O. R. Tambo's international terminal (Terminal A), the domestic terminal (Terminal B) is connected by a busy and fairly long walkway. ■TIP→ Allow 10–15 minutes' walking time between international and domestic terminals.

Cape Town International is 19 km (12 miles) southeast of the city, and Durban International is 16 km (10 miles) north of the city. If you are traveling to or from either Johannesburg or Cape Town airport (and, to a lesser extent, Durban) be aware of the time of day. Traffic can be horrendous between 7 and 9 in the morning and between about 3:30 and 6 in the evening.

The other major cities are served by small airports that are really easy to navigate. Port Elizabeth is the main airport for the Eastern Cape, George serves the Garden Route, and the closest airports to Kruger National Park are the small airports at Nelspruit, Hoedspruit, and Phalaborwa. Most airports are managed by the Airports Company of South Africa.

International Airports Cape Town International Airport (*CPT*). ✉ *Matroos-fontein, Cape Town* ☎ *021/937–1200* ⊕ *www.capetown-airport.com.* **Durban International Airport** (*DUR*). ✉ *King Shaka Dr., La Mercy, Durban* ☎ *032/436–6585* ⊕ *www.kingshakainternational.co.za.* **O. R. Tambo International Airport** (*JNB*). ✉ *O. R. Tambo Airport Rd., Johannesburg* ☎ *011/921–6911* ⊕ *www.johannesburg-airport.com.*

FLIGHTS

South Africa's international airline is South African Airways (SAA), which offers nonstop service between Johannesburg and New York–JFK (JFK) and Washington–Dulles (IAD), though some flights from Dulles make a stopover in Dakar, Senegal. Delta also offers nonstop service from the United States to South Africa. Flight times from the U.S. East Coast range from 15 hours (from Atlanta to Johannesburg on Delta) to almost 20 hours (on Delta via Amsterdam). When booking flights, check the routing carefully; some involve stopovers of an hour or two, which may change from day to day. European airlines serving South Africa are British Airways, KLM, Virgin Atlantic, Lufthansa, and Air France.

Three major domestic airlines have flights connecting South Africa's principal airports. SA Airlink and SA Express are subsidiaries of SAA, and Comair is a subsidiary of British Airways. Comair and SAA serve Livingstone, Zambia (for Victoria Falls); Air Zimbabwe and SAA serve Victoria Falls airport in Zimbabwe.

Recent years have seen an explosion of low-cost carriers serving popular domestic routes in South Africa with regularly scheduled flights. Kulula.com and Mango provide reasonably priced domestic air tickets if you book in advance. Phakalane Airways provides service to airports in the Northern Cape. The only downside is that they have fewer flights per day and aren't always cheaper than SAA.

Airlines Air France ☎ *0861/340–340 in South Africa, 800/237–2747 in the U.S.* ⊕ *www.airfrance.co.za.* **British Airways** ☎ *011/441–8600 in South Africa, 800/247–9297 in the U.S.* ⊕ *www.britishairways.com.* **Delta** ☎ *800/241–4141 in the U.S., 011/408–8200 in South Africa* ⊕ *www.delta.com.* **KLM** ☎ *0860/247–747 in South Africa, 866/434–0320 in the U.S.* ⊕ *www.klm.com.* **Lufthansa** ☎ *0861/842–538 in South Africa, 800/645–3880 in the U.S.* ⊕ *www.lufthansa.com.* **South African Airways** ☎ *0860/003–146 in South Africa, 800/521–4845 in the U.S.* ⊕ *www.flysaa.com.* **United** ☎ *011/463–1170 in South Africa, 800/864–8331 in the U.S.* ⊕ *www.united.com.* **Virgin Atlantic** ☎ *011/340–3400 in South Africa, 800/862–8621 in the U.S.* ⊕ *www.virgin-atlantic.com.*

6

Domestic Airlines Air Zimbabwe ☎ *263/457–5021* ⊕ *www.airzimbabwe. aero.* **British Airways Comair** ☎ *011/921–0222 in South Africa, 0860/435–922 in South Africa (toll-free), 800/247–9297 in the U.S.* ⊕ *www.britishairways. com.* **Kulula** ☎ *086/158–5852 in South Africa* ⊕ *www.kulula.com.* **Mango** ☎ *011/086–6100 in Johannesburg, 021/815–4100 in Cape Town, 086/101–0002 in South Africa (toll-free)* ⊕ *www.flymango.com.* **Phakalane Airways.** Phakalane Airways provides air connections between Kimberley, Upington, and Springbok in conjunction with the Northern Cape Provincial Department. ✉ *Springbok* ☎ *053/492–0001* ⊕ *www.phakalaneairways.co.za.* **SA Airlink** ☎ *011/451–7300 in South Africa, 010/590–3170 in South Africa* ⊕ *www.flyairlink.com.* **SA Express** ☎ *086/172–9227 in South Africa (toll-free)* ⊕ *www.flyexpress.aero.*

CHARTER FLIGHTS

Charters are common for getting to safari lodges and remote destinations throughout southern Africa. These aircraft are well maintained and are almost always booked by your lodge or travel agent. The major charter companies run daily shuttles from O. R. Tambo to destinations such as Kruger Park. On-demand flights are very expensive for independent travelers, as they require minimum passenger loads. If it's just two passengers, you will be charged for the vacant seats. Keep in mind that you probably won't get to choose the charter company you fly with. The aircraft you get depends on the number of passengers flying and can vary from very small (you will sit in the copilot's seat) to a much more comfortable commuter plane.

Because of the limited space and size of the aircraft, charter carriers observe strict luggage regulations: luggage must be soft-sided and weigh no more than 57 pounds (and often less); on many charter flights the weight cannot exceed 33 pounds.

Charter Companies African Ramble ☎ *084/359–2929, 083/375–6514* ⊕ *www.aframble.co.za.* **Federal Air** ☎ *011/395–9000* ⊕ *www.fedair.com.* **Wilderness Air** ⊕ *www.wilderness-air.com.*

CAR TRAVEL

South Africa has a superb network of multilane roads and highways. Distances are vast, so guard against fatigue (a definite factor for jet-lagged drivers), which is an even bigger killer than alcohol. Toll roads, scattered among the main routes, charge anything from R10 to R60.

You can drive in South Africa for up to six months on any English-language license. South Africa's Automobile Association publishes a range of maps, atlases, and travel guides, available for purchase on its website (⊕ *www.aa.co.za*). The commercial website Drive South Africa (⊕ *www.drivesouthafrica.co.za.*) has everything you need to know about driving in the country, including road safety and driving distances. ⚠ Carjackings can and do occur with such frequency that certain high-risk areas are marked by permanent carjacking signs

GASOLINE

Service stations (open 24 hours) are positioned at regular intervals along all major highways in South Africa. There are no self-service stations. In return, tip the attendant R2–R5 (more if you've filled the tank). South Africa has a choice of unleaded or leaded gasoline, and many vehicles operate on diesel—be sure you get the right fuel. Gasoline is measured in liters, and the cost is higher than in the United States. When driving long distances, check your routes carefully, as the distances between towns—and hence gas stations—can be more than 100 miles.

PARKING

In the countryside, parking is mostly free, but you will almost certainly need to pay for parking in cities, which will probably run you about R5–R8 per hour. Many towns have an official attendant (who should be wearing a vest of some sort) who will log the number of the spot you park in; you're asked to pay up front for the amount of time you expect to park. If the guard is unofficial, acknowledge them on arrival, ask them to look after your car, and pay a few rand when you return (they depend on these tips). At pay-and-display parking lots you pay in advance; other garages expect payment at the exit. Many (such as those at shopping malls and airports) require that you pay for your parking before you return to your car (at kiosks near the exits to the parking areas). Your receipt ticket allows you to exit. Just read the signs carefully.

RENTAL CARS

Rates are similar to those in the United States. Some companies charge more on weekends, so it's best to get a range of quotes before booking your car.

For a car with automatic transmission and air-conditioning, you'll pay slightly less for a car that doesn't have unlimited mileage. When comparing prices, make sure you're getting the same thing. Some companies quote prices without insurance, some include 80% or 90% coverage, and some quote with 100% protection. Get all terms in writing before you leave on your trip.

There's no need to rent a 4x4 vehicle, as all roads are paved, including those in Kruger National Park.

You can often save some money by booking a car through a broker, who will access the car from one of the main agencies. Smaller, local agencies often give a much better price, but the car must be returned in the same city. This is pretty popular in Cape Town but not so much in other centers.

To rent a car you need to be 23 years or older and have held a driver's license for three years. Younger international drivers can rent from some companies but will pay a penalty. You need to get special permission to take rental cars into neighboring countries (including Lesotho and Swaziland). Most companies allow additional drivers, but some charge.

CAR-RENTAL INSURANCE

In South Africa it's necessary to buy special insurance if you plan to cross borders into neighboring countries, but CDW and TDW (collision damage waiver and theft-damage waiver) are optional on domestic rentals. Any time you are considering crossing a border with your rental vehicle, you must inform the rental company ahead of time to fulfill any paperwork requirements and pay additional fees.

Emergency Services General emergency number ☎ *112 from mobile phone, 10111 from landline, 107 for Cape Town only.*

Local Agencies Car Mania ☎ *021/447–3001* ⊕ *www.carmania.co.za.* **Value Car Hire** ☎ *021/386–7699* ⊕ *www.valuerentalcar.com.*

Major Agencies Avis ☎ *0861/021–111, 011/387–8431* ⊕ *www.avis.co.za.* **Budget** ☎ *800/472–3325* ⊕ *www.budget.co.za.* **Europcar** ☎ *0861/131–000, 011/479–4000* ⊕ *www.europcar.co.za.* **Hertz** ☎ *021/935–4800* ⊕ *www.hertz.co.za.* **National Car Rental** ☎ *877/222–9058* ⊕ *www.nationalcar.com.*

ABOUT THE RESTAURANTS

South Africa's cities and towns are full of dining options, from chain restaurants like the popular Nando's to chic cafés. Indian food and Cape Malay dishes are regional favorites in Cape Town, while traditional smoked meats and sausages are available countrywide. In South Africa dinner is eaten at night and lunch at noon. Restaurants serve breakfast until about 11:30; a few serve breakfast all day. If you're staying at a game lodge, your mealtimes will revolve around the game drives—usually coffee and *rusks* (similar to biscotti) early in the morning, more coffee and probably muffins on the first game drive, a huge brunch in the late morning, no lunch, tea and something sweet in the late afternoon before the evening game drive, cocktails and snacks on the drive, and a substantial supper, or dinner, at about 8 or 8:30.

Many restaurants accustomed to serving tourists accept credit cards, usually Visa and American Express, with MasterCard increasingly accepted.

Most restaurants welcome casual dress, including jeans and sneakers, but draw the line at shorts and a halter top at dinner, except for restaurants on the beach.

ABOUT THE LODGES AND HOTELS

Be warned that lodging terminology in South Africa can be misleading. The term *lodge* is a particularly tricky one. A guest lodge or a game lodge is almost always an upmarket, full-service facility with loads of extra attractions. But the term *lodge* when applied to city hotels often indicates a minimum-service hotel, like the City and Town Lodges and Holiday Inn Garden Courts. A backpacker lodge, however, is essentially a hostel.

A *rondavel* can be a small cabin, often in a rounded shape, and its cousin, the *banda,* can be anything from a basic stand-alone structure to a Quonset hut. Think very rustic.

Be sure you understand the hotel's cancellation policy. Some places allow you to cancel without any kind of penalty—even if you prepaid to secure a discounted rate—if you cancel at least 24 hours in advance. Others require you to cancel a week in advance or penalize you the cost of one night. Small inns and B&Bs are most likely to require you to cancel far in advance. Always have written confirmation of your booking when you check in. ■TIP→ **Most hotels allow children under a certain** age to stay in their parents' room at no extra charge, but others charge for them as extra adults, and some don't allow children under 12 at all. Ask about the policy on children before checking in, and make sure you find out the cutoff age for discounts.

In South Africa, most accommodations from hotels to guesthouses do include breakfast in the rate. Most game lodges include all meals, or they may be all-inclusive (including alcohol as well). All hotels listed have private bath unless otherwise noted.

WHAT IT COSTS IN SOUTH AFRICAN RAND				
	$	$$	$$$	$$$$
Restaurants	under R100	R100–R150	R151–R200	over R200
Hotels	under R1,500	R1,500–R2,500	R2,501–R3,500	over R3,500

Restaurant prices are the average cost of a main course at dinner or, if dinner is not served, at lunch. Hotel prices are the lowest cost of a standard double room in high season.

COMMUNICATIONS

6

INTERNET

Most hotels have Wi-Fi. Stores such as Woolworths, restaurants such as Wimpy, and most airports offer a countrywide Wi-Fi service called AlwaysOn (⊕ *www.alwayson.co.za*) that allows you 30 minutes of free Wi-Fi per day. If you need more time, you can pay for it.

PHONES

The country code for South Africa is 27. When dialing from abroad, drop the initial 0 from local area codes.

CALLING WITHIN SOUTH AFRICA

When making a phone call in South Africa, always use the full 10-digit number, including the area code, even if you're in the same area. For directory assistance, call 1023. For operator-assisted national long-distance calls, call 1025. For international operator assistance, dial 10903#. These numbers are free if dialed from a Telkom (landline) phone but are charged at normal cell-phone rates from a mobile—and they're busy call centers. Directory inquiry numbers are different for each cell-phone network. Vodacom is 111, MTN is 200, and Cell C is 146. These calls are charged at normal rates, but the call is timed only from when it is actually answered.

CALLING OUTSIDE SOUTH AFRICA

When dialing out from South Africa, dial 00 before the international code. So, for example, you would dial 001 for the United States, since the country code for the United States is 1.

Internet calling like Skype also works well from the United States, but it's not always functional in South Africa, unless you're on a reliable high-speed Internet connection, which isn't available everywhere. However, if you have a South African "free" cell phone (meaning you can receive calls for free; all phones using an SA SIM card do this), someone in the United States can call you from their Skype account, for reasonable per-minute charges, and you won't be charged.

Access Codes AT&T Direct ☎ *800/288–2020 from South Africa* ⊕ *www.att. com.* **MCI Worldwide Access** ☎ *0800/990–011 from South Africa.* **Sprint International Access** ☎ *0800/990–001 from South Africa.*

MOBILE PHONES

Cell phones are ubiquitous and have quite extensive coverage. There are four cell-phone service providers in South Africa—Cell C, MTN, Virgin Mobile, and Vodacom—and you can buy these SIM cards, as well as airtime, in supermarkets for as little as R10 for the SIM card. (If you purchase SIM cards at the airport, you will be charged much more.) Bear in mind that your U.S. cell phone may not work with the local GSM system and/or that your phone may be blocked from using SIM cards outside of your plan if your phone is not unlocked. Basic but functional GSM cell phones start at R100, and are available at the mobile carrier shops as well as major department stores like Woolworths.

Cellular Abroad rents and sells GMS phones and sells SIM cards that work in many countries, but they cost a lot more than local solutions. Mobal rents mobiles and sells GSM phones (starting at $49) that will operate in 150 countries. Per-call rates vary throughout the world. Vodacom is the country's leading cellular network.

The least complicated way to make and receive phone calls is to obtain international roaming service from your cell-phone service provider before you leave home, but this can be expensive. Any phone that you take abroad must be unlocked by your company for you to be able to use it.

Contacts Cell C ☎ *084/140* ⊕ *www.cellc.co.za.* **Cellular Abroad** ☎ *800/287–5072 in the U.S., 800/3623–3333 abroad* ⊕ *www.cellularabroad.com.* **Mobal** ☎ *888/888–9162 in the U.S.* ⊕ *www.mobal.com.* **MTN** ☎ *083/173* ⊕ *www.mtn. co.za.* **Virgin Mobile** ☎ *0741/000–123* ⊕ *www.virginmobile.co.za.* **Vodacom** ☎ *082/111* ⊕ *www.vodacom.co.za.*

EMERGENCIES

If you specifically need an ambulance, you can get one by calling the special ambulance number or through the general emergency number. If you intend to scuba dive in South Africa, make sure you have DAN membership, which will be honored by Divers Alert Network South Africa (DANSA).

Emergency Contacts DANSA ☎ *0800/020–111 for emergency hotline, 27/828–106010 from outside S.A.* ⊕ *www.dansa.org.* **General emergency** ☎ *10111 from landline, 112 from mobile phone, 107 for Cape Town only.*

HEALTH AND SAFETY

The drinking water in South Africa is treated and, except in rural areas, is safe to drink. Many people filter it, though, to get rid of the chlorine, as that aseptic status does not come free. You can eat fresh fruits and salads and have ice in your drinks.

It is always wise for travelers to have medical insurance for travel that will also help with emergency evacuation (most safari operators require emergency evacuation coverage and may ask you to pay for it along with your tour payments). If you don't want general travel insurance, many companies offer medical-only policies.

Although the majority of visitors experience a crime-free trip to South Africa, it's essential to practice vigilance and extreme care. Do not walk alone at night, and exercise caution even during the day. Avoid wearing jewelry (even costume jewelry), don't invite attention by wearing an expensive camera around your neck, and don't flash a large wad of cash. If you are toting a handbag, wear the strap across your body; even better, wear a money belt, preferably hidden from view under your clothing. When sitting at airports or at restaurants, especially outdoor cafés, make sure to keep your bag on your lap or between your legs. Even better, loop the strap around your leg, or clip the strap around the table or chair.

Carjacking is another problem, with armed bandits often forcing drivers out of their vehicles at traffic lights, in driveways, or during a fake accident. Always drive with your windows closed and doors locked, don't stop for hitchhikers, and park in well-lighted places. At traffic lights, leave enough space between you and the vehicle in front so you can pull into another lane if necessary. In the unlikely event you are carjacked, don't argue, and don't look at the carjacker's face. Just get out of the car, or ask to be let out of the car. Do not try to keep any of your belongings—they are all replaceable, even that laptop with all that data on it. If you aren't given the opportunity to leave the car, try to stay calm, ostentatiously look away from the hijackers so they can be sure you can't identify them, and follow all instructions. Ask again, calmly, to be let out of the car.

Many places that are unsafe in South Africa will not bear obvious signs of danger. Purchase a good map and obtain comprehensive directions from your hotel or rental-car agent. Taking the wrong exit off a highway into a township could lead you straight to troubles. Many cities are ringed by "no go" areas. Learn from your hotel or the locals which areas to avoid. If you sense you have taken a wrong turn, drive toward a public area, such as a gas station, or building with an armed guard, before attempting to correct your mistake, which could just compound the problem. When parking, don't leave anything visible in the car; stow it all in the trunk—this includes clothing or shoes. As an added measure, leave the glove box open, to show there's nothing of value inside (take the rental agreement with you).

Before setting out on foot, ask your hotel concierge which route to take and how far you can safely go. Walk with a purposeful stride so you look like you know where you're going, and duck into a shop or café if you need to check a map, speak on your mobile phone. ⚠ **Don't walk while speaking on a cell phone.**

Lone women travelers need to be particularly vigilant about walking alone and locking their rooms. South Africa has one of the world's highest rates of rape. If you do attract someone who won't take a firm but polite "*No*" for an answer, appeal immediately to the hotel manager, bartender, or someone else who seems to be in charge. If you have to walk a short distance alone at night, such as from the hotel reception to your room in a dark motel compound or back from a café along a main street, have a plan, carry a whistle, and know what you'll do if you are grabbed.

MONEY MATTERS

Rand is the South African currency: 100 cents equal 1 rand. Dollar/rand exchange rate varies from day to day, but for the past couple years has hovered around a trading rate of US$1 to R8. Credit cards are widely accepted in shops, restaurants, and hotels, and there are plenty of ATMs at banks, service stations, and shopping malls.

VISITOR INFO

The official South Africa Tourism website and SouthAfrica.info are full of general country information.

⇨ *For Cape Town, Johannesburg, and Durban visitor information, see Visitor Info in each city's section below.*

Visitor Info SouthAfrica.info ⊕ *www.southafrica.info.* **South African Tourism** ☎ *800/593–1318 in U.S., 011/895–3000 in South Africa* ⊕ *www.southafrica.net.*

MUST-SEE PARKS

Unfortunately, you probably won't be able to see all of South Africa in one trip. So the chapter is broken down into Must-See Parks (Kruger National Park, Sabi Sand Game Reserve, KwaZulu-Natal Parks, Kgalagadi Transfrontier Park) and If You Have Time Parks (Tswalu Kalahari Reserve, Madikwe, Kwandwe, Addo Elephant Park, Pilanesberg Game Reserve) to help you better organize your time. We suggest that you read about all of them and then choose for yourself.

FIND YOUR CAUSE

The African Conservation Foundation (⊕ *www.africanconservation. org*) was established in 1999 to work as a link between like-minded conservation organizations with the goal of sharing resources and information. If you're looking for an organization to support and/or volunteer with, the website has a comprehensive list of available organizations.

KRUGER NATIONAL PARK

Game
★★★★★

Park Accessibility
★★★★★

Getting Around
★★★★★

Accommodations
★★★★★

Scenic Beauty
★★★★

Visiting Kruger is likely to be one of the greatest experiences of your life, truly providing ultimate "Wow!" moments. You'll be amazed at the diversity of life forms—the tallest (the giraffe), the biggest (the elephant), the funkiest (the dung beetle), the toothiest (the crocodile), and the glitziest (the lilac-breasted roller).

6

But it's not all game and safari. If you're into ancient human history, there are also major archaeological sites and fascinating San (Bushman) rock paintings. (There is ample evidence that prehistoric humans (*Homo erectus*) roamed the area between 500,000 and 100,000 years ago.) Founded in 1898 by Paul Kruger, president of what was then the Transvaal Republic, the park is a place to safari at your own pace, choosing between upscale private camps or simple campsites.

Kruger lies in the hot lowveld, a subtropical section of Mpumalanga and Limpopo provinces that abuts Mozambique. The park cuts a swath 80 km (50 miles) wide and 320 km (200 miles) long from Zimbabwe and the Limpopo River in the north to the Crocodile River in the south. It is divided into 16 macro eco-zones, each supporting a great variety of plants, birds, and animals, including 145 mammal species and almost 500 species of birds, some of which are not found elsewhere in South Africa. In 2002 a treaty was signed between South Africa, Zimbabwe, and Mozambique to form a giant conservation area, the Great Limpopo Transfrontier Park. It's a complex ongoing process, but once all the fences between Kruger, the Gonarezhou National Park in Mozambique, and the Limpopo National Park in Zimbabwe are finally removed, the Peace Park will be the largest conservation area in the world.

WHEN TO GO
Kruger National Park is hellishly hot in midsummer (November–March), but the bush is green, the animals are sleek and glossy, and the birdlife is prolific, even though high grass and dense foliage make spotting animals more difficult. Winter (May–September) is the high

season. The bush is at its dullest, driest, and most colorless, but the game is much easier to spot, as many trees are bare, the grass is low, and animals congregate around the few available permanent water sources. However, temperatures can drop to almost freezing at night and in the very early morning. The shoulder months of April and October are also good, and less crowded.

GETTING HERE AND AROUND

You can fly to Kruger Mpumalanga International Airport (KMIA), at Mbombela (Nelspruit); Skukuza Airport in Kruger itself; Hoedspruit Airport, close to Kruger's Orpen Gate; or Phalaborwa Airport (if you're going to the north of Kruger) from either Johannesburg or Cape Town. You can also drive to Kruger from Johannesburg in about six hours; if you drive, a 4x4 isn't necessary since all roads are paved.

Airports Hoedspruit Airport (*HDS*). ⊠ *Eastgate Airport, Hoedspruit* ☎ *015/793–3681* ✆ *eastgaterecep@kapama.co.za* ⊕ *www.eastgateairport. co.za.* **Kruger Mpumalanga International Airport (KMIA)** ☎ *013/753–7500* ⊕ *www.kmiairport.co.za.* **Phalaborwa Airport** (*PHW*). ⊠ *Access Rd., near Phalaborwa Gate, Phalaborwa.* **Skukuza Airport** (*SZK*). ⊠ *Skukuza* ⊕ *www. skukuzaairport.com.*

MONEY MATTERS

Kruger accepts credit cards, which are also useful for big purchases, but you should always have some small change for staff tips (tip your cleaning person R20 per hut per day) and for drinks and snacks at the camp shops, although camp shops also accept credit cards.

PLANNING YOUR TIME

How and where you tackle Kruger will depend on your time frame. With excellent roads and accommodations, it's a great place to drive yourself. If you don't feel up to driving or self-catering, you can choose a private lodge in Kruger itself or just outside the park and take the guided drives—although it's not quite the same as lying in bed and hearing the hyenas prowling around the camp fence or a lion roaring under the stars.

If you can spend a week here, start in the north at the very top of the park at the Punda Maria Camp, then make your way leisurely south to the very bottom at Crocodile Bridge Gate or Malelane Gate. With only three days or fewer, reserve one of the southern camps such as Berg-en-Dal or Lower Sabie and just plan to explore these areas. No matter where you go in Kruger, be sure to plan your route and accommodations (advance booking is essential). Game-viewing isn't an exact science: you might see all the Big Five plus hundreds of other animals, but you could see much less. Try to plan your route to include water holes and rivers, which afford your best opportunity to see game. Old Africa hands claim that the very early morning, when the camp gates open, is the best time for game-viewing, but it's all quite random—you could see a leopard drinking at noon, a breeding herd of elephants midmorning, or a lion pride dozing under a tree in the middle of the afternoon. You could also head out at dawn and find very little wildlife. Be sure to take at least one guided sunset drive; you won't likely forget the thrill of catching a nocturnal animal in the spotlight.

Visitor Information South African National Parks ☎ *012/428–9111* ✉ *reservations@sanparks.org* 🌐 *www.sanparks.org.*

WHERE TO STAY

It's impossible to recommend just one camp in Kruger. One person might prefer the intimacy of Kruger's oldest camp, Punda Maria, with its whitewashed thatch cottages; another might favor big, bustling Skukuza. A great way to experience the park is to stay in as many of the camps as possible. The SANParks website (🌐 *www.sanparks.org*) has a comprehensive overview of the different camps. The bushveld camps are more expensive than the regular camps, but offer much more privacy and exclusivity—but no shops, restaurants, or pools. If you seek the ultimate in luxury, stay at one of the private luxury lodges in the concession areas, some of which also have walking trails.

Reservations for park-operated accommodations should be made through **South African National Parks.** If air-conditioning is a must for you, be sure to check the website to confirm its availability in the accommodation of your choice. **■TIP→ Book your guided game drives and walks when you check in. Opt for the sunset drive. You'll get to see the animals coming to drink plus a thrilling night drive.**

6

LUXURY LODGES

$$$$ Fodor's Choice ★ 🏨 **Jock Safari Lodge.** This lodge, one of South Africa's loveliest, is set among 14,826 acres of private concession in southwest Kruger. Formerly owned by the National Parks Board, it's been managed as a private concession since 2000. Had Sir Percy Fitzpatrick, author of the famous *Jock of the Bushveld* and his canine superstar still been alive, they would have highly approved of today's camp, which is authentic and steeped in history. Twelve comfortable, spacious suites, each with a plunge pool, have stunning views over the Biyamiti River. The food, service, and rangers are superb, but the game-viewing is spectacular—think night drives in Kruger. **■TIP→ The nearby Fitzpatrick's Camp is great for families, and the rustic Explorer Camp offers one of South Africa's best two-day hiking trails.** **Pros:** authentic safari experience. **Cons:** busy in season. [$] *Rooms from: R10200* ✉ *Kruger National Park* ☎ *041/509–3000* ✉ *reservations@shamwarigroup.com* 🌐 *www.jocksafarilodge.com* 🛏 *12 suites* 🍴 *All meals.*

$$ FAMILY 🏨 **Protea Hotel Kruger Gate.** Set in its own small reserve 110 yards from the Paul Kruger Gate, this comfortable hotel is a luxury alternative to the sometimes bare-bones accommodations of Kruger's rest camps. It has two major advantages: fast access to the good game-viewing south-central portion of the park, plus an authentic bushveld feel. Rangers lead guided walks through the surrounding bush, and you can even sleep overnight in a tree house, or book a guided game drive (note that all these activities cost extra). Rooms, connected by a raised wooden walkway through indigenous forest, have Spanish-tile floors and standard hotel furniture. Self-catering chalets sleep six. **Pros:** good for families. **Cons:** you can't get away from the fact that this is a hotel with a hotel atmosphere. [$] *Rooms from: R2100* ✉ *Kruger Gate, Skukuza*

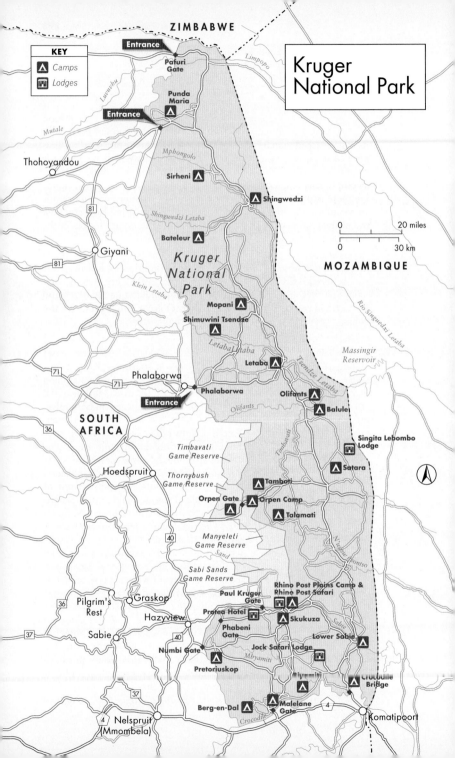

WALKING KRUGER

Kruger's seven wilderness trails accommodate eight hikers each. On three-day, two-night hikes, led by an armed ranger and local tracker, you walk in the mornings and evenings, with an afternoon siesta. You can generally get closer to animals in a vehicle, but many hikers can recount face-to-face encounters with everything from rhinos to lions.

Be prepared to walk up to 19 km (12 miles) a day. No one under 12 is allowed; those over 60 must have a doctor's certificate. Hikers sleep in rustic two-bed huts and share a reed-wall bathroom (flush toilets, bucket showers). Meals are simple (stews and barbecues); you bring your own drinks. In summer, walking is uncomfortably hot (and trails are cheaper); in winter, nights can be freezing—bring warm clothes and an extra blanket. Reserve 13 months ahead, when bookings open. The cost is about R3,430 per person per trail.

Bushman Trail. In the southwestern corner of the park, this trail takes its name from the San rock paintings and sites found in the area. The trail camp lies in a secluded valley dominated by granite hills and cliffs. Watch for white rhinos, elephants, and buffalo. Check in at Berg-en-Dal.

Metsi Metsi Trail. The permanent water of the nearby N'waswitsontso River makes this one of the best trails for winter game-viewing. Midway between Skukuza and Satara, the trail camp is in the lee of a mountain in an area of gorges, cliffs, and rolling savanna. Check in at Skukuza.

Napi Trail. White rhino sightings are common on this trail, which runs through mixed bushveld between Pretoriuskop and Skukuza. Other possibilities are black rhinos, cheetahs, leopards, elephants, and, if you're lucky, nomadic wild dogs. The camp is tucked into dense riverine forest at the confluence of the Napi and Biyamiti rivers. Check in at Pretoriuskop.

Nyalaland Trail. In the far north of the park, this trail camp sits among ancient baobab trees near the Luvuvhu River. Walk at the foot of huge rocky gorges and in dense forest. Look for highly sought-after birds: Böhm's spinetail, crowned eagle, and Pel's fishing owl. Hippos, crocs, elephants, buffalo, and the nyala antelope are almost a sure thing. Check in at Punda Maria.

Olifants Trail. This spectacularly sited camp sits on a high bluff overlooking the Olifants River and affords regular sightings of elephants, lions, buffalo, and hippos. The landscape varies from riverine forest to the rocky foothills of the Lebombo Mountains. Check in at Letaba.

Sweni Trail. East of Satara, this trail camp overlooks the Sweni Spruit and savanna. The area attracts large herds of zebras, wildebeests, and buffalo with their attendant predators: lions, spotted hyenas, and wild dogs. Check in at Satara.

Wolhuter Trail. You just might come face-to-face with a white rhino on this trail through undulating bushveld, interspersed with rocky kopjes, midway between Berg-en-Dal and Pretoriuskop. Elephants, buffalo, and lions are also likely. Check in at Berg-en-Dal.

6

☎ *013/735–5671* ✉ *sales@phkrugergate.co.za* ⊕ *www.proteahotels. com* ⤳ *96 rooms, 7 suites* ❙⦿❙ *Some meals.*

$$$$ ⛺ **Rhino Post Safari Lodge.** This lodge comprises eight spacious suites on stilts overlooking the Mutlumuvi riverbed. Each open-plan suite built of canvas, thatch, wood, and stone has a bedroom, private wooden deck, bathroom with a deep freestanding bath, twin sinks, a separate toilet, and an outdoor shower protected by thick reed poles. **Pros:** bang in the middle of Kruger Park. **Cons:** canvas makes the suites very hot in summer and very cold in winter; you need to be walking-fit for this camp. $ *Rooms from: R7860* ✉ *Kruger National Park* ☎ *035/474– 1473* ✉ *res@isibindi.co.za* ⊕ *www.isibindiafrica.co.za* ⤳ *8 suites* ❙⦿❙ *All meals.*

$$$$ ⛺ **Singita Lebombo Lodge.** Named for the nearby Lebombo mountain range, the breathtakingly beautiful Singita Lebombo—winner of numerous international accolades and eco-driven in concept—is Bauhaus in the bush, with a uniquely African feel. Built "to touch the ground lightly," the lodge hangs seemingly suspended on the edge of a cliff, and wooden walkways connect the aptly named "lofts" (suites)—which you'll never want to leave, so gorgeous and comfortable are they— with spectacular views of the river and bushveld below. Outdoor and indoor areas fuse seamlessly. Organic materials (wood, cane, cotton, and linen) are daringly juxtaposed with steel and glass. Service and food are superb. **Pros:** stunning avant-garde architecture; excellent game; great curio shop and spa; lovely riverside bush breakfasts. **Cons:** avoid if you prefer a traditional safari lodge; very pricey. $ *Rooms from: R34600* ✉ *Kruger National Park* ☎ *021/683–3424 for reservations, 013/735–5471 for lodge* ✉ *enquiries@singita.com* ⊕ *www.singita.co.za* ⤳ *15 suites* ❙⦿❙ *All-inclusive.*

PERMANENT TENTED CAMPS

$ ⛺ **Berg-en-Dal.** This rest camp lies at the southern tip of the park, in a

FAMILY basin surrounded by rocky hills. It's known for its white rhinos, leop-

Fodor's Choice ards, and wild dogs, but there's plenty of other game, too. A dam

★ (often nearly dry in winter) by one side of the perimeter fence offers good game-viewing, including a close look at cruising crocodiles and munching elephants. It has thoughtful landscaping, which has left much of the indigenous vegetation intact, making for more privacy, plus an attractive pool and well-stocked grocery-curio shop, and kids can run around safely here. Accommodation options run from 65 chalets to 23 family cottages, and two guesthouses. **Pros:** you can sit on benches at the perimeter fence and watch game come and go all day. **Cons:** always crowded (although chalets are well spaced out). $ *Rooms from: R1060* ✉ *Kruger National Park* ☎ *012/428–9111* ✉ *reservations@sanparks. org* ⊕ *www.sanparks.org* ⤳ *90 suites* ❙⦿❙ *No meals.*

$ ⛺ **Crocodile Bridge.** Situated in Kruger's southeastern corner, this award-

FAMILY winning small rest camp sits on the scenic Crocodile River and doubles as an entrance gate, which makes it a convenient stopover if you arrive near the park's closing time and are too late to make it to another camp. The road leading from the camp to Lower Sabie is famous for sightings of general game as well as buffalo, rhinos, cheetahs, and lions, but it's often crowded on weekends, holidays, and during school vacations. A hippo pool lies just 5 km (3 miles) away. Accommodations range from bungalows and safari tents to campsites. ■ TIP➔ **Two of the bungalows are geared toward travelers with disabilities. Pros:** adjacent to one of best game roads in park. **Cons:** close proximity to the outside world of roads and farms. $ *Rooms from: R1160* ✉ *Kruger National Park* ☎ *012/428–9111* ✍ *reservations@sanparks.org* ⊕ *www.sanparks.org* ⤴ *28 suites* ⦿| *No meals.*

$ 🏠 **Letaba.** Overlooking the frequently dry Letaba River, this lovely old
FAMILY   camp sits in the middle of elephant country in the park's central section. There's excellent game-viewing on all the roads round the camp: be careful in early morning and at sundown that you don't bump into a hippo. The camp itself has a real bush feel: all the huts are thatch (ask for one overlooking the river), and the grounds are full of old trees. The restaurant and snack bar look out over the broad, sandy busy-with-game riverbed. Campsites, on the camp's perimeter, offer lots of shade for your tent or trailer. **Pros:** camp has a real bush feel. **Cons:** far from southern entrance gates, so you'll need more traveling time. $ *Rooms from: R1040* ✉ *Kruger National Park* ☎ *012/428–9111* ✍ *reservations@sanparks.org* ⊕ *www.sanparks.org* ⤴ *118 suites* ⦿| *No meals.*

$ 🏠 **Lower Sabie.** One of the most popular camps in Kruger, Lower Sabie
FAMILY   has tremendous views over a broad sweep of the Sabie River and sits in one of the best game-viewing areas of the park (along with Skukuza and Satara). White rhinos, lions, cheetahs, elephants, and buffalo frequently come down to the river to drink, especially in the dry winter months. Long wooden walkways curve around the restaurant and shop where you can sit and look out over the river. Ancient trees full of birds line the camp perimeter along the river (spot the dozing hippos) and there are lots of animal drinking holes within a few minutes' drive. Guests have a range of options to stay in, ranging from huts and bungalows to safari tents; there is one family cottage. **Pros:** great location; superb game in vicinity. **Cons:** camp and restaurant always crowded. $ *Rooms from: R1160* ✉ *Kruger National Park* ☎ *012/428–9111* ✍ *reservations@ sanparks.org* ⊕ *www.sanparks.org* ⤴ *109 suites* ⦿| *No meals.*

$ 🏠 **Mopani.** Built in the lee of a rocky kopje overlooking a lake, this camp in the northern section is one of Kruger's biggest. The camp is a landscaped oasis for birds, people, and a few impalas and other grazing animals amid not very attractive surrounding mopane woodlands. If it's hippos you're after, from your veranda feast your eyes on a cavalcade of these giants frolicking in the lake. Constructed of rough stone, wood, and thatch, the camp blends well into the thick vegetation. Shaded wooden walkways connect the public areas, all of which overlook the lake, and the view from the open-air bar is awesome. The à la carte restaurant (reserve before 6 pm) serves better food than most of the other camps, and the cottages are better equipped and larger than their counterparts elsewhere in Kruger. Ask for accommodations overlooking the lake when you book. Mopani lacks the intimate charm of some of the smaller camps, and the surrounding mopane woodland doesn't attract much game, but it's a really comfortable camp to relax in for a night or two if you're driving the length of the park. **Pros:** lovely accommodation; right on big lake; good restaurant and bar; easy to get

"[This] matriarch [in Kruger National Park] decided that her charges were threatened by our presence! She charged our vehicle. While contemplating my demise, I [snapped] the attached photo." —Linda R. Hansen, Fodors.com member

bookings. **Cons:** not much game in immediate vicinity. [$] *Rooms from: R1060* ✉ *Kruger National Park* ☎ *012/428–9111* ✍ *reservations@sanparks.org* 🌐 *www.sanparks.org* 🛏 *45 bungalows, 12 cottages, 45 guest cottages, 1 guesthouse.*

$ 🏨 **Olifants.** In the center of Kruger, Olifants has the best setting of all the camps: high atop cliffs on a rocky ridge with panoramic views of the distant hills and the Olifants River below. A lovely thatch-sheltered terrace allows you to sit for hours with binoculars and pick out the animals below. Lions often make kills in the river valley, and elephants, buffalo, giraffes, kudu, and other game come to drink and bathe. ■ **TIP→ Try to book one of the thatch rondavels overlooking the river.** It's a charming old camp, graced with wonderful indigenous trees. The only drawback, particularly in summer, however, is there's no pool. **Pros:** stunning location. **Cons:** huts in the middle of the camp have no privacy; high malaria area. [$] *Rooms from: R1260* ✉ *Olifants Camp Rd., Kruger National Park* ☎ *012/428–9111* ✍ *reservations@sanparks.org* 🌐 *www.sanparks.org* 🛏 *109 suites* 🍴 *No meals.*

$ 🏨 **Orpen.** Don't dismiss this tiny, underappreciated rest camp on Kruger's western border in the center of the park because of its proximity to the Orpen Gate. It may not be the most attractive camp—the rooms, arranged in a rough semicircle around a large lawn, look out toward the perimeter fence, about 150 feet away—but there's a permanent water hole where animals come to drink, and plenty of game is in the vicinity, including cheetahs, lions, and rhinos. The two-bedroom huts are a bit sparse, without bathrooms or cooking facilities (although there are good communal ones), but there are three comfortable family cottages with bathrooms and kitchenettes. And it's a blissfully quiet camp, as there are so few accommodations. **Pros:** great game-viewing. **Cons:** close to main gate. [$] *Rooms from: R1080* ✉ *Kruger National Park* ☎ *012/428–9111* ✉ *reservations@sanparks.org* 🌐 *www.sanparks.org* 🛏 *15 suites* 🍴 *No meals.*

$ FAMILY 🏨 **Pretoriuskop.** This large, nostalgically old-fashioned camp, close to the Numbi Gate in southwest Kruger, makes a good overnight stop or touring base. The rocky koppies and steep ridges that characterize the surrounding landscape provide ideal habitat for mountain reedbuck and klipspringers—antelope not always easily seen elsewhere in the park. The area's *sourveld*—so named because its vegetation is less sweet and attractive to herbivores than other kinds of vegetation—also attracts browsers like giraffes and kudu, as well as white rhinos, lions, and wild dogs. There's not a lot of privacy in the camp—accommodations (rondavels, bungalows, cottages, and guesthouses) tend to overlook each other—but there is some shade, plus a great swimming pool. **Pros:** good restaurant for snacks and toasted sandwiches. **Cons:** bleak and bare in winter; barracks-style feel. [$] *Rooms from: R1120* ✉ *Kruger National Park* ☎ *012/428–9111* ✉ *reservations@sanparks.org* 🌐 *www.sanparks.org* 🛏 *135 suites* 🍴 *No meals.*

6

$ 🏨 **Punda Maria.** It's worth visiting this lovely little camp in Kruger's far north, because it offers one of the park's best bush experiences. It's a small enclave, with tiny whitewashed thatch cottages in terraces on a hill. It's Kruger's best birding camp: at a tiny, stone birdbath just behind the barbecue site, dozens of birds come and go all day. A nature trail winds through the camp—also great for birding, as is the Punda/Pafuri road, where you can spot lots of raptors. A guided walking tour takes you to one of South Africa's most interesting archaeological sites—the stone Thulamela Ruins, dating from 1250 to 1700. **Pros:** very attractive camp; Kruger's best birding area. **Cons:** very far north; game less abundant than the south. [$] *Rooms from: R1030* ✉ *Punda Maria Camp Rd., Kruger National Park* ☎ *012/428–9111* ✉ *reservations@sanparks.org* 🌐 *www.sanparks.org* 🛏 *31 suites* 🍴 *No meals.*

$$$$ 🏨 **Rhino Post Plains Camp.** Overlooking a water hole amid an acacia knobthorn thicket deep in the heart of the Timbitene Plain, Plains Camp has four comfortably furnished tents with wooden decks and great views of the plains. A deck with a bar and plunge pool is great for postwalk get-togethers, and there's a small tented dining area. Daily walks with an ranger (who is armed) bring you into close contact with the bush and its denizens. The camp is simple, unpretentious, very friendly, and has great food. **Pros:** right in the middle of Kruger; great game; fabulous night drives when everyone else in the Kruger camps is confined to barracks. **Cons:** surroundings a bit bleak, especially in winter; not much privacy between tents. [$] *Rooms from: R7860* ✉ *Off the Marula Loop, Kruger National Park* ☎ *035/474–1473* ✉ *res@isibindi.co.za* 🌐 *www.isibindiafrica.co.za* 🛏 *4 suites* 🍴 *All meals.*

$ FAMILY 🏨 **Satara.** With some of the best guaranteed game viewing in Kruger (especially on the N'wanetsi River Road, also known as S100), this large camp sits in the park's central section. The knobthorn veld surrounding the camp provides the best grazing in the park and attracts large concentrations of plains game, which in turn attract predators—lions, cheetahs, leopards, hyenas, and wild dogs. Despite its size, Satara is very appealing, possibly because of its tremendous birdlife and general layout. Cottages and two- or three-bed thatch rondavels arranged in large circles, face inward onto a central, open, grassy area. Campsites are secluded, with an excellent view of the bush, although they don't have much shade. **Pros:** good shop, restaurant, pool; great guided sunset drives. **Cons:** early booking essential. [$] *Rooms from: R1160* ✉ *Kruger National Park* ☎ *012/428–9111* 📧 *reservations@sanparks.org* 🌐 *www.sanparks.org* 🛏 *165 suites* 🍴 *No meals.*

$ FAMILY 🏨 **Shingwedzi.** This attractive thatch-and-stone camp sits in northern Kruger beside the Shingwedzi River and near the Kanniedood (Never Die) Dam. Consequently there's more game around this camp than anywhere else in the region—especially when you drive the Shingwedzi River Road early in the morning or just before the camp closes at night. Be careful you don't bump into a hippo. (You'll face a hefty fine if you get back to camp late after the gates have officially closed.) Comfortable accommodations are of two types: A and B (literally). **■ TIP→ Try for one of the A units, with an additional two-bed loft; some also have fully equipped kitchenettes.** **Pros:** game-busy river road; in winter, gorgeous bright pink impala lilies. **Cons:** some accommodations are grouped in a circle around a big bare open space that affords little individual privacy. [$] *Rooms from: R1030* ✉ *Kruger National Park* ☎ *012/428–9111* 📧 *reservations@sanparks.org* 🌐 *www.sanparks.org* 🛏 *81 suites* 🍴 *No meals.*

$ FAMILY 🏨 **Skukuza.** Skukuza is highly popular because it lies in an area teeming with game, including lions, cheetahs, and hyenas, and sits on a bank of the crocodile-infested Sabie River, with good views of dozing hippos, elephants, and grazing waterbuck. More like a small town than a rest camp, it has a gas station, police station, airport, post office, car-rental agency, grocery store, and library. Visit the museum and education center to learn something about the park's history and ecology. Even if you don't stay here, it's worth a visit to stroll along the banks of the Sabie River to spot game and birds. **■ TIP→ If you can book one of the guesthouses (pricey but worth it), you'll have exclusivity and privacy.** **Pros:** in middle of the park's best game areas; great river location. **Cons:** usually crowded with regular visitors and busloads of day-trippers. [$] *Rooms from: R1140* ✉ *Kruger National Park* ☎ *012/428–9111* 📧 *reservations@sanparks.org* 🌐 *www.sanparks.org* 🛏 *257 suites* 🍴 *No meals.*

$ 🏨 **Tamboti.** Kruger's first tented camp, close to the Orpen Gate, is superbly sited on the banks of the frequently dry Tamboti River, among huge trees. Communal facilities make it a bit like an upscale campsite; nevertheless, it's one of Kruger's most popular camps, so book well ahead. From your tent you may well see elephants digging in the riverbed for water just beyond the barely visible electrified fence. Each of the walk-in, permanent tents has its own deck overlooking the river. **■ TIP→ When you book, ask for a tent in the deep shade of large riverine trees—worth it in the midsummer heat. All kitchen, washing, and toilet facilities are in two shared central blocks.** **Pros:** great game. **Cons:** always fully occupied, shared bathrooms. [$] *Rooms from: R1240*

South Africa's Tribes

ZULU

The Zulu are the largest tribe in South Africa. They're a patriarchal society, and in a traditional Zulu village there are several households, each with its own cattle herds under the authority of a senior male. The men often have more than one wife, and the "great wife" is usually the mother of his male children. An estimated 10 million Zulu live in the KwaZulu-Natal province, where they migrated more than a thousand years ago. Because of the clashes with the British forces, including the bloody battles of the Anglo-Zulu War (1878), which resulted in the demise of the Zulu Kingdom, Zulus are often stereotyped as being a war-mongering people, but this is far from the case. While the Zulu have historically proven to be highly adept in battle, it's not because of some innate ferocity, but rather an ability to plan and strategize. Today, it's their musical prowess that has had a major impact on popular culture. Kwaito, for example, a style of music blending dance, hip-hop, and rap, is dominated by Zulu musicians. More traditional Zulu music has been incorporated into the music of western musicians, including Paul Simon and the soundtrack for the Broadway musical *The Lion King.* One of the more famous Zulu singing groups today

is Ladysmith Black Mambazo, which has toured the world with its popular collection of traditional Zulu anthems.

XHOSA

The Xhosa people have lived in the Eastern Cape Province since the 15th century, when they migrated here from East and Central Africa. They're the second most populous tribe in South Africa (about 8 million people), next to the Zulu. A typical Xhosa village is made up of several *kraals,* or cattle enclosures, surrounded by family huts. In the 18th century, the Xhosa clashed with the Boers over land; both groups were farmers and eventually war broke out over who had dominion over what. Eventually, the Boers and British colonizers united in a policy of white rule, subjugating black Africans through the passage of the Native Land Act of 1913, which confined black Africans to only 13% of the land in South Africa. This laid the foundation for apartheid, which similarly restricted blacks to areas called Homelands. The Homelands were difficult to farm, overcrowded, and disease-ridden, and remain to this day a shameful part of South Africa's apartheid past. It wasn't until Xhosa tribesman Nelson Mandela was elected president of South Africa in 1994 that the Homelands were abolished.

6

✉ *Kruger National Park* ☎ *012/428–9111* ✐ *reservations@sanparks. org* ⊕ *www.sanparks.org* ⇄ *40 suites* ⑩ *No meals.*

BUSHVELD CAMPS

Smaller, more intimate, more luxurious, and consequently more expensive than regular rest camps, Kruger's bushveld camps are in remote wilderness areas of the park that are often off-limits to regular visitors. Access is limited to guests only. As a result you get far more bush and fewer fellow travelers. Night drives and day excursions are available in most of the camps. There are no restaurants, gas pumps, or grocery stores, so bring your provisions with you (though you can buy wood

Singita Lebombo Lodge, Kruger National Park

Sweni Lodge, Kruger National Park

Protea Hotel Kruger Gate, Kruger National Park

Rhino Post Plains Camp, Kruger National Park

for your barbecue). All accommodations have fully equipped kitchens, bathrooms, ceiling fans, and large verandas, most with air-conditioning. Cottages have tile floors, cheerful furnishings, and cane patio furniture and are sited in stands of trees or clumps of indigenous bush for maximum privacy. Many face directly onto a river or water hole. There's only a handful of one-bedroom cottages (at Biyamiti, Shimuwini, Sirheni, and Talamati), but it's worth booking a four-bed cottage and paying the extra, even for only two people. The average cottage price for a couple is R1000 per night with extra people (up to five or six) paying R290 each. If you have a large group or are planning a special celebration, you might consider reserving one of the two bush lodges, which must be booked as a whole: **Roodewal Bush Lodge** sleeps 16, and **Boulders Bush Lodge** sleeps 12. Reservations should be made with South African National Parks.

$ 🖾 **Bateleur.** Hidden in the northern reaches of the park, this tiny camp, the oldest of the bushveld camps, is one of Kruger's most remote destinations. Shaded by tall trees, it overlooks the dry watercourse of the Mashokwe Spruit. A raised platform provides an excellent game-viewing vantage point (don't forget to apply mosquito repellent if you sit here at dawn or dusk), and it's only a short drive to two nearby dams, which draw a huge variety of animals, from lions and elephants to zebras and hippos. The main bedroom in each fully equipped cottage has air-conditioning; elsewhere in each cottage there are ceiling fans, a microwave, and a TV. **Pros:** private and intimate; guests see a lot at the camp's hide; no traffic jams. **Cons:** long distance to travel; there's a TV, which can be a pro or a con depending on your point of view. $ *Rooms from: R950* ⊠ *Kruger National Park* ☎ *012/428–9111* ✍ *reservations@ sanparks.org* ⊕ *www.sanparks.org* ⤴ *7 suites* ⏐◯⏐ *No meals.*

$ 🖾 **Biyamiti.** Close to the park gate at Crocodile Bridge, this larger-than-average, beautiful, sought-after bush camp overlooks the normally dry sands of the Biyamiti River. It's popular because it's close to the southern gates, and the game is usually prolific. A private sand road over a dry riverbed takes you to the well-sited cottages, where big shade trees attract a myriad of birds and make you feel almost completely cocooned in the wilderness. Find time to sit in the hide, because the surrounding vegetation is mixed combretum woodland, which attracts healthy populations of kudu, impalas, elephants, lions, and black and white rhinos. **Pros:** easily accessible; lots of game; variety of drives in area. **Cons:** difficult to book because of its popularity. $ *Rooms from: R1350* ⊠ *Biyamiti Camp Rd., Kruger National Park* ☎ *012/428–9111* ✍ *reservations@sanparks.org* ⊕ *www.sanparks.org* ⤴ *15 suites* ⏐◯⏐ *No meals.*

$ 🖾 **Shimuwini.** Birders descend in droves on this peaceful bushveld camp set on a lovely dam on the Letaba River. Towering trees provide welcome shade, as well as sheltering dozens of resident and migratory birds. Away from the river, the riverine forest becomes mopane woodland where the beautiful roan antelope and rare sable antelope roam. Resident leopards patrol the territory, and elephants frequently browse in the mopane. ■**TIP**➔ Be sure to visit the huge, ancient baobab tree near the camp—shimuwini is the Shangaan word for "place of the baobab," and there are lots of baobabs in the surrounding area. Cottages have one, two, or three bedrooms. **Pros:** lovely situation overlooking permanent lake. **Cons:** only one access road so coming and going gets monotonous; game can be sparse. [$] *Rooms from: R1120* ✉ *Shimuwini Camp Rd., Kruger National Park* ☎ *012/428–9111* ✉ *reservations@sanparks.org* 🌐 *www.sanparks.org* 🛏 *15 suites* 🍴 *No meals.*

$ 🏨 **Sirheni.** Remote and lovely, Sirheni lies on the edge of the Sirheni Dam in an isolated wilderness area in Kruger's far north. It's a long drive to get here but well worth the effort, because there's permanent water and game—including lions and white rhinos—often drink at the dam, particularly in the dry winter months. Try to spot the resident leopard, which often drinks at the dam in the evening. You can watch the sun set over the magnificent bush from one of two secluded viewing platforms at either end of the camp, but be sure to smother yourself with mosquito repellent. **Pros:** permanent water hole; superb bird-watching. **Cons:** high malaria area; no electrical plug points; no cell-phone reception (which can be a pro or con). [$] *Rooms from: R1120* ✉ *Sirheni Camp Rd., Kruger National Park* ☎ *012/428–9111* ✉ *reservations@sanparks.org* 🌐 *www.sanparks.org* 🛏 *15 cottages* 🍴 *No meals.*

$ 🏨 **Talamati.** On the banks of the normally dry N'waswitsontso River in Kruger's central section, this peaceful camp in the middle of a wide, open valley has excellent game-viewing. Grassy plains and mixed woodlands provide an ideal habitat for herds of impalas, zebras, and wildebeests, as well as lions, cheetahs, and elephants. You can take a break from your vehicle and watch birds and game from a couple of raised viewing platforms inside the perimeter fence. The cottages are well equipped and comfortable, with cane furniture and airy verandas. **Pros:** peaceful; good plains game; couple of good picnic spots in vicinity; bigger camps near enough to stock up on supplies. **Cons:** a bit bland. [$] *Rooms from: R1200* ✉ *Talamati-camp Rd., Kruger National Park* ☎ *012/428–9111* ✉ *reservations@sanparks.org* 🌐 *www.sanparks.org* 🛏 *15 suites* 🍴 *No meals.*

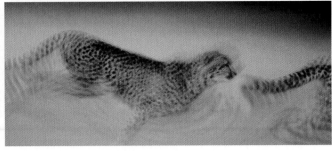

SABI SAND GAME RESERVE

Game
★★★★★
Park Accessibility
★★★★★
Getting Around
★★★★★
Accommodations
★★★★★
Scenic Beauty
★★★

This is the most famous and exclusive of South Africa's private reserves. Collectively owned and managed, the 153,000-acre reserve near Kruger is home to dozens of private lodges, including the world-famous MalaMala and Londolozi. Sabi Sand fully deserves its exalted reputation, boasting perhaps the highest game density of any private reserve in southern Africa.

Although not all lodges own vast tracts of land, the majority have traversing rights over most of the reserve. With an average of 20 vehicles watching for game and communicating by radio, you're bound to see an enormous amount of game and almost certainly the Big Five, and since only three vehicles are allowed at a sighting at a time, you can be assured of a grandstand seat. Sabi Sand is the best area for leopard sightings. It's a memorable experience to see this beautiful, powerful, and often elusive cat padding purposefully through the bush at night, illuminated in your ranger's spotlight. There are many lion prides, and occasionally the increasingly rare wild dogs will migrate from Kruger to den in Sabi Sand. You'll also see white and black rhinos, zebras, giraffes, wildebeests, and most of the antelope species, plus birds galore.

The daily program at each lodge rarely deviates from a pattern, starting with tea, coffee, and muffins or rusks before an early-morning game drive (usually starting at dawn, later in winter). You return to the lodge around 10 am, at which point you dine on an extensive hot breakfast or brunch. You can then choose to go on a bush walk with an armed ranger, where you learn about some of the minutiae of the bush (including the Little Five), although you could also happen on giraffes, antelopes, or any one of the Big Five. But don't worry—you'll be well briefed in advance on what you should do if you come face-to-face with, say, a lion. The rest of the day, until the late-afternoon game drive, is spent at leisure—reading up on the bush in the camp library,

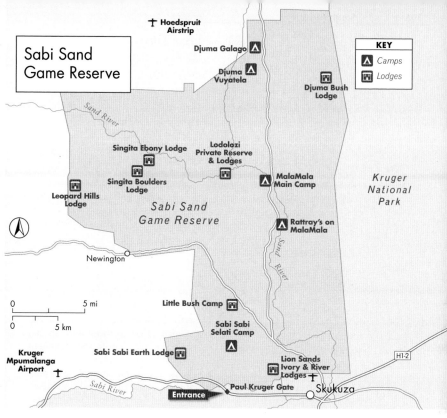

Sabi Sand Game Reserve

KEY
Camps
Lodges

Hoedspruit Airstrip

Djuma Galago

Djuma Vuyatela

Djuma Bush Lodge

Sand River

Singita Ebony Lodge

Lodolozi Private Reserve & Lodges

Singita Boulders Lodge

Leopard Hills Lodge

MalaMala Main Camp

Kruger National Park

Sabi Sand Game Reserve

Rattray's on MalaMala

Sand River

Newington

0   5 mi
0   5 km

Little Bush Camp

Sabi Sabi Selati Camp

Kruger Mpumalanga Airport

Sabi Sabi Earth Lodge

Lion Sands Ivory & River Lodges

H1-2

Sabi River

Entrance   Paul Kruger Gate   Skukuza

snoozing, swimming, or having a spa treatment. A sumptuous after-noon tea is served at 3:30 or 4 before you head back into the bush for your night drive. During the drive, your ranger will find a peaceful spot for sundowners, and you can sip the drink of your choice and nibble snacks as you watch one of Africa's spectacular sunsets. As darkness falls, your ranger will switch on the spotlight so you can spy noctur-nal animals: lions, leopards, jackals, porcupines, servals (small spotted cats like bonsai leopards), civets, and the enchanting little bush babies. You'll return to the lodge around 7:30, in time to freshen up before a three- or five-course dinner, with at least one dinner in a *boma* (open-air dining area) around a blazing fire. Often the camp staff entertains after dinner with local songs and dances—an unforgettable experience. Children under 12 aren't allowed at some of the camps; others have great kids' programs.

GETTING HERE AND AROUND
Kruger Mpumalanga International Airport (KMIA), at Nelspruit, and Hoedspruit airport, close to Kruger's Orpen Gate, serve Sabi Sand Reserve. You can also drive yourself to the reserve and park at your lodge.

Airports Hoedspruit Airport (HDS). ✉ *Eastgate Airport, Hoedspruit* ☎ *015/793–3681* ✉ *eastgaterecep@kapama.co.za* 🌐 *www.eastgateairport.co.za.*

Kruger Mpumalanga International Airport (KMIA) ☎ *013/753–7500* 🌐 *www.kmiairport.co.za.*

Visitor Info Sabi Sand Reserve ☎ *012/343–1991* 🌐 *www.sabisand.co.za.*

DJUMA PRIVATE GAME RESERVE

This 17,297-acre reserve sits right up against Kruger in the northeast corner of the world-famous Sabi Sand Reserve. Expect classic bushveld terrain—dams, rivers, ancient riverine trees, grassland, and plains. There are no fences separating Kruger from Sabi Sand, so game wanders freely back and forth, and no matter where you are in the Sabi Sand Reserve, you'll be treated to some of South Africa's best game-viewing. Djuma is no exception. The Big Five are all here, plus hundreds of birds. The reserve's rangers are famous for their dedication and knowledge, which they share in a friendly, very informal way.

EXPLORING

FAMILY **Djuma Private Game Reserve.** Shangaan for "roar of the lion," Djuma is in the northeast corner of the Sabi Sands Game Reserve. Your hosts are husband-and-wife team Jurie and Pippa Moolman, who are passionate about their work (Jurie has a B.S. in ecology). Although there's a good chance of seeing the Big Five during the bush walk after breakfast and the twice-daily game drives, Djuma also caters to those with special bushveld interests, such as bird-watching or tree identification. Djuma's rangers and trackers are also adept at finding seldom-seen animals, such as wild dogs, spotted hyenas, and genets. You'll find none of the formality that sometimes prevails at the larger lodges. For example, members of the staff eat all meals with you and join you around the nighttime fire. In fact, Djuma prides itself on its personal service and feeling of intimacy. ✉ *Sabi Sand Game Reserve* ☎ *013/735–5555* 🌐 *www.djuma.com* 🛏 *Vuyatela: 5 suites; Galago 5 rooms* 🍴 *No meals.*

WHERE TO STAY

BUDGET LODGE

$$ 🏨 **Galago.** A delightful and affordable alternative to other upscale lodges, Galago, which means "lesser bush baby" in Shangaan, is a converted U-shape farmhouse whose five rooms form an arc around a central fireplace. There's a big, shady veranda where you can sit and gaze out over the open plain before cooling off in the plunge pool. You can bring your own food and do your own cooking or bring your own supplies and hire the camp's chef (R650 per day) to cook it for you. Game drives and walks are led by your own ranger. As you must rent the whole, it's the perfect camp for a family safari or friends' reunion. **Pros:** real value for money. **Cons:** hire a cook or you'll spend your time working. [$] *Rooms from: R2300* ✉ *Djuma Private Game Reserve, Sabi Sand Game Reserve* ☎ *013/735–5555* ✉ *reservations@djuma.com* 🌐 *www.djuma.com* 🛏 *5 rooms* 🍴 *No meals.*

PERMANENT CAMP

$$ 🏨 **Vuyatela.** Djuma's vibey, most upscale camp mixes contemporary
FAMILY African township culture with modern Shangaan culture, making it very different from most of the other private camps. Bright colors, trendy

designs, hand-painted napkins, and candy-wrapper placemats combine with traditional leather chairs, thatch, and hand-painted mud walls. Look out for some great contemporary African township art, both classic and "naïf" artifacts, and especially for the chandelier made with old Coca-Cola bottles above the dining table. The camp is unfenced, and it's quite usual to see kudu nibbling the lawns or giraffes towering above the rooftops. Accommodations are in beautifully decorated chalets with private plunge pools. **Pros:** amazing African art; legendary hosts; trips to authentic villages. **Cons:** funky township style (corrugated iron, recycled metals, in-your-face glitzy township feel) may not be to everyone's taste. [$] *Rooms from: R2900* ✉ *Djuma Private Game Reserve, Sabi Sand Game Reserve* ☎ *013/735–5555 for reservations, 013/735–5118 for lodge* ✍ *reservations@djuma.com* 🌐 *www.djuma.com* 🛏 *5 suites* 🍴 *No meals.*

LION SANDS PRIVATE GAME RESERVE

Situated along the Sabie River, this reserve has one of the best locations in the Sabi Sand Game Reserve. All of the lodges overlook the river, which is a magnet for all kinds of game. You'll be able to peer into Kruger Park, on the other side of the river, and watch game meander along the riverbanks among big riverine trees. You may never want to leave your personal deck, or the big viewing decks even for an exciting game drive or guided walk, because you're bound to spot animals, birds, and crocs from camp.

6

EXPLORING

Fodor's Choice ★ **Lion Sands Private Game Reserve.** Separated from Kruger National Park by the Sabie River, the reserve has been owned and operated by the More family for four generations. Purchased in 1933 as a family retreat, it was opened to the public in 1978 with two lodges and 10,000 acres of undisturbed wildlife that's available only to its guests. Accommodations range from the ultraluxe Ivory Lodge to the more economical River Lodge, and then there's the once-in-a-lifetime Chalkley Treehouse (yes, it really is a bed on a platform in a tree, but it's nothing like the treehouse in your backyard), or the 1933 Lodge, the More family's vacation home that's perfect for larger groups and comes complete with personal chef, guide, pool, gym, and wine cellar. The family is so committed to keeping the reserve as close to its original state as possible that they employ a full-time ecologist, the only reserve in the Sabi Sand group to do so. ✉ *Lion Sands Private Game Reserve, Sabi Sand Game Reserve* ☎ *013/735–5330* ✍ *res@lionsands.com* 🌐 *www.lionsands.com* 🍴 *All meals.*

WHERE TO STAY

LUXURY LODGES

$$$$ Fodor's Choice ★ 🏨 **Lion Sands Ivory Lodge.** Ivory Lodge offers the ultimate in luxury, privacy, and relaxation. Suites are really more like villas, as each has its own private entrance, separate sitting room and bedroom joined by a breezeway, and superb views overlooking the Sabi River and Kruger—the spacious deck comes equipped with a telescope and a plunge pool. Suites are decorated in contemporary African-European style with

wood-burning fireplaces, a butler's passageway—you'll have a personal butler—and an indoor and outdoor shower, as well as a freestanding tub. You won't even know if Brangelina or Ewan is in the next villa, and you won't care. ■ **TIP→ For something even more special (if possible), inquire about spending the night at the Chalkley Treehouse.** **Pros:** exclusivity; great views; brilliant game-viewing. **Cons:** the temptation of abundant great food; it's so decadent, you might forget to leave. [$] *Rooms from: R32950* ✉ *Lion Sands Private Game Reserve, Sabi Sand Game Reserve* ☎ *031/735–5330* ✉ *res@lionsands.com* 🌐 *www.lionsands.com* 🛏 *6 suites* 🍴 *All meals* ☞ *No children under 12 years old.*

$$$$ 🏨 **Lion Sands River Lodge.** Set on one of the longest and best stretches of river frontage in Sabi Sand, you can watch the passing animal and bird show from your deck or from the huge, tree-shaded, wooden viewing area that juts out over the riverbank facing Kruger National Park. The guest rooms are comfortable and attractively Africa-themed, with honey-color stone floors with pebble inlays, cream-color wooden furniture, embroidered white bed linens, and lamps and tables of dark indigenous wood. The food is imaginative and tasty, the young staff enthusiastic, and the rangers highly qualified. After an exhilarating game drive, take a bush walk, go fishing, or relax with a beauty treatment at Lalamuka Spa (*lalamuka* means "unwind" in Shangaan). There's a resident senior ecologist, plus a classy and interesting curio shop. **Pros:** fabulous river frontage; well-managed. **Cons:** some chalets quite close together so not much privacy. [$] *Rooms from: R17560* ✉ *Lion Sands Private Game Reserve, Sabi Sand Game Reserve* ☎ *013/735–5330* ✉ *res@lionsands.com* 🌐 *www.lionsands.com* 🛏 *20 rooms* 🍴 *All meals* ☞ *No children under 10 years old.*

LONDOLOZI RESERVE

Since its inception in 1974 (it was a family farm and retreat before that), Londolozi has become synonymous with South Africa's finest game lodges and game experiences. (*Londolozi* is the Zulu word for "protector of all living things.") Brother-and-sister Bronwyn and Boyd Varty, the third generation of the Varty family, are now in charge with a mission to reconnect the human spirit with the wilderness and to carry on their family's quest to honor the animal kingdom. The Big Five are all here, as are the world-famous leopards of Londolozi. (You are guaranteed to see at least one.) There are five camps, each representing a different element in nature: Pioneer Camp (water), Tree Camp (wood), Granite Suites (rock), Varty Camp (fire), and Founders Camp (earth). Each is totally private, hidden in dense riverine forest on the banks of the Sand River. The Varty family live on the property, and their friendliness and personal attention, along with the many staff who have been here for decades, will make you feel part of the family immediately. The central reception and curio shop are at Varty Camp.

EXPLORING

Fodor's Choice ★ **Londolozi Game Reserve.** Formerly a family farm and retreat since 1926, Londolozi today is synonymous with South Africa's finest game lodges and game experiences. Dave and John Varty, grandsons of the original owner, Charles Varty, put the reserve on the map with glamorous marketing and a vision of style and comfort that grandfather Charles could never have imagined. Now younger generation, brother-and-sister team Bronwyn and Boyd Varty, are carrying on their family's quest to honor the animal kingdom. Game abounds; the Big Five are all here, and the leopards of Londolozi are world famous. There are five camps, each representing a different element in nature: Pioneer Camp (water), Tree Camp (wood), Granite Suites (rock), Varty Camp (fire), and Founders Camp (earth). ✉ *Londolozi Reserve, Sabi Sand Game Reserve* ☎ *011/280–6655* ✍ *news@londolozi.co.za* 🌐 *www.londolozi.com* 🍴 *All meals.*

WHERE TO STAY

PERMANENT CAMPS

$$$$ FAMILY 🏨 **Founders Camp.** This recently refurbished, inviting camp has 10 stone-and-thatch suites in individual chalets set amid thick riverine bush; some chalets are linked by interconnecting skywalks, which is great for families or groups traveling together. Decorated in warm, comforting earth tones, each chalet has its own wooden viewing deck and plunge pool. Old family photographs decorate the walls and tables in this camp, reminding you of Londolozi's 40-year-old history. Relax on the huge thatch dining and viewing deck that juts out over a quiet backwater of the Sand River, and watch the mammals and birds go by. ■ **TIP→ Ask your ranger about Londolozi's unique on-site photography studio and its user-friendly services.** **Pros:** quick, safe access between family rooms; children over 4 welcome. **Cons:** lodges are in quite close proximity to one another. [$] *Rooms from: R20900* ✉ *Londolozi Reserve, Sabi Sand Game Reserve* ☎ *011/280–6655* 🌐 *www.londolozi.com* 🛏 *10 suites* 🍴 *All-inclusive.*

$$$$ 🏨 **Pioneer Camp.** The most secluded of all of Londolozi's camps, Pioneer's three private suites overlook the river and are perfect for getting away from others. It can also be adapted into a temporary family homestead for 12 if you want to rent the whole place. Suites have a modern Ralph Lauren feel, and your floor-to-ceiling glass sliding panels offer great wilderness views. Super-elegant bathrooms and classy bedrooms meld contemporary chic and classic African styles; clean, uncluttered furnishings blend perfectly with faded sepia photographs, old hunting prints, and scuffed safari treasures. The black-and-white outside showers come straight from a modern lifestyle magazine. In winter, sink deeply into your comfortable armchair in front of your own blazing fireplace; in summer, sit outside in your outdoor dining room and listen to Africa's night noises. There are inside and outside dining areas, viewing decks, and a gorgeous S-shape pool nestling in the surrounding bush. ■ **TIP→ There's a user-friendly photography studio on site.** **Pros:** authentic romantic-safari atmosphere; only three suites; intimate atmosphere. **Cons:** with only three suites it's best if you know all other guests. [$] *Rooms from: R30700* ✉ *Londolozi Reserve, Sabi*

Sand Game Reserve ☎ *011/280–6655* ✐ *reservations@londolozi.com* ⊕ *www.londolozi.com* ➥ *3 suites* ⦿ *All-inclusive* ☞ *No children under 12 years old.*

$$$$ ⍓**Tree Camp.** The first Relais & Chateaux game lodge in the world,
Fodor's Choice this gorgeous camp (think leopards, lanterns, leadwoods,and leopard
★ orchids) is tucked into the riverbank overlooking indigenous forest. The lodge is themed in chocolate and white, with exquisite leopard photos on the walls, airy and stylish interiors, and elegant yet simple furnishings. Huge bedrooms, en-suite bathrooms, and plunge pools continue the elegance, simplicity, and sophistication. From your spacious deck you look out onto a world of cool-green forest dominated by ancient African ebony and marula trees. Treat yourself to a bottle of bubbly from the Champagne Library and then dine with others while swapping bush stories or alone in your private sala. **Pros:** the viewing deck; state-of-the-art designer interiors. **Cons:** stylishness nudges out coziness. **$** *Rooms from: R28700* ✉ *Londolozi Reserve, Sabi Sand Game Reserve* ☎ *011/280–6655* ✐ *reservations@londolozi.com* ⊕ *www. londolozi.com* ➥ *6 suites* ⦿ *All-inclusive.*

$$$$ ⍓**Varty Camp.** This camp's fire has been burning for more than eight
FAMILY decades, making Varty Camp the very soul and center of Londolozi. It's also the largest of Londolozi's camp, centered on a thatch A-frame lodge that houses a dining room, sitting areas, and lounge. Meals are served on a broad wooden deck that juts over the riverbed and under an ancient jackalberry tree. The thatch rondavels, which were the Varty family's original hunting camp, now do duty as a library, a wine cellar, and an interpretive center, where you can listen to history and ecotourism talks—don't miss the Londolozi Leopard presentation. If you're looking for romance, have a private dinner on your veranda and go for a moonlight dip in your own plunge pool. In suites, the pool leads right to the riverbed. All rooms are decorated in African ethnic chic—in creams and browns and with the ubiquitous historic family photographs and documents—and have great bushveld views. Families are welcome (children must be over 4), and the fascinating kids' programs should turn any couch potato into an instant wannabe ranger. **Pros:** friendly atmosphere; great game; all chalets are interleading. **Cons:** lots of kids might not be for you. **$** *Rooms from: R17900* ✉ *Londolozi Reserve, Sabi Sand Game Reserve* ☎ *011/280–6655* ✐ *reservations@londolozi. com* ⊕ *www.londolozi.com* ➥ *10 suites* ⦿ *All-inclusive.*

MALAMALA GAME RESERVE

This legendary game reserve (designated as such in 1929) is tops in its field. The first and only community-owned game reserve in Sabi Sand, it continues to be managed by the legendary Rattray family in partnership with the N'wandlamharhi Community. It's the largest privately owned Big Five game area in South Africa, and includes an unfenced 30-km (19-mile) boundary with Kruger National Park, across which game cross continuously. The variety of habitats range from riverine bush, favorite hiding place of the leopard, to open grasslands, where cheetahs hunt.

You'll be delighted with incomparable personal service, superb food, and discreetly elegant, comfortable accommodations, where you'll rub shoulders with statesmen and stateswomen, aristocrats, celebrities, and returning visitors alike. Mike Rattray, a legend in his own time in South Africa's game-lodge industry, describes MalaMala as "a camp in the bush," but it's certainly more than that, although it still retains that genuine bushveld feel of bygone days. Both the outstanding hospitality and the game-viewing experience keep guests coming back.

MalaMala's animal-viewing statistics are impressive: the Big Five are spotted almost every day. At one moment your well-educated, friendly, articulate ranger will fascinate you with the description of the sex life of a dung beetle, as you watch the sturdy male battling his way along the road pushing his perfectly round ball of dung with wife-to-be perched perilously on top; at another, your adrenaline will flow as you follow a leopard stalking impala in the gathering gloom. Along with the local Shangaan trackers, whose eyesight rivals that of the animals they are tracking, the top-class rangers ensure that your game experience is unforgettable.

EXPLORING

Fodor'sChoice **MalaMala Private Game Reserve.** This legendary game reserve (designated
★ as such in 1929), is tops in its field. The first and only community-owned game reserve in Sabi Sand, it continues to be managed by the legendary Rattray family in partnership with the N'wandlamharhi Community. Expect incomparable personal service, superb food, and discreetly elegant, comfortable accommodations where you'll rub shoulders with aristocrats, celebrities, and returning visitors alike. It retains the genuine bushveld feel of bygone days, and its outstanding hospitality and the game-viewing experience keep guests coming back. MalaMala constitutes the largest privately owned Big Five game area in South Africa and includes an unfenced 30-km (19-mile) boundary with Kruger National Park, across which game crosses continuously. MalaMala's statistics are almost unbelievable: the Big Five are spotted almost every day. ⊠ *Mala Mala Game Reserve, Sabi Sand Game Reserve* ☎ *011/442–2267* ⊕ *www.malamala.com* ⦿ *All meals.*

WHERE TO STAY
PERMANENT CAMPS

$$$$ 🛈 **Main Camp.** Stone and thatch air-conditioned rondavels with separate his-and-her bathrooms are decorated in creams and browns and
FAMILY furnished with cane armchairs, colorful handwoven tapestries and rugs, terra-cotta floors, and original artwork. Public areas have a genuine safari feel, with plush couches, animal skins, and African artifacts. Shaded by ancient jackalberry trees, a huge deck overlooks the Sand River and its continuous passing show of animals. Browse in air-conditioned Monkey Room for books and wildlife videos, sample the magnificent wine cellar, sun yourself by the pool, or stay fit in the well-appointed gym. The food (among the best in the bush) is tasty, wholesome, and varied, with a full buffet at both lunch and dinner. Children are welcomed with special programs, activities, and goody-filled backpacks; children under five are not allowed on game

drives. One guest room is geared toward travelers with disabilities. **Pros:** authentic; sweeping wilderness views; amazing game viewing. **Cons:** rondavels are a bit old-fashioned, but that goes with the ambience. [$] *Rooms from: US$1480* ✉ *Mala Mala Game Reserve, Sabi Sand Game Reserve* ☎ *011/442–2267 for reservations, 013/735–9200 for lodge* ✍ *maincamp@malamalacamp.co.za* 🌐 *www.malamala.com* 🛏 *8 suites, 9 rooms* 🍴 *All-inclusive.*

$$$$ Fodor'sChoice ★ 🏨 **Rattray's on MalaMala.** The breathtakingly beautiful Rattray's merges original bushveld style with daring contemporary ideas. Stay in one of eight opulent *khayas* (think Tuscan villas) with spacious his-and-her bathrooms, dressing rooms, and private heated plunge pools. The entrance hall, with art by distinguished African wildlife artists such as Keith Joubert, leads to a huge bedroom with a wooden four-poster bed, lounge with comfy furniture, writing desks (for crucial nightly journal entries), antique Persian rugs, and a dining nook. Floor-to-ceiling windows with insect-proof sliding doors face the Sand River and lead to massive wooden game-viewing decks. Public areas include viewing and dining decks, an infinity pool, lounge areas, a library, and an impressive wine cellar. **Pros:** superb game-viewing; tantalizing views over the river. **Cons:** Tuscan villas in the bush may not be your idea of Africa; no children under 16 (though this may be a pro for some). [$] *Rooms from: US$2050* ✉ *Mala Mala Game Reserve, Sabi Sand Game Reserve* ☎ *011/442–2267 for reservations, 013/735–3000 for lodge* ✍ *reception@rattrayscamp.co.za* 🌐 *www.malamala.com* 🛏 *8 suites* 🍴 *All-inclusive.*

SABI SABI PRIVATE GAME RESERVE

Founded in 1978 at the southern end of Sabi Sand, the multi-award-winning Sabi Sabi Private Game Reserve was one of the first reserves to offer photo safaris and to link ecotourism, conservation, and community. Superb accommodations and abundant game lure guests back to Sabi Sabi in large numbers.

EXPLORING

Fodor'sChoice ★ **Sabi Sabi Private Game Reserve.** There's a strong emphasis on ecology at Sabi Sabi: guests are encouraged to look beyond the Big Five and to become aware of the birds and smaller mammals of the bush. There are four very different lodges, each individually remarkable: Bush Lodge, famous for its friendly hospitality and ever-busy water hole; Little Bush Lodge, an intimate, back-to-nature tented camp; Selati, haunt of celebs and royalty, themed on an old Kruger Park railway line; and the daringly innovative Earth Lodge. ✉ *Sabi Sand Game Reserve* ☎ *011/447–7172 Reservations* ✍ *res@sabisabi.com* 🌐 *www.sabisabi.com* 🍴 *All meals.*

WHERE TO STAY

$$$$ FAMILY 🏨 **Little Bush Camp.** Sabi Sabi's delightful little camp is tucked away in the bushveld on the banks of the Msuthlu River and combines spaciousness with a sense of intimacy. At night glowing oil lanterns lead you along a wooden walkway to your comfortable thatch-roof room or suite decorated in earthy tones of brown, cream, and white. After your action-packed morning game drive—during which you'll see game

"This was the first rhino that I had seen in person. 'HUGE!' was my first impression." —adkinsek, Fodors.com member

galore—and your delicious brunch, relax on your secluded wooden deck with plunge pool overlooking the bush, or go active and take a guided game walk with your armed ranger. In the evening dine out under the stars—if you're a city slicker, you may never have seen such bright ones. **Pros:** perfect for families. **Cons:** there may be other families. $ *Rooms from: R19400* ⊠ *Sabi Sabi Private Game Reserve, Sabi Sand Game Reserve* ☎ *011/447-7172 for reservations, 013/735-5080 for lodge* ✎ *res@sabisabi.com (reservations), littlebush@sabisabi.com (camp)* ⊕ *www.sabisabi.com* ⇄ *6 suites* |◎| *All meals.*

$$$$ 🍴 **Sabi Sabi's Bush Lodge.** Bush Lodge overlooks a busy water hole (lions
FAMILY are frequent visitors) and the dry course of the Msuthlu River. The thatch, open-sided dining area, observation deck, and pool all have magnificent views of game at the water hole. Thatch suites are connected by walkways that weave between manicured lawns and beneath enormous shade trees where owls and fruit bats call at night. All have a deck overlooking the dry river course (where you may well see an elephant padding along) and outdoor and indoor showers. Roomy, comfortable chalets are Africa-themed, each with a personal wooden deck. **Pros:** always prolific game around the lodge; roomy chalets. **Cons:** big and busy might not be your idea of relaxing getaway. $ *Rooms from: R19400* ⊠ *Sabi Sabi Private Game Reserve, Sabi Sand Game Reserve* ☎ *013/735-5656 lodge* ⊕ *www.sabisabi.com* ⇄ *25 suites* |◎| *All meals.*

$$$$ 🍴 **Sabi Sabi's Earth Lodge.** This avant-garde, eco-friendly lodge was the first to break away from the traditional safari style and strive for a contemporary theme. It's a luxurious cross between a Hopi cave dwelling and a medieval keep, but with modern touches. You won't spot your mud-domed suite, hidden from view by bush-covered hummocks, until

you're practically at the front door. Rough-textured, dark brown walls encrusted with orange seeds and wisps of indigenous grasses cocoon the gorgeous suites, which have a huge living area, a mega bedroom and bathroom, private veranda, and plunge pool. The dining boma, fashioned from branches, is lit at night by scores of flickering lanterns. A personal butler takes care of your every need, and there's a meditation garden. **Pros:** stunning architecture and design. **Cons:** if you favor traditional safari accommodation, this is not for you. $ *Rooms from: R25400 ⊠ Sabi Sabi Private Game Reserve, Sabi Sand Game Reserve* ☎ *013/735–5261 lodge* ⊕ *www.sabisabi.com* ⤳ *13 suites* ⦿ *All-inclusive.*

$$$$ ⌁ **Sabi Sabi Selati Camp.** For an *Out of Africa* experience and great game,
Fodor's Choice   you can't beat Selati, an intimate, stylish, colonial-style camp that was
★   formerly the private hunting lodge of a famous South African opera singer. The early-1900s atmosphere is created by the use of genuine train memorabilia—old leather suitcases, antique wooden chairs, nameplates, and signals—that recall the old Selati branch train line, which once crossed the reserve in the 1870s. At night the grounds flicker with the lights of the original shunters' oil lamps. Dinner is held in the boma, whereas brunch is served in the friendly farmhouse kitchen. Glitterati and European royalty have stayed at the spacious Ivory Presidential Suite, with its Persian rugs and antique furniture. **Pros:** unique atmosphere; Ivory Presidential Suite superb value for money; secluded and intimate. **Cons:** some old-timers preferred the camp when it was just lantern-lit with no electricity. $ *Rooms from: R19400 ⊠ Sabi Sabi Private Game Reserve, Sabi Sand Game Reserve* ☎ *011/447–7172 for reservations, 013/735–5771 for lodge* ✉ *res@sabisabi.com (reservations), selati@sabisabi.com (lodge)* ⊕ *www.sabisabi.com* ⤳ *8 suites* ⦿ *All meals.*

SINGITA

Although Singita (Shangaan for "the miracle") offers much the same thrilling Sabi Sand bush and game experiences as other lodges, superb service really puts it head and shoulders above many of the rest of the herd.

EXPLORING

Fodor's Choice   **Singita Sabi Sand.** Expect low-key opulence, a comforting organic atmo-
★   sphere, truly spacious accommodations, superb food and wine with a resident sommelier (wine can be shipped home), and a variety of public spaces—little private dining nooks to a huge viewing deck built round an ancient jackalberry tree, comfortable library with TV and internet, and an attractive poolside bar—really do put this gorgeous lodge head and shoulders above the rest of the herd. Whether you fancy a starlit private supper, a riverside breakfast, a bike ride though the bush, or just chilling alone in your megasuite, you've only to ask. Forget the usual lodge curio shop and take a ride to the on-site Trading Post where objets d'art, handmade jewelry, classy bush gear, and artifacts from all over Africa are clustered together in a series of adjoining rooms that seem more like someone's home than a shop. ⊠ *Singita Sabi Sand, Sabi Sand*

Game Reserve ☎ *021/683–3424* ✉ *enquiries@singita.com* 🌐 *www.singita.co.za* 🍴 *All meals.*

WHERE TO STAY

LUXURY LODGES

$$$$ Fodor's Choice ★ 🏨 **Boulders Lodge.** Expect traditional Africa at its most luxurious. Terracotta polished stone floors blend with cow-skin rugs, hide-covered armchairs, hand-carved tables, and carefully chosen artifacts. From every side there are stunning bushveld views. Luxuriate in a sumptuous suite with leather and wicker armchairs, a zebra-skin ottoman, and desks and tables fashioned from organic wood shapes. A herd of impalas could easily fit into the bathroom, with its claw-foot tub, his-and-her basins, and an indoor and outdoor shower. All doors lead out onto a big wooden deck with a horizon pool, sun loungers, and bushveld views. **TIP→ Request Room 11 or 12, which overlook a water hole.** **Pros:** spacious accommodation; superb food. **Cons:** a bit of a walk from the suites to the main lodge; refuse the crackling log fire if you're at all congested. [$] *Rooms from: R34600* ✉ *Singita Sabi Sand, Sabi Sand Game Reserve* ☎ *021/683–3424 for reservations, 013/735–9800 for lodge* ✉ *enquiries@singita.com* 🌐 *www.singita.co.za* 🛏 *12 suites* 🍴 *All-inclusive.*

$$$$ 🏨 **Ebony Lodge.** If Ernest Hemingway had built his ideal home in the African bush, this would be it. From the moment you walk into the main lounge with its genuine antique furniture, leather chairs gleaming with the polish of years of use, old photographs and paintings, mounted game trophies, and hand-carved doors and windows, you'll be transported to Old Africa at its best. Your room gives exactly the same feel—beautiful antiques, a claw-foot bathtub, a four-poster bed, and a dressing room big enough to swing a leopard by the tail. Write in your journal at the antique desk or laze on your deck next to the pool and soak up the stunning views. **Pros:** the mother lodge of all the Singita properties; cozy library. **Cons:** the beds are very high off the ground—if you've short legs or creak a bit, ask for a stool. [$] *Rooms from: R34600* ✉ *Singita Sabi Sand, Sabi Sand Game Reserve* ☎ *021/683–3424 for reservations, 013/735–9800 for lodge* ✉ *enquiries@singita.com* 🌐 *www.singita.co.za* 🛏 *9 suites* 🍴 *All-inclusive.*

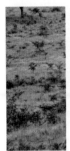

KWAZULU-NATAL PARKS

Game
★★★★
Park Accessibility
★★★★★
Getting Around
★★★★★
Accommodations
★★★★★
Scenic Beauty
★★★★

The province of KwaZulu-Natal is a premier vacation destination for South Africans, with some of the finest game reserves in the country, including the Hluhluwe-Imfolozi Game Reserve. The reserve is small compared to Kruger, but here you'll see the Big Five and plenty of plains game, plus an incredibly biologically diverse mix of plants and trees. The nearby Mkuze and Ithala game reserves are even smaller but are still worth a visit for their numerous bird species and game.

KwaZulu-Natal's best private lodges lie in northern Zululand and Maputaland, a remote region close to Mozambique. These lodges are sufficiently close to one another and Hluhluwe-Imfolozi Game Reserve to allow you to put together a bush experience that delivers the Big Five and a great deal more, including superb bird-watching opportunities and an unrivaled beach paradise.

WHEN TO GO
Summers are hot, hot, hot. If you can't take heat and humidity, then autumn, winter, and early summer are probably the best times to visit.

GETTING HERE AND AROUND
The Richards Bay airport is the closest to the Hluhluwe-iMfolozi area—about 100 km (60 miles) south of Hluhluwe-iMfolozi and about 224 km (140 miles) south of Ithala.

There are daily flights from Johannesburg to Richards Bay; flight time is about an hour. Private lodges will arrange your transfers for you.

If you're traveling to Hluhluwe-iMfolozi from Durban, drive north on the N2 to Mtubatuba, then cut west on the R618 to Mambeni Gate. Otherwise, continue up the N2 to the Hluhluwe exit and follow the signs to the park and Memorial Gate. The whole trip takes about three hours, but watch out for potholes.

If you're headed to Ithala from Durban, drive north on the N2 to Empangeni, and then head west on the R34 to Vryheid. From here cut east on the R69 to Louwsburg. The reserve is immediately northwest of the village, from which there are clear signs. The journey from Durban takes around 5 hours and from Hluhluwe-iMfolozi about 2½ hours. Roads are good, and there are plenty of gas stations along the way.

Airport Richards Bay Airport ⊠ *Fish Eagle Rd., Richards Bay* ☎ *035/786–0986.* **Upington International Airport** ☎ *054/337–7900* ⊕ *www.upingtonairport.com.*

HLUHLUWE-IMFOLOZI GAME RESERVE

Renowned for its conservation successes—most notably with white rhinos—this reserve is a wonderful place to view the Big Five and many other species. Until 1989 it consisted of two separate parks, Hluhluwe in the north and iMfolozi in the south, separated by a fenced corridor. Although a road (R618) still runs through this corridor, the fences have been removed, and the parks now operate as a single entity. Hluhluwe and the corridor are the most scenic areas of the park, notable for their bush-covered hills and knockout views, whereas iMfolozi is better known for its broad plains.

GETTING HERE AND AROUND

If you're traveling to Hluhluwe-Imfolozi from Durban, drive north on the N2 to Mtubatuba, then cut west on the R618 to Mambeni Gate. Otherwise, continue up the N2 to the Hluhluwe exit and follow the signs to the park and Memorial Gate. The whole trip takes about three hours, but watch out for potholes.

TIMING

Compared to Kruger, Hluhluwe-Imfolozi is tiny—less than 6% of Kruger's size—but such comparisons can be misleading. You can spend days driving around this park and still not see everything, or feel like you're going in circles. Probably the biggest advantage Hluhluwe has over Kruger is that game-viewing is good year-round, whereas Kruger has seasonal peaks and valleys. Another bonus is its proximity to Mkuze Game Reserve and the spectacular coastal reserves of iSimangaliso Greater St. Lucia Wetland Park. The park is also close enough to Durban to make it a worthwhile one- or two-day excursion.

EXPLORING

Hluhluwe-iMfolozi Park. Reputedly King Shaka's favorite hunting ground, Zululand's Hluhluwe-iMfolozi (pronounced "shloo-*shloo*-ee im-fuh-*low*-zee") incorporates two of Africa's oldest reserves: Hluhluwe and iMfolozi, both founded in 1895. In an area of just 906 square km (350 square miles), Hluhluwe-iMfolozi delivers the Big Five plus all the plains game and species like nyala and red duiker that are rare in other parts of the country. Equally important, it encompasses one of the most biologically diverse habitats on the planet, with a unique mix of forest, woodland, savanna, and grassland. You'll find about 1,250 species of plants and trees here—more than in some entire countries.

The park is administered by Ezemvelo KZN Wildlife, the province's official conservation organization, which looks after all the large game reserves and parks as well as many nature reserves. Thanks to its conservation efforts and those of its predecessor, the highly regarded Natal Parks Board, the park can take credit for saving the white rhino from extinction. So successful was the park at increasing white rhino numbers that in 1960 it established its now famous Rhino Capture Unit to relocate rhinos to other reserves in Africa. The park is currently trying to do for the black rhino what it did for its white cousins. Poaching in the past nearly decimated Africa's black rhino population, but as a result of the park's remarkable conservation program, 20% of Africa's remaining black rhinos now live in this reserve—and you won't get a better chance of seeing them in the wild than here. ☎ *033/845–1002* ⊕ *www.kznwildlife.com* 🖱 *R130.*

ACTIVITIES

BUSH WALKS

Armed rangers lead groups of eight on two- to three-hour bush walks departing from Hilltop or Mpila Camp. You may not spot much game on these walks, but you do see plenty of birds, and you learn a great deal about the area's ecology and tips on how to recognize the signs of the bush, including animal spoor. Walks depart daily at 5:30 am and 3:30 pm (6 and 3 in winter) and cost R250. Reserve a few days in advance at **Hilltop Camp** reception (☎ *035/562–0848*).

GAME DRIVES

A great way to see the park is on game drives led by rangers. These drives (R300 per person) hold several advantages over driving through the park yourself: you sit high up in an open-air vehicle with a good view and the wind in your face, a ranger explains the finer points of animal behavior and ecology, and your guide has a good idea where to find animals like leopards, cheetahs, and lions. Game drives leave daily at 5:30 am in summer, 6:30 am in winter. The park also offers three-hour night drives, during which you search with powerful spotlights for nocturnal animals. These three-hour drives depart at 7, and you should make advance reservations at **Hilltop Camp reception** (☎ *035/562–0848*).

WILDERNESS TRAILS

The park's **Wilderness Trails** are every bit as popular as Kruger's, but they tend to be tougher and more rustic. You should be fit enough to walk up to 16 km (10 miles) a day for a period of three days and four nights. An armed ranger leads the hikes, and all equipment, food, and baggage are carried by donkeys. The first and last nights are spent at Mndindini, a permanent tented camp. The other two are spent under canvas in the bush. While in the bush, hikers bathe in the iMfolozi River or have a hot bucket shower; toilet facilities consist of a spade and toilet-paper roll. Trails, open March through October, are limited to eight people and should be reserved a year in advance (R3,430 per person per trail).

Fully catered two- or three-night **Short Wilderness Trails** (R2,250 per person) involve stays at a satellite camp in the wilderness area. You'll sleep in a dome tent, and although there's hot water from a bucket shower, your toilet is a spade.

If that sounds too easy, you can always opt for the four-night **Primitive Trail.** On this trek hikers carry their own packs and sleep out under the stars, although there are lightweight tents for inclement weather. A campfire burns all night to scare off animals, and each participant is expected to sit a 90-minute watch. A ranger acts as guide. The cost is R2,400 per person.

A less rugged wilderness experience can be had on the **Base Camp Trail,** based out of the tented Mndindini camp, where you're guaranteed a bed and some creature comforts. The idea behind these trails is to instill in the participants an appreciation for the beauty of the untamed bush. You can also join the Mpila night drive if you wish. Participation is limited to eight people and costs about R3,900 per person.

The **Explorer Trail,** two nights and three days, combines the most comfortable Base Camp trail with the Primitive Trail. On this trail you sleep out under the stars at a different spot each night. The cost is R2,350 per person.

WHERE TO STAY

Hluhluwe-iMfolozi offers a range of accommodations in government-run rest camps, with an emphasis on self-catering (only Hilltop has a restaurant). The park also has secluded bush lodges and camps, but most foreign visitors can't avail themselves of these lodgings, as each must be reserved in a block, and the smallest accommodates at least eight people. Conservation levies are R80 per person.

PERMANENT CAMPS

$$ FAMILY **Hilltop Camp.** This delightful lodge in the Hluhluwe half of the park matches some of South Africa's best private lodges. Perched on the crest of a hill, with panoramic views over the park, self-contained chalets have high thatch ceilings, rattan furniture, and small verandas. Unless you plan to cook, forgo the more expensive chalets with fully equipped kitchens and eat at the restaurant. If you're on a tight budget, opt for a basic rondavel with two beds, a basin, and a refrigerator; toilet facilities are communal. **TIP→ Chalets with best views are No. 40 upward.** A restaurant, pub, convenience store, and a gas station are on site. **Pros:** floodlit water hole. **Cons:** watch out for marauding monkeys. [$] *Rooms from: R2188* ✉ *Hluhluwe* ☎ *033/845–1000/1 for central reservations, 035/562–0848* 🌐 *www.kznwildlife.com* 🛏 *20 rondavels, 49 chalets, 2 lodges* 🍴 *No meals.*

$$ **Mpila Camp.** In the central iMfolozi section of the park, Mpila is reminiscent of some of Kruger's older camps. Choose among fully equipped one-room chalets with en-suite bathroom, kitchenette and deck, three-bedroom cottages (these come with a cook who will prepare the food you've brought with you) self-catering chalets, and the Safari Tented camp, with two- and four-bed self-catering tents with en-suite bathrooms. Three luxurious lodges with resident chef and ranger are also available. Gas is available, but you can only buy curios and sodas at the camp shop, so stock up with groceries before you arrive. **Pros:** free-roaming game; lovely location. **Cons:** electricity only 7 am–10 pm;

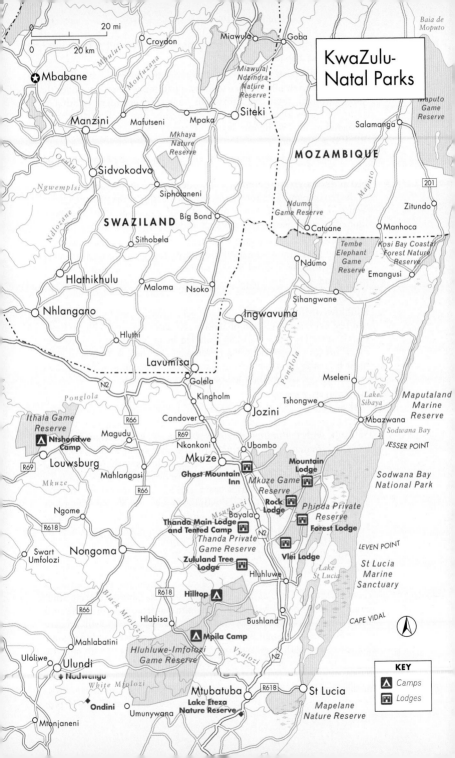

watch out for hyenas stealing your braai meat. $ *Rooms from: R1640* ✉ *Hluhluwe iMfolozi* ☎ *033/845–1000/1 for central reservations, 035/550–8476/7 for reception* ⊕ *www.kznwildlife.com* ⤴ *2 cottages, 18 chalets, 13 safari tents, 2 lodges* ○| *No meals.*

LUXURY LODGES

$$$$
FAMILY
Zululand Tree Lodge. About 16 km (10 miles) from Hluhluwe-iMfolozi Park, this lodge lies in a forest of fever trees on the 3,700-acre Ubizane Game Reserve and makes a great base from which to explore Hluhluwe, Mkuze, and St. Lucia. Built of thatch and wood, the open-sided lodge sits on stilts overlooking the Mzinene River. Rooms are in separate cottages, also on stilts, along the riverbank. The rooms themselves are small but tastefully decorated. A qualified ranger will take you for a bush walk or a game drive (which is included in your stay) through the small reserve or a little farther afield for a game drive in nearby Hluhluwe-iMfolozi. **Pros:** bird's-eye views over lovely surroundings; friendly staff. **Cons:** smelly crocodile pool in front of dining deck. $ *Rooms from: R4560* ✉ *1020 Main Rd., Hluhluwe* ☎ *035/562–1020* ⊕ *www.ubizane.co.za* ⤴ *24 rooms* ○| *All meals.*

UMKHUZE KZN PARK

6

Wildlife—and amazing birdlife—abounds in this 400-square-km (154-square-mile) reserve in the shadow of the Ubombo Mountains. Lying between the uMkhuze and Msunduzi rivers, it makes up the northwestern spur of the iSimangaliso Wetland Park, a UNESCO World Heritage Site. It has been a protected area since 1912.

EXPLORING

uMkhuze KZN Park. If you're a birder, then you'll find yourself in seventh heaven in this reserve, 48 km (30 miles) north of Hluhluwe-iMfolozi, which is famous for its birds: more than 420 bird species have been spotted here, including myriad waterfowl drawn to the park's shallow pans in summer. Several blinds, particularly those overlooking Nsumo Pan, offer superb views. Don't miss out on the amazing 3-km (2-mile) walk through a spectacular rare forest of towering, ancient fig trees. This is a good place to spot rhinos and elephants although lions, cheetah and leopard, are much harder to find. However, there's is plenty of other game, including hippos, zebras, giraffes, kudus, and nyalas. ■ TIP➜ **There are variant spellings of Mkuze in the area; you may also see Mkuzi or Mkhuzi.** ✉ *Off N2, Mkuze* ☎ *035/573–9004* ⊕ *www. kznwildlife.com* ⤴ *R40 per vehicle plus R40 per person* ☉ *Daily 6–6.*

WHERE TO STAY

$$
Ghost Mountain Inn. Swaths of scarlet bougainvillea run riot in the lush gardens of this family-owned country inn with tastefully furnished rooms that each have a small veranda. It was here that Rider Haggard wrote some of his adventure stories, inspired perhaps by the mysterious lights and elusive flickering flames that give the mountain its spooky name. Large, invitingly restful public areas have terra-cotta tiles and comfortable cane furniture. Don't miss the enthusiastic Zulu dancing before a succulent barbecue under the stars. The friendly staff can arrange tours to the neighboring game reserves and cultural sights

or will fix you up to go bird-watching or fishing. **Pros:** good value for money; generous buffet; good curio shop. **Cons:** hotel-like atmosphere; tour buses overnight here. [$] *Rooms from: R2020* ✉ *Fish Eagle Rd., uMkhuze* ☎ *035/573–1025* 🌐 *www.ghostmountaininn.co.za* 🛏 *50 rooms* 🍴 *Breakfast.*

ITHALA GAME RESERVE

The topography of this reserve, from mountaintop to deep river valleys, incorporates varied terrain and plant life, and makes for superior game-viewing in relation to its relatively small size. Thousands of years of human habitation have also provided archaeological and historical interest.

> **SELF-GUIDED TRAILS**
>
> An unusual feature of Ithala is its self-guided walking trails, in the mountainside above Ntshondwe Camp. The trails give you a chance to stretch your limbs if you've just spent hours cooped up in a car. They also let you get really close to the euphorbias, acacias, and other fascinating indigenous vegetation that festoon the hills. Ask at the camp reception for further information.

EXPLORING

Ithala Game Reserve. Close to the Swaziland border, Ithala (sometimes spelled "Itala"), founded in 1972 and run by KZN Wildlife, is a rugged region that drops 3,290 feet in just 15 km (9 miles) through sandstone cliffs, multicolor rocks, granite hills, ironstone outcrops, and quartz formations. Because it's a small reserve (296 square km [114 square miles]) and has no lions, it's often bypassed, even by South Africans. The other four of the Big Five are here—it's excellent for black and white rhinos—and you could spot cheetahs, hyenas, giraffes, and an array of antelope among its 80 mammal species. It's also an excellent spot for birders. The stunning landscapes and the relaxed game-viewing make this area a breath of fresh air after the Big Five melee of Kruger. ✉ *Pongola* ☎ *033/845–1002* 🌐 *www.kznwildlife.com* 🎟 *R40 per person and R40 per vehicle.*

WHERE TO STAY

Although Ithala has several exclusive bush camps, these are booked up months in advance by South Africans, making the chalets at its main camp the only practical accommodations for foreign visitors.

$$ Fodor's Choice ★ 🏨 **Ntshondwe Camp.** Arriving at the award-winning Ntshondwe Camp is nothing short of dramatic. The meandering road climbs from open plains to the top of a plateau dotted with granite formations, which at the last minute magically yield the rest camp at the foot of pink and russet cliffs. The two-, four-, and six-bed self-catering chalets, which blend perfectly with the surroundings, have a simply furnished spacious lounge, a fully equipped kitchen, and a large veranda surrounded by indigenous bush. A magnificent game-viewing deck juts out over a steep slope with views of a water hole and surrounding valleys. A gas station, store (with great curios), and restaurant are all on the premises. **Pros:** tarred road access; game drives; self-guided walks. **Cons:** busy conference and wedding venue. [$] *Rooms from: R1680* ✉ *Ithala Game*

Reserve ☎ *033/845–1000/1* 🌐 *www.kznwildlife.com* 🛏 *67 chalets, 1 lodge* 🍴 *No meals.*

PHINDA PRIVATE GAME RESERVE

Where Phinda excels is in the superb quality of its rangers, who can provide fascinating commentary on everything from local birds to frogs. It's amazing just how enthralling the love life of a dung beetle can be! There are also Phinda adventures (optional extras) down the Mzinene River for a close-up look at crocodiles, hippos, and birds; big-game fishing or scuba diving off the deserted, wildly beautiful Maputaland coast; and sightseeing flights over Phinda and the highest vegetated dunes in the world.

EXPLORING

FAMILY **Phinda Private Game Reserve.** This eco-award-winning flagship &Beyond reserve, established in 1991, is a heartening example of tourism serving the environment with panache. *Phinda* ("*pin*-duh") is Zulu for "return," referring to the restoration of 220 square km (85 square miles) of overgrazed ranchland in northern Zululand to bushveld. It's a triumph. Today Phinda has a stunning variety of five healthy ecosystems: sand forest (which grows on the fossil dunes of an earlier coastline), savanna, bushveld, open woodland, and verdant wetlands. The Big Five are all here, plus leopards, cheetahs, spotted hyenas, hippos, giraffes, impalas, and the rare, elusive, tiny Suni antelope. Birdlife is prolific and extraordinary, with some special Zululand finds: the pink-throated twin spot, the crested guinea fowl, the African broadbill, and the crowned eagle. The reserve is a little more than two hours drive from Richards Bay or four hours by road from Durban. ☎ *011/809–4300* 🌐 *www.andbeyond.com.*

WHERE TO STAY

LUXURY LODGES

$$$$ Fodor's Choice ★ 🏨 **Forest Lodge.** Hidden in a rare sand forest, this fabulous lodge overlooks a small water hole where nyala, warthogs, and baboons frequently come to drink. A real departure from traditional safari lodges, it's very modern, with a vaguely Japanese Zen feel, thanks to glass-panel walls, light woods, and a deliberately spare, clean look. The effect is stylish and very elegant, softened by modern African art and sculpture. Suites use the same architectural concepts as the lodge, where walls have become windows, and rely on the dense forest (or drapes) for privacy. **Pros:** magical feeling of oneness with the surrounding bush. **Cons:** being in a glass box could make some visitors nervous; not for traditional tastes. [$] *Rooms from: R12000* ✉ *Phinda Game Reserve* ☎ *011/809–4300* 🌐 *www.andbeyond.com* 🛏 *16 suites* 🍴 *All-inclusive.*

$$$$ FAMILY 🏨 **Mountain Lodge.** This attractive thatch lodge sits on a rocky hill overlooking miles of bushveld plains and the Ubombo Mountains. Wide verandas lead into the lounge and bar, with their high ceilings, dark beams, and cool tile floors. In winter guests can snuggle into cushioned wicker chairs next to a blazing log fire. Brick pathways wind down the hillside from the lodge to elegant split-level suites with mosquito nets, thatch roofs, and large decks overlooking the reserve. Children are

Hilltop Camp, Hluhluwe Game Reserve

Mpila Camp, Hluhluwe Game Reserve

Interior of Chalet, Hilltop Camp, Hluhluwe GR

Rock Lodge   Mountain Lodge, Phinda Private Game Reserve

Forest Lodge

welcome, although those under five are not allowed on game drives and 6- to 11-year-olds are permitted only at the manager's discretion. **Pros:** great mountain views; very family-friendly. **Cons:** rather bland interiors; pricey if you take the kids (pricey even if you don't take the kids). $ *Rooms from: R12000* ✉ *Phinda Game Reserve, off R22, Hluhluwe* 📞 *011/809–4300* ⊕ *www.andbeyond.com* 🔄 *25 suites* 🍽 *All-inclusive.*

$$$$ 🏨 **Rock Lodge.** If you get tired of the eagle's-eye view of the deep valley below from your private veranda, you can write in your journal in your luxurious sitting room or take a late-night dip in your own plunge pool. All of Phinda's activities are included—twice-daily game drives, nature walks, riverboat cruises, and canoe trips along the Mzinene River. Scuba diving, deep-sea fishing, and spectacular small-plane flights are extras. Don't miss out on one of Phinda's legendary bush dinners: hundreds of lanterns light up the surrounding forest and bush, and the food is unforgettable. **Pros:** personal plunge pools; amazing views. **Cons:** stay away if you suffer from vertigo. $ *Rooms from: R14340* ✉ *Phinda Game Reserve* 📞 *011/809–4300* ⊕ *www.andbeyond.com* 🔄 *6 suites* 🍽 *All-inclusive.*

$$$$
Fodor's Choice
★

🏨 **Vlei Lodge.** Your suite at this comfortable lodge, tucked into the shade of a sand forest, is so private it's hard to believe there are other guests. Made of thatch, teak, and glass, they have a distinct Asian feel and overlook a marshland on the edge of an inviting woodland. The bedrooms and bathrooms are huge, and each has a private plunge pool (one visitor found a lion drinking from his) and outdoor deck. The lounge-living area of the lodge has a dining area, and a large terrace under a canopy of trees, where breakfast is served. The bush braai, with its splendid food and fairy-tale setting, is a memorable occasion after an evening game drive. **Pros:** superb views over the floodplains. **Cons:** lots of mosquitoes and other flying insects. $ *Rooms from: R14340* ✉ *Phinda Game Reserve* 📞 *011/809–4300* ⊕ *www.andbeyond.com* 🔄 *6 suites* 🍽 *All-inclusive.*

THANDA PRIVATE GAME RESERVE

One of KwaZulu-Natal's newer game reserves, Thanda offers a more intimate nature experience than some. Game may sometimes be elusive, but the highly experienced and enthusiastic rangers work hard to find the Big Five and other wildlife. Enjoyable cultural interactions with local people are a highlight of any visit.

EXPLORING

Thanda Private Game Reserve. In wild, beautiful northern Zululand, the multi-award-winning 150-square-km (60-square-mile) Thanda reserve, which turned 10 in 2014, continues to restore former farmlands and hunting grounds to their previous pristine state, thanks to a joint venture with local communities and the king of the Zulus, Goodwill Zwelitini, who donated some of his royal hunting grounds to the project. Game that used to roam this wilderness centuries ago has been reestablished, including the Big Five. *Thanda* ("*tan*-duh") is Zulu for "love," and its philosophy echoes just that: "for the love of nature, wildlife, and dear ones." There's a main lodge, a private villa, and a small tented camp and opportunities to interact with the local people. ✉ *D242, off N2, Hluhluwe* 🌐 *www.thanda.com.*

GETTING HERE AND AROUND

Road transfers from Richards Bay and Durban airports can be arranged with the reserve.

WHERE TO STAY

LUXURY LODGE

$$$$ FAMILY **Thanda Main Lodge.** This exquisite lodge blends elements of royal Zulu with an eclectic pan-African feel. Domed, beehive-shap dwellings perch on the side of rolling hills and overlook mountains and bushveld. Inside, contemporary Scandinavian touches meet African chic—from the "eyelashes" of slatted poles that peep out from under the thatch roofs to the embedded mosaics in royal Zulu red and blue that decorate the polished, honey-color stone floors. A huge stone fireplace divides the bedroom area from the comfortable and roomy lounge, whilst outside there's a personal plunge pool, private deck, and cushioned *sala* (outdoor covered deck). Dine on a superb meal with other guests or alone in your private boma under the stars. **Pros:** luxury unlimited. **Cons:** some might say it's Hollywood in the bush. 💲 *Rooms from: R12500* ✉ *Off N2 and D242, Hluhluwe* ☎ *035/573–1899* 🌐 *www.thanda.com* *9 chalets* *All-inclusive.*

PERMANENT CAMP

$$$$ FAMILY **Thanda Tented Camp.** Perfect for a family or friends' reunion (although great for individual travelers too), this intimate, luxurious camp deep in the bush brings you into close contact with your surroundings. You might wake up in your spacious safari tent with en-suite bathroom and private veranda to find a warthog or nyala grazing outside. The camp has its own vehicle, ranger, and tracker, and a huge sala with pool and sundeck. Jabula (meaning "happiness" in isiZulu) Tent is the ultimate bush honeymoon getaway. **Pros:** five-star luxury on a bonsai scale; solar power. **Cons:** not for the nervous type; no a/c; no children. 💲 *Rooms from: R7100* ✉ *Off N2, D242, Hluhluwe* ☎ *035/573–1899* 🌐 *www.thanda.co.za* *15 tents* *All-inclusive.*

KGALAGADI TRANSFRONTIER PARK

Game
★★★★
Park Accessibility
★★★
Getting Around
★★★★★
Accommodations
★★★★
Scenic Beauty
★★★★★

If you're looking for true wilderness, remoteness, and stark, almost surreal landscapes and you're not averse to forgoing luxury and getting sand in your hair, then this uniquely beautiful park within the Kalahari Desert is for you.

In an odd little finger of the country jutting north between Botswana in the east and Namibia in the west lies South Africa's second-largest park after Kruger. The "reborn" Kgalagadi was officially launched in 2000 as the first transfrontier, or "peace park," in southern Africa by merging South Africa's vast Kalahari Gemsbok National Park with the even larger Gemsbok National Park in Botswana. The name Kgalagadi (pronounced "kala-*hardy*") is derived from the San language and means "place of thirst." It's now one of the largest protected wilderness areas in the world—an area of more than 38,000 square km (14,670 square miles). Of this awesome area, 9,600 square km (3,700 square miles) fall in South Africa, and the rest fall in Botswana.

Passing through the Twee Rivieren Gate, you'll encounter a vast desert under enormous, usually cloudless skies and a sense of space and openness that few other places can offer. With the rest camp to the left, just a little farther down the dirt road to the right is the dry Nossob River, lined by camel-thorn trees, which winds its way to Botswana, into which the park continues.

The Kgalagadi Transfrontier is less commercialized and developed than Kruger. The roads aren't paved, and you'll come across far fewer people and cars. There's less game on the whole than in Kruger, but because there's also less vegetation, the animals are much more visible. Also, because the game and large carnivores are concentrated in two river-beds (the route that two roads follow), the park offers unsurpassed game-viewing and photographic opportunities. Perhaps the key to really appreciating this barren place is in understanding how its creatures have adapted to their harsh surroundings to survive—like the gemsbok, which has a sophisticated cooling system allowing it to tolerate extreme changes in body temperature. There are also insects in the park that inhale only every half hour or so to preserve the moisture that breathing expends.

The landscape—endless dunes punctuated with blond grass and the odd thorn tree—is dominated by two *wadis* (dry riverbeds): the Nossob (which forms the border between South Africa and Botswana) and its tributary, the Auob. The Nossob flows only a few times a century, and the Auob flows only once every couple of decades or so. A single road runs beside each riverbed, along which windmills pump water into man-made water holes, which help the animals to survive and provide good viewing stations for visitors. There are 82 water holes, 49 of which are along tourist roads. Park management struggles to keep up their maintenance; it's a constant battle against the elements, with the elements often winning. Similarly, the park constantly maintains and improves tourist roads, but again it's a never-ending struggle. A third road traverses the park's interior to join the other two. The scenery and vegetation on this road change dramatically from two river valleys dominated by sandy banks to a grassy escarpment. Two more dune roads have been added, and several 4x4 routes have been developed. From Nossob camp a road leads to Union's End, the country's northernmost tip, where South Africa, Namibia, and Botswana meet. Allow a full day for the long and dusty drive, which is 124 km (77 miles) one way. It's possible to enter Botswana from the South African side, but you'll need a 4x4. The park infrastructure in Botswana is very basic, with just three campsites and mostly 4x4 terrain.

The park is famous for its gemsbok, the desert-adapted springbok, and its legendary, huge, black-maned Kalahari lions. It also has leopards, cheetahs, eland, blue wildebeests, jackals, and giraffes, as well as meerkats and mongooses. Rarer desert species, such as the elusive aardvark and the pretty Cape fox, also make their home here. Among birders, the park is known as one of Africa's raptor meccas; it's filled with bateleurs, lappet-faced vultures, pygmy falcons, and the cooperatively hunting red-necked falcons and gabar goshawks.

The park's legendary night drives (approximately R200 per person) depart most evenings around 5:30 in summer, earlier in winter (check when you get to your camp), from Twee Rivieren Camp and Nossob. The drives set out just as the park gate closes to everyone else. You'll have a chance to see rare nocturnal animals like the brown hyena and the bat-eared fox by spotlight. The guided morning walks—during which you see the sun rise over the Kalahari and could bump into a lion—are also a must. Reservations are essential and can be made when you book your accommodations.

WHEN TO GO

The park can be superhot in summer and freezing at night in winter (literally below zero, with frost on the ground). Autumn—from late February to mid-April—is perhaps the best time to visit. It's cool after the rains, and many of the migratory birds are still around. The winter months of June and July are also a good time. It's best to make reservations as far in advance as possible, even up to 11 months if you want to visit at Easter or in June or July, when there are school vacations.

GETTING HERE AND AROUND

Upington International Airport is 260 km (162 miles) south of Kgalagadi Transfrontier Park; many lodgings provide shuttle service, or you can rent a car at the airport. If you reserve a car through an agency in Upington, you can pick it up from the Twee Rivieren Camp. If you drive from Johannesburg, you have a choice of two routes: either via Upington (with the last stretch a 60-km [37-mile] gravel road) or via Kuruman, Hotazel, and Vanzylrus (with about 340 km [211 miles] of gravel road). The gravel sections on both routes are badly corrugated, so don't speed.

Airport Information Upington International Airport ✉ *Diedricks St., Upington* ☎ *054/337–7900.*

VISITOR INFORMATION

There's a daily conservation fee, but Wild Cards, available at the gates or online, are more economical for stays of more than a few days. Reservations for all accommodations, bush drives, wilderness trails, and other park activities must be made through South African National Parks.

EXPLORING

Kgalagadi Transfrontier Park. Originally called Kalahari Gemsbok National Park when it was first incorporated in 1931, Kgalagadi was combined with Botswana's Gemsbok National Park to create this internationally protected area of nearly 9 million acres. Unlike Kruger, South Africa's other mammoth national park, this is a desert park, with sparse vegetation and even sand dunes. The game seen here is mostly concentrated around two roads, which follow the park's two (mostly) dry riverbeds. Black-maned Kalahari lions, springbok, oryx, pygmy falcons, and martial eagles are among the star animal attractions. You will not find the broad range of animals that you see in Kruger, but because of the sparse vegetation and limited grazing areas, they are more visible here. Among the noteworthy plant species are plenty of beautiful camel-thorn acacia trees. The park has several lodges and more rustic rest camps for accommodations, but its isolation means that it's never as crowded as Kruger. ✉ *Twee Rivieren Rest Camp, Kgalagadi Transfrontier Park* ☎ *054/561–2000* ⊕ *www.sanparks.co.za* ✉ *R248 per person per day.*

WHERE TO STAY

Accommodations within the park are in three traditional rest camps and several highly sought-after wilderness camps (try to reserve these if possible) that are spread around the park. All of the traditional rest camps have shops selling food, curios, and some basic equipment, but Twee Rivieren has the best variety of fresh fruit, vegetables, milk, and meat, and is the only camp with a restaurant. Twee Rivieren is also the only camp with telephone and cell-phone reception (although cell-phone reception quickly disappears as you head into the dunes) and 24-hour

"This giraffe was photographed during my first day on safari. A beautiful animal in the perfect location. I was hooked." —wlbox, Fodors.com member

electricity; the other camps have gas and electricity, but the electricity runs only part of the day, at different times in each camp.

For all national park accommodations, contact South African National Parks (✉ *reservation@sanparks.org*), or you can reserve directly through the park if you happen to be there and would like to stay a night or add another night onto your stay.

For a private luxury lodge, !Xaus, owned by the Khomani San community, is deep in the west of the park. Because it's roughly 50 km (32 miles) in from the gate, guests are met by a vehicle at the Kumqwa rest area, where they park their car. From there it is exactly 91 dunes to the lodge in a 4x4—and well worth it.

BOOKING

South African National Parks. Usually safest to book through this central booking office in Pretoria, although often when that office says "full," the camp itself has vacancies. ☎ *012/428–9111 in Pretoria, 021/552–0008 in Cape Town* ⊕ *www.sanparks.org.*

A limited number of campsites (R195) are available at Nossob (20) and Twee Rivieren (24). All campsites have a *braai* and access to electricity and water, and there are communal bathroom facilities and a basic communal kitchen. Before you arrive, be sure to arm yourself with the "blue camping plug"—available from any camping–RV shop—to plug into the electrical system and a long extension cord. Try to find a shady spot.

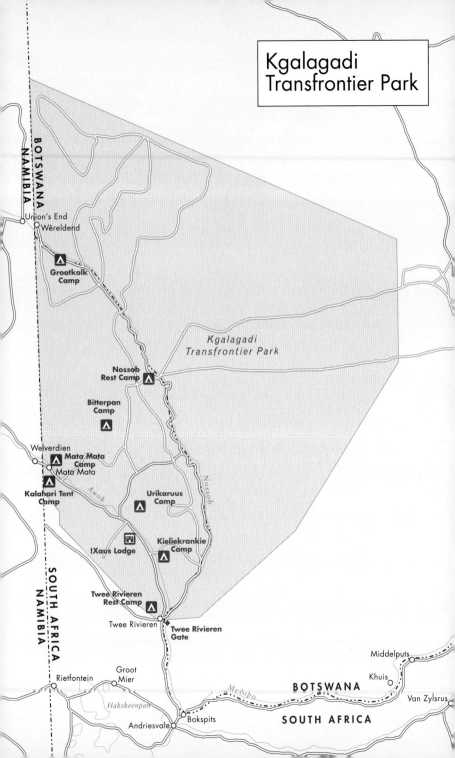

CLOSE UP

San Culture and Language

Also called the /Xam, the hunter-gatherer San (Bushmen) have a culture that dates back more than 20,000 years, and their genetic origins are more than 1 million years old, contemporary humans' oldest. Fast-forward a few years—about 2,000 years ago, to be inexact—when Korana or Khoi (Khoe) herders migrated south, bringing their livestock and settling along the Orange (Gariep/Garieb), Vaal, and Riet rivers. During the 18th and 19th centuries, the Griquas—thought to be part Khoi and part slave—moved into the Northern Cape with their cattle and sheep.

At one time 20 to 30 languages pertaining to various clans flourished, but colonialism brought with it devastating results for the San's native tongue. It lost out to Tswana and Afrikaans. In the nick of time in the 1870s, British doctor Wilhelm Bleek, who spoke /Xam, and Lucy Lloyd recorded the last activities of /Xam culture and tradition. (Some of these records can be found at the McGregor Museum in Kimberley.)

Still, thousands of Northern Cape residents today acknowledge an ancestral connection to the largest San or /Xam group of the 18th and 19th centuries. The two biggest remaining groups are the !Xu and Khwe, who live at Schmidtsdrift, 80 km (50 miles) from Kimberley. Among the best-known groups in South Africa today are the Khomani San.

6

LUXURY LODGE

$ **!Xaus Lodge.** If you want to experience one of South Africa's most
Fodor's Choice beautiful and isolated parks without hassle, then this luxury lodge
★ owned by the Khomani San and Mier communities and jointly managed with SANParks is the place for you. You'll be picked up in a 4x4 from Twee Rivieren, fed, watered, taken on game drives and desert walks, and introduced to the local San. Located deep in the desert 32 km (20 miles) from the Auob River Road along a track that crosses the red dunes of the Kalahari, this enchanting lodge overlooks an amazingly scenic saltpan. The twin-bed, en-suite chalets perch on sand dunes overlooking the pan, which is 1 km in circumference; each chalet has a private deck. A fan will keep you cool in summer, and a gas heater, hot-water bottle, blankets and warm sheets will help you stay warm on winter nights. A welcome swimming pool is set in a deck overlooking the pan. The attractive rustic furniture and eye-catching artwork throughout this delightful, unique lodge are all made by local craftspeople and artists. Activities include game drives in an open safari vehicle, walks with San trackers, and a chance to watch San artists at work. At night the stars and planets are bright and clear, especially at new moon; a telescope brings ancient tradition and modern technology together as the San interpret for you their legends of the night sky. But !Xaus (pronounced "*kaus*") comprises so much more than its activities: it is solitude, peace, and silence as you "listen" to day turn into night, plus interaction with the cheerful and willing staff, the majority of whom come from the surrounding local communities. **Pros:** unique wilderness

!Xaus Lodge, Kgalagadi Transfrontier Park

setting; only private lodge in area; opportunities to interact with the local people. **Cons:** It doesn't get much more remote than this; not a Big Five destination. $ *Rooms from: R3670* ✉ *Dune 92 Kgalagadi, Kgalagadi Transfrontier Park* ☎ *021/701–7860* ⊕ *www.xauslodge.co.za* ⏎ *12 chalets* ⦿ *All-inclusive.*

NATIONAL PARK ACCOMMODATIONS
REST CAMPS

$ 🛏 **Nossob Rest Camp.** In the central section of the park, this camp is on the Botswana border, 166 km (103 miles) from Twee Rivieren. Basic brick chalets come with an outside braai and real bush atmosphere and sleep three to six people. Guesthouses have showers but no tubs. Most of the chalets are less than 50 yards from the fence, and there's also a stunning blind overlooking the water hole. You can see game without even leaving camp, but watch out for marauding jackals here; although they're not dangerous or aggressive, they're always on the lookout for unattended food. A small shop sells the basics. There's no electricity in the camp, and the generators are turned off at 11. **Pros:** riverbed location in a desert landscape makes it a great place to see predators, particularly lions; predator information center. **Cons:** barren, unattractive camp; no phone reception. $ *Rooms from: R750* ✉ *Kgalagadi Transfrontier Park* ☎ *012/428–9111* ⊕ *www.sanparks.org* ⏎ *15 chalets, 1 cottage, 2 guesthouses, 21 campsites* ⦿ *No meals.*

$ 🛏 **Twee Rivieren Rest Camp.** On the Kgalagadi's southern boundary, this
FAMILY camp is home to the park's headquarters. It's the biggest of the camps and has the most modern facilities; all units have fully equipped kitchens, and the camp shop here is the best. You can choose from a couple of

types of accommodations, from a two-bedroom, six-bed family cottage to a bungalow with two single beds and a sleeper couch. Try for units 1–16, which look out over the dunes. Take a guided morning walk *and* a night drive—worth every penny. There are educational exhibits on the Kalahari's animal and plant life. From Upington to Twee Rivieren is 260 km (161 miles) on a relatively good road; only the last 52 km (32 miles) are gravel. **Pros:** modern, well-equipped chalets; on-site grocery store selling basics; not-to-be-missed guided morning and night drives; 24-hour electricity. **Cons:** the biggest and noisiest camp in the park; not particularly attractive [$] *Rooms from: R1110* ✉ *Kgalagadi Transfrontier Park* ☎ *012/428–9111* ✍ *reservations@sanparks.org* 🌐 *www.sanparks.org* 🛏 *1 cottage, 30 bungalows* 🍴 *No meals.*

WILDERNESS CAMPS

Kgalagadi is the first national park to provide accommodation deep in the wilderness, where several unfenced wilderness camps with their own water holes for game-viewing put you deep in the heart of the Kalahari. These enchanting camps are very popular, so make your reservations well in advance—11 months ahead, if possible. Each camp is slightly different, but all have the same facilities and are similarly priced. All have an equipped kitchen with a gas-powered refrigerator, solar-powered lights, gas for hot water, and a deck with braai facilities. You do need to supply your own water and firewood.

6

Because all of these camps are unfenced (which is part of their desirability and charm), it's probably best not to walk outside your accommodation at night. There's a very real chance of face-to-face encounters with nocturnal hunters like lions, leopards, and hyenas.

$ 🏨 **Bitterpan.** This camp overlooks an enormous expanse of sand and a water hole, where you can watch game come and go from your deck or from the communal areas. Four double cabins with their own bathrooms border a narrow walkway that leads to a large communal kitchen, dining room, and braai area. Bitterpan is accessible only by 4x4, and only guests here may use the road from Nossob to Urikaruus. **Pros:** spectacular game-viewing from your accommodation; beautiful desert scenery; only four cabins. **Cons:** 4x4s only; no children under 12; communal kitchen and eating area (cross fingers you share the camp with amenable visitors); it's a long drive to get here from any starting point; guests have to bring their own drinking water and firewood. [$] *Rooms from: R1165* ✉ *Kgalagadi Transfrontier Park* ☎ *012/428–9111* 🌐 *www.sanparks.org* 🛏 *4 cabins* 🍴 *No meals.*

$ 🏨 **Grootkolk.** Surrounded by camelthorn trees and close to the Nossob River bed, this lovely camp has good game-viewing, with lions, cheetahs, hyenas, and lots of antelope, including oryx and springbok, and it can book up months in advance. All four well-sited rustic desert cabins have a good view of the water hole, which is spotlighted for a couple of hours every night. Although the road to Grootkolk is heavily corrugated, you can negotiate it with a two-wheel-drive vehicle. **Pros:** spotlighted water hole; sublime wilderness; ceiling fans in the cabins. **Cons:** 4x4s or 2x4s only; no children under 12; chalets are made from canvas and sandbags, so if you prefer something more substantial, stay away.

[$] *Rooms from: R1350* ✉ *Kgalagadi Transfrontier Park* ☎ *012/428–9111* 🌐 *www.sanparks.org* 🛏 *4 cabins* 🍴 *No meals.*

$ 🏨 **Kalahari Tent Camp.** Many visitors say that this good game-viewing camp overlooking the Auob River bed and water hole is one of the most beautiful places in the park, so try to stay for more than one night. Your accommodation consists of a large walk-in tent with a spacious and attractive bedroom, shower, and toilet. There's a separate, fully equipped kitchen tent, also suitable as a dining room, and the terrace between these two tents has excellent views over the riverbed and its wildlife. At night, look out for jackals, lions, a resident family of meerkats, and spare-wheel-cover-eating hyenas around the tents—just be sure to stay in your tent at night and avoid walking around. The secluded honeymoon unit has a king-size bed and a bath and shower. **Pros:** near Mata Mata, which has a shop and gas; excellent game-viewing; family-friendly; lovely honeymoon tent; ceiling fans in the tents, pool. **Cons:** guests must bring their own drinking water and firewood. [$] *Rooms from: R1355* ✉ *Kgalagadi Transfrontier Park* ☎ *012/428–9111* ✉ *reservations@sanparks.org* 🌐 *www.sanparks.org* 🛏 *10 tents, 4 family tents, 1 honeymoon tent* 🍴 *No meals.*

FAMILY

$ 🏨 **Kieliekrankie.** Perched high on a big sand dune only 8 km (5 miles) from the game-rich Auob River road, this small camp overlooks seemingly infinite red Kalahari sands, creating an amazing sense of space and isolation. The four cabins have stunning views over the desert and come with a kitchen tent, bedroom, bathroom, and deck with braai. **Pros:** easily accessible with a sedan; you can start your game drives before residents of the other camps reach the area so you have the game to yourself for a while; the red Kalahari sands are unforgettable. **Cons:** no children under 12; guests must bring their own drinking water and firewood. [$] *Rooms from: R1350* ✉ *Kgalagadi Transfrontier Park* ☎ *012/428–9111* 🌐 *www.sanparks.org* 🛏 *4 cabins* 🍴 *No meals.*

$ 🏨 **Urikaruus.** Four cabins with kitchens, bedrooms, and bathrooms are built on stilts among camelthorn trees overlooking the Auob River. You'll easily spot game as it comes to drink at the water hole close to the cabins. **Pros:** accessible with a sedan; stunning location; game to yourself on early-morning and late-afternoon drives; cabins have their own kitchens. **Cons:** no children under 12; guests must bring their own drinking water and firewood. [$] *Rooms from: R1350* ✉ *Kgalagadi Transfrontier Park* ☎ *012/428–9111* 🌐 *www.sanparks.org* 🛏 *4 cabins* 🍴 *No meals.*

IF YOU HAVE TIME

Although this chapter goes into great detail about the must-see parks in South Africa, there are many others to explore if you have time. Here are a few good ones to consider.

NORTHERN CAPE

TSWALU KALAHARI RESERVE

250 km (155 miles) southeast of Kgalagadi Transfrontier Park; 262 km (163 miles) northeast of Upington; 145 km (90 miles) northwest of Kuruman.

Near the Kgalagadi Transfrontier Park is the malaria-free Tswalu Kalahari Reserve, at 1,000 square km (386 square miles) the largest privately owned game reserve in Africa; it's the perfect place to photograph a gemsbok against a red dune and big blue sky. Initially founded as a conservation project by the late millionaire Stephen Boler (how he made his money is a story in itself), primarily to protect and breed the endangered desert rhino, he left it to the Oppenheimer family (of De Beers diamonds fame) in his will. Today it spreads over endless Kalahari dunes covered with tufts of golden veld and over much of the Northern Cape's Korannaberg mountain range. Its initial population of 7,000 animals has grown, and it's now home to lions, cheetahs, buffalo, giraffes, and a range of antelope species—including rare species such as roan and sable antelope, black wildebeests, and mountain zebras. For (sadly) financial reasons a fence keeps the lion and the sable antelope separate in this massive reserve. There's not as much game as in some of Mpumalanga's private reserves because the land has a lower carrying capacity (the annual rainfall is only about 9¾ inches). But when you do see the animals, the lack of vegetation makes sightings spectacular.

GETTING HERE AND AROUND

The lodge operates a direct flight between its Johannesburg airport hangar and Tswalu (this has to be booked directly through the reserve). It's also easy (and cheaper) to fly to Kimberley or Upington and be picked up from there by the lodge. Daily charter flights are available from Johannesburg, Durban, and Cape Town with Airlink and Federal Air. Road transfers from Kimberley or Upington can be arranged, or you can book a charter flight from Johannesburg.

EXPLORING

FAMILY **Tswalu Kalahari Reserve.** This reserve northeast of Upington is one of the most child-friendly game reserves in southern Africa. Children are welcomed and well catered to, with lots of freedom and special activities. No other game reserve offers such flexibility, and the dedication of the field guides and butlers here allows you to plan your days as you please: you might prefer a champagne breakfast in your stunning accommodation to going out on a game drive, or you may want to sleep under the stars on the "Malori" open deck. The reserve plays a particularly important conservation role: backed by funds from the De Beers family, its desert black rhino population represents one third of South Africa's entire remaining animals. In addition to rhino sightings, the interactive experience with the meerkats is a highlight when staying at Tswalu, as are visits to 380,000-year-old rock engravings from the earliest residents of these phenomenal landscapes.

A stop on your game drive from one of the many spacious hills affords a peace and serenity not often experienced in Africa, as you sip sundowners on red dunes while the typically sensational sunsets are the cherry on top. The reserve is a must-visit if you're in the area, and there are easy connections via Johannesburg by charter flight. Kuruman is the nearest town. ✉ *Kuruman* ☎ *053/781–9331* 🌐 *www.tswalu.com.*

WHERE TO STAY

$$$$ FAMILY 🏨 **The Motse.** Tswalu's main lodge is made up of freestanding thatch-and-stone suites clustered around a large main building with a heated natural-color pool and a floodlighted water hole. The décor—in keeping with the unusual and unique Tswalu experience—is minimalist and modern, echoing the landscape in colors and textures. But this makes it sound drab, and it's not. Indeed, it's beautiful. **Pros:** special children's room and babysitting services and nannies available; unique desert landscape; same great wildlife as Tarkuni; wonderful library with rare books. **Cons:** no elephants; sable antelopes kept separate from the lions, making the experience feel a little manufactured. [$] *Rooms from: R10600* ✉ *Tswalu Kalahari Reserve* 🌐 *www.tswalu.com* 🛏 *8 suites* 🍴 *All meals.*

$$$$ FAMILY 🏨 **Tswalu Tarkuni Lodge.** In a private section of Tswalu, Tarkuni is an exclusive, self-contained house decorated similarly to The Motswe and offering a comparable level of luxury. Perfect for small groups and families, Tarkuni sleeps 10 and comes with its own chef, game vehicle, and tracker. The food is almost as memorable as the scenery, and every meal is served in a different location: on a lantern-lighted dune or alongside a crackling fire in the lodge's boma. Apart from guided walks and drives, horseback trails (not included in the rate) that you traverse with a qualified guide offer close encounters with wildlife. Two sets of bunk beds, plus an adjoining nanny's quarters, are geared toward children. **Pros:** this is excellent value, and if there are 10 of you, it works out to be far more affordable than most other luxury lodges; a children's paradise; black-maned Kalahari lions, occasional wild dogs, cheetahs, and one third of South Africa's endangered desert black rhino population; if you're a fan of TV's *Meerkat Manor,* you'll be in a seventh heaven. **Cons:** no elephants. [$] *Rooms from: US$5711* ✉ *Tswalu Kalahari Reserve* 🌐 *www.tswalu.com* 🛏 *1 house* 🍴 *All meals.*

EASTERN CAPE

ADDO ELEPHANT NATIONAL PARK

72 km (45 miles) north of Port Elizabeth.

GETTING HERE AND AROUND

The closest airport to Addo Elephant Park is Port Elizabeth (PLZ) airport. Flights arrive daily from all of South Africa's main cities via South African Airways, SA Express, SA Airlink, British Airways, and the budget airlines Mango and Kulula. Flights from Cape Town take roughly 1 hour and from Johannesburg 1½ hours.

Traveling by car is the easiest and best way to tour this area, as public transport is limited. Some roads are unpaved but in decent condition. Most lodges will organize airport transfers for their guests

EXPLORING

Addo Elephant National Park. Smack in the middle of a citrus-growing and horse-breeding area, Addo Elephant National Park is home to a staggering 700 elephants not to mention plenty of buffalo, black rhino, leopards, spotted hyena, hundreds of kudu and other antelopes, and lions. At present the park has about 400,000 acres, but it's expanding all the time and is intended to reach a total of about 600,000 acres, including a fully ncorporated marine section. The most accessible parts of the park are the original, main section and the Colchester, Kabouga, Woody Cape, and Zuurberg sections. The original section of Addo still holds most of the game and is served by Addo Main Camp. The Colchester section, in the south, which has one SANParks camp, is contiguous with the main area. The scenic Nyati section is separated from the main section by a road and railway line. Just north of Nyati is the mountainous Zuurberg section, which doesn't have a large variety of game but is particularly scenic, with fabulous hiking trails and horse trails. It is also the closest section of the park to Addo Elephant Back Safaris. You can explore the park in your own vehicle, in which case you need to heed the road signs that claim "dung beetles have right of way." Addo is home to the almost-endemic and extremely rare flightless dung beetle, which can often be seen rolling its unusual incubator across the roads. Watch out for them (they're only about 2 inches long, but have sharp spines that can puncture tires), and watch them: they're fascinating. Instead of driving you could take a night or day game drive with a park ranger in an open vehicle from the main camp. A more adventurous option is to ride a horse among the elephants. Warning: no citrus fruit may be brought into the park, as elephants find it irresistible and can smell it for miles. ✉ *Addo Elephant National Park* ☎ *042/233–8600* 🌐 *www.addoelephantpark.com* 🎫 *R50* 🕒 *Daily 7–7 (may vary with seasons).*

WHERE TO STAY

$ 🏨 **Addo Elephant National Park Main Camp.** One of the best SANParks rest camps, this location has a range of self-catering accommodations, such as safari tents, forest cabins, rondavels, cottages, and chalets, and a shop that sells basic supplies as well as souvenirs. An à la carte restaurant with reasonable prices is open for all meals, and a floodlit waterhole is nearby, which allows great nighttime game viewing opportunities. Prices are calculated according to a complicated SANParks formula, which works by unit price, not per person. Camping rates are R230 for up to two people. Note that these are the minimum rates even if there's only one person booking the accommodation. There's also a conservation levy, which is paid per person per day in the park. **Pros:** great value; you get to enter the game area before the main gates open and go on night drives. **Cons:** the shop has only basic supplies; the rondavels have shared cooking facilities. [$] *Rooms from: R1300* ✉ *Addo Elephant National Park* ☎ *012/428–9111* 🌐 *www.addoelephant.com* 🛏 *65 suites* 🍴 *No meals.*

6

"Addo Elephant Park: [these elephants were lined up] all in a row, drinking water in an orderly way. Small to big." —JAK, Fodors.com member

$$$$ **Gorah Elephant Camp.** A private concession within the main section of Addo, this picturesque colonial-themed camp has accommodations in spacious, luxurious safari tents with thick thatch canopies and furnished in antiques from the colonial era. Each tent has an en-suite bathroom with shower and a private deck with uninterrupted views. The lodge itself is a gracious old farmhouse with an interesting history dating all the way back to 1856. The whole camp is completely unfenced and overlooks a water hole, so it's possible to watch elephants, buffalo, and other animals from your lunch table or the veranda, while you may be woken at night by the sound of marauding lions and hyenas passing close to the tents. Everything at Gorah is understated yet seriously stylish, including the swimming-pool area, and the cuisine and service are outstanding. Dinner is served by romantic candlelight, either on the veranda or in the splendid dining room. The camp is run partly on solar power and partly by a generator at certain times of day, so Wi-Fi is not accessible at all times and only in the main lodge building. The lodge operates two game drives a day within the private concession area and the rest of Addo. **Pros:** the food and service are top-notch; guests are not required to sit together at meals; the location and colonial style are special. **Cons:** rooms don't have bathtubs; rooms can get cold at night in winter; you often have to leave the private concession area to find the best game. *Rooms from: R10000 ✉ Addo Elephant National Park ☎ 044/501–1111 res@hunterhotels.com www.hunterhotels.com 11 tents All inclusive.*

$$ **Fodor's Choice ★** **Hitgeheim Country Lodge.** This lovely lodge is set on a steep cliff overlooking the Sundays River and the town of Addo. Classically decorated rooms graced with lovely antiques are in separate thatch buildings, all with verandas overlooking the river. The bathrooms are spacious and luxuriously appointed with large tubs and enormous shower stalls. Some rooms have indoor and outdoor showers. Birds frolic in the natural vegetation that has been allowed to grow up to the edge of the verandas, and tame buck often wander around the garden. Hitgeheim (pronounced "hitch-ee-hime") is situated on an eco-reserve and you can go for walks to observe birdlife and perhaps view some of the 11 indigenous antelope species found here. The food is fabulous, and most guests opt to stay for the four-course dinners (R325, guests only), although simpler dinner options can be tailor-made to your preferences. The lodge has its own game-viewing vehicle and guide, which can be booked at an extra cost, and can also organize elephant-back riding and day-trips to the nearby Big Five game reserves. **Pros:** personal touches, such as a turndown service and luxury bath products by the South African company Charlotte Rhys; very friendly and helpful owners; very reasonable prices. **Cons:** not for independent travelers, as the owners like to arrange your activities for you; the restaurant is not open to nonguests. $ *Rooms from: R2500* ✉ *Addo Elephant National Park ✛ 18 km (11 miles) from Addo Main Gate on R335, then follow R336 to Kirkwood* ☎ *042/234–0778* ⊕ *www.hitgeheim-addo.co.za* ⤳ *8 suites* ⧉ *Breakfast.*

$$$$ 🏨 **River Bend Lodge.** Situated on a 34,594-acre private concession within **FAMILY** the Nyati section of Addo, River Bend perfectly balances the feel of a sophisticated, comfortable country house with all the facilities of a game lodge. The spacious public rooms, filled with antiques and comfy couches, are in a beautifully renovated farmhouse and outbuildings. The guest rooms are in individual cottages with private verandas dotted around the lovely gardens; some have outdoor showers and each is uniquely decorated with a different color scheme. In addition to the usual game drives, you can tour the adjacent citrus farm. There's also a safari villa that sleeps six. **Pros:** kids are welcome, and there's an enclosed playground; the food is excellent, especially the seven-course dinner menu; all food and drinks are included in the rack rates. **Cons:** décor is more English colonial than African; only the honeymoon suite has a plunge pool; it's not the most exciting section of the park in terms of game. $ *Rooms from: R11000* ✉ *Zuurberg, Addo Elephant National Park* ☎ *042/233–8000* ✍ *reservations@riverbendlodge.co.za* ⊕ *www.riverbendlodge.co.za* ⤳ *8 suites* ⧉ *All meals.*

KWANDWE PRIVATE GAME RESERVE
38 km (24 miles) northeast of Grahamstown.

GETTING HERE AND AROUND
Kwandwe is a 30-minute drive from Grahamstown, and air and road shuttles are available from Port Elizabeth, which is a 1½-hour drive.

EXPLORING
Kwandwe Private Game Reserve. Kwandwe Private Game Reserve is tucked away in the Eastern Cape, near the quaint, historic cathedral city of Grahamstown. Little more than a decade ago, the area was ravaged farmland and goat-ridden semidesert. Today it is a conservation

triumph—more than 55,000 acres of various vegetation types and scenic diversity, including rocky outcrops, great plains, thorn thickets, forests, desert scrub, and the Great Fish River—that's home to more than 7,000 mammals, including the Big Five. Your chances of seeing the elusive black rhino are very good, and it's likely you'll see fauna you don't always see elsewhere, such as black wildebeest and the endangered blue crane (*Kwandwe* means "place of the blue crane" in Xhosa). If you come in winter, you'll see one of nature's finest floral displays, when thousands of scarlet, orange, and fiery-red aloes are in bloom, attended by colorful sunbirds. The reserve also has a strong focus on community development, as evinced by the Community Centre and village within the reserve, both of which are worth a visit. ✉ *Grahamstown* ☎ *046/603–3400* ✍ *reservations@kwandwe.co.za* 🌐 *www.kwandwe.com.*

WHERE TO STAY

There are four great places to stay within the reserve; guests can choose between classic colonial or modern chic. You'll be cosseted, pampered, well fed, and taken on some memorable wildlife adventures. Kwandwe is a member of the prestigious Relais & Châteaux group. All the lodges listed here have cable TV in a communal area as well as a safari shop, and massages are available upon request. The child-friendly lodges have movies and games. In the single-use lodges, these are hidden away in a cupboard, so you can keep their existence a secret from your brood unless a rainy day makes them essential.

$$$$ 🏨 **Ecca Lodge.** This classy lodge combines understated modern elegance with vibrant African colors. High, white, open-rafter, wooden ceilings top wood paneled walls, and the furnishings complement and enhance the views outside the huge windows and viewing decks. Velvet cushions and rugs echo the African sky at dawn, and the pillars of rough-hewn rock recall the koppies that dot the reserve. Your bedroom may qualify as one of the biggest you will ever sleep in. Keep the curtains facing your king-size bed open at night so that you're woken by a dazzling sunrise. Chill by the rim-flow lodge pool, or just hang out at your private plunge pool with only the birds and the sounds of the wilderness to keep you company. You'll dine in a big, airy dining room with an interactive kitchen or on the deck beneath the trees, looking out over the undulating hills and valleys of the reserve. If you find time, watch DVDs or read in the library or games room, or just sit on your massive wraparound deck and listen to the silence. **Pros:** superb food; an extensive self-service bar; magnificent open outdoor and indoor showers. **Cons:** some guides are young and slightly inexperienced; service can be a little disorganized; the lounge can feel big and impersonal. [$] *Rooms from: R9875* ✉ *Kwandwe Private Game Reserve* ☎ *046/603–3400* ✍ *reservations@kwandwe.co.za* 🌐 *www.kwandwe.com* 🛏 *6 rooms* 🍴 *All meals.*

$$$$ 🏨 **Great Fish River Lodge.** If you have an artistic eye, you'll immediately
Fodor's Choice ★ notice how the curving thatch roof of the main buildings echoes the mountain skyline opposite. Steps lead down to the public areas—dining room, comfortable lounges, and library—that sprawl along the banks of the Great Fish River. Floor-to-ceiling windows bathe the stone walls, Persian rugs, fireplaces, deep armchairs, bookcases, and old prints and

photographs in clear light. At night the stars provide a dazzling display as lions call over the noise of the rushing river. All the spacious en-suite bedrooms overlook the river, and you'll be hard put to tear yourself away from your personal plunge-pool-with-a-view to go chasing game. The décor is Africa-inspired, with earth-tone fabrics. Pewter and glass add understated sophistication to the furnishings, while ostrich egg-shells, animal hides, and horns reference the lodge's surroundings. **Pros:** spectacular river views; unusual habitats (it's not often you find lions clambering up and down rocky outcrops); ultrafriendly staff. **Cons:** avoid if you're a bit unsteady as there are lots of tricky steps; also avoid if you don't like open camps and predators potentially wandering around the lodge at night. [$] *Rooms from: R9875* ✉ *Kwandwe Private Game Reserve* ☎ *046/603–3400* 📧 *reservations@kwandwe.co.za* 🌐 *www.kwandwereserve.co.za* 🛏 *9 suites* 🍴 *All meals.*

$$$$ 🏨 **Melton Manor.** Slightly bigger than Uplands, the Manor accommodates up to eight guests and offers the same superb service and exclusivity. It's a farmhouse in contemporary style with handmade clay chandeliers, cowhide rugs, vintage ball-and-claw armoires, and huge bathrooms with claw-foot tubs. Built around a small central lawn with a swimming pool, the four spacious rooms look outward into the bush for privacy. You have your own chef and game ranger, and you call the shots. This is a great option for families, as you can take the little ones on game drives or leave them behind with babysitters. It's also a good deal for three couples traveling together (and a great deal for four). **Pros:** exclusivity deluxe; great food; great service. **Cons:** as you're in your own group you miss out on the opportunity to meet other lodge guests; unlike other Kwandwe lodges, there are no private plunge pools and decks; you can only book for a minimum of four people. [$] *Rooms from: R7900* ✉ *Kwandwe Private Game Reserve* ☎ *046/603–3400* 📧 *reservations@kwandwe.co.za* 🌐 *www.kwandwereserve.co.za* 🛏 *4 rooms* 🍴 *All meals.*

$$$$ 🏨 **Uplands Homestead.** If you're a small family or a bunch of friends and want to have a genuine, very exclusive, *Out of Africa* experience, then stay at this restored 1905 colonial farmhouse. There are three spacious en-suite bedrooms with balconies furnished in early Settlers style, and you'll have your own tracking and guiding team, plus a dedicated chef. The game experience is excellent, and you'll have memorable moments sitting around a blazing log fire as you swap fireside tales in the evening. Try one of Kwandwe's specialist safaris that range from learning about carnivore research to walking trails and excursions revealing the colorful past of this area, which is steeped in cultural, military, and archaeological history. **Pros:** perfect for that special family occasion or friends' reunion; great food and service. **Cons:** can only be booked for families or parties of up to six; the colonial nostalgia might be a little overwhelming for some. [$] *Rooms from: R7900* ✉ *Kwandwe Private Game Reserve* 📧 *reservations@kwandwe.co.za* 🌐 *www.kwandwereserve.co.za* 🛏 *3 rooms* 🍴 *All meals.*

NORTH WEST

PILANESBERG GAME RESERVE
200 km (124 miles) northwest of Johannesburg.

The 150,000-acre Pilanesberg Game Reserve is often called the Pilanesberg National Park. It isn't actually a South African national park these days, though it was one in the days when Bophutatswana was independent Bantustan. The game reserve is centered on the caldera of an extinct volcano dating back 1.3 billion years that may well have once been Africa's highest peak. Concentric rings of mountains surround a lake filled with crocodiles and hippos. Open grassland, rocky crags, and densely forested gorges provide ideal habitats for a wide range of plains and woodland game, including rare brown hyenas and cheetahs, and wildebeests and zebras, which are abundant in this reserve. Since the introduction of lions in 1993, Pilanesberg (pronounced "pee-*luns*-berg") can boast the Big Five. One of the best places in the country to see rhinos, it's also a bird-watcher's paradise, with a vast range of grassland species, waterbirds, and birds of prey. It's also malaria-free and an excellent choice for game-viewing if you're short on time and can't make it all the way to Kruger National Park, for instance. You can drive around the park in your own vehicle or join guided safaris with Pilanesberg Mankwe Safaris. The entertainment and resort complex of Sun City is nearby.

GETTING HERE AND AROUND
To get to the Pilanesberg from Johannesburg, get on the N4 highway to Krugersdorp and take the R556 off-ramp and follow the signs. The drive is about 2½ to 3 hours. There is a shuttle from Johannesburg to Sun City, just outside the park, but public transportation in and around the park is limited, so you'll need to rent a car or hire a transfer company.

EXPLORING
Pilanesberg Game Reserve. The 150,000-acre Pilanesberg Game Reserve is centered on the caldera of an extinct volcano. Concentric rings of mountains surround a lake filled with crocodiles and hippos. Open grassland, rocky crags, and forested gorges provide ideal habitats for a wide range of plains and woodland game, especially wildebeests and zebras, which are plentiful here. The Pilanesberg boasts the Big Five—you have a great chance of seeing elephants and rhinos here on almost any single drive—and is malaria-free. It's a bird-watcher's paradise, with a vast range of grassland species, waterbirds, and birds of prey. The entertainment and resort complex of Sun City is nearby. ⊠ *Pilanesberg Game Reserve, Sun City* ☎ *014/555–1600* ⊕ *www.pilanesbergnationalpark.org* 🖃 *R20 per vehicle, R65 per person* ⊙ *Mar., Apr., Sept., and Oct., daily 6 am–6:30 pm; May–Aug., daily 6:30–6; Nov.–Feb., daily 5:30 am–7 pm.*

WHERE TO STAY
$$$$ 🛏 **Bakubung Bush Lodge.** Abutting Pilanesberg, this lodge sits at the head of a long valley with terrific views of a hippo pool that forms the lodge's central attraction—it's not unusual to have hippos grazing 100 feet from the terrace restaurant. Despite this, the lodge never

Continued on page 352

AFRICAN MUSIC & DANCE

Talking drums echo in the forests and over the plains. The pounding of hands on taut animal-skin–covered logs is heard and interpreted by tribes' versed in jungle telegraphy. This form of dialogue is outlawed, but the art survives and modern African music is born. The beat is the essential component of the music, and by extension, of African dance.

African music and dance are all about conveying moods and emotions. They're also an integral part of ritual and ceremony. Rhythm is the key. Interlocking rhythms follow a time-honored, prescribed pattern. Drumming as a spiritual release and a team-building exercise has now become cool in Europe and the United States. African singing is easily recognized for its polyphony, where several parts, or voices, take turns producing wonderful harmonies. African choirs, like the Soweto Gospel Choir (above), are world-famous. Praise-singers are common in ceremonies where high-ranking African dignitaries are present. Dance is polycentric—different parts of the body are used independently—and conveys images of love, war, coming of age, welcome, and rites of passage.

Musicologists lament that traditional forms of indigenous music and dance are being replaced by Western genres, but fortunately, African rhythms are eternal.

THE SOUNDS OF AFRICA

When you think traditional African music, think percussion (drums and xylophones), strings (the mouth bow), and winds (horns and whistles). You should also think of trumpets, guitars, pianos, or saxophones, as these have been absorbed into African jazz.

DJEMBE DRUMS

Djembe drums, originally from Mali, come in various sizes and are copied and manufactured all over the world.

TALKING DRUMS

These drums are among the oldest instruments in West Africa. They are typically hourglass-shaped, with goat- or lizard-skin drum heads. The two heads are joined by strings or thongs, and their sound can be manipulated. The player, who puts the drum under his shoulder and beats the drum with a stick, can also tighten or loosen the connectors to create a sound similar to speech. Messages can thus be conveyed over considerable distances.

MBIRA

The *mbira*, or thumb-piano, has been played for more than 1,000 years at religious and social events. It consists of 22 to 28 metal keys or strips mounted atop a resonating box or shell.

KHOISAN MOUTH BOW

Derived from the hunting bow of the Kalahari Bushmen, the instrument dates back more than 40,000 years. You can still find them—usually as tourist souvenirs—all over the continent.

CONCERTINA

Though the concertina arrived with European settlers, it was absorbed into township music, as well as Boeremusiek (Afrikaans folk music). Present-day Afrikaans dance bands use the instrument in *sakkie-sakkie*, a style of music that accompanies sakkie, a South African dance.

MARIMBAS

Marimbas, or African xylophones, are found all over Southern and East Africa; the bigger the instrument, the deeper the sound. Originally part of the Lozi and Chopi tribal traditions in Zambia and Mozambique, they're now used in everything from pop songs to national anthems.

KUDU HORN

Made from the horn of the male greater kudu antelope, this instrument was originally used in hunting. Today you'll probably hear it only when you're called to meals at your safari lodge.

PENNYWHISTLE

The tin or pennywhistle, once used by cattle herders, is now an integral part of African music, specifically *kwela* (street music with jazz undertones).

6

IN FOCUS AFRICAN MUSIC & DANCE

MUSICIANS

Music and political activism have always gone hand in hand in South Africa. Under Apartheid, black music was ignored by music companies and radio stations, though it continued to thrive underground. American swing jazz had a huge influence on the music community in the 1950s, which soon evolved into an African jazz form known as *mbaqanga*, or "home-made."

In the 1960s, radio exposure forced the government to restrict lyrics and censor all songs considered subversive. This resulted in many jazz musicians leaving the country, among them Hugh Masekela and Miriam Makeba. After the collapse of Apartheid in the '90s, many of the exiled artists finally returned home. Today South Africa's Yvonne Chaka Chaka is one of the country's best known vocalists, singing everything from disco to R&B; her fans call her Princess Africa.

LADYSMITH BLACK MAMBAZO

Formed in 1964 by Joseph Shabalala, the Grammy-award–winning vocal group (*above*) came to world prominence when it joined Paul Simon on his 1986 album *Graceland*. The group performed at Nelson Mandela's inauguration in 1994 and continues to record and perform today, spreading a message of peace, love, and harmony.

MIRIAM MAKEBA

The late Miriam Makeba (*below*) began her professional career in the 1950s when she joined the Manhattan Brothers and later started her own, all-female group, the Skylarks. Her international hits "Pata Pata" and "The Click Song" focused world attention on South Africa's Apartheid policy. She performed with Harry Belafonte and Paul Simon and became known worldwide as Mama Africa.

HUGH MASEKELA

After much musical success in the 1950s, Masekela (*left*) fled South Africa in 1961 and studied music in London and New York. He had several hits in the United States, including "Grazin' in the Grass," which sold four million copies in 1968. Maseleka has performed with everyone from Louis Armstrong to Paul Simon and is considered by many to be a master of African music.

AFRICAN DANCING

Gumboot dancers perform during a New Year's eve carnival in Johannesburg, South Africa

Wherever groups of people come together in Africa, be it at weddings, funerals, or parties, you can be sure that there will be dancing. It's an essential part of the African psyche, one that is a form of expression and release for many Afri- cans. The South Africa protest dance, the *toi-toi*, is synonymous with marches and strikes. Dancing is also synonymous with rhythm, and rhythm means drums. The drum symbolizes life and emotion; it beats as the heart of the community.

GUMBOOT DANCING

Gumboot dancing started in the late 1800s as a form of communication between mine workers. Today this ground-stomping dance is a spectacular art form that's performed all over Southern Africa. The dance is a specialty of Black Umfolozi, a troupe from Zimbabwe, and "Gumboots," a track from Paul Si- mon's *Graceland* album, featured South Africa's Boyoyo Boys.

KWAITO DANCING

The 1990s and the release of Nelson Mandela saw the cre- ation of *kwaito*, a form of hip-hop music cre- ated on computers and synthesizers. It's widely known as the voice of the ghetto. The hugely popular kwaito dance, a kind of synchronized group tap-dancing, soon followed.

South Africa's leading kwaito group, Mandoza, performs before thousands of fans on the sand at Durban's North Beach

really succeeds in creating a bush feel, perhaps because it's such a big convention and family destination. Its brick buildings feel vaguely institutional. Nevertheless, the guest rooms, particularly the executive studios, are very pleasant, thanks to light pine furniture, colorful African bedspreads, and super views of the valley. The lodge conducts game drives in open-air vehicles, as well as ranger-guided walks. A shuttle bus (R60 round-trip) runs to Sun City, 10 km (6 miles) away. **Pros:** malaria-free; resident hippos; cheerful atmosphere. **Cons:** close to a main gate; always crowded. [$] *Rooms from: R4430* ✉ *Bakubung, Pilanesberg Game Reserve* ☎ *014/552–6000 for lodge, 014/552–4006 for reservations* 🌐 *www.legacyhotels.co.za* 🛏 *76 rooms, 66 chalets* 🍴 *Some meals.*

$$$$ FAMILY 🏨 **Kwa Maritane Bush Lodge.** The greatest asset of this hotel, primarily a time-share resort, is its location: in a bowl of rocky hills on the edge of the national park. The resort has a blind overlooking a water hole and connected to the lodge via a tunnel. Guest rooms have high thatch ceilings and large glass doors that open onto a veranda. It's best to secure a unit far from the noise of the reception, dining, and pool areas. You can pay to go on day or night game drives in open-air vehicles or to go on guided walks with an armed ranger—both worthwhile. The breakfasts at the restaurant are legendary. **Pros:** malaria-free; you've got the best of both worlds: bushveld on your doorstep and Sun City only 20 minutes away by free shuttle bus; lovely swimming pools. **Cons:** you can't get away from the hotel feel; busy during school holidays; it gets noisy around reception, pool, and dining areas. [$] *Rooms from: R5316* ✉ *Kwa Maritane, Pilanesberg Game Reserve* ☎ *014/552–5100 for hotel, 014/552–5161 for reservations* 🌐 *www.legacyhotels.co.za* 🛏 *90 rooms* 🍴 *Some meals.*

$$ 🏨 **Manyane.** In a thinly wooded savanna east of Pilanesberg's volcanic ridges, this resort offers affordable accommodations in the Sun City area for those travelers who want to experience the region but can't pay five-star prices. Manyane is simple but well located, efficiently run, and clean. Thatch roofing helps soften the harsh lines of bare tile floors and brick. You can choose from a two- or four-bed chalet with a small, fully equipped kitchen and bathroom; there are also furnished tents with electricity, and the camping facilities are also very popular. Self-guided nature trails lead from the chalets, providing interesting background on the geology and flora of the park. You can also take advantage of the outdoor chess and trampoline. **Pros:** accommodations are very basic but a good value; there is a good restaurant if you want a break from self-catering; lovely pool, which is a delight on a hot day. **Cons:** more downmarket than other options in the area; can be full of noisy campers and late-night revelers. [$] *Rooms from: R1760* ✉ *Manyane, Pilanesberg National Park* ☎ *014/555–1000* 🌐 *www.manyaneresort-pilanesberg.com* 🛏 *14 4-bed chalets, 10 2-bed chalets* 🍴 *No meals.*

$$$$ 🏨 **Tshukudu Bush Lodge.** Tshukudu Bush Lodge is built into the side of a steep, rocky hill and overlooks open grassland and a large water hole where elephants bathe. If you watch long enough, you might see most of the Big Five from your veranda. Winding stone stairways lead up the hill to thatch cottages with private balconies, wicker furniture, African materials, and black-slate floors. Fireplaces and mosquito nets

are standard, and sunken bathtubs have spectacular views of the water hole. At night you can use a spotlight to illuminate game at the water hole below. **Pros:** malaria-free; luxurious and secluded accommodation; high on a hill with great views. **Cons:** it's a 132-step climb to the main lodge from the parking area, so avoid it if you're not sound of wind and limb; game good, but not as abundant as Kruger. $ *Rooms from: R8630* ⊠ *Tshukudu, Pilanesberg Game Reserve* ☎ *014/552–6255* ⊕ *www.legacyhotels.co.za* ⮌ *6 cottages* ⦿⧵ *All-inclusive.*

MADIKWE GAME RESERVE
300 km (186 miles) northwest of Johannesburg (or farther, depending on which gate you enter).

Just as leopards and Sabi Sand Game Reserve are synonymous, think of Madikwe Game Reserve and wild dogs in the same way. This is probably your best chance in South Africa to have an almost guaranteed sighting of the "painted wolves."

More than two decades ago the 765-square-km (475-square-mile) area bordering Botswana was a wasteland of abandoned cattle farms, overgrown bush, and rusting fences. A brilliant and unique collaboration between the North West Parks Board, private enterprise, and local communities changed all that when Operation Phoenix—one of the most ambitious game relocation programs in the world—relocated more than 8,000 animals of 27 different species to Madikwe. Soon after, it became one of the fastest-growing safari destinations in South Africa.

Madikwe today is teeming with game. Spot the Big Five, plus resident breeding packs of the endangered painted wolves—the wild dogs of Africa. On your morning, evening, or night game drive, you also might spot cheetahs, hippos, lions, elephants, and buffalos, but you'll certainly see zebras, wildebeests, and several kinds of antelope (South Africans refer to all antelope generically as "buck," whether they're male or female). Birders can spot more than 350 birds. Be dazzled by the crimson-breasted shrike, the lilac-breasted roller, yellow- and red-billed hornbills, blue waxbills, and many more.

GETTING HERE AND AROUND
Madikwe is an easy drive on good roads from Johannesburg. Go to Sun City via Hartbeespoort Dam and follow the signs to Madikwe, which is about an hour's drive from Sun City (though your trip could be an hour longer if your lodge is in the north of the park). Ask at your lodge for detailed instructions. You'll be driven around in an open game vehicle by a staff member of your lodge; guided bush walks are also available. No day visitors are allowed.

EXPLORING
Madikwe Game Reserve. This 187,500-acre game reserve in the North-West Province (about four hours from Johannesburg) close to the Botswana border is open only to overnight visitors, who can choose from more than 20 lodges to stay at, most of them five-star. The reserve is famous for its wild dog population, but is also known for cheetah, the Big Five, and its general game, such as zebra, wildebeest, giraffe, and impala. It was established in 1991 and is fast becoming one of the most popular private reserves in the country, because of its abundance

of game, proximity to Johannesburg, and the fact that it is malaria-free (so is very safe for children). ✉ *Madikwe Game Reserve* 🌐 *www.parksnorthwest.co.za/madikwe.*

WHERE TO STAY

In the south, choose between the ultraluxurious Tuningi Lodge, where a 300-year-old fig tree stands sentinel over a busy water hole, or either of Jaci's delightful lodges. Madikwe Safari Lodge, managed by the More family of Mpumalanga's Lion Sands, is another example of this company's high standards of luxury, service, and game-viewing.

Tau Lodge in the north of the reserve is more like a small resort than a private safari lodge, but the accommodations are excellent, the food is good, and the game drives are well done. Always check for special offers at any of the Madikwe lodges. You can often get very affordable rates, especially off-season.

$$$$ FAMILY 🏨 **Jaci's Lodges.** The two lodges that make up Jaci's Lodges are family owned and have a longstanding reputation for friendliness, superb game drives, and comfortable accommodations that has made them synonymous with the name Madikwe Game Reserve. **Jaci's Safari Lodge** sits in the southeast reserve on the edge of the Marico River. You'll stay in one of eight roomy tented suites with outdoor showers, handcrafted mosaic baths, and a private deck looking out over the bushveld and river below. There are also two suites that sleep about 10 each if you have a bigger family group. The welcoming public areas are bright and cheerful with a seamless fusion of contemporary and African décor. This is probably one of the most child-friendly lodges in South Africa. Take the older kids with you on guided game drives (6 to 12 years, younger by special arrangement). The eight rooms of the secluded **Jaci's Tree Lodge**, built of rosewood and thatch and perched on stilts connected by wooden walkways, have views through the riverine trees across the Marico River. You may not want to leave your leafy aerie and its surrounding birdsong. **Pros:** friendly, welcoming atmosphere; great children's activities and facilities; great game-viewing. **Cons:** if children aren't your thing, stay away from Jaci's Safari Lodge; pricey. [$] *Rooms from: R9590* ✉ *Madikwe Game Reserve* ☎ *083/700–2071* ✉ *jacisreservations@madikwe.com* 🌐 *www.madikwe.com* 🛏 *8 tented suites per camp, 2 family suites at Safari Lodge* 🍴 *All meals.*

$$$$ FAMILY 🏨 **Madikwe Safari Lodge.** This stunning 5-star lodge in the central eastern region of the park is managed by the More family of Lion Sands, and their attention to detail, reputation for fine food and excellent service, and thrilling game drives are readily apparent. Michelle Obama, Beyonce, and Jay-Z have all spent family time here. The lodge comprises three different lodges: Lelapa, the largest, with 12 suites; Kopano and Dithaba both with 4 suites each. Imagine a happy union between Middle Earth and Great Zimbabwe—adobe and thatch buildings with pointed roofs, house nooks, crannies, viewing decks, bars, and dining areas. The suites are huge, with floor-to-ceiling windows, a lounge area with a comfy sofa, and an open fireplace. Your room includes a king-size bed, dressing area, bathroom with his-and-her basins and large tub, and an indoor-outdoor shower. Earth tones are complemented by bright cushions and throws. Sit out on your large wooden deck and watch the amazing birdlife, or dip into the plunge pool on those very hot days. Kids are welcome and a visit to the fascinating Eco House, which houses all kinds of interesting natural exhibits, is a must. **Pros:** malaria-free; superb accommodation; great food; excellent game-viewing. **Cons:** not as scenically beautiful as the Mpumalanga and KwaZulu-Natal reserves; long walks between suites. $ *Rooms from: R13960* ⊠ *Madikwe Game Reserve* ☎ *018/350–9902* ⊕ *www.madikwesafarilodge. co.za* ⤢ *20 suites* ⵏ *All meals.*

$$$$ ⌂ **Tuningi Safari Lodge.** A 300 year-old fig tree dominates the ultraluxurious Tuningi Lodge overlooking a busy water hole that will keep you entranced all day. In winter especially this water hole is a pachyderm Times Square, with elephants coming and going all day and night. The lodge is themed around African-colonial chic with a huge comfortable lounge overlooking the pool. Your spacious villa decorated in earth tones with lots of wood everywhere has a king-size bed, a bathroom with a sunken bath, and an open fireplace (wonderful in winter). Tuningi is child-friendly and has special children's programs. If you want some quiet time, dedicated rangers and staff will take care of the kids and if you're traveling with family or in a small group seeking privacy, then the family unit of Little Tuningi fits the bill. **Pros:** superb accommodation, service, and food. **Cons:** pricey but look out for special offers, particularly in the off-season. $ *Rooms from: R9000* ⊠ *Madikwe Game Reserve* ☎ *011/781–5384* ⊕ *www.seasonsinafrica. com* ⤢ *2 family units, 4 double suites* ⵏ *All meals.*

GATEWAY CITIES

South Africa's two hub cities are Johannesburg and Cape Town. It's almost certain that you'll arrive and leave the country from one of these two cities. Make the most of your time in transit—there's a lot you can do in 24 hours.

JOHANNESBURG

Johannesburg is South Africa's most-visited city by far, and it's well worth a stopover of at least two or three days. There's plenty to see here, including the Apartheid Museum and Constitution Hill in the city, not to mention the nearby city of Soweto, and the Cradle of Humankind UNESCO World Heritage Site about 90 minutes away.

Ask a *jol* (lively party) of Jo'burgers what they love about their hometown, and they may point to its high-paced energy; its opportunity; afternoon thunderstorms in the summer; the Pirates versus Chiefs derby (the Orlando Pirates and Kaizer Chiefs are South Africa's most loved—and hated—soccer teams); spectacular sunsets; jacaranda blooms carpeting the city in purple in October and November; a great climate; the dog walks around Emmarentia Dam; the fast-paced lifestyle; the can-do attitude; the down-to-earth nature of its people; and the city's rich history. For many, Johannesburg is the gateway to the rest of Africa, and it may very well be the continent's most cosmopolitan city.

Johannesburg's origins lie in the discovery of gold. The city sits at the center of a vast urban industrial complex that covers most of the province of Gauteng (the *g* is pronounced like the *ch* in Chanukah), which means "Place Where the Gold Is" in the Sotho language and is home to the world's deepest gold mines (more than 3.9 km [2.4 miles] deep). More than 100 years ago it was just a rocky piece of unwanted Highveld land. But in 1886 an Australian, George Harrison, officially discovered gold, catapulting Johannesburg into a modern metropolis that still helps to power the country's economy (though gold mining has been winding down in recent years).

Despite its industrial past, Jozi remains a green city, with more than 10 million trees and many beautiful parks and nature reserves, which is all the more exceptional considering it is the largest city in the world not built on a river or near a significant water source.

In addition, local government has invested in an extensive new public transportation system that serves the local working population and tourists alike. This includes the Gautrain rapid rail system that connects Johannesburg with Pretoria and the O. R. Tambo International Airport, moving Jo'burg steadily toward its goal of being—as the city's government is eager to brand it—"a world-class African city."

WHEN TO GO

Jo'burgers boast that they enjoy the best climate in the world: not too hot in summer (mid-September–mid-April), not too cold in winter (mid-April–mid-September), and not prone to sudden temperature changes. Summer (especially during December and January) may have the edge, though: it's when the gardens and open spaces are at their most beautiful.

GETTING HERE AND AROUND

It's difficult but not impossible to see the Johannesburg area without a car. A good bet is to rent one, decide what you want to see, and get a good road map or rent a GPS navigator. If you're reluctant to drive yourself, book a couple of full-day or half-day tours that will pick you up from your hotel or a central landmark. The City Sightseeing bus can give you an excellent overview of the city and enable you to hop on and off at most of Johannesburg's attractions. Spend a half day or a full day doing this.

AIR TRAVEL

O. R. Tambo International Airport is about 19 km (12 miles) from the Johannesburg city center and is linked to the city by a fast highway, which is always busy but especially so before 9 am and between 4 and 7 pm. The best way to travel to and from it is via the Gautrain, a high-speed train that connects Sandton, Johannesburg, and Pretoria directly with O. R. Tambo. It takes about 30 minutes to travel from the airport to Sandton. The train runs from between 5 or 5:30 am and 9 or 9:30 pm every day, depending on the station.

Alternatively, Magic Bus offers private transfers to all major Sandton hotels (R575 per vehicle for one or two people, R630 for three people, R670 for four to seven people). The journey takes 30 minutes to an hour. Getthere Transfers and Tours charges R450 from the airport to anywhere in Johannesburg for the first rider and R30 for each additional person (R500 to Pretoria and R50 for each additional person). Airport Link will ferry you anywhere in the central Johannesburg area for R490 per person.

Wilro Tours runs from the airport to Sandton (R835 for one to three people, R1,230 for four to seven).

In addition, scores of licensed taxis line up outside the airport terminal. By law they must have a working meter. Expect to pay about R500 for a trip to Sandton. Negotiate a price before you get into a taxi.

Lines at the airport can be long: plan to arrive two to three hours before an international departure and at least an hour before domestic departures. The airport has its own police station, but luggage theft has still been a problem in recent years. Keep your belongings close to you at all times.

If your hotel or guesthouse does not have a shuttle, ask a staff member to arrange for your transportation with a reliable company. Most lodgings have a regular service they use, so you should have no problem arranging this in advance.

Prices vary, depending on where you are staying, but plan on R400–R500 for a ride from your hotel or guesthouse in Sandton, Rosebank, or the city center to the airport. Some companies charge per head, whereas others charge per trip, so be sure to check that in advance. The Gautrain is less expensive, quick, and safe, but you'll have to handle your own luggage. Most guesthouses or hotels will be able to drop you at the closest Gautrain station.

Airport Contacts O. R. Tambo International Airport ☎ *086/727–7888* ⊕ *www.acsa.co.za.*

Airport Transfers Airport Link ☎ *011/794–8300, 083/625–5090* ⊕ *www. airportlink.co.za.* **Gautrain** ☎ *0800/428–87246* ⊕ *www.gautrain.co.za.* **Getthere Transfers and Tours** ☎ *076/632–4235.* **Legend Tours and Transfers** ☎ *021/704–9140* ⊕ *www.legendtours.co.za.* **Magic Bus** ☎ *011/548–0822* ⊕ *www.megabus.co.za.*

CAR TRAVEL

Traveling by car is the easiest way to get around Johannesburg, as the city's public transportation is not that reliable or extensive, though this is changing (the Gautrain, for example, is incredibly reliable). The general speed limit for city streets is 60 kph (37 mph); for main streets it's often 80 kph (50 mph), and for highways it's 100 kph or 120 kph (62 mph or 75 mph). But be warned that Johannesburg drivers are known as the most aggressive in the country, and minibus taxis are famous for ignoring the rules of the road, often stopping for passengers with little or no warning. Most city roads and main countryside roads are in good condition, with plenty of signage. City street names are sometimes visible only on the curb, however. Avoid driving in rush hours, 7 to 8:30 am and 4 to 6:30 pm, as the main roads become terribly congested. Gas stations are plentiful in most areas. (Don't pump your own gas, though; stations employ operators to do that for you.)

If you plan to drive yourself around, get a *good* map of the city center and northern suburbs or buy or rent a GPS (available at the airport and most car-rental agencies). MapStudio prints excellent street guides, available at bookstores and many gas stations and convenience stores.

Rental agencies have offices in the northern suburbs and at the airport.

TAXI TRAVEL

Minibus taxis form the backbone of Jo'burg's transportation for ordinary commuters, but you should avoid using them since they're often not roadworthy, drivers can be irresponsible, and it's difficult to know where they're going without consulting a local. Car taxis, though more expensive, are easier to use. They have stands at the airport and the train stations, but otherwise you must phone for one (be sure to ask how long it will take the taxi to get to you). Taxis should be licensed and have a working meter. Meters usually start at R50 (includes first 3 km [2 miles]) and are about R13 per kilometer (½ mile) thereafter. Expect to pay about R500 to the airport from town or Sandton and about R300 to the city center from Sandton. Uber is a popular, safe, and inexpensive taxi service, but it can be accessed only from a smartphone app.

Contacts Maxi Taxi ☎ *011/648–1212, 011/648–1200.* **Quick Cab** ☎ *086/166–5566.* **Rose Taxis** ☎ *011/403–9625, 011/403–0000* ⊕ *www.rosetaxis.com.* **Uber** ⊕ *www.uber.com/cities/johannesburg.*

⇨ *For information on airlines or roadside assistance or car-rental companies, see the Planning section at the beginning of the chapter.*

TIMING

If you have only one day in Jo'burg, take a tour of Soweto and visit the Apartheid Museum, then stop by Constitution Hill if you have a chance. Spend the evening having dinner at an African-style restaurant, such as Moyo. If you have a second day, focus on what interests you most: perhaps a trip to the Cradle of Humankind, where you can explore the sites of some of the world's most significant paleontological discoveries; a trip to Cullinan, where you can visit a working diamond mine; or a fun day or two at Sun City.

TOURS

Township tours (to Soweto in particular) are offered by a number of local operators. One of the best options is to do a Soweto tour with the City Sightseeing bus, which partners with local operators for tours of Soweto. For more recommendations of reputable tour operators, inquire at Johannesburg Tourism.

Fodor's Choice
★

City Sightseeing Bus. The City Sightseeing bus is a great and very safe way to see the Johannesburg city center and all its main attractions. The bus departs from 12 locations every 30 minutes from 9 to 5 every day, but the best places to catch it are either at Gold Reef City or Park Station (accessible via the Gautrain). Adults and kids alike will love the experience; there's a special children's soundtrack, and the adult commentary is available in 16 languages. The total trip takes about two hours if you don't get off (though you should consider at least getting off at the Apartheid Museum and Constitution Hill); you can get a one- or two-day pass. There is also an option to pair it with a Soweto tour, also highly recommended. You can buy your tickets at O. R. Tambo, at Gold Reef City, or Park Station (or you can wait and buy tickets on any City Sightseeing bus), but there's a discount for purchasing them online. ☎ *0861/733–287* ⊕ *www.citysightseeing.co.za* 🎫 *From R150.*

SAFETY

Johannesburg is notorious for being a dangerous city—it's quite common to hear about serious crimes such as armed robbery and murder. That said, it's safe for visitors who avoid dangerous areas and take reasonable precautions. Do not leave bags or valuables visible in a car, and keep the doors locked, even while driving (to minimize the risk of smash-and-grab robberies or carjackings); don't wear flashy jewelry or carry large wads of cash or expensive equipment. ⚠ **Don't visit a township or squatter camp on your own. Unemployment is rife, and foreigners are easy pickings. If you wish to see a township, check with reputable companies, which run excellent tours and know which areas to avoid.** The Apartheid Museum and Constitution Hill within the city and the Cradle of Humankind just outside are perfectly safe to visit on your own.

⚠ **If you drive yourself around the city, it's safest to keep your doors locked and windows up, and to not leave valuables such as bags, cameras, or phones on the seat or visible.**

VISITOR INFORMATION

The helpful Gauteng Tourism Authority has information on the whole province, but more detailed information is often available from local tourism associations—for example, the Soweto Accommodation Association lists more than 20 lodgings. Joburg Tourism has a good website, with information about Johannesburg and up-to-date listings of events happening around the city.

Contacts City of Johannesburg ⊕ *www.joburg.org.za.* **Gauteng Tourism Authority** ☎ *011/085-2500* ⊕ *www.gauteng.net.* **Joburg Tourism** ☎ *011/214-0700* ⊕ *www.joburgtourism.com.* **Soweto.co.za** ☎ *011/312-9228* ⊕ *www.soweto.co.za.*

EXPLORING

The Greater Johannesburg metropolitan area is massive—more than 1,600 square km (618 square miles)—incorporating the large municipalities of Randburg and Sandton to the north. Most of the sights are just north of the city center, which degenerated badly in the 1990s but is now being revamped.

To the south, in Ormonde, are the Apartheid Museum and Gold Reef City; the sprawling township of Soweto is just a little farther to the southwest. Johannesburg's northern suburbs are its most affluent. On the way to the shopping meccas of Rosebank and Sandton, you can find the superb Johannesburg Zoo and the South African Museum of Military History, in the leafy suburb of Saxonwold.

TOP ATTRACTIONS

Fodor'sChoice
★ **Apartheid Museum.** The Apartheid Museum takes you on a journey through South African apartheid history—from the entrance, where you pass through a turnstile according to your assigned skin color (black or white), to the myriad historical, brutally honest, and sometimes shocking photographs, films, video displays, documents, and other exhibits. It's an emotional, multilayered journey. As you walk chronologically through the apartheid years and eventually reach the country's first steps to freedom, with democratic elections in 1994, you experience a taste of the pain and suffering with which so many South Africans had to live. A room with 121 ropes with hangman's knots hanging from the ceiling—one rope for each political prisoner executed in the apartheid era—is especially chilling. ⊠ *Northern Pkwy. and Gold Reef Rd., Ormonde* ☎ *011/309-4700* ⊕ *www.apartheidmuseum.org* ⊑ *R70* ⊘ *Daily 9–5.*

Fodor'sChoice **Constitution Hill.** Overlooking Jo'burg's inner city and suburbs, Constitu-
★ tion Hill houses the **Constitutional Court,** set up in 1994 with the birth
of democracy, as well as the austere **Old Fort Prison Complex** (also
called Number Four), where thousands of political prisoners were incar-
cerated, including South African Nobel Peace laureates Albert Luthuli
and Nelson Mandela, and iconic Indian leader Mahatma Gandhi. The
court decides on the most important cases relating to human rights,
much like the Supreme Court in the United States. Exhibits in the visitor center portray the country's journey to democracy. You can walk
along the prison ramparts (built in the 1890s), read messages on the
We the People Wall (and add your own), or view the court itself, in
which large, slanting columns represent the trees under which African
villagers traditionally met to discuss matters of importance. If the court
isn't in session, you can walk right into the courtroom, where many of
the country's landmark legal decisions have been made in recent years
and where the 11 chairs of the justices are each covered in a different
cowhide, representing their individuality. A small but good shop carries interesting titles about South African history. Group tours of the
Old Fort Prison Complex are given every hour on the hour from 9 to
4 and include a visit to the Women's Jail, where there are photographs
and exhibits of how women were treated in the prison system and how
they contributed to the struggle against apartheid. You can also take
a private tour, which departs at any time. ⊠ *Joubert and Kotze sts.,
entrance on Joubert St., Braamfontein, City Center* ☎ *011/381–3100*
⊕ *www.constitutionhill.org.za* ✉ *Court free; Old Fort group tour R50,
private tour R70* ☽ *Court Thurs.–Tues. 9–5 (last entry at 4), Wed. 9–1.
Old Fort group tours on the hr, daily 9–4; private tours by appt.*

Fodor'sChoice **Hector Pieterson Memorial and Museum.** Opposite Holy Cross Church, a
★ stone's throw from the former homes of Nelson Mandela and Archbishop Desmond Tutu on Vilakazi Street, the Hector Pieterson Memorial and Museum is a crucial landmark. Pieterson, a 13-year-old scholar,
was the first victim of police fire on June 16, 1976, when schoolchildren
rose up to protest their second-rate Bantu (black) education system. The
memorial is a paved area with benches for reflection, an inscribed stone
and simple water feature; inside the museum are grainy photographs
and films that bring that fateful day to life. A total of 562 small granite
blocks in the museum courtyard are a tribute to the children who died
in the Soweto uprisings. ⊠ *Khumalo and Phela sts., Orlando West,
Soweto* ☎ *011/536–2253* ⊕ *www.joburg.org.za* ✉ *R30* ☽ *Mon.–Sat.
10–5, Sun. 10–4:30.*

WORTH NOTING

FAMILY **Gold Reef City.** This theme park lets you step back in time to 1880s
Johannesburg and see why it became known as the City of Gold. One of
the city's most popular attractions, it has good rides that kids will enjoy
and is based on the history of Jo'burg. In addition to riding the Ana-
conda, a scary roller coaster on which you hang under the track, feet
in the air, you can (for an additional fee) descend into an old gold mine
and see molten gold being poured. The reconstructed streets are lined
with operating Victorian-style shops and restaurants. And for those
with money to burn, the large, glitzy Gold Reef Village Casino beckons

across the road. ✉ *Northern Park Way, Shaft 14, Ormonde, 6 km (4 miles) south of city center* ☎ *011/248–6800* 🌐 *www.goldreefcity.co.za* 🎟 *R165, R90 for mine tour* 🕓 *Wed.–Sun. (except for school holidays, when it's open daily) 9:30–5; mine tours hourly 10–4.*

WHERE TO EAT

Jo'burgers love eating out, and there are hundreds of restaurants throughout the city to satisfy them. Some notable destinations for food include Melrose Arch, Parkhurst, Sandton, and Greenside. Smart-casual dress is a good bet. Many establishments are closed on Sunday night and Monday.

There's no way to do justice to the sheer scope and variety of Johannesburg's restaurants in a few examples. What follows is a (necessarily subjective) list of some of the best. Try asking locals what they recommend; eating out is the most popular form of entertainment in Johannesburg, and everyone has a list of favorite spots, which changes often.

$$$ AFRICAN Fodor's Choice ★

🍴 **Moyo.** From the food and décor to the music and live entertainment, Moyo is strongly African in theme. The focus of the rich and varied menu is pan-African, incorporating tandoori cookery from northern Africa, Cape Malay influences such as lentil bobotie, Moroccan-influenced tasty *tagines* (stews with lamb, chicken, fish, or seven vegetables), and ostrich burgers and other dishes representing South Africa. Diners are often entertained by storytellers, face painters, and musicians. The restaurant has six locations in South Africa. At night or in winter, the branch at Melrose Arch is the better bet of the two Jo'burg outposts. In summer and during the day, the Zoo Lake branch (✉ *1 Prince of Wales Dr., Parkview* ☎ *011/646–0058*) is nicer. [$] *Average main: R180* ✉ *Melrose Arch, High St., Shop 5, Melrose North* ☎ *011/684–1477* 🌐 *www.moyo.co.za* ✍ *Reservations essential.*

$$ ITALIAN Fodor's Choice ★

🍴 **Tortellino d'Oro.** This small and unpretentious restaurant and deli has legendary food, especially the pasta. Run by an Italian family, Tortellino's is popular for both lunch and dinner. Try the Parma ham and melon as an antipasto, and then get a pasta for your main course, such as the tortellini, which is filled with a mixture of ham, mortadella sausage, chicken, and Parmesan cheese then served with mushroom cream, Napoletana, or butter and sage sauce. The service is as outstanding, as is the food, and there's an excellent wine list. Be sure to book ahead. [$] *Average main: R120* ✉ *Oaklands Shopping Center, Pretoria St. at Victoria St., Oaklands* ☎ *011/483–1249* 🌐 *www.tortellino.co.za* ✍ *Reservations essential* 🕓 *No dinner Sun.*

$$ AFRICAN

🍴 **Wandie's Place.** Wandie's Place isn't the only good township restaurant, but it's the best known and one of the most popular spots in Jo'burg. The décor is eclectic township (a bit makeshift), and the walls are adorned with signatures and business cards of tourists who have crossed its path. The waiters are smartly dressed in bowties, and the food is truly African. Meat stews, *imifino* (a leafy African dish), sweet potatoes, beans, corn porridge, traditionally cooked pumpkin, chicken, and tripe are laid out in a buffet in a motley selection of pots and containers. The food is hot, the drinks are cold, and the conversation flows. You may end up here with a tour bus, but it's big enough to cope.

It's not that difficult to find, and parking is safe, but it's probably better to organize a visit on a guided trip. [$] *Average main: R120* ✉ *618 Makhalamele St., Dube* ☎ *011/982–2796* 🌐 *www.wandiesplace.co.za.*

WHERE TO STAY

Most, if not all, of the good hotels are in the northern suburbs. Many of them are linked to nearby malls and are well policed. Boutique hotels have sprung up everywhere, as have bed-and-breakfasts from Melville to Soweto. Hotels are quieter in December and January, when many locals take their annual vacations and rates are often cheaper. But beware: if there's a major conference, some of the smaller hotels can be booked months in advance.

All the hotels we list offer no-smoking rooms, and many have no-smoking floors.

Hotel reviews have been shortened. For full information, visit Fodors.com.

$$ HOTEL 🏨 **Clico Boutique Hotel.** This small, upmarket guesthouse in central Rosebank is an old Cape Dutch house with a gracious garden that offers good value in an area known for expensive accommodations. **Pros:** 24-hour manned security and CCTV cameras; free Wi-Fi throughout the hotel; restaurant serves breakfast daily, and lunch and dinner are available upon request. **Cons:** Some of the on-site parking spaces are difficult to negotiate; noise from the pool activity can travel to the suites; dining at lunch and dinner times needs to be booked in advance. [$] *Rooms from: R1936* ✉ *27 Sturdee Ave., at Jellicoe Ave., Rosebank* ☎ *011/252–3300* 🌐 *www.clicohotel.com* 🛏 *9 suites, including 1 room with kitchen* 🍴 *Breakfast.*

$$ HOTEL 🏨 **Crowne Plaza Johannesburg–The Rosebank.** Notable for its quirky public spaces—Louis XVI reproduction armchairs, white shaggy rugs, and the very popular Circle Bar with its beaded booths—The Rosebank Crowne Plaza is an "it" spot for late-night revelry. **Pros:** hip nightspot; great spa and gym. **Cons:** popular with partying locals; bathrooms in deluxe suites lack privacy. [$] *Rooms from: R1700* ✉ *Tyrwhitt and Sturdee aves., Rosebank* ☎ *011/448–3600* 🌐 *www.therosebank.co.za* 🛏 *294 rooms, 24 suites.* 🍴 *Breakfast.*

$$$$ HOTEL Fodor's Choice ★ 🏨 **Four Seasons The Westcliff.** The iconic Westcliff, now under the Four Seasons banner and with a $56 million revamp has been transformed into the paragon of a luxurious urban resort, while renowned chef Dirk Gieselmann has been whisked from France to oversee both the new View and Flame restaurants. **Pros:** great location; spectacular views over Johannesburg; impeccable service. **Cons:** all this luxury and service comes at a high cost; rather formal atmosphere, which may not be to everyone's liking; rooms spread out along a steep hill, sometimes requiring a shuttle. [$] *Rooms from: R3795* ✉ *67 Jan Smuts Ave., Westcliff* ☎ *011/481–6000* 🌐 *www.fourseasons.com/johannesburg* 🛏 *81 rooms, 36 suites* 🍴 *Breakfast.*

$$$ HOTEL 🏨 **InterContinental Johannesburg O.R. Tambo Airport.** A few paces from international arrivals and adjacent to the car-rental companies, this is a good choice for those who have a one-night layover. **Pros:** ideal for those who don't need to go into Johannesburg or who have a layover

before a connecting flight; free Wi-Fi; free meet-and-greet service with escort to the hotel. **Cons:** large and impersonal; you won't see much of Johannesburg without leaving the hotel. $ *Rooms from: R3850* ✉ *O. R. Tambo Airport, Kempton Park* ☎ *011/961–5400* ⊕ *www.ihg. com* ⇋ *138 rooms, 2 suites* ⎮◎⎮ *Breakfast.*

$$$
HOTEL
Fodor'sChoice
★

⬚ **The Orient Hotel.** This exquisite, Asia-themed boutique hotel is aimed at the discerning traveler who is looking for an unusual and memorable experience and wants to be out of the center of the Johannesburg business district. **Pros:** superb cuisine; majestic surroundings; extraordinary service. **Cons:** no Wi-Fi; poor mobile phone reception; need a car to get around. $ *Rooms from: R3000* ✉ *Francolin Conservancy, Crocodile Valley Rd., Pretoria* ☎ *012/371–2902* ⊕ *www.the-orient.net* ⇋ *10 suites* ⎮◎⎮ *Breakfast.*

$$$$
HOTEL
Fodor'sChoice
★

⬚ **The Saxon Hotel, Village & Spa.** In the exclusive suburb of Sandhurst, adjacent to the commercial and shopping center of Sandton, the Saxon Hotel has repeatedly received awards for its excellence. **Pros:** possibly the most exclusive address in Gauteng; exceptional spa on site; good for business travelers or high-profile folk who'd rather not see anyone else in the corridors. **Cons:** some might find the atmosphere a bit snooty; children under 14 not welcome in restaurant; pricey. $ *Rooms from: R5210* ✉ *36 Saxon Rd., Sandhurst* ☎ *011/292–6000* ⊕ *www.saxon. co.za* ⇋ *53 suites* ⎮◎⎮ *Breakfast.*

SHOPPING

Whether you're after designer clothes, high-quality African art, or glamorous gifts, Johannesburg offers outstanding shopping opportunities. At the city's several markets, bargaining can get you a great price.

Fodor'sChoice
★

African Craft Market. Located between the Rosebank Mall and the Zone, the African Craft Market has a huge variety of African crafts from Cape to Cairo, all displayed to the background beat of traditional African music. Drive a hard bargain here—the vendors expect you to! If you want to save your shopping until the end of your trip, then this should be your destination. It's the best place in Jo'burg to buy African crafts, and it's an entertaining place to visit as well. ✉ *Mall of Rosebank, Cradock Ave. and Baker St., Rosebank* ☎ *072/614–5506* ⊕ *www. rosebankmall.co.za/art-crafts-rosebank-mall* ☉ *Daily 9–6.*

Rooftop Market. Rosebank's Rooftop Market has become a Sunday tradition in the city. More than 600 stalls sell African and Western crafts, antiques, books, food, art, trinkets, CDs, jewelry, and clothes. Frequently, African musicians, dancers, and other entertainers delight the crowds. ✉ *The Mall of Rosebank, 50 Bath Ave., Rosebank* ☎ *011/442–4488* ⊕ *www.craft.co.za* ☉ *Sun. 9–5.*

SIDE TRIP FROM JOHANNESBURG

CRADLE OF HUMANKIND

72 km (45 miles) northwest of Johannesburg.

This UNESCO World Heritage Site stretches over an area of about 470 square km (181 square miles), with about 300 caves. Inside these caves, paleoanthropologists have discovered thousands of fossils of hominids

"[This] person [was] waiting to sell his goods to a tourist. The colors were so vivid and alive." —larrya, Fodors. com member

and other animals, dating back some 4 million years. The most famous of these fossils are Mrs. Ples, a skull more than 2 million years old, and Little Foot, a skeleton more than 3 million years old. Although the Cradle does not have the world's oldest hominid fossils, it has the most complete fossil record of human evolution anywhere on earth, has produced more hominid fossils than anywhere else, and has been designated a UNESCO World Heritage Site.

Archaeological finds at the Cradle of Humankind include 1.7-million-year-old stone tools, the oldest recorded in southern Africa. At Swartkrans, near Sterkfontein, a collection of burned bones tells us that our ancestors could manage fire more than a million years ago.

Not all the fossil sites in the Cradle are open to the public, but a tour of the Sterkfontein Caves and the visitor center provides an excellent overview of the paleontological work in progress, and a trip to Maropeng, a much larger visitor center 10 km (6 miles) from the Sterkfontein Caves, provides even more background. Special tours to fossil sites with expert guides can be booked via tour operator Palaeo-Tours.

GETTING HERE AND AROUND
Public transportation to the Cradle of Humankind area is limited, so using a rental car or taking an organized tour is best. Some hotels in the area will arrange transportation on request. The Cradle of Humankind is about a 90-minute drive from Johannesburg or Pretoria, but isn't well signposted, so use a GPS or download instructions on how to get there from the Maropeng website if you don't visit on a guided tour.

Maropeng Visitor Centre. Maropeng is the official visitor centre of the Cradle of Humankind World Heritage Site and offers much more than information about the region: it's a modern, interactive museum dedicated to the history of humanity. It provides information about the various fossil sites in the area. About a 90-minute drive from either Johannesburg or Pretoria, it's one of the area's top attractions. It's best visited in parallel with the nearby fossil site of Sterkfontein Caves (about 5 km [3 miles] away), but to visit both you'll need to set aside at least half a day. ⊠ *Off R563 Hekpoort Rd., Sterkfontein* ☎ *014/577–9000* ⊕ *www.maropeng.co.za.*

CAPE TOWN

A favorite South African topic of debate is whether Cape Town really is part of Africa. That's how different it is, both from the rest of the country and the rest of the continent. And therein lies its attraction. South Africa's most urbane, sophisticated city sits in stark contrast to the South Africa north of the Hex River Valley. Here, the traffic lights work pretty much consistently and good restaurants are commonplace. In fact, dining establishments in the so-called Mother City always dominate the country's "best of" lists.

What also distinguishes this city is its deep sense of history. Nowhere else in the country will you find structures dating back to the 17th century. South Africa as it is known today began here.

A visit to Cape Town is synonymous with a visit to the peninsula south of the city, and for good reason. With pristine white-sand beaches, hundreds of mountain trails, and numerous activities from surfing to paragliding to mountain biking, the accessibility, variety, and pure beauty of the great outdoors will keep nature lovers and outdoor adventurers occupied for hours, if not days. A week exploring just the city and peninsula is barely enough.

Often likened to San Francisco, Cape Town has two things that the former doesn't: Table Mountain and Africa. The mountain, or tabletop, is vital to Cape Town's identity. It dominates the city in a way that's difficult to comprehend until you visit. In the afternoon, when creeping fingers of clouds spill over Table Mountain and reach toward the city, the whole town seems to hold its breath—because in summer it brings frequent strong southeasterly winds. Meanwhile, for all of its bon-vivant European vibe, Cape Town also reflects the diversity, vitality, and spirit of Africa, with many West and Central Africans and Zimbabweans—many of them having fled from conflicts elsewhere—calling this city home.

WHEN TO GO

Whatever activities you hope to accomplish in Cape Town, head up Table Mountain as soon as the wind isn't blowing. Cape Town wind is notorious, and the mountain can be shut for days on end when there are gales. Summer (October–March) is the windiest time of the year, and from December to April winds can reach 60 km (37 miles) an hour. But they will often happen in the winter months, too—just less frequently. If you're planning to visit Robben Island during peak season, it's also wise to book well in advance. One of the best months to visit is April, when the heat and wind have abated and the Cape is bathed in warm autumnal hues. Winter rains can put off visitors, but this time of the year holds its own surprises: the countryside is a brilliant green, and without fail the best sunny and temperate days come between the rainy spells. Whales are seen in False Bay in spring (late August to early September), when wildflowers are also in bloom.

GETTING HERE AND AROUND

AIR TRAVEL

Cape Town International Airport is about 19 km (12 miles) from the city center. It should take about 20 minutes to get from the airport to the city; during rush hour it can easily be double that. Private airport-transfer operators abound, and there is now public bus service to and from the airport. All major car-rental companies have counters at Cape Town International, and driving to the City Bowl or V&A Waterfront is straightforward in daylight. If your flight arrives after dark, consider prearranging transportation through your hotel. There are tourist information desks in both the domestic and international terminals. ⇨ *For information about airlines that fly to Cape Town, see Air Travel in Travel Smart.*

Contacts Cape Town International Airport ⊠ *Matroosfontein* ☎ *021/937–1200, 086/727–7888 for flight info* ⊕ *www.airports.co.za.*

AIRPORT TRANSFERS

Metered taxis and shuttle services (usually minivans) are based inside the domestic baggage hall and outside the international and domestic terminals and can also be phoned for airport drop-offs. Rates vary depending on the operator, number of passengers, destination, and time of arrival. The fare for one person to the city center is R300 in a metered taxi; a group of up to four will usually pay the same rate. A surcharge of up to R50 is sometimes levied from 10 pm until early morning, and some services charge more for arrivals than for departures to cover waiting time. For single travelers, a prearranged shared shuttle is the most economical, costing about R150–R180 per person; however, there may be numerous drop-offs, so this can be slow. MyCiti, a public bus, also serves the airport, and for R90 it's the cheapest way to or from the airport and City Centre. ⚠ **Reports of overcharging are common, so discuss the fare before entering any taxi.**

Rikkis provides inexpensive, unmetered fares (R220 to City Centre, for example) from the airport. ⇨ *For contact information, see Taxi Travel.*

Recommended shared-van services include Legend Tours and Transfers or Magic Bus Airport. Citi Hopper provides both shared-van transfers and private-car transfers.

Airport Transfers Citi Hopper ☎ *021/936–3460/1, 082/773–7678* ⊕ *www.citihopper.co.za.* **Legend Tours and Transfers** ☎ *021/704–9140* ⊕ *www. legendtours.co.za.* **Magic Bus Airport Transfers** ☎ *021/505–6300* ⊕ *www. magicbus.co.za.*

CAR TRAVEL

Although many locals drive, tourists may find public transportation (MyCiti buses) or taxis a better option; save the rental car for when you are getting out of town. Cape Town's roads are excellent, but getting around can be a bit confusing. Signposting is inconsistent, switching between Afrikaans and English, between different names for the same road (especially highways), and between different destinations on the same route. Sometimes the signs simply vanish. ⚠ **Cape Town is also littered with signs indicating "Cape Town" instead of "City Centre," as well as "Kaapstad," which is Afrikaans for Cape Town.** A good one-page map is essential and available from car-rental agencies and tourism information desks. Among the hazards are pedestrians running across highways, speeding vehicles, and minibus taxis. Roadblocks for document and DWI checks are also becoming more frequent.

Parking in the city center is a nightmare. There are simply not enough parking garages, longer-stay parking spaces are scarce, and most hotels charge a small fortune for parking. There are numerous pay-and-display (i.e., put a ticket in your windshield) and pay-on-exit parking lots around the city, but parking is strictly enforced. Prices range from R6 to R12 per half hour. For central attractions like Greenmarket Square, the Company's Garden, the South African National Gallery, and the Castle of Good Hope, look for a lot around the Grand Parade on Darling Street. The Sanlam Golden Acre Parking Garage on Adderley Street offers covered parking, as does the Parkade on Strand Street, but Queen Victoria Street alongside the South African Museum (and Company's Garden) is always bound to have a few spaces.

The main arteries leading out of the city are the N1, which bypasses the city's Northern Suburbs en route to Paarl and, ultimately, Johannesburg; and the N2, which heads out past Khayelitsha and through Somerset West to the Overberg and the Garden Route before continuing on through the Eastern Cape to Durban and beyond. Branching off the N1, the N7 goes to Namibia. The M3 splits off from the N2 near Observatory, leading to the False Bay side of the peninsula via Claremont and Constantia; it's the main and quickest route to the beaches of Muizenberg, Kalk Bay, St. James, and Simon's Town. Rush hour sees bumper-to-bumper traffic on all major arteries into the city from 6 to 9, and out of the city from 4 to 6:30.

TAXI TRAVEL

Taxis are expensive compared with other forms of transportation but offer a quick way to get around the city center. Don't expect to see the throngs of cabs you find in London or New York, as most people in Cape Town use public transportation or their own cars. You'll be lucky to hail one on the street. Taxis rarely use roof lights to indicate availability, but if you flag down an occupied cab, the driver may radio another car for you. Your best bet is to summon a taxi by phone or head to one of the major taxi stands, such as those at Greenmarket Square or either end of Adderley Street (near the Slave Lodge and outside the train station). Expect to pay R50–R70 for a trip from the City Centre to the Waterfront. For lower rates at night, try prebooking the Backpacker Bus, a shuttle service on Adderley Street. In addition to the companies listed here, ask your hotel or guesthouse which company it recommends. Lodging establishments often have a relationship with particular companies and/or drivers, and this way you may be assured of safe, reliable service.

Rikkis are London taxi-style cars that provide a cheaper alternative to metered taxis. Service is door-to-door, and they operate 24 hours a day, covering the entire city and airport.

To the airport from the City Bowl will cost R220, with the cost rising the farther out you are.

Contacts Backpacker Bus ☎ 021/424–1184 ⊕ www.backpackerbus.co.za. **Excite Taxis** ☎ 021/448–4444. **Rikkis** ☎ 0861/745–547 ⊕ www.rikkis.co.za. **Unicab** ☎ 0861/710–711 ⊕ www.unicab.co.za.

SAFETY

There's no reason for paranoia in Cape Town, but there are a few things to look out for. Women and couples are strongly advised not to walk in isolated places after dark. If you want to walk somewhere in the evening, make sure you do so in a large group, stay vigilant at all times, and keep flashy jewelry and expensive cameras hidden, or better yet, at the hotel, much as you would anywhere else. It's difficult for any youthful-looking tourist to pass a street corner in the city's nightlife district without being offered hard drugs or cannabis. Resist.

Street kids and roving teens are blamed for much of the petty crime in the city, but sophisticated crime syndicates are often involved, and many of Cape Town's fraudsters are smartly dressed. Windows will be smashed to snatch cell phones lying on car seats, and phones may even be pulled out of people's hands while in use, so don't talk on your cell phone while walking. Watch your pockets at busy transportation hubs and on trains. It's better to sit in a crowded car; if you suddenly find yourself alone, move to another one. Public transportation collapses after dark. Unless you're at the Waterfront or in a large group, use metered taxis.

Trendy nightlife areas like Long Street and Kloof Street (which leads on via a dogleg from Long Street), are frequented by both teens and adults. These areas are safe, but one should always be vigilant at night. The predominantly gay nightlife scene around Greenpoint has seen some ugly incidents in recent times, so make sure you know where you're going and with whom.

Despite thousands of safe visits every year, Lion's Head—the peak below Table Mountain—and the running trails around Newlands Forest have been the sites of several knifepoint robberies in daylight. Just be wise and never completely off guard. The handful of incidents in recent years have happened around sunrise or sunset.

Drivers quickly discover that poor signposting is a general issue in Cape Town, especially in the black townships, where most streets still have numbers rather than names and many are not signed at all. Carry a good map and use a GPS.

Visit township attractions only as part of an organized tour with a reputable operator.

As in other major cities, drug use is a problem in Cape Town, including both IV drugs and ingestibles. The drug of choice for children on the street is glue, and increasingly "tic" or methamphetamine. You will undoubtedly come across many people begging in Cape Town, including kids. Please do not give cash directly to children, as this often supports either a glue habit or adults lurking in the background. If you are concerned and wish to contribute, consider supporting people who sell *The Big Issue* magazine (associated with a worthy organization of the same name) or giving food instead of money.

TOUR OPTIONS

Numerous companies offer guided tours of the city center, the peninsula, the Winelands, and any place else in the Cape (or beyond) that you might wish to visit. They differ in type of transportation used, focus, and size. For comprehensive information on touring companies, head to one of the Cape Town Tourism offices or ask for recommendations at your hotel.

Cape Town on Foot. Owner Ursula Stevens seems to be busy, leading walks through Cape Town, around the Cape of Good Hope, and up the West Coast—all guided by the seven books she has written on the areas. So her commentary comes straight from the horse's mouth. City walking tours last about 2½ hours and cover major historical attractions, architecture, and highlights of modern-day Cape Town. Bo-Kaap tours include the Bo-Kaap Museum. ⊕ *www.wanderlust.co.za.*

City Sightseeing. The hop-on, hop-off red City Sightseeing bus is a pleasant way to familiarize yourself with Cape Town; a day ticket costs R125, and there are two routes to choose from. The Red Route runs through the city, and you can get on and off at major museums, the V&A Waterfront, Table Mountain Cableway, Two Oceans Aquarium, and other attractions. The Blue Route takes you farther afield—to Kirstenbosch National Botanic Gardens, Hout Bay, and Camps Bay, to name a few destinations. Tickets are available at the Waterfront outside the aquarium or on the bus. ⊕ *www.citysightseeing.co.za.*

VISITOR INFORMATION

From October to March, the office in City Centre is open weekdays 8–6, Saturday 8:30–2, and Sunday 9–1; from April to September, it's open weekdays 8–5:30, Saturday 8:30–1, and Sunday 9–1. The branch at the Waterfront is open daily 9–7.

Cape Town Tourism ⊠ *The Pinnacle Building, Burg and Castle sts., Cape Town Central* ☎ *021/487–6800, 0861/322–223 in S.A. only* ⊕ *www.capetown.travel.*

EXPLORING

TOP ATTRACTIONS

FAMILY

Fodor'sChoice

★

Kirstenbosch National Botanical Gardens. Spectacular in each season, these world-famous gardens showcase stunning South African flora in a magnificent setting, extending up the eastern slopes of Table Mountain and overlooking the sprawling city and the distant Hottentots Holland Mountains. No wonder the gardens are photographed from every angle. And now they can be seen from the Tree Canopy Walkway, opened in June. The Gardens aren't just enjoyed by out-of-town

"After a day of [enduring the] constant baying from the colony of Jackass Penguins, this one decided to get away from the crowd for a quiet stroll on the beach." —Stacy Freeman, Fodors.com member

visitors; on weekends Capetonians flock here with their families to lie on the lawns and read their newspapers while the kids run riot. Walking trails meander through the gardens, and grassy banks are ideal for a picnic or afternoon nap. The plantings are limited to species indigenous to Southern Africa, including fynbos—hardy, thin-leaved plants that proliferate in the Cape. Among these are proteas, including silver trees and king proteas, ericas, and *restios* (reeds). Magnificent sculptures from Zimbabwe are displayed around the gardens, too. Garden highlights include a large cycad garden, the Bird Bath (a beautiful stone pool built around a crystal-clear spring), and the fragrance garden, which is wheelchair-friendly and has a tapping rail and Braille interpretive boards. Free 90-minute guided tours take place daily at 10 (except Sunday). Those who have difficulty walking can enjoy a comprehensive tour lasting one hour (R50, hourly 9–3) in seven-person (excluding the driver) golf carts. Another wheelchair trail leads from the main paths into the wilder section of the park, getting close to the feel of the mountain walks. Concerts featuring the best of South African entertainment—from classical music to township jazz to rock and roll—are held Sunday in summer, starting an hour before sunset. But get there early, as the space fills quickly with picnicking music lovers. A visitor center by the conservatory houses a restaurant, bookstore, and coffee shop. Unfortunately, muggings have become increasingly more common in the gardens' isolated areas, and women are advised not to walk alone in the upper reaches of the park far from general activity. ✉ *Rhodes Dr., Newlands* ☎ *021/799–8783* ⊕ *www.sanbi.org* 🖃 *R50* ⊙ *Apr.–Aug., daily 8–6; Sept.–Mar., daily 8–7.*

Fodor'sChoice   **Robben Island.** Made famous by its most illustrious inhabitant, Nelson
★   Mandela, this island, whose name is Dutch for "seals," has a long and
sad history. At various times a prison, leper colony, mental institution, and military base, it is finally filling a positive, enlightening, and
empowering role in its latest incarnation as a museum.

Declared a UNESCO World Heritage Site on December 1, 1997, Robben Island has become a symbol of the triumph of the human spirit. In
1997 around 90,000 made the pilgrimage; in 2006 more than 300,000
crossed the water to see where some of the greatest South Africans spent
much of their lives. Visiting the island is a sobering experience, which
begins at the modern Nelson Mandela Gateway to Robben Island, an
impressive embarkation center that doubles as a conference center.
Interactive exhibits display historic photos of prison life. Next make
the journey across the water, remembering to watch Table Mountain
recede in the distance and imagine what it must have been like to have
just received a 20-year jail sentence. Boats leave on the hour (every other
hour in winter), and the crossing takes 30 minutes.

Tours are organized by the Robben Island Museum. (Other operators advertise Robben Island tours but just take visitors on a boat trip
around the island.) As a result of the reconciliation process, most tour
guides are former political prisoners. During the 2½-hour tour you walk
through the prison and see the cells where Mandela and other leaders
were imprisoned. You also tour the lime quarry, Robert Sobukwe's
place of confinement, and the leper church. Due to increased demand
for tickets during peak season (December–January), make bookings
at least three weeks in advance. Take sunglasses and a hat in summer.
■ TIP➔ You are advised to tip your guide only if you feel that the tour
has been informative. ✉ *Nelson Mandela Gateway, V&A Waterfront*
☎ *021/413–4220* ⊕ *www.robben-island.org.za* ☑ *R280* ☉ *Nov.–Apr.,
daily 8–3; May–Sept. or Oct., daily 9–1. The last boat generally leaves
the island at 6 pm in summer and 4 pm in winter. Hours and boat
departures vary. As the phone isn't always answered and the website
isn't always functioning, it can be best to get a tour operator to handle
queries for you.*

Table Mountain. Table Mountain truly is one of southern Africa's most
beautiful and impressive natural wonders. The views from its summit
are awe-inspiring. The mountain rises more than 3,500 feet above the
city, and its distinctive flat top is visible to sailors 65 km (40 miles) out
to sea. Climbing up the step-like Plattekloof Gorge—the most popular
route up—will take two to three hours, depending on your fitness level.
There is no water along the route; you *must* take at least 2 liters (½
gallon) of water per person. Table Mountain can be dangerous if you're
not familiar with the terrain. Many paths that look like good routes
down the mountain end in treacherous cliffs. ⚠ Do not underestimate
this mountain: every year local and foreign visitors to the mountain get
lost, some falling off ledges with fatal consequences. It may be in the
middle of a city, but it is not a genteel town park. Because of occasional
muggings near the Rhodes Memorial (east) of the mountain, it's unwise
to walk alone on that side. It's recommended that you travel in a group
or, better yet, with a guide. If you want to do the climb on your own,

wear sturdy shoes or hiking boots; always take warm clothes, including a windbreaker or fleece; travel with a mobile phone; and let someone know of your plans. Consult the staff at a Cape Town Tourism office for more guidelines. Another (much easier) way to reach the summit is to take the cable car, which affords fantastic views. Cable cars depart from the Lower Cable Station, which lies on the slope of Table Mountain near its western end; the station is a long way from the city on foot, and you're better off traveling by car, tuk-tuk, or taxi. ⊠ *Tokai Manor House, Tokai Rd., Table Mountain National Park* 🕾 *021/712–2337, 021/712–0527* ⊕ *www.sanparks.org* 🖃 *Free* ⊙ *Park daily dawn–dusk. Parking lots: Oct.–Mar., daily 8–7; Apr.–Sept., daily 8–6.*

FAMILY

Fodor's Choice

★

Two Oceans Aquarium. This aquarium is widely considered one of the finest in the world. Stunning displays reveal the marine life of the warm Indian Ocean and the icy Atlantic. It's a hands-on place, with a touch pool for children and opportunities for certified divers to explore the vast, five-story kelp forest or the predator tank, where you share the water with a couple of large ragged-tooth sharks (*Carcharias taurus*) and get a legal adrenaline rush (for an additional fee, of course). If you don't fancy getting wet, you can still watch the feeding in the predator tank every day at 3. But there's more to the aquarium than just snapping jaws. Look for the endangered African penguins, also known as jackass penguins because of the awkward braying noise they make; pulsating moon jellies and spider crabs; and a new frog exhibit. ⊠ *Dock Rd., V&A Waterfront* 🕾 *021/418–3823* ⊕ *www.aquarium.co.za* 🖃 *R112* ⊙ *Daily 9:30–6.*

WORTH NOTING

Long Street. The section of Long between Orange and Strand streets is lined with magnificently restored Georgian and Victorian buildings. Wrought-iron balconies and fancy curlicues on these colorful houses evoke the French Quarter in New Orleans. In the 1960s, Long Street played host to bars, prostitutes, and sleazy hotels. Today antiques dealers, the Pan-African Market, funky clothing outlets and a plethora of cafes, bars, and restaurants make this one of the best browsing streets in the city; by night, some of its older reputation remains true. Lodgings here range from backpackers' digs to the posh Grand Daddy. At the mountain end is Long Street Baths, an indoor swimming pool and old Turkish *hammam* (steam bath). ⊠ *Long St., between Orange and Strand sts., Cape Town Central.*

WHERE TO EAT

Cape Town is the culinary capital of South Africa and quite possibly the continent. It certainly has the best restaurants in southern Africa. Nowhere else in the country is the populace so discerning about food, and nowhere else is there such a wide selection of high-quality restaurants. Western culinary history here dates back to the 17th century—Cape Town was founded specifically to grow food—and that heritage is reflected in the city's cuisine and the fact that a number of restaurants operate in historic townhouses and 18th-century wine estates.

6

$$$
EUROPEAN
Fodor's Choice
★

✕ **Aubergine.** One of Cape Town's oldest and most consistent fine-dining establishments, Aubergine has a timber-and-glass interior that matches chef-owner Harald Bresselschmidt's classic-with-a-twist cuisine. Using the freshest South African produce prepared with classical European methods, the chef cooks with wine in mind, and Aubergine's cellar and pairings are unsurprisingly superb. Purists who appreciate dishes that allow natural flavors to shine will thoroughly enjoy a languorous multicourse meal. The seafood on the menu is wonderful: the octopus with baby fennel, plum tomatoes, and eggplant in lemon-thyme crème fraîche is divine, and the beet-cured klingklip takes this often ho-hum fish to unexpected heights. Meanwhile, meat dishes like a Wagyu beef carpaccio with Jersualem artichokes are sublime. Lunch and winter specials are more affordable ways of enjoying this fine restaurant. $ *Average main: R195* ✉ *39 Barnet St., Gardens* ☎ *021/465–4909* ⊕ *www. aubergine.co.za* ⟐ *Reservations essential* ⊗ *Closed Sun. No lunch Mon., Tues., and Sat.*

$$$
FRENCH
Fodor's Choice
★

✕ **Bistro Bizerca.** With its superb cuisine and excellent service, diners adore this French bistro located in an old Cape Dutch building on Heritage Square. Using classic French techniques but drawing on local produce and adding some fusion twists, dishes like the signature raw Norwegian salmon salad with ginger, soy, and shallots are served in a warm wood-floored dining room with a vertical garden feature, as well as in a lovely outside courtyard. The culinary magic is mostly found in the form of daily specials presented chalkboard-style, including dishes like a duo of tuna with avocado wasabi-and-jalapeño dressing, or the veal tongue with Gruyère and local *waterblommetjies* (water lily). Lunch is buzzier than dinner, but the food is splendid every time. In the summer enjoy a tapas and drinks menu from 3 to 6 during the week in the courtyard. $ *Average main: R160* ✉ *Heritage Sq., 98 Shortmarket St., Cape Town Central* ☎ *021/423–8888* ⊕ *www.bizerca.com* ⟐ *Reservations essential* ⊗ *Closed Sun. No lunch Sat.*

$$$$
ECLECTIC
Fodor's Choice
★

✕ **La Colombe.** Among South Africa's most lauded fine-dining restaurants, La Colombe recently moved its award-winning French-Asian cuisine to a new location on the Silvermist organic wine estate overlooking the Constantia wine valley. Return visitors will be happy to know that favorites like the seared scallops and pork belly starter and foie gras–topped meat dishes remain, although with a slightly increased focus on the creative Asian twists: the scallops are now miso-seared, and the pork belly done Asian barbeque–style and served with a lemongrass and ginger velouté. For more traditional tastes, dishes like the aged beef in a black pepper–café au lait sauce are sure to delight. The new space is both intimate and cool, the simple white-painted timber offset by charcoal finishes and black beams, all flooded with light and stunning views during the day, and elegantly refined in the evening. The lunch menu is à la carte, while dinner is a 4-course affair (a gourmand tasting menu will be offered as well). However you order, consider pairing your meal with selections from the excellent wine list, and conclude with one of the spectacular desserts and the chef's signature petit fours. Understated smooth service and the bucolic location will ensure that La Colombe will remain a favorite Cape Town splurge. $ *Average* *main: R465* ✉ *Silvermist Mountain Lodge, Main Rd., Constantia Nek, Constantia* ☎ *021/795–0125* 🌐 *www.lacolombe.co.za* ✍ *Reservations essential.*

$$$$ JAPANESE Fodor's Choice ★ 🍴 **Nobu.** World-famous chef Nobuyuki "Nobu" Matsuhisa's exceptional contemporary Japanese cuisine with a South American twist may be costly by local standards, but the cost here is entirely worth it when compared with the bill at one of Nobu's sister New York or London branches. Food is the main event in this vast, modern space, in the Waterfront's One&Only resort. If your budget allows, the omakase multicourse tasting menu is the way to go for a divine culinary experience in which the chef will surprise you with his choices for the evening. Do not miss dishes like the signature Alaskan black cod with miso. The spinach salad with dried miso and truffle oil is sublime, the kingklip tempura heavenly, and the sushi excellent, including an unusually diverse range of choices for Cape Town. There is a stellar selection of sake and, of course, excellent local wines. [$] *Average main: R475* ✉ *One&Only Cape Town, Dock Rd., V&A Waterfront* ☎ *021/431–4511* 🌐 *www.oneandonlyresorts.com* ✍ *Reservations essential* 🕓 *No lunch.*

$$$ ECLECTIC Fodor's Choice ★ 🍴 **The Pot Luck Club.** A playful and inventive tapas-style venture from Cape Town star chef Luke Dale Roberts, this hip eatery on the sixth floor of an old silo is perfect for enjoying fine-dining nibbles set against gorgeous views in a stylish yet comfortable atmosphere. The menu changes regularly, but the smoked beef filet and truffle café au lait, and Korean fried chicken with pineapple-and-miso slaw remain favorites. Think of each plate as a half portion, and come with a crew to maximize how many you can taste. The cocktails are equally delicious, the service is friendly and efficient, and the atmosphere, with its amazing views of the harbor and mountain and funky lighting, is very relaxed. The all-you-can-drink sparkling-wine brunches (Sunday only) are also a fantastic treat. [$] *Average main: R190* ✉ *Old Biscuit Mill, 375 Albert Rd., Silo Top Floor, Woodstock* ☎ *021/447–0804* 🌐 *www.thepotluckclub.co.za* ✍ *Reservations essential* 🕓 *Closed Sun.*

$$$$ MODERN EUROPEAN 🍴 **The Roundhouse.** Known for its exceptional natural beauty, Cape Town is surprisingly short on restaurants with killer views: the Roundhouse is helping close that gap. Converted from its origins as an 18th-century Table Mountain–side hunting lodge, this unique fine-dining restaurant overlooking Camps Bay specializes in creative and surprising flavor combinations—think mussels with oak-smoked butter and kombu gel—served by an excellent and exceptionally suave team of waiters. The Somerset Room offers sea views, but can be noisy. The private room for up to eight guests may better suit big groups. The adjacent "Rumbullion" picnic area from which diners can enjoy breathtaking mountain and sea views serves a more casual burger-and-pizza-style menu, and is an excellent place to while away a summer afternoon. Hours vary with season, so best to call and check. [$] *Average main: R595* ✉ *The Glen, Round House Rd., Table Mountain National Park* ☎ *021/438–4347* 🌐 *www.theroundhouserestaurant.com* ✍ *Reservations essential* 🕓 *Closed Mon. No dinner Sun. Rumbuillion closed May–Sept.*

6

$ ✕ **Skinny Legs & All.** Serving delicious, organic fare from breakfast
CAFÉ   through lunch, this unpretentious yet design-conscious café is a great
addition to Cape Town's downtown food scene. Starting the day with
the only muffin in town worth eating (a carrot-coconut concoction,
perfectly spiced and not too sweet), breakfast also includes items like
raw muesli with sheep's milk yogurt, fresh scones, and French toast with
vanilla-infused compote. Lunch usually includes some kind of risotto,
soup in the winter, and several salad options in the summer. Though the
menu changes regularly, expect dishes like a cinnamon-spiced quinoa
salad with roasted eggplant and toasted almonds, wild mushroom par-
cels with wild rice, or the Lumberjack sandwich of roasted chicken and
avocado with homemade coriander mayo. Free Wi-Fi, plenty of reading
material, and some great art on the walls complete the picture. $ *Aver-*
age main: R85 ✉ *70 Loop St., Cape Town Central* ☎ *021/423–5403*
⊕ *www.skinnylegsandall.co.za* ☉ *Closed Sun.*

$$$$ ✕ **The Test Kitchen.** Star chef Luke Dale Roberts put South Africa on the
ECLECTIC   culinary map when he opened this deceptively casual-looking eatery in
Fodor's Choice   Cape Town's trendy Woodstock neighborhood in 2009. Serving varying
★   tasting menus of truly mind-blowing inspiration, Roberts is working
some serious foodie magic here, and you'll be lucky if you can get a
table (it's typically booked four months in advance). The wonders begin
with dishes like pickled fish served with carrots prepared three ways
and honeycomb, a meal that brilliantly showcases Roberts' genius for
texture and working sweet against savory. The journey continues with
creations like a "Southern-style foie gras" of bourbon, molasses, and
oak-smoked duck. Expect the unexpected (both in taste sensation and
the arrival of little yummies you didn't order), and don't neglect the
cocktails, which are also brilliant. The relaxed ambience created by
exposed brick, funky lamps, friendly staff, and a totally open service
area acts as a great foil to the cuisine coming out of this kitchen. $ *Av-*
erage main: R590 ✉ *The Old Biscuit Mill, 375 Albert Rd., Shop 104A,*
Woodstock ☎ *021/447–2337* ⊕ *www.thetestkitchen.co.za* ⌖ *Reserva-*
tions essential ☉ *Closed Sun. and Mon.*

$$$ ✕ **Willoughby & Co.** Though unfortunately inside the mall, this buzzing
JAPANESE   hive of activity consistently churns out what many say is the city's best
sushi, thus adding a certain joy to a trip to the V&A. Expect an array
of fanciful and decadent signature rolls such as the creamy rock-shrimp
maki (a tuna-style roll graced with large chunks of tempura fried cray-
fish in a spicy mayo-based sauce) and the rainbow nation roll (salmon,
avocado, and tuna topped with caviar and a few squizzles of delicious
sesame-oil and sweet chili sauces). The traditional sashimi is also excel-
lent, as is the Japanese Kitchen menu. There will almost inevitably be a
line during normal dinner hours; however, it goes quickly (especially if
you sit at the sushi bar, which is the place to be) and you're likely to be
offered free tastes of various new vintages while waiting. $ *Average main:*
R150 ✉ *Victoria Wharf, Shop 6132, V&A Waterfront* ☎ *021/418–6115*
⊕ *www.willoughbyandco.co.za* ⌖ *Reservations not accepted*

WHERE TO STAY

Finding lodging in Cape Town can be a nightmare during peak travel season (December–January), as many of the more reasonable accommodations are booked up. It's worth traveling between April and August, if you can, to take advantage of the "secret season" discounts that are sometimes half the high-season rate. Other reduced rates can be scored by booking directly online, checking the "Best Available Rate" at large hotels, or simply asking if any specials or discounts are available.

First-time, short-term, or business visitors will want to locate themselves centrally. The historic city center is a vibrant and pedestrian-friendly place by day, but at night can feel a bit deserted and edgy, depending on where you are. Night owls may prefer to stay amid the nonstop action of Long Street or Kloof Street, or at the V&A Waterfront, with its plethora of pedestrian-friendly shopping and dining options (though be aware that locals don't consider the Waterfront the "real" Cape Town). Boutique hotels and bed-and-breakfasts in Gardens are often within walking distance of attractions and dining but will be quieter and often enjoy lovely views. Options along the Atlantic Seaboard are also close to the action and (mostly) pedestrian-friendly, with the added advantage of sea and sunset views. Staying farther out on the Cape Peninsula, whether the False Bay or Atlantic side, provides the closest thing in Cape Town to a beach-vacation atmosphere despite the cold ocean waters. The Southern Suburbs, especially around Constantia or Tokai, can make a good base from which to explore the area's wine estates as well as the peninsula, but you'll be dependent on a car for everything, and should plan on 25 to 45 minutes to get into town.

LODGING ALTERNATIVES

When South Africans travel, they often stay in guesthouses or B&Bs. Among them you will find some of the most elegant and professionally run establishments available, offering everything a hotel does but on a smaller, more personal scale. If you prefer a bit more anonymity or want to save money, consider renting a fully furnished apartment, especially if you're staying two or more weeks. Airbnb has listings in Cape Town, and several agencies can help you make bookings.

Cape Stay. Cape Stay offers a huge selection of accommodations to suit different needs, from very simple and affordable apartments to luxurious villas to special rates at well known hotels, covering both Cape Town and popular Western Cape destinations. ⊕ *www.capestay.co.za.*

CAPSOL Property & Tourism Solutions. CAPSOL has more than 2,000 high-quality, furnished, fully stocked villas and apartments along the Atlantic seaboard from Cape Town to Bakoven, including Clifton, Bantry Bay and Camps Bay. Apartments range from R1,600–R30,000 per night, most with a minimum 3-night stay depending on season. ⊠ *The Penthouse, 13 Totnes Ave., Camps Bay* ☎ *021/438–9644* ⊕ *www.capsol.co.za.*

HOTELS AND RESORTS

Hotel reviews have been shortened. For full information, visit Fodors. com.

$ ⊞ **The Bay Atlantic Guesthouse.** This unpretentious, value-oriented guest-

B&B/INN house is extremely well located a couple of blocks from Camps Bay's lively main drag. **Pros:** great location and views for money; friendly, homey space. **Cons:** decor is old-fashioned; rooms without views are underwhelming. $ *Rooms from: R1400* ⊠ *3 Berkley Rd.* ☎ *021/438–4341* ⊕ *www.thebayatlantic.com* ⟿ *7 rooms* ⦿| *Breakfast.*

$$$$
HOTEL
Fodor's Choice
★

🔲 **Belmond Mount Nelson Hotel.** This distinctive pink landmark has been the grande dame of Cape Town since it opened its doors in 1899 to accommodate passengers just off the Union-Castle steamships. **Pros:** aesthetically, this is the real colonial deal; guests include movie stars and diplomats; excellent restaurant. **Cons:** breakfast restaurant Oasis lacks the charm of the rest of the hotel. $ *Rooms from: R7565* ⊠ *76 Orange St., Gardens* ☎ *021/483–1000* ⊕ *www.belmond.com/mount-nelson-hotel-cape-town* ⟿ *133 rooms, 65 suites* ⦿| *Breakfast.*

$$
B&B/INN

🔲 **Blackheath Lodge.** Conveniently located on a quiet street in upper Sea Point, this small, stylish Victorian-era hotel with great concierge-level owner-rendered service is an extremely good value. **Pros:** excellent service; 24-hour minibar; nice location. **Cons:** no bathtubs in rooms; no gym. $ *Rooms from: R1950* ⊠ *Blackheath Rd.* ☎ *021/439–2541* ⊕ *www.blackheathlodge.com* ⟿ *15 rooms* ⦿| *Breakfast.*

$$
B&B/INN

🔲 **Cape Heritage Hotel.** Built as a private home in 1771, this centrally located boutique hotel has teak-beam ceilings, foot-wide yellow-wood floorboards, and numerous other details that recall its gracious past. **Pros:** excellent eateries in adjoining Heritage Square; free uncapped Wi-Fi in rooms and public areas; great location in Cape Town's historic district. **Cons:** bordered by one busy road; parking isn't free. $ *Rooms from: R2390* ⊠ *90 Bree St., Cape Town Central* ☎ *021/424–4646* ⊕ *www.capeheritage.co.za* ⟿ *17 rooms* ⦿| *Breakfast.*

$$$$
HOTEL
Fodor's Choice
★

🔲 **Cellars-Hohenort Hotel & Spa.** With acres of gardens and spectacular views across the Constantia Valley, this idyllic getaway makes the world beyond disappear. **Pros:** exquisite gardens; two pools (one for children); fantastic breakfast in lovely Conservatory Restaurant. **Cons:** need a car to get around; more modern rooms are less spectacular; a lot of stairs to access best rooms. $ *Rooms from: R5000* ⊠ *93 Brommersvlei Rd.* ☎ *021/794–2137* ⊕ *www.cellars-hohenort.com* ⟿ *52 rooms, 1 suite* ⦿| *Breakfast.*

$$$$
HOTEL

🔲 **The Dock House Boutique Hotel.** Victorian splendor meets modern glam at this stunning boutique hotel perched over Cape Town's trendy and ever-popular V&A Waterfront. **Pros:** the hotel's elegant interior has been featured in décor magazines; close to activities, dining, and shopping; excellent room service. **Cons:** guests have to walk outside to reach the gym and spa; those wishing to socialize with other guests should look elsewhere. $ *Rooms from: R6830* ⊠ *Portswood Close, Portswood Ridge, V&A Waterfront* ☎ *021/421–9334* ⊕ *www.dockhouse.co.za* ⟿ *5 rooms, 1 suite, 2 villas* ⦿| *Breakfast.*

$$$$
HOTEL
Fodor's Choice
★

🔲 **Ellerman House.** Built in 1906 for shipping magnate Sir John Ellerman, what may be Cape Town's finest hotel sits high on a hill up from Sea Point in Bantry Bay, graced with stupendous views of the sea, and an art collection that puts the National Gallery to shame. **Pros:** stunning national art collection; free transfers within 15 km, hand-finished laundry packed in tissue paper; free, fully stocked guest pantry. **Cons:** Kloof Road is busy; often booked a year in advance. $ *Rooms from:*

R10000 ✉ *180 Kloof Rd., Bantry Bay, Sea Point* ☎ *021/430–3200* 🌐 *www.ellerman.co.za* 🛏 *11 rooms, 2 suites, 2 villas* 🍴 *Breakfast.*

$$$$ RESORT FAMILY 🏨 **One&Only Cape Town.** In the spirit of founding investor Sol Kerzner's "go big or go home" philosophy, the One&Only Cape Town is a splendid tribute to excess with its four-story glass window views onto Table Mountain from the aptly named Vista Bar and decadent island spa surrounded by a moat. **Pros:** conveniently located in the heart of the Watefront; oceans of space and great views from all rooms; excellent personalized service; great kids' programs. **Cons:** Marina Rise guests must walk through the lounge in their swimsuit/robe to reach the pool or spa; lacks the intimacy of a smaller hotel. [$] *Rooms from: R7215* ✉ *Dock Rd., V&A Waterfront* ☎ *021/431–5888* 🌐 *www.oneandonlyresorts.com* 🛏 *131 rooms* 🍴 *Breakfast.*

$$$$ HOTEL 🏨 **Pod.** This sexy designer boutique hotel enjoys a great location on a quiet corner just a block from Camps Bay's main drag. **Pros:** excellent breakfast; spa with shower for use by late check-outs; eco-friendly additions like door sensor to switch a/c off and tree planting for guests of three nights or more. **Cons:** classic rooms are small; no on-site restaurant after breakfast. [$] *Rooms from: R5150* ✉ *3 Argyle Rd.* ☎ *021/438–8550* 🌐 *www.pod.co.za* 🛏 *17 rooms* 🍴 *Breakfast.*

$$$$ RESORT Fodor's Choice ★ 🏨 **Tintswalo Atlantic.** Visitors attracted to the Cape Peninsula for its natural grandeur will think they've died and gone to heaven when arriving at this discreetly luxurious boutique hotel. **Pros:** unique mind-blowing location; stupendous breakfast; gorgeous beach chic décor. **Cons:** must drive to all activities and sights; [$] *Rooms from: R8520* ✉ *Chapman's Peak Dr., Km 2, Hout Bay* ☎ *021/201–0025* 🌐 *www.tintswalo.com* 🛏 *10 island suites, 1 presidential suite* 🍴 *Some meals.*

$$$$ HOTEL Fodor's Choice ★ 🏨 **Twelve Apostles Hotel & Spa.** If you fancy taking a helicopter to the airport or lazing in a bubble bath while looking out floor-to-ceiling windows at sea and mountains, then this award-winning, luxurious hotel and spa may be for you. **Pros:** wonderfully attentive staff; Table Mountain is your back garden; sports buddy program provides a companion for runs or mountain biking in surrounding area. **Cons:** overlooks a road that gets busy; nearest off-site restaurant is at least 10 minutes by car; views from some rooms partially blocked by overhanging beam. [$] *Rooms from: R5685* ✉ *Victoria Rd.* ☎ *021/437–9000* 🌐 *www.12apostleshotel.com* 🛏 *55 rooms, 15 suites* 🍴 *Breakfast.*

SIDE TRIP FROM CAPE TOWN

THE CAPE WINELANDS

Although the Cape Winelands region is largely thought of as the wine centers of Stellenbosch, Franschhoek, and Paarl, today these areas make up only about 33% of all the land in the Cape under vine. This wine-growing region is now so vast, you can trek to the fringes of the Karoo Desert, in the northeast, and still find a grape. There are around 18 wine routes in the Western Cape, ranging from the Olifants River, in the north, to the coastal mountains of the Overberg and beyond. There's also a well-established Winelands brandy route, and an annual port festival is held in Calitzdorp, in the Little Karoo.

South African Wine

The South African wine industry is booming. Buried by sanctions during apartheid, South African wines were largely unknown internationally. But today there's enormous interest in South African reds *and* whites. Although South Africa has a reputation for delivering good quality at the bottom end of the market, more and more ultrapremium wines are emerging. Good-quality wines at varied prices are readily available—even in supermarkets.

Currently white wine production outstrips red, but the quality continually improves for both, and they regularly win international awards. Particularly notable is pinotage, South Africa's own grape variety, a cross between pinot noir and cinsaut (formerly hermitage). Chenin blanc is the country's most widely planted variety and is used in everything from blends to bubbly (known in South Africa as "Méthode Cap Classique").

The industry is transforming itself slowly. The illegal *dop* (drink) or tot system, in which farmers pay some of laborers' wages in wine, is finally on its way out, and there's a concerted effort among producers to uplift their laborers' quality of life. Many international companies refuse to import wine from farms that don't secure their workers' rights, and many farms are working at black empowerment. Tukulu, Riebeek Cellars, Thandi Wines, Ses'Fikile (which translated means "we have arrived"), M'hudi, and Freedom Road are just some of the pioneers. Three farms that deserve a special mention when it comes to transformation are Bosman Family Vineyard (Wellington), Solms-Delta Wine Estate (Franschhoek), and Van Loveren Family Cellar (Robertson). Tragically, South Africa has one of the highest incidences of fetal alcohol syndrome, a legacy left over from the dop system.

If you're serious about wine, arm yourself with *John Platter's Wine Guide* or visit ⊕ www.winemag. co.za (the new digital form of *Wine* magazine), featuring local wineries. For an in-depth read and fantastic photos, pick up *Wines and Vineyards of South Africa* by Wendy Torein or *New World of Wine from the Cape of Good Hope: The Definitive Guide to the South African Wine Industry* by Phyllis Hands, David Hughes, and Keith Phillips. *Wines of the New South Africa: Tradition and Revolution* by Tim James is also recommended reading.

The secret to touring the Cape Winelands is not to hurry. Dally over lunch on a vine-shaded veranda at a 300-year-old estate, enjoy an afternoon nap under a spreading oak, or sip wine while savoring the impossible views. Of the scores of wineries and estates in the Cape Winelands, the ones listed here are chosen for their great wine, their beauty, or their historic significance. It would be a mistake to try to cover them all in less than a week. You have nothing to gain from hightailing it around the Cape Winelands other than a headache. If your interest is more aesthetic and cultural than wine-driven, you would do well to focus on the historic estates of Stellenbosch and Franschhoek. Most Paarl wineries stand out more for the quality of their wine than for their beauty.

GETTING HERE AND AROUND

Driving yourself is undoubtedly the best way to appreciate the area. Each wine route is clearly marked with attractive road signs, and there are complimentary maps available at the tourism bureaus and at most wine farms. Roads in the area are good, and even the dirt roads leading up to a couple of the farms are nothing to worry about.

The best way to get to the Cape Winelands is to take the N2 out of Cape Town and then the R310 to Stellenbosch. Outside of rush hour, this will take you around 45 minutes. Expect some delays during the harvest months (generally late January through late March), when tractors ferry grapes from farms to cellars on the narrower secondary roads. On your way back to Cape Town, stick to the R310 and the N2. Avoid taking the M12, as it gets very confusing, and you'll end up in suburbs that aren't on tourist maps.

The major car-rental agencies have offices in the smaller towns, but it's best to deal with the Cape Town offices. Besides, you'll probably want to pick up a car at the airport. Since driving yourself around limits the amount of wine you can taste, unless you have a designated driver, it's best to join a tour, take a taxi, or—do it in style—rent a limo from Cape Limousine Services. Limos cost about R1,500 for the first hour and R600 per hour thereafter, so they're relatively cost-effective if you have a group of four or five.

Paarl Radio Taxis will transport up to three people at about R10 per kilometer (half mile). Waiting time is around R60 per hour. Larger groups can arrange transportation by minibus. Daksi Cab, based in Stellenbosch, works on a trip rate rather than a per-kilometer basis. A trip to a local restaurant costs around R90 regardless of the number of people. Daksi also provides shuttle service to the airport.

There's no regular bus service to the Cape Winelands suitable for tourists. If you are based in Stellenbosch, however, and don't want to drive to the wineries, you can make use of the Vine Hopper, a minibus that follows a fixed route to six wine farms. Tickets cost around R240 for a one-day ticket and R420 for a two-day ticket, and you'll be given a timetable so that you can get on and off as you please.

We do not recommend Cape Metro trains to Stellenbosch and Paarl because of an increase in violent muggings.

Contacts Cape Limousine Services ✉ *Capri Village, 20 Tobago Way, Sunnydale, Fish Hoek* ☎ *021/785–3100.* **Daksi Cab** ☎ *084/400–4480* ⊕ *www. daksicab.co.za.* **Paarl Radio Taxis** ☎ *021/872–5671.* **Vine Hopper** ✉ *Black Horse Centre, Dorp St. and Mark Rd., Stellenbosch* ☎ *021/882–8112* ⊕ *www. vinehopper.co.za.*

TOURS

Most tours of the Cape Winelands are operated by companies based in Cape Town; most have half- or full-day tours, but they vary by company and might include a cheese tasting or cellar tour in addition to wine tasting. Expect to pay around R580 for a half day and R800 for a full day, including all tasting fees. Though you stop for lunch, it is not included in the cost.

BEACH ESCAPES

So you've had your fill of exploring the bush, tracking animals and birds, and immersing yourself in wilderness. Now maybe you've got time to head for the beach. Summer is the best time to catch a tan, but people also head to Durban in winter as well as in summer.

DURBAN

Durban isn't slick or sophisticated, but 320 days of sunshine a year entices visitors and locals alike to the vast stretches of beautiful beach that hug the coastline. The proximity to the beach has given the province's largest city a laid-back vibe that makes it a perfect vacation destination.

Durban has the pulse, the look, and the complex face of Africa. It may have something to do with the summer heat, a clinging sauna that soaks you with sweat in minutes. If you wander into the Indian District or drive through the Warwick Triangle—an area away from the sea around Julius Nyerere (Warwick) Avenue—the pulsating city rises up to meet you. Traditional healers tout animal organs, vegetable and spice vendors crowd the sidewalks, and minibus taxis hoot incessantly as they trawl for business. It is by turns colorful, stimulating, and hypnotic.

It's also a place steeped in history and culture. Gandhi lived and practiced law here, and Winston Churchill visited as a young man. It's home to the largest number of Indians outside India; the massive Indian townships of Phoenix and Chatsworth stand as testimony to the harsh treatment Indians received during apartheid, though now thousands of Indians are professionals and businesspeople in Durban.

⚠ Street names have all been updated, but the old ones remain in brackets, as some maps and locals still refer to streets by the old names

WHEN TO GO

The height of summer (December and January) brings heat, humidity, higher prices, and crowds, who pour into "Durbs," as it's fondly known, by the millions. Locals know never to brave the beach on holidays or over the Christmas season except for an hour or two from 6 am—one of the nicest times there. June and July are Durban's driest months, and although you can never predict the weather, expect warm, dry days and cool nights.

GETTING HERE AND AROUND

AIR TRAVEL

About 17 km (11 miles) from Umhlanga and about 32 km (20 miles) north of Durban, King Shaka International Airport operates under the management of the Airports Company South Africa.

South African Airways (SAA) flies to Durban via Johannesburg. Domestic airlines serving Durban are SAA, BA/Comair, Kulula, SA Express, SA Airlink, and Mango. Perhaps the easiest way to book a ticket to or from Durban is online. Kulula and Mango are the budget-priced airlines, so expect to buy your own snacks and drinks on board. SAA is usually the more expensive option, unless you're looking for a ticket at short notice (next day or two), when it may turn out to offer the lowest price.

The most inexpensive ground transfer into Durban and back is the Airport Shuttle Service, which costs R70 and departs every 30 to 45 minutes after incoming flights arrive and leaves the city center every hour. Its drop-off points are flexible within the city and include all hotels on the North Beach and South Beach, the Central Business District, the International Convention Centre, and the Moses Mabhida Stadium. On request, the driver is likely to drop you anywhere en route. Call ahead and the bus will pick you up at any hotel in the city; there's no need to reserve for the trip into Durban. A taxi ride into Durban will cost around R4450. If you plan to go farther afield, call Magic Transfers or catch a cab from outside the terminal building.

Airports Airports Company South Africa ☎ *011/921–6262* ⊕ *www. acsa.co.za.* **King Shaka International Airport** ☎ *011/921–6262* ⊕ *kingshakainternational.co.za.*

Airport Transfers Airport Shuttle Service ☎ *031/465–5573.* **Aqua Tours** ☎ *082/410–7116* ⊕ *www.aquatours.co.za.* **Magic Transfers** ☎ *031/263–2647.*

CAR TRAVEL

Durban is relatively easy to navigate because the sea is a constant reference point. Downtown Durban is dominated by two parallel one-way streets, Dr. Pixley kaSeme Street (West Street) going toward the sea and Anton Lembede Street (Smith Street) going away from the sea, toward Berea and Pietermaritzburg; together they get you in and out of the city center easily. Parking downtown is a nightmare; head for an underground garage whenever you can. As with the rest of South Africa, wherever you go, self-appointed car guards will ask if they can watch your car. The going rate for a tip—if you want to give one—is R5, depending on how long you're away. The guards directly outside

Joe Kool's, between North and South beaches, are said to be very trust-worthy. ⚠ Don't leave your keys with anyone.

The M4 (Ruth First Highway), which stretches north up to the Dol-phin Coast—from Umhlanga to Ballito, about 40 km (25 miles) and beyond—is a particularly pretty coastal road, offering many views of the sea through lush natural vegetation and sugarcane fields. It's much nicer than the sterile N2 highway, which takes a parallel path slightly inland and offers no views.

Avis, Budget, Europcar, and Tempest have rental offices at the airport. Rates start at around R400 per day, including insurance and 200 km (125 miles), plus R2.10 per additional kilometer (half mile), or about R500 for the weekend. Avis offers unlimited mileage to international visitors, as long as you can produce your return ticket, international driver's license, and passport as proof.

TAXI TRAVEL

Taxis are metered and start at R5, with an additional R12 per kilo-meter (half mile); after-hours and time-based charges apply. Fares are calculated per vehicle for up to four passengers. Expect to pay about R50 from City Hall to North Beach and R400 to Durban International Airport. The most convenient taxi stands are around City Hall, in front of the beach hotels, and outside Spiga d'Oro on Florida Road in Morn-ingside. Some taxis display a "for-hire" light, whereas others you simply hail when you can see they're empty.

There's no need to contact a taxi yourself. They will either be easy to find or your hotel or restaurant can call one for you. Once a driver has dropped you off, he or she will usually give you a card so you have contact details for the return trip.

Contacts Umhlanga Cabs ☎ *031/561–1846.*

SAFETY AND PRECAUTIONS

Durban has not escaped the crime evident in every South African city. Particularly in the city center but also elsewhere, smash-and-grab thieves roam the streets, looking for bags or valuables in your car, even while you're driving, so lock any valuables in the trunk and keep your car doors locked and windows up at all times. Although there's no need to be fearful, be observant wherever you go. Hire a guide to take you around Durban, don't wander around the city center or outside your hotel alone at night, and keep expensive cameras and other pos-sessions concealed. The Durban Beachfront (with recently upgraded security features), Umhlanga, and the outlying areas are safe to explore on your own, though you'll need a taxi or car to get between them. If you plan to take a dip while you're at the beach, ask a neighboring beachgoer or lifeguard to keep an eye on your belongings, or put them in a locker—available in the vicinity of North and South beaches and on Umhlanga Main Beach.

TOUR OPTIONS

Durban Tourism. Three-hour walking tours depart from the Tourist Junc-tion on weekdays at 9:30 and 1:30; the Oriental Walkabout explores the Indian District, including Victoria Market and several mosques, and the Historical Walkabout covers major monuments and museums. Reservations are essential; a two-person minimum applies. Durban Tourism can also provide details of various guided township tours by local tour operators, which offer an insight into the social history and modern-day challenges of the townships. ☎ *031/322–4164* ⊕ *www. durbanexperience.co.za* 🖃 *R100.*

Isle of Capri. This company offers sightseeing cruises around Durban Bay or out to sea, plus whale- and dolphin-watching tours. Boats depart from Wilson's Wharf on Margaret Mncadi Avenue. ✉ *14–18 Boatman's Rd., Canal Rd., Victoria Embankment* ☎ *031/305–3099* ⊕ *www. isleofcapri.co.za.*

VISITOR INFORMATION

The Tourist Junction, in the restored old Durban Station building provides information on almost everything that's happening in Durban and KwaZulu-Natal.

Contacts Durban Tourism Office ✉ *90 Florida Rd.* ☎ *031/322–4164* ⊕ *www. durbanexperience.co.za* ⊙ *Weekdays 8:30–5.* **Durban Tourism Beach Office** ✉ *1 K. E. Masinga Rd., Beachfront* ☎ *031/322–4173* ⊕ *www.durbanexperience. co.za.*

EXPLORING

TOP ATTRACTIONS

FAMILY **KwaZulu-Natal Sharks Board.** Most of the popular bathing beaches in KwaZulu-Natal are protected by shark nets maintained by this shark-research institute, the world's foremost. Each day, weather permitting, crews in ski boats check the nets, releasing healthy sharks back into the ocean and bringing dead ones back to the institute, where they are dissected and studied. One-hour tours are offered, including a shark dissection (sharks' stomachs have included such surprising objects as a boot, a tin can, and a car license plate!) and an enjoyable and fascinating audiovisual presentation on sharks and shark nets. An exhibit area and good curio shop are also here. You can join the early morning trip from Durban harbor to watch the staff service the shark nets off Durban's Golden Mile. Depending on the season, you will more than likely see dolphins and whales close at hand. Booking is essential for trips to the shark nets, and a minimum of six people is required; no one under age six is allowed. ■TIP→ Book well in advance for this—it may turn out to be a highlight of your trip. ✉ *1a Herrwood Dr., Umhlanga* ☎ *031/566–0400* ⊕ *www.shark.co.za* 🖃 *Presentation R45, boat trips R300* ⊙ *Presentation Tues., Wed., and Thurs. at 9 and 2, Sun. at 2. Boat trips to shark nets, daily (weather dependent) 6:30–8:30 am.*

FAMILY **uShaka Marine World.** This aquatic complex combines the uShaka Sea World aquarium and the uShaka Wet 'n Wild water park. The largest aquarium in the Southern Hemisphere, it has a capacity of nearly six million gallons of water, more than four times the size of Cape Town's aquarium. Enter through the side of a giant ship and walk down several stories to enter a "labyrinth of shipwrecks"—a jumble of five different fake but highly realistic wrecks, from an early-20th-century passenger cruiser to a steamship. Within this labyrinth are massive tanks, housing more than 350 species of fish and other sea life and the biggest variety of

"The direct eye contact with one of the most majestic mammals alive was just awe inspiring. [It was a] true sense of connection with nature." —jspiegel, Fodors.com member.

sharks in the world, including ragged-tooth and Zambezi (bull sharks). Try to catch the divers hand-feeding fish and rays in the morning. The complex includes dolphin, penguin, and seal shows, and a variety of reptiles and amphibians populate the Dangerous Creatures exhibit.

The extensive water park comprises slides, pools, and about 10 different water rides. The intensity ranges from toddler-friendly to adrenaline junkie. Durban's moderate winter temperatures make it an attraction pretty much year round, though it's especially popular in summer. ■ TIP → Avoid on public holidays, and call ahead during winter when hours may change. ⊠ *1 King Shaka Ave., Beachfront* ☎ *031/328–8000* ⊕ *www.ushakamarineworld.co.za* ✉ *Sea World R149; Wet 'n Wild R149; combo ticket R199. Dangerous Creatures Exhibit R40* ☾ *Daily 10–5.*

BEACHES

The sea near Durban, unlike that around the Cape, is comfortably warm year-round: in summer the water temperature can top 27°C (80°F), whereas in winter 19°C (65°F) it's considered cold. The beaches are safe, the sand is a beautiful golden color, and you'll see people swimming year-round. KwaZulu-Natal's main beaches are protected by shark nets and staffed by lifeguards, and there are usually signs giving the wind direction, water temperature, and warnings about any dangerous swimming conditions. Directly in front of uShaka Marine World, **uShaka Beach** is an attractive public beach. The **Golden Mile**, stretching from South Beach all the way to Snake Park Beach, is packed with people who enjoy the waterslides, singles' bars, and fast-food joints. A little farther north are the **Umhlanga beaches,** and on the opposite side of the bay are the less commercialized but also less accessible and safe beaches on **Durban's Bluff.** Another pretty beach and coastal walk, just north of the **Umhlanga Lagoon,** leads to miles of near-empty beaches backed by virgin bush. ⚠ You should not walk alone on deserted beaches or carry jewelry, phones, or cameras, and never walk the beaches at night.

WHERE TO EAT

Durban's dining public is fickle by nature, and restaurants tend to change hands fairly often. But don't be discouraged—Durban offers some superb dining options, provided you eat to its strengths. Thanks to a huge Indian population, it has some of the best curry restaurants in the country.

Durbanites eat lunch and dinner relatively early because they're early risers, particularly in summer, when it's light soon after 4. They're also generally casual dressers—you'll rarely need a jacket and tie, and jeans are rarely frowned upon.

$$
SEAFOOD
✕ **Cargo Hold.** You might need to book several weeks in advance to secure a table next to the shark tank at here, but if you do it'll be one of your most memorable dining experiences. Enjoy a duo of carpaccios—smoked ostrich or peppered beef—while massive ragged-tooth sharks drift right by your table and sandsharks stir up the sandy bottom. Aside from the array of fish dishes like salmon trout in a phyllo pastry wrap or *peri-peri* (spicy chili-pepper sauce) calamari with basmati rice, Cargo Hold also serves meat dishes like slow-braised lamb shank in tomato, honey, lemon, and Dijon mustard. The restaurant is done up like a shipwreck; both floors have tank frontage. ■TIP➜ **The view of the shark tank is best from the bottom floor, so ask for this when booking.** The restaurant is part of the building known as the Phantom Ship, accessed from the promenade next to the ship's giant propeller; you don't need to pay admission to uShaka Marine World to eat here. $ *Average main: R130* ✉ *uShaka Marine World, 1 King Shaka Ave., Beachfront* ☎ *031/328–8037* ⊕ *www.ushakamarineworld.co.za/ restaurants/cargo-hold* ⌕ *Reservations essential.*

$$$
SOUTH AFRICAN
Fodor's Choice
★
✕ **Havana Grill.** Attention to detail and freshly prepared, quality food combine to make this one of Durban's finest restaurants. It offers spectacular sea vistas (ask for a table with a view when making your reservation) and a contemporary interior, with white, leather-upholstered chairs, wall-length couches, and antelope horns on the walls. Steak—prepared and aged in the in-house butchery—and seafood are specialties. Try the tasting platter for starters (minimum of two people sharing): a mix of nachos; jalapeños stuffed with cheese; grilled calamari; bruschetta; lamb and spring rolls. For mains, consider the grain-fed ribeye steak with a duo of peppercorn and red wine sauce; seasonal varieties of venison; or line-caught fish (likely swordfish, dorado, or Cape salmon). There's a good basic domestic wine list, but take the opportunity to make a selection from a walk-in cellar lined with lesser-known wines. $ *Average main: R150* ✉ *Suncoast Casino & Entertainment World, Shop U2, 20 Suncoast Bd., Beachfront* ☎ *031/337–1305* ⊕ *www.havanagrill.co.za* ⌕ *Reservations essential* ⌕ *No children after 6 pm.*

6

$$$
FRENCH
Fodor's Choice
★

✕ **Ile Maurice.** One of Umhlanga's culinary gems, this restaurant was built up over many years by the charming Mauvis family. Today ownership is shared by Jean Mauvis and Christian Lenferna de la Motte. The soft-hued interior and pretty veranda that overlooks the Umhlanga beach hark back to the area's colonial roots. On the menu you'll find classic French Mauritian fare such as soupe de poisson à la mauricienne and octopus curry. Although seafood is a specialty, meat-lovers have plenty to choose from, with filet de chateau a popular option. A well-considered wine list complements the menu. $ *Average main: R150* ⊠ *9 McCausland Crescent, Umhlanga* ☎ *031/561–7609* ⊕ *www. ilemauricerestaurant.co.za* ⌂ *Reservations essential* 🎩 *Jacket required* ⊘ *Closed Mon.*

WHERE TO STAY

Many of Durban's main hotels lie along the Golden Mile, but there are some wonderful boutique hotels and bed-and-breakfasts (especially in Berea, Morningside, and Umhlanga) that offer a more personalized experience.

Hotel reviews have been shortened. For full information, visit Fodors. com.

$$$$
HOTEL
Fodor's Choice
★

🏨 **Beverly Hills Hotel.** In a high-rise building right on the beach, this upscale hotel is popular with both vacationers and businesspeople and has a longstanding reputation for gracious hospitality. **Pros:** unbeatable sea views; hotel has its own demarcated piece of beach with lounge chairs; great cocktail bar. **Cons:** some rooms are smaller than you might expect; prices increase in-season. $ *Rooms from: R6018* ⊠ *54 Lighthouse Rd.* ☎ *031/561–2211* ⊕ *www.tsogosunhotels.com/deluxe/ beverly-hills-hotel/* 🛏 *88 rooms, 7 suites, 8 garden villas* ❚◎❚ *Breakfast.*

$$
RESORT
FAMILY

🏨 **Cabana Beach.** Families who want a traditional beach vacation can't do better than this large resort, where children under 18 stay free, the bathing beach is directly in front of the hotel, and there are tons of activities to keep kids happy. **Pros:** at main swimming beach; adults-only pool; within walking distance to village. **Cons:** basic, no-frills, no-fuss interiors; teeming with children in-season. $ *Rooms from: R1800* ⊠ *10 Lagoon Dr.* ☎ *031/561–2371* ⊕ *www.tsogosunhotels.com/resorts/ cabana-beach/* 🛏 *217 apartments* ❚◎❚ *No meals.*

$$
HOTEL

🏨 **Durban Hilton.** This massive luxury hotel adjacent to the International Convention Centre is a short taxi ride from the city center and beachfront and is favored by business people and conference-goers. **Pros:** close to convention center; good gym; beauty salon offers unusual treatments such as the bamboo massage. **Cons:** not within walking distance of restaurants; unsafe to walk outside hotel after dark. $ *Rooms from: R2590* ⊠ *12–14 Walnut Rd.* ☎ *031/336–8100* ⊕ *www.hilton. com* 🛏 *327 rooms, 16 suites* ❚◎❚ *No meals.*

$$
HOTEL

🏨 **Garden Court Marine Parade.** You can't beat the location of this pleasant hotel midway between South and North beaches and only a five-minute drive from the city center. **Pros:** central location on Golden Mile; sea views; friendly staff. **Cons:** hotel lobby and bar area lack atmosphere; recommended restaurants a taxi ride away; inadvisable to walk in area after dark. $ *Rooms from: R1799* ⊠ *167 Tambo (Marine)*

Parade ☎ *031/337–3341* 🌐 *www.tsogosun.com* 🛏 *346 rooms, 6 suites* 🍴 *Breakfast.*

$$$$ HOTEL FAMILY Fodor's Choice ★ 🏨 **Oyster Box.** The iconic multi-award-winning Oyster Box hotel has achieved a perfect marriage between old colonial and African contemporary style in its luxurious accommodations and offers an eye-popping range of services and complimentary extras. **Pros:** fabulous food and service; spa includes complimentary healthful buffet; free shuttle to Gateway Shopping Centre; free snacks and treats all over the place; kids' vacation club. **Cons:** lots of steps and only one elevator; insufficient signage to rooms and public areas. [$] *Rooms from: R5875* ✉ *2 Lighthouse Rd., Umhlanga* ☎ *031/514–5000* 🌐 *www.oysterboxhotel.com* 🛏 *69 rooms, 17 suites* 🍴 *Breakfast.*

$$ HOTEL 🏨 **Suncoast Hotel and Towers.** This hotel mostly attracts business people and gamblers, but it's a stone's throw from the beach and has some great sea views. **Pros:** closest hotel to Moses Mabhida Stadium; spa; access to beach. **Cons:** smallish rooms. [$] *Rooms from: R2220* ✉ *20 Battery Beach Rd., Beachfront* ☎ *031/314–7878* 🌐 *www.tsogosunhotels.com/deluxe/suncoast-towers/pages/overview.aspx* 🛏 *165 rooms, 36 suites* 🍴 *Breakfast.*

$$$ HOTEL Fodor's Choice ★ 🏨 **Teremok Marine.** Translated from Russian as "little hideaway," this delightful boutique lodge has individually styled rooms, each offering a different sensory experience—its own specific body-product fragrance, mood CD, candy—and the three rooms at the top have beautiful ocean views. **Pros:** close to Umhlanga village and one block from the sea; personalized service; free Internet; free transfers to village; complimentary laundry service. **Cons:** 1 km (½ mile) from nearest restaurants; open-plan bathrooms in all but one room. [$] *Rooms from: R3250* ✉ *49 Marine Dr.* ☎ *031/561–5848* 🌐 *www.teremok.co.za* 🛏 *8 rooms* 🍴 *Breakfast.*

$$$ HOTEL 🏨 **Tsogo Sun Elangeni & Maharani.** Overlooking North Beach along the Golden Mile, this combination of two adjacent high-rise hotels is a two-minute drive from the city center and attracts a mix of business, conference, and leisure travelers. **Pros:** tour and travel desk; business center; sea views; discounted rates on weekends. **Cons:** not for those who prefer an intimate hotel experience; breakfast not included in price during peak times; minimum-stay requirements in peak season. [$] *Rooms from: R2600* ✉ *63 Tambo (Snell) Parade, Beachfront* ☎ *031/362–1300* 🌐 *www.tsogosunhotels.com* 🛏 *734 rooms, 19 suites* 🍴 *Multiple meal plans.*

RWANDA AND
UGANDA

WELCOME TO RWANDA AND UGANDA

TOP REASONS TO GO

★ **Gorilla Trekking.**
Navigate your way through emerald foliage, bamboo forests, and gauzelike mists to behold the world's largest living primates on their own turf. Their sheer size and eerily humanlike interactions will leave you spellbound.

★ **Volcanoes National Park.**
This slice of the Virunga Mountains may be synonymous with gorilla trekking, but its active volcanoes, caves, and grasslands offer stunning views and rewarding hikes. You can spot buffalo, hyena, golden monkeys, and some 200 bird species in its environs.

★ **Kigali.** Arguably East Africa's safest and most future-focused city, Rwanda's capital is a patchwork of palm tree–lined boulevards, artisan coffee shops, international restaurants, and a downtown dotted with new buildings.

★ **Kampala.** Uganda's capital city is regionally renowned for its dancing-till-dawn nightlife, bustling markets, and white-knuckle motorbike taxi rides. Cafés and an active National Theatre offer more low-key entertainment options.

1 Rwanda. Trekking mountain gorillas in this landlocked country of undulating hills, terraced farmlands, volcanic mountain chains, and dense rain forests is an experience unlike any other. You'll witness awe-inspiring panoramas, a plethora of primates, friendly local people, and one of Africa's most promising capitals.

2 Uganda. Uganda's dramatically diverse landscapes, from the snow-capped Rwenzori Mountains to the mist-cloaked hillsides of Bwindi Impenetrable National Park, make it an award-winning destination among travelers.

93

GETTING ORIENTED

At 26,338 square km (10,169 square miles), Rwanda encompasses 5 volcanoes, 23 lakes, and a spectacular assortment of wildlife. Biological diversity is concentrated in three national parks: Nyungwe National Park, which has the largest mountain rain forest in Africa; Volcanoes National Park, home to the critically endangered mountain gorillas; and Akagera National Park, the largest protected wetland in Central Africa. Uganda, Rwanda's larger northern neighbor, spans 236,040 square km (146,675 square miles), with Kenya to the east, the Democratic Republic of the Congo to the west, and South Sudan to the north. "The Pearl of Africa" has 10 national parks, more than 1,000 species of birds, and 13 types of primates, including mountain gorillas.

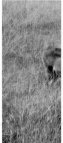

By Lauren Everitt and Anne-Marie Weeden

Looking into the eyes of a mountain gorilla, trekkers will experience a profound sense of recognition that no lion or elephant encounter, however thrilling, can match. Experiencing the exchange in the lush landscapes of this magnificent animal's own territory can humble even the most seasoned traveler.

Fewer than 900 mountain gorillas remain, and more than half of them live in the Virunga Moutains, a string of volcanoes that straddles Uganda, Rwanda, and the Democratic Republic of the Congo. The rest reside in Uganda's Bwindi Impenetrable National Park. Instability in the Congo makes Rwanda and Uganda the best places to behold the world's largest living primates. Though the required permit seems expensive, a golden hour with these fascinating animals will likely rank as an all-time travel high. Each gorilla group offers a new experience: Rwanda's Susa group was famously studied by primatologist Dian Fossey and has multiple silverback males and several sets of twins. Other groups are known for power struggles and female snatching. Some trekkers find the experience so exhilarating they go back for a second day.

In 1981, the Virunga gorilla population dipped to 254 individuals. Now, the gorillas' numbers are on the rise, thanks in large part to robust conservation efforts by both countries. Those include attracting high-dollar, conservation-conscious visitors rather than hordes of viewers, who might damage the environment. Revenue from the permit goes to preserving the endangered primates and supporting nearby communities.

Picking a country for your trek will depend on your priorities. Rwanda's pricier permits, US$750, are offset by the close proximity of the gorillas to the country's main airport, a two-hour drive on excellent roads. The Rwandan trek is generally gentler, and the less dense foliage is more photo-friendly. Meanwhile, Uganda offers two gorilla-spotting locations and a bargain off-season permit price of US$350 (normally US$600). Both Uganda parks are a solid seven-hour drive from the main airport. However, the journey presents excellent sightseeing opportunities for travelers with flexible itineraries. The upshot: If you're pressed for time and prefer easier gorilla access, pick Rwanda. If you've got a few days for exploring the surrounding countryside or prefer to go during the off-season, Uganda is your best bet.

It's worth noting that Rwanda offers more than just gorillas: The primeval forests of Nyungwe National Park are inhabited by more than 75 different mammals, including hundreds of chimpanzees and nearly 300 bird species. Akagera National Park in the northeast offers a savanna safari experience without the usual khaki-clad crowds.

Rwanda has made massive strides in security and national development in the two decades since the infamous 1994 genocide and is now among the safest countries in Africa. A sense of order prevails: violent crime is nearly nonexistent, and police can be spotted at most major intersections. New roads and tidy villages characterize the countryside. Citizens are required to participate in a monthly day of community service, and you'll be hard-pressed to find litter on the streets, particularly plastic bags, which are banned. You'll find new businesses, homes, and roadways under construction in every corner of the country.

Uganda has earned a tourism reputation as the "Pearl of Africa." The country has 10 national parks and a dazzling array of landscapes, which range from dry savannas to dense forests to snow-capped mountains. Visitors can observe lions prowling the grasslands one day and go white-water rafting down the Nile the next. Ugandans are also notoriously friendly, and English is widely spoken.

Regardless of which country you choose for your gorilla trek, it's a heady experience you'll never find in a zoo, as mountain gorillas don't survive in captivity. All told, you'll witness one of mankind's closest relatives in his natural habitat and contribute to its preservation.

PLANNING

WHEN TO GO

Gorilla trekking occurs year-round, but the optimal time is during the two dry seasons: June through September (the long dry season) and December through February (the short dry season). Travelers willing to brave a wet and muddy hike in October and November or between March to May will be rewarded by lower lodging prices, fewer crowds, and often shorter treks as gorillas keep to the lower slopes during the rainy seasons. Uganda slashes its gorilla permits from US$650 to US$350 from April to May. Rwanda does not, but lodges in both countries offer low-season rates. Rest assured, whenever you go, your gorilla encounter will not disappoint.

GETTING HERE AND AROUND

AIR TRAVEL

Kigali International Airport serves as the primary gateway for Rwanda's gorilla safaris. There are no direct flights from the United States, but many carriers offer one-stop itineraries. Brussels Airlines departs from Washington, D.C., with a stopover in Brussels. Ethiopian Airlines also flies from Washington, D.C., to Kigali by way of Addis Ababa. Lufthansa offers a flight from Chicago to Kigali via Brussels. Other airlines that fly to Kigali include Air France, KLM, South African Airways, and Turkish Airlines.

Most visitors arrive in Uganda via Entebbe International Airport, which has more than a dozen international carriers including: Turkish Airlines, Qatar Airways, British Airways, Emirates, Brussels Airlines, Ethiopian Airlines, and South African Airways. Again, there are no direct flights from the U.S. Emirates and Qatar offer one-stop itineraries from Washington, D.C., to Entebbe via Dubai and Doha, respectively. British Airways flies from New York to Entebbe through London.

INTERNAL FLIGHTS

Two popular operators offer internal air transfers around Uganda. The Entebbe-based company, Aerolink Uganda Limited, is known for its affordable daily scheduled service plying a circuit that includes many of the national parks. Fly Uganda, operating from their private hub at Kajjansi Airfield (roughly halfway between Kampala and Entebbe), offer private charter and scheduled flights in a fleet of various aircraft, serving airstrips around the country. ■TIP→ **For a special treat, ask about their scenic flights over Kampala or the Source of the Nile, a great way to take in this area.**

Airlines AeroLink Uganda Limited. ✉ *Entebbe International Airport, Entebbe, Central Region, Uganda* ☎ *0317/333–000, 0776/882–205* ⊕ *www. aerolinkuganda.com.* **Air France** ✉ *Paris, France* ☎ *800/237–2747* ⊕ *www. airfrance.us.* **British Airways** ✉ *Harmondsworth, England* ☎ *800/247–9297* ⊕ *www.britishairways.com.* **Brussels Airlines** ✉ *Belgium* ☎ *866/308–2230 for reservations* ⊕ *www.brusselsairlines.com.* **Emirates** ✉ *United Arab Emirates* ☎ *800/777–3999* ⊕ *www.emirates.com.* **Ethiopian Airlines** ✉ *Rwanda* ☎ *800/445–2733* ⊕ *www.flyethiopian.com.* **Fly Uganda.** ✉ *Gate One, Kajjansi Airfield, Kajjansi, Central Region, Uganda* ☎ *0772/712–557, 0772/712–553, 0772/712–554* ⊕ *www.flyuganda.com.* **KLM** ✉ *Netherlands* ☎ *866/434–0320* ⊕ *www.klm.com.* **Lufthansa** ✉ *Cologne, Germany* ☎ *800/645–3880 for reservations* ⊕ *www.lufthansa.com.* **Qatar Airways** ✉ *Qatar* ☎ *877/777–2827 for reservations* ⊕ *www.qatarairways.com.* **South African Airways** ✉ *Johannesburg, South Africa* ☎ *800/722–9675 for reservations* ⊕ *www.flysaa.com.* **Turkish Airlines** ✉ *Turkey* ☎ *800/874–8875* ⊕ *www.turkishairlines.com.*

AIRPORTS AND TRANSFERS

Kigali International Airport, previously known as Gregoire Kayibanda Airport, is approximately 10 km (6 miles) or a 15-minute drive from central Kigali. Uniformed taxi drivers are in abundance around the airport and will zip you downtown for a negotiable fee of around Rwf10,000 (US$15). Be warned that pricier hotels like Kigali Serena

Hotel draw higher fare quotes. Uganda's Entebbe International Airport is 40 km (25 miles) from central Kampala. Airport taxis charge around Ush70,000 (US$27) for one way. Safari operators and hotels in both countries often include airport pickup in their fees or as an add-on service.

Airport Contacts Entebbe International Airport ⊠ *5536 Kampala Rd., Entebbe, Uganda* ☏ *256/041–435–30000* ⊕ *entebbe-airport.com.* **Kigali International Airport** ⊠ *KN5 Rd., Kanombe, Kigali, Rwanda.*

ESSENTIALS

HEALTH AND SAFETY

Visitors to Uganda and Rwanda are required to present proof of yellow fever vaccination upon arrival at the airport. Hepatitis A and B vaccinations are recommended. Adventurous eaters and travelers to rural areas should also consider the Typhoid vaccine. Malaria is a risk in both countries, so consult with your doctor on antimalarial tablet options. At the very least, sleep under a mosquito net at night and wear insect repellent during the day. Avoid tap water and opt for bottled instead. Petty theft and muggings do occur, so don't wander around alone at night, particularly in urban areas.

MONEY MATTERS

Rwanda's official currency is the Rwandan franc (Rwf). At this writing the exchange rate is approximately Rwf690 to US$1. Uganda's shilling (Ush) has an exchange rate of Ush2,630 to US$1. Although larger hotels and tour companies may accept U.S. dollars and credit cards, expect to pay in francs or shillings at local shops and restaurants. You can withdraw the local currency at ATMs, found in large cities, or exchange your U.S. dollars at the airport and local banks. ■ TIP➔ **US$50 and US$100 bills will fetch better exchange rates, as will newer notes. Bills printed before 2005 may not be accepted.**

PASSPORTS AND VISAS

Tourist visas are not required in Rwanda for stays shorter than 90 days. For Uganda, a single-entry, three-month tourist visa (US$50) can be obtained from the Uganda Embassy in Washington, D.C., or the Uganda Mission to the U.N. in New York City. You will need to mail in an application form, two passport-size photos, and the correct visa fee two months before travel. Processing time is three working days. Although not recommended, you can also secure a visa at Entebbe International Airport, where you must pay in cash. For both countries, your passport must be valid for six months from the date of intended travel and contain at least one blank page.

TOUR OPERATORS

The complex logistics of planning a gorilla-tracking safari means all but the hardiest of independent travelers would be advised to rely on the services of a reputable tour operator with local expertise. The following list includes a selection of established, high-end operators with local offices in either Uganda or Rwanda, or both. All offer tailor-made

tours; some also provide scheduled group departures as a more affordable alternative.

Classic Africa Safaris. This Uganda-based safari operator (with strong representation in the United States) has some of the best vehicles and guides
in the country. Offering customized tours of Uganda and Rwanda, they
also boast carbon neutral status. ✉ *Plot 26, Eric Magala Rd., Entebbe,
Central Region, Uganda* ☎ *0414/320–121* ⊕ *www.classicuganda.com.*

Journeys Discovering Africa. One of the few upmarket East Africa operators with fully owned operations in both Rwanda and Uganda, Journeys
Discovering Africa receive glowing feedback for their customized private tours and affordable group safaris. ✉ *51 Elmwood Ave., Harrow,
Middlesex, England* ☎ *0800/088–5470 in the U.K. (toll-free), 888/428–
2772 in the U.S. (toll-free)* ⊕ *www.journeysdiscoveringafrica.com.*

Thousand Hills Expeditions. Named for the *milles collines* (thousand hills)
of Rwanda, this established safari operator offers personalized travel
of both Rwanda and Uganda, for private and small group safaris.
✉ *1000 Rue de L'Akanyaru, Kivyovu, Kigali, Rwanda* ☎ *0280/311–
000, 0788/351–000* ⊕ *www.thousandhillsexpeditions.com.*

Volcanoes Safaris. This established safari operator, with sales offices
in the United Kingdom and the United States, offers luxury gorilla
and chimp tracking safaris of Uganda and Rwanda. Their itineraries
focus largely on their own lodges, but they are well-regarded upmarket properties in stunning locations. ✉ *27 Lumumba Ave., Kampala,
Central Region, Uganda* ☎ *0114/346–464, 0772/741–718* ⊕ *www.
volcanoessafaris.com.*

Wild Frontiers. This experienced safari outfitter offers personalized and set departure safaris of Uganda from its base in Entebbe, Uganda. The company operates its own network of upmarket lodges, can set up private mobile camps, and runs an equally tight ship with their Murchison Falls National Park and Lake Victoria based boat operations, providing well-guided launch cruises and sport fishing in both locations. They also offer day trips to Ngamba Island Chimpanzee Sanctuary and the Uganda Wildlife Education Centre in Entebbe. ✉ *Nsamizi Rd., Entebbe, Central Region, Uganda* ☎ *0414/321–479, 0772/502–155* ⊕ *wildfrontiers.co.ug.*

VISITOR INFORMATION

Rwanda's Tourism and Conservation Department has a decent website (⊕ *www.rwandatourism.com*) that will give you a helpful overview of possible destinations and activities, but don't expect a timely response to personal inquiries. For more candid and thorough reviews, your best bet is Living in Kigali (⊕ *www.livinginkigali.com*), which has restaurant and site suggestions and tips for traveling outside the city.

The Uganda Tourism Board runs its own site (⊕ *www.visituganda.com*) with a helpful FAQ, directories, and site suggestions. Many safari operators and high-end lodges provide comprehensive information for guests on their websites and will answer individual concerns.

DINING AND LODGING PRICE INFORMATION

WHAT IT COSTS IN U.S. DOLLARS			
$	$$	$$$	$$$$
Hotels	under $250	$251–450	$451–$600	over $600
Restaurants	under $12	$12–$20	$21–$30	over $30

Most safari prices refer to an all-inclusive per-person rate excluding tax (a few only operate on a half-board rate), assuming double occupancy. Hotel rates refer to double occupancy excluding tax.

VOLCANOES NATIONAL PARK, RWANDA

Game
★★★★★

Park Accessibility
★★★

Getting Around
★★★

Accommodations
★★★★★

Scenic Beauty
★★★★★

Imagine slashing your way through undergrowth, sidling around bamboo forests, and peering through eucalyptus leaves to catch a glimpse of the massive and majestic silverback mountain gorilla.

He makes eye contact, grunts, then proceeds to pick his nose. Two teenage gorillas, drunk off bamboo sap, roll past in a wrestling match, brushing your leg as they go by. A mother gorilla carts her two-week-old baby around piggyback and throws a cautious glance your way. Visitors describe the hour-long encounter with gorillas in Volcanoes National Park as surreal. Set against the backdrop of the Virunga Mountains, each peak topped by saucer-shape clouds, a visit with mankind's not-so-distant relatives certainly seems to defy reality.

Volcanoes National Park is one of only four places on earth where visitors can commune with the critically endangered mountain gorillas. The park encompasses a 160-square-kilometer (62-square-mile) slice of the Virunga Mountains, including a string of nine volcanoes that extends into neighboring Uganda and the Democratic Republic of the Congo. The ecologically rich Virunga region is home to more than half of the world's mountain gorilla, which number fewer than 900.

Volcanoes was gazetted in 1925, making it the first national park in Rwanda. Tourism activities were suspended during the Rwanda Civil War but resumed in 1999. Now travelers can visit one of 10 habituated gorilla groups by purchasing a permit for US$750. A maximum of eight people are allowed to visit each group daily.

Gorillas may be the headline act, but there's plenty more to see and do in the park. Hiking enthusiasts can navigate a network of trails through the Virunga Mountains, including summiting the 3,711-meter (12,175-foot) Mount Bisoke, with its crater lake and rewarding cross-border views of the Democratic Republic of the Congo. History and mammal buffs can visit the grave and research center of prominent primatologist Dian Fossey, whose life and work inspired the movie *Gorillas in the Mist*.

A visit with the park's population of golden monkeys is worth the US$100 permit. These hyper, cherub-cheeked primates swing through the bamboo forests, occasionally swooping down to the forest floor for a particularly choice bamboo shoot. Be warned that catching them on camera can prove tricky. Volcanoes is also home to forest elephants, buffalo, spotted hyenas, and nearly 200 bird species.

WHEN TO GO

The best time for gorilla trekking is during Rwanda's two dry seasons: from December to early February and from June to September. The drier months make for a more pleasant (and less muddy) hike. Note that this is high season, so secure your gorilla permit well in advance and prepare to pay more for lodging. The temperate climate can be fickle regardless of when you go, so pack a jacket for cool evenings and a rain poncho.

GETTING HERE AND AROUND

Most tour operators will provide transport for the two-hour trip from Kigali to Musanze, the country's bustling gorilla tourism hub. Independent travelers can catch a public bus from Kigali's Nyabugogo bus station to Musanze for less than US$5. ■ TIP→ **All gorilla trekkers are required to secure gorilla permits in advance. Less than 100 permits are available each day, so visitors are advised to purchase them early from tour operators or by emailing the Rwanda Development Board.** All trekkers must arrive at the park's headquarters in the nearby village of Kinigi at 7 am, where they're assigned to a gorilla group. Transportation for the trek is required. Tour operators will generally provide a vehicle, or trekkers can rent a 4x4 and driver in Musanze from US$80.

EXPLORING

Red Rocks Rwanda. A 7-km (4-mile) trip from gorilla-tourism hub Musanze, this cultural exchange center offers an eclectic mix of diversions for the post-primate-safari crowd. Get your cultural fix via an extensive itinerary of activities that includes classes in weaving traditional baskets, brewing banana beer, and cooking local cuisine. You can also arrange for heritage and wooden-bike tours, instruction in dance and drumming, or a home stay with a local family. The extensive grounds include a gift shop run by women from the local community, a bar, a boma pit, an outdoor dance pavilion, several campsites, and six guest rooms. All profits from the activities are channeled back to the community, as are 50% of the accommodation fees. Activities should be booked 48 hours in advance to ensure availability. ✉ *Nyakinama, Musanze, Rwanda* ☎ *250/789–254–315.*

WHERE TO STAY

LUXURY LODGES

$$$$ ⊞ **Virunga Lodge.** Perched on a 2,300-meter (7,500-foot) ridge between Lake Ruhondo and Lake Bulhera, this remote lodge offers a bush-chic experience and breathtaking views. The inviting common area, characterized by deep-cushion couches, a roaring central fireplace, and a small bar, doubles as an international living room, where gorilla trekkers from

all over the globe swap stories about their great-ape encounters. Guests retire to tile-roofed bandas tucked out of sight from each other. Kitenge quilts and handcrafted teak furniture lend an exotic fairy-tale aura. The lodge may be charmingly rustic, but its amenities are decidedly sophisticated: complimentary massages, shoe cleaning, free laundry, and an in-person wake-up call with your hot beverage of choice. The all-inclusive cuisine is impressive and features a traditional Rwandan dinner option. **Pros:** massive bathrooms with lake-and-mountain views; secluded and spacious patios; well-appointed common area with communal dinner. **Cons:** staff can be scarce; no in-room electrical outlets; 45-minute drive to gorilla trekking. $ *Rooms from: US$1260* ⊠ *Mwiko Village, Burera District, Rwanda* ☎ *250/782–574–363* ⊕ *www.volcanoessafaris.com* ⤴ *8 rooms, 2 suites* ○| *All-inclusive.*

BUDGET ACCOMMODATIONS

$ Villa Gorilla. This Rwandan-owned boutique hotel is a top pick for ape trekkers looking for local flavor without scrimping on comfort. From chilled tree-tomato juice and warm towels on arrival to in-room flower arrangements and a reflexively responsive staff, Villa Gorilla exudes hospitality. The pastel orange exterior and living room–style reception extend the warm welcome. Bedrooms feature straw-mat floors, carved gorilla figurines, and woven baskets. The volcanoes views from the garden patio and boma pit serve as a reminder that this isn't your average weekend escape. The staff are well-versed in gorilla treks and will ensure you're on time for yours. **Pros:** five-minute drive to park headquarters; welcoming and responsive staff; meals included with room. **Cons:** noise from the lobby filters into the rooms; only one wine choice. $ *Rooms from: US$200* ⊠ *Kinigi, Musanze District, Northern Province, Rwanda* ☎ *250/788–592–924* ⊕ *www.villagorillarwanda. com* ⤴ *4 rooms, 3 cottages* ○| *All meals.*

$ **Waterfront Resort Lake Kivu.** This intimate inn on the shores of Lake Kivu is well worth the hour drive from Volcanoes National Park for a post–gorilla trek chill-out; the gentle shush of waves and the chants of local fisherman are all that punctuate its botanical garden–worthy grounds. The lobby's ivy-wrapped stone arches frame the lake's shimmering surface, while the property's private beach and tiki-hut lawn tables offer a perfect perch for drying off after a leisurely swim. The immense rooms feature plush beds with down pillows and French doors that open onto shoreline views; animal-hair rungs and decorative gourds add a traditional flourish. ■ TIP→ **Upgrade to the lakeshore bungalows to enjoy more space, uninterrupted views, and an open-sky shower.** **Pros:** stunning grounds with palm trees, tropical flowers, and thatched-roof lounge areas; spacious rooms with comfortable beds; private beach. **Cons:** mediocre food; Wi-Fi only in lobby; no drinking water provided in rooms. $ *Rooms from: US$80* ⊠ *Gisenyi, Rubavu, Rwanda* ☎ *250/789–528–772* ⊕ *www.waterfrontresortlk.com* ⤴ *7 rooms, 3 cottages* ○| *Breakfast.*

NYUNGWE FOREST NATIONAL PARK, RWANDA

Game
★★★

Park Accessibility
★★★

Getting Around
★★★

Accommodations
★★

Scenic Beauty
★★★★★

Nyungwe National Park may be most famous for chimpanzee trekking, but this stretch of 1,020 square km (394 square miles) in southwestern Rwanda teams with a dazzling array of flora and fauna and an impressive spread of hiking trails. Meander though and you'll feel as though you've wandered onto the set of *Jurassic Park*. You'll spot 100-year-old trees, fern-fringed waterfalls, and over-size driver ants to the accompaniment of a cacophony of bird calls.

Nestled in the Albertine Rift, a biodiversity-rich area of East Africa, Nyungwe is home to nearly 300 bird species, more than 75 different mammals, and some 1,000 plant types. It was recognized as a national park in 2005 and remains Africa's largest protected mountain rain forest. Trails cut through the park's closed-canopy forests, bamboo thickets, and orchid-filled swamps. Be warned that the weather can be wet—it is a rain forest after all. The park receives more than 2,000 mm (79 inches) of precipitation annually and provides water to approximately 70% of the county. In 2006, an exploring team claimed to find the furthest source of the Nile River in Nyungwe.

Most visitors come to witness the park's 500-some-odd chimpanzees or its "super group" of several hundred black-and-white colobus monkeys, whose clever antics and aerial acrobatics will keep your camera clicking. But chimps and giant troupes aren't the only show in town. With 13 species, the park has one of the highest primate diversity concentrations in the world. You'll see L'Hoest's monkeys frolicking around the roads, and, if you're really lucky, the reclusive owl-faced monkey.

Primate trekking can be costly (a chimpanzee pass is US$90 for foreigners), but visitors can also opt for a reasonably priced guided hike for US$40. The 13 trails range from the 2-km (1.2-mile) Karamba Trail (an excellent choice for birders) to the rigorous Mount Bigugu Trail that leads to the park's highest point. Hardy trekkers can also take in an impressive waterfall on the four-hour Isumo Trail or spend three days camping along the Congo Nile Trail. In 2010, the park opened the Canopy Walk, a 200-meter (656-foot) walkway suspended 50 meters (164 feet) above the ground. The "hanging trail" affords magnificent views of the treetop canopy and up-close bird encounters. Nyungwe is a little-known birders' paradise, though spotting them typically requires the help of a trained guide, who can be secured at one of the park's three reception centers.

WHEN TO GO

Late June through early September is dry season and high season at Nyungwe for good reason: the rain forest receives a reprieve from daily downpours, meaning you can explore all day. But even during the wet season, from March to May, showers generally arrive in the afternoon, leaving plenty of time for morning hiking and an outdoor lunch. Plus, you'll enjoy less competition for tours and discounted rates at some hotels.

GETTING HERE AND AROUND

Nyungwe National Park is approximately 225 km (140 miles), or four to five hours driving, from Kigali. Many visitors choose to hire a car and driver. Budget travelers can take one of three bus lines from Kigali's central bus station, Nyabugogo, to the park for Rwf5,000 (US$7), though quarters are cramped, and drivers can be reckless. Alternately, you can fly into Kamembe Airport, a half-hour drive from the park's western edge, and arrange for pickup with your lodge. For transport inside the park, your best bet is to hire a car from Kigali or ask for recommended drivers at your accommodation. Most activities depart from the park's Uwinka Reception Center. To get there from nearby Gisakura village, the location of our lodging suggestions, you'll need to use a private car or a public bus. Note that chimpanzee trekking requires a 4x4.

WHERE TO STAY

LUXURY LODGES

$$$ Nyungwe Forest Lodge. You'll forget you're next to a rain forest in this
Fodor's Choice   lavish retreat—until you slide back the glass balcony doors to let in for-
★   est breezes and birdsong. Nyungwe Forest Lodge is luxury plopped on a tea plantation with easy access to the national park. The award-winning architecture harmonizes with the surrounding environment, and stilt-supported cottages connected via boardwalk lead to a lobby bedecked with chandeliers, lily ponds, sleek sofas, slate floors, and regional curios. High-flying trekkers from the United States and Europe are no doubt attracted to the chocolate-on-the-nightstand turndown service, forest-view balconies, and flawlessly functional amenities. The warmed infinity pool and full-service spa are an added sell. No restaurants are nearby, but the included meal package has some of the best cuisine in

the country. **Pros:** rooms are practically suites with private balconies; close proximity to the park; the meal plan is wide-ranging and good. **Cons:** short and expensive wine list; in-room Wi-Fi is spotty at best. [$] *Rooms from: US$590* ✉ *Gisakura, Rwanda* ☎ *27/41–509–3000* 🌐 *www.nyungweforestlodge.com* 🛏 *22 rooms, 2 suites* 🍴 *All meals.*

BUDGET ACCOMMODATIONS

$ 🏨 **Nyungwe Top View Hill Hotel.** Stunning views of mist-veiled mountains, excellent service, and convenient access to Nyungwe National Park, all for US$200, make this hilltop hotel a best-value option. The circular, thatch-roof reception building has a restaurant and bar for tired and thirsty trekkers. Carved masks and Imigongo cow dung paintings mingle with contemporary IKEA-esque furniture in the public areas. The two-room cottages feature a living room with fireplace and private balconies. Thoughtful touches set this stay apart: tea and warm towels on arrival, a complimentary shoe-cleaning service, an evening fire, and an impressive number of bed warmers each night. The staff will cheerily recommend park excursions and phone ahead to ensure availability. **■ TIP→ Nearby dining options are scarce, so spring for the all-inclusive option for an extra US$50 per person.** **Pros:** spacious cottages; helpful staff; stunning balcony views from every room. **Cons:** hotel can be drafty; rooms show some wear; entrance road is steep and rocky. [$] *Rooms from: US$200* ✉ *Gisakura, Rwanda* ☎ *250/787–109–335* 🛏 *12 cottages* 🍴 *Breakfast.*

7

IF YOU HAVE TIME IN RWANDA

AKAGERA NATIONAL PARK

This 1,122-square-km (433-square-mile) park along Rwanda's north-eastern border with Tanzania is the safari scene's best-kept secret. You can experience prime safari lands without the Land Rover wagon circles that surround wildlife in Kenya and Tanzania. The borders encompass a labyrinth of lakes and papyrus swamps teeming with hippos and crocodiles, plus savannas dotted by giraffes, zebras, elephants, and nearly a dozen varieties of antelope.

Originally established in 1934, Akagera has weathered a tumultuous history. The park lost half its territory and all of its lions in the wake of the 1994 genocide. Now, however, the park has experienced a rebirth. Nonprofit African Parks partnered with the Rwandan government to spend approximately US$10 million on restoring the country's only protected savanna environment. Lions will be reintroduced in 2015, and the park already has a new thatch-roof reception center, a café, and a luxury tented lodge. It also offers camping facilities, guided game drives, boat cruises, and fishing trips. Akagera is still off the main tourist circuit. If you're seeking solitude and a one-on-one experience with nature, it doesn't get better than this.

GETTING HERE AND AROUND

The park is self-drive, so your best option is to rent a 4x4 in Kigali. Akagera is 2½ hours from the capital city. Rental fees are at least US$200 per day and typically include gas and a driver-guide. If you're comfortable driving yourself, you can find 4x4s starting from US$65 per day. Visitors are encouraged to hire a guide for a daily fee of US$30. Should you opt to forego the guide, pick up the helpful guidebook for US$3 from the reception center just inside the Kiyonza Entrance Gate. It takes approximately six hours to drive from the park's southern entrance to the northernmost exit gate, so plan for a long day trip from Kigali or an overnight at one of the campsites.

WHERE TO STAY

$$ 🏕 **Ruzizi Tented Lodge.** Akagera visitors flock to this solar-powered tented lodge on the shores of Lake Ihema to commune with nature without forgoing warm showers, three-course meals, and a fully stocked bar. Monkeys scamper along the raised wooden walkways that connect each tent with the thatched-roof reception area. Guests simply follow this boardwalk to a lakeside breakfast or a grilled dinner under the stars. Each "tent" has a desk, two-person couch, plush bed, and freestanding bathroom with rainfall shower. Pull back the flaps for shoreline views and the occasional bathing elephant. All of the lodge's profits go to conservation activities in the park. **Pros:** camping without the hassle; excellent showers; private deck with lakeside views. **Cons:** no Wi-Fi; drinking water gets expensive; wildlife may keep you up at night. $ *Rooms from: US$300* ✉ *Akagera National Park, Rwanda* 📠 *250/787–113–300* ⊕ *www.ruzizilodge.com* ⟿ *7 tents, 1 family tent, 1 luxury tent* ⊗ *Closed 2 wks in Nov.* 🍴 *Some meals.*

KIGALI, RWANDA

Kigali is a fascinating example of a future-focused African city. Once the wasteland of civil war and genocide, Rwanda's capital has transformed itself into a model of urban development. In the two decades after the genocide, exiles have flocked to the city flush with education, investment dollars, and entrepreneurial ideas. Foreigners have jumped in the mix, opening sushi joints, yoga studios, bakeries, artisan coffee shops, and even a co-working space for start-ups. The nightlife is also picking up, and you'll find dance clubs, sports bars, and live music.

With a population of approximately 1 million people, the city is the commercial and governmental hub for the rest of the country. Its trash-free boulevards, smooth roads, LED streetlights, and meticulously manicured medians are a closer approximation of Europe than East Africa. It's an image the country is keen to expand. Construction on an ultramodern convention center and adjoining IT complex is currently underway, and a slick new master plan calls for an overhaul of the business district and more urban housing.

Even without gleaming new buildings, the city is something to behold. The undulating skyline of red-roofed houses, terraced farm plots, and brilliant green foliage is stunning. Kigali is also safe: violent crime is rare, particularly against foreigners, and police do their job, including handing out speeding tickets. You'll rarely find yourself hassled, and negotiating traffic will be your biggest obstacle. Some expatriates say that they feel safer raising their kids in Kigali than in U.S. cities.

GETTING HERE AND AROUND

Kigali is relatively easy to navigate. The ubiquitous motorbike taxis, called "motos," are a cheap and convenient mode of transport and a ride from the airport to the city center costs less than US$3. Note that moto fares are negotiable, and their safety record is questionable. Professionally run taxis are marked and metered, though they are generally the most expensive option. An airport transfer to town can run upward of US$15. Unmarked private taxis are also available, but be prepared to negotiate the fare in advance. If you plan to stay in Kigali for several days, you may want to rent a car from US$65 per day. The roads are generally in excellent condition, but be warned that other drivers, pedestrians, and motos can make driving a stressful experience.

EXPLORING

Kigali Genocide Memorial Centre. Visitors should not miss this well-conceived tribute to the victims of the 1994 genocide, which saw an estimated 1 million people killed in the span of 100 days. Outside, a terraced series of mass graves entombs some 250,000 victims. Inside, an informative exhibition walks visitors through the historical lead-up to the Rwandan genocide and the global community's faltering response. A display of skulls and bones alongside personal effects personifies the tragedy. A second section explores mankind's capacity for cruelty with a display on genocides from around the world. The exhibition ends with enlarged black-and-white photos of child genocide victims, ranging from 8 months to 17 years. Each picture is accompanied by a placard listing the child's favorite foods and activities and his or her final moments. There is no entrance fee, but donations are encouraged. The audio guide is worthwhile for US$15. ⊠ *KG 14 Ave., Gisozi, Kigali, Rwanda* ⊕ *www.kigaligenocidememorial.org/old* ☎ *Free* ⊗ *Daily 8–4.*

Presidential Palace Museum. Former Rwandan President Juvenal Habyari-mana's home offers an intimate look at the actors and spaces that gave rise to the 1994 genocide. The president's assassination is said to have sparked the killing spree. The remains of his private plane, which was shot down over his home, are still on display outside the museum walls. The sunroom where the president's wife and her infamous coterie, the *akuzu,* plotted the genocide still has the original furniture and carpet. A tour guide will point out artifacts of the president's paranoia: censors on the stairs, a secret escape route, and a bathroom safe once stuffed with cash. Other highlights include a Rwanda-shape pool for the president's 8-meter (26-foot) pet python and a witchcraft consultation room next to the house's Catholic chapel. Much of the furniture was looted during the genocide but pieces such as Habyarimana's imposing desk, an elephant-foot table, and the still-working German refrigerator illustrate the leader's extravagant tastes. The full tour takes one hour and costs US$12. ⊠ *Kanombe, Kigali, Rwanda* ⊗ *Daily 8–6.*

WHERE TO EAT

$$
ECLECTIC
✕ **Heaven.** Founded by American couple Alissa and Josh Ruxin, this oasis of gourmet cuisine is a favorite among foreign residents and affluent Rwandans for weekend brunch, evening cocktails, and special-occasion dinners. The wooden terrace with thatched-roof and recessed lighting affords spectacular hillside views, while art from the adjoining gallery bedecks the brick walls. The international menu ranges from Chinese stir-fry to pumpkin risotto to goat *brochettes* (a Rwandan staple). Herbs and greens are grown on-site and organic produce is used when possible. Local favorites are given a decidedly foodie twist, such as the *urwagwa* sour cocktail, which pairs regional banana beer with citron and lemongrass. Spring for the seven-course tasting menu to sample your way through the chef's best work for US$36. $ *Average main: US$17* ⊠ *7 KN 29 St., Kigali, Rwanda* ☎ *250/788–486–581* ⊕ *www.heavenrwanda.com.*

$$$$
ECLECTIC
Fodor's Choice
★
✕ **Paladar Venceremos.** This intimate home-based restaurant feels like an elegant outdoor dinner party. The six-course prix-fixe menu features fusion fare, such as porcini mushroom soup with truffle oil, filet mignon with pancetta brown sauce, and lavender flower sorbet. Le Cordon Bleu–trained chef Carlos Caula sources nearly all ingredients locally, and everything from the pasta to the pastry crust is made in-house. Guests are served on the chef's spacious flagstone-and-tile patio with sweeping city views. Lit candles, light strands, wicker-and-wood-furniture, and sparing décor exude an earthy elegance and keep the focus on the food. Dinner is served promptly at 7:30 pm on Friday and Saturday. The weekday lunch offers a wallet-friendly selection of artisan sandwiches, soups, and salads. Scout out the menu online and

call ahead with any special dietary preferences. The wine selection is limited, so bring your own libation for a corkage fee of Rwf5,000 (US$7). [$] *Average main: US$40* ✉ *61 KG 9 Ave., Nyarutarama, Kigali, Rwanda* ☎ *250/786–790–635* 🌐 *www.venceremoscafe.com* ✍ *Reservations essential* 💳 *No credit cards* 🕒 *No dinner weekdays.*

$ AFRICAN 🍴 **Republika Lounge.** Kigali's fickle social scene finally found a staple in this hilltop African fusion restaurant that has been in business for more than decade, a true feat in this city. Americans, Europeans, and Kigali's elite flock to the brother-and-sister-run Republika Lounge for happy hour, late-night drinks, and a belt-loosening tapas spread. Sample your way through Rwanda and East African cuisine and don't miss the cassava-leaf *sombe,* fried plantains imported from Burundi, curried coconut fish, and the eatery's famed *liboké* (a steamed chicken dish), all of which come served in glazed earthenware pottery. More traditional eaters won't be disappointed with the garlic fries or the steak and mashed potatoes. Sculpted tree trunks inside and sweeping city views outside make it feel as though you're dining in an opulent tree house. [$] *Average main: US$11* ✉ *Ave. KN 6, St. KN 43, Kivyovu, Kigali, Rwanda* ☎ *250/788–303–030* 🕒 *Closed Sun.*

WHERE TO STAY

Hotel reviews have been shortened. For full information, visit Fodors.com

$$ HOTEL 🏨 **Kigali Serena Hotel.** The crème de la crème of Kigali accommodations, the city's only five-star hotel draws an elite crowd with its open-air restaurants, heliconia-and-palm-fringed pool, up-to-date business center, and fully equipped gym. **Pros:** central location; wide array of amenities; excellent on-site dining options. **Cons:** spotty service; atmosphere can feel stifled; small standard rooms. [$] *Rooms from: US$450* ✉ *KN 3 Ave., Nyarugenge, Kigali, Rwanda* ☎ *250/788–184–500* 🌐 *www.serenahotels.com* 🛏 *123 rooms, 25 suites* 🍽 *Breakfast.*

$ HOTEL 🏨 **Golf Hills Residence.** More American McMansion than African accommodation, this boutique hotel with golf course views and bend-over-backward service is a convenient base for safari-goers. **Pros:** great value; quiet and clean rooms for a restful night; accommodating staff. **Cons:** 10-minute ride to town and top tourist destinations; few restaurants and nightspots in immediate area. [$] *Rooms from: US$80* ✉ *KG 415 St., Nyarutarama, Kigali, Rwanda* ☎ *250/787–113–300* 🌐 *www.golfhillsresidence.com* 🛏 *16 rooms, 1 suite* 🍽 *Breakfast.*

7

BWINDI IMPENETRABLE
NATIONAL PARK, UGANDA

Home to nearly half the world's remaining population of critically endangered mountain gorillas, Bwindi is one of only three places in the world where one can spend a magical hour in the company of these gentle giants.

Game
★★★★★

Park Accessibility
★★★

Getting Around
★★★

Accommodations
★★★★

Scenic Beauty
★★★★★

Once part of a much larger forest stretching as far as Rwanda and beyond, the park is now an oasis of 128 square miles of pristine rain forest in southwest Uganda. Designated a UNESCO World Heritage Site, Bwindi is one of the largest African forests encompassing both lowland and montane species. It has an incredibly rich ecosystem: more diversity of tree and fern species than anywhere else in the region, around 202 species of butterfly, 120 mammal species, and the only place one can find gorillas and chimpanzees in the same forest.

Since the first group was habituated for tourism nearly quarter of a century ago, a total of 11 gorilla families (out of an estimated 408 individuals) are now used for tourism. Small groups of tourists set off on bracing hikes every morning for a bucket list encounter with a Silverback and his clan. Visitors pay $600 per gorilla-tracking permit, but as one of the most unusual and exclusive wildlife encounters, it does not disappoint. Permits are strictly controlled to minimize contact between gorillas and the outside world (their DNA makes them susceptible to human ailments—so you won't be allowed to track if you're ill) and the funds raised go toward conservation activities in Bwindi, and all over Uganda.

A portion also supports nearby communities, and many local people now work in tourism: from serving as porters on gorilla tracking expeditions to guiding visitors on other local tourism initiatives: forest hikes, community walks, and living history encounters with the Batwa tribe. In some areas, the relationship between community and conservation is even more symbiotic, with local people donating land for use as wildlife buffer zones in exchange for collecting "bed night" fees from lodges. Bwindi today is a leading example of eco-tourism done well.

WHEN TO GO

Bwindi experiences rainfall year-round (it is a rain forest after all). The wettest months are March through May and October through November, with comparatively drier weather from June to August and from December to February. Daytime temperatures are fairly constant, hovering around 75°F (24°C), but nights can be chilly, with lows of around 50°F (10°C). Low-season discounts apply to most lodge rates (and often gorilla permits, too) in April, May, and November. Permit availability can be tricky in peak months of July through September.

GETTING HERE AND AROUND

Lying about 500 km (300 miles; 10-hour drive) from Kampala, Bwindi is served by scheduled/charter flights via airstrips around the park. There are four distinct sectors for tracking: Buhoma, Ruhija, Rushaga, and Nkuringo. ■TIP→ Securing your permit in advance from Uganda Wildlife Authority is vital, as this dictates where you track, and therefore where you stay. Some of the best accommodation is at Buhoma and Nkuringo, but don't rule out tracking elsewhere if you plan carefully: Ruhija tracking is viable from Buhoma; Rushaga can be reached from Nkuringo. If driving, you'll need a 4x4 because roads can be difficult, especially in the wettest months. Because of this, and the permit permutations, most people travel with a tour operator.

Contacts AeroLink Uganda Limited. ☎ 0317/333–000, 0776/882–205 ⊕ www.aerolinkuganda.com. **Fly Uganda.** ☎ 0772/712–557 ⊕ www.flyuganda.com.

Uganda Wildlife Authority. The UWA is in charge of managing Uganda's national parks and wildlife reserves, including issuing various primate tracking permits: gorilla tracking in Bwindi Impenetrable National Park ($600 per permit); and chimpanzees in Kibale ($150 per permit, $220 for habituation), and Kyambura Gorge in Queen Elizabeth National Park ($50 per permit). If traveling in April, May, or November, ask about green-season gorilla permit discounts. Sometimes there are great deals to be had. If organizing your own safari, contact the UWA up to a year in advance to secure permits (more if booking on behalf of a large group). Once arranged, you can obtain your Wildlife Card (loaded with permits and any other prepaid fees) in person at their reservations office in Kampala. All eminently doable, but the complexity of this process is another reason the vast majority prefer to let a tour operator take the strain. ⊠ Plot 7 Kira Rd., Kamwokya, Kampala, Sao Tome & Principe ☎ 0414/355–400 ⊕ www.ugandawildlife.org ☉ Weekdays 8–5, Sat. 9–noon.

WHERE TO STAY

LUXURY LODGES

$$$$ 🏠 **Buhoma Lodge.** The cottages at Buhoma Lodge, located within Bwindi Impenetrable National Park, rise up on stilts out of the hillside, ensuring that views from the highest rooms—long, sweeping vistas down the mist-clad valley—are some of the best this side of the forest. ■TIP→ Ask for cottage no. 2 or 4 to guarantee the panoramas, but be prepared for steps. Inside the rooms, cream walls and bedspreads offset Congolese masks and woven-basket décor, and the *kitenge* robes and paper-bead curtain ties are a nice local touch. Bathtubs have recently been added to some of the en suites, much appreciated after a hard day's gorilla tracking. The public areas comprise a cozy lounge and dining room. Charcoal braziers are lit every night as waiters serve up tasty four-course dinners, and a craft shop supports local women's groups. **Pros:** a smiling staff and professional management; great ambience at night; two-minute walk from the briefing point for gorilla tracking. **Cons:** no hair dryers allowed; close to park offices so some passing traffic. [$] *Rooms from: US$660* ✉ *Bwindi Impenetrable National Park, Buhoma, Western Region, Uganda* ✥ *400 meters on right after park gate* ☎ *0414/321–479, 0772/721–155* 🌐 *www.ugandaexclusivecamps.com* 🛏 *9 double/twin cottages, 1 family cottage* 🍴 *All meals.*

$$$$ 🏨 **Clouds Mountain Gorilla Lodge.** Not only the most exclusive lodge in Bwindi, Clouds also has one of the greatest views in Uganda: high on a ridge, verdant hills tumble away to a valley below, under distant volcanic peaks. At dawn, when mist sits low in the valleys, they really do look like islands in the clouds. Each cottage is crafted, grotto-like, from lumps of igneous rock. Inside, the effect is light and airy by day and cozy by night: vast picture windows frame the landscape; contemporary Ugandan art adorns the walls; and plump cream couches face onto a two-way hearth, its flames stoked by your personal butler. What's more, the lodge is a shining example of community conservation—it is run as a partnership between local people, the lodge operator, and the African Wildlife Foundation. So you can feel pampered *and* worthy. **Pros:** a butler at your beck and call; romantic surroundings; excellent meals full of fresh produce grown on site. **Cons:** rates are pricey; not all cottages have the view. ■ **TIP→ Ask for Safari or Rafiki if this is important to you.** [$] *Rooms from: US$1220* ✉ *Nkuringo, Western Region, Uganda* ✥ *Entrance on left, opposite UWA Ranger post at northern end of Nkuringo village* ☎ *0414/251–182* 🌐 *www.wildplacesafrica.com* 🛏 *6 double cottages, 2 family cottages* 🍴 *All-inclusive.*

FAMILY

Fodor's Choice ★

$$$$ 🏨 **Volcanoes Bwindi Lodge.** This quirkily decorated eco-lodge is on the edge of Bwindi in its own reserve of secondary forest, creating a 50-acre gorilla-friendly buffer zone between the park and the nearby village of Buhoma. Some guests have been lucky enough to observe the Rushegura group of gorillas within the lodge grounds. The eight thatched bandas, all named after local gorillas, are the epitome of shabby chic: patchwork-upholstered chairs, bathroom vanity units made from recycled tin, striped kilims on the floor, and hand-sewn quilts on the beds. Each guest is entitled to a complimentary massage, conducted in a charming, though slightly chilly, cabin on the grounds. Other activities include: craft shop and orphanage visits, a tea plantation tour, and a visit to the local community hospital. **Pros:** friendly, competent staff with great attention to detail; great location; strong eco-credentials. **Cons:** fairly average food for a lodge of this caliber; lots of steps in and out of the lodge. [$] *Rooms from: US$660* ✉ *Buhoma, Western Region, Uganda* ✥ *Look for lodge sign on left as you enter Buhoma village*

☎ *0414/346–464, 0772/741–720* ⊕ *www.volcanoessafaris.com* ⇔ *8 double/twin cottages* ⊟ *No credit cards* ⦿ *All-inclusive.*

PERMANENT TENTED CAMPS

$$$$ 🏕 **Sanctuary Gorilla Forest Camp.** A standout property in northern Bwindi, Sanctuary Gorilla Forest Camp delivers impeccable service in a classic forest setting. Eight canvas tents on dark-wood platforms occupy their own private clearings inside the impenetrable forest itself. Cow-horn and glass-bead decorated cushions adorn twin queen beds; matching white robes and a hair dryer (a rare find in Bwindi) hang in the en-suite bathroom. Walkie-talkies make it all too easy to order up drinks without leaving your tent; and the candelit bathtub offering forest views and complimentary Africology bathcare products is delightful. If that doesn't help you unwind, the spa will: facials, mani/pedis, and various massages in a secluded room. The main lounge and restaurant offer superlative fare, with a popular high tea station offering hot drinks and fruit smoothies every afternoon. **Pros:** super-smooth service; excellent menu full of fresh ingredients; forest location. **Cons:** closeness of surrounding forest around the tents obscures views and invites the occasional creepy crawlie. $ *Rooms from: US$1310* ⊠ *Bwindi Impenetrable National Park, Buhoma, Western Region, Uganda* ⊹ *500 meters on right after park gate* ☎ *0414/340–290, 0776/340–290* ⊕ *www. sanctuaryretreats.com* ⇔ *8 luxury tents* ⦿ *All-inclusive.*

BUDGET ACCOMMODATIONS

$
Fodor's Choice
★
🏕 **Nkuringo Gorilla Camp.** This eco-friendly little camp has graduated from humble beginnings as a hiker's bunkhouse to a charming property offering exceptional value for this area. Guests choose from en-suite rooms or cute cottages painstakingly constructed using local materials, with an attention to detail rarely seen in this price bracket. Intricately folded banana palms line the roof, bright *kitenge* cushions bring warmth and color, and woven elephant grasses hide the rainwater collection butts (the camp is carbon-neutral and the nearest water source is a one-hour round trip). The family cottage surveys Bwindi itself, and of the four remaining cottages, two have balconies overlooking the distant Virungas. ■**TIP➔ Ask for Nyiragongo or Nyamugira for the view of the Virungus.** A communal dining room evokes the spirit of bunkhouses past, but this area is pegged for upgrade soon. **Pros:** impeccable green credentials; incredible value; great for walkers and adventurers. **Cons:** basic dining facilities; the high altitude (2,161 meters [7,090 feet]) means it can be chilly at night; no Wi-Fi. $ *Rooms from: US$250* ⊠ *Nkuringo, Western Region, Uganda* ⊹ *On righthand side on bend in road, just before Nkuringo village* ☎ *0774/805–580, 0792/805–580, 0702/805–580* ⊕ *www.gorillacamp.com* ⇔ *1 family cottage, 4 double cottages, 4 double rooms* ⦿ *All meals.*

7

SPORTS AND THE OUTDOORS

CANOEING

If visiting Southern Bwindi (Rushaga or Nkuringo sectors), nearby Lake Mutanda beckons for a rather special experience: paddling across its waters in a traditional dug-out canoe. The backdrop is stunning. The island-studded lake is overlooked by distant volcanic peaks and the Virunga massif that straddles the Uganda/Rwanda border. Canoeing can be combined with a guided hike from nearby Rubuguri to the lakeshore. A peaceful diversion from the hectic pace of safari itineraries, canoeing offers far more insight into the charms and challenges of daily life than driving by in your 4x4 vehicle.

Edirisa Canoe Trekking. A social enterprise with a sense of adventure, Edirisa offers their unique blend of hiking, paddling, and community on canoe-trekking expeditions (using dug-outs, naturally). This Kabale-based nonprofit allows visitors to experience authentic Uganda, while providing employment and promoting local culture. Enthusiastic young guides accompany guests, with assistance from Bakiga and Batwa elders along the way. Single or multiday options are available, including the epic five-day Buhoma-Kabale trek along the **Gorilla Highlands** trail. Accommodation is extremely basic—you camp in tents—but there is no better way to see the real Uganda. ✉ *The Home of Edirisa, Nyerere Ave., Plot 1, Kabale, Uganda* ☎ *0752/558–558, 0776/558–123, 0752/558–222* ⊕ *www.canoetrekking.com.*

HIKING

Various trails exist at Bwindi, through the forest and nearby scenery. Shorter hikes of three hours with park rangers are available: in Buhoma and Rushaga we recommend the different (but similarly monikered) Waterfall Trails; birders can head to Ruhija for the ornithologically rewarding Mubwindi Swamp hike. Longer forays—arranged by private outfitters—include the four- to five-hour Ivy River Trail from Buhoma to Nkuringo (or vice versa, for a more gentle gradient). From Nkuringo, the Kashasha River Trail offers a strenuous seven- to eight-hour loop, or you can strike out on the multiday Gorilla Highlands Trail to scenic Lake Bunyonyi.

Nkuringo Walking Safaris. This pioneering trekking company, with offices in Entebbe and a base at Nkuringo on the south side of Bwindi Impenetrable National Park, offers various guided day hikes through Bwindi and surrounding farmland, alongside dug-out canoe trips on Lake Mutanda. Their professional guides are trained to identify local flora and fauna, and will also share insights into local everyday life and farming practices. Their hiking packages are an excellent value and can be combined with your choice of accommodation in the area (so you can scale the comfort factor up or down as required). ✉ *Nkuringo Gorilla Camp, Nkuringo, Western Region, Uganda* ☎ *0774/805–580, 0702/805–580* ⊕ *www.nkuringowalkingsafaris.com.*

KIBALE NATIONAL PARK, UGANDA

Game
★★★★★
Park Accessibility
★★★★
Getting Around
★★★★
Accommodations
★★★★
Scenic Beauty
★★★★★

This 296-square-mile tract of forest is home to one of the greatest variety and concentration of primates on the continent, and its population of nearly 1,500 chimpanzees makes it a great place to track these endangered apes.

Kibale weaves a rich tapestry of rain forest life: as many as 13 primate species reside here; around 335 bird species are found, including six that are endemic to the region; and nearly 230 different species of tree create a varied canopy, some towering more than 130 feet (50m).

Chimpanzee-tracking excursions set out from the Kanyanchu Headquarters twice a day. Accompanied by a forest ranger you will hike along forest trails in search of man's closest relatives (chimps share 98.7% of our DNA). Once located, the group spends a maximum of one hour with these fascinating great apes. You can watch them feed, groom, play, and sometimes even hunt together. There is no guarantee of a sighting, but chances are generally high, with a success rate of more than 90%.

Those with a real passion for primates (and the stamina to match) can join a "chimpanzee habituation" experience. This unique opportunity to observe chimpanzees from dawn until dusk allows visitors to gather deeper insight into their behavior. Nocturnal primates may also be seen, with varying degrees of success, on the guided walk that departs Kanyanchu every evening at nightfall. Birders will love exploring Kibale, and neighboring Bigodi Wetland Sanctuary, in search of such key species as green-breasted pitta, brown-chested alethe, and little greenbul. Bigodi is also a great place for monkey-spotting; the guided nature trail in this community-run conservation project takes around three hours to complete.

Outside the park, rolling panoramas of tea plantations and ancient volcanic craters dominate the landscape between Kibale and Fort Portal, with plenty of informal hiking opportunities offering a pleasant way to pass an afternoon. Ask your lodge or guide for details of local routes;

7

many are self-guided and offer the chance to witness everyday rural life in one of the prettiest regions of Uganda.

WHEN TO GO

Kibale is a rain forest, with the chance of wet weather year-round. If you avoid March through May and September through November you will miss the worst of it, though dry-season months can make the chimp tracking more arduous, as the apes travel farther in search of fruiting trees. Temperatures are fairly constant, with average daytime highs around 80°F (27°C) and nights dropping to about 59°F (15°C). Be sure to secure chimp permits well in advance at any time of year.

GETTING HERE AND AROUND

Located in western Uganda, Kibale lies about 16 miles (26 km) south-east of the town of Fort Portal on the Kamwenge Road. The park is about a five- or six-hour drive from Kampala or Entebbe respectively, and three hours from northern Queen Elizabeth National Park. Drive times will be reduced once the last stretch of road is surfaced; roadwork was ongoing at this writing. If you prefer to fly, you can choose from a small charter to Fort Portal airstrip (its limited length excludes all but the tiniest light aircraft), or charter to Kasese, two hours south, in a wider choice of planes. Chimp tracking or habituation permits should be secured in advance from the Uganda Wildlife Authority.

Contacts AeroLink Uganda Limited. ☎ *0317/333–000, 0776/882–205* ⊕ *www.aerolinkuganda.com.* **Fly Uganda.** ☎ *0772/712–557* ⊕ *www.flyuganda. com.* **Uganda Wildlife Authority.** ☎ *0414/355–400* ⊕ *www.ugandawildlife.org.*

EXPLORING

Bigodi Wetland Sanctuary. This community-run conservation project managed by the Kibale Association for Rural and Environmental Development (KAFRED) offers a guided nature trail through Magombe Wetland, near Bigodi. Thanks to more open terrain, it frequently delivers better bird-watching and monkey-spotting than neighboring Kibale. Here, red colobus are common, with a chance of seeing black and white colobus, grey-cheeked mangabey, L'Hoest's and red-tailed monkeys. Serious birders will enjoy the knowledgeable guides, who can identify the wetland's 200-odd species with ease. The 5-km (3-mile) trail takes three to four hours, and if you don't have waterproof boots consider renting a pair from KAFRED. If you want to sample more of their particular blend of community tourism, traditional lunches, homestays, and village walks are also on offer. ✉ *KAFRED Office, Fort Portal-Kamwenge Rd., near Kibale National Park, Bigodi, Western Region, Uganda* ⊕ *From Kanyanchu HQ in Kibale Forest, head southeast on Kamwenge Rd. After couple of miles, you reach village of Bigodi. KAFRED office is on right at start of trading center* ☎ *0772/468–113* ⊕ *www.bigodi-tourism.org* ✉ *US$25* ⊙ *Daily 7:30 am–6 pm.*

WHERE TO STAY

LUXURY LODGES

$$$$ Fodor'sChoice ★ **Kyaninga Lodge.** Overlooking a cobalt-blue crater lake, the design of this fairy-tale property provides serious wow factor: Kyaninga took 130 men, seven years and more than 1,000 hand-carved logs to build. Eight chaletlike cottages perch high on the crater rim; intricate wooden walkways connect each building; while landscaped gardens and orchards (the source of delicious homemade preserves at breakfast) fan out across the valley below. Since it opened it's taken no time to become the number-one choice in the area. Kibale is nearby, but a variety of activities closer to home will keep guests happy for days: crater hikes; wild swimming in Lake Kyaninga; birding in the forest; trekking to the edge of the Albertine Rift; and even a round of golf at Toro Golf Club with a top Uganda player (sponsored by Kyaninga). **■TIP→ If you struggle with steps ask for Cottage 4 or 5, as they are closest to the lodge.** **Pros:** stunning property; friendly staff; much of their tasty food grown on site. **Cons:** farther from Kibale than most; lots of steps to climb. [$] *Rooms from: US$680* ✉ *Lake Kyaninga near Fort Portal, Western Region, Uganda* ✣ *Turn north at Mpanga Bridge, about 2 km (1.2 miles) outside Fort Portal town on Kampala Road (signed for lodge). Follow road for 1.8 km (1.1 miles) and turn left at Kyaninga Lodge signpost. Follow road for another 6 km (3.7 miles) until you reach lodge* ☎ *0794/304–211, 0772/999–750* 🌐 *www.kyaningalodge.com* 🛏 *8 double/twin cottages* 💳 *No credit cards* 🍴 *All meals.*

$$$$ FAMILY **Ndali Lodge.** A Ugandan "Downton Abbey," Ndali is a bit of an institution, offering a charming blend of warm hospitality and colonial history. If you like country-house style (interpreted here in a uniquely African way), appreciate fine wines and good company, and cannot imagine taking a walk without several large dogs bounding along beside you, then you'll love Aubrey & Clare Price's home—for a home is what it is. Traditional thatch cottages, built by Aubrey and his father in the heart of his grandfather's 1920s tea estate, enjoy panoramic views either side: the mighty Rwenzoris to the west, their glacial peaks occasionally visible on a clear morning; and the enchanting Lake Nyinambuga—so pretty they put it on a local banknote. By night the lodge is at its most romantic, lit entirely by candles. **Pros:** the home-away-from-home feel; fantastic walking country; great for kids. **Cons:** 100% solar power means no hair dryers; spotty Wi-Fi; if dogs aren't your thing, forget it. [$] *Rooms from: US$720* ✉ *Lake Nyinambuga, Kabata, near Kibale National Park, Fort Portal, Western Region, Uganda* ✣ *Take Kamwenge Rd. (also for Kibale National Park) and fork right at cluster of signs at Kasiisi (after just under 12 km [7.5 miles]). After about the same distance again, having passed through scruffy Rwaihamba trading center, you reach turn-off for Ndali on right-hand side, by small school* ☎ *0772/221–309, 0772/487–673* 🌐 *www.ndalilodge.com* 🛏 *8 cottages* 💳 *No credit cards* 🍴 *All meals.*

PERMANENT TENTED CAMPS

$ ⛶ **Primate Lodge Kibale.** Right behind the Park Headquarters, Primate Lodge Kibale is convenient for those early mornings when tracking chimps or birding. En-suite tents and stone cottages occupy small clearings within the forest itself, making the lodge a mecca for birding groups that can spend their time just wandering around the grounds. Unfortunately, other aspects of the lodge experience are rather underwhelming: one gets the feeling the location has bred a degree of complacency. That said, if you're booked for chimp habituation (with a reporting time of 6:30 am), for the night forest walk, or you simply want to clock up the birding hours, the time gained from staying right next to the trailhead could make all the difference. **Pros:** location next to trailhead; great for birders. **Cons:** better value can be found elsewhere; Wi-Fi available only when generator on. $ *Rooms from: US$198* ⊠ *Kanyanchu, Kibale National Park, Fort Portal, Western Region, Uganda* ✛ *Take Kamwenge Rd. from Fort Portal toward Kibale National Park. Pass through park, and look for turn on left just before leaving forest. The lodge is by Kanyanchu Park HQ* ☎ *0414/267–153, 0701/426–368* ⊕ *www.ugandalodges.com* ⇆ *8 safari tents, 7 cottages* ○| *All meals.*

QUEEN ELIZABETH NATIONAL PARK, UGANDA

Game
★★★

Park Accessibility
★★★★

Getting Around
★★★★

Accommodations
★★★★

Scenic Beauty
★★★★★

Serving up a rich diversity of game and scenery, Queen Elizabeth National Park (QENP) is a rewarding safari stopover between the primate hubs of Kibale and Bwindi.

For the purposes of safari planning, the park is divided into two sectors. The northern sector, Mweya, straddles the Equator; the euphorbia-studded valley framed by the Rwenzoris and the Kichwamba Escarpment to the north and south, with Lakes George and Edward to the east and west.

Despite the lack of the wildlife volumes of parks like the Serengeti in Tanzania, the variety of habitat in QENP provides a wealth of activities: popular launch cruises ply the bird-lined Kazinga Channel (the park has more than 600 species); the geologically intriguing Explosion Crater Drive offers panoramic views; guided hikes in Kyambura Gorge, though no substitute for Kibale, provide the chance of spotting chimpanzees; and the kob breeding grounds of Kasenyi Plains, which attract lions, hyenas, and leopards, offer more traditional wildlife-viewing. Cat-crazed visitors can ask about Lion Monitoring at Mweya Visitor Centre. This researcher-accompanied activity uses radio technology to get you up close, though availability is weather- (and researcher-) dependent.

To the south, the Ishasha sector is a wilder, more remote destination. Far from the crowds, there are no gimmicks, just plain, old-fashioned wilderness. Rolling plains are home to herds of elephants, kob, and topi, and local lion prides are known for climbing the giant fig trees. These show-stealing cats are usually given top billing for any foray into this sector, but Ishasha's beauty is best savored slowly. Spend time appreciating the full abundance of life on the savanna, and the discovery of telltale tails dangling from a tree will not be the only reward.

Nearby, communities have developed several worthwhile tourism activities. Visit a working salt lake at Katwe or participate in a craft workshop with Kikorongo Community Group in the north, or tour Deo's Homestead near Ishasha for insight into the challenges of farming near wildlife. Such community interactions offer a welcome change of pace,

7

as well as a fascinating contrast to the wealth of wildlife in this beautiful park.

WHEN TO GO

Located in the Albertine rift at a lower altitude than most of Uganda, the climate in QENP is warm and constant, with mean annual temperatures of 59°F to 84°F (15°C to 29°C). Biannual wet seasons March through May and August through November are better for photography, with (generally short) storms producing interesting light and clearer skies. Drier periods in January and February and June and July are dusty and hot, with controlled burning by park authorities toward the end of these seasons making wildlife-viewing feel positively postapocalyptic.

GETTING HERE AND AROUND

Around 400 km (250 miles) from Entebbe, Mweya is a seven hour drive on tarmac roads. Ishasha lies two hours (100 km [60 miles]) farther south on murram. Kibale is three hours (160 km [100 miles]) north; and Ishasha is two hours (60 km [40 miles]) from northern Bwindi. AeroLink will drop off at Mweya airstrip at no extra charge, and their scheduled stop at Kihihi serves Ishasha. Private charters from Fly Uganda are also available. Mweya Visitor Centre (at the tip of the peninsula) is a good resource. Head here to book UWA boat cruises or lion monitoring. Rangers for game drives on Kasenyi Plains are collected from Kasenyi gate, and in Ishasha from the UWA bandas near the start of the southern circuit.

EXPLORING

Fodor's Choice
★
Explosion Crater Drive. A stunning three-hour diversion along rocky tracks in northern Queen Elizabeth National Park, the Explosion Crater Drive runs between the Queen's Pavillion (turn off the Kikorongo-Katunguru highway at the Equator Markers) and the Kabatoro Gate (aka the Main Gate) on the Katwe public road. There is no need to prebook, or take a ranger, but a competent 4x4 driver and vehicle is most definitely required. Known for its scenic vistas rather than wildlife-viewing potential (though elephants are relatively common, lions are not unheard of, and the crater environment is great for spotting birds of prey), the drive traverses the Katwe crater field. This area of the park is littered with steep-sided volcanic craters, each containing its own micro-habitat from ancient rainforest to a sulfurous lake. It's enough to make geologists of us all. ⊠ *Explosion Crater Dr., Queen Elizabeth National Park, Western Region, Uganda* ☎ *0414/355–400, 0414/355–403* ⊕ *www.ugandawildlife.org* ✉ *Included in park entry fee* ⊙ *Daily 6:30–6:30.*

Kyambura Gorge. The forested ridges of Kyambura Gorge form a deep cleft in the savanna landscape between Maramagambo Forest and Lake George, creating a natural boundary between Queen Elizabeth National Park and neighboring Kyambura Wildlife Reserve. Offering the chance to spot chimps on guided forest walks, the chimpanzee trackling in Kyambura Gorge is more active than most; you may have to cross the river by fallen log (slippery when wet!) and the steep sides of the gorge can be difficult at best. But it's a mysterious, primeval place, and worth the 2.5 km (1.6 miles) drive from the Katunguru highway just for the view alone. Chimp permits (USD$50) can be arranged with the UWA locally, but limited availability means it's best to secure them in advance from their HQ in Kampala. Visiting the viewing platform is free, provided one has paid park entry fees. ⊠ *Fig Tree Camp, Kyambura Gorge, Queen Elizabeth National Park, Western Region, Uganda* ☎ *0414/355–400* ⊕ *www.ugandawildlife.org* ⊗ *Daily 6:30–6:30.*

WHERE TO STAY

LUXURY LODGES

$$ 🏠 **Mweya Safari Lodge.** Big groups love the location of this "hotel-in-the-bush," situated on the Mweya peninsula overlooking Kazinga Channel (a popular water hole for big game), in the heart of Queen Elizabeth National Park. Staying here means you're well placed for early-morning game drives or the unmissable wildlife launch cruise; the lodge has its own fleet of very smart boats just for this purpose. Choose from accommodations to suit all tastes: simple en-suite rooms, deluxe rooms with air-conditioning, suites and cottages, and a few stylish safari tents (a recent welcome addition). A pool, health club, massage area, business center, and vast gift shop ensure you need never leave. The manicured lawns and shrubbery may feel too tame for safari aficionados, yet the professional staff and central location means Mweya is still the busiest property in the park. **Pros:** located in the park; rooms to suit all budgets/styles. **Cons:** with 46 rooms, 4 tents, and 4 cottages, it can feel big and impersonal; restaurant switches to buffet meals in busy periods. $ *Rooms from: US$402* ⊠ *Mweya Peninsula, Queen Elizabeth National Park, Western Region, Uganda* ✦ *Gate on left after passing through UWA checkpoint on Mweya peninsula, inside Queen Elizabeth National Park* ☎ *0312/260–260, 0414/255–992* ⊕ *www.mweyalodge. com* ⤳ *32 standard rooms, 12 deluxe rooms, 2 suites, 4 safari tents, 4 cottages* ⊗ *Multiple meal plans.*

$$$$ 🏠 **Volcanoes Kyambura Gorge Lodge.** This masterpiece of design, con-
Fodor's Choice verted from an old coffee station, sometimes feels more like a hip New
★ York loft than a safari lodge, but the combination of whimsical upcycling chic with local building materials is part of its eclectic charm. A hanging curtain of recycled mortar trays (themselves recycled from cooking skillets) divides the lounge from the bar, traditional Karamojong tobacco carriers are repurposed as hanging baskets, and a patchwork installation of plastic jerrycans hangs on the wall. Eight bandas are decorated in a similar contemporary style, each with a different color palette; rooms overlook the forested gorge (great for birders), or the rolling savanna of the national park (complete with passing elephants). Massages are conducted in a converted packing shed, near a cute little rock pool. Guests interested in learning more about the lodge's eco-credentials should take the coffee tour. **Pros:** stylish contemporary design; impressive commitment to community and conservation; staff are eager to please. **Cons:** for those who prefer traditional lodge design, it may feel a little too modern; food can be below par. $ *Rooms from: US$944* ⊠ *Kyambura, Western Region, Uganda* ✦ *Turn off (at lodge sign) at Kyambura trading center on Bushenyi-Katunguru Rd.*

Continue through village and then turn left at lodge sign ☎ *0414/346–464, 0772/741–720* 🌐 *www.volcanoessafaris.com* 🛏 *8 twin/double bandas (cottages)* 💳 *No credit cards* 🍴 *All-inclusive.*

PERMANENT TENTED CAMPS

$$$$ Fodor's Choice ★ 🏨 **Ishasha Wilderness Camp.** Steeped in classic safari style, this intimate camp will make you feel as if you have stumbled onto the set of *Out of Africa*. Located on the banks of the Ntungwe River, in the remote southern sector of Queen Elizabeth National Park, its rooms are constructed from canvas, net, and wood, reminiscent of old-school safari tents but with *plenty* of comfort. For those wanting to escape modern life, it's perfect. Hot water needs ordering in advance and Wi-Fi is limited to set times, but dinners are served on white linen under the stars, so life still feels privileged. It's not unusual to spot wildlife while in camp: colobus monkeys in the trees, a hippo in the shallows, elephants crossing. And this sense of being surrounded by wild things is perhaps the greatest privilege of all. **Pros:** a classic safari experience; remote, wilderness location; some of the best lodge food in Uganda. **Cons:** too cut-off for some tastes; no hot running water; limited connectivity. [$] *Rooms from: US$720* ✉ *Ishasha Sector, Queen Elizabeth National Park, Uganda* ☎ *0414/321–479, 0772/721–155* 🌐 *www.ugandaexclusivecamps.com* 🛏 *10 tented rooms* 🍴 *All meals.*

BUDGET ACCOMMODATIONS

$$ 🏨 **Kyambura Game Lodge.** Phoenix-like, this lodge has *literally* risen from the ashes, having been restored after a 2012 bushfire destroyed most of its structures. It now offers better value than ever before. Overlooking a small volcanic crater on the boundary of Queen Elizabeth National Park, eight neatly thatched cottages enjoy an enviable sunset view. Families love the pool, and the fire pit and local dance troupe add to the ambience come nightfall. Quirky design touches in a rustic style, and the team's easy hospitality, elevate the guest experience beyond the ordinary. **Pros:** great service and rooms for the price; beautiful sunset views. **Cons:** frequent call-to-prayer from nearby mosque and road noise can disturb light sleepers; average food; road between lodge and park in terrible condition. [$] *Rooms from: US$364* ✉ *Kyambura, Western Region, Uganda* ✥ *Turn off main Bushenyi-Katunguru Rd. at Kyambura trading center (cluster of signs on corner, including one for Volcanoes lodge). After about 100 meters, turn left at sign for Kyambura Game Lodge* ☎ *0414/322–789, 0703/614–337, 0702/526–636* 🌐 *www.kyamburalodge.com* 🛏 *8 double/twin cottages* 🍴 *All meals.*

SPORTS AND THE OUTDOORS

BOATING

In the northern sector of Queen Elizabeth National Park, the Kazinga Channel attracts all manner of game. Herds of elephants and buffalo throng the banks; smaller herbivores such as warthog and kob are also present; pods of hippo and solitary crocs bask in the shallows; and a significant proportion of the park's staggering 610 bird species can be seen here. With such natural bounty, it's no wonder the two-hour boat cruise along its banks is far and away the highlight activity in this sector of the park. The Uganda Wildlife Authority and Mweya Safari Lodge both operate boats for this purpose from the jetty below the lodge.

Fodor'sChoice ★ **Mweya Safari Lodge Boats.** With a variety of comfortable, modern craft, the slick river operations from Mweya Safari Lodge offer several scheduled or private Kazinga Channel cruises a day, leaving at 9, 11, 2, and 4:15 pm subject to demand. Choose from the 38-seat *Hippo* or 10-seat *Sunbird*. Both are thoughtfully equipped with a cash bar, or book yourself on the luxury 12-seat *Kingfisher* boat, where the price includes drinks and nibbles. ⊠ *Mweya Jetty, Mweya Peninsula, Queen Elizabeth National Park, Uganda* ☎ *0392/796–773, 0752/798–882* ⊕ *www.mweyalodge.com* 🖅 *From $28.*

UWA Mweya Boats. The Uganda Wildlife Authority operate their own boat cruises along the Kazinga Channel. Two-hour trips depart daily at 9, 11, 3, and 5 from the UWA jetty below Mweya Safari Lodge. There is a relatively large minimum requirement of 10 passengers, and their craft are older than the lodge boats. However, the guides certainly know their stuff, and departures are often fully booked during peak season. Book ahead at their offices in Kampala, or take your chances locally at the Katunguru HQ and Mweya Visitor Centre. ⊠ *Plot 7 Kira Rd., Kampala, Uganda* ☎ *0414/355–400* ⊕ *www.ugandawildlife.org* 🖅 *US$30* ⊙ *Kampala reservations office closed Sat. afternoon and Sun. The boats and park offices operate daily.*

7

IF YOU HAVE TIME IN UGANDA

Although the must-see parks in Uganda are described in detail above, there are still other places worth exploring if you have time.

LAKE MBURO NATIONAL PARK

Roughly halfway between Kampala and Bwindi, Lake Mburo National Park is underrated; its unique variety of game and birdlife, plenty of opportunities to get out of the car, and excellent lodges means it offers far more than just a convenient stopover en route to the gorillas.

This little park is made up of wetlands (including the eponymous lake itself), open savanna, and acacia woodland, studded with rocky outcrops. Its range of habitats supports around 315 bird species, including certain southern varieties for whom the park is the most northerly part of their range. Bird-watchers will appreciate the Lake Mburo boat cruise, a shoe-in for the elusive African finfoot.

For wildlife-lovers, the park delivers a wealth of smaller herbivores: large gatherings of impala not found anywhere else in Uganda mingle with zebra, topi, oribi, and bushbuck; herds of the largest living antelope, the eland, take up seasonal residence; and dainty klipspringers hide out on rocky *koppies*. Local leopard and hyena populations are on the increase, with plenty of smaller predators, such as genet and white-tailed mongoose, also present. This makes for interesting nocturnal viewing, as the park is one of the few places allowing such game drives. Other novel activities include horseback safaris and nature walks that offer a different perspective on wildlife-viewing and allow you to appreciate the peaceful serenity of the bush.

GETTING HERE AND AROUND

City traffic allowing, this park is now less than a four-hour drive (230 km [140 miles]) from Kampala, with newly resurfaced highways making the journey relatively pleasant. A handy café/crafts pit stop can be made at the Equator (75 km [47 miles] south of Kampala). The Nshara gate is reached by turning off the Masaka-Mbarara highway about 20 km (12 miles) past Lyantonde; turn off for the more westerly Sanga gate 37 km (23 miles) shy of Mbarara, at the town of the same name. No public transport exists beyond the main highway, and a 4x4 is recommended for navigating the park and approach roads. If you have to fly in, charters to nearby Mbarara airstrip are available, just more than an hour from the park.

WHERE TO STAY

LUXURY LODGES

$$$

FAMILY

Fodor's Choice

★

Mihingo Lodge. High up on a *kopje* (rocky outcrop), the cottages at this superb boutique lodge blend seamlessly into the landscape, each offering a different view of the surrounding bush. Guests in Kings cottage have spotted leopard on the adjacent rock, Klipspringer has its own water hole, and Tree (as the name suggests) has its own tree growing up through the hardwood platform. Its eco-creds go further than design: the lodge is carbon-neutral and has pioneered a local predator compensation scheme. Mihingo offers plenty of romantic nooks: the sundeck below the rainwater infinity pool, the tower with near 360-degree views, and secret sundowner spots out on the rock. In addition to standard walks and game drives, Mihingo offers horseback safaris, bushcraft courses, and activity books for kids, and every night, bushbabies are fed from a viewing platform below the bar. Kids love it. **Pros:** a true eco-lodge; delicious buffet meals; vast array of activities to satisfy young and old. **Cons:** often overlooked as off the mainstream safari trail; limited Wi-Fi; holiday weekends can see it filled with expats. [$] *Rooms from: US$520* ✉ *Lake Mburo National Park, Uganda* ✣ *From Nshara gate of Lake Mburo NP, drive 5 km (3 miles) and then turn left onto Ruroko track. Follow for around 6 km (4 miles) until you see right turn signed for Mihingo* ☎ *0752/410–509* 🌐 *www.mihingolodge.com* 🛏 *12 cottages* 🍴 *All meals.*

BUDGET ACCOMMODATIONS

$$ Fodor's Choice ★ 🏨 **Rwakobo Rock.** A gem of a budget lodge, Rwakobo Rock is deservedly popular with the adventure crowd. Hearty, home-cooked fare is served up under the open thatch of their main building on the side of the eponymous rock. Simply furnished thatched cottages are tucked away in hidden corners; their interiors decorated in the black and white colors of the local Hima tribe. Recycled bottles of filtered water harvested via rainwater catchment speak to the young owner's environmental stance. A fire-pit smolders and hammocks dot the property, encouraging a chilled-out vibe that's hard to ignore. When not exploring Lake Mburo National Park, you can hire a mountain bike for a two-wheel safari, head out on a nature walk, or have a microadventure on the rock. The view from the top is awesome. **Pros:** relaxed, informal style offering great value; climbers will love bouldering on the rock. **Cons:** poorly lit paths to the rooms; watch your step—occasionally herds of cattle come through the lodge, with slippery consequences. [$] *Rooms from: US$250* ✉ *Near Nshara Gate, Lake Mburo National Park, Uganda* ✣ *Turn off main Masaka-Mbarara Hwy. following signs for Nshara gate of Lake Mburo National Park. The lodge is on right after 8 km, just 1.5 km from Nshara Gate* ☎ *0755/211–771* 🌐 *www.rwakoborock.com* 🛏 *9 twin/double cottages* 🍴 *All meals.*

MURCHISON FALLS NATIONAL PARK

Historically a highlight of the East African safari circuit, at 1,483 square miles Murchison Falls National Park is the largest of Uganda's reserves, offering an abundance of wildlife against a superbly scenic backdrop.

Bisected by the Nile River, many of the activities gravitate around the water. Delta cruises offer peaceful contemplation of papyrus-lined channels (and a good chance of spotting Shoebill); half-/full-day sportfishing trips can be arranged; and the most popular activity is the launch cruise to Murchison Falls. Here, 300 cubic meters of water per second explodes through a narrow gorge, creating the most powerful stretch of water in the world. Active adventurers can prearrange to be dropped by boat at the base of the Falls, known as the Devil's Cauldron, for a steep hike up to the Top of the Falls where dramatic vistas await. The viewpoints can also be accessed by vehicle, from the south and north banks.

North-bank game tracks promise rewarding wildlife-viewing: herds of elephant, buffalo, and critically endangered Rothschild's giraffe; smaller herbivores include Uganda kob, Jackson's hartebeest, oribi and warthog; elusive predators such as spotted hyena, lion, leopard, and jackal; and an impressive bird list of more than 450 species. Lion Monitoring, where visitors accompany researchers to locate local prides, is also available here. Most activities are centered on Paraa in the heart of the park, but the southerly Budongo Forest provides a worthy diversion for excellent chimpanzee tracking and bird-watching.

GETTING HERE AND AROUND

The park lies five- to six-hours' drive (320 km [185 miles]) northwest of Kampala. Schedule and charter flights fly in from Entebbe airport or Kajjansi airfield, landing at Bugungu, Pakuba or Chobe airstrips as required. Kichumbanyobo gate in the south, just north of Masindi town, is best for access to Budongo Forest, and can also be used for the most efficient access to south bank lodges, along with the westerly Bugungu gate. From Paraa, a car ferry crosses the Nile in both directions, so those heading to north bank lodges may prefer to enter from Wangkwar or Tangi gates, both accessed from the main Karuma-Pakwach highway, and enjoy game drives en route to their accommodation.

WHERE TO STAY

LUXURY LODGES

$$$

Fodor's Choice ★

Baker's Lodge. The launch of Baker's Lodge has been eagerly anticipated, and the pedigree of its parent company, which specializes in intimate, organically styled properties elsewhere in Uganda, suggests it will deliver. Located in a grove of sausage trees at the water's edge, the lodge has 180-degree views of the Nile. The property has its own boat operations, plying popular launch cruises; and after time on the water, guests can arrive at camp by river. This simple act feels remarkably glamorous, reminiscent of the way early explorers, such as the camp's namesake, Samuel Baker, would have experienced this area. The camp was preparing for a soft launch at the time of writing with 6 of the eventual 10 wooden and canvas rooms ready for use; the remaining rooms and a pool will be developed in 2015. **Pros:** beautiful riverfront location delivering understated luxury with a light environmental footprint. **Cons:** admirable eco-credentials means hair dryers will be a no-no; still some construction to go at the time of this writing. $ *Rooms from: US$560* ⊠ *Near Murchison Falls National Park, Paraa, Western Region, Uganda* ⊹ *Head south from ferry crossing in Murchison Falls National Park and take exit road to Mubako gate (on right after UWA offices up hill from jetty). After passing primary school look for lodge sign on right-hand side of road* ☎ *0772/721–155, 0414/321–479* ⊕ *www.ugandaexclusivecamps.com* ⇱ *8 tented rooms* ⊚| *All meals.*

$$

Paraa Safari Lodge. This centrally located lodge, overlooking the Nile as it wends its way to Lake Albert, is popular with all those who like their creature comforts in the bush. Built in the 1950s, it's one of the more historic properties in Uganda. With more than 50 rooms, it's also a lot bigger than most, with amenities galore. A vast pool with swim-up bar is a big hit on a hot afternoon; guests in the deluxe rooms are grateful for the air-conditioning; and if you fancy hosting a business conference mid-safari, this is the place to do it. The north bank location also comes with benefits: no need to wait for the ferry crossing when you want to head out on a game drive. The lodge works hard to offset its footprint: it supports the Giraffe Conservation Foundation and nearby Paraa Primary School. **Pros:** high level of personal comfort; great pool and views; close to game tracks. **Cons:** a far cry from the intimacy and romance of a smaller lodge; not all rooms have river views. [$] *Rooms from: US$349* ✉ *North bank of the Nile, Murchison Falls National Park, Paraa, Western Region, Uganda* ✣ *Found at north bank of Nile, at Paraa ferry crossing and boat jetty* ☎ *0312/260–260, 0414/255–992* 🌐 *www.paraalodge.com* 🛏 *36 standard rooms, 15 deluxe rooms, 2 suites, 3 safari tents, 1 cottage* 🍴 *All meals.*

BUDGET ACCOMMODATIONS

$ FAMILY Fodor's Choice ★ 🏨 **Murchison River Lodge.** Since it opened a few years ago, this budget boutique lodge has found its niche. Local expats and price-conscious tourists love its laid-back, unpretentious style. With a philosophy celebrating the simpler things in life, they've got the recipe just right: kids love the pool, and home-cooked, healthy meals are served by smiling staff. Life here generally mirrors the slow pace of the river drifting by. Family cottages are set back overlooking acacia woodland and thatched safari tents dot the bush and bank closer to the river, but the main restaurant and bar area, lined with comfy couches crafted from salvaged railway sleepers, takes the lion's share of the view. Despite the proximity of the park and all of its alluring activities, it's tempting to while away days just looking out over the papyrus-filled islands of the Nile, watching for passing elephant. **Pros:** simple pleasures done well; great value; a warm and welcoming staff. **Cons:** no Wi-Fi and poor phone reception; due to environmental considerations, the three tents with river views have chemical toilets (the rest have flush). [$] *Rooms from: US$200* ✉ *Near Murchison Falls National Park, Paraa, Western Region, Uganda* ✣ *From Paraa: Head south and take first right turn (signed for Murchison River Lodge) after leaving the river. Continue along road, through Mubako gate, until you see lodge on right. From Bulisa: Turn east toward park and Bugungu gate. Turn left after 10 km (signed for lodge). Follow this track, and signs, through fields until you reach lodge* ☎ *0714/000–085, 0782/007–552* 🌐 *murchisonriverlodge.com* 🛏 *4 family cottages, 6 en-suite safari tents* 🍴 *All meals.*

SPORTS AND THE OUTDOORS

BOATING

The undisputed highlight of Murchions Falls National Park are the many ways visitors can "mess about on the river": cruises to the Falls, exploring the Nile delta, sundowner trips with chilled drinks onboard, and even sport-fishing expeditions for keen anglers. Watching the sun set (or rise) over this ancient river, to a backing track of hippo snorts and birdcalls, is stirring stuff. Three different outfitters—the park authorities and two private operators with lodges in the area—offer boat cruises from Paraa with varying degrees of choice. Book a scheduled departure for the best value, or ask about private cruising rates for an exclusive experience tailored to your interests.

7

Paraa Safari Lodge Boats. Sleek, new boats are the hallmark of the Paraa Safari Lodge river operations; their variously sized watercrafts include the double-decker *African Queen,* the 14-seat *Paraa Voyager,* or the 10-seat *Jewel of the Nile.* Their scheduled trips head upstream to the Falls from their jetty on the north bank, with regular departures at 8:30 am and 2:30 pm, subject to demand. In addition, they also offer launch cruises to the Nile delta area. ⊠ *North bank, Murchison Falls National Park, Paraa, Western Region, Uganda* ☎ *0772/788–880, 0752/788–880* ⊕ *www.paraalodge.com.*

UWA Murchison Boats. Operating from their south bank jetty at Paraa, the Uganda Wildlife Authority offers daily cruises upstream to Murchison Falls, departing at 8 am and 2 pm. Their large boats are somewhat older than those of the private outfitters operating in the same area, and a minimum of 10 passengers are required for the craft to depart, but their seasoned guides and this remarkable stretch of river ensure the excursion is still excellent value. You can secure your place on one of their cruises by visiting their central reservations office in Kampala, or the local park offices at Paraa. ⊠ *South bank, Murchison Falls National Park, Paraa, Western Region, Uganda* ☎ *0414/355–400, 0414/355–405* ⊕ *www.ugandawildlife.org* 🎟 *US$30* ⊙ *Closed Sat. afternoon and Sun.*

Fodor's Choice   **Wild Frontiers Murchison Boats.** This established safari outfitter, and
★   operator of nearby Baker's Lodge, provides scenic wildlife cruises and sport-fishing trips with their fleet of boats stationed at the Paraa jetty. Scheduled and private departures include trips to the Falls and the Nile delta—the latter providing many a Shoebill sighting—and sunset/sunrise cruises offer great value. ■TIP➔ When booking your Falls cruise, ask about their Falls & Sundowner option. The later departure time of 3:30 pm generally means better wildlife sightings and a more peaceful river setting. They have a variety of comfortable craft, offer the most flexibility for customized trips, and their skippers and guides are well trained, with a knack for knowing just when to turn off the engines and glide silently past the riverbanks, enjoying the natural sounds of the bush. ⊠ *South bank, Murchison Falls National Park, Paraa, Western Region, Uganda* ⊕ *wildfrontiers.co.ug* 🎟 *From US$20 per person to more than a US$1,000 per day for a large group on an exclusive booking.*

JINJA AND THE RIVER NILE

The age-old quest to locate the source of the Nile finally ended at Jinja, now the self-appointed adventure capital of East Africa where today's modern explorers avail themselves of a veritable smorgasbord of white-knuckle activities.

Back in 1862, John Hanning Speke declared Ripon Falls to be the source of the Nile. Today, the laid-back town of Jinja overlooks this mighty river as it flows out of Lake Victoria, at the start of its 6,800-km (4,200-mile) journey to the Mediterranean. Thanks to a 1950s hydro-power dam, Ripon Falls are now completely submerged; visitors can still view the official "source" in a 30-minute boat trip, but all that remains is a suggestive ripple on the water's surface, so it can be rather an anticlimax.

The river remains the reason behind why people come, but for a cluster of adventure activities rather than a history lesson. An industry fueled by sheer adrenaline has sprung up around the Nile's greatest asset: a series of dramatically churning white-water rapids that mark its course. White-water rafting is the main attraction, but visitors can choose from a smorgasbord of other thrills (and possible spills): kayaking; river-boarding; jetboat trips; bungee jumping; ATV safaris; horseback riding; and mountain biking. For fans of more serene outdoor pursuits, the "lake" of flat water at Bujagali, created by the recent addition of a second hydropower dam, offers stand-up paddleboarding, sit-on kayak trips, birding, and sunset cruises.

GETTING HERE AND AROUND
A two- to three-hour drive (80 km [50 miles]) east of Kampala, Jinja can be reached by the more direct (but juggernaut-choked) Jinja Road through Mabira Forest, or the more peaceful Gayaza Road route. The final approach to Jinja for both options involves crossing the Nile over the Owen Falls Dam. Enjoy the views but don't take any pictures—cameras can be confiscated because this is an important government installation. Bujagali, with its community of adventure companies and budget camps, lies 12 km (7 miles) north of Jinja on the east bank. Charter and scheduled flights from Fly Uganda are available to nearby Jinja Airstrip.

Contacts Fly Uganda. ☎ *0772/712–557* ⊕ *www.flyuganda.com*

WHERE TO STAY
LUXURY LODGES
$$$$ ⚇ **Wildwaters Lodge.** If this world-class lodge, part of the respected
Fodor'sChoice Lemala group, does not enchant you with its magical location, it will
★ win you over with its service and superb cuisine. Midstream on its private island in the mighty River Nile, powerful rapids thunder past its natural-rock swimming pool. Raised wooden walkways crisscross the riverine forest on the island, and each spacious cottage boasts a private deck with outdoor bathtub. Five-course dinners are a culinary treat, made all the more special by the backdrop; moonlight playing on the constant motion of whitewater. Recently the lodge team renovated the old Brady steam engine from the *African Queen*, used in the classic Hepburn/Bogart movie of the same name, and now you can take a riverboat tour in the modern-day version as a serene alternative to white-water rafting and other adventure activities in the area. **Pros:** one of the best lodges in Uganda, Wildwaters has become a destination in itself; an excellent spot to wind down after a safari. **Cons:** slightly off the main safari trail; some people find the roar of the rapids too noisy. $ *Rooms from: US$720* ⊠ *Kalagala Falls, River Nile, Jinja, Central Region, Uganda* ⊕ *From Jinja Rd.: Turn north at Nile Breweries and continue for 26 km (16 miles) till you get to Kangulamira town. Turn right here just before Petrocity fuel station. Travel 3 km (2 miles) until you reach lodge parking area. The lodge guard will then radio lodge to send a boat. Alternatively: Take Gayaza Rd. northeast from Kampala. At Kayunga town, turn right toward Jinja. Turn left in Kangulamira town just after Petrocity fuel station, then follow directions as above.*

☎ *0312/237–438, 0772/237–400* ⊕ *www.wild-uganda.com* ⇆ *10 cottage suites* ❍| *All meals.*

SPORTS AND THE OUTDOORS
WHITE-WATER RAFTING

None of Jinja's activities is more popular than rafting the mighty Nile. Trips tackle a sequence of white-water rapids, graded between 3 and 5, with names such as Super Hole and the ominous-sounding Bad Place. At local beauty spot Itanda Falls, a Class VI rapid necessitates a portage via surrounding rocks that fall within a nature reserve. As a result, a US$15 "green fee" may be added to the activity cost. Three established, reputable companies offer similarly priced one-day packages, including transport from Kampala if required, lunch on the river, and beers afterward to toast the excitements of the day. Two-day or longer expeditions are also available.

Adrift East Africa. Adrift was set up by New Zealander Cam McCleay, who left his native New Zealand to pioneer several expeditions along this river, styling himself as a modern-day explorer, with various adventures along the way. His team is made up of smart professionals, managing bookings for rafting and Wildwaters Lodge from their central-Kampala base in Kololo. They also operate the Nile High Bungee from their riverside camp off the Bujagali Road. If staying at Wildwaters Lodge, they will collect you from, and drop you back at the lodge. ⊠ *14 York Terrace, Kololo, Kampala, Uganda* ☎ *256/312–237–438 for main office, 256/772–454–206 (mobile)* ⊕ *www.adrift.ug* ✉ *One-day rafting package USD$125 per person.*

Nalubale Rafting. The folks at Nalubale Rafting are a friendly and enthusiastic bunch, with a laid-back base in Jinja town and the cheap and cheerful Nile River Camp at Bujagali. Groups of volunteers, students, and independent travelers paddle confidently under supervision from their professional river guides; families are well catered for on their "Fish'n'Flip" trips; and they conjure up an impressive riverside lunch spread for hungry rafters. If you hunger for something worthy of a modern-day explorer, they occasionally run six-day Jinja-Karuma rafting expeditions. ⊠ *Kiira Rd. 38, Eastern Region, Jinja, Uganda* ☎ *256/782–638–938 (mobile)* ⊕ *www.nalubalerafting.com* ✉ *From USD$125 per person; Fish'n'flips from $30.*

Nile River Explorers. The bustling NRE base in Jinja town, and their camp at Bujagali, is a hip hang out for backpackers. As rafting goes, they offer similar standards of professionalism and flair to that provided by the other operators. Their typical clientele like to raft hard and party harder, and the company's enduring popularity ensures there is rarely a day when they are not on the river. In addition to rafting, they have a network of connections that are well set up to book you almost any other activity in the area. ⊠ *Plot 41, Wilson Ave., Eastern Region, Jinja, Uganda* ☎ *256/772–422–373* ⊕ *www.raftafrica.com* ✉ *From USD$125*

KAMPALA AND ENTEBBE, UGANDA

Visitors to Uganda looking for a base as the start or end of their gorilla safari have a choice between two very different destinations: the bustling sprawl of the country's capital Kampala, or the simple serenity of Entebbe, its international airport hub.

Entebbe is a peaceful, sleepy town, situated at the tip of a peninsula extending south of Kampala into Lake Victoria. Just a couple of miles from the country's only international airport, overnighting here is definitely convenient for anyone with early or late flight arrival/departure times. Entebbe's proximity to the airport, and Kajjansi Airfield a few miles up the road, also makes it handy for the domestic air services to the national parks. Charming, boutique guesthouses or mediocre business hotels typify the accommodation here. If these are not your style they become significantly more appealing when you realize that the 40-km (25-mile) journey between Kampala and Entebbe can take more than 90 minutes to complete.

If the bright lights of Kampala do beckon—and if time is not a precious commodity—then Uganda's dynamic capital offers an impressive roll call of positive qualities: a far wider range of fashionable eateries dot the city, it delivers a better quality of high-end hotel, the nightlife is buzzing, the city is host to a growing arts scene, and shopping mavens will love the craft markets and souvenir shops. Aside from the Kasubi Tombs—a burial ground for members of the Buganda royal family, at this writing still under reconstruction after a fire gutted the main structures in 2010—there is a distinct lack of any substantial tourist attractions, but for many, Kampala's own brand of vibrant urban chaos is a sight in itself. This really is a tale of two cities.

Whatever you choose, a Chinese company has started construction of a tolled superhighway between Kampala and Entebbe. Estimates suggest it should be finished in 2016, and once completed, the new toll road should significantly reduce the time it takes to get between the two destinations. Until then, your overnight stop of choice will probably be based on a complex trade-off between personal preferences, traffic jams, and flight times.

GETTING HERE AND AROUND

Entebbe International Airport (EBB) serves Entebbe (5 km [3 miles]) and Kampala (40 km [25 miles]). (⇨ *See international flights at the start of this chapter.*) Regional services from RwandAir, Precision Air, and Kenya Airways serve destinations in Rwanda, Tanzania, and Kenya respectively (as did Air Uganda until their operating license was revoked). A positive new development for those planning Tanzania/Uganda safaris is the daily service from the Serengeti, operated by Coastal Aviation and eliminating the need to route via Dar es Salaam/Arusha. From Entebbe, licensed airport taxis are available at all hours from the stand just outside arrivals, though it's less stressful to prebook a hotel or tour company driver to meet your flight. Most Entebbe properties include this in their rates.

EXPLORING

FodorsChoice   **Ngamba Island Chimpanzee Sanctuary.** Delivering a different experience
★   to tracking wild chimps, this island sanctuary in Lake Victoria offers
the chance for visitors to observe its population of rescue chimps, and
the opportunity to get up close and personal with our primate cousins.
Lying 23 km (14 miles) southeast of Entebbe, the sanctuary was established in 1998 by the Chimpanzee Sanctuary & Wildlife Conservation
Trust. Its mission to care for chimps rescued from captivity, each with
its own sad story. A small corner of its 50 hectares is fenced off for day-
trippers to observe feeding sessions from a viewing platform—an excellent photographic opportunity in itself. But the real appeal lies in getting
behind-the-scenes: overnight visitors (the island has a small tented
camp) can opt for the Caregiver experience. Be prepared for extensive
medical requirements, but the chance to hold and care for these tragic
chimps will melt your heart. ⊠ *Chimpanzee Sanctuary & Wildlife Conservation Trust, Plot 1, Bank Close, Entebbe, Central Region, Uganda*
☎ *0414/320–662, 0758/221–880* ⊕ *www.ngambaisland.com* ⊠ *Half-
day speedboat trips from US$145 per person; Caregiver Experience
US$200 per person (except transfers, entry fee and accommodation).*

Uganda Wildlife Education Centre. On the lakeshore in Entebbe, the
Uganda Wildlife Education Centre plays a multifaceted role: it's an
animal rescue center, veterinary institution and tourist attraction all
rolled into one. But perhaps its most significant role is as an education
facility for future generations. Referred to as UWEC (pronounced "*ooh-
eck*"), the former Entebbe zoo is home to an array of Ugandan species,
usually inclusive of a few school trips. Facilities for the animals may
feel a little cramped, but the team place great importance on putting
conservation first, making it a pleasant enough place to while away a
spare morning or afternoon in Entebbe. ■**TIP➔ To get the most out
of your visit, book the Behind-the-Scenes tour ($70) for a chance to
enter some of the enclosures and meet the animals, or the Chimpanzee
Close-up ($260), for a cuddle with one of the orphaned chimpanzees in
their care.** ⊠ *Plot 56/57 Lugard Ave., Entebbe, Central Region, Uganda*
☎ *0414/320–520, 0718/329–299* ⊕ *www.uweczoo.org* ⊠ *$15.*

WHERE TO EAT

ENTEBBE

$ ✕**Faze 3.** A lively choice for Entebbe nights out, and handy for diners
ECLECTIC   stopping off en route to the airport for late-night flights, Faze 3 boasts
a mind-boggling selection of dishes. Their menu encompasses a wide
range of cuisines. The choices include starters and snacks, light salads,
pita pockets and sandwiches, as well as filling mains comprising continental classics, authentic curries and a popular selection of meaty feasts
served sizzlingly hot on cast-iron skillets. Well-trained staff provide
snappy service and there is plenty of seating inside and out. The best
place to sit is definitely on the vast terrace overlooking the lake, to enjoy
the cool breezes and views. If you're in a large group, it's best to book
a table here in advance, especially on Wednesday, Friday, and Saturday
night and Sunday afternoon, when live music dials up the party vibe.

$ *Average main: US$10* ⊠ *106 Circular Rd., Entebbe, Central Region, Uganda* ☎ *0778/609–595, 0312/671–345, 0414/598–080.*

$

PIZZA

✕**Goretti's Beachside Pizzeria.** A cold beer, crisp pizza, and curling your toes in the sand are a few of life's simple pleasures. Enjoy all three simultaneously at Goretti's Beachside Pizzeria, a popular haunt for tourists and locals alike. Diners sit in plastic chairs at tables placed among swaying palms on the beach itself. The shoreline location makes up for slow and sometimes unenthusiastic service. Because of the views (and the greater possibility of insects after dusk), lunchtime is the best time to appreciate the charm of this simple restaurant shack. Grilled meat or fish is also available, but wood-fired pizza is what they do best. Just be sure to allow a couple of hours, during which you can gaze out over Lake Victoria while availing yourself of their uncomplicated drinks menu: local beers, soft drinks, the usual spirits, and boxed South African wine by the glass. $ *Average main: US$10* ⊠ *Nambi Rd., Entebbe, Central Region, Uganda* ☎ *0772/308–887, 0773/100–500* ⊕ *www. gorettistoursandtravel.com/pizzeria* ⊟ *No credit cards.*

$$$

ITALIAN

Fodor's Choice

★

✕**Mediterraneo.** Restauranteur Stefano Ginetti has created a stylish addition to his similarly monikered Nairobi eateries: from its location within the grounds of Villa Kololo (a quirky boutique hotel), Kampala's Mediterraneo serves up world-class Italian food to a fashionable crowd. Tiered hardwood decks encircle a leafy courtyard, creating intimate spaces decorated with vintage bric-a-brac. An expert kitchen team turns out exquisitely simple food using fresh local produce and specialist ingredients, flown in where necessary. The *breseola della valtellina* is the genuine article; veal Scaloppini is served with real Fontana cheese; and *aragosta all griglia* uses rock lobster from the Kenyan coast. The pasta in their ravioli, agnolotti, or pappardelle dishes is made from scratch, and the wood-fired pizzas taste just like they do in Naples. A Chef's Special menu is switched up regularly, keeping things fresh. The well-curated wine list includes French, South African, and (of course) Italian labels. $ *Average main: US$21* ⊠ *Villa Kololo, 31 Acacia Ave., Kampala, Central Region, Uganda* ☎ *0414/500–533, 0701/098–732* ⊕ *www.villakololo.com* ⚐ *Reservations essential.*

KAMPALA

$$

ECLECTIC

Fodor's Choice

★

✕**The Bistro.** This stylish, modern restaurant in the heart of buzzing Kisementi delivers accomplished fusion cuisine with considerable flair, transforming effortlessly from convivial café by day to happening eatery by night. Customers love the laid-back atmosphere of the Bistro's shaded terrace. Inside, statement décor and white-linen tablecloths create a more formal dining experience. First-class service has long been a hallmark; as has the eclectic menu, which artfully combines burgers, salads, wraps, pasta, and grills with the likes of noodles, curries, sushi, and tapas, with all dietary needs and preferences represented. It doesn't stop there: a dedicated breakfast menu, crowd-pleasing desserts, freshly pressed juices, Arabica coffee and creamy shakes, quaffable wine, and expertly mixed cocktails complete the panoply of choice. Happy Hour (known here as "Gin o'clock") runs Monday through Thursday from 4 to 7; a three-piece band entertains diners on Friday night; and wine tasting takes place the last Wednesday of the month. $ *Average main:*

7

US$13 ✉ *15 Cooper Rd., Kisementi, Kampala, Central Region, Uganda* ☎ *0757/247–876* ✍ *Reservations essential.*

$$ INDIAN 🍴 **Khazana: The Verandah.** A new outpost of the popular Khana Khazana restaurant in Kololo, the Verandah is its stylish southside sister, serving up classic Indian cuisine in a white-stucco loggia overlooking a fountain. Petal-strewn water features, ornately decorated wall alcoves and Nehru-collared waitstaff add to the subcontinental style of this high-caliber curry house. Its more central counterpart has been a long-standing favorite of the Kampala dining scene, and if anything, the Verandah looks set to eclipse this: the food and service is frequently better here than at the original. The history of India's relationship with Uganda is reflected in this country's love affair with Indian cuisine, and no one should visit without sampling at least one Indian meal. At these prices, the Khazana restaurants may be among the more expensive places to do so, but they're by far the best. [$] *Average main: US$18* ✉ *Plot No. 7921/7922 Tank Hill Rd., Muyenga, Kampala, Central Region, Uganda* ☎ *0752/224–003, 0752/224–004* ✍ *Reservations essential.*

$$ AFRICAN 🍴 **The Lawns.** The only restaurant in Kampala with a license to serve game, the Lawns is about the closest Uganda has to the legendary carnivore experience enjoyed by Kenyan safari-goers *(⇨ See Chapter 4)*. Unashamedly celebrating the wildest cuts of meat, with dishes like ostrich burgers, smoked kudu steak or whole crocodile tail (preorder 2–3 hours), this barn-size venue is not for vegetarians. ■ **TIP→ Order the tasting platter to sample four different exotic meats, and cocktail-lovers should check out the lengthy list of martini recipes.** More domestic grilled meats are available for traditionalists. Happy hour runs weekdays 5–7, and a live band plays every Saturday night. Sunday is unique for the live grill experience, where meat is carved tableside. All game is sourced legally from registered South African game ranches. Don't be put off by the wild rabbits nibbling the gardens—they're strictly pets and not for the pot. [$] *Average main: US$20* ✉ *Plot 34 Impala Ave., Kololo, Kampala, Central Region, Uganda* ☎ *0414/250–337, 0312/515–373* 🌐 *www.thelawns.co.ug* ✍ *Reservations essential.*

WHERE TO STAY

Hotel reviews have been shortened. For full information, visit Fodors.com

ENTEBBE

$ B&B/INN Fodor's Choice ★ 🏨 **The Boma.** This popular boutique hotel with a reputation for great service is tucked away on a leafy residential street in Entebbe, a few minutes' drive from the airport. **Pros:** colonial style and professional service at an affordable price; rate includes airport transfers if required; superb service. **Cons:** can get booked up quickly; incoming/outgoing guests can make it noisy at night. [$] *Rooms from: US$165* ✉ *Plot 20A Gowers Rd., Entebbe, Uganda* ✥ *Turn off airport road at AAR Victoria Medical Centre (and Boma sign)* ☎ *0772/467–929* 🌐 *www.boma.co.ug* 🛏 *16 double/twin rooms* 💳 *No credit cards* 🍽 *Breakfast.*

$ B&B/INN 🏨 **Karibu Guesthouse.** An unpretentious guesthouse in a peaceful area of Entebbe, Karibu lives up to its name (it means "you're welcome" in

Swahili) with friendly, well-trained staff and some of the best food this side of Kampala. **Pros:** 10 minutes from airport; lovers of French cuisine will appreciate the food. **Cons:** some airport/guest noise at night; no swimming pool. [$] *Rooms from: US$145* ✉ *84 Nsamizi Rd., Entebbe, Uganda* ✣ *From Entebbe airport, take main highway to Kampala. After 5 km the road bends to right and you see Lake Victoria Hotel on right. Turn left here (signed Karibu) and then turn right, up hill, at T-junction. At next T-junction, turn left. Karibu is signed on left side after 800 meters* ☎ *0777/044–984, 0788/714–587* 🌐 *www.karibuguesthouse.com* 🛏 *7* 🍴 *Breakfast.*

KAMPALA

$$ HOTEL 🏨 **The Emin Pasha Hotel.** With its city-center location on top of Nakasero Hill, this well-established boutique hotel oozes colonial style, attracting a glamorous mix of Ugandan socialites, well-heeled safari-goers, international diplomats, and the East African business crowd. **Pros:** stylish alternative to the business hotels that dominate the capital; very comfortable room experience; *the* place to be seen in Kampala society. **Cons:** its popularity means the public areas can get crowded. [$] *Rooms from: US$270* ✉ *27 Akii Bua Rd., Nakasero, Kampala, Uganda* ☎ *0414/236–977, 0312/264–712* 🌐 *www.eminpasha.com* 🛏 *16 rooms, 4 suites* 🍴 *Breakfast.*

$$$ HOTEL 🏨 **Kampala Serena Hotel.** Towering above sculpted water features and landscaped gardens like a modern-day Moorish palace, the Kampala Serena sets *the* standard for hotel service in Uganda. **Pros:** international standards; central location; extremely professional. **Cons:** too large and impersonal for some tastes; full of business travelers; prices high if you're not on an expense account (a glass of house wine is around $12); the building has a macabre history: before it was extensively renovated by the Serena chain the property was the infamous Nile Hotel, associated with state-sanctioned torture that took place under the bloody regimes of Obote and Amin. [$] *Rooms from: US$447* ✉ *Kintu Rd., Kampala, Uganda* ☎ *0414/309–000, 0312/309–000* 🌐 *www.serenahotels.com* 🛏 *140 rooms, 12 suites* 🍴 *Breakfast.*

$$ RESORT FAMILY 🏨 **Lake Victoria Serena Resort.** Despite its neither-here-nor-there location, visitors to this pastel-hue citadel on Lake Victoria happily trade the plush comfort of the rooms and extensive facilities for its remote position. **Pros:** well-appointed rooms with lake views; comfortable spot to wind down post-safari; reliable service. **Cons:** a long way from anywhere; guests complain of poor Wi-Fi in rooms; bland, business style. [$] *Rooms from: US$322* ✉ *Lweza-Kigo Rd., off Entebbe Rd., Kampala, Uganda* ✣ *From Entebbe: Turn right off Entebbe road in Kajjansi trading center (after footbridge). At T-junction, turn left, and continue until you pass turn-off for Lweza estate. After this, turn right onto Kigo Rd. Continue along this road until you reach property. From Kampala: Turn left off Entebbe road in Kajjansi trading center (before footbridge). Then follow the directions as above* ☎ *0417/121–000* 🌐 *www.serenahotels.com* 🛏 *114 rooms, 10 suites* 🍴 *Breakfast* ☞ *At this writing a 9-hole, on-site golf course is scheduled for completion in 2015.*

7

BOTSWANA

WELCOME TO BOTSWANA

TOP REASONS TO GO

★ **The Okavango Delta.** Whether you're drifting dreamily in a *mokoro* (canoe) through crystal-clear, papyrus-fringed channels or walking among ancient trees on one of the many islands, your everyday world is guaranteed to fade from your consciousness.

★ **Big Game.** You won't find huge herds as in the Serengeti, but you'll come face-to-face with more critters than you ever knew existed. And there won't be hordes of other visitors blocking your view or diluting the experience.

★ **Birding.** Marvel at more than 900 species—many endemic—that crowd the game reserves. A sighting of a Pel's fishing owl, one of the world's rarest birds, will have Audubon twitching in his grave.

★ **Walking with the Bushmen.** Far from being lifeless, deserts are miracles of plenty, you just have to be in the right company—that of the Kalahari Bushmen. Listen to their dissonant music and watch them dance a dance as old as time.

1 The Okavango Delta. The Okavango Delta is formed by the Okavango River, which descends from the Angolan highlands and then fans out over north-western Botswana. It's made up of an intricate network of channels, quiet lagoons, and reed-lined backwaters. There *is* big game, but the magical scenery of this recently declared UNESCO World Heritage site is equally impressive.

2 Moremi Game Reserve. In the southeastern sector of the Okavango lies this spectacular reserve where the life-giving waters of the Okavango meet the vast Kalahari. Teeming with game and birds, it's one of Africa's greatest parks, and, unlike the Masai Mara or Kruger Park, sees hardly any people. You'll love the Garden of Eden atmosphere even if you do encounter the odd snake or two.

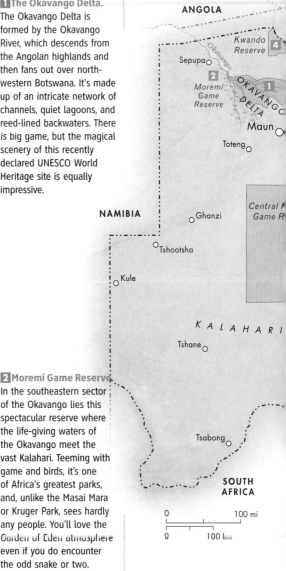

3 **Chobe National Park.**
Huge herds of elephants roam this 11,700-square-km (4,500-square-mile) park that borders the Chobe River in northeast Botswana. Although it's one of Africa's great game reserves, its lack of roads and often almost inaccessible conditions—especially in the rainy season—means you'll need a 4x4 to tackle it on your own.

GETTING ORIENTED

Botswana is roughly the size of France or Texas, and nearly 18% is reserved for conservation and tourism. The Moremi Game Reserve, the first such reserve in Southern Africa created by an African community on its own tribal lands, is a major draw. One hundred kilometers (62 miles) west of Victoria Falls in Botswana's northeast corner is Chobe National Park, known for its elephants. The wide and tranquil Chobe River is surrounded by a natural wilderness of floodplain, dead lake bed, sand ridges, and forest. Downstream it joins the mighty Zambezi on its journey through Zimbabwe and Mozambique. Upstream, where it's known as the Linyanti, it forms the border between Botswana and Namibia. In this area, the Linyanti Reserve, which borders Chobe National Park, is a huge private concession, as is the Kwando Reserve, to the west.

4 **Kwando, Selinda, and Linyanti Reserves.**
These three neighboring private concessions lie on Botswana's northern border tracking the Kwando River until it becomes the Linyanti and finally the Chobe River. It's an area crisscrossed by thousands of ancient game trails traversed by wildlife that move freely between the Okavango Delta to the west, Chobe National Park to the east, and the open Namibian wilderness to the north.

8

Updated by
James Gifford

More than half a century ago Botswana was a Cinderella among nations. Then the Fairy Godmother visited and
bestowed upon her the gift of diamonds. The resulting economic boom transformed Botswana into one of Africa's richest countries (as measured by per capita income). In 1966
the British Protectorate of Bechuanaland was granted independence and renamed Botswana, and the first democratic
president, the internationally respected Sir Seretse Khama,
guided his country into a peaceful future.

Where other nations' celebrations quickly turned sour, Botswana's independence brought an enduring tide of optimism. The country side-
stepped the scourge of tribalism and factional fighting that cursed much
of the continent and is considered one of Africa's most stable democra-
cies. The infrastructure is excellent, and the country is extremely safe.
Another big bonus is that nearly everybody speaks English—a legacy
from when Botswana was a British protectorate.

Although cities such as Gaborone (pronounced "*ha*-bo-ronee"), the
capital, have been modernized, Botswana has little in the way of urban
excitement. But outside the cities it's a land of amazing variety: the
Kalahari Desert lies in stark contrast to the lush beauty of the Okavango
Delta, one of Botswana's most magnificent and best-known regions.
Botswana is passionate about conservation, and its legendary big
game goes hand-in-hand with its admirable conservation record. Once
a hunting mecca for the so-called Great White Hunters (i.e., Ernest
Hemingway), shooting now is with cameras, not rifles. The government effectively banned all commercial hunting on nonprivately owned
land in 2014.

Botswana's policy of low-impact, high-cost tourism ensures the wilderness remains pristine and exclusive. The great rivers—the Chobe, the
Linyanti, and the Kwando—are teeming with herds of elephants and
packs of wild dogs, otherwise known as the elusive "painted wolves"

FAST FACTS

Size At 581,730 square km (224,607 square miles), it's roughly the size of France or Texas.

Capital Gaborone.

Number of National Parks Seven. Chobe National Park (including the Savuti and Linyanti areas); Moremi Game Reserve; Central Kalahari Game Reserve; Khutse Game Reserve; Kgalagadi Transfrontier Park; Magkadikgadi Pans National Park; Nxai Pan National Park.

Number of Private Reserves As new private reserves or concessions are established regularly, it's difficult to estimate. Outside of Moremi Game Reserve, the Okavango Delta is made up of a large number of private concessions and this system of leased land allocation is used throughout the country, mostly as buffer zones surrounding the national parks.

Population 2 million.

Big Five All here, although rhinos have only been reintroduced relatively recently through the collaborative efforts of the government, Wilderness, &Beyond, and Desert & Delta Safaris.

Language The national language is Setswana, but English is the official language and is spoken nearly everywhere.

Time Botswana is on CAST (Central African Standard Time), which is two hours ahead of Greenwich Mean Time and seven hours ahead of North American Eastern Standard Time.

8

of Africa. The Savuti Channel, which was dry for decades, is now flowing again and is a mecca for water birds. The golden grass of the Savuti plains is still home to huge prides of lions that hunt under skies pulsing with brilliant stars. Then there are the vast white pie-crust surfaces of the Makgadikgadi Pans (the nearest thing on earth to the surface of the moon), once a mega inland lake where flamingos still flock to breed and strange prehistoric islands of rock rise dramatically from the flaky, arid surface.

If you'd like to meet some of the most fascinating people, the stark and desolate Central Kalahari Game Reserve is home to the fastest disappearing indigenous population on earth, the Kalahari San Bushmen.

PLANNING

WHEN TO GO

The best time to visit Botswana is in the autumn and winter months (April–September), the dry season; however, it's also the most expensive time. In the Delta during the winter months the water comes in from the Angolan highlands, and the floodplains, channels, lakes, and inland waterways are literally brimming with sparkling, fresh water. Elsewhere, because it's the dry season, the grass and vegetation are sparse, and it's much easier to see game, which often have no choice but to drink at available water holes or rivers. But be warned: it can be bitterly cold, particularly early in the morning and at night. Dress in layers, which you can discard or add to as the sun goes up or down.

During the green season (October–February), aptly named since it's when the bush is at its most lush and is populated with lots of baby animals, you'll find great economy deals offered by most of the lodges, but it can be very hot, especially in October and early November when temperatures can reach up to 35°C (95°F) or more. The rains tend to arrive from November onwards and can continue until late March or early April, which helps to cool things down but can impact on your activities. If you're a birder (Botswana has more than 400 species of birds), this is the best time to visit because all the migratory birds have returned; the green vegetation also provides an attractive backdrop for keen photographers. Generally speaking, though, unless you can stand great heat, don't mind getting wet, or are a devoted bird-watcher, stick with fall and winter.

GETTING HERE AND AROUND

AIR TRAVEL

AIRPORTS

In this huge, often inaccessible country, air travel is the easiest way to get around. Sir Seretse Khama Airport, 15 km (9½ miles) from Gaborone's city center, is Botswana's main point of entry. Kasane International Airport is 3 km (2 miles) from the entrance to Chobe National Park, and small but very busy Maun Airport, the gateway to the Okavango Delta, is 1 km (½ mile) from the city center of this northern safari capital. All three are easy to find your way around in and rarely crowded.

Airports Kasane International Airport ⊠ *Upper Rd., Kasane* ☎ *625–0133.* **Maun Airport** ⊠ *Mathiba I St., Maun* ☎ *686–0238.* **Sir Seretse Khama Airport** ⊠ *Airport Rd., Phakalane, Gaborone* ☎ *395–1191.*

FLIGHTS

Air Botswana has scheduled flights from Johannesburg to Gaborone and Maun on a daily basis. The airline also flies Johannesburg to Kasane on Tuesday and from Cape Town to Gaborone and Maun on Thursday and Sunday. SA Airlink also has daily flights from Johannesburg to Gaborone, Maun, and Kasane.

Mack Air, Wilderness Air and Delta Air fly directly between Johannesburg's Lanseria airport and Maun on private charters.

Airlines Air Botswana ☎ *395–1921* ⊕ *www.airbotswana.co.bw.* **Delta Air** ☎ *686–0044* ✎ *schedules@deltabotswana.com* ⊕ *www.deltal.com.* **Mack Air** ☎ *686–0675* ✎ *reservations@mackair.co.bw* ⊕ *www.mackair.co.bw.* **SA Airlink** ☎ *27-11/451–7300 in South Africa, 395–1820* ⊕ *www.flyairlink.com.* **Wilderness Air** ☎ *686–0778* ⊕ *www.wilderness-air.com.*

CHARTER FLIGHTS

Air charter companies operate small planes from Kasane and Maun to all the camps. Flown by some of the youngest looking pilots in the world, these flights, which your travel agent will arrange, are reliable, reasonably cheap, and average between 25 and 50 minutes. Maximum baggage allowance is 12 kilograms (26 pounds) in a soft sports/duffel bag (no hard cases allowed), excluding the weight of camera equipment (within reason). Because of the thermal air currents over Botswana, and because most flights are around midday, when thermals are at their strongest, flights can sometimes be very bumpy. Take air-sickness pills if you're susceptible to motion sickness; then sit back and enjoy the fabulous bird's-eye views. You're sure to spot elephants and hippos from the air.

CAR TRAVEL

All the main access roads from neighboring countries are paved, and cross-border formalities are user-friendly. Maun is easy to reach from South Africa, Namibia, and Zimbabwe, but the distances are long and not very scenic. Gaborone is 360 km (225 miles) from Johannesburg via Rustenburg, Zeerust, and the Tlokweng border post. Driving in Botswana is on the left-hand side of the road. The "Shell Tourist Map of Botswana" is the best available map. Find it at Botswana airports or in airport bookstores.

Forget about a car in the Okavango Delta unless it's amphibious. Only the western and eastern sides of the Delta panhandle and the Moremi Game Reserve are accessible by car; but it's wisest to always take a 4x4 vehicle. The road from Maun to Moremi North Gate is paved for the first 47 km (29 miles) up to Shorobe, where it becomes gravel for 11 km (7 miles) and then a dirt road.

A 4x4 vehicle is also essential in Chobe National Park. The roads are sandy and/or very muddy, depending on the season.

ESSENTIALS

8

COMMUNICATIONS

Botswana phone numbers begin with the 267 country code, which you don't dial within the country. (There are no internal area codes in Botswana.)

HEALTH AND SAFETY

There are high standards of hygiene in all the private lodges, and most hotels are usually up to international health standards. But malaria is rife, so don't forget to take those antimalarials. Botswana has one of the highest AIDS rates in Africa, but it also has one of Africa's most progressive and comprehensive programs for dealing with the disease. All the private lodges and camps have excellent staff medical programs; you're in no danger of contracting the disease unless you have sex with a stranger. As in most cities, crime is prevalent in Gaborone, but simple safety precautions such as locking up your documents and valuables and not walking alone at night will keep you safe. On safari, there's always potential danger from wild animals, but your ranger will brief you thoroughly on the dos and don'ts of encountering big game.

The American embassy is in Gaborone, the country's capital city.

Most safari companies include emergency medical evacuation insurance for public liability to the nearest hospital, but you must have your own travel and medical insurance as well. There are two 24-hour emergency rescue companies: Medical Rescue International, which will require confirmation with your insurance company before evacuation, and Okavango Air Rescue, which will liaise with your insurance after your safe evacuation.

Embassies U.S. Embassy ✉ *Embassy Dr., Government Enclave, Gaborone* ☎ *395-3982, 373-2222 after hours* ⊕ *botswana.usembassy.gov* ⊗ *Mon.–Thurs. 7:30–5, Fri. 7:30–1:30.*

Emergencies Ambulance ☎ *997.* **Medical Rescue** ☎ *992.* **Police** ☎ *999.*

Emergency Services Medical Rescue International ☎ *390-1601.* **Okavango Air Rescue** ☎ *686-1616.*

MONEY MATTERS

The pula and the thebe constitute the country's currency; one pula equals 100 thebe. You'll need to change your money into pula, as this is the only legally accepted currency. However, most camp prices are quoted in U.S. dollars.

There are no restrictions on foreign currency notes brought into the country as long as they're declared. Travelers can carry up to P10,000 (about US$1,600), or the equivalent in foreign currency, out of the country without declaring it. Banking hours are weekdays 9–3:30, Saturday 8:30–12:30. Hours at Barclays Bank at Sir Seretse Khama International Airport are Monday–Saturday 6 am–10 pm.

■TIP➜ Though the national currency is the pula, you can use U.S. dollars or euros as tips. Your information folder at each lodge will give helpful suggestions on whom and what to tip.

PASSPORTS AND VISAS

All visitors, including infants, need a valid passport to enter Botswana for visits of up to 90 days.

ABOUT THE HOTELS AND LODGES

Most camps accommodate 12 to 20 people, so the only traffic you'll encounter among the Delta's waterways is that of grazing hippos and dozing crocodiles. Even in the northern part of Chobe, where most vehicles are, rush hour consists of buffalo and elephant herds trekking to the rivers. Prices are highest June through October. Check with individual camps for special offers.

A word about terminology: "Land camps" are in game reserves or concessions and offer morning and evening game drives. If you're not in a national park, you'll be able to go out for night drives off-road with a powerful spotlight to pick out nocturnal animals. "Water camps" are deep in the Okavango Delta and often accessible only by air or water. Many camps offer both a land and a true water experience, so you get the best of both worlds.

There's limited local cuisine in Botswana, so the food is designed to appeal to a wide variety of visitors. Nevertheless, it's very tasty. Most camps bake their own excellent bread, muffins, and cakes and often make desserts such as meringues, éclairs, and homemade ice cream. And

The Bayei people live along the tributaries of the Okanvago and Chobe Rivers.

you'll find plenty of tasty South African wine and beer. Don't expect TVs or elevators, even at very expensive camps.

⇨ *For information on converters and electricity while on Safari, see Electricity, in the Planning Your Safari chapter.*

MOBILE SAFARIS

Often incorrectly viewed only as a cost-cutting measure, the range of mobile safari options in Botswana is staggering. At the top end, your large walk-in en-suite tent will have Persian rugs, antique furniture and flush toilets; at the other extreme, you will help with the cooking and even setting up camp. The most popular option lies somewhere in the middle—a nonparticipatory safari with en-suite tents, hot-water bucket showers, and a talented chef who can create delicious three course meals that would rival many lodges all on an open fire. As well as feeling closer to nature (lions can easily walk through your camp at night), mobile safari guides tend to be the most knowledgeable in the country and spending 10 days with the same guide as you move through different habitats gives you a greater depth of understanding. It also gives the guide the opportunity to tailor the focus of game drives to your specific interests, helped by the inherent flexible nature of mobiles. The one downside is that although you will have your own private campsite, you will probably be in the national parks so will see other vehicles during the day.

DINING AND LODGING PRICES

Most lodging prices are quoted in U.S. dollars, and you can use dollars, euros, or South African rand as tips wherever you stay. The average price per person per night at private lodges is US$500–US$1,000, which includes accommodations, all game activities, all meals, soft drinks, and good South African wine. Camps arrange transfers from the nearest airport or airstrip.

■TIP→ It's important to note that there are few budget lodging options available in Botswana, and most of the camps we write about fall into the "luxury" category.

WHAT IT COSTS IN U.S. DOLLARS			
$	$$	$$$	$$$$
Hotels	under $250	$250–$450	$451–$600	over $600
Dining	under $12	$12–$20	$21–$30	over $30

Prices in the restaurant reviews are the average cost of a main course at dinner or, if dinner isn't served, at lunch; taxes and service charges are generally included. Prices in the lodging reviews are the lowest cost of a standard double room in high season.

GOING GREEN

In such a pristine, finely balanced environment, it's vital to limit the impact on the flora and fauna, and many safari companies are now installing ecologically sound practices. Gone are the days of camps accruing mountains of empty, plastic water bottles—almost all lodges (and some mobile operators) will give you metal water bottles to fill and reuse with filtered drinking water from their reverse osmosis plants. Solar power is also slowly taking over from noisy, diesel-guzzling generators. In addition, the major companies run a range of community initiatives aimed at ensuring the local Batswana population see the benefits from the unique habitat and its wildlife, creating a framework for long-term sustainable tourism.

VISITOR INFORMATION

Visit Botswana Tourism's website for tour operator and travel agency information. To be listed on the website, these organizations must satisfy and adhere to the high standards demanded by Botswana Tourism.

Contacts **Botswana Tourism Organization** ⊕ *www.botswanatourism.co.bw.*

MUST-SEE PARKS

You'd probably like to see all of Botswana, but we know that's not always possible. The chapter has been broken down by Must-See Parks (Okavango Delta, Moremi Game Reserve, Chobe National Park, and the Kwando, Linyanti and Selinda Reserves) and If You Have Time Areas (Central Kalahari Game Reserve, Makgadikgadi Pans and Tuli Block) to help you better organize your time. We suggest, though, that you read about all of them and then choose which one is best for you.

THE OKAVANGO DELTA

Game
★★★★★
Park Accessibility
★★★
Getting Around
★★★★
Accommodations
★★★★★
Scenic Beauty
★★★★★

There's no place on earth like the Okavango. The world's largest inland delta, the Okavango was formed by the Okavango River, which floods down from the Angolan highlands once a year and fans out into northwestern Botswana in a meandering complex network of papyrus-lined channels, deep, still pools (where crocodiles and hippos lurk), secret waterways (where reeds and grass almost meet over your head), palm-fringed islands, and natural lagoons.

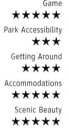

8

This watery network covers an area of more than 15,000 square km (5,791 square miles). This vast area is sometimes referred to as the Swamps, but this gives a false impression because there are no murky mangroves or sinister everglades here. It's just open, crystal-clear waters where you'll discover an unparalleled experience of being in one of the world's last great wilderness areas. Often, the only way to get around this network of waterways is by boat.

The *mokoro*, a canoelike boat synonymous with the Okavango, was introduced to the Delta in the mid-18th century, when the Bayei people moved down from the Zambezi. The Bayei invented the mokoro as a controllable craft that could be maneuvered up- or downstream. These boats were traditionally made from the trunks of the great jackalberry, morula, and sausage trees. Today, because of the need to protect the trees, you may find yourself in the modern equivalent: a fiberglass canoe. Either way, a skilled poler (think gondolier) will stand or sit at the rear of the narrow craft guiding you through the Delta's waterways—he'll be on full alert for the ubiquitous and unpredictable hippos but may be a bit more laid-back when it comes to the mighty crocs that lie in the sun. (Powerboats are an option in deeper waters.) Bird-watching from these boats is a special thrill: the annual return of thousands of gorgeous carmine bee-eaters to the northern Delta and Linyanti in September and October is a dazzling sight, as is a glimpse of the huge orange-color

Pel's fishing owl. ■ TIP→ Don't miss the chance to go on a guided walk on one of the many islands.

Although most camps are now both land- and water-based, in a water camp—usually an island surrounded by water—you'll almost certainly see elephants, hippos, crocs, and red *lechwes* (beautiful antelope endemic to the Swamps), and you may catch a glimpse of the rare, aquatic sitatunga antelope. You'll almost certainly hear lions but may not always see them; if you're very lucky, you may see a pride swimming between islands. On the other hand, if you're in a land-and-water camp, you'll see lots of game. Remember that you'll see plenty of animals elsewhere in Botswana. You're in the Delta to experience the unforgettable beauty.

GETTING HERE AND AROUND

You'll fly into Maun and then be transferred by your tour operator to a small plane that'll bring you to an airstrip in the Delta. Distance from the airstrip to camps varies, but normally won't be much longer than 20–25 minutes and this is often an exciting game drive through the bush. Roads are bumpy—but you're in a game vehicle.

WHERE TO STAY

LUXURY LODGES

$$$$ **Delta Camp.** This enchanting camp is set deep on an island in the Okan-
FAMILY vango. Reed chalets, each with a private bathroom, are furnished with wood furniture and upturned mekoro; they look like something straight out of *The Swiss Family Robinson*. Each chalet faces northeast to catch the first rays of the sun as it rises above the palm trees, and below your windows are shallow, bird-filled pools, with deep waterways only paces from your front door. Family-owned for many years, the camp has an intimate, relaxed atmosphere; the goal here is to experience the tranquility of the environment. Activities include guided mokoro trails into the maze of waterways and game walks on adjacent islands with a professional, licensed guide. In addition to being completely solar-powered, the lack of motorboats is a major conservation plus, as the emphasis is on preserving the pristine purity of the environment. This adds immeasurably to the relaxed, peaceful atmosphere that pervades this lovely camp. **Pros:** splendid isolation; no noises from motorboats; accepts children of all ages. **Cons:** if you want to go powerboating, this is not the place; comfortable but not luxurious accommodation. $ *Rooms from: US$885 ⊠ Okavango Delta ☎ 686–1154 ⊕ www.deltacampbotswana. com ⇄ 10 tents ⦿ All meals.*

$$$$ **Jao Camp.** Spectacular Jao (as in "now"), a pure Hollywood-meets-Africa fantasy, is on a densely wooded island in a private concession bordering the Moremi Wildlife Reserve. Land and water activities are available, depending on the seasonal water levels, so you can take a day or night game drive in an open 4x4, glide in a mokoro through rippling meadows of water lilies, chug along hippo highways in a motorboat, or go on a guided walk. You'll see lots of predators, especially lions, which live here in the highest concentration in the country, according to a wildlife census. Accommodations are individual spacious tents

with superb views over the vast floodplains. Private bath facilities include an indoor and outdoor shower, flush toilet, and Victorian claw-foot tub. Rare African artifacts decorate the multitiered wood interior of the main building. The food is delicious and the standard of service is superb. **Pros:** African fantasy deluxe; superb service; gorgeous views; extensive spa. **Cons:** lots of steps; game not always on tap. [$] *Rooms from: US$2232* ✉ *Jao Concession, Okavango Delta* ☎ *27–11/807–1800 in South Africa* 🌐 *www.wilderness-safaris.com* 🛏 *9 tents* 🍴 *All meals.*

A HAZARDOUS HERBIVORE

They may look cute and harmless, but hippos are responsible for more human fatalities than any other large animal in Africa. Though they're not threatening creatures by nature and quickly retreat to water at any sign of danger, the trouble occurs when people get between a hippo and its water.

$$$$ 🏨 **Kwetsani Camp.** Perched on high wooden stilts amid a forest canopy on a small island surrounded by enormous open plains, Kwetsani is one of the loveliest of the delta camps. The public areas overlooking the floodplains are built around huge, ancient trees, with a giant jackalberry dominating the bar. Each spacious room, made of canvas, wood, and slatted poles, is set like a child's building block in the middle of a large wooden deck built high into the trees. Polished wooden floors; coir mats; comfy armchairs; butlers' tables with tea, coffee, and biscuits; billowing mosquito nets; cow-hide covered ottomans; and indoor and outdoor showers all contribute to a warm, homey atmosphere. After enjoying a game drive or mokoro trip, end your day with a sundowner (cocktail) party by the lagoon lighted by flickering lanterns, with entertainment by the best in local talent—snorting hippos, whooping hyenas, and keening waterbirds. **Pros:** gorgeous views; genuine delta feel. **Cons:** game can be sporadic. [$] *Rooms from: US$1369* ✉ *Jao Concession, Okavango Delta* ☎ *27–11/807–1800 in South Africa* 🌐 *www.kwetsani.com* 🛏 *5 Tents* 🍴 *All meals.*

$$$$ FAMILY 🏨 **Sandibe Okavango Safari Lodge.** A land and water camp run by &Beyond, Sandibe clings to the edge of a pristine channel of the Santantadibe River. Go fishing, take a mokoro ride through tunnels of interlacing papyrus, walk on a palm-studded island, or track big game in an open-sided vehicle. Watch out for some Okavango-specific animals like the secretive sitatunga—a rare, aquatic antelope. The camp, which is set in a lush forest, was completely rebuilt in 2014 and has a unique modern design full of light, curves, and cavernous archways with wooden shingled roofs echoing the plated armor of a pangolin. It'll be difficult to tear yourself away from your cozy stilted cottage with its free-standing fireplace, split-level viewing deck, and plunge pool. However, the main lodge has a massage sala with delta views that might do for awhile. After a splendid dinner, enjoy a nightcap around a crackling fire under a star-studded sky. Like the other &Beyond camps, Sandibe welcomes children of all ages and has a special kids program. **Pros:** beautiful, stylish accommodation; great game. **Cons:** might be

"Obviously not happy with our encroachment, this hippo signals that we should move away before his splashing turns into a charge." —hslogan, Fodors.com member

too modern for some. $ *Rooms from: US$1940* ✉ *Okavango Delta* ☎ *27–11/809–4300* ⊕ *www.sandibe.com* ⇨ *12 cottages* ⦿ *All meals.*

$$$$ 🏨 **Vumbura Plains.** If it's old-style African safari ambience you're looking for, then this camp is not for you. These state-of-the-art buildings are all about space, shape, light, and texture on a grand scale. Public areas are decorated with rag rugs, beaded throws, enticing hanging chairs and some exquisite indigenous African artwork. The art deco–style carved wooden bar divides the lounge area from the dining area, which is decorated with dry hollow palm trunks and hanging lamps that mimic the local sausage trees. Sip your coffee or after-dinner drinks in deep padded L-shape sofas by firelight on the deck as frogs pipe and fireflies dance. ⚠ There are many steps and long up-and-down boardwalks between the widely spaced rooms. If this seems a bit challenging, you may want to stay someplace else. Each en-suite room has a huge wooden outside deck, with comfortable lie-out chairs, a *sala* (thatched, outdoor daybed area), and plunge pool, and the enclosed living spaces have floor-to-ceiling windows and mesh doors that capture every source of light, from the early rays of dawn to the blazing sunset. Curl up with a book in your cushioned, sunken lounge, snooze in your king-size bed, or cool off in the emperor-size, mosaic-floor shower. Suspended woven rugs divide the sleeping and bathroom areas, and the décor of cream, grey, soft browns, and moss green melds with the outside environment. Vumbura has the same community relationship with the Okavango Community Trust as its neighbor, Duba Plains. ■ TIP➔ Don't miss out on the superb curio shop; it's one of the best in Botswana. **Pros:** Manhattan in the bush; awesome game. **Cons:** not for the traditionalist;

Vumbura Plains

Kwetsani

Jao

rooms have an open floor plan. $ *Rooms from: US$2232* ✉ *Vumbura Concession, Okavango Delta* ☎ *27–11/807–1800* 🌐 *www.wilderness-safaris.com* 🛏 *14 rooms* 🍴 *All meals.*

PERMANENT TENTED CAMPS

$$$$ **Abu Camp.** You will want for nothing at this lavish camp where the main draw is its opportunity for immersion into a resident elephant herd—from riding atop to walking among their towering tree-trunk legs to sharing a mud bath. At night, a sleep-out deck above the herd even allows you to be lulled to sleep by their nocturnal rumblings. Neutral tones permeate the elegant décor of each of the six individually appointed chalets, whose verandas are replete with roll-top baths overlooking a natural lagoon, while striking, curved, canvas-covered roofs improve ventilation. Two communal lounge areas and a small gym are linked by an expansive deck where gourmet meals are served under the shade of a huge sycamore fig in a fine-dining experience that would rival many top restaurants (the bush dinner is a nine-course Moroccan tapas extravaganza!). There are no set times here: meals are served wherever and whenever you desire and itineraries are tailored to the whims of each individual guest. **■ TIP→ Ask for Tent 2 when booking—it's the only one with a plunge pool.** **Pros:** a once-in-a-lifetime opportunity to get up close to elephants; break from the typical safari mold. **Cons:** it isn't cheap; lion sightings can be sporadic. $ *Rooms from: US$2650* ✉ *Okavango Delta* ☎ *27–11/807–1800 in South Africa* 🌐 *www.abucamp.com* 🛏 *6 tents* 🍴 *All-inclusive.*

$$$$ **Camp Okavango.** Most people involuntarily draw a breath when they walk from the airstrip into this sprawling campsite. Its location on remote Nxaragha ("Na-*ra*-ka") Island in the heart of the permanent delta makes it accessible only by plane or water. Built by an eccentric American millionaire many years ago (she used to jet off to Los Angeles to get her hair done), this water camp combines style, comfort, and a year-round water wilderness experience. Huge trees arch over an outdoor lounge with sweeping lawns leading down to the water, where hippos snort all night. Your tent, with private bathroom, is built on a raised wooden platform that overlooks the delta. It's set among groves of ancient trees and is so well separated that you might believe you're the only one in camp. Common areas with worn flagstones have comfortable colonial-style furniture, and elegant dinners are served in the high-thatch dining area, where an original sycamore-fig mokoro is suspended over the long wooden dining table. A camp highlight: chilled drinks from a bar set up in the middle of a lagoon tended by a wading barman. **Pros:** a truly authentic water camp. **Cons:** no game-viewing by road; unlikely to see much game other than elephants and hippos. $ *Rooms from: US$895* ✉ *Shinde Concession, Okavango Delta* ☎ *27–11/394–3873 in South Africa* 🌐 *www.desertdelta.com* 🛏 *11 tents, 1 suite* ⏲ *Closed for one month between Jan. and Mar.* 🍴 *All meals.*

$$$$ **Chitabe Camp and Chitabe Lediba.** Be sure to have your camera at the ready in this exclusive concession that borders the Moremi Wildlife Reserve; you'll want to take pictures of everything. With just four tents, Lediba is run as a smaller sister to the eight-room Chitabe Camp but is otherwise similar in all aspects. Spacious, comfortable tents on stilts

8

CLOSE UP

The People of Botswana

BATSWANA

Although the term is also used to describe all Botswana citizens, the Batswana (or Tswana) people represent the largest ethnic group in Botswana, comprising around three-quarters of the country's population; many Batswana also reside in South Africa. Living mainly in thatch-roof *rondavels* made of mud and cow dung, they're pastoralists and are tied to the land and their cattle, which are used in negotiating marriages and other rites of passage. Despite the inevitable impact of development, they remain family-oriented and still live in villages with the *kgosi* (chief) as the primary decision-maker.

BAKALANGA

The second largest population group in the country, also known as the Kalanga are mainly agricultural-ists and have actually been ruled by other groups for the last 600 years. Despite this, their traditions and language have remained intact and a large number reside in neighboring Zimbabwe.

BAYEI AND BANOKA

The Bayei moved to the southern Okavango Delta from the Chobe River in the mid-18th century where they met and exchanged skills with the hunter-gatherers known as the Banoka (or River Bushmen). The Bayei are expert fishermen, and they use nets and traps to fish along the water-ways and floodplains. Their boats, known as *mekoro* (singular *mokoro*) were dug-out canoes carved from tree trunks, and formed an essential part of their daily life, serving as both transportation along the rivers and an important tool for fishing—they even used the slender craft when hunting hippo with rudimentary harpoons.

SAN BUSHMEN

Without doubt the most well known of Botswana's ethnic peoples, the Kalahari-dwelling San attracted huge publicity after international organizations fought government attempts to relocate them outside the Central Kalahari Game Reserve, where it is estimated they had lived for 20,000 years. The situation is more complicated than it sounds as modernization had impacted their hunter-gatherer lifestyle leading to larger permanent homesteads, the introduction of domestic livestock, and allegedly bows and arrows being upgraded to rifles. Conversely, although the Botswana government sensibly doesn't allow any of their policies to favor a single ethnic group, hunter-gathering is not regarded as a form of land use and they don't have the traditional land rights granted to other ethnic groups, placing them at a significant disadvantage. They are also not recognized in the power structure accorded to other chiefs. Although still awaiting a definitive resolu-tion, some of the original settlers have now returned, and impor-tantly their involvement in multiple tourism projects enables them to keep practicing their traditional way of life. At many of the camps in the Kalahari and Makgadikgadi, you will get first-hand experience of their music, dancing, and ingenious survival techniques.

are connected by raised wooden walkways that put you safely above the ground and give you a Tarzan's-eye view of the surrounding bush. You'll sleep in a luxurious, East African–style tent with wooden floors, a fine-art wildlife print hanging above two comfortable single beds, oversize armchairs and a private shower. A separate thatch dining room, bar, and lounge area, also linked by wooden walkways, looks out over a floodplain. Unfortunately, there are no vistas of water. The camp lies within the known territories of several packs of wild dogs, so you have a good chance of seeing these fascinating "painted wolves." The area has a variety of habitats, from marshlands and riverine areas to open grasslands and seasonally flooded plains. Although it's on one of the most beautiful islands in the delta, it's not really a water camp because it doesn't offer water activities. **Pros:** very good chance to see wild dogs. **Cons:** no water activities. $ *Rooms from: US$1498* ✉ *Chitabe Concession, Okavango Delta* ☏ *27–11/807–1800 in South Africa* ⊕ *www. wilderness-safaris.com* ↪ *12 tents* ⍾ *All meals.*

$$$$ ⛺ **Duba Plains.** Built on an island that can be reached only by plane, Fodor's Choice this tiny camp is shaded by ebony, fig, and garcinia trees, and sur-★   rounded by vast plains—which are flooded from about May to early October, depending on the rains—the camp is ideal for true wilderness buffs. When the water is high, the game compete with the camp for dry ground, and lions and hyenas become regular dusk-to-dawn visitors. You can watch hundreds of buffalo, lions, leopards, elephants, hippos, and the athletic, semi-aquatic red lechwe antelope from one of only three 4x4 open-game vehicles in the reserve. The Duba lion prides are among the few to hunt by day—they have a taste for buffalo— and if you're really lucky, you might find yourself and your vehicle bang in the middle of one of these spectacular hunts. The area is also a birder's paradise, with an abundance of waterfowl. En-suite tents with ceiling fans and gleaming Rhodesian teak furniture complement stupendous views. There's a comfy lounge and bar in the public area as well as a small pool. The camp is in the Kwedi Reserve, a massive wildlife sanctuary that also encompasses the Vumbura concession and has been ceded by the Botswana Government and the Tawana Land Board to the people who live in the north of the delta. The aim is that the local people benefit from the wildlife that tourists come to see in their "backyard," so to speak. Annual payments are made to a trust called the Okavango Community Trust, which represents the interests of all the people living in the five villages to the north of the Okavango. **Pros:** some of the delta's best game-viewing with lions hunting by day; maximum of 3 vehicles in the whole concession. **Cons:** accommodation is quite basic, but comfortable. $ *Rooms from: US$1620* ✉ *Okavango Delta* ☏ *27–87/354–6591 in South Africa* ⊕ *www.dubaplains.com* ↪ *6 tents* ⍾ *All-inclusive.*

$$$$ ⛺ **Eagle Island Camp.** You'll find this camp deep in the central delta on Xaxaba (pronounced "ka-*ka*-ba") Island, which is surrounded by pristine waterways, tall palm trees, and vast floodplains. At dawn and dusk hippos chortle, birds call, and hyenas whoop. Activities here are foot- and water-based. You'll glide through high, emerald-green papyrus tunnels in a mokoro; go powerboating on wide lagoons; or enjoy

sundowners as you float silently in your mokoro on crystal-clear water as the sun sets in a blaze of red and gold. Or have a front-row seat for the same nightly spectacle—a sunset—in the Fish Eagle Bar, which juts out over the water. Large walk-in tents are decorated in traditional African style with four-poster beds and lamps fashioned out of Botswana baskets and carved African pots. Sit out on your huge veranda, or snooze in the inviting canvas hammock. Dine in style in the elegant dining room where local artwork adds to the classic safari ambience. The main viewing deck overlooks vast expanses of water complete with dozing hippos. At this writing the camp is scheduled for a complete refurbishment in the first half of 2015. **Pros:** gorgeous views of the delta; genuine delta water experience. **Cons:** this is a water camp, so no game drives. [$] *Rooms from: US$1733* ✉ *Okavango Delta* ☎ *27–21/483–1600 in South Africa* 🌐 *www.belmondsafaris.com* 🛏 *11 tents, 1 suite* 🍴 *All-inclusive.*

DID YOU KNOW?

Wondering where Nxabega Okavango Safari Camp got its interesting name? *Nxabega* (pronounced "Na-becka") means "place of the giraffe" in the language of the Bayei, who live nearby in the most remote parts of the Delta. Needless to say, giraffes aren't the only animals here. The Okavango has lions, elephants, antelopes, hippos, and many other species.

$$$$ 🏨 **Kanana Camp.** The simple natural charm of Kanana makes you feel part of the delta, not cocooned away from it. Game drives, mokoroing, boating, and bush walks (there are resident Pel's fishing owls on nearby islands) are all part of the experience, but a visit to the Thapagadi Lagoon is a must. The lagoon is home to a fantastic heronry, where maribou, open-billed and yellow-billed storks nest with all kinds of herons, cormorants, pelicans, darters, and egrets—you'll never forget the sounds of this avian community. Safari tents (where tea and coffee are brought at dawn by a cheerful staff member) with wooden decks overlook dense reed beds and a papyrus-thick floodplain. Dark-wood furniture is complemented by colorful rugs and throws, while the bathroom features a glass-walled shower and twin basins. You'll fall asleep to the sound of hippos munching, squelching, and splashing outside your tent and awake to tumultuous birdsong. Public areas are built around a massive ancient fig tree, where green pigeons feast as you enjoy imaginative food on the dining deck. With 360-degree views of the surrounding floodplain, the über-romantic, raised sleep-out deck located a short drive from camp is an unforgettable experience. **Pros:** superb birding in the nearby heronry; private sleep-out deck. **Cons:** predators not on tap. [$] *Rooms from: US$890* ✉ *Kanana Private Concession, Okavango Delta* ☎ *686–1226* 🌐 *www.kerdowneybotswana.com* 🛏 *8 tents* 🍴 *All meals.*

$$$$ Fodor's Choice ★ 🏨 **Little Vumbura.** This "goldilocks" of the safari circuit appears to have it all: situated on its own, tiny private island, Little Vumbura has a genuine water camp feel, yet just a five-minute boat drive away lies the predator-packed Vumbura concession. Conical, canvas roofs peek above tall, wispy papyrus in an almost seamless transition between artifice

and nature. Inside the en-suite tents, grass mats decorate a wooden floor on which sits a writing desk, armchair, and twin beds, splashed with aquamarine cushions, while wooden sliding doors reveal your outside deck furnished with a futon. The inviting open-walled lounge has ethnic ornaments and wicker furniture colored by multiple shades of cobalt and sapphire, echoing the surrounding waters. A winding walkway climbs up to a small look-out library with hanging chairs below which mekoro sit ready among the lapping waves. Sip your pre-dinner drink on a floating deck beneath countless twinkling stars, warmed by a crackling fire. Your only dilemma will be whether to leave your intimate, cocooned environment to track the predators that roam the mainland. **Pros:** best of both land and water activities; tranquil, relaxed ambience. **Cons:** separate shower room is a bit small; can get booked up a long way in advance. $ *Rooms from: US$1498* ⊠ *Vumbura Concession, Okavango Delta* ☎ *27–11/807–1800 in South Africa* ⊕ *www. littlevumbura.com* ⏎ *6 tents* ⏐◯⏐ *All-inclusive.*

$$$$ ⬚ **Macatoo Camp.** Be prepared to get wet as you gallop through knee-deep, crystal-clear floodwaters among herds of giraffe on your chosen steed at Macatoo Camp. Wade past oblivious, munching elephants, before arriving at the tree house—a deck built into the canopy of a gigantic strangler fig, where dry clothing materializes and brunch is hoisted 5 meters from the ground via an ingenious dumb-waiter pulley system. A laid-back atmosphere pervades the unpretentious camp—eight simple but comfortably furnished en-suite tents sit on elevated decks, and the mess tent's sumptuous leather sofas will soothe weary limbs while you gaze at monochrome prints reminding you of the day's adventures. A honeymoon tent with roll-top bath and his-and-hers basins is available for a supplement. After the morning's exertions, recline on rattan loungers beneath swaying weaver nests or cool off in the communal plunge pool overlooking an emerald floodplain. Shorter afternoon rides are more sedate or you can opt for a game drive, mokoro excursion, or guided walk—activities also available to nonriders. Bush dinners can be a treat when a live termite mound doubles up as a delicious pizza oven. **Pros:** an alternative safari perspective; stable of 50 horses ensures a match for your riding style. **Cons:** riders must be experienced; no plug sockets in rooms. $ *Rooms from: US$925* ⊠ *Okavango Delta* ☎ *686–1523* ⊕ *www.africanhorseback.com* ⏎ *8 tents* ⏐◯⏐ *All-inclusive.*

$$$$ ⬚ **Nxabega Okavango Safari Camp.** Renowned for its beauty, Nxabega
FAMILY (pronounced "*na*-becka") is in the very heart of the delta and offers both a water and a land experience. The camp overlooks wetlands, delta channels, and grassy floodplains, which host lion, leopard (rarely seen), elephant, and buffalo, as well as several unique bird species; African ebony and strangler figs shade the main camp. Because it's a private concession, you can take a night drive in an open vehicle and spot big predators as well as the small nocturnal ones like civets (black-and-white badger-looking creatures), bush babies (similar to furry, flying squirrels), and genets (small spotted cats). En-suite safari tents are on raised teak platforms, each with a private veranda overlooking the water and bush. The main lodge is made of thatch and wood; the high-roofed and

paneled dining room has an almost medieval banquet-hall feel. The food is excellent but don't worry, you'll lose some of those extra calories by taking a guided walk on one of the nearby islands to track game and spot birds. Boat excursions and bush walks are offered, and the staff will even arrange wilderness picnics or breakfast in bed. Like many of the larger safari companies, &Beyond, which runs Nxabega Camp, has a community and sustainable development program in the region which they operate through the nonprofit Africa Foundation. **Pros:** guests have the opportunity to experience game drives and water excursions. **Cons:** no sweeping views of the delta. [$] *Rooms from: US$1380* ✉ *Okavango Delta* ☎ *27–11/809–4300 in South Africa* 🌐 *www.nxabega.com* 🛏 *9 tents* 🍴 *All-inclusive.*

$$$$ 🏨 **Shinde Camp.** Ker & Downey's oldest camp, and possibly its loveliest, lies in a vast palm-dotted area in the heart of the northern delta. Surrounded by lagoons and waterways encrusted with white, yellow, and purple water lilies, and home to hundreds of birds, it's also home to lots of game. Your large tent, outfitted with wing-back chairs, an armoire, and chests with leather straps, has polished wooden floors both inside and outside on your viewing deck. Spacious bathrooms have brass fittings and walk-in showers. A spiraling wooden ramp connects the dining area, built high in the trees at the top of the lodge, with a lookout deck and lounge in the middle and a boma under huge old trees at the bottom. If you want even more exclusivity and private pampering, opt for Shinde Enclave, which accommodates up to six guests with a private guide and waiter. **Pros:** perfect for those looking for the out-of-Africa experience; great predators; superb birdlife. **Cons:** lots of steps. [$] *Rooms from: US$995* ✉ *Shinde Concession, Okavango Delta* ☎ *686–1226* 🌐 *www.kerdowneybotswana.com* 🛏 *8 tents* 🍴 *All meals.*

$$$$ FAMILY 🏨 **Xaranna Okavango Delta Camp.** In 2008 she was the brash new princess on the block, dazzling the eye with bright pink, sage green, and white canvas décor. Today, however, Xaranna is undisputably the Queen of the Delta, her pointed canvas roofs tethered by poles are now weathered, her soft furnishings have gently blended their colors, and her whole appearance now graciously complements the awesome natural beauty of the surroundings. This is a water-based camp in a permanent channel of the Okavango, so although you'll see game, don't expect it to be readily available especially when the water is high from April to October. Enjoy your water wilderness experience—the beauty of the wide lagoons, the arching papyrus hippo water paths, and the glorious sunsets. Tents are huge with a living room, bedroom, dressing room, and bathroom with both indoor and outdoor showers. During the day, cool off in your personal plunge pool and lie in your decadently comfortable sala, gazing out at a sweeping lily-studded horizon as water birds crisscross the sky. **Pros:** some of the best accommodation in the Delta; great food; superb service. **Cons:** not reknowned for big game. [$] *Rooms from: US$1630* ✉ *Okavango Delta* ☎ *27–11/809–4300 in South Africa* 🌐 *www.xaranna.com* 🛏 *9 tents* 🍴 *All meals.*

MOREMI GAME RESERVE

Game
★★★★★

Park Accessibility
★★★

Getting Around
★★★★

Accommodations
★★★★★

Scenic Beauty
★★★★

Prolific wildlife and an astonishing variety of bird life characterize this reserve, which has become well known because it's the first in Southern Africa to be proclaimed by the local people (the Batswana) themselves. As there are no fences, the big game—and there's lots of it—can migrate to and from Chobe National Park in the north.

Sometimes it seems as if a large proportion of Botswana's 150,000 elephants have made their way here, particularly in the dry winter season. Be prepared to check off on your game list lions, cheetahs, leopards, hyenas, wild dogs, buffalo, hippos, dozens of different antelopes, zebras, giraffes, monkeys, baboons, and more than 400 kinds of birds.

WHEN TO GO

If you're a birder, choose the hot summer months (November–April) because dozens of returning migrants flock here in the thousands. The return of the Carmine bee-eaters and Woodland kingfishers is a dazzling sight, as are the hosts of wading water birds, from storks of all kinds to elegant little sandpipers. Although during the South African school vacations (July and December) there are more vehicles than normal, traffic is mostly light, and in the Moremi, unlike many of Africa's other great reserves, you'll often be the only ones watching the game. The dry season (May–October) is the best game-viewing time as the vegetation is sparse and it's easier to spot game. Also, because there's little or no surface water, animals are forced to drink at the rivers or permanent water holes. However, during the other months—known as the green season or rainy season—you'll often get fantastic offers by individual lodges, with greatly reduced rates. But be warned, summer temperatures can soar to the mid-80s (Fahrenheit) and higher, so make sure your lodge of choice has a pool and at least a fan.

Moremi Game Reserve

GETTING HERE AND AROUND

Self-driving is possible in the Moremi, but a 4x4 is essential because
road conditions are poor (sometimes impassable in the rainy season)
and distances from cities are long. Unless you have lots of time, are a
really experienced 4x4 driver and camper, and are prepared for only
limited camping facilities, it's recommended that you stick to an all-
inclusive fly-in package.

WHERE TO STAY

National-park amenities are better than in the old days, with new ablution blocks at the campsites. But remember, you have to bring all your
own supplies and drinking water, and roads are very bad, especially
in the wet season. The campsites aren't fenced and lions, hyenas, and
all sorts of game frequent them. If you're an overseas visitor, we suggest you stick to the private lodges. They might be pricey, but they're
worth every penny.

LUXURY LODGING

$$$$ ⛺ **Chief's Camp.** Chief's Camp is in the exclusive Mombo Concession
of the Okavango Delta's Moremi Game Reserve, the first area to rein-
troduce both white and black rhino species back into Botswana and
probably the greatest predator viewing in the whole country. Built with

wood from commercially grown forests using the skills of local builders, the main lodge sits under a canopy of jackalberry, sausage, and rain trees and comprises a split-level deck, with a generous pool overlooking a waterlogged floodplain—at high flood, you can mokoro straight from the lodge. Under a large thatch roof, a plush lounge and bar are adjacent to the dining area where imaginative à la carte dinners are served. If you are in need of some pampering, head to the dedicated spa treatment room for a range of massage and beauty treatments. Children under 9 years old are not allowed. **Pros:** always has repeat customers; great friendly atmosphere; chance to see rhinos. **Cons:** have to book up a long way in advance. $ *Rooms from: US$2430* ⌧ *Chief's Island, Moremi Game Reserve* ☎ *27–11/438–4650* ⊕ *www.sanctuaryretreats. com* ⌁ *12 tents* ⦿| *All-inclusive.*

$$$$
Fodor's Choice
★
Mombo Camp and Little Mombo. On Mombo Island, off the northwest tip of Chief's Island, this legendary camp is surrounded by wall-to-wall game. Although there is plenty of surface water in the area (marshes and floodplains), it's strictly a land-activity camp. The camp has exclusive use of a large area of Moremi, so privacy is assured. Its great wildlife, including all of the large predators, has made this area one of Botswana's top wildlife documentary locations—*National Geographic* and the BBC have both filmed here. The stunning camp has identical guest rooms divided into two distinct camps: Mombo has nine rooms, Little Mombo only three. These camps are among the best known, most expensive, and most sought-after in Botswana, so be sure to book months in advance. Each spacious room is built on a raised wooden platform with wonderful views over the open plains (you're almost guaranteed to see game as you sit there), and although the en-suite rooms have a tented feel, they are ultra luxurious. The dining room, lounge, and bar are also built on big wooden decks overlooking the magnificent animal-dotted savanna. The atmosphere is friendly, and the personal attention, food, and guides all excellent. **Pros:** brilliant big-five game-viewing; one of the best safari lodges in Botswana; 100% solar-powered. **Cons:** very, very pricey; often fully booked. $ *Rooms from: US$2577* ⌧ *Chief's Island, Moremi Game Reserve* ☎ *27–11/807–1800 in South Africa* ⊕ *www. wilderness-safaris.com* ⌁ *12 rooms* ⦿| *All-inclusive.*

$$$$
Xigera Camp. The cry of the fish eagle permeates this exceptionally lovely, solar-powered camp (pronounced "*kee*-jer-ah"), which is set on the aptly named Paradise Island amid thickets of old trees in one of the most beautiful parts of the reserve. Spacious rooms of timber and canvas are built on a high wooden platform overlooking a floodplain. Reed blinds separate the sleeping area from the bathroom with a reed-walled shower and separate toilet; you can also shower under the stars. Raised wooden walkways connect rooms to the main lodge, which sprawls beside a lagoon where a small wooden drawbridge joins the island to the mainland. At night this bridge becomes a thoroughfare for lions and hyenas, and it's not uncommon to see one of these nocturnal visitors walk by as you sip your postprandial drink by the blazing fire. The food is varied and excellent, and the staff is ultra-friendly and attentive. **Pros:** lovely setting; camp bridge often has lions crossing, which some may view as a con; very good food; indoor and outdoor showers. **Cons:**

"At Vumbura camp, the resident elephant was quite friendly and curious." —Kim Freedman, Fodors.com member

less luxurious than some other camps. $ *Rooms from: US$1369* ⊠ *Moremi Game Reserve* ☎ *27–11/807–1800* ⊕ *www.wilderness-safaris.com* ⤴ *10 rooms* ⦿ *All-inclusive.*

PERMANENT TENTED CAMPS

$$$$ ⛺ **Camp Moremi.** You get the best of both water and land at Camp Moremi. You'll see lions, elephants, giraffes, zebras, all kinds of antelope, and often the elusive leopard, cheetah, and wild dog. The rare Pel's fishing owl regularly plummets down to the shallow pool below the Tree Lodge to snag a fish. Bird-watching is excellent throughout the year; ask for a powerboat ride to the heronries on nearby lagoons. Huge African ebony trees, home to two-legged, four-legged, winged, and earthbound creatures, dominate the campsite on the edge of a lovely lagoon. From the high viewing platform in the trees you can look out on a limitless horizon as the sun sets over the smooth, calm waters. Tastefully decorated, comfortable tents are well spaced to ensure privacy. Camp Moremi's timber-and-thatch tree lodge has a dining area, bar, lounge, library, and sundeck with great views of Xakanaxa Lagoon. **Pros:** excellent location in great game area; well established with ancient trees; Pel's fishing owl known to frequent camp. **Cons:** tents are comfortable but not very luxurious. $ *Rooms from: US$895* ⊠ *Moremi Game Reserve* ☎ *27–11/394–3873 in South Africa* ⊕ *www.desertdelta.com* ⤴ *12 tents* ⊙ *Closed for one month between Jan. and Mar.* ⦿ *All meals.*

$$$$ ⛺ **Belmond Khwai River Lodge.** As you sit on the wooden deck jutting out over the narrow Khwai River, eating brunch or chilling out, you may just forget the outside world. Floating water lilies, tiny bejeweled kingfishers dipping and swooping in front of you, and the sounds of gently

Mombo Camp

Mombo

Xigera

lapping water relax even the most driven work junkie. Bigger than some of the other safari lodges and one of the oldest, Khwai is renowned for its personal attention and friendly service. Although the lodge is just a stone's throw (across the river) from Moremi, most of your activities will be in the predator-rich Khwai Community Concession—lion, leopard, wild dog, and spotted hyena are regularly seen. You can also spot plenty of wildlife from the lodge itself and the excitement of seeing a hippo or elephant stroll past the viewing deck outside your deluxe tent is not something you'll easily forget. **Pros:** romantic bar with fabulous sunset views; great game-viewing, especially in dry season. **Cons:** the concession is not private and can get busy in peak season. [$] *Rooms from: US$1733* ✉ *Moremi Game Reserve* ☎ *27–21/483–1600 in South Africa* 🌐 *www.belmondsafaris.com* 🛏 *14 tents, 1 suite* 🍴 *All-inclusive.*

$$$$ 🏨 **Camp Xakanaxa.** For a genuine bush-camp experience—no unnecessary frills—it would be hard to beat this old-fashioned camp (pronounced "ka-*kan*-ah-ka"). From the moment you walk through the rustic reception area, a feeling of unpretentious warmth and relaxation envelops you; it's no wonder that visitors return again and again. Each spacious tent has wooden floors, plenty of storage space, a huge comfy bed, reading lamps, a megasize bathroom under the stars (read: no roof), and a viewing deck. The staff, many with more than 10 years of experience, get everything right, from their attentive service to the superb, wholesome, home-cooked food. Even the resident croc who sunbathes under her very own sign ("Beware crocodile") has been here since she was a tiny whippersnapper. Wooden-decked public areas sprawl along the water, and elephants and hippos wander past your tent most nights. **Pros:** authentic, unpretentious, *Out of Africa* experience; heaps of return guests; superb value. **Cons:** the only bad thing we can say is that it's not drop-dead luxury. [$] *Rooms from: US$895* ✉ *Moremi Game Reserve* ☎ *27–11/394–3873 in South Africa* 🌐 *www.desertdelta.com* 🛏 *12 tents* 🕒 *Closed 1 month Jan.–Mar.* 🍴 *All-inclusive.*

Fodor's Choice ★

CHOBE NATIONAL PARK

Game
★★★★

Park Accessibility
★★★★

Getting Around
★★★★

Accommodations
★★★★★

Scenic Beauty
★★★★

This 12,000-square-km (4,500-square-mile) reserve is the second largest national park in Botswana, and it has four very different ecosystems: Serondela in the extreme northeast with fertile plains and thick forests; the Savuti Channel in the west, which is now once again spilling its contents into Savuti marsh; the Linyanti Swamps in the northwest; and the arid hinterland in between.

The whole area, however, is home to a shifting migratory population of more than 50,000 elephants. In addition to spotting Chobe's great pachyderm herds, you should see lions, leopards, hyenas, wild dogs, impalas, waterbucks, kudus, zebras, wildebeests (gnus), giraffes, and warthogs. Watch closely at the water holes when prey species come down to drink and are most vulnerable—they are so palpably nervous that you'll feel jumpy, too. Lions in this area are often specialized killers; one pride might target giraffes, another zebras, another buffalo, or even young elephants. But lions are also opportunistic, and you could see them pounce on anything from a porcupine to a lowly scrub hare. Bird life along the river is awesome and the major must-sees are the slaty egrets, rock pratincoles, pink-throated longclaws, and lesser gallinules.

The northern section of the park comprises riverine bush devastated by the hordes of elephants coming down to the perennial Chobe River to drink in winter. Fortunately, the wide sweep of the Caprivi floodplains, where hundreds of buffalo and elephants graze silhouetted against almost psychedelic sunsets, softens this harsh, featureless landscape where it faces neighboring Namibia.

Chobe can be crowded, unlike the rest of Botswana, because there are simply too many vehicles on too few roads, particularly in the dry season. One of the quieter parts of the park is around the Ngwezumba River, an area of forests and pans in the more remote middle of the park; the drawback here is that game is harder to find.

8

In the southwestern part of the park lies the fabled Savuti area, famous for its predators. Savuti offers a sweeping expanse of savanna brooded over by seven rocky outcrops that guard a lush marsh, courtesy of the now-flowing Savuti Channel. Savuti is dramatically different from elsewhere in Botswana; there are open spaces, limitless horizons, wide skies, and unending miles of waving tall grass punctuated by starkly beautiful dead trees—the legacy of the relentless drought. After exceptional rains and an above-average flood in 2010, the Savuti Channel started flowing again, attracting thousands of plains animals and attendant predators. Your chances of seeing wild dogs are high. Like Chobe National Park overall, Savuti is famed for its elephants, but breeding herds are only there for a two- to three-month period before the first rains. The rest of the year, Savuti is the domain of the bull elephants: old grandfathers, middle-aged males, and feisty young teenagers. The old ones gaze at you with imperturbable dignity, but it's the youngsters who'll make your adrenaline run riot when they kick up the dust and bellow belligerently as they make a mock charge in your direction.

A SUNSET CRUISE

A sundowner cruise on the Chobe River is an unforgettable experience. If your own lodge offers this experience, you'll most likely be in a smallish boat, but if they don't, try to avoid the big, noisy "Booze Cruise" excursions sold by the travel companies in the area. Instead, opt for a smaller boat with an experienced local guide and boatman.

And while you're in the Savuti area looking for leopards and the tiny acrobatic klipspringer antelopes, be sure to pay a visit to the striking rock paintings, early humans' attempts to represent the wildlife all around. In summertime thousands of migrating zebras and wildebeests provide the equivalent of fast food for the lion prides, hungry hyenas, and cheetahs that follow the herds. The Cape buffalo herds also arrive in summer along with thousands of returning bird migrants. The raptors are spectacular. You'll see falcons, eagles, kestrels, goshawks, ospreys, and sparrow hawks. In the northwest of the park are the Linyanti Swamps, also famous for their game concentrations, and in particular wild dogs. ■TIP→ Early morning and late afternoon are the best game-spotting times.

WHEN TO GO
In the rainy season, roughly October through April, much of the game moves away from the permanent water provided by the rivers so you should visit May through September to find out why this place is unique.

GETTING HERE AND AROUND
You can fly straight to Kasane from Johannesburg where your lodge will meet and transfer you. Most lodges are 10 minutes from the airport.

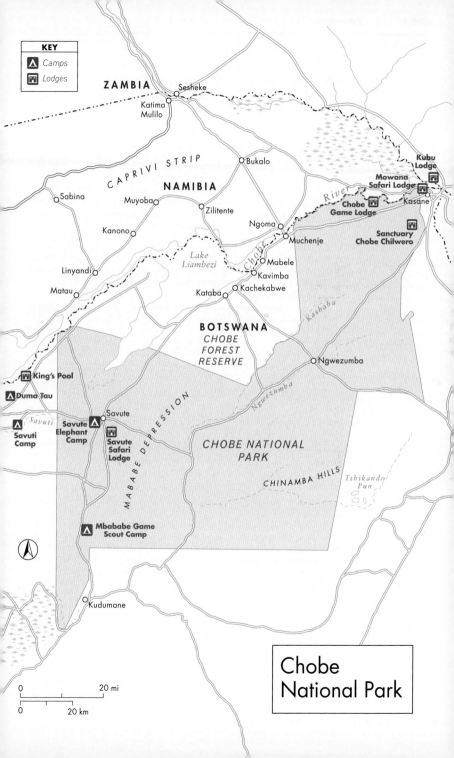

KEY
⛺ Camps
🏛 Lodges

ZAMBIA
Sesheke
Katima Mulilo

CAPRIVI STRIP

NAMIBIA
Sabina
Muyoba
Zilitente
Bukalo
Kanono
Ngoma
Muchenje
Lake Liambezi
Mabele
Linyandi
Kavimba
Matau
Kataba
Kachekabwe

River
Kubu Lodge
Mowana Safari Lodge
Chobe Game Lodge
Kasane
Sanctuary Chobe Chilwero
Chobe

Kashaba

BOTSWANA
CHOBE FOREST RESERVE
Ngwezumba

King's Pool
Duma Tau
Savuti
Savuti Camp
Savute
Savute Elephant Camp
Savute Safari Lodge

MBABE DEPRESSION

Ngwezumba

CHOBE NATIONAL PARK

CHINAMBA HILLS
Tshikando Pan

Mbababe Game Scout Camp

Kudumane

0 ——— 20 mi
0 ——— 20 km

Chobe National Park

WHERE TO STAY

LUXURY LODGES

$$$$ FAMILY 🏨 **Chobe Game Lodge.** The only permanent lodge in Chobe National Park, this grand old dame—Liz Taylor and Richard Burton got married for the second time here in the '70s—still offers one of Botswana's most sophisticated stays, although the feel is more hotel-like than lodge-like. Terracotta tiles, Rhodesian teak furniture, tribal artifacts, and the ubiquitous, beautiful handwoven Botswana baskets give the feel of Africa. The solid Moorish-style buildings—with their graceful high arches and barrel-vaulted ceilings—insulate the not-so-intrepid traveler from too-close encounters of the animal kind: baboon mothers have been known to teach their young how to turn a doorknob! The gorgeous gardens are a riot of color and attract lots of small fauna. There's a well-stocked curio shop with great clothes and wildlife books. Don't miss out on the well-run daily activities from game drives to river cruises. **Pros:** well-run operation; lovely views and gardens. **Cons:** hotel-like atmosphere; lots of tour groups. [$] *Rooms from: US$895* ✉ *Chobe National Park* ☎ *27–11/394–3873* 🌐 *www.chobegamelodge.co.bw* 🛏 *43 rooms, 4 suites* 🍴 *All-inclusive.*

$$$ FAMILY 🏨 **Kubu Lodge.** If you want to escape the real world for a while, then this small, quiet attractive lodge on the banks of the Chobe, which prides itself on its seclusion, is right for you; it has no phones, radios, or TV. Situated where Botswana, Namibia, Zimbabwe, and Zambia meet, the 11 en-suite thatch chalets are on stilts and are unpretentiously but comfortably furnished in earth tones. After your Chobe National Park game drive or boat cruise, come back and take a leisurely saunter around the Kubu Lodge Nature Trail—be on the lookout for dozens of birds and the endemic Chobe bushbuck—or go next door to the Crocodile Farm and eyeball Nelson, one of the oldest and biggest crocs in captivity. **Pros:** very affordable. **Cons:** 9 km (5½ miles) from Chobe National Park; activities are additional costs. [$] *Rooms from: US$440* ✉ *KuGo Road 1, Kasane* ☎ *625–0312* 🌐 *www.kubulodge.net* 🛏 *11 chalets* ⏲ *Closed Feb.* 🍴 *All meals* ☞ *Rates per room based on two people sharing.*

$$$ FAMILY 🏨 **Mowana Safari Lodge.** Built round an 800-year-old baobab tree situated among lovely private gardens on the banks of the Chobe River, you'll find this lodge just 8 km (5 miles) from the entrance to Chobe National Park. Like its older sister, Chobe Safari Lodge, farther downstream, this lodge is more like a hotel than a safari lodge. That's not to say that you still won't get your full safari experience; you'll just be a bit cocooned away from the actual wilderness. Pleasantly decorated with an ethnic African theme, all 116 air-conditioned rooms overlook the river, on which you'll probably spend a fair amount of time boating, bird-watching, game-viewing and fishing. Morning, evening, and night drives are available, but because the river roads are few and many game vehicles use the same roads, your game-viewing can become rather crowded. You can take a short flight or helicopter ride over the nearby Victoria Falls, go white water rafting on the Zambezi, or try a host of other activities. Children under 12 stay free. **Pros:** great location; excellent excursions. **Cons:** big and bustling, more like a hotel than a

"This baby baboon loved running up and down the branch of the tree they were sitting in while Mommy sat still. . . . I hope she grows into those ears!" —GlenRidgeDoug, Fodors.com member

lodge. $ *Rooms from: US$461* ✉ *President Ave., Kasane* ☎ *625–0300* ⊕ *www.crestamowana.com* ⇦ *112 rooms, 4 suites* ⏍ *All meals.*

$$$$
FAMILY
▦ **Sanctuary Chobe Chilwero.** Easily accessible from both the Zimbabwe and Zambian side of Vic Falls, this lodge is perched on a small hill on the border of Chobe National Park (Chilwero means "high view" in Setswana, the national language). Its 15 spacious thatch cottages are the ultimate in luxury: en-suite bathrooms with claw-foot baths, private gardens with hammocks, and viewing decks with stunning vistas of the Chobe River. Catch up on the real world (if you can bear to!) in the communications center, or pamper yourself with a beauty treatment at the stylish spa. All the Chobe activities are available, from walking safaris and fishing to game drives, day trips to the nearby Vic Falls, and the must-not-miss sunset cruises. Although you're not really in a wilderness area, the privacy and exclusivity of the lodge will persuade you that you are miles away from civilization. **Pros:** lovely views; intimate atmosphere; great spa. **Cons:** situated near busy town, which means you are not in the bush. $ *Rooms from: US$1118* ✉ *Kasane* ☎ *27–11/438–4650 in South Africa* ⊕ *www.sanctuaryretreats.com* ⇦ *15 cottages* ⏍ *All-inclusive.*

$$$$
▦ **Savute Safari Lodge.** As your small plane flies over this attractive lodge, you can see the wide meanders of the Savuti Channel before it melts into the Savuti marsh. The exterior of the main building and the safari suites are traditional thatch and timber; inside the recently refurbished rooms, the neutral tones of the soft furnishings complement the view outside your windows. A wall of glass patio doors leads to your oversize veranda, from which you can watch game drinking from the river in

Savuti Camp

Savuti Camp

Savuti Camp

front of camp. Scrumptious late-morning brunches and candlelit buffet dinners are served on a raised open-sided deck almost within touching distance of the gray, ghostly shapes of elephants who saunter past on their nocturnal wanderings. In winter, you will appreciate the cozy bar's open fireplace as you sip your apéritif and swap stories of the day's events. **Pros:** elephants galore; great predator sightings; good wilderness feel. **Cons:** if you have an elephant phobia, stay away. $ *Rooms from: US$895* ⊠ *Savuti, Chobe National Park* ☎ *27–11/394–3873 in South Africa* ⊕ *www.desertdelta.com* ⊃ *12 tents* ⦿ *All-inclusive.*

PERMANENT TENTED CAMPS

$$$$ ⛺ **Savuti Camp.** This intimate camp has only seven walk-in tents, which are raised on stilts above the broad Savuti Channel. Several bridges allow you to traverse both sides of the river in search of the many resident predators—lions, leopards, cheetahs, and wild dogs can all be spotted here—during day and night game-drives. Although the flowing channel has provided more elephant drinking points compared to a few years ago when this was a single waterhole in a dry riverbed, you should still see plenty of pachyderms especially in the dry season. The elevated thatched main area (including a bar, pool and viewing decks) has wicker furniture with plush, crimson cushions matching the stunning sunsets reflected in the water below. Spacious, comfortable en-suite rooms with snug armchairs and writing desks continue the burgundy-color theme. For something a bit more adventurous, you can spend the night on one of two sleep-out decks located a short boat ride away from camp, with just a mosquito net separating you from a giant dome of sparkling stars. **Pros:** good predators; opportunity to sleep under the stars. **Cons:** very dry and hot in the summer. $ *Rooms from: US$1369* ⊠ *Linyanti Reserve* ☎ *27–11/807–1800 in South Africa* ⊕ *www.wilderness-safaris.com* ⊃ *7 tents* ⦿ *All-inclusive.*

$$$$ ⛺ **Savute Elephant Camp.** In the thriving Savuti region, splendid, spacious, air-conditioned, twin-bed tents are elegantly furnished with cane and dark-wood furniture, an impressive bed canopy with mosquito net, and a roomy bathroom with his-and-her sinks. For cold winter mornings and evenings, the air-conditioning unit even features a built-in heater function. Your private viewing deck with comfortable chairs and an inviting chaise longue overlooks the resurgent Savuti Channel, a magnet for thirsty elephants in the dry season. As the camp is in Chobe National Park, night drives and walking are against regulations, but you'll still see plenty of game and birds during the day. If you can manage to be here at full moon, the sight of masses of great, gray shapes gleaming in the moonlight is truly unforgettable. **Pros:** great location; good predators all year round. **Cons:** no night drives; décor exactly the same as the other Belmond camps. $ *Rooms from: US$1733* ⊠ *Chobe National Park* ☎ *27–21/483–1600 in South Africa* ⊕ *www.belmondsafaris.com* ⊃ *12 tents* ⦿ *All-inclusive.*

8

KWANDO RESERVE

Game
★★★★★

Park Accessibility
★★★

Getting Around
★★★★

Accommodations
★★★

Scenic Beauty
★★★

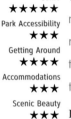

The Kwando Reserve is a 2,300-square-km (900-square-mile) private concession that has more than 80 km (50 miles) of river frontage. It stretches south from the banks of the Kwando River, through open plains and mopane forests to the Okavango Delta.

It's an area crisscrossed by thousands of ancient game trails traversed by wildlife that move freely between the Okavango Delta, Chobe, and the open Namibian wilderness to the north. As you fly in to the reserve, you'll see this web of thousands of interlacing natural game trails—from hippo highways to the tiny paths of smaller animals. This should clue you in to Kwando's diverse animal life: elephants, crowds of buffalo, zebras, antelope of all kinds, wild dogs, lions, and wildebeests. Participants on one night drive came upon a running battle between a pack of 14 wild dogs and two hyenas who had stolen the dogs' fresh kill. The noisy battle ended when a loudly trumpeting elephant, fed up with the commotion, charged the wild dogs and drove them off. There's a sheer joy in knowing you are one of very few vehicles in a half-million acres of wilderness.

If you have children older than six years, Kwando is a good option (for under-12s, you will need to book a private vehicle). The safari starts with a safety briefing, and kids get their own tents next to mom and dad (or you can share). Kids learn to track and take plaster casts of spoor, sit up in the tracker's seat on the vehicle to follow game, cook marshmallows over the boma fire, and make bush jewelry. Kids can eat on their own or with you, and if you want an afternoon snooze, they'll be supervised in a fun activity. The program's available at both Kwando camps; the price is the same per night as for an adult.

WHEN TO GO

Visit May through September. You'll see loads of game, especially predators, and fewer than 40 other guests in the whole reserve.

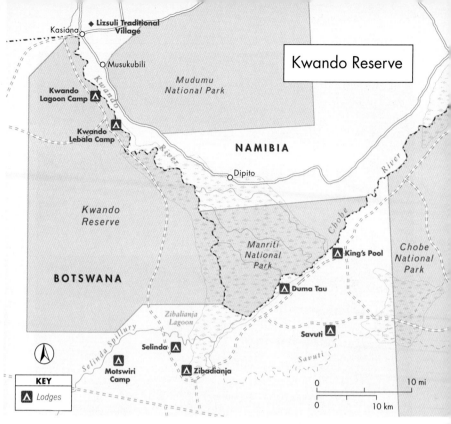

GETTING HERE AND AROUND

Guests fly directly into Kwando Reserve from Maun; the flight takes about 35–40 minutes. Transfer to lodges will take between 10 and 30 minutes.

VISITOR INFO

Contact **Kwando Safaris.** ☎ 686-1449 ⊕ www.kwando.co.za.

WHERE TO STAY

LUXURY LODGING

$$$$
FAMILY
Fodor's Choice
★

🖼 **Kwando Lagoon Camp.** The camp perches on the banks of the fast-flowing Kwando River, quite literally in the middle of nowhere. Canvas and thatch chalets with separate lounge area and floor-to-ceiling views nestle on grassy slopes under the shade of giant jackalberry trees that are hundreds of years old. After a night spent next to one of these mighty trees, a major source of natural energy, people say you wake up rejuvenated, your body buzzing with new life. From the thatch dining and bar area you can watch herds of elephants only yards away as they come to drink and bathe, or hippos snoozing in the sun. You might also spot a malachite kingfisher darting like a bejeweled minijet over the water. Go for a morning or evening game drive, drift along the

Kwando Lebala Camp

Kwando Lebala Camp

Kwando Lagoon Camp

river in a double-decker boat, or go spinner- or fly-fishing for tiger fish and bream. The emphasis in the camp is on informality, simplicity, and soaking up the wilderness experience. **Pros:** exclusivity; solar-powered; good chance to see wild dogs. **Cons:** tracking predators off-road is a slow, methodical process. [$] *Rooms from: US$1206* ✉ *Kwando Reserve* ☎ *686–1449* 🌐 *www.kwando.co.za* 🛏 *8 tents* 🍴 *All-inclusive.*

$$$$ FAMILY 🏨 **Kwando Lebala Camp.** Lebala Camp is 30 km (18 miles) south of Lagoon Camp and looks out over the Linyanti wetlands. The secluded tents, built on raised teak decks, are magnificent. All have private bathrooms with Victorian claw-foot tubs. If you want to get even closer to nature, bathe in your own outdoor shower or just sit on your sundeck and look out at the endless vistas. On morning or evening game drives you'll see loads of game, and if you fancy a freshly caught fish supper, try your hand at spinner-fishing. **Pros:** superb predator-viewing. **Cons:** no water activities; single pursuit of predators may not suit all. [$] *Rooms from: US$1206* ✉ *Kwando Reserve* ☎ *686–1449* 🌐 *www.kwando.com* 🛏 *8 tents* 🍴 *All-inclusive.*

8

LINYANTI RESERVE

Concessions can be leased for up to 15 years. It's a spectacular wildlife area comprising the Linyanti marshes, open floodplains, rolling savanna, and the Savuti Channel. Because it's a private concession, open vehicles can drive where and when they like, which means superb game-viewing at all hours of the day.

Basic choices for viewing wildlife are game drives (including thrilling night drives with spotlights), boat trips, and walks with friendly and knowledgeable Motswana guides. Even in peak season there's a maximum of only six game vehicles driving around at one time, allowing you to see Africa as the early hunters and explorers might have first seen it. The Savuti Channel is a huge river that has appeared in several *National Geographic* documentaries. Take lots of pictures, and for once you won't bore your friends with the results: hundreds of elephants drinking from pools at sunset, hippos and hyenas nonchalantly strolling past a pride of lions preparing to hunt under moonlight, and thousands of water and land birds everywhere.

WHEN TO GO

Summers are very hot and winters very cold. The shoulder seasons (April and September) are the best.

GETTING HERE AND AROUND

Flights from Maun take about 40 minutes; don't be shocked when you land on a dirt airstrip in the middle of the bush. Your transportation to and from the lodge and on all game drives will be in an open-sided vehicle.

WHERE TO STAY

PERMANENT TENTED CAMPS

$$$$ FAMILY **Duma Tau.** Rebuilt in 2012, this welcoming camp, imaginatively decorated and furnished, is in raised tent chalets with a spectacular view over Osprey Lagoon. The light, spacious rooms have whitewashed wood floors, earthy tones, and split-level outside decks. A giant, antiquated Hessian map of Bechuanaland serves as a backdrop to your writing desk, behind which lies your bathroom and indoor shower. The art-deco-meets-safari-chic theme continues in the main lounge with an eclectic mix of chairs, sofas, and weathered trunks. Although the watery view from the elevated bar is impressive, for an alternative aspect descend to one of several floating decks and hides along the water's edge. The food is creatively served and tastes superb. Before you set out on your early-morning game drive, try a plate of piping-hot porridge, a danish straight from the oven, or a freshly baked muffin. **Pros:** great predator-viewing; solar-powered. **Cons:** public areas can be cold in winter. [$] *Rooms from: US$1498* ✉ *Linyanti Reserve* ☎ *27–11/807–1800 in South Africa* 🌐 *www.dumatau.com* 🛏 *10 chalets* 🍴 *All-inclusive.*

$$$$ **King's Pool.** Despite its traditional thatch roof and African artifact adornments, there is a modern feel to this camp's main area, overlooking the Linyanti River. Twisting, dead tree trunks are mounted on

stands in pools of water creating sculptures that cleverly mirror the local habitat in times of flood. Beyond the inviting wooden bar, two sunken, semicircular alcoves filled with earth-color cushions and each set around a fire, inevitably delay diners before they finally succumb to the appetizing smells emanating from the individually laid, bleached-wood tables above. Take a break from your game-viewer and relax on a couch aboard the *Queen Silvia* barge (only when the water is high) as you watch elephants swim across to Namibia. Or you can take a guided bush walk, a fishing trip, or a visit to the sunken blind where you're eye-level with splashing elephant feet. The massive hand-carved door of your megasize thatch-and-canvas-ceiling chalet leads into an entrance hall, bedroom with four-poster bed, a huge bathroom with his-and-hers basins and double tiled showers, and a sitting area with access to your outside deck and plunge pool. Don't miss the fascinating curio shop with classy artifacts from all over Africa. **Pros:** classy, comfortable, and 100% solar-powered. **Cons:** very grand—you may prefer something simpler; game less reliable in the wet season. $ *Rooms from: US$2232* ✉ *Linyanti Reserve* ☎ *27–11/807–1800 in South Africa* ⊕ *www.wilderness-safaris.com* ⇨ *9 tents* ⦿ *All-inclusive.*

SELINDA RESERVE

Sandwiched between the Kwando and Linyanti concessions, this 1,300-square-km (500-square-mile) reserve trades the river frontage of its neighbors for the Zibadianja Lagoon, a sprawling, permanent body of water fed by the Kwando River and presided over by towering African mangosteen and jackalberry trees. It is also the location for the seasonal and intriguing Selinda Spillway. After a multidecade arid period the spillway sprang to life in 2009 as water from the Kwando River flooded the Linyanti Swamps, filling this narrow, west-flowing channel until it eventually joined up with the Okavango River. The Okavango, which tends to flood a couple of months before the Linyanti Swamps, flows in the opposite direction, leading to the remarkable phenomenon that the Selinda Spillway can flow in both directions at the same time.

Game-viewing is on a par with the Kwando and Linyanti reserves: lions, leopards and wild dogs are all sighted regularly in the dry season, along with the usual plains game.

WHEN TO GO
The dry season (May–October) has the best game viewing, but be aware October can get very hot.

GETTING HERE AND AROUND
Flights from Maun take about 45 minutes; the transfer time to the lodges varies depending on the camp.

WHERE TO STAY

PERMANENT TENTED CAMPS

$$$$

Fodor's Choice ★

Zarafa Camp. This intimate, luxury tented camp is set on the banks of Zibadianja Lagoon. A heavy, ornate wooden door guards the entrance to your spacious living area equipped with Wi-Fi, a well-stocked bar, writing desk and leather sofa. But the real opulence of Zarafa lies in the details: sparkling plunge pools, gleaming claw-foot copper baths, free-standing fireplaces for those chilly winter nights, a cooling system above the bed for summer, and semi-pro DSLR cameras with telephoto lenses and Swarovski binoculars to use free of charge. Power is 100% solar; furniture was created using recycled wood from Indonesia's 2004 tsunami; and a bio-gas tank converts table leftovers to cooking gas for the next scrumptious meal. Activities (day and night drives, walks, and sunset cruises) and meals can be taken whenever and wherever you wish. For ultimate seclusion, opt for the Dhow suites—an adjacent two-bedroom villa with your own private chef, butler, pool and even a humidor. **Pros:** understated luxury; flexible timetables; reliable game. **Cons:** rooms can be a bit hot in summer; very pricey. $ *Rooms from: US$2430* ⊠ *Selinda Reserve* ☎ *686–4001* ⊕ *www.greatplainsconservation.com* ⌨ *4 tents, 1 villa* ⦿ *All-inclusive.*

IF YOU HAVE TIME

By all means, do your Big Five, big-park thing, but if you can make the time, explore the following parks and areas.

THE CENTRAL KALAHARI GAME RESERVE

The second largest national park in Africa has its own unique beauty that's only enhanced by its vastness, emptiness, grandeur, and desolation. You won't see the prolific game of Chobe or Moremi, but there's unusual wildlife, such as the elusive brown hyena, stately gemsbok, pronking springbok, bat-eared foxes, African wild cats, cheetahs, leopards, and porcupines. And if you're very lucky, you may spot the huge, black-maned Kalahari lions, which dwarf their bush counterparts. Deception Valley—so-called because from a distance a dry riverbed appears to run deep and full—lies on the northern border of the reserve.

WHEN TO GO

Summers are very hot and winters very cold. Temperatures are most comfortable in the shoulder seasons (April and September). Game-viewing is best just after the rains (around April) when large herds of gemsbok and springbok converge on the pans.

GETTING HERE AND AROUND

Although self-drives are possible here, it's not advised. Instead, fly in from Maun. Your lodge can and will arrange all your transportation to and from the airstrip for you in an open-sided game vehicle.

WHERE TO STAY

$$$$

Fodor's Choice

★

Deception Valley Lodge. Situated on private land bordering the Central Kalahari Game Reserve, this striking thatch-and-stone lodge was the first to be built in the Central Kalahari and is arguably still the best. Built largely by hand by the desert-dwelling Naru people, the main lounge has deep-red sofas and kilims with wooden sliding doors leading out onto a wraparound deck, which faces a busy water hole. You'll sleep in a large thatch bungalow where the roomy lounge has polished wooden floors, more kilims, wrought iron, wood chairs, a deep comfy sofa, and framed bushman memorabilia. Your bedroom will have a hand-carved headboard, crisp white linens, and plump duvets. There's a separate en-suite bathroom with a claw-foot bath and outside shower. Enjoy delicious food (try the tender oryx filet marinated in Worcestershire sauce, olive oil, and herbs) including homemade bread and rolls, before sitting out under the blazing desert stars for a nightcap. Although you'll be taken on game drives and birding expeditions, the absolute highlight of your stay at this unique lodge will be a walk with the San Bushmen themselves. Dressed in skins and thong sandals, with their bows and arrows over their shoulders, and carrying spears and digging sticks, they'll lead you through the dry grass and bush on a three-hour walk through one of the most remote areas on earth. You'll be shown how to trap a bird or animal, how to make fire, which plants and trees will heal and sustain you, and at the end of the walk, they will dance and sing for you. This is pure magic. **Pros:** if you're looking for solitude, this is the place; great curio shop. **Cons:** there's game here, but it's not

8

always easy to find. $ *Rooms from: US$607* ✉ *Central Kalahari Game Reserve* ⊕ *www.dvl.co.za* ⤳ *7 chalets, 1 suite* ⦿ *All-inclusive.*

$$$$ ⛺ **Kalahari Plains Camp.** This is one of Wilderness Safari's newer camps, its first in the great Kalahari Desert, and 100% solar-powered. Situated in the desolate northern part of the Central Kalahari Game Reserve, which is one of the largest game reserves in the world and bigger than Switzerland, overlooking a huge pan, you'll stay in one of 10 en-suite innovatively insulated canvas tents designed to keep you cool in summer and warm in winter. Accommodation is basic but comfortable and if you can stand the desert sun you can sunbathe on your rooftop deck, or sleep under the dazzling desert stars. Game is particularly abundant during and just after the rains (roughly October through April) when seasonal herds of plains game move in and are followed by opportunistic predators: great black-maned Kalahari lions, leopards, and cheetahs. Other desert specialists include shy brown hyenas, endearing bat-eared foxes, and tenacious honey badgers, while birdlife is spectacular with over 220 species including threatened species such as the lappet-faced vulture and the Kori bustard, one of the world's heaviest flying birds. **Pros:** stunning desert scenery all year round; abundant game in season; interpretive walks with the local San Bushmen. **Cons:** tents get very hot in summer, even with the insulation; water is quite salty. $ *Rooms from: US$776* ✉ *Central Kalahari Game Reserve* ☎ *27–11/807–1800 in South Africa* ⊕ *www.wilderness-safaris.com* ⤳ *10 tents* ⦿ *All meals.*

THE MAKGADIKGADI PANS

These immense salt pans in the eastern Kalahari—once the bed of an African superlake—provide some of Botswana's most dramatic scenery. Two of these pans, Ntetwe and Sowa, the largest of their kind in the world, have a flaky, pastrylike surface that might be the nearest thing on earth to the surface of the moon. In winter (May–September) these huge bone-dry surfaces, punctuated by islands of grass and lines of fantastic palm trees, dazzle and shimmer into hundreds of dancing mirages under the midday sun. In summer months (October–April) the last great migration in Southern Africa takes place here: more than 20,000 zebras and wildebeests with predators on their heels come seeking the fresh young grass of the rainwater-flooded pans. Waterbirds also flock here from all over the continent; the flamingos are particularly spectacular.

You can see stars as never before, and if you're lucky, as the San Bushmen say, even hear them sing. Grab the opportunity to ride 4x4 bikes into an always-vanishing horizon; close your eyes and listen as an ancient San Bushman hunter tells tales of how the world began in his unique language—the clicks will sound strange to your ears—or just wander in wonder over the pristine piecrust surface of the pans.

WHEN TO GO

May through September you will experience the surreal, dry winter landscapes, but there is less game. October through February are the months of the migration with game galore.

"Wild dogs are endangered; there are only about 800 left in Botswana. We [saw] a pack of 7 adults and 4 puppies getting ready to go on a hunt. This puppy was very interested in our jeep!" —DAleffi, Fodors.com member

GETTING HERE AND AROUND

Just like the Central Kalahari Game Reserve, self-drives are possible here but not advised. Instead, have your lodge arrange your transportation. Flights from Maun take about 40 minutes and don't be shocked when you land on a dirt airstrip in the middle of the bush. Your transportation to and from the lodge and on all game drives will be in an open-sided vehicle.

WHERE TO STAY
LUXURY LODGING

$$$$ ⛺ **Camp Kalahari.** Offering all the Makgadikgadi activities, Camp Kala-
FAMILY   hari represents a more down-to-earth and affordable option in this area and is ideally suited to families. Spacious guest tents with wooden verandas are decorated with grass mats, Persian kilims, canopied iron bedsteads, and polished trunks. The covered bathroom lies behind an ingenious, head-high paneled wall of dried palm fronds allowing light to enter from the back of the bedroom giving it an airy, roomy feel. Go on a walk with the fascinating San bushmen who will charm you with their language of clicks and quirky sense of humor, speed across the flat-as-a-pancake salt pans on a quad bike, or visit a colony of habituated meerkats. When you return to the paraffin-lamp lit main area, a fire will be beckoning as you wash your hands with water from a copper pitcher and sit among an eclectic mix of handmade African, wooden furniture, colonial antiques, and emerald aloes nestling in golden ammo casings. **Pros:** 100% solar-powered; accepts children of all ages; horseback-riding options. **Cons:** not fancy; no power in rooms. $ *Rooms from:*

US$682 ✉ *Makgadikgadi Pans* ☎ *27–11/447–1605 in South Africa* 🌐 *www.unchartedafrica.com* 🛏 *10 tents* 🍴 *All-inclusive.*

$$$$ 🏨 **Jack's Camp.** If you're bold-spirited, reasonably fit, and have kept your childlike sense of wonder, then Jack's is for you. A cross between a Fellini movie, a Salvador Dalí painting, and *Alice in Wonderland,* this camp doesn't offer the cocooned luxury of some of the Okavango camps; it offers a more rugged, pioneer feel reminiscent of a 1940s-style safari. East African safari tents on wooden decks set in a palm grove have ancient Persian rugs, antique brass-hinged chests, teak and canvas furniture, stately four-poster beds, a flush toilet that resembles a throne, and indoor and outdoor showers. Meals are taken under a huge baobab tree or in a large, open-sided tent. The camp's highly qualified rangers are respected throughout Botswana for their love and commitment to this amazing area. You won't find the Big Five here, but you will find unique desert-adapted animals and plants like the brown hyena, meerkats, salt bushes, and desert palms. You can also explore the pans on quads or learn about the unique ecosystem from the enigmatic San Bushmen. **Pros:** exclusivity and isolation. **Cons:** no shaded walkways; the desert locale can be dusty; summer days are blisteringly hot, winter nights can be freezing. [$] *Rooms from: US$1490* ✉ *Makgadikgadi Pans* ☎ *27–11/447–1605* 🌐 *www.unchartedafrica.com* 🛏 *10 tents* 🍴 *All-inclusive.*

$$$$ Fodor's Choice ★ 🏨 **San Camp.** It's all about the view from this collection of snow-white tents looking out over the surreal, stark landscape of Botswana's Makgadikgadi salt pans. Recline amidst a sea of Persian rugs and matching cushions as you munch on miniature tea-time scones, gazing out at the infinite horizon, or make the most of the therapeutic effect of nature's minimalism in the neighboring yoga tent. Accommodation is in six en-suite tents, lit by paraffin lanterns with solar-powered hot water and furnished in old East African style. The whole camp was completely revamped and relaunched in 2011 and what it may lack in sumptuousness, it makes up for in service. Guides are knowledgeable and personable, and the food, exquisitely prepared, is always served with a smile. Guided activities include fascinating walks with San Bushmen, desert quad excursions, stargazing, and nocturnal wildlife spotting, along with safari game drives. **Pros:** friendly, knowledgeable staff; unique location. **Cons:** no power in tents. [$] *Rooms from: US$1228* ✉ *Makgadikgadi Pans* ☎ *27–11/447–1605 in South Africa* 🌐 *www.unchartedafrica.com* 🛏 *6 tents* 🕒 *Closed during the rainy season (Oct. 15–Apr. 16)* 🍴 *All-inclusive.*

TULI BLOCK

This ruggedly beautiful corner of northeastern Botswana is easily accessible from South Africa and well worth a visit. Huge, striking red-rock formations, unlike anywhere else in Botswana, mingle with acacia woodlands, riverine bush, hills, wooded valleys, and open grassy plains. Be sure to visit the Motloutse ruins, where ancient baobabs stand sentinel over Stone Age ruins that have existed here for more than 30,000 years, as majestic black eagles soar overhead.

Continued on page 487

(top) Weaving pandanu vegetal carpets. (bottom) Botswana basket.

AFRICAN ARTS & CULTURE
by Kate Turkington

African art is as diverse as its peoples. If you're a collector, an artist, or just an admirer, you'll find everything from masks and carvings to world famous rock art, hand-painted batiks, and hand-woven cloths.

African art is centered on meaning. Its sculptures, carvings, and masks symbolize the powerful spirit world that underpins most African societies. Christianity and the Westernization of many African communities has stifled much of the traditional craftsmanship by imposing new themes and, in the past, denigrating traditional religions. Fortunately, wooden masks—some genuine, some not, some beautiful, some seriously scary—wire and bead tribal necklaces, beadwork, woven baskets, and much, much more continue to be big sellers all over Southern and East Africa.

If you're looking for something a little funky or unique, check out the handmade bead-and-wire animals, birds, cars, and mobiles for sale along South Africa's roads and in Tanzania's markets.

TYPES OF CRAFTS AND ART

High-quality crafts abound, from handwoven cloths in East Africa, to stunning soapstone and wood carvings at Victoria Falls, handwoven baskets in Botswana and Zululand, leatherwork, pottery and embroidery in Namibia, and jewelry just about everywhere.

BOTSWANA BASKETS

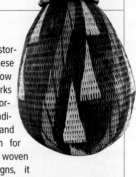

Once used for storage purposes, these baskets are now sought-after works of art that incorporate many traditional designs and patterns. Known for the intricately woven geometric designs, it can take up to six weeks to make a basket. Zulu baskets, from South Africa's KwaZulu province, can be made of brightly colored wire or grass and palm coils. For either type, expect to pay anywhere from US$20 to US$300.

MASKS

Masks were often worn by tribal elders in rites of passage (birth, initiation, weddings, and funerals) and can range from frightening depictions of devils and evil spirits, to more gentle and benign expressions. A few dollars will buy you a readily available tourist mask; an authentic piece could run you hundreds, sometimes thousands of U.S. dollars.

BEADWORK

Each color and pattern has meaning. Green is for grass or a baby, red is for blood or young women, and white is for purity. By looking at a women's beadwork you can tell how many children she has (and what sex), how old she is or how long she's been married. Beading is used in headdresses, necklaces, rings, earrings, wedding aprons, barrettes, and baskets. Expect to pay US$10 for a Zulu bracelet or US$200 for a Masai wedding necklace.

WEAVING

The striking red handmade robes of East Africa's Masai people are a fine example of a centuries-old African weaving tradition. Fabrics, like kekois and Masai cloaks, are usually made of cotton. Handpainted or batik cloths are more expensive than factory printed ones. A cotton kekoi will cost you US$15, a red Masai cloth US$20, a batik US$30.

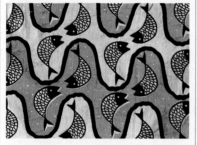

ROCK ART

Engravings (made by scratching into a rock's surface), paintings, and finger paintings are found all over sub-Saharan Africa, particularly in South Africa. The rock paintings in the Drakensburg Mountains in Kwa-Zulu Natal, are regarded as the world's finest. Central Namibia has the world's largest open-air art gallery at Twyfelfontein where thousands of paintings and engravings line the sides of the rocks and mountain. Materials came from the immediate environment: ocher (red iron-oxide clay) for red, charcoal for black, and white clay for white. Many images illustrate the activities and experiences of the African shamans. The shamans believed that when an image was drawn, power was transferred to the people and the land.

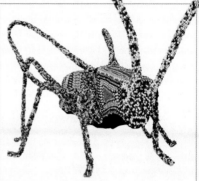

WIRECRAFT FIGURES

Wire-and-bead animals and all kinds of previously unimagined subjects are now contemporary works of art. First made and sold in South Africa, you can now buy them just about anywhere. A palm-sized critter usually sells for US$10, but a nearly-life-sized animal can cost up to US$450; you'd pay three times more in a European or U.S. gallery. Tip: Beaded key rings (US$5) make great easy-to-pack gifts.

PAINTING

Painting in acrylics is a fairly recent medium in Africa. Keep an eye out for Tinga Tinga paintings (above) at curio shops or stalls in Kenya and Tanzania. Prices range from $10 to $50; you can expect to pay upwards of $100 online. The semi-impressionistic wildlife paintings of Keith Joubert are particularly sought-after. Consult his website (⊕ www.keith-joubert.com) for locations of his exhibitions.

SMART SHOPPING TIPS

So where should you buy all of this amazing handiwork? And what do you do when you've found that piece you want to take home? Read on for helpful tips and locations across our Safari coverage.

■ Local markets, roadside stalls, and cooperatives often offer the cheapest, most authentic crafts.

■ Safari lodge shops can be pricey, but stock really classy souvenirs (often from all over Africa) and cool safari gear.

■ A universal rule for bargaining is to divide the seller's first price by half, then up it a bit.

■ If possible, carry your purchases with you. Try to get breakables bubble-wrapped and pack securely in the middle of your main suitcase. Pack smaller purchases in your carry-on.

■ Mail your dirty clothes home or donate them to a local charity so you'll have more room for purchases.

■ Only ship home if you've bought something very big, very fragile, or very expensive.

AFRICAN BEADS

Small discs, dating from 10,000 B.C., made from ostrich eggshells are the earliest known African beads. The introduction of glass beads came with the trade from around 200 B.C. Subsequently, European and Arab traders bartered beads for ivory, gold, and slaves. In many African societies, beads are still highly prized for both everyday and ceremonial ornamentation.

Still relatively unknown to foreign travelers, the Tuli Block is home to huge elephant herds, the *eland*—Africa's largest and highest-jumping antelope—zebras, wildebeests, leopards, and prolific bird life. Try to catch a glimpse of the elusive and diminutive klipspringer antelope perching on top of a rock zealously guarding his mountain home. Gareth Patterson, southern Africa's "Lion Man," lived here alone with three young lions over a period of years, successfully reintroducing them to the wild after having brought them down from Kenya after George "Born Free" Adamson was brutally murdered there by poachers. If the Limpopo River is full, you'll be winched into Botswana over the river in a small cage—a unique way of getting from one country to another. If the river is dry, you'll be driven over in an open-sided game vehicle.

MASHATU GAME RESERVE

Mashatu offers a genuine wilderness experience on 90,000 acres that seem to stretch to infinity on all sides. There are wall-to-wall elephants—breeding herds often with tiny babies in tow—as well as aardvarks, aardwolves (a relative of the hyena), lots of leopards, wandering lions, and hundreds of birds. All the superb rangers are Batswana—most were born in the area, and some have been here for more than 15 years. They have a bottomless reservoir of local knowledge.

WHEN TO GO

Summers are very hot and winters very cold. The shoulder seasons (April and September) are the best.

GETTING HERE AND AROUND

Mashatu is an easy five-hour drive from Johannesburg and Gaborone. You'll be met at Pont Drift, the South African–Botswana border post, where you leave your car under huge jackalberry trees at the South African police station before crossing the Limpopo River by 4x4 vehicle or cable car—depending on whether the river is flooded.

If you'd rather fly, South African Airlink flies daily from O.R. Tambo International Airport, Johannesburg, to Polokwane, where you can pick up a self-drive or chauffeur-driven car from Budget Rent a Car for the just-under-two-hour drive to Pont Drift.

Airlines South African Airlink ✉ *South Africa* ☎ *27–11/451–7300 in South Africa* ⊕ *www.flyairlink.co.za.*

Car Rentals Budget ✉ *Natlee Centre, Mathiba Rd., Maun Airport, Maun* ☎ *267/686–37* ⊕ *www.budget.co.za.*

WHERE TO STAY

$$$ 🏕 **Mashatu Main Camp.** A sister camp to South Africa's world-famous

Fodor's Choice Mala Mala Camp, the professionalism of the staff here is so unobtru-

★ sive you only realize later how superbly and sincerely welcomed, entertained, and informed you have been during your stay. Accommodations are in tasteful family suites where earth-pattern and -color fabrics pick up and enhance the terra-cotta floor tiles. Furniture of natural basket weave, russet-and-cream handwoven wool rugs, and pine-paneled ceilings promote the overall atmosphere of quiet good taste. Comfort is assured by air-conditioning in the hot summer months which have a heating function for the cold winter ones. The thatched outdoor dining area overlooks a large water hole where elephants, zebras, wildebeests, and other Mashatu regulars drink. **Pros:** game galore, particularly lions and leopards; superb service and guiding. **Cons:** suites lack personal viewing decks. $ *Rooms from: US$485* ✉ *Mashatu Game Reserve* ☎ *27–31/761–3440 in South Africa* ⊕ *www.mashatu.com* 🛏 *14 suites* ⦿| *All-inclusive.*

$$ ⛺ **Mashatu Tent Camp.** This small and intimate camp offers the same excellent service as Main Camp but with a firsthand bush experience. The camp is deep in the wilderness, and as you lie in your tent and listen to a lion's roar, a hyena's whoop, or a leopard's cough, you'll feel part of the heartbeat of Africa. Eight spacious tents with carpeted floors, each with a tiny veranda overlooking the surrounding bush, provide an unparalleled back-to-nature feeling. A fenced walkway leads to an en-suite bathroom where the stars are your roof. Knowledgeable, local rangers will open your ears and your eyes to the environment: on one night game-drive guests saw a male leopard up a tree jealously guarding his impala kill from a female leopard who was looking for a slice of the action, while a hopeful hyena lurked nearby. There's plenty of water in the vicinity, so the game is also plentiful—once two guests were trapped in their tent when a pride of lions killed a zebra outside it. This camp may not be for everyone, but for something truly different, real, and very special, a stay here won't soon be forgotten. **Pros:** true wilderness experience; splendid isolation. **Cons:** very close to nature; don't come here if you are fearful of critters big or small. $ *Rooms from: US$350* ✉ *Mashatu Game Reserve* ☎ *27–31/761–3440 in South Africa* ⊕ *www. mashatu.com* 🛏 *8 tents* ⦿| *All-inclusive.*

MAUN

The little town of Maun serves as the gateway to the Okavango Delta and the Moremi Game Reserve. And, despite the city's rapid development in the last decade, it has kept the feel of a pioneer border town. The name comes from the San word *maung,* which means the "place of short reeds," and Maun became the capital of the Tawana people in 1915; it's now Botswana's fifth-largest town. Although there are now shopping centers and a paved road to Gaborone, Botswana's capital, cement block houses and mud huts still give Maun a rural feel, especially as goats and donkeys litter the roads.

The town spreads along the banks of the Thamalakane River, and it's possible to take mokoro trips into the Delta directly from Maun. It's also a good base from which to explore the Tsolido hills and the Makgadikgadi Pans by road.

The bustling airport has new runways and planes of all sizes taking off and landing at all hours of the day, delivering tourists to and from the tourist camps in the Delta and Moremi. Maun itself is by no means a tourist destination—at best you'd probably stay a night or even two before setting off farther afield. There are a handful of supermarkets, so you can stock up on supplies if you're setting off on a road trip, but in general most camps are accessible only by air, so you'll probably only see the airport.

GETTING HERE AND AROUND

Many visitors to Botswana will find themselves with a layover in Johannesburg before or after their safari. It's a massive metropolitan area— more than 1,300 square km (800 square miles)—that epitomizes South Africa's paradoxical makeup: it's rich, poor, innovative, and historical all rolled into one. Most of the sights and many of the city's good hotels and major malls are in the northern suburbs (Greenside, Parkhurst, Sandton, and Rosebank, among many others). Some notable destinations for food include Melrose Arch, Parkhurst, Sandton, the South (for its Portuguese cuisine), Melville, and Chinatown in the CBD (Central Business District).

For some ideas and suggestions to help determine where you should stay, eat, and, if you have time, sightsee, see Johannesburg *(Chapter 6 South Africa).*

If you don't fly to Gaborone, your first entry into Botswana will probably be by air into Maun, the gateway to the Delta. At best, you'd spend only a night here, though most visitors are picked up at Maun airport immediately on arrival by their respective tour operators and whisked away to their lodges by charter planes.

A local taxi is your best bet for getting around, as there's no public transportation. Taxis are usually available outside Maun airport. It's possible to hire a fully equipped 4x4 for camping, but generally speaking, you're better off and safer (the roads in the Delta are sometimes impassable) to fly between Maun and the tourist camps. Make sure your tour package includes all local flights.

8

SAFETY AND PRECAUTIONS

Crime has increased in recent years, so take good care of your belongings and utilize your hotel's safe. Don't walk alone at night. If you must leave the hotel, have the concierge or front desk call a taxi for you.

TIMING

Most people will be here only a night, if not just a few hours, so use the time to relax or stock up on supplies at one of the local grocery stores if you're self-driving.

ESSENTIALS

Banks Barclays Bank ✉ *Old Mall, Tsheko-Tsheko Rd.* ☎ *686–0210.* **First National Bank** ✉ *1–2 Ngami Centre, Koro St.* ☎ *686–0919.* **Standard Chartered Bank** ✉ *Mokoro Complex, Old Mall, Tsaro St.* ☎ *686–0209.*

Medical Assistance Delta Medical Centre ✉ *Old Mall, Tsheko-Tsheko Rd.* ☎ *686–1411* 🌐 *www.deltamedicalcentre.net.* **Doctors Inn** ✉ *Moeti Rd.* ☎ *686–5115, 7364–6408 for emergency.* **General Emergency Number** ☎ *911.* **Medi-Help Clinic** ✉ *New Mall, Sir Seretse Khama Rd.* ☎ *686–4084.*

Rental Cars Avis ✉ *Mathiba I Rd.* ☎ *686–0039, 7583–6018* 🌐 *www.avis.com.* **Maun Self Drive 4x4** ✉ *16–17 Nkwe Rd.* ☎ *686–1875, 7130–3788* 🌐 *www.maunselfdrive4x4.com.*

EXPLORING

Nhabe Museum. Housed in a former British military building, Nhabe Museum has a few permanent displays of Ngamiland's history and artifacts, including musical instruments and hunting tools. More interesting are the rotating exhibitions featuring the work of local Botswana painters, photographers, sculptors, woodworkers, and weavers. ✉ *Sir Seretse Kharma Rd., Town Center* ☎ *686–1346* 🎫 *Free* 🕒 *Mon.–Sat. 9–4:30.*

WHERE TO EAT

$ STEAKHOUSE 🍴 **Chaplin's.** Maun's newest restaurant, at this writing, also presents the best food in town. A small interior with open kitchen has a vintage theme—the front of a 1955 Mercedes protrudes from one wall while the rear of the vehicle has been converted into a sofa. Known for its excellent pizzas and mouthwatering burgers, the menu has recently been extended and it also has great specials. Service here is top-notch. [$] *Average main: US$10* ✉ *Nkwe Rd.* ☎ *7696–8484* 🕒 *Closed Sat. morning and Sun.*

$ FRENCH 🍴 **French Connection.** This alfresco restaurant, under new ownership, adds a refreshing, French twist to its dishes distinguishing it from the steak-and-burger menus of its rivals. Generous portions and imaginative specials attract locals and tourists alike for lunch and especially on Friday and Saturday evenings. [$] *Average main: US$10* ✉ *Mophane Ave.* ☎ *680–0625* 🕒 *Closed Sun. No dinner Mon.–Thurs.*

$ CAFE 🍴 **Hilary's Coffee Shop.** If you've time for a cup of coffee and a quick snack in between flights or before you set out on safari, leave the airport and turn right. You'll find the coffee shop behind the offices of Okavango Wilderness Safaris. Hilary has run this coffee shop for years, and everything you eat here is home baked, including the best breakfast options in Maun. Grab a sandwich or a salad and be sure to try her homemade whole-wheat bread. ⓈAverage main: US$10 ✉ Mathiba Rd., just before the Avis Rent-a-Car office ☎ 686–1610 ⊘ Closed Sun. No lunch Sat.

$ ✕ **Motsana.** The café at the Gothic-looking Motsana center serves tasty
CAFÉ sandwiches, delicious pancakes, lip-smacking milkshakes, and a handful of simple main courses. Wander round the curio shops while you wait for your food or make use of the free Wi-Fi. In winter, a projector and screen transforms the stage into a cinema on Thursday night when dinner is also served. ⓈAverage main: US$10 ✉ Shorobe Rd. to Moremi ☎ 680–0405 ⊕ www.motsana.com ⊘ Closed Sun. No dinner.

$ ✕ **Sports Bar and Restaurant.** This is one of Maun's liveliest eateries and
STEAKHOUSE where you can get a really good pizza and good spare ribs. Friday night is party night with live music and game rangers, expats, and local yuppies dancing their hearts out. It's a bit out of town so you will need transport. ⓈAverage main: US$10 ✉ Sir Seretse Khama Rd. ☎ 686–2676 ⊘ No lunch.

WHERE TO STAY

Hotel reviews have been shortened. For full information, visit Fodors. com.

$ 🏕 **Audi Camp.** This lively tented camp offers a budget option for the
RESORT Okavango Delta. **Pros:** affordable lodging; excellent service and staff;
FAMILY good value excursions. **Cons:** not much privacy; only four en-suite tents; all activities extra. ⓈRooms from: US$75 ✉ Shorobe Rd., 12 km (7½ miles) from Maun ☎ 686–0599 ⊕ www.audicamp.com ⇆ 22 tents, 1 self-catered house ⦿ Breakfast.

$ 🏕 **Riley's Hotel.** A Maun institution, this comfortable modern hotel,
HOTEL on the banks of the Thamalakane River, is a far cry from the seven dusty rooms built by the legendary Harry Riley in the middle 1930s. **Pros:** central location; clean and comfortable. **Cons:** bland hotel-like rooms; indifferent service. ⓈRooms from: US$169 ✉ Tsheko-Tsheko Rd. ☎ 686–0204 ⊕ www.crestahotels.co.bw ⇆ 51 rooms ⦿ Breakfast.

$ 🏕 **Thamalakane River Lodge.** Situated en route to Moremi Game Reserve,
B&B/INN this lovely lodge sits on the bank of the Thamalakane River. **Pros:**
FAMILY good restaurant; closest accommodation in Maun to Moremi Game Reserve. **Cons:** if you're not en route to Moremi, it's a bit out of the way. ⓈRooms from: US$204 ✉ Shorobe Rd. ☎ 27–74/148–3766 in South Africa ✎ reservations@thamalakane.com ⊕ www.thamalakane. com ⇆ 18 chalets, 8 tents ⦿ Breakfast.

8

NAMIBIA

9

WELCOME TO NAMIBIA

TOP REASONS TO GO

★ **The world's oldest living desert.** The Namib is everything you might imagine a "real" desert to be.

★ **A memorable drive.** The road from Swakopmund to Walvis Bay is one of the most beautiful and unusual routes in the world.

★ **Water-hole wonders.** Arm yourself with binoculars, drinks, a picnic, and patience. Open your car windows and wait for the game to come. You won't be disappointed.

★ **Ride the Desert Express.** During this two-day train journey between Windhoek and Swakopmund, you'll stop to walk in the desert, visit the world's biggest outdoor rock-art gallery, watch lions being fed, and view a spectacular desert sunset (or sunrise).

★ **Etosha National Park.** One of Africa's largest and most spectacular game parks, Etosha has cheap and cheerful self-catering accommodations, an excellent road network, and superb game-viewing.

1 Namib-Naukluft Park. At nearly 50,000 square km (19,300 square miles) and bigger than Switzerland, this park, which harbors the oldest desert in the world, is one of the largest national parks in Africa. Expect classic desert scenery (including towering, truly awesome sand dunes), but also windswept gravel plains, rocky outcrops and inselbergs, and some of the earth's strangest living things, from plants and insects to mammals and reptiles.

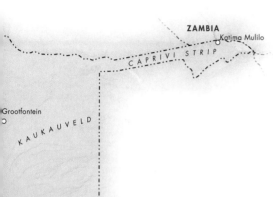

ZAMBIA

Katima Mulilo

CAPRIVI STRIP

Grootfontein

KAUKAUVELD

Gobabis   BOTSWANA

NAMALAND

SOUTH
Karasburg   AFRICA

River

0   100 mi

0   100 km

GETTING ORIENTED

Namibia is a big country, four times as large as the United Kingdom and bigger than Texas, but its excellent road network means you can get around very easily. The country is bordered by the icy Atlantic on the west, the Kalahari Desert on the east, the Kunene River to the north, and the Orange River to the south. Although South Africa, Botswana, and Angola are its immediate neighbors, if you're traveling by road, it's easiest to access Namibia from South Africa. By all means drive yourself, but punctuate this self-drive with a fly-in safari into one of the more remote lodges on the Skeleton Coast or Damaraland. This way you'll get to see Namibia's true vastness and remoteness.

9

2 Damaraland. Situated in northwest Namibia, Damaraland is a different desert from Namib. It's barren and inhospitable, but there's life and plenty of it, including *Welwitschia mirabilis*, reputed to be the world's longest-living plant; colorful lichen fields; camelthorn and candelabra trees; salt bushes; and the ubiquitous shepherd's tree. And, of course, there are the amazing desert elephants.

3 Etosha National Park. Regarded as one of Africa's great national parks, Etosha is dominated by Etosha Pan: a landscape of white, salty plains. The numerous water holes make this park ideal for game-viewing. If you're looking to do a self-drive, this is the place to come—the roads are good, and there are plenty of affordable accommodations.

Updated by Colleen Blaine

Many countries in Africa boast teeming wildlife and gorgeous scenery, but few, if any, can claim such limitless horizons; such untamed wilderness; such a pleasant climate; so few people (fewer than two per square mile); the oldest desert in the world; a wild, beautiful coastline; one of Africa's greatest game parks; plus—and this is a big bonus—a well-developed infrastructure and tourist facilities that are among the best in Africa. Welcome to Namibia.

A former German colony, South West Africa, as it was then known, was a pawn in the power games of European politics. Although the Portuguese navigators were the first Europeans to arrive, in 1485, they quickly abandoned the desolate and dangerous Atlantic shores of the "Coast of Death," as they called it. By the late 1700s British, French, and American whalers were using the deepwater ports of Lüderitz and Walvis (Whalefish) Bay, which the Dutch, now settled in the Cape, then claimed as their own. A few years later, after France invaded Holland, England seized the opportunity to claim the territory, together with the Cape Colony. Then it became Germany's turn to throw its hat into the ring. In the wake of its early missionaries and traders, Germany claimed the entire country as a colony in 1884, only to surrender it to the South African forces fighting on the Allied side during World War I. South Africa was given a League of Nations mandate to administer the territory after the war, and despite a 1978 UN resolution to revoke that mandate, South Africa held on to Namibia for 10 years. A bitter and bloody bush war with SWAPO (South West African People's Organization) freedom fighters raged until Namibia finally won its independence on March 21, 1990, after 106 years of foreign rule. Although most of the earlier colonial influences have now vanished, everywhere you go in Namibia today you'll find traces of the German past—forts and castles, place names, cuisine, and even German efficiency.

Often called the "Land God Made in Anger" because of its stark landscapes, untamed wilderness, harsh environment, and rare beauty,

FAST FACTS

Size Namibia covers 824,292 square km (318,259 square miles)

Capital Windhoek

Number of National Parks 20: Etosha, Kaudom, Mamili, Mudumu, Namib-Naukluft, and Waterberg National Parks, Ai-Ais & Fish River Canyon, and Skeleton Coast Park are among the most visited.

Number of Private Reserves There are more than 400 privately owned game reserves.

Population Slightly more than 2 million

Big Five In Etosha you can see all of the Big Five.

Language English is the official language, but it's usually spoken as a second language. Afrikaans is spoken by many residents of various races, and there's a large population of German-speaking people. The most widely spoken indigenous languages are Kwanyama (a dialect of Owambo), Herero, and a number of Nama (San) dialects.

Time Namibia, like Botswana, is on CAST (Central African Standard Time), which is two hours ahead of Greenwich Mean Time and seven hours ahead of North American Eastern Standard Time (six hours during eastern daylight saving time).

Namibia was carved out by the forces of nature. The same continuous geological movements produced not only spectacular beauty but also considerable mineral wealth: alluvial diamonds, uranium, gold, lead, zinc, silver, copper, tungsten, and tin—still the cornerstone of Namibia's economy. In addition it is also a significant resource of semiprecious stones (tourmaline, citrine, amethyst, topaz and aquamarine) and mineral specimens to buyers and collectors alike. Humans have lived here for thousands of years; the San (Bushmen) are the earliest known residents, although their hunting-gathering way of life is now almost extinct. Today most Namibians work in agriculture, from subsistence farms to huge cattle ranches and game farms.

Namibia prides itself on its conservation policies and vision. In many conservation areas, local communities, the wildlife, and the environment have been successfully integrated. Wilderness Damaraland Camp, for example, is an internationally acclaimed role model in linking tourism with community development projects. Hunting, a controversial issue for many people, is carefully controlled so that the impact on the environment is minimal and the revenue earned is substantial and can often be ploughed back into sustainable conservation.

PLANNING

WHEN TO GO

Namibia has a subtropical desert climate with nonstop sunshine throughout the year. It's classified as arid to non-arid, and, generally speaking, it gets wet only in the northwest and then only during the rainy season (October–April), which is the hottest season. The south is warm and dry, although temperatures vary dramatically between night and day, particularly in the desert, where the air is sparkling, and pollution practically unheard of. Days are crystal clear and perfect for traveling. Elsewhere the weather is clear, dry, crisp, and nearly perfect, averaging 25°C (77°F) during the day, but in the desert areas it can drop to freezing at night, especially in winter. (Bring warm clothes for after the sun goes down.)

The climate can be breathtakingly varied along the Skeleton Coast because of the Atlantic and its cold Benguela current, which makes the night cool and damp and brings thick morning coastal fog. Days are usually bright and sunny, and in summer, extremely hot, so dress in layers.

Etosha's best season is winter (May–September), when the weather is cooler, the grass shorter, and game easier to see. But if you can stand the heat, consider a summer visit to see the return of thousands of water-birds, as well as the tens of thousands of animals, to the lush feeding grounds around Okuakuejo.

GETTING HERE AND AROUND

AIR TRAVEL
Namibia's main point of entry is Hosea Kutako International Airport, near Windhoek. The smaller Eros Airport handles local flights and charters. Once in the country you can make use of scheduled flights or charter flights that service all domestic destinations. Walvis Bay—the nearest airport for Namib-Naukluft and the Skeleton Coast—now has a small international airport with flights to and from Windhoek, Johannesburg, and Cape Town.

The national carrier is Air Namibia, which operates international flights between Windhoek and Frankfurt, Johannesburg, and Cape Town, and internal flights to most of Namibia's major tourist destinations. South African Airways (SAA) and British Airways (BA) operate links to Johannesburg and Cape Town. SA Express Airways flies between Johannesburg or Cape Town and Walvis Bay.

All camps in Etosha National Park have their own landing strips. Have your tour operator arrange charters or fly-in safaris for you. Air Namibia flies directly to Mokuti on the regularly scheduled flight between Windhoek and Victoria Falls. Chartered flights and fly-in safaris also use the Ongava airstrip, as well as any of the many lodge-owned airstrips around the country.

Airlines Air Namibia ☎ *061/299–6333* ⊕ *www.airnamibia.com.* **SA Express Airways** ☎ *27–11/978–1111 in Johannesburg* ⊕ *www.flyexpress.aero.* **South African Airways** ☎ *27–11/978–5313 in Johannesburg* ⊕ *www.flysaa.com.*

CAR TRAVEL
FROM SOUTH AFRICA
Driving to Namibia from South Africa is possible, and there's an excellent road network for all in-country tourist attractions, but be warned that the trip is tiring and time-consuming because of the huge distances

involved. The Trans-Kalahari Highway links Johannesburg to Windhoek and Gaborone. From Johannesburg to Windhoek on this road it's 1,426 km (884 miles). To allow free access to game, there are no fences in the Kalahari, so don't speed, and look out for antelope as well as donkeys and cows on the road. You can also drive from Johannesburg to Windhoek (1,791 km [1,110 miles]) via Upington, going through the Narochas (Nakop) border post (open 24 hours). This is a good route if you want to visit the Augrabies Falls and Kgalagadi Transfrontier Park in South Africa first. You can also drive from Cape Town to Namibia along the N7, an excellent road that becomes the B1 as you cross into Namibia at the Noordoewer border post (open 24 hours). It's 763 km (473 miles) from Cape Town to Noordoewer, 795 km (493 miles) from Noordoewer to Windhoek. Border posts are efficient and friendly. Make sure you have all your paperwork to hand over—you'll need a current international driver's license.

FROM BOTSWANA

Coming from Botswana, Namibia is entered at the Buitepos on the Trans-Kalahari Highway if coming from Gabarone, or through Ngoma on the Caprivi Strip if coming from the Okavango Delta. Border posts aren't open 24 hours, and opening times should be confirmed before traveling. Cross-border charges (CBCs) must be paid by all foreign-registered vehicles entering Namibia, and cost about N$220 per vehicle (more for buses and motor homes). Tourists driving a rental car must also pay the CBC and will receive a CBC certificate for every entry into Namibia.

TO ETOSHA NATIONAL PARK

You can drive from Windhoek, via Otjiwarongo and Tsumeb, and arrive at the park on its eastern side by the Von Lindequist Gate, 106 km (66 miles) from Tsumeb and 550 km (341 miles) north of Windhoek. Alternatively, you can drive from Windhoek via Otjiwarongo and Outjo and come in the Anderson Gate, south of Okaukuejo, 120 km (74½ miles) from Outjo, 450 km (279 miles) north of Windhoek. The latter is the more popular route. The newest option is to drive through Kamanjab to access the park's recently opened western side through the Galton Gate, 476 km (296 miles) north of Windhoek. All three drives are long, hot, and dusty, so you might want to fly to your camp's landing strip if you're short on time. Travel time will depend on your driving and choice of vehicle, so check with your car-rental company.

DRIVING TIPS

If you're not staying at a private lodge in Etosha that provides transportation, you'll need to rent a vehicle. Air-conditioning is a must at any time of the year, as are spare tires in good condition. You can pick up rental cars at the town nearest whichever park you're visiting or at Etosha itself, but it's better to book them before you leave home. For driving on the main roads, a two-wheel-drive vehicle is fine. In some areas, though, including parts of the Namib-Naukluft Park and Damaraland, four-wheel drive is essential. In Etosha a two-wheel-drive car is fine; don't exceed the speed limit of 60 kph (37 mph). Always check the state of the roads with the nearest tourist office before you set off, and never underestimate the long distances involved. Don't drive at night unless you absolutely have to. Roads are unlighted, and animals like to bed down on the warm surfaces. If you hit an animal, even a small one, it could be the end of you and your vehicle, not to mention the critter. Don't speed on gravel roads. It's very easy to skid or roll your vehicle—at least one tourist per year dies this way. Don't drive off marked roads: Namibia's "empty" landscapes are incredible fragile habitats that cars can scar for hundreds of years. Make sure you have plenty of water and *padkos,* Afrikaans for "road food." Try out the ubiquitous *biltong,* Namibia's upgraded version of jerky. Finally, keep in mind that gas stations sometimes only accept cash and can be few and far between.

Automobile Associations Automobile Association of Namibia (AAN) ✉ *Windhoek* ☎ *061/224–201* ⊕ *www.aa-namibia.com.*

TRAIN TRAVEL

The Desert Express travels between Windhoek, the capital of Namibia, and Swakopmund, the country's premier coastal resort. The train departs from Windhoek on Friday and from Swakopmund on Saturday. Longer journeys to Etosha are also available.

Train Information Desert Express ✉ *Windhoek Railway Station, Bahnhof St., Windhoek* ☎ *011/913–2442* ⊕ *www.jbtours.co.za.*

ESSENTIALS

COMMUNICATIONS

The country code for Namibia is 264. When dialing from abroad, drop the initial 0 from local area codes.

CALLING WITHIN NAMIBIA

Namibian telephone numbers vary and are constantly changing; many have six digits (not including the area and country code), but some have fewer or more digits.

CALLING OUTSIDE NAMIBIA

You can use public phones for direct international calls. Buy Telecards in different denominations from post offices and telecom offices.

MOBILE PHONES

There's cell-phone reception in all major towns. Enable your own for international roaming before you leave home, or buy a local SIM card when you arrive (a much cheaper option, and very easy to do). The two major cell networks are MTC, and the newer (government-owned) TN Mobile. A SIM card will cost around N$10–N$20, and the prepaid rate varies from about N$1–N$3 per minute. Airtime is available in most supermarkets, convenience stores, and some bookshops.

HEALTH AND SAFETY

Malaria is endemic in the east, north, and northeast, so antimalarials are essential. Never venture into the desert without water, a sun hat, and sunblock. AIDS is a major problem, as elsewhere in Africa; sex with a stranger puts you at risk. In towns, don't walk alone at night, and lock your valuables, documents, and cash in the hotel or lodge safe. In game areas, never walk after dark unless accompanied by an armed guide.

"[T]he stark beauty [of the Namibian desert] was beyond words. The Deadvlei trees have stood for almost a thousand years, and we were speechless when we saw them." —jeep61, Fodors.com member

Because there's comparatively little traffic, self-driving visitors are often tempted to speed. Don't. Gravel roads can be treacherous.

Be sure you have comprehensive medical insurance before you leave home. There's a high standard of medical care in Namibia. Consult your hotel or the white pages of the telephone directory under medical practitioners. If you get sick, go to a private clinic rather than a government-run one.

Windhoek and Otjiwarongo have excellent private clinics. Both cities have a Medi-Clinic, and Windhoek has the Roman Catholic Hospital.

Embassies U.S. Embassy ⌧ *14 Lossen St., Windhoek* ☎ *061/295-8500* ⊕ *windhoek.usembassy.gov.*

Emergency Services International SOS ☎ *112 from mobile phone, 061/128-5501 in Windhoek, 064/463-676 in Swakopmund, 064/400-700 in Walvis Bay, 081/128-5501 in Tsumeb* ⊕ *www.internationalsos.com.* **Netcare 911** ☎ *061/223-330* ⊕ *www.medpages.co.za.*

Hospitals Medi-Clinic ⌧ *Corner of Heliodoor and Eros sts., Eros Park, Windhoek* ☎ *061/433-1000* ⌧ *Franziska van Neel St., Swakopmund* ☎ *064/441-220* ⌧ *Sonn St., Otjiwarongo* ☎ *067/303-734 for emergencies, 065/130-3734 for general info.* **Roman Catholic Hospital** ⌧ *92 Karl Werner List St., Windhoek* ☎ *061/270-2004* ⊕ *www.rcchurch.na.*

MONEY MATTERS

Namibia's currency is the Namibian dollar (N$), which is linked to the South African rand. (Namibia's currency can't be used in South Africa except unofficially at border towns.) At this writing, the Namibian dollar was trading at about N$10 to US$1. *Bureau de change* offices at the airports often stay open until late.

There are main branches of major banks near or in the city center of Windhoek, Swakopmund, and Walvis Bay, plus several easy-to-find ATMs. Ask at your accommodation for more information. Major credit cards are accepted everywhere but at street markets, with Visa being the preferred card. South African rand are accepted everywhere. In more rural or remote areas, carry Namibian dollars or South African rand. Note that some gas stations take only cash.

Tipping: Tipping is tricky and depends on where you're staying and what services you've received. Your in-room lodge-information package often makes tipping suggestions. Tips can be given in U.S. or Namibian dollars or South African rand. Most lodges suggest US$10 per person per day for your guide and US$5 per person per day for your tracker.

PASSPORTS AND VISAS

All non-nationals, including infants, need a valid passport to enter Namibia for visits of up to 90 days. Business visitors need visas.

ABOUT THE RESTAURANTS

You won't find much truly Namibian food (although local venison, seafood, and Namibian oysters are superb); the cuisine is mainly European, often German, though international variety and standards increasingly are found in the larger towns. Lodges usually serve good homestyle cooking—pies, pastries, fresh vegetables, lots of red meat, mouthwatering desserts, and the traditional *braai* (barbecue). Because of its past as a German colony, Namibia is known for its lager. South African wine, which is excellent, is readily available. ⇨ *For information on South African wine, see the box in the South Africa chapter.*

ABOUT THE HOTELS AND LODGES

Namibia's private camps, lodges, and other accommodations are often up to high international standards. Even deep at tented camps, there are en-suite bathrooms and private verandas, but don't expect TVs. Most private lodges are all-inclusive (Full American Plan), including transfers, meals, activities, and usually drinks. Camps offer at least two activities a day.

At the national park camps, self-catering (with cooking facilities) accommodations are basic, clean, comfortable, and much cheaper than private lodges outside the park. In Etosha each camp has a restaurant with adequate food, a shop selling basic foodstuffs and curios, a post office, a gas station, and a pool. Most rooms have private toilets, baths or showers, air-conditioning, a refrigerator, and a *braai*. Linens are provided. Some bigger bungalows have a full kitchen.

In Windhoek and Swakopmund, a large array of lodgings, from large upmarket hotels to intimate boutique hotels and family-run B&Bs, are yours to choose from. All urban lodging rates include breakfast, but rarely any other meals.

WHAT IT COSTS				
	$	$$	$$$	$$$$
Hotels	under $250	$250–$450	$451–$600	over $600
Restaurants	under $12	$12–$20	$21–$30	over $30

Prices in the restaurant reviews are the average cost of a main course at dinner or, if dinner isn't served, at lunch; taxes and service charges are generally included. Prices in the lodging reviews are the lowest cost of a standard double room in high season.

VISITOR INFORMATION

The Namibia Tourism Board (NTB) can provide a free map and a free copy of *Welcome to Namibia—Official Visitors' Guide*, which gives useful information plus accommodation lists, but doesn't provide detailed personalized advice. It's open weekdays 8–5. For more hands-on assistance, check out the tourist information centers (all run by different agencies, from the City of Windhoek to private companies) located in Windhoek and Swakopmund. Namibia Wildlife Resorts (NWR) offers information on accommodation in the national parks, which you can also book through them.

Contacts Namibia Tourism Board (NTB). ⊠ *Channel Life Towers, 39 Post St. Mall, 1st fl., Windhoek* ☎ *061/290–6000* ⊕ *www.namibiatourism.com.na.* **Namibia Wildlife Resorts** (NWR). ⊠ *Independence Ave., 181 Gathemann Building, Windhoek* ☎ *061/285–7200* ⊕ *www.nwr.com.na.* **City Tourism Office** ⊠ *39 Post St. Mall, Windhoek* ☎ *061/290–2092, 061/290–2596* ⊕ *www.windhoekcc.org.na.*

MUST-SEE PARKS

You probably won't be able to see all of Namibia in one trip, so we've broken down the chapter by Must-See Parks (Namib-Naukluft Park, Damaraland, Etosha National Park) and If You Have Time Parks (the Skeleton Coast and the Caprivi Strip) to help you organize your time. We suggest that you read about all of them and then choose for yourself.

NAMIB-NAUKLUFT PARK

Game
★★
Park Accessibility
★★★★
Getting Around
★★★★
Accommodations
★★★★★
Scenic Beauty
★★★★★

Namib-Naukluft Park, south of Walvis Bay, is the fourth-largest national park in the world and is renowned for its beauty, isolation, tranquillity, romantic desert landscapes, and rare desert-adapted plants and creatures.

Covering an area of 12.1 million acres, it stretches 400 km (248 miles) long and 150 km (93 miles) wide, along the southern part of Namibia's coastline from Walvis Bay to Lüderitz, and accounts for a tenth of Namibia's surface area. The Namib Desert is considered the world's most ancient desert, at more than 55 million years old. To examine the park properly, it's best to think of it as five distinct areas: the northern section—between the Kuiseb and Swakops rivers—synonymous with rocky stone surfaces, *inselbergs* (granite islands), and dry riverbeds; the middle section, the 80-million-year-old heart of the desert and home of Sesriem Canyon and Sossusvlei, the highest sand dunes in the world; Naukluft (meaning "narrow gorge"), some 120 km (74½ miles) northwest of Sesriem, which has wall-to-wall game and birds and is the home of the Kuiseb Canyon; the western section, with its lichen-covered plains, prehistoric plants, and bird sanctuaries of Walvis Bay and Sandwich Harbour; and the southern section, where, if you're traveling up from South Africa by road, it's worth having a look at Duwisib Castle, 72 km (45 miles) southwest of Maltahöhe beside the D286—an anachronistic stone castle built in 1909 by a German army officer who was later killed at the Somme. The park's southern border ends at the charming little town of Lüderitz.

The kind of wildlife you'll encounter will depend on which area of the park you visit. In the north look out for the staggeringly beautiful *gemsbok* (oryx), the quintessential desert antelope, believed by some to be the animal behind the unicorn myth. Well-adapted for the desert, they obtain moisture from roots, tubers, and wild melons when water is scarce, and adapt their body temperatures and brains through specialized nasal blood vessels. Also found in the park are more than 50 species of mammals, including springboks, zebras, leopards, caracals, Cape and bat-eared foxes, aardwolves, and klipspringers as well as cheetahs, spotted hyenas, black-backed jackals, and the awesome lappet-face vultures, the biggest in Africa.

There are almost 200 species of birds, from the startlingly beautiful crimson-breasted shrike to soaring falcons and buzzards. You'll notice huge haystacks weighing down tall trees and telephone poles. These are the condominiums of the sociable weavers, so called because they nest communally, sometimes with thousands of fellow weavers.

You'll be able to observe some of the earth's strangest creatures in the sand dunes: the dune beetle, which collects condensed fog on its back into a single droplet that it then rolls down its back into its mouth; the golden mole (thought until recently to be extinct), which "swims" beneath the sand, ambushing beetles and grubs on the surface; the sidewinding adder; and the sand-diving lizard that raises one foot at a time above the hot sand in a strange stationary dance.

Don't overlook the amazing desert-adapted plants including the nara melon, still harvested and eaten by the locals, the baffling geophytes, plants that disguise themselves as stones, and the mind-boggling *Welwitschia mirabilis,* the Namib's most famous, and the world's oldest, living plant.

WHEN TO GO
Temperatures can be extremely variable, with days generally hot (sometimes exceeding 104°F [40°C]) and nights that can descend to freezing. Given these extremes, the dunes are best visited early in the morning, especially in the summer (September–March). The park is open throughout the year, and in winter you can visit the dunes during the day, though note that it can still get warm, especially when you're climbing the dunes.

GETTING HERE AND AROUND
At its closest, the Namib-Naukluft is approximately 200 km (124 miles) from Windhoek and can be accessed by many roads, both major and minor. Entry permits for the park, including Sossusvlei and Sandwich Harbour, are required, and can be obtained from the Ministry of Environment Tourism offices in Windhoek, Swakopmund, or Sesriem. The park is officially split into four sections: Sesriem and Sossusvlei; Namib; Naukluft; and Sandwich Harbour. Entrance is between sunrise and sunset only. The distance between Sesriem and Sossusvlei is 65 km (40 miles), the last 5 km (3 miles) of which require a 4x4. The dunes are easily accessible by foot from the sedan car park. Sandwich Harbour is accessible only with a 4x4, and an experienced guide is highly recommended.

SAFETY AND PRECAUTIONS
Stay on existing roads and tracks, and always have plenty of water available (at least a liter per person in case the car breaks down and it takes time for help to arrive). The lichen and gravel plains are extremely fragile and tire tracks can last for hundreds of years. Avoid disturbing nesting raptors if mountain climbing. Campsites, which are mostly concentrated in the northern section of the park, have very limited facilities. You must be fully independent when camping. Bring firewood, water,

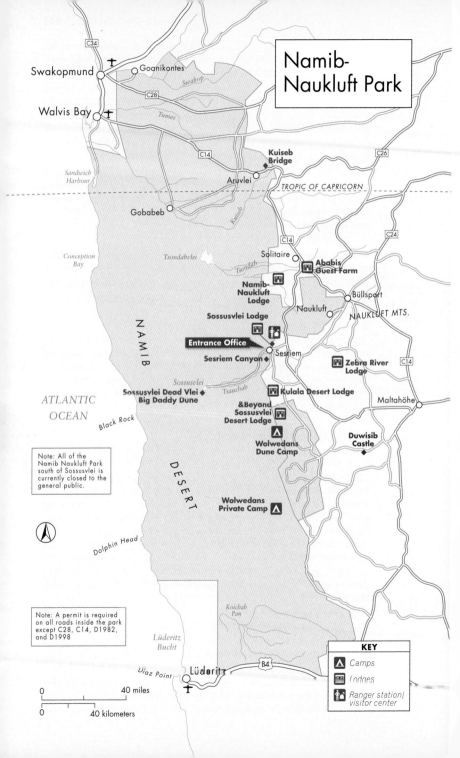

and food. Always carry water, sunblock, and a hat, regardless of the season. If traveling in an open vehicle, always take a thick jacket (i.e., a Windbreaker) as the wind while driving can be freezing (even in summer in the early morning before sunrise). At Sesriem Canyon there are ablution blocks with potable water. Private campsites at guest farms or lodges also often have water. Always be sure to inquire ahead of time and make use of dedicated campsites. Community campsites may not always have water, so if you plan to visit these, bring water for washing up and cooking as well as for drinking.

TIMING
Those only intending to visit Sossusvlei should plan on at least two nights so as to have an entire day to climb the dunes and visit Dead Vlei. Climbing the dunes should be done very early in the morning to avoid the heat. If you're planning to hike the Namib-Naukluft Trail as well, five days total should suffice.

EXPLORING

Even if you're not a romantic, the Sossusvlei's huge, star-shape desert dunes, which rise dramatically 1,000 feet above the surrounding plains and sprawl like massive pieces of abstract sculpture, are guaranteed to stir your soul and imagination. The landscape has continuously shifting colors—from yellow-gold and ocher to rose, purple, and deep red—that grow paler or darker according to the time of day. The dunes have their own distinctive features, ranging from the crescent-shape barchan dunes—which migrate up to 2 or 3 yards a year, covering and uncovering whatever crosses their path—to the spectacular, stationary star-shape dunes, formed by the multidirectional winds that tease and tumble the sands back and forth. Park gates open an hour before sunrise, so if you can, try to be among the dunes as the sun comes up—it's a spectacular sight.

TOP ATTRACTIONS
Big Daddy Dune. If you're in good shape, you can hike to the top of Big Daddy, the highest sand dune in the world at 360 meters (1,181 feet). But it's tough going: more than an hour of very hot trudging and wading through ankle- and sometimes knee-deep sand to climb the major route up to Dead Vlei (where ghostly skeletons of ancient trees jut up from a flat, sandy, dried-up lake) and Big Daddy (the hub of Sossusvlei) from the parking area. If you don't feel up to any physical exertion at all, then sit in the shade of camelthorn trees at the bottom of the dunes and watch the birdlife, or focus your binoculars on the distant climbers. ⊠ *70 km (43 miles) from the Sesriem gate, Namib-Naukluft Park* ☉ *Sunrise to sunset.*

Elim Dune. If you're fairly fit, it's well worth climbing the towering Elim Dune, the nearest sand dune to Sesriem, about 5 km (3 miles) away; it will take you more than an hour, but the superb views of the surrounding desert and gravel plains are infinitely rewarding. Be warned: dune climbing is exhausting, so make discretion the better part of valor. If you're driving yourself, check with your car-rental company for distances and times, which can vary according to the state of the roads.

9

Keep in mind that a 4x4 will give you more access and better viewing, and with a 4x4 you can park just below Dead Vlei. ✉ *5 km (3 miles) from Sesriem, Namib-Naukluft Park* ⏲ *Sunrise to sunset.*

Sesriem Canyon. About 4 km (2½ miles) from Sesriem Gate, your entry point to Sossusvlei, is Sesriem Canyon, named after the six *rieme* (thongs) that were tied to the buckets of the early Dutch settlers when they drew up water from the canyon. A narrow gorge of about 1 km in length, the Sesriem Canyon is the product of centuries of erosion. Plunging down 30–40 meters at its end are a series of pools that fill with water during the rains, which only happens during the wetter months and not very often. If you are lucky you will get to cool off in the pools; otherwise climbing down into the canyon offers you a wonderful escape from the heat of desert as you wander along in the deep shade. ✉ *Near entry to Sossusvlei, Namib-Naukluft Park* ⏲ *Sunrise to sunset.*

WHERE TO STAY

LUXURY LODGES

$$$$ Fodor's Choice ★ 🏨 **&Beyond Sossusvlei Desert Lodge.** This gorgeous glass and stone lodge has a spectacular setting in the NamibRand Nature Reserve. Its ultra-luxurious desert villas, facing a vast golden-yellow plain with misty mountains on the horizon, are built of natural rock and look out over a plain ringed by peaks. Huge desert-facing suites have private patios and sundecks and big open fireplaces to keep you warm on chilly desert nights. Shower in your megasize bathroom (even your toilet has an incomparable view) or outside in your own little walled garden. You can lie in bed and watch the stars through the skylight overhead or climb up to the observatory behind the lodge. In 2012 the area was awarded the coveted International Dark Sky Reserve status and with the observatory's state-of-the-art telescope and the lodge's resident astronomer you can experience an enthralling tour through the heavens. The food is as creative as the lodge itself; and you can enjoy the experience of dining on fresh, succulent seafood such as mahimahi under the stars. You can explore the area on an eco-friendly quad bike, go for guided nature walks or drives, spot some native desert birds and animals, or just sit and gaze at the incredible views. **Pros:** fantastic service; lodge observatory with resident astronomers; more than the usual activities available including guided or unguided nature walks, a game drive to a petrified dune, expeditions to San caves to view paintings, the highly recommended quad biking tour to see the thousands of mysterious, unexplained fairy circles as the sun sets and even a day trip to visit the famous Sossusvlei. **Cons:** the dressing room/area is in the hallway of the suites; no coffee or tea appliances in the rooms. [$] *Rooms from: US$768* ✉ *Namib-Naukluft Park* ☎ *2711/809–4300* 🌐 *www.andbeyondafrica.com* 🛏 *10 villas* 🍴 *All-inclusive.*

$$$ 🏨 **Kulala Desert Lodge.** In the heart of the Namib and set on a 91,000-acre wilderness reserve that borders the Namib-Naukluft Park, this lodge offers magnificent views of the famous red dunes of Sossusvlei, superb mountain scenery, and vast open plains. The tented, double-layer canvas, thatch-roofed chalets (*kulala*) sit on a wooden platform

Kulala Desert Lodge

Sossusvlei Wilderness

Sossusvlei Desert Lodge

overlooking the dry riverbed and desert landscape. In summer you can request a bedroll from reception to sleep on your roof under the stars. The expanded veranda at the main lodge overlooks a water hole and is the perfect place to watch or photograph the magnificent desert sunset. Activities include desert excursions, morning and evening game drives, trips to Sossusvlei, birding, and guided walks. For an additional fee you can splurge on a hot-air balloon trip or helicopter ride over the desert—a once-in-a-lifetime opportunity. **Pros:** located on a 91,000-acre reserve, this is the lodge closest to the dune belt at Namib-Naukluft Park and has its own private entrance to the Sossusvlei area; great staff. **Cons:** décor can seem stark to some; if you choose the half-board option you must pay for activities and extras like bottled water. [$] *Rooms from: US$468* ✉ *Namib-Naukluft Park* ☎ *2711/807–1800 in South Africa* 🌐 *www.wilderness-safaris.com* 🛏 *23 chalets* 🍴 *Multiple meal plans.*

$$$ 🏨 **Wolwedans Private Camp.** This simple wood and canvas camp, in the serene and secluded NamibRand Nature Reserve, gives its guests up-close access to the surrounding desert habitat. The reserve is a reflection of the diversity of the Namib Desert with its steep mountain ranges, vast savannas, glorious red sand dunes, and clay pans. Here you might possibly see the oryx, as well as more than 100 bird species including the rare dune lark. The reserve is sparsely developed and off-limits to large vehicles such as tour buses and 4x4s. What's more, a percentage of your park entry fee goes directly into conserving the integrity of the reserve. The camp itself is made up of just three en-suite doubles that share a library, kitchen, chef, butler and numerous outdoor spaces from which to enjoy the views. **Pros:** beautiful, private, and intimate location with outdoor salas and decks to enjoy the views; fully equipped kitchen and open-plan design; guided activities include drives, flights, walks, and hot-air ballooning. **Cons:** you won't meet any other guests; some activities are at extra charge. [$] *Rooms from: US$486* ✉ *Namib-Naukluft Park* ☎ *061/230–616* 🌐 *www.wolwedans.com* 🛏 *3 rooms* 🍴 *All meals* ☞ *Minimum stay two nights.*

PERMANENT TENTED CAMPS

$$$ 🏨 **Wolwedans Dune Camp.** For seclusion and green, conscientious travel in a ridiculously pretty setting, Wolwedans Dune Camp is unbeatable. Set against an 820-foot-high sand dune facing a mountain that turns different shades of pink in the setting sun, this is an intimate camp. Guests, who've included Brad Pitt, Angelina Jolie, and their brood, sit around one long communal table for breakfast and dinner prepared by alumni of Wolwedans' excellent Desert Academy. Take a game drive with the well-informed guides and learn about the unique desert fauna and flora of the NamibRand, from the heat-adapted oryx and tok-tok beetles to Pale Chanting Goshawks and the remarkable camelthorn tree. Progressive in their long-term approach to conservation and energy, the Wolwedans group recycles, grows as much of their own produce as possible, and runs their camps on a solar-hybrid system, which saves you from having to hear a diesel generator all night. **Pros:** privacy or company as you want it; excellent service; a clean conscience thanks to Wolwedans's in-depth greening efforts; outstanding lunch and dinner menus. **Cons:** there's only one honeymoon table for couples who

aren't in the mood to socialize over dinner; if your time is limited a trip to the Sossusvlei Dunes takes the better part of a day. $ *Rooms from: US$480 ⊠ Namib-Naukluft Park ☎ 061/230–616 ⊕ www.wolwedans. com ➷ 6 tents ⦿ All-inclusive.*

BUDGET ACCOMMODATIONS

$ ⌂ **Ababis Guest Farm.** Ostriches and cows rub unlikely shoulders at this intimate, historic guesthouse at a farm on the northern side of the Naukluft Mountains, near the tiny town of Solitaire. It was established in 1898 as an outpost of the German Imperial Stud Farm at Nauchas. Today it's an ideal base for exploring the area, whether on foot or by 4x4—although it's a day-long trip (and an expensive one) to Sossusvlei and back. With long hikes and short strolls around the farm, the area is ideal for hikers and very popular with German tourists. There are seven en-suite rooms with private verandas, and the English-and-German-speaking hosts will escort you on game drives, to nearby San paintings, or to the Naukluft plateau. You'll dine well on home-cooked food, and there's a surprisingly good wine selection. **Pros:** charming, homey environment; self-guided hikes and walking. **Cons:** only two rooms have a/c and the rest are quite hot; most excursions at extra cost. $ *Rooms from: US$198 ⊠ Namib-Naukluft Park ☎ 063/683–080, 063/293–362 ⊕ www.ababis-guestfarm.com ➷ 7 rooms ⦿ Multiple meal plans.*

$ ⌂ **Namib Naukluft Lodge.** Resembling children's building blocks set down by a giant hand in the middle of nowhere, this pinkish-brown desert-tone lodge sits in the midst of a wide plain of desert, backed by gorgeous granite hills. Awesome views go with the territory. You can choose to sit on your private veranda and watch the fiery desert sunset, sip a sundowner by the pool, or enjoy a meal in the open-air restaurant. The lodge will arrange outings and activities for you—don't miss out on an easy walk in the world's oldest desert. **Pros:** shuttle available from Windhoek and Swakopmund to the lodge; friendly service; stunning location. **Cons:** relatively long drive to Sossusvlei; no-frills accommodation; some expected activities are at extra cost. $ *Rooms from: US$196 ⊠ Namib-Naukluft Park ☎ 061/372–100 ⊕ www.namib-naukluft-lodge.com ➷ 16 rooms ⦿ All meals.*

$ ⌂ **Sossusvlei Lodge.** If you want to be on the spot when the park gates open at first light, then this hotel right at the Sesriem entrance is the right choice for you. Its décor—in shades of terra-cotta, burnt sienna, and apricot—blends perfectly with the desert surroundings. You may feel like a well-to-do Bedouin in your spacious and luxurious tented room, imaginatively constructed of concrete, ironwork, canvas, and leather. After a hot, dusty day in the desert, it's wonderful to wallow in the swimming pool, which faces the dunes, and later gaze at the dazzling brilliance of the night skies. There's a good restaurant serving light meals and an excellent wine list. **Pros:** great, convenient location for early-morning drives; many of the rooms have a good view on the water hole; consistent service. **Cons:** some might feel the style verges on a housing development; no bathtubs. $ *Rooms from: US$194 ⊠ Namib-Naukluft Park ☎ 063/293–636, 021/930–4564 ⊕ www.sossusvleilodge. com ➷ 45 rooms ⦿ All meals.*

9

$ FAMILY **Zebra River Lodge.** From this delightful lodge, where personal attention and friendly service are outstanding (the lodge gets lots of repeat visitors), you can drive yourself to Sesriem and Sossusvlei (90 km [56 miles] to the gate) or to Naukluft. The comfortable and unpretentious lodge has its own canyon—popular with geologists and archeologists—hiking trails, and perennial springs. Fifteen guest rooms, all with views of the swimming pool and bush beyond, are tastefully furnished and built with stone making them a welcome refuge from the hot days. **Pros:** the farm is of international importance for its fossils and birds with more than 118 species seen on the property; very peaceful. **Cons:** far from Sossusvlei; activities are at additional cost. [$] *Rooms from: US$186* ✉ *D850, Maltahohe District* ☎ *063/693–265* 🌐 *www.zebra-river-lodge.com* 🛏 *15 rooms* 🍴 *All meals.*

Continued on page 518

The Sossusvlei salt pans.

THE NAMIBIA DUNES

by Kate Turkington

Be prepared for sand like you've never seen it before: in dunes that roar, rumble, and ramble. We guarantee the sight will stir your soul and imagination.

Namibia's dunes, which rise dramatically more than 1,000 meters (3,281 feet) above the surrounding plains, are said to be the world's highest. But don't think that if you've seen one sandy ridge you've seen them all. Expect great variety here. There are crescent-shaped dunes that migrate up to 2 or 3 meters (7 to 10 feet) a year, covering and uncovering whatever's in their path. There are also fossil dunes made of ancient sand that solidified millions of years ago, and star-shaped dunes formed by multidirectional winds teasing and tumbling the sand.

Amid this unique landscape live some of the world's strangest, most well-adapted creatures. The golden mole, for instance, spends its life "swimming" under the sand, popping up to the surface to grab unwary insects. Certain types of beetles collect condensed droplets of water on their backs and then roll the liquid down to their mouths; still other beetles dig trenches to collect moisture. As its name suggests, the side-winding adder moves itself from side to side over the sand, while, contrary to its name, the sand-diving lizard stands motionless, one foot raised, as if in some ancient ritual dance. And then there's the quintessential desert antelope: the beautiful gemsbok (oryx), which is believed by some to be the animal behind the unicorn myth.

WHERE DID THE DUNES COME FROM?

The formation and structure of sand dunes is extremely complex, but basically there are three prerequisites for dunes: plenty of loose sand, plenty of wind, and a flat surface with no obstacles like trees or mountains to prevent dunes building up. Namibia has these three things in abundance.

EXPLORING THE DUNES

Gemsbok in the desert dunes of Namib-Naukluft Park.

WHERE ARE THE DUNES?

Enormous Namib-Naukluft Park—renowned for its isolated, romantic desert scapes—stretches 400 km (250 miles) along the southern part of Namibia's coastline, from Walvis Bay to Lüderitz, and accounts for a tenth of the country's surface area. Sossusvlei, the 80-million-year-old heart of the desert, is in the middle section of the park. It's a great entry point from which you can start your adventures. This desert is thought to be the oldest desert in the world. Although its geological base area is relatively stable, the dunes themselves are continuously sculpted by the desert winds.

DUNE EXPLORER

Sure, you could explore the dunes on your own, but you really can't beat the know-how of an experienced guide; ask your lodge to arrange this. Look to climb "Big Daddy," a dune that's as tall as a seven-story building, or Dune 7 (about 1,256 feet) or Dune 45 (557 feet). You could also just climb to the halfway point of Big Daddy or simply sit in the shade at the bottom of a dune and watch the distant climbers exert themselves.

WHEN TO GO

Sunset and sunrise are the best times to visit (be at the gates of Sesriem when it opens at 5 am or camp in the park), because the colors of the dunes change in spectacular fashion from yellow-gold and ocher to rose, purple, and deep red. Keep in mind that midday temperatures can peak at over 40°C (104°F) in summer.

THE SLOW PACE

Sip sundowners as the sun sinks, go hot-air ballooning at dawn, or simply marvel at the life that is found in this harsh environment. You won't see big game, but you will see a wealth of unique birds, insects, plants, and geological formations. Whatever you do, make sure you take a moment to appreciate the soul-searing and soul-searching silence.

ADRENALINE JUNKIES WELCOME

(top) Preparing to sandboard. (bottom) Sandboarding.

Looking for some excitement? Adrenaline junkies can try their hand (or feet) at skydiving, dune-buggying, paragliding, sandboarding, or dune-boarding (for the more advanced). The less adventurous (but romantic) can take day, moonlight, sunrise, or sunset horseback or camel rides through the riverbeds and up into the moonlike landscape.

If you have time for just one thing, make it sandboarding because it will certainly get your heart pumping. Once you are ferried up the dunes by quad bike, your operator will arm you with the necessary equipment: a sandboard—a flat piece of hardboard, a safety hat, gloves, and elbow guards. It's also a good idea to wear long pants and long sleeves to avoid a sandburn. Beginners should head to the smaller dunes to practice (i.e. sliding down on your stomach) to get the feel of it. As you get better and more adventurous, head to the top of a high dune, but be advised, you can reach speeds of up to

80 kph (50 mph). Once you get the hang of this, try standing up. Hey, if Cameron Diaz survived, so will you.

If you get really advanced, there's always dune-boarding. You use all the same gear as sandboarding, except your board is similar to a regular surfboard on which you stand up and "surf" down the dunes.

9

IN FOCUS THE NAMIBIA DUNES

DAMARALAND

Game
★★★
Park Accessibility
★
Getting Around
★★
Accommodations
★★
Scenic Beauty
★★★★★

Stretching 600 km (370 miles) from just south of Etosha to Usakos in the south and 200 km (125 miles) from east to west, this stark, mountainous area is inland from Skeleton Coast National Park.

You can drive into Damaraland from the park via the Springbokwater Gate or drive from Swakopmund to Uis, where you can visit the Daureb Craft Centre and watch the craftspeople at work, or make it part of your customized safari. A good base for touring southern Damaraland is the little town of Khorixas. From here you can visit the Organ Pipes, hundreds of angular rock formations, or watch the rising or setting sun bathe the slopes of Burnt Mountain in fiery splendor. You'll find yourself surrounded by a dramatic landscape of steep valleys; rugged cliffs of red, gray, black, and brown; and towering mountains, including Spitzkoppe (Namibia's Matterhorn, which towers nearly 610 meters [2,000 feet] above the plains), where Damara guides will show you the Golden Snake and the Bridge—an interesting rock formation—and the San paintings at Bushman's Paradise. There are more spectacular rock paintings at Brandberg Mountain, especially the famous White Lady of Brandberg at Tsisab Gorge, whose depiction and origin have teased the minds of scholars for decades. (Is she of Mediterranean origin? Is "she" really a "he" covered in white initiation paint?)

Other stops of interest are the Petrified Forest, 42 km (25 miles) west of Khorixas, where the corpses of dead trees lie forever frozen in a bed of sandstone. The first UNESCO World Heritage Site in Namibia, Twyfelfontein, 90 km (56 miles) west of Khorixas, is also the biggest outdoor art gallery in the world, where thousands of rock paintings and ancient rock engravings are open to the sky. It's extremely rare for this many paintings and engravings to be found at the same site. As you approach, you'll see scattered boulders everywhere—a closer examination will reveal thousands of rock paintings and engravings. Get yourself a local, knowledgeable guide when you arrive, and try to give yourself a full day here. Start early (it's hard to pick out some of the art in full sunshine), bring binoculars, wear sturdy shoes, and bring water (at least a gallon) and a hat.

Northern Damaraland consists of concession areas that have been set aside for tourism, with many tourist operators working hand in hand with the local communities. This is a desert of a different kind from the classic sand dunes of the Namib. It's a landscape of almost unsurpassed rugged beauty formed by millions of years of unending geological movement. Vivid brick-red sediments complement gray lava

slopes punctuated by black fingers of "frozen" basaltic rock creeping down from the jagged rocky horizons. Millions of stones, interspersed with clumps of silvery-gray shrubs and pioneer grass, litter the unending slopes, hillsides, and mountain faces. There seem to be as many rocks, huge and small, as there are grains of sand on the beaches of the windswept, treacherous Skeleton Coast, some 90 km (56 miles) to the west. But there's life, and plenty of it, in this seemingly inhospitable landscape, including dozens of *Welwitschia mirabilis*—plants that can live for up to 1,000 years. Stop at a 500-year-old "youngster" and consider that when this plant was a newborn, Columbus was sailing for the New World and the Portuguese to Namibia.

The landscape is also dotted with colorful lichen fields, dark-green umbrella-shape camelthorn trees, candelabra euphorbias raising their prickly fleshy arms to the cloudless sky, saltbushes, and the ubiquitous shepherd's tree. Also here is the *moringa* tree—the "enchanted" tree, so-called because according to San legend, the god of thunder, not wanting moringa trees in heaven, pulled them all up and threw them out. They fell upside down into the earth, looking like miniature baobab trees. In the middle of this rocky desert rubble is Slangpost, a small, verdant oasis in the middle of what seems to be nowhere (not even the mountains have a name in this part of the world; they're referred to simply as the "no-name mountains"). Look out for traces of the amazing desert elephants (sometimes called the desert-adapted elephants), their huge footprints trodden over by the healthy herds of goats and sheep belonging to the local Damara farmers. Your best chance of seeing the elephants is along the surprisingly green and fertile dry Huab River bed, where they browse on the large seedpods of the Ana tree and whatever else they find edible. The great gray shapes silhouetted against the dry river's sandy mounds ringed by mountains and sand dunes are an incredible sight.

The Kaokoveld, north of Damaraland, although enticing because it's pristine and rarely visited, is also inhospitably rugged. Self-drives are for the really intrepid, do-it-yourself explorer.

WHEN TO GO

The area can be visited throughout the year. However, during the rainy season (January–April), roads and tracks may be difficult to negotiate, or not accessible at all due to flooding. Come May the area has a special splendor with waves of green grass growing on the plains and hills. From May to September the days will be cooler and more bearable, but nights can be very cold, especially for the camper. From October to December nights can be cool and days very hot.

GETTING HERE AND AROUND

One can access Damaraland from the coast (Swakopmund and Walvis Bay) by traveling via Henties Bay and Uis on the C35, or farther up the coast, accessing the park from Springbokwater on the C39. Coming from Windhoek, drive via Omaruru (C33) and Uis (C36) to Damaraland. From the north, travel via Kamanjab (C35) and Outjo (C39) to Khorixas. Good gravel roads can be traveled between attractions. The area is extremely fragile, and vehicles must always stay on existing roads and tracks. It's not advised to travel on to smaller tracks without the company of an experienced Namibian guide, as tourists frequently lose their way in these parts.

SAFETY AND PRECAUTIONS

Don't travel faster than 80 kph (50 mph) on gravel roads. Always fill up your tank when a gas station is available (e.g., Kamanjab, Outjo, Khorixas, and Uis). Smaller towns such as Palmwag and Sesfontein may not have gas available, so it's also advisable to take additional gas in a can if you plan to travel long stretches between places where gas isn't available. Always bring sufficient water.

TIMING

Four days is a suggested minimum, especially if you plan to visit Burnt Mountain, the Organ Pipes, Twyfelfontein, and the Petrified Forest, which can easily take a full day or a day and a half to explore. A half-day or full-day drive to view the desert-adapted elephant and other wildlife in the Huab River is also a highlight. Additionally, a day trip to the Welwitschia plains and Messum Crater is worthwhile.

WHERE TO STAY

LUXURY LODGES

$$$$ ⛺ **Damaraland Camp.** A joint community venture with the Torra Conservancy (the local community), this desolate camp is on the Huab River in central Damaraland, midway between Khorixas and the coast. Perched on a raised wooden platform, the views from the gorgeous and spacious adobe-style, thatch units take in a landscape of craggy beauty formed by millions of years of unending geological movement. You'll drive with an experienced ranger in an open 4x4 to see the famous *Welwitschia* plant and track desert elephants. After a day in the desert, cool off in the natural rock pool and watch the desert birds, or relax with a drink in the spacious, airy lodge, where stunning and surreal views are the name of the game. Pros: one of Namibia's most pristine wilderness areas; solar-powered and using eco-building techniques; impressive community-based, responsible tourism model. **Cons:** game drives are

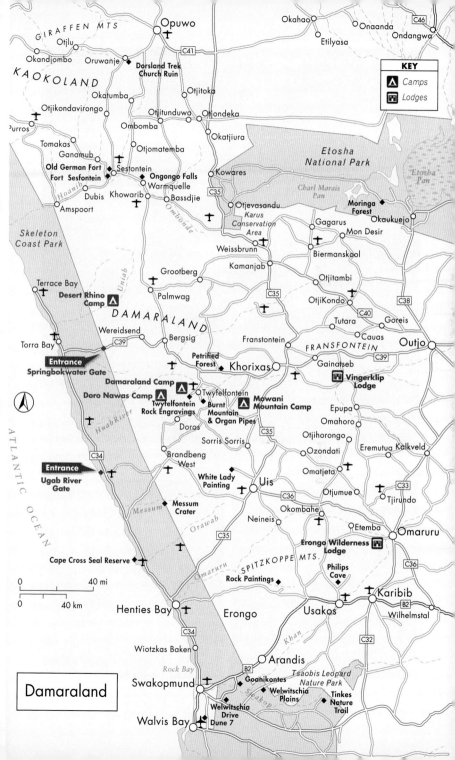

Doro Nawas

Vingerklip Lodge

Damaraland Camp

additional for those on half-board basis; rough entrance road means leaving your 2x4 vehicle in a parking area about 45 minutes away on arrival. [$] *Rooms from: US$661* ✉ *Damaraland* ☎ *27–11/807–1800 in South Africa* 🌐 *www.wilderness-safaris.com* 🛏 *10 tents* 🍴 *Multiple meal plans.*

$$$ 🏨 **Doro Nawas Camp.** Blending into the backdrop and set amid stony slopes, rugged boulders, the distant Entendeka Mountains, and the pink and russet sandstone cliffs of Twyfelfontein to the south (where you can visit some of the most famous San rock paintings and engravings in the world), this is classic Damaraland. What's more, this camp may be your best bet to see the long-legged desert elephants. You'll stay in a sturdy en-suite stone, canvas, and thatch unit with an indoor and outdoor shower. You can relax in the rim-flow style pool after a day's activities, or climb up to the roof area of the main building to sip sundowners or watch the blazing stars. The staff seem genuinely thrilled to meet you and this carries through to their service. **Pros:** guided walking trails; great community-based, responsible tourism model; amazing location close to rock art at Twyfelfontein; ability to sleep under the stars on your room deck—in your big cozy bed. **Cons:** half-board clients must pay for guided trips to see the elephants. [$] *Rooms from: US$506* ✉ *Namib-Naukluft Park* ☎ *27–11/807–1800 in South Africa* 🌐 *www.wilderness-safaris.com* 🛏 *17 chalets* 🍴 *Multiple meal plans.*

$$ 🏨 **Mowani Mountain Camp.** A scenic, centrally located locale from which to explore Damaraland's desolate attractions, Mowani Mountain Camp is perched on a pile of giant round boulders in sight of the impressive Brandberg Mountain. Each of the 12 rooms and the luxury suites are set back, almost camouflaged in the boulders with views either of the hilltop vista or the valley where guides will take you to look for desert elephants. Conveniently located close to the area's major attractions—the Brandberg Mountains, the White Lady rock art, Twelfontein's rock-art gallery, the Organ Pipes, the Burnt Mountain, the Petrified Forest—Mowani's mix of well-appointed rooms and stunning natural setting (toast the day at the sundowner rock or take a plunge between the rocks in the pool) make for a memorable stay. **Pros:** the sundowner rock; convenient to local attractions; excellent campsites with private bathrooms should you prefer a collapsible tent to a permanent camp. **Cons:** the "donkey" boilers for hot water, while authentically rustic and charming, aren't always that reliable; activities are extra if you're not on fully inclusive plan. [$] *Rooms from: US$255* ✉ *Namib-Naukluft Park* ☎ *061/232–009* 🌐 *www.mowani.com* 🛏 *13 rooms, 2 suites* 🍴 *All meals.*

9

PERMANENT TENTED CAMPS

$$$$ 🏨 **Desert Rhino Camp.** If it's rhinos you're after, especially the rare black rhino, then this remote tented camp, formerly Palmwag Rhino Camp, in the heart of the private 1 million–acre Palmwag Reserve is a must. Because there are freshwater springs everywhere, you'll see not only the desert-adapted black rhino, but plenty of other game, too, including desert elephants, giraffes, zebras, kudu, and possibly lions, leopards, and cheetahs. The camp collaborates with the Save the Rhino Trust, and one of the highlights of your stay will be tracking the rare

black rhino on foot. (If this is not your idea of fun, go tracking in an open vehicle instead.) You'll likely feel very close to the desert in your spacious tent with en-suite bathroom, flush toilet, and hot water on demand for your bucket shower. **Pros:** amazing educational experience on rhinos and their ecology; evening meals taken together by the fire pit allow guests to mingle. **Cons:** some visitors could find this experience overly rustic. $ *Rooms from: US$661* ✉ *Namib-Naukluft Park* ☎ *27–11/807–1800 in South Africa* ⊕ *www.wilderness-safaris.com* ⇆ *8 tents* ⎮◎⎮ *All-inclusive.*

BUDGET ACCOMMODATIONS

$ ⚏ **Erongo Wilderness Lodge.** Discover an absolute closeness to nature at this tranquil lodge completely surrounded by colossal granite boulders. Hugging the Erongo Mountain Range in a 200,000-hectare (500,000-acre) conservancy, the tented chalets staggered among the boulders glow in the afternoon sun. With perfectly angled sunset-view decks, stone stairways, and unique indoor/outdoor bathrooms, the lodge makes a sublimely peaceful retreat. Have dinner under the stars, or relax next to the fireplace and enjoy a decadent dessert. Wake up early to go for the three-hour nature walk with one of the fantastic guides and climb to the top of the biggest boulder to enjoy the true beauty of the area. Around the lodge you may spot the rosy-faced lovebirds and Damara dik-diks that visit the water hole. **Pros:** incredibly peaceful; attentive and warm staff; spectacular views. **Cons:** some chalets are far from main lodge with many steps to navigate; not everyone will appreciate the open-air bathroom. $ *Rooms from: US$195* ✉ *Omaruru Conservancy, Erongo, Damaraland* ☎ *061/239–199* ⊕ *www.erongowilderness-namibia.com* ⇆ *9 chalets, 1 family chalet* ⎮◎⎮ *Some meals.*

$ ⚏ **Vingerklip Lodge.** In a dramatic locale in Damaraland's Valley of the Ugab Terraces, this lodge is set against the backdrop of a mighty stone finger pointing toward the sky. Take time while you're here to listen to the silence. The 360-degree views from the Sundowner Terrace are magnificent. The friendly and knowledgeable staff organize tours to the well-known sights in the vicinity such as the petrified forest, a Himba village, and the rock engravings at Twyfelfontein. Bungalows cling to the side of a rocky hill and are clean and comfortable, but it's the remarkable views that you'll always remember, especially if you stay in the Heaven's Gate room. **Pros:** drop-dead gorgeous views; great food. **Cons:** rooms are not large; service can vary; bit too far to use as a base to explore Damaraland attractions. $ *Rooms from: US$114* ✉ *Damaraland* ☎ *061/255–344 for booking office, 067/290–319 for lodge* ✐ *reservations@vingerklip.com.na* ⊕ *www.vingerklip.com.na* ⇆ *24 bungalows* ⎮◎⎮ *Some meals.*

ETOSHA NATIONAL PARK

Game
★★★★★
Park Accessibility
★★★★★
Getting Around
★★★★★
Accomodations
★★★★★
Scenic Beauty
★★★★★

This photogenic, startlingly beautiful park takes its name—meaning Great White Place—from a vast flat depression that was a deep inland lake 12 million years ago. The white clay pan, also known as the Place of Mirages, covers nearly 25% of the park's surface.

Although it's usually dry, in a good rainy season it floods and becomes home to many water birds, including tens of thousands of flamingos that feed on the blue-green algae of the pan. Although the park is never crowded with visitors like some of the East African game parks, the scenery here is no less spectacular: huge herds that dot the plains and gather at the many and varied water holes. The dust devils, mirages, and terrain that changes from densely wooded thickets to wide-open spaces and from white salt-encrusted pans to blond grasslands, will keep you captivated for hours.

The game's all here—the Big Five—large and small, fierce and gentle, beautiful and ugly. But one of Etosha's main attractions isn't the numbers of animals that you can see (more than 114 species), but how easily you can see them. The game depend on the natural springs that are found all along the edges of the pan, and as the animals have grown used to drinking at these water holes for decades, they're not put off by vehicles or game-seeking visitors. On the road from the Von Lindequist Gate, the eastern entrance to Etosha, look out for the smallest of all African antelope, the Damara dik-dik. If you see a diminutive "Bambi" sheltering under a roadside bush, that's it. The Namutoni area and the two Okevi water holes—Klein Namutoni and Kalkheuwel—probably provide the best chances to see leopards. Don't miss the blackface impala, native to Etosha, and one of the rarest of antelope and an endangered species. Bigger and more boldly marked than its smaller cousin, the impala, you'll find it drinking in small herds at water holes all over the park.

9

The real secret of game-watching in the park is to settle in at one of the many water holes, most of which are on the southern edges of the pan, and wait. And wait. Each water hole has its own unique personality and characteristics. Even if the hole is small and deep, like Ombika, on the western side, you'll be amazed at what may arrive. Old Africa hands maintain that you should be up at dawn for the best sightings, but you can see marvelous game at all times of day. The plains, where you'll likely spot cheetahs, are also home to huge herds of zebras and wildebeests, and you may see the silhouettes of giraffes as they cross the skyline in stately procession. Watch out for herds of springbok "pronking"—an activity wherein these lovely little antelope bounce and bound high into the air as they run. Zoologists argue over the reason for this behavior. Some say it's to avoid predators, others that it's to demonstrate agility, strength, and stamina; most visitors like to believe that pronking is just for fun. Salvadora, a constant spring on the fringe of Etosha Pan near Halali, is a favorite watering point for some of these big herds. Watch out also for the stately eland, Africa's largest antelope. As big as a cow, although more streamlined and elegant, this antelope can jump higher than any other African antelope—amazing when you consider its huge size. And where there's water, there's always game. Predators, especially lions, lurk around most of the water holes looking for a meal. Plan to spend at least half a night sitting on a bench at the floodlighted Okaukuejo water hole. You really are within spitting distance of the game. Bring a book, write in your journal, or just sit while you wait. You may be amazed at the variety of animals that come down to drink: black and white rhinos, lions, jackals, and even the occasional leopard. This is a particularly good place to look out for black rhinos, which trot purposefully up to drink and in so doing scare all but the bravest of other game away. Groot Okevi water hole, close to Namutoni, is also good for black rhinos.

Don't overlook the more than 340 dazzling varieties of bird—the crimson-breasted shrike is particularly gorgeous—and watch for ostriches running over the plains or raptors hunting silently overhead. There are many endemics, including the black-faced and bare-cheeked babblers, violet wood-hoopoe (look for them in Halali camp), Rüppell's parrot, Bradfield's swift, and the white-tailed shrike.

Be aware of the trees, shrubs, and plants as well. Just east of Okaukuejo is the legendary Haunted or Ghost Forest, where moringa trees have morphed into twisted, strange, and grotesque shapes: you may feel as if you're in Snow White's forest or deep in Middle Earth.

WHEN TO GO

The best time to visit is from April to September, when the temperatures are cooler, and the increasingly thirsty animals gather at water holes, making it easiest to see them (the driest time of year when this will be the case is August to September). May to August is the coolest time of year, and nights can be downright freezing—be sure to bring adequate warm clothes for night drives. Bird watchers will want to visit in the summer (November to March) when the migratory birds (both intra-African and Palaearctic) flock in the park's many habitats after

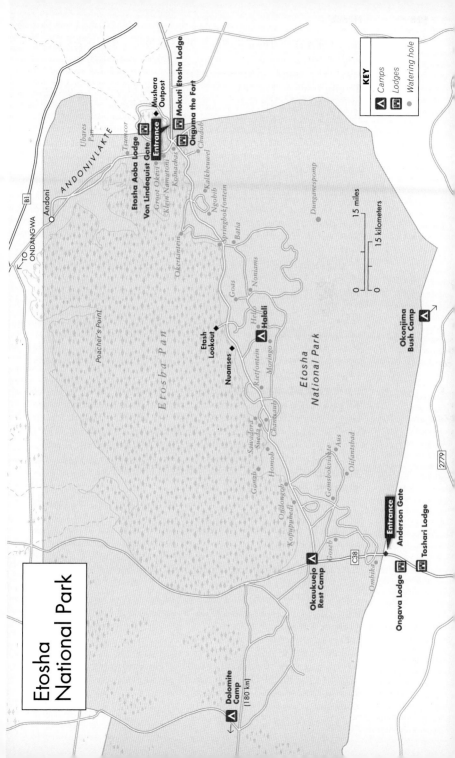

Etosha National Park

KEY
- ⌂ Camps
- ⌂ Lodges
- • Watering hole

TO ONDANGWA

B1

Andoni

ANDONIVLAKTE

Ubares Pan

Mushara Outpost ◆
Mokuti Etosha Lodge

Tsumcor

Entrance
Etosha Aoba Lodge
Von Lindequist Gate
Onguma the Fort
Groot Okevi
Klein Namutoni
Koinachas
Chudob

Kalkheuwel

Ngobib
Springbokfontein
Batia

Okerfontein

Goas
Nomams

Dungatespomp

Poacher's Point

Etosha Pan

Etosh Lookout ◆
Nuamses ◆
Rietfontein
Moringo

Hello
Halali ⌂

Okonjima Bush Camp ⌂

Etosha National Park

Charitsaub

Salvadora
Sueda

Gonab
Homob
Ogdongob
Kapupuhedi

Gemsbokvlakte
Aus
Olifantsbad

0   15 miles
0   15 kilometers

Okaukuejo Rest Camp ⌂

Goseb
C38
Ombika

Entrance
Anderson Gate

Ongava Lodge
Toshari Lodge

2779

Dolomite Camp ⌂
(180 km)

the summer rains. The main Etosha Pan can become a huge expanse of shallow water filled with flamingos, wildfowl, and waders.

GETTING HERE AND AROUND

Tourists coming from the Oshakati area via the B1 can access the park through King Nehale Gate (northeast); coming from Tsumeb also via the B1 through the Von Lindequist Gate (east); coming from Outjo via the C38 through the Anderson Gate (south) from sunrise to sunset; and coming from Kamanjab via the C35 through the Galton Gate (west) (but note that if you are heading east to Okaukuejo, it is almost a five-hour drive through the park). Tourists may not drive in the park after sunset or before sunrise, and thus need to allow time to arrive at their respective rest camps if moving around close to these times. Namibia Wildlife Resorts (NWR) also offers guided night drives, which can be booked directly at the camps. If you're staying at Onkoshi, you need to report to reception at Namutoni to be transferred to Onkoshi, as only guests with 4x4 vehicles are able to travel along this section of road (at this writing the road is being prepared for all-vehicle access in the near future).

ADMISSION

The park gates are open from sunrise to sunset, and the daily entrance fee is N$80 for foreign visitors and N$10 for a passenger vehicle with fewer than 10 seats. You pay for your vehicle entry permit and for any balance remaining on your prebooked accommodations (which include personal entry fees) at the reception of the rest camp closest to the gate through which you enter.

SAFETY AND PRECAUTIONS

Motorists aren't allowed to travel faster than 60 kph (37 mph) inside the park, nor are they allowed to exit their vehicles unless they're at the rest camps or toilets. Always be on the lookout for animals, which can cross the road at random, and often are concealed by bushes before emerging. Refrain from making noise and getting too close to any animals, especially elephants, as they could panic and charge your car.

TIMING AND TOURING TIPS

Two to three days will allow you to visit the eastern and central parts of the park, as well as Okaukuejo. Taking in the "newer" western part of the park properly will require at least two days due to its relative isolation from the rest of the park—it's only 180 km (112 miles) to the next camp, but the speed limit is 60 kph (37 mph). Throughout most of the park there are numerous water holes to visit, but that's best done in the early morning and late afternoon when the animals are more active and temperatures are cooler.

The park is huge—22,270 square km (8,598 square miles), 300 km (186 miles) wide, and 110 km (68 miles) long. The western part, which makes up a third of the overall park, is open to the public through the Galton Gate, but if you plan to drive through to Okaukeujo you need to arrive by 1 pm otherwise they will not allow access (unless you have a booking at the NWR's Dolomite Camp in the west). If you prefer to visit the park on one of the many safaris offered by various tour companies, make sure you choose one with an open vehicle or pop-top with few passengers—you probably don't want to find yourself in an air-conditioned 75-seater bus. That said, the best way to see the park is to drive yourself so you can stop at your leisure (don't exceed the 60 kph speed limit, and stick to marked roads). A two-wheel-drive car is fine, as the roads are good, but the higher up you sit, the better your view, so opt for the more expensive *combis* (vans) or 4x4s if possible. In addition to patience, you'll need drinks, snacks, field guides to the animals and birds, binoculars, and your camera. There are more than 40 water holes, with Rietfontein, Okaukuejo, Goas, Halali, Klein Namutoni, and Chudob regarded as the best for game-watching and taking pictures, but nothing is certain in the bush. Keep your eyes and ears open, and you may come across game at any time, in any place. Arm yourself with the MET map of Etosha (available in the camps), which shows the names and locations of the water holes and indicates which roads are open.

WHERE TO STAY

If you wish to stay inside Etosha itself you can lodge at one of the NWR rest camps (book months in advance, especially for the peak periods of July to September and around Christmas and Easter, though you may want to avoid the crowds at these times). The rest camps of Halali, Onkoshi, Dolomite, Namutoni, and Okaukuejo have pools, grocery-curio-liquor stores, gas stations, and restaurants serving breakfast, lunch, and dinner. There are also numerous full-service private lodges and guest farms near the park.

LUXURY LODGES

$$ ⊤ **The Mushara Outpost.** If you're a fan of old-fashioned luxury, warm service, and accommodation that combines the authenticity of the bush with a stylish and comfortable interior, then this is an excellent option. Situated close to the Von Lindequist Gate on the eastern side of Etosha, the Outpost is perfectly placed to take advantage of the park's game-thick eastern section, especially if you opt for the fully inclusive rate that includes two game drives; and they have recently introduced guided bush walks. The lodge has a comfortable rambling feel to it with a large farm-style main house. The eight luxury tents made from canvas and wood are delightfully well-appointed on the inside, ensuring that after a day of game drives you'll be able to relax and recharge your batteries while sitting on your deck among the shady trees. **Pros:** rooms are bright and comfortable; bathrooms feature glass convertible showers that go from indoor to outdoor with the zip of canvas; excellent service. **Cons:** laundry services are an additional charge; no children under 12. $ *Rooms from: US$370* ⊠ *Etosha National Park* ☎ *061/240–020 for bookings, 067/229–106 for lodge* ⊕ *www.mushara-lodge.com* ⇄ *8 tents* ⊠ *All-inclusive.*

$$ ⊤ **Okonjima Bush Camp.** Located about halfway between Windhoek and Etosha, this camp is an excellent stopover point on your way to the park. Nestled among the Omboroko Mountains, this lovely but very busy lodge is also home to the environmental-award-winning Africat Foundation (⊕ *www.africat.org*), which has rehabilitated and cared for leopards and cheetahs for many years. You can get a close look at these magnificent cats feeding, and there are also guided San and Bantu walking trails. A bonus is the spacious blind, within walking distance of your thatch room, where you can sit and watch some of the smaller animals and hundreds of birds. In addition to lodging in the farmhouse with either garden or mountain views, there's a villa that sleeps up to 12, a suite that sleeps four, and a bush camp of eight thatch chalets with a canvas "front wall" that can be lifted during the day so you can enjoy the view. (If you're looking for ultimate exclusivity, treat yourself to the gorgeous Bush Suite.) The Plains Camp (with an additional 30 rooms) is better for families and is not as personal as the Bush Camp, Suite or Villa. **Pros:** numerous activities including cheetah/leaopard-tracking, self-guided walking trails, and bird-watching; great service; kitchen facilities are available. **Cons:** some of the garden rooms—in the Plains Camp—are small and dark; sometimes there is a bit of herding of guests for activities. $ *Rooms from: US$430* ✉ *Etosha National Park* ☎ *067/687–034, 81–276–23 (mobile)* ⊕ *www.okonjima.com* ⤳ *8 rooms, 2 villas* ◉ *All meals.*

$$$$ ▦ **Ongava Lodge.** On the southern boundary of Etosha close to the Anderson Gate, this lodge has its own surrounding game reserve. Each unit features its own plunge pool, sala, outdoor shower and bath with magnificent views, and wood decks, which cling to the side of a steep, rocky outcrop. Some units overlook a couple of busy water holes. The stunning main area has stone floors and sweeping thatch roofs, as well as myriad spots from which to gaze at the neverending plains beyond. Take a guided walk and sneak up on some zebras and wildebeests, go rhino tracking, or sit in a hide at the water hole just before sunset and listen to the soft twittering calls of hundreds of sand grouse as they come to drink. Lions often stray in from Etosha and join the evening party. If you want to be more on the wild side, you can stay at Ongava Tented Camp, a small, intimate site nestled deep in the bush. You'll sleep in a walk-in tent on a slate base under a thatch awning with a private bathroom. After a day spent game-watching, it's great to cool off in the outside shower or in the plunge pool. If you want even more exclusivity and luxury, opt for Little Ongava, which has three gorgeous suites. **Pros:** great location by the entrance of Etosha; large luxurious rooms; great wildlife viewing from the lodge water hole; guided walks include white rhino tracking. **Cons:** pool on the small side; there are many stairs to the lodge. $ *Rooms from: US$674* ✉ *Etosha National Park* ☎ *27–11/807–1800 in South Africa* ⊕ *www.wilderness-safaris. com* ⤳ *13 units, 1 family room, 6 tented units, 3 suites* ◉ *All-inclusive.*

$$ ▦ **Onguma: The Fort.** This flagship lodge in the Onguma Game Reserve

Fodor's Choice

★

on the eastern border of Etosha National Park's Fischer Pan is the epitome of luxury and style. Unlike any other lodge in Namibia this lodge blends a unique Moroccan-style fort architecture with subtle hints of color and raw African textures. The wide deck of the main lodge looks out over the stark expanse of the pan and a water hole, which is visited by many animals that have wandered across from Etosha. You get a strong sense that you're at the edge of civilization here. The 13 exquisitely appointed suites stretch to either side of the lodge with equally astonishing pan views, outdoor showers, and cool stone interiors. The staff are like a well-oiled machine and you feel as though you are a VIP at a royal palace. **Pros:** arresting view of the pan; stunning swimming pool and sundowner area; extensive wine cellar and first-class food. **Cons:** no walking around after dark or between room and lodge (but they provide a golf cart transport). [$] *Rooms from: US$284* ✉ *Etosha National Park* ☎ *061/237–055* 🌐 *www.onguma.com* 🛏 *11 bush suites, 1 sultan suite, 1 honeymoon suite* 🍴 *All meals.*

BUDGET ACCOMMODATIONS

$ 🏨 **Etosha Aoba Lodge.** This small, family-owned, ultrafriendly lodge is 10 km (6 miles) east of the Von Lindequist Gate—about a 30-minute drive from the park. After a hot, dusty day in the park, you can slip into crisp white bed linens in your cool thatch chalet, or sip a cocktail on your mini-veranda while listening to the noises of the night. The owners emphasize excellent cuisine made with fresh, local produce; you'll dine under the thatch roof of the main building. Most visitors have their own vehicles, but the lodge can arrange trips into the park for you. The lodge gets many repeat visitors. **Pros:** lodge is set in a beautiful natural forest; great night drive with bush stargazing for budding astronomers; fabulous food and wine tastings every night. **Cons:** rooms are on the small side. [$] *Rooms from: US$162* ✉ *Etosha National Park* ☎ *061/237–055 bookings, 067/229–100 lodge* 🌐 *www.etosha-aoba-lodge.com* 🛏 *10 chalets* 🍴 *Breakfast.*

$ FAMILY 🏨 **Mokuti Etosha Lodge.** Since this lodge is in its own park a stone's throw from the Von Lindequist Gate, you may well wake up and find an antelope or warthog munching the grass outside your room. Despite being one of Namibia's largest lodges, the rooms are smallish and rather sparsely furnished, but you'll be out most of the day game-viewing. You can take a walk, either guided or on your own, and be quite safe. Follow the paths, and you may come face-to-face with a giraffe or any number of gorgeous birds. Don't miss the amazing reptile park, where you can meet pythons, scorpions, tortoises, and the odd crocodile. To catch sight of the bigger game, take an early-morning or afternoon tour into Etosha from the lodge. Air Namibia flies to and from Mokuti five days a week. **Pros:** a stone's throw from Etosha gate; all the amenities of a big hotel, including tennis and billiards. **Cons:** rooms lack views and the character of a smaller lodge. [$] *Rooms from: US$115* ✉ *Etosha National Park* ☎ *061/207–5360 for ookings, 067/229–084 for lodge* 🌐 *www.mokutietoshalodge.com* 🛏 *90 rooms, 8 luxury rooms, 8 luxury family rooms* 🍴 *Breakfast.*

$ FAMILY 🏨 **Toshari Lodge.** This pleasant and affordable lodge about 25 km (15½ miles) south of Etosha's Anderson Gate makes a great base for exploring the park. If you're fed up with self-driving, then let an experienced guide take you on the lodge's 7½-hour drive in an open game vehicle with a great picnic included (30 people maximum; six people max per vehicle). Cheerful well-appointed double rooms with fans and mosquito nets are set among green lawns and old mopane and seringa trees. The restaurant serves excellent home-cooked food and has a good wine list specializing in fine South African wines. You can also dine in the boma under the unbelievably brilliant Namibian stars. Kids under 6 stay free

CLOSE UP

Namibia's Tribes

HERERO

The Herero came to Namibia during the 17th century from East Africa. They're traditionally pastoralists, with cattle playing a major role in their nomadic lifestyle. Today, though, most Herero are farmers or merchants in Namibia's urban hubs; some have also become professionals. Herero women are known for their stylish dress—full-length colorful gowns and unique, wide-brim hats. Ironically, this style of dress was adopted from missionaries that introduced German colonial rule to Namibia in the early part of the 20th century. The Herero–German War (1904–07) was a cruel episode in the history of Southern Africa as German military policy was to annihilate or confine Herero to labor camps so Europeans could establish farms. Issues regarding the treatment of the Herero during this time are still being battled out in the legal system: the German government has issued an official apology, but the Herero feel they deserve more for the death of an estimated 65,000 tribe members, and are seeking financial reparations through the international courts.

HIMBA

The Himba, a matriarchal tribe closely related to the Herero, are famous for covering their faces and hair with a light mixture of ochre, herbs, and animal fat to shield them from the hot sun. They wear very little clothing due to the harsh desert climate. The tribe lives mainly in the Kunene region of northern Namibia and, like the Herero, the Himba are a nomadic people who breed cattle as well as goats. Himba women do most of the work in the tribe—they bear children, take care of the children, tend to the livestock, and even build homes. In the 1980s and '90s, Himba culture was endangered due to severe draught and the war in nearby Angola. Recently they had to battle modernization and fight against a proposed hydroelectric dam, which threatened to flood their homesteads and destroy their pastures. However, with help from the international community, the Himba have successfully blocked the dam and managed to maintain control of their land and their traditions.

---

with their parents. **Pros:** convenient location; clean comfortable rooms with a/c; great campsite, walking trails, and water hole. **Cons:** not a luxury lodge; due to proximity to the main road between Outjo and the Anderson Gate, some traffic noise can be heard in the campsites (though not the rooms). $ *Rooms from: US$78* ✉ *Etosha National Park* ☎ *067/333–440, 067/333–440* ⊕ *www.etoshagateway-toshari.com* ⊋ *27 chalets, 3 family rooms, 7 luxury rooms* ⊙ *Breakfast.*

NATIONAL PARKS ACCOMMODATIONS

$ **Dolomite Camp.** This is the place for those looking for something unique and far from the madding crowds. Opened in 2011, the newest of Etosha's camps is also the only one in the previously off-limits western section of the park. The camp, set among the Dolomite hills synonymous with its name, sports a bar, sunset deck, and an infinity pool perfect for scoping out the scorched plains and hills while cooling off. Tented deluxe chalets with mesmerizing views are elegantly

Namibia's Herero women are known for their colorful gowns and wide-brimmed hats.

appointed and some have plunge pools. Having been untouched by tourists for almost 50 years, this section of the park has allowed animals like black rhinos and black-faced impalas to breed successfully. You may also be lucky enough to see roan antelope, Moneiro's hornbills, and Hartmann's zebras—species specific to the area. **Pros:** no crowds; a newer, better-designed camp than the other NWR offerings; completely unspoiled wilderness; more personal service than any other NWR camp. **Cons:** far from the rest of the park and the Etosha Pan; long uneven pathways from chalets to lodge could be off-putting for some. $ *Rooms from: US$135* ✉ *Etosha National Park* ☎ *061/285–7200* ⊕ *www.nwr. com.na* ⇆ *20 chalets* ⚬| *Some meals.*

$ 🛏 **Halali.** Etosha's smallest NWR camp with self-catering and non-self-catering chalets as well as a campsite has undergone a renovation that has vastly improved most of the chalets (though the cheapest category is still very small). If you're a bird-watcher, this place merits a giant check mark on your list. Rare violet wood hoopoes and bare-cheeked babblers frequent the camp, and if you walk up the rocky path to the pleasant floodlighted water hole and are prepared to sit and wait, there's a good chance you'll spot lions, elephants, and black rhinos. In peak season it can be maddeningly busy. Halali, which is roughly halfway between Okuakuejo and Namutoni, is in the only area of the park with hills. Halali offers its own game drives, and its small convenience store is useful, even if the stock is somewhat limited and costly—overlook the disarray and you will find something you need. Rather go for the bush chalets or family room as the double room options are unacceptably small. **Pros:** prime location in the middle of Etosha; one of the quieter and less trafficked camps. **Cons:** mosquito nets are not all in

Ongava Lodge

Halali

Namutoni

great shape; electricity can go out, which renders a/c useless; service can be disappointing; only offer an expensive buffet option for dinners. ⓢ *Rooms from: US$115* ✉ *Etosha National Park* ☎ *061/285–7200, 061/285–7200* ⊕ *www.nwr.com.na* ⮐ *61 chalets* ⎮◯⎮ *Breakfast.*

$ ⌂**Okaukuejo.** On the western side of Etosha, this is the biggest and noisiest national-park camp. The staff aren't always the most hospitable, but a floodlighted water hole—regarded as one of the finest in Africa—makes up for service shortfalls. Climb the spiral staircase to the top of the round tower for a good view of the surrounding countryside, and then settle down to an all-night game-watching vigil. Recently renovated, pleasantly furnished, and spotlessly clean accommodations range from a premier water-hole chalet, water-hole and bush chalets, and double rooms, some of which have self-catering facilities. There is also a campsite, which during peak season can be bustling and noisy with not quite enough ablutions There are mail facilities at the camp, as well as a restaurant, gas station, and store to stock up on provisions. **Pros:** famously great water hole; can sit on your deck and view the water hole from certain chalets. **Cons:** this popular camp can be busy and noisy; service can vary. ⓢ *Rooms from: US$140* ✉ *Etosha National Park* ☎ *061/285–7200, 061/285–7200* ⊕ *www.nwr.com.na* ⮐ *35 water-hole chalets, 25 bush chalets, 40 double rooms, 2 family chalets* ⎮◯⎮ *Breakfast.*

9

IF YOU HAVE TIME

Although the must-see parks in Namibia are described in great detail above, there are still other places worth exploring if you have time.

THE SKELETON COAST

This wildly beautiful but dangerous shore, a third of Namibia's coastline, stretches from the Ugab River in the south to the Kunene River, the border with Angola, in the north. The Portuguese seafarers who explored this area in the 15th century called this treacherous coast with its cold Benguela current and deadly crosscurrents the "Coast of Death." Its newer, no-less-sinister name, the Skeleton Coast, testifies to innumerable shipwrecks, lives lost, bleached whale bones, and the insignificant, transient nature of humans in the face of the raw power of nature. Still comparatively unknown to tourists, this region has a stark beauty and an awesomely diverse landscape—gray gravel plains, rugged wilderness, rusting shipwrecks, desert wastes, meandering barchan dunes, distant mountains, towering walls of sand and granite, and crashing seas. You'll rarely see more than a handful of visitors in this inaccessible and rugged coastal area. This isn't an easy ride, as distances are vast, amenities scarce or nonexistent, and the roads demanding. Don't exceed 80 kph (50 mph) on the gravel roads, and never drive off the road on the ecologically vulnerable salt pans and lichen fields: the scars left by vehicles can last for hundreds of years and do irreparable damage.

Skeleton Coast National Park extends along this rugged Atlantic coast and about 40 km (25 miles) inland; the 200-km (125-mile) stretch of coast from Swakopmund to the Ugab River is the National West Coast Tourist Recreational Area. You can drive along a coastal road right up to Terrace Bay, and for the first 250 km (155 miles) from Swakopmund north to Terrace Bay you'll find not sand dunes but glinting gravel plains and scattered rocks. Stop and sift a handful of gravel: you may well find garnets and crystals among the tiny stones. In other places the plains are carpeted with lichens—yellow, red, orange, and many shades of green. In the early morning these lichen fields look lushly attractive, but during the heat of midday they seem dried up and insignificant. But don't whiz by. Stop and pour a drop of water on the lichens and watch a small miracle as they unfurl and come alive. If you're a birder, the salt pans on the way from Swakopmund to Henties Bay are worth a visit; you might spot a rare migrant wader there. The famous Namibian oysters are farmed here in sea ponds—don't leave Namibia without tasting these. The surreal little seaside holiday town of Henties Bay is like a deserted Hollywood back lot in winter, but in summer is full of holidaying Namibian fisherfolk from Swakopmund, Windhoek, and Tsumeb.

You'll smell the hundreds of thousands of Cape fur seals (*Arctocephalus pusillus pusillus*) at the Cape Cross seal colony, north of Henties Bay, long before you get there, but stifle your gags and go goggle at the seething mass on land and in the water. If you visit in late November or early December, you can "ooh" and "aah" at the furry baby seal pups, as well as the marauding jackals looking for a fast-food snack. Farther north the dunes begin, ending in the north at the Kunene River, Namibia's border with Angola. This northern stretch of coast from the Ugab River to the Kunene River is managed by the government as a wilderness area and accounts for a

third of Namibia's coastline. But if it's lush green pastures and abundance of game you want, then this raw, rugged, harsh, and uncompromising landscape isn't for you. What you'll find are dramatically different scenery—big skies and unending horizons—an absence of tourists ("crowds" around here means one or two vehicles), and some wildlife: brown hyenas, springbok, oryx, jackals, and, if you're really lucky, a cheetah or rhino. The sight of a majestic oryx silhouetted against towering sand dunes or a cheeky jackal scavenging seal pups on the beaches is extremely rewarding. The best activity, however, is just concentrating on the freedom, beauty, and strange solitude of the area.

WHEN TO GO

The northern Skeleton Coast experiences the same weather year-round: moderate temperatures with mist, wind, and hardly any rain. For anglers, the best time to visit is November to March. For the inland Kaokoveld, the dry winter season from May to August is best. The rainy summer months of January to March can bring extremely high temperatures and flash floods.

GETTING HERE AND AROUND

You can drive (a 4x4 gives you more flexibility) from Swakopmund north through Henties Bay via the Ugab Gate, with its eerie painted skulls and crossbones on the gates, or from the more northerly Springbokwater Gate. You must reach your gate of entry before 3 pm. Always stick to the marked roads and avoid driving on treacherous salt pans. Look out for an abandoned 1960s oil rig lying next to the road between the Ugab River and Terrace Bay.

The Uniab River valley, between Torra Bay and Terrace Bay, is your best chance of spotting big game such as rhinos and occasionally elephants. Once you get to Terrace Bay, 287 km (178 miles) north of Henties Bay, that's the end of your car trip: it's the last outpost. If you want to explore further, then a fly-in safari is your only option.

Many parts of the Skeleton Coast can be visited only with a dedicated operator, and the lengths of tours vary. If you intend to spend time only in Torra Bay or Terrace Bay, two to three days will suffice. Bear in mind that this coastline doesn't conform to the usual "beach holiday" image: Namibia's beaches are wild and desolate, offering a welcome respite from the hot inland areas during summer months and a wonderful destination for fishermen.

The C34 road runs parallel to the coast, and then a rough track continues up past Torra Bay to the ranger station (Ministry of Environment and Tourism). Driving the C34 is straightforward, although fog can

CLOSE UP

From Portugal to the Skeleton Coast

More than 500 years ago, a daring little band of Portuguese sailors, inspired by the vision of their charismatic leader, Prince Henry the Navigator—who, contrary to what you might expect from his name, never left his native land—set sail from the School of Navigation at Sagres, the farthest western point of Europe, to find fame, fortune, and new lands for the Crown. Facing unknown dangers and terra incognita—the maps of the time were little more than fanciful sketchbooks filled with dragons and warnings that "here be monsters"—the intrepid sailors pushed back the edges of the known world nautical mile by nautical mile until they entered the waters of the southwest coastline of Africa on tiny, frail caravels. In 1485, Captain Diego Cão and his battered crew finally dropped anchor off a desolate beach thousands of miles from home and safety. There, on the lonely windswept sands, they erected a cross both in honor of their heavenly king, whom they credited with protecting and directing them during their arduous journey, as well as to King John I, their earthly monarch. North of Swakopmund, as you marvel at thousands upon thousands of the Cape fur seals at Cape Cross, you can see a replica of that cross (the original is in the Berlin Oceanographic Museum). Sadly, the courageous Captain Cão never made it home: he's buried nearby on a rocky outcrop.

make the surface slick and the road is mostly gravel, so keep speeds below 80 kph (49 mph). You can purchase your entry permit either at the Ugab or Springbokwasser Gates. There are several short detours to points of interest, but off-road driving is strictly prohibited.

WHERE TO STAY
LUXURY LODGES

$$$$ **Serra Cafema.** This astonishingly different and dramatically sited
Fodor's Choice camp in the extreme northwest of Namibia on the Angolan border is
★ the most remote camp in Southern Africa. After a dry, dusty, but magnificently beautiful drive from the airstrip, you are guaranteed to gasp with awe as you first catch sight of the camp from a high sand dune. Built amid a grove of ancient albida trees on the banks of the wide Kunene River, it seems like a desert mirage. Only the nomadic Himba people share this area, and a visit to a local village is an eye-opening experience and one of the highlights of a stay here. Another day, ride a quad bike over the billowing sand dunes and spot the Atlantic from a high vantage point. Although tents (on raised platforms) are luxurious and have private bathrooms, don't come here if you aren't tough. The flight from Windhoek is long and bumpy, and the terrain harsh and demanding, but the experience—staying by a wide river in the midst of the oldest desert in the world—is almost surreal. This is one-of-a-kind Africa. Stay for three nights to make the most of the experience: go walking, boating, birding, or quad biking; do a nature drive; or just sit by the rushing river and contemplate. **Pros:** surreal remote wilderness area (malaria-free zone); gorgeous camp and rooms with views of Kunene River; a wealth of activities beyond game drives; outstanding

service. **Cons:** you may find yourself torn between activities and relaxing in your lovely tent; not a lot of wildlife; arduous travel to get here. [$] *Rooms from: US$1095* ✉ *Skeleton Coast* ☎ *27–11/807–1800 in South Africa* 🌐 *www.wilderness-safaris.com* 🛏 *8 tents* 🍴 *All-inclusive.*

NATIONAL PARKS ACCOMMODATIONS

$ 🏨 **Terrace Bay.** An isolated outpost and government resort and the northernmost point in the park to which you can drive, this may well be the most remote spot on earth you ever visit. Surrounded by gravel plains, it's a popular spot for anglers and people who want to get to know the desert. Don't miss the surprising Uniab River delta, a lush green oasis in a miniature canyon a couple of miles from Terrace Bay. It's also a good stop if you're going on into Damaraland. The accommodations, once part of a diamond-mining operation, are simple and basic, though each bungalow has a refrigerator, shower, and toilet. The four-room family chalet has all the modern conveniences, including air-conditioning and a fully equipped kitchen. Breakfast and dinner are provided, and there's a small shop that stocks basic groceries, beer, wine, and some fishing equipment. The resort does not accommodate day visitors. **Pros:** the angling is awesome, so be sure to bring a permit and your rod; remote desolate coast. **Cons:** rooms are clean and comfortable but nothing special; activities for nonfishermen are limited. [$] *Rooms from: US$85* ✉ *Skeleton Coast* ☎ *061/285–7200* 🌐 *www.nwr.com.na* 🛏 *20 rooms, 2 family chalets* 🍴 *Some meals.*

CAPRIVI STRIP

This lovely unspoiled area—one of Namibia's best-kept secrets—lies in northeast Namibia (and is sometimes simply referred to as "northeast Namibia") at the confluence of the Zambezi and Chobe rivers, and serves as a gateway to Zimbabwe's Victoria Falls and Botswana's Chobe National Park. Because it's relatively unknown as a tourist area, you'll get the feeling here that you're truly alone with nature.

Think of the Caprivi Strip as a long finger of land at the top of the country pointing eastward for 450 km (280 miles) toward Zimbabwe and Zambia; in many ways, because of its rivers, marshes, and forests, the area is much more like those countries than the rest of Namibia. This part of Namibia is the closest thing to Botswana's Okavango Delta, and it shelters much of the same game: elephants, the aquatic lechwe and the rare sitatunga antelope, the uncommon roan and sable antelope, and, hardly ever seen in Namibia, big buffalo herds. However, you're unlikely to see predators.

You've got to be fairly determined to get here because the journey can be circuitous, to say the least. You can fly in to Katima Mulilo, the vibey little main town (which is closer to Gaborone, Botswana, or Lusaka, Zambia, than it is to Windhoek), pick up a vehicle, and drive. Visit the Caprivi Art Centre near the African market, where you'll find beautifully crafted baskets, carvings, and handmade pottery. There's a main road across the strip, the B8, but it's relatively busy with commercial traffic to and from Zambia and Botswana. Or you can fly into Livingstone in Zambia, cross the Sesheke border (over the Zambezi River), and continue by road and river to your chosen lodge. (To give you some idea: to get to Susuwe Island Lodge, you fly from Johannesburg into Livingstone, then take a small plane to the Namibian immigration post at Katimo Mulilo, then fly to the Immelman airstrip nearby, the once infamous Doppies SADF forward base, and travel by road and river to the lodge.) However you get here, the destination is well worth every last mile for a remote, water-wilderness experience. Your best bet is to choose a lodge and then let it make all your travel arrangements for you.

Neither the Caprivi Strip's Mudumu National Park or Mahango National Park is easily accessible—particularly in the wet season—but if you're a do-it-yourself adventure type, you might enjoy a visit to either park. You'll see plenty of game, including hippos, elephants, buffalo, roan and sable antelope, kudu, zebras, and maybe even wild dogs. Mahango is great for bird-watching, with more species than any other Namibian park.

WHEN TO GO
For bird-watchers the best time to visit is summer (December–February), but be forewarned that the heat and humidity can be unbearable. Toward the end of summer, the Zambezi, Chobe, and Linyanti rivers usually flood, making access to Lake Liambezi and the Mamili National Park difficult. Access will be by 4x4, and will require negotiating completely submerged roads. Otherwise, the Caprivi can be visited for most of the year, but inquire at the lodge you're interested in how negotiable their roads are during the rainy season (November–April/May). The winter months of April to October are great for game-viewing, and far more pleasant what with the cooler temperatures and lack of rainfall.

GETTING HERE AND AROUND
The B8 road from Katima Mulilo to Kasane is paved, and the Namibia/Kasane Bridge has been renovated. The immigration office in Kasane is open from 7:30 to 4. Roads from Katima Mulilo to Victoria Falls and through Gaborone to Johannesburg are all paved and in good condition. The Sesheke Bridge between Namibia and Zambia opened in 2004, completing the TransCaprivi Highway, and linking the port of Walvis Bay with Zambia's capital, Lusaka. The Wenela Border Post is open from 6 to 6. Immigration and customs facilities are also available at Lianshulu Lodge, open from 8 to 5. The Ngoma border is open from 7 to 6. Day trips can be taken across the border in Chobe National Park. ■TIP→ A 4x4 vehicle is required for some of the parks. One can travel on the main roads by sedan car.

TIMING
To explore Caprivi from east to west and to enjoy its peace and quiet, at least a week should be set aside.

WHERE TO STAY
LUXURY LODGES
$$ Impalila Island Lodge. At the crossroads of four countries—Namibia, Botswana, Zambia, and Zimbabwe—this all-inclusive lodge is famous for its hospitality, accommodations, food, and activities. Raised wood-and-thatch chalets, furnished with polished local mukwa wood, open onto wide verandas overlooking the Mambova Rapids at the confluence

of the Zambezi and Chobe rivers. The main thatch dining and bar area is built around two huge baobab trees. After your day's activities, relax on the wooden deck and boast about your tiger-fishing skills, or tick off your mammal and bird lists. Don't miss a guided boat trip to the banks of Botswana's Chobe National Park for game-viewing, or a tranquil mokoro trip in the papyrus-fringed channels. **Pros:** great food; with more than 450 bird species, this place is wonderful for birders; fantastic river safaris in Chobe National Park. **Cons:** game drives into Chobe must be prearranged at extra cost. $ *Rooms from: US$395* ⌂ *Caprivi Strip* ☎ *27–11/781–1661 in South Africa* ✉ *res3@anthology.co.za* ⊕ *www.africananthology.co.za* ⇨ *8 chalets* ⎮◎⎮ *All-inclusive.*

$$$
Fodor's Choice
★

🏠 **Ntwala Island Lodge.** East of Susuwe Island Lodge is the breathtaking, daringly beautiful Ntwala Island Lodge. Only 80 km (50 miles) upstream from Victoria Falls, the four art-deco-meets-Africa chalets are built on an untouched Namibian cluster of small islands linked by floating wooden walkways. You can fly in from Namibia or Botswana, but there's also a road option. Drive to Kasane in Botswana, and then board a small boat that skirts rapids and dodges hippos as it takes you to your very own Treasure Island. A gray, mosaic-edge, kidney-shape pool surrounded by white sand shimmers outside your cream-color, tile-roof chalet, just a couple of yards from the rushing Zambezi. The braying of trumpeter hornbills, the liquid notes of the robins, and the startled calls of francolins greet you. The chalets are spectacular by any standard, with huge rooms, circular wooden canopies echoing the circular bed platforms, carved half-moon chests, handwrought light fittings of metal feathers, and bathrooms big enough to host a party. Freestanding canvas and wooden screens are topped by metal Prince of Wales's feathers, matching the metal curlicue towel rails and bath-accessories trolley. Try your hand at tiger-fishing, marvel at the industry of the reed cormorants as they continuously crisscross the sky carrying nesting material to their heronry, or watch the sunset herds of elephants and buffalo, the unique Chobe bushbuck, a group of impala, and if you're really lucky, in the dry season, some thirsty lions. **Pros:** known as the most luxurious and intimate of the Islands in Africa lodges; huge beautiful rooms with private plunge pools, outdoor showers, and great views; each suite has its own boat and guide. **Cons:** aluminum building materials at the main lodge can rob the luxurious "African feeling" for some; insects at night can be irritating (the consequence of the proximate river). $ *Rooms from: US$595* ⌂ *Caprivi Strip* ☎ *27–11/234–6500 in South Africa* ⊕ *www.ntwala.natureworkshop.com* ⇨ *4 luxury suites* ⎮◎⎮ *All-inclusive.*

$$
🏠 **Susuwe Island Lodge.** This is classic Africa: a solid structure of wood and stone built before the designer-chic lodge invasion. This six-chalet lodge—completely upgraded in 2014—is at the eastern end of the Caprivi Strip (before the strip widens on its way to Botswana) on a small island in a teak forest in the Bwabwata National Park. Here, the deep, clear waters of the Kwando River lap the island's edges, and swamp boubous whistle their melodious calls. Take the time to climb to the highest viewing deck—up in that bird-rich canopy your inner spirit will be restored. A brass lizard, frozen in time, scurries up a wooden

stair rail, while a long-lashed giraffe with bead earrings adorns the outside of one door. Two mekoro act as bookcases; a tiny, tiled elephant watches you from a corner of the stone floor; and in your emperor-size chalet, you'll find candles in carved logs, faded kilims, and a personal plunge pool beside the rushing river. This river trip is one you won't likely forget. Though elephants are around, this is not Big Five country; it's a place to unwind, which is a perfect way to end a safari. **Pros:** more than 8,000 elephants and other exciting game inhabit this area, which is a mix of savanna, wetlands, and woodlands; game drives, boat cruises, and walks are all included; each suite has its own lounge, private plunge pool, and river-facing deck. **Cons:** some game-viewing vehicles lack canvas canopies. $ *Rooms from: US$368* ⊠ *Caprivi Strip* ☎ *061/224–420 in Windhoek* ⊕ *www.caprivicollection.com* ⤢ *6 chalets* ❧ *All-inclusive.*

BUDGET LODGINGS

$ 🏨 **Protea Hotels Zambezi River.** Just 2 km (1 mile) from Katimo Mulilo, is the town's best hotel, where the rooms spread along the banks of the Zambezi River amid colorful bougainvillea bushes and flame trees. But far from the traditional sounds of Africa, the sounds you are most likely to hear are rap, hip-hop, and hard rock from the radios in the Zambian riverside villages just across the river. It's a convenient stopover offering recently renovated, clean, comfortable tiled rooms with windows and double doors facing the river. (Look for the Cape clawless otters playing in the river.) Food is quick and palatable, but don't hold your breath for something special. Short cruises on the river are available. **Pros:** conveniently located 20 minutes from the airport; modern conveniences like satellite TV, a/c, and room service. **Cons:** though clean and comfortable, this outlet of the Protea chain lacks the charm of a smaller hotel; inconsistent service. $ *Rooms from: US$152* ⊠ *Caprivi Strip* ☎ *066/251–500* ⊕ *www.proteahotels.com* ⤢ *38 rooms* ❧ *Breakfast.*

WATERBERG PLATEAU PARK

This lovely game reserve, established in 1972 when several rare and endangered species were introduced from other areas of Namibia and South Africa, is one of the most peaceful and relatively unknown wilderness areas in Namibia. About 91 km (56 miles) east of Otjiwarongo, it's also an ideal stopover on the way from Windhoek to Etosha. The plateau is a huge, flat-top massif rising abruptly from the surrounding plain and offering superb views of the park, the outstanding rock formations, and the magnitude of the plateau itself. Edged with steep-sided, rugged, reddish-brown cliffs, the plateau is covered with red Kalahari sand that supports a range of dry woodland vegetation, from the red syringa trees and Kalahari apple leaf to the kudu bush. You're not allowed to drive yourself, but game-viewing tours operate every morning and evening from the beautifully landscaped Waterberg Camp (book in advance through the NWR; you can join a tour even if you're not a guest of the camp). Although you won't see the big numbers of game that you'll find in Etosha, you could spot the rare roan and sable antelope, Cape buffalo, white and black rhinos, giraffes, hyenas, leopards, and cheetahs. But game-spotting isn't an exact science, so there

"As the sun began to descend over the edge of the Waterberg Plateau, a golden light glazed these two grazers. One was cautious, the other sprung." —Britton Upham, Fodors.com member

are no guarantees. The park is a wonderful place to hike, whether on the much-sought-after, three-day, accompanied Waterberg Wilderness Trail (book through the NWR at the Waterberg Camp [formerly the Bernabé de la Bat Rest Camp] in advance) or on a short 3-km (2-mile) walk around camp.

WHEN TO GO

The park can be visited throughout the year. During the rainy season (December–April) the last stretch of road (which is gravel) must be negotiated very carefully as the surface can be slippery when wet.

GETTING HERE AND AROUND

The park is located about 300 km (186 miles) northeast of Windhoek. Visitors can't drive up onto the plateau in their own vehicles but can explore by foot on self-guided wilderness trails. Daily guided game drives (about four hours) include visits to fantastic hides on the plateau that offer excellent views of water-hole life. Daily game drives can be booked at the Waterberg Camp.

SAFETY AND PRECAUTIONS

Don't feed the animals, and keep your belongings safely away from inquisitive baboons. Lock your bungalow when leaving, as baboons may try to enter an unlocked room. Bring warm clothing for winter weather: game drives in the early morning or late afternoon can be very chilly—even in summer, and especially when it's rained.

TIMING

There are hikes of differing lengths, so inquire how much time you'll need for your chosen route from NWR. If not hiking, then a minimum stay of two nights is recommended so you'll have one whole day to climb the mountain, go on a game drive, relax at the pool, and explore the walking-trails around the camp.

WHERE TO STAY

NATIONAL PARKS ACCOMMODATIONS

$ **Waterberg Camp.** Previously known as Bernabé de la Bat Rest Camp, this NWR property is located on the escarpment's wooded slopes. Take a dip in the camp's natural spring–fed swimming pool at the foot of the towering sandstone cliffs or the new pool bar, then relax in front of your bungalow and watch the sun set over the plateau. Surrounding the camp is one of the largest varieties of plant species in Southern Africa. It's best to book accommodations in advance at NWR in Windhoek, although you can take a chance (particularly in the low season) and book when you arrive at the park office between 8 am and sunset. Camping is also available. There is a restaurant and small shop selling basic groceries and drinks; and should the shop fail to deliver, there's a grocery store in town. **Pros:** guided game drives on the plateau where you can see rare animals; beautiful self-guided walks on the plateau and nature trails in the park. **Cons:** not all self-catering kitchens are well stocked; service is inconsistent; walking trails are not always well maintained. [$] *Rooms from: US$66* ✉ *Waterberg Plateau Park* ☎ *061/285–7200* 🌐 *www.nwr.com.na* 🛏 *23 bush chalets, 34 rooms, 8 premier chalets, 2 family chalets* 🍴 *Breakfast.*

WINDHOEK

The pleasant if provincial little capital city of Windhoek lies almost exactly in the center of the country and is surrounded by the Khomas Highland and the Auas and Eros mountains. With its colonial architecture, sidewalk cafés, shopping centers, and shady parks, it's by no means a hardship to spend a day or two here.

It's very likely that you'll have to take a connecting flight through Windhoek on route to your safari destination, so you'll likely spend at least one overnight here.

Settled by the Germans in the 1890s, it's an easy town to explore on foot (though summers are blisteringly hot). Main sights, which are clustered around the downtown area, include the National Gallery (where you can often purchase works in the temporary exhibits), the remarkably good craft center, and some old German architecture. The city has a population of about 250,000 and growing, most of which resides in the largely black township of Katutura. If you have a few free hours, a visit to Katutura makes an interesting half-day expedition that gives visitors at least an idea of how the majority of urban Namibians live. Windhoek is also home to the country's brewing industry—a holdover from its days as a German colony—and a guided visit to the brewery is possible.

GETTING HERE AND AROUND

Namibia's main point of entry is Hosea Kutako International Airport. It's a small, bustling, modern airport that's a scenic 45-km (28-mile) drive from Windhoek. The smaller Eros Airport handles local flights and charters. Once in the country you can make use of scheduled flights or charter flights that service all domestic destinations.

Licensed shuttle companies (look for a sticker that shows they're registered with the NTB) offer service from Hosea Kutako International Airport to Windhoek's city center; the pickup and drop-off point is at the taxi stand on Independence Avenue, next to the Tourist Information Center. Expect to pay N$250–N$300 each way. Many larger hotels run a courtesy shuttle service to and from the airport. "Radio taxis" (taxis with radio contact to the dispatch) are available, but negotiate the price before you get in. Check on current fares at the airport information counter.

Intercape Mainliner runs buses between Windhoek and Swakopmund, as do other smaller and reliable shuttle services. Information on these is available at the Tourist Information Center in both cities.

If you're only in Windhoek for 24 hours or so, you won't need a car. It's an easy city to walk around in, and taxis are available everywhere. Always negotiate with the driver before getting into the taxi. Hotels also provide shuttle service.

9

That said, if you plan to drive to Swakopmund or any of the parks, you can rent a car here. Gas is on sale in all towns, but if you're planning a long journey between towns, fill up in Windhoek before you leave.

If you've got three days or so to spare and you're headed to or from the coastal resort of Swakopmund, then consider traveling on the Desert Express. The train departs from Windhoek on Friday around midday, and from Swakopmund on Saturday around 3 pm, arriving the next day around 10:30 am. Your first stop on the outward journey from Windhoek is Okapuka Ranch, where you'll watch lions being fed, after which you get back on the train and enjoy a splendid dinner yourself. The train parks in a siding for the night, then leaves early in the morning so you can catch a spectacular sunrise over the desert. Later, you get a chance to walk in the Namib when the train stops in the dunes between Swapkopmund and Walvis Bay. If you do the return journey, you'll be taken to see the San rock paintings at Spitzkoppe. The train has 24 air-conditioned, small but comfortable cabins with en-suite facilities. Longer journeys to Etosha are available. One-way fares from Windhoek to Swakopmund start at N$3,500 per person sharing, and are all-inclusive of meals and activities.

African Extravaganza specializes in shuttle services, scheduled safaris, charter tours and fly-ins, self-drive options, day excursions, and transfers. But as Windhoek is a small town and easy to walk around in, your best bet is to stay in the city and see what's going on there. Ask your hotel concierge or guesthouse owner for up-to-date information, or check out the Tour and Safari Association website (⊕ *www.tasa.na*) for a comprehensive list of registered operators describing their specialties.

HEALTH AND SAFETY

If you need medical attention in Windhoek, consider the Medi-Clinic, an excellent private clinic, or the Roman Catholic Hospital. Ask at your accommodation for the nearest pharmacy.

Pickpockets work the city center, particularly the markets and the Post Street Mall. Lock your valuables away in the hotel safe, and carry only what you need. Never travel with expensive jewelry. Don't walk alone at night, and stick to well-lighted areas.

VISITOR INFORMATION

The very helpful Tourist Information Bureau (run by the City of Windhoek) at the Post Street Mall provides information on Windhoek and environs; it's open weekdays 7:30–1 and 2–4:30. It also operates a kiosk on Independence Avenue next to the main taxi stand and opposite the Kalahari Sands and Casino. Also on Independence Avenue is the Tourist Information Center run by the Leading Lodges of Africa; here you can book accommodations, car rentals, and get advice about travel throughout the country. There's also a luggage storage facility and a small café with Wi-Fi.

The head office of the Namibia Wildlife Resorts (NWR) is also on Independence Avenue. Here you can get information on NWR lodging in all the parks and make bookings. Finally, the Namibia Tourism Board (NTB) has general information on Windhoek as well as the rest of Namibia, but isn't tailored to individual consultation. It's open weekdays 8–5.

Additionally, Windhoek City Tours now has a bus tour on the ubiquitous double-decker red buses that ply cities from London to Tokyo. Leaving twice daily at 9:30 and 2:30, the bus (N$185) is a pleasant zero-effort way to get your bearings and catch all the major sights in about two hours, with live commentary. Tickets and information are available at the Leading Lodge's Tourist Information Center on Independence Avenue.

ESSENTIALS

Airports Eros Airport ☎ 061/295–5501 ⊕ www.airports.com.na. **Hosea Kutako International Airport** ☎ 061/295–5600 ⊕ www.airports.com.na.

Bus Line Intercape Mainliner ☎ 061/227–847 ⊕ www.intercape.co.za.

Car Rentals Avis ☎ 061/233–166 ⊕ www.avis.co.za. **Budget** ☎ 062/228–720 ⊕ www.budget.co.za. **Hertz** ☎ 062/256–274 ⊕ www.hertz.co.za.

Tour Operator African Extravaganza ☎ 061/372–100, 061/372–100 ⊕ www.african-extravaganza.com.

Visitor Information Namibia Tourism Board (NTB). ✉ Channel Life Tower, 39 Post St. Mall, 1st fl. ☎ 061/290–6069 ⊕ www.namibiatourism.com.na. **Namibia Wildlife Resorts** (NWR). ✉ 189 Independence Ave. ☎ 061/285–7200 ⊕ www.nwr.com.na. **City Tourist Office** ✉ Post St. Mall ☎ 061/290–2092, 061/290–2596 ⊕ www.windhoekcc.org.na. **Windhoek City Tours** ✉ 117 Independence Ave. ☎ 061/275–300 ⊕ www.senseofafrica-namibia.com.

EXPLORING

TOP ATTRACTIONS

Namibia Crafts Centre. On Tal Street in the old breweries building behind the Kalahari Sands and Casino hotel, the Namibia Crafts Centre boasts some truly beautiful and unique pieces of work. Dozens of stalls showcase the work of more than 1,500 rural craftspeople, and include items such as particularly fine woven baskets, striking and original beadwork, distinct Caprivian pots, handmade contemporary jewelry, eye-catching prints, and much more. Be sure to check out the Omba Arts Trust stall, where changing exhibits of truly stunning work done by women from disadvantaged communities can be viewed and purchased. ✉ 40 Tal St. ☎ 061/242–2222 ⌚ Weekdays 9–5:30, weekends 9–1:30.

National Gallery. This small but lovely museum features contemporary Namibian art. The somewhat ho-hum permanent exhibit downstairs features German-Namibian painters from the 20th century. Head upstairs, where cool contemporary lithographs by young Namibian artists line the walls, and regularly changing temporary exhibits feature very good work by Namibian and other African artists, most of which is for sale. A small café and shop adjoin. ✉ Corner of John Meinart St. and Robert Mugabe Ave. ☎ 061/231–160 ⊕ www.nagn.org.na ✉ Suggested donation N$20 ⌚ Tues.–Fri. 8–5.

Post Street Mall. At this open-air market known for its colorful sidewalk displays of curios, crafts, and carvings of all kinds, international tourists and businesspeople rub shoulders with Herero women in full traditional Victorian dress. Keep an eye out for the meteorites mounted on slender steel columns. These meteorites hit the earth during the Gibeon meteorite shower, which rained down some 600 million years ago, the heaviest such shower known on earth. ■TIP➔ There are some curios and beadwork on sale here but be sure to check out the sidewalk curio market farther down on Independence Avenue. ⊠ *Post St.* ☺ *Mon.–Sat. 9–5.*

WORTH NOTING

Alte Feste Museum. Literally the "old fort," the oldest existing building in Windhoek (1890) once garrisoned the first contingent of German colonial troops. Now this somewhat decrepit edifice serves as the National Museum's historical display center, with exhibits from the colonial and postcolonial periods, including numerous military items and an interesting section on Namibia's first democratic election and important patriots of the Namibian revolution. A somewhat flashier exhibit on Namibian rock compiled in cooperation with the University of Cologne is the most recent addition. ⊠ *Robert Mugabe Ave.* ☎ *061/293–4437* ⊕ *www.namibiantourism.com.na* 🗺 *Free* ☺ *Summer, daily 9–6; winter, daily 9–5.*

Bushman Art Gallery. This souvenir and curio shop on bustling Independence Avenue distinguishes itself from the rest with its fairly sizable collection of cult objects (religious, ceremonial, drums, etc.) and domestic utensils of local bushman and Himba tribes (not for sale). A large assortment of other carvings and antiques from around Africa adorn the walls and display cases. ⊠ *187 Independence Ave.* ☎ *061/228–828, 061/229–131* ⊕ *www.bushmanart-gallery.com* 🗺 *Free* ☺ *Daily 9–5.*

Christuskirche. The Lutheran Christ Church is a good representation of German colonial architecture—a mixture of art nouveau and neo-Gothic dating from 1896. Although the church is sometimes locked, you can obtain a key from the nearby church office at 12 Fidel Castro Street (down the hill from the church). ⊠ *Robert Mugabe Ave.* ☎ *061/244–588* ☺ *Church office weekdays 7:30–1.*

House of Gems. For a uniquely Namibian gift, visit this long-standing attraction in the heart of Windhoek. House of Gems is a small unassuming shop that has been around for more than 40 years and houses a magnificent collection of Namibian crystals and semiprecious stones. Browse the raw crystals and marvel at the many colors or purchase an exquisitely cut tourmaline, topaz, amethyst, or aquamarine for a reasonable price. ⊠ *131 Werner List St. (former Stubel St.)* ☎ *061/225–202* ⊕ *www.namrocks.com.*

Katutura. Created in the late 1950s for the forced evictions of blacks from the town center, Windhoek's vast African township now houses an estimated 60% of the city's population and makes for an interesting trip. Be sure to visit the Oshetu Market ("our market"), where northern Namibian fare like mopane worms and dried patties of a type of local spinach are sold, and whose bustling meat market includes a barbeque area where the adventurous can try succulent slices of all types of roasted meat, dipped by locals in a mixture of salt and chili. Most tours will include a visit to Penduka, an NGO (non-governmental organization) set up by the UN to empower women. Here you can meet the women who have learned to manufacture beads and fabrics for sale. ■ **TIP→ Be sure to go with a guide, who can both navigate the dirt roads and provide commentary on what you're seeing; Katutura Face to Face Tours are one of several companies that run tours.** ✉ *7716 Sussex St.* ☎ *061/265–446* 🌐 *www.namibweb.com/katuturatours* 🎫 *Tours N$400–500 per person* 🕙 *Tours last 3–4 hrs.*

National Museum of Namibia—Owela Display Centre. With displays on everything from archeology to natural history to ethnology, this rather musty but endearing museum makes up in information (on densely formatted placards) for what it lacks in style, and it's next door to the larger National Museum of Namibia. The exhibit on the San, including refreshingly critical commentary on the bushman as a social construct, and a discussion on the exploitation of that concept, is worth noting. ✉ *Robert Mugabe St.* ☎ *061/276–825* 🎫 *Suggested donation N$20* 🕙 *Daily 8–5.*

Tintenpalast. The handsome circa-1912 (Palace of Ink) is fronted by beautiful formal gardens. Formerly the administration offices of the German colonial government, the two-story building now houses the National Assembly. One-hour tours are given weekdays at 9, 10, and 3. Nearby is the **Office of the Prime Minister,** decorated in mosaics, indigenous woods, and murals. Security guards will give informal tours on request. ✉ *Robert Mugabe Ave.* ☎ *061/288–9111* 🎫 *Free* 🕙 *Weekdays 9–5.*

WHERE TO EAT

$$ EUROPEAN

🍴 **Am Weinberg.** Located in one of Windhoek's older homes (built in 1901), this fine-dining establishment has fabulous views of the city from an unexpectedly relaxed and homey vantage—think warm mustard-color walls, slate-tile floors, and hurricane lamps. The food is upscale European, with French and Italian classics. The mains focus, however, is on perfectly cooked steaks and game meat, such as the herb-crusted springbok loin. There are also a few fish options, including a delicious and rich Marseilles-style bouillabaisse. The wine list befits an ex–wine estate, but mark-ups are significant. Early arrivals can enjoy sundowners from the bar on a lower terrace that enjoys great views. [$] *Average main: US$17* ✉ *13 Jan Jonker Rd., Klein Windhoek* ☎ *061/236–050* 🌐 *www.amweinberg.com.*

$ CAFÉ

🍴 **Craft Café.** This bustling café with lovely outdoor seating serves up generous portions of delicious and (mostly) healthy fare, including huge open-face sandwiches on fresh bread, gorgeous salads, quiches, and freshly squeezed fruit and vegetable juices. It's not all good for you, though: delightful cakes and sweet treats are also baked fresh daily, and all manner of smoothies and milkshakes can be had. Conveniently located upstairs at the Craft Centre, the café's shaded balcony underneath a fig tree is a great place to take a load off. [$] *Average main: US$5* ✉ *40 Tal St.* ☎ *061/249–974* 🌐 *www.craftcafe-namibia.com.*

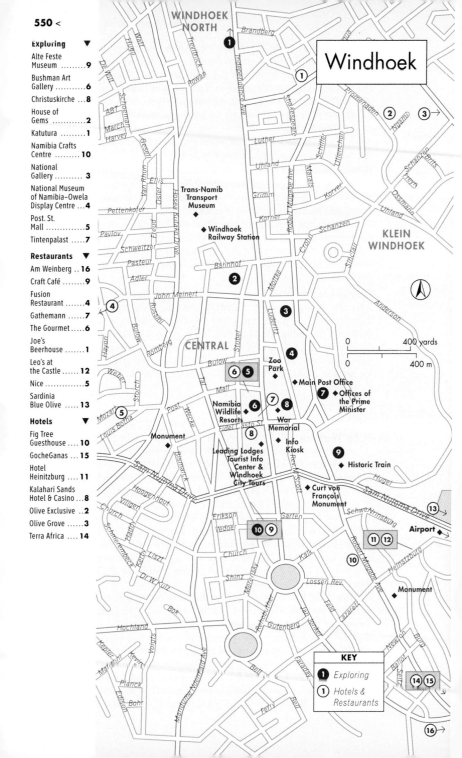

Windhoek

WINDHOEK
NORTH

KLEIN
WINDHOEK

Trans-Namib
Transport
Museum

Windhoek
Railway Station

CENTRAL

Zoo
Park

Main Post Office

Offices of
the Prime
Minister

Namibia
Wildlife
Resorts

War
Memorial

Info
Kiosk

Monument

Leading Lodges
Tourist Info
Center &
Windhoek
City Tours

Historic Train

Curt von
François
Monument

Airport

Monument

KEY

❶ *Exploring*

① *Hotels &
Restaurants*

0   400 yards

0   400 m

$ AFRICAN 🍴 **Fusion Restaurant.** Located in the quiet suburban neighborhood of Windhoek West, Fusion offers first-timers a gentle introduction to dishes from a variety of African cuisines. Softening and melding flavors from traditional recipes, the chef makes dishes like the delicious Senegalese *bourakhe* (a lamb and prawn stew in spinach with peanut butter) extremely accessible to Western palates. The food here is lovingly presented, and the atmosphere and service are friendly and unpretentious. A gallery of local art (for sale), and a huge garden complete the picture. [$] *Average main: US$8* ✉ *Corner of Simpson and Beethoven sts., Windhoek West* ☎ *081/214–8404* 🌐 *www.letseat.at/fusion_namibia.*

$$ AFRICAN 🍴 **Gathemann.** This Windhoek favorite (whose expat Swiss owner/chef doubles as the Swiss Honorary Consul) blends traditional Germanic dishes with an exciting lineup of new creations using local ingredients. Aside from the usual selection of Namibian game and fish, try the giant seasonal *omajova* mushrooms, oysters from Walvis Bay, *mahangu* (pearl millet) creations, green asparagus from Swakopmund, and wine from Namibia's Kristell Kellerei wine farm in Omaruru. Centrally located in the middle of Windhoek, it's an excellent option for an alfresco meal and a favorite with the Windhoek locals. The place to sit is on the terrace overlooking Independence Avenue and the colonial-era Zoo Park. [$] *Average main: US$13* ✉ *175 Independence Ave.* ☎ *061/223–853.*

$$ ECLECTIC 🍴 **The Gourmet.** The massive menu at this popular and conveniently located eatery ensures something for everyone. You'll find German specialties like schnitzels and *spätzelpan* next to a huge selection of pizzas, the ever-popular steaks and game meats, some tasty vegetarian options, a huge array of sweet and savory crepes, and even a few pan-African dishes (the Malawian *msamba* veggie dish is great). Located in the old (very German) Kaiserkrone Hotel just off the Post Street Mall in a leafy courtyard, The Gourmet may not be exactly gourmet, but it is a good value and is a perfect option for lunch. [$] *Average main: US$14* ✉ *Kaiserkrone Centre, Post St. Mall* ☎ *061/232–630* 🕒 *Closed Sun.*

$$ GERMAN FAMILY 🍴 **Joe's Beerhouse.** Tuck into generous portions of German and Namibian food at this popular Windhoek institution. Venison is a specialty (try the kudu steak or gemsbok filet), but if the Teutonic urge strikes, opt for the sauerkraut and pork filet or their pork roast pan. Vegetarian food is also available. Although the interior is fun-filled with Joe's personal collection of memorabilia, it's also pleasant to sit outside in the boma by a roaring fire and quaff *glühwein* (mulled wine) or Camelthorn Brewery's Sundowner beer, a local lager. There's a great play area for kids and despite the vast amount of people in the restaurant the service is fairly prompt. [$] *Average main: US$14* ✉ *160 Nelson Mandela Ave.* ☎ *061/232–457* 🌐 *www.joesbeerhouse.com* ✍ *Reservations essential.*

$$ EUROPEAN 🍴 **Leo's at the Castle.** Doubtless the priciest restaurant in town, Leo's is also arguably Windhoek's only true fine-dining establishment. Literally in a castle on a hill, Leo's small chandelier-dazzled dining room has fabulous views across the city. Inside, it's all champagne and taupe elegance, with red roses in simple sterling vases, and sepia prints of early-20th-century photographs of the castle. The cuisine is haute all the way and gorgeously prepared and presented. The seasonal menu is not large but focuses on meat, with a couple fresh fish and vegetarian

options. The wine list is an impressive tome. In warm weather, the outside seating is its own delight. $ *Average main: US$13* ⊠ *Hotel Heinitzburg, 22 Heinitzburg St.* ☎ *061/249–597* ⊕ *www.heinitzburg. com* ⚲ *Reservations essential.*

$$ ×**Nice.** Windhoek's newest and hippest place to wine and dine is the
ECLECTIC restaurant showcase for the Namibian Institute of Culinary Education
Fodor'sChoice (NICE). With an emphasis on local ingredients and a multitude of influ-
★ ences, trainees supervised by head chefs produce delicious fare, such as tomato-based seafood ragout, or oryx loin with poached pear, pilaf, and a red wine reduction. When in season try dishes featuring local delicacies like kalahari truffles. Simpler fare like fish 'n' chips can also be had, and the desserts are excellent. With varied seating options— indoor, pondside dining, seating at the popular bar—the gorgeous space is elegant-cool all the way; it's the renovated family home of the owner. With trainees, however, does come inconsistent service so sit back relax and just enjoy the vibe. Connected to the Wolwedans Group with their properties in the Namibrand private reserve, NICE produces young talented cooks who get poached by other lodges throughout Namibia. $ *Average main: US$12* ⊠ *2 Mozart St. (corner of Hosea Kutako Dr.)* ☎ *061/300–710* ⊕ *www.nice.com.na.*

$ ×**Sardinia Blue Olive.** The Sardinia Blue Olive is Windhoek's offering
ITALIAN of classic Italian cuisine but with a touch of Namibian-inspired mains like oryx and lamb shank. Despite being 250 miles from the ocean their seafood is impressive and the deep-dish pizzas are as cheesy as it gets. Try their calamari starter with crispy squidheads in a light lemon garlic sauce. The space is lacking in décor and theme, but it's always bustling and the crowd creates the vibe. Good service and decent wine list. $ *Average main: US$11* ⊠ *Schoemans Building, Sam Nujoma Dr.* ☎ *061/258–183* ⚲ *Reservations essential* ☺ *Closed Mon.*

WHERE TO STAY

Hotel reviews have been shortened. For full information, visit Fodors. com.

$ ⬚ **Fig Tree Guesthouse.** This small and lovely guesthouse is very cen-
B&B/INN trally located on Robert Mugabe Avenue, just a 5- to 10-minute walk from downtown Windhoek. **Pros:** all rooms have fridges and micro-waves; rooms have printers; small, intimate B&B in convenient central location. **Cons:** not many rooms so can get fully booked in season; rooms lack a view and some can be a bit dark. $ *Rooms from: US$83* ⊠ *11 Robert Mugabe Ave.* ☎ *061/400–966* ⊕ *www.figtree.com.na* ⬚ *8 rooms* ⦿ *Multiple meal plans.*

$ ⬚ **GocheGanas.** Just on the outskirts of Windhoek, this well-appointed
B&B/INN lodge has all the safari charm and sophistication of a luxury lodge. **Pros:** close to Windhoek but far enough away to feel like a real safari lodge; wellness village, spa, and hot pool; excellent service. **Cons:** limited wine selection; restaurant feels a little sparse and hollow. $ *Rooms from: US$234* ⊠ *20 km along D1463 to South of Windhoek* ☎ *061/224–909* ⊕ *www.gocheganas.com* ⬚ *13 suites, 1 family suite* ⦿ *Some meals.*

$$ 🏨 **Hotel Heinitzburg.** This is your chance to stay in a turn-of-the-20th-century castle, a white fort with battlements set high on a hill and com-
HOTEL missioned by a German count for his fiancée in 1914. **Pros:** lavishly decadent interior styling; great, personalized service; 5-minute drive from city center. **Cons:** rooms don't have tons of natural light (it's a castle after all); the décor and bathrooms are a little dated. $ *Rooms from: US$269* ✉ *22 Heinitzburg St.* ☎ *061/249–597* ⊕ *www.heinitzburg.com* ⇒ *16 rooms* ⦿ *Breakfast.*

$ 🏨 **Kalahari Sands and Casino.** Known locally as the Sands, this hotel has
HOTEL rooms that are pleasant with a recent décor-uplift giving the property just enough character to make it comfortable and elegant. **Pros:** centrally located; most of downtown Windhoek is within walking distance; impressive breakfast buffet. **Cons:** navigating the entrance and parking area (if self-driving) can be confusing; the area is popular with vagrants. $ *Rooms from: US$143* ✉ *Gustav Voigts Centre, 129 Independence Ave.* ☎ *061/280–0000 for hotel, 2711/780–7810 for central reservations* ⊕ *www.suninternational.com* ⇒ *167 rooms, 5 suites* ⦿ *Breakfast.*

$ 🏨 **Olive Exclusive Boutique Hotel.** Windhoek's premier boutique hotel, the
HOTEL Olive Exclusive, with it's six large suites each decorated thematically
Fodor's Choice according to each of Namibia's regions, is an upmarket treat either
★ before or after your safari. **Pros:** beautifully appointed and spacious suites; in-house spa therapist; excellent restaurant. **Cons:** the view onto the hills of Windhoek and a flourishing olive grove is decent, but could seem spoiled by shabby housing on one side; you need a car to get around. $ *Rooms from: US$198* ✉ *22 Promenaden St., Klein Windhoek* ☎ *061/239–199* ⊕ *www.theolive-namibia.com* ⇒ *7 suites* ⦿ *Multiple meal plans.*

$ 🏨 **Olive Grove.** Located about a 10-minute drive north of the city center,
B&B/INN this elegant guesthouse is incredibly popular for its stylish simplicity and great service. **Pros:** great food; helpful and friendly staff; in-house spa therapist. **Cons:** must drive to city center; downstairs "patio" rooms lack views and can be a bit dark; pool is for plunging only. $ *Rooms from: US$68* ✉ *20 Promenaden Rd.* ☎ *061/239–199* ⊕ *www.olivegrove-namibia.com* ⇒ *11 rooms* ⦿ *Breakfast.*

$ 🏨 **Terra Africa.** The feeling of being in someone's home starts upon enter-
B&B/INN ing the lounge decorated with African art and strewn with magazines by a fireplace, and continues thanks to the personalized and friendly service here. **Pros:** extremely friendly and helpful staff; charming pool and garden area; homey comforts like a fireplace in the lounge. **Cons:** rooms vary significantly in size and view; must drive to city center; nearby road can be noisy. $ *Rooms from: US$133* ✉ *6 Kenneth McArthur St., Olympia* ☎ *061/252–100* ⊕ *www.terra-africa.com* ⇒ *10 rooms* ⊙ *Closed Dec. 22–Jan. 3* ⦿ *Breakfast.*

9

BEACH ESCAPES

You don't come to Namibia for beaches, but if you do fancy a dip in the freezing Atlantic waters, Swakopmund, the country's only real beach resort, is your best bet.

SWAKOPMUND

Although the desert continues to sweep its remorseless way toward the mighty Atlantic and its infamous Skeleton Coast, humans have somehow managed to hang on to this patch of coastline, where Swakopmund clings to the edge of the continent. The first 40 German settlers, complete with household goods and breeding cattle, arrived here with 120 German colonial troops on the *Marie Woermann* in the late 19th century. Today, instead of the primitive shelters that the early settlers built on the beach to protect themselves from sand and sea, stands Swakopmund, or "Swakops," as the resort town is affectionately known. There's something surreal about Swakops. On the one hand, it's like a tiny European transplant, with its seaside promenade, sidewalk cafés, fine German colonial buildings, trendy bistros, friendly and neat-as-a-pin pensions, and immaculate boarding houses and hotels. On the other hand, this little town is squashed between the relentless Atlantic and the harsh desert, in one of the wildest and most untamed parts of the African continent—something you might understandably forget while nibbling a chocolate torte or sipping a good German beer under a striped umbrella.

Swakops makes for a different, unique beach escape because of its history and surreal surroundings. It's one of the top adventure centers in Africa, second only to Victoria Falls in Zimbabwe. Adrenaline junkies can try their hand (or feet) at skydiving, sandboarding, kayaking, dune-buggying, paragliding, or wave-skipping in a light aircraft. The less adventurous (but romantic) can take day, moonlight, sunrise, or sunset horseback or camel rides through the riverbeds and up into the moonlike landscape. The curious can partake in one of the fabulous "little five" living-desert tours through the dunes that represent the northern extent of the Namib-Naukluft (⇨ *see Essentials below*). There are also lots of curio shops and commercial art galleries, making Swakops great for shopping, and the dining options are improving all the time.

WHEN TO GO

Keep in mind that the town is packed with vacationing Namibians and South Africans at Christmas, New Year's, and Easter, so avoid these times if you can. The sea keeps temperatures relatively comfortable year-round, and positively chilly outside of summer.

GETTING HERE AND AROUND

The closest airport, handling domestic and international flights, is about a 45-minute drive from Swakopmund at Walvis Bay. ⇨ *For more information on flights and carriers, see Air Travel in the Planning section, above.*

Intercape Mainliner runs buses between Windhoek and Swakopmund. The Town Hoppers shuttle service also runs a daily shuttle between Windhoek and Swakopmund for N$270 one-way. For an additional fee, they'll provide door-to-door pickup and/or drop-off. There are no reliable bus services within Swakopmund for visitors.

If you have the time, it's worth renting a car to drive from Windhoek to Swakopmund. It's a very scenic and easy four-hour drive, about 368 km (228 miles) on the B1, a good paved road. Once in Swakopmund, it's easy to find your way around. With a car, you'll also be able to visit the Cape Cross seal colony and drive farther north toward the Skeleton Coast, or drive 30 km (19 miles) south to Walvis Bay, where numerous outdoor activities originate. *(⇨ For more information on Walvis Bay, see Walvis Bay section below.)* A two-wheel-drive vehicle is fine, but if you intend on visiting Sandwich Harbour or Sossusvlei in Namib-Naukluft Park, then four-wheel drive will give you more access and better viewing (and is essential for Sandwich Harbour).

If you arrange to rent a car in advance at any of the reliable agencies, you'll be met at Walvis Bay Airport. The car-rental agencies also have offices in Swakopmund.

⇨ *For more information on train travel between Windhoek and Swakopmund, see Windhoek's Getting Here and Around section, above.*

SAFETY AND PRECAUTIONS

Swakops is a very safe little town, but you should always be aware of potential pickpockets. Lock your valuables away in the hotel safe, and carry only what you need. Never travel with expensive jewelry. Don't walk alone at night, and stick to well-lighted areas.

Cottage Private Hospital is a private clinic. Ask at your accommodation about the nearest pharmacy.

TIMING

Swakopmund is both a pleasant place in itself and offers a surprising array of activities and good shopping, as well as some culinary variety if you've been on safari for a while. Visitors generally stay two nights, but three to four nights is better if you really want to partake in a few of the outdoor activities for which this area is famous (several of which happen in Walvis Bay, a 40-minute drive south), as well as relax and stroll around the town itself.

VISITOR INFORMATION

Namib-I, the tourist information center, provides excellent national and local information, maps, and more.

CONTACTS

Airport Walvis Bay Airport ☎ *064/271-072* ⊕ *www.airports.com.na.*

Bus Line Intercape Mainliner ☎ *061/227-847* ⊕ *www.intercape.co.za.*

Car Rentals Avis ✉ *Swakopmund Hotel and Entertainments Centre, 2 Theo-Ben Guribab Ave.* ☎ *064/402-527.* **Crossroads 4x4 Hire** ✉ *3 Moses Garoëb St.* ☎ *064/403-777* ⊕ *www.crossroads4x4hire.com.* **Hertz** ✉ *Walvis Bay Airport, Walvis Bay* ☎ *064/200-853* ⊕ *www.hertz.co.za.* **Town Hoppers Shuttle** ✉ *Antonius Building, Nathanael Maxuilili St., Shop 12* ☎ *064/407-223, 081/210-3062* ⊕ *www.namibiashuttle.com.*

Emergency Contacts Ambulance/Hospital ☎ *064/412-200.* **Police** ☎ *064/10111.*

Hospital Cottage Medi-Clinic ✉ *Franziska van Neel St.* ☎ *064/412-200* ⊕ *www.mediclinic.co.za.*

Visitor Information Namib I Tourist Information ✉ *28 Sam Nujoma Ave., corner of Hendrik Witbooi St.* ☎ *064/404-827.*

EXPLORING

TOP ATTRACTIONS

Kristall Galerie. This sizable gallery houses the largest known quartz-crystal cluster in the world—an awesome natural wonder more than 520 million years old and weighing 14,000 kilograms. Numerous smaller but no less beautiful chunks of Namibian minerals and gems, including a wide variety of quartz crystals, rainbow tourmalines, and other semiprecious stones, are also on display. Some great souvenirs can be had in the adjoining large gift shop and high-end jewelry boutique to allow you to take home a unique piece of Namibia. ✉ *Corner of Tobias Hainyeko and Theo-Ben Gurirab aves.* ☎ *064/406-080* ⊕ *www.namibiagemstones.com* 🎟 *N$20* ⊗ *Mon.–Sat. 9–4:45.*

FAMILY **The Living Desert Snake Park.** With more than 25 species of Namibian snakes, lizards, chameleons, and scorpions, this small museum will excite herpetologists large and small. Several of Southern Africa's most dangerous snakes can be seen in the flesh here, including the black mamba and puff adder. Snake feedings take place on Saturday at 10. ✉ *59 Sam Nujoma Ave., corner of Otavi Bahnhof* ☎ *064/405-100, 081/128-5100* 🎟 *N$30* ⊗ *Weekdays 9–5, Sat. 9–1.*

Swakopmund Dunes. Though you may have already visited higher or more visually stunning dunes, the Swakop dunes have the unique distinction of being the subject of a truly fascinating tour that introduces visitors to the numerous—and normally invisible—creatures thriving in this surreal ecosystem. Both Chris Nel, the operator of Living Desert Namibia tours, and Tommy Collard, of Tommy's Tours *(⇨ see Tour Operators, below, for contact information)*, are passionate and well-informed characters who tend to leap out of 4x4s to catch the desert's perfectly camouflaged lizards, geckos, and snakes. A visit here is a

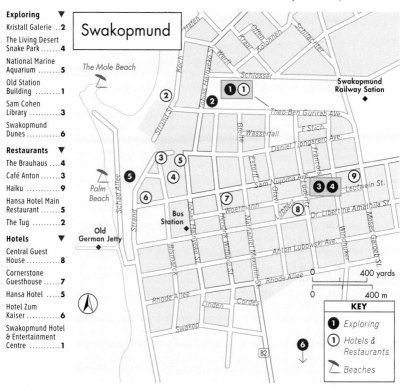

unique, educational, and often humorous experience. ⊠ *Swakopmund Dunes.*

WORTH NOTING

FAMILY **National Marine Aquarium.** The small, attractive aquarium showcases great displays of marine life in its tanks, including a huge main tank that can be viewed from different angles. ■ TIP→ **The bigger fish, especially the sharks, are fed around 3 pm so try to time your visit for then.** It's a worthwhile attraction if you are travelling with kids and is a great way to spend half an hour or so. ⊠ *South Strand St. (at the southern end)* ☎ *064/410–1000* ⊠ *N\$30* ⊘ *Tues.–Sun. 10–4.*

Old Station Building. Probably Swakops's most notable landmark, the gorgeous, historic Old Station Building was built in 1901. Declared a national monument in 1972, this magnificent example of German colonial architecture came to life again in the early 1990s, when it was restored and renovated in a style evoking the charm and nostalgia of the old railway days. Don't miss the huge bustling lobby—a remnant of the building's former life as a railway station. Today, the building houses the Swakopmund Hotel and Entertainment Centre, which includes a movie theater, casino, spa, and two restaurants. ⊠ *2 Theo-Ben Gurirab Ave.* ⊕ *www.legacyhotels.co.za.*

9

Sam Cohen Library. As in Windhoek, there are lots of historic German buildings dating to the turn of the 20th century, most of them in perfect condition. The railway station, the prison, the Woermann House, the Kaserne (barracks), the Lutheran church, and the district court look more like illustrations from some Brothers Grimm fairy tale than the working buildings they once were. You can usually purchase a book with detailed information about these buildings from the Sam Cohen Library, which is worth a visit for its impressive collection of Africana books, archives of old newspapers (many in German), and vast photo collection (though note the N$50 users fee to browse the archives). This library began its life with 5 books and now has over 10,000 volumes. ☒ *Sam Nujoma St., corner of Windhuker St.* ☎ *064/402–695* ☞ *Free (N$50 browsing fee)* ☉ *Weekdays 8–1 and 3–5, 2nd Sat. of the month 9–1.*

BEACHES

Though Namibia is hardly a beach destination, if you really want some sand and sun time, head to the Mole and adjacent Palm Beach, Swakops's most popular beaches (in front of the lighthouse). Keep in mind that this isn't Mauritius or the Caribbean: the sea can be treacherous, and the temperature usually runs in the lower 50s. Both of these beaches are a short walk from the center of town, and there are numerous cafés and restaurants along here to stop for a quick drink or bite to eat. The beach is sheltered by a breakwater, so its calm waters attract crowds, especially on the weekends; if you do swim out, beware of the strong currents just off the breakwater. There's a paved walkway that heads north along the beach if you need to stretch your legs. You can also head to the jetty at the southern end of the beach for a stroll. The southern side of the jetty is for walkers, while the northern side is reserved for fishing.

The Mole Beach. The designated swimming beach at Swakopmund, The Mole, is actually a failed engineering project. In 1899 the South Africans controlled the closest harbor at Walvis Bay, so attempts were made to build a harbor at Swakopmund. The engineer, FW Ortloff, failed to take into account the force of the Benguela current flowing down the length of Namibia and dumping desert sands on the shore. The result is the promontory you see today with The Mole now forming a secluded swimming beach. A short walk from the center of town, the beach is serviced by a number of restaurants and small cafés; the closest hotel is the Hotel Zum Kaiser. The Atlantic Ocean is generally cold and rough, and unfortunately the town closed its heated Olympic-size swimming pool so if you're set on swimming, you'll have to brave it. Lifeguards are on duty during the summer. **Amenities:** lifeguards (in summer), toilets, parking (no fee). **Best for:** swimming, sunsets. ☒ *A. Schad Promenade.*

Palm Beach. At a manageable 500 meters (1,640 feet), Palm Beach, which stretches along the western side of Swakopmund and effectively forms the western border, is the recommended beach for gentle walking. Swimming isn't encouraged due to rough waters and strong currents (and the icy Atlantic waters). Instead stroll from the north, starting at the Mole beach, and watch the sun go down in the west. Enjoy a sundowner on Swakopmund's famous jetty and if you're hungry try the festive scene at the famous Tug restaurant. The palms the beach is named after are set back against the access road offering limited shade. Busy in summer, but quiet in winter, Palm Beach is also often in fog due to the cold air of the Atlantic hitting the heat of the desert. Set just back off Beach Road, Hotel Zum Kaiser (previously known as Swakopmund Boutique Hotel) is the closest accommodation to the beach. **Amenities:** food and drink, parking, toilets. **Best for:** walking, sunsets. ⊠ *A. Schad Promenade.*

SHOPPING

African Art Jewellers. A cut above the rest, the original and African-inspired designs and materials used by this fine jeweler are worth checking out. ⊠ *1 Hendrik Witbooi St.* ☎ *064/405–566* ⊙ *Weekdays 8:30–1 and 2–6, Sat. 8:30–1.*

Art Africa. A lovely emporium of high-quality crafts and curios from all over Namibia, as well as other parts of Africa. Items include rural art, contemporary jewelry, ceramics, leather products, masks, baskets, and funky whimsical crafts. ⊠ *Shop 6, The Arcade, Sam Nujome St.* ☎ *064/463–454* ⊙ *Weekdays 8:30–6, Sat. 8:30–1 and 4–6, Sun. 10–6.*

Die Muschel. This beautiful book and coffee shop in the center of Swakopmund, specializes in gorgeous coffee table books of African landscapes, people, and animals, as well as a great selection of field guides, maps, and other books about Namibia and Southern Africa. It's a perfect spot to buy postcards and find a new book to read for the rest of your trip. ⊠ *Corner of Brauhaus Arcade and Tobias Hainyeko St.* ☎ *064/402–874* ⊕ *www.muschel.iway.na* ⊙ *Weekdays 8:30–6, Sat. 8:30–1 and 4–6, Sun. 10–6.*

Peter's Antiques. This store has been described as the best shop in Africa for its superbly eclectic collection of pieces from all over sub-Saharan Africa. Those not in the market are still welcome to browse the shop like a museum. ⊠ *24 Tobias Hainyeko St.* ☎ *064/405–624* ⊕ *www.peters-antiques.com* ⊙ *Weekdays 9–1 and 3–6, Sat. 9–1 and 5–6, Sun. 5–6.*

WHERE TO EAT

$ ╳ **The Brauhaus.** A Swakopmund institution, the original Brauhaus
GERMAN burned to the ground in 2009 in an electrical fire, but the current edifice is an exact replica of its predecessor, minus many of the beloved beer steins and other decorative memorabilia. The beer is flowing once again, and the big wooden tables invite long sit-downs over hearty lunches and dinners featuring dishes like schnitzel, bratwurst, and *rösti* (similar to a potato pancake). The German fare is excellent but if goulash and sauerkraut don't do it for you, there is a large selection of steaks and game meat, as well as seafood and even a few pasta and vegetarian options. A lively gathering place on Saturday afternoons, this is the place to mingle with the (mostly Germanic) locals. $ *Average main: US$10* ⊠ *The Arcade 22, Sam Nujoma Ave.* ☎ *064/402–214* ⊕ *www.swakopmundbrauhaus.com* ⊙ *Closed Sun., except mid-Dec.–mid-Jan.*

$ ╳ **Café Anton.** This is a good place to take a break after perusing the
CAFÉ curio market around the lighthouse. Sit on the palm-shaded terrace overlooking the lighthouse and the sea and watch the world go by while you eat a breakfast of scrumptious home-baked cake or pastry, or enjoy

a late afternoon tea with hazelnut triangles, custard-filled danishes, or croissants. The chocolate-drenched Florentiner cookies are divine, and the Black Forest cake is made exactly as it is in Germany and the apple strudel is legendary. A small selection of light lunch options like toasted sandwiches and soups is served until 2 pm. $ *Average main: US$4* ✉ *Schweizerhaus Hotel, 1 Bismarck St., overlooking the Mole* ☎ *064/400–331* ⊕ *www.schweizerhaus.net.*

$$ ✕ **Haiku.** For those returning from days and nights book-ended by the
SUSHI ubiquitous bounty of meat that is safari cuisine, this sushi joint will offer a delightful though costly alternative. The owners take pains to import the majority of their grocery ingredients from Japan and also have nonlocal fish flown in on a regular basis. Inventive combinations and rolls like the white-pearl starter (crab mixed with sushi rice with a ponzu wasabi sauce) and the black-dragon roll (spicy tuna with mango and avo) are recommended. Portions are not large, but everything is fresh and lovingly prepared. $ *Average main: US$14* ✉ *37 Tobias Hanyeko St.* ☎ *064/406–406* ⊘ *Closed Mon.*

$$ ✕ **Hansa Hotel Main Restaurant.** If you're looking for a special-occasion
EUROPEAN dinner and you appreciate good, rich food such as venison, steak, and Namibian seafood delicacies, then you can't do better than this rather formal, highly rated restaurant with an excellent wine list. Start with the game consommé with marrow dumplings before moving on to the giant prawns in honey-lemon butter or the springbok loin. Your surroundings are a perfectly restored 1905 German colonial building (the hotel itself has earned plenty of accolades), which lends itself to a certain old-world charm with the service to match. $ *Average main: US$13* ✉ *3 Hendrik Witbooi St.* ☎ *064/414–200* ⊕ *www.hansahotel.com.na* ⌂ *Reservations essential.*

$$ ✕ **The Tug.** It's all about location at the Tug, which, as its name suggests,
SEAFOOD is actually an old tugboat that has been raised up and moored next to the jetty. Swakops is known for its fresh seafood—especially the local oysters—which is quite good here. Creative seafood alternatives include venison or ostrich stir-fry. ■ **TIP→ Try to reserve a sea-view table so you can watch the ocean crashing just beneath you, but reserve at least a week in advance.** The outside deck is also a coveted location for a summer sundowner and it's always bustling with visitors and locals alike; alternatively enjoy an after-dinner drink in the bar which is feels like you are in the boat's bridge. $ *Average main: US$14* ✉ *The Strand, Swakopmund* ☎ *064/402–356* ⊕ *www.the-tug.com* ⌂ *Reservations essential* ⊘ *No lunch weekdays.*

WHERE TO STAY

Several of the lodging establishments listed don't have air-conditioning, but because of the cool climate, this is actually standard practice in the smaller guesthouses. They all have fans for use in summer, and it's rarely so hot that the average person would consider air-conditioning necessary. For much of the year, having a heater indoors is more of an issue.

Hotel reviews have been shortened. For full information, visit Fodors. com.

$ B&B/INN **Central Guest House.** This charming and extremely conveniently located old house is an owner-managed B&B with six rooms. **Pros:** personalized and helpful service; convenient location; lovely old house. **Cons:** exterior is a bit stark; rooms lack any particular view. [$] *Rooms from: US$66* ✉ *Corner of Lüderitz and Lutwein sts.* ☎ *064/407–189* 🌐 *www.guesthouse.com.na* 🛏 *6 rooms* 🍴 *Breakfast.*

$ B&B/INN **Cornerstone Guesthouse.** Walking into Cornerstone one is struck by the lovely manicured garden and the pleasantly homey (and exceedingly clean) ambience. **Pros:** great breakfast; personalized friendly service; lovely garden. **Cons:** one room looks onto parking area instead of garden; often fully booked. [$] *Rooms from: US$62* ✉ *40 Hendrik Witbooi St., Swakopmund* ☎ *064/462–468* 🌐 *www.cornerstoneguesthouse.com* 🛏 *6 rooms* 🍴 *Breakfast.*

$ HOTEL Fodor's Choice ★ **Hansa Hotel.** This old-world grand dame gives guests a Belle Époque feeling with the hushed solicitude, gleaming brass, thick carpets, and manicured garden. **Pros:** lovely extras like a house library with a great selection of books; gorgeous old bar with a fireplace; amazing restaurant. **Cons:** could be a bit stuffy for the younger crowd; bathrooms feel a little cramped. [$] *Rooms from: US$97* ✉ *3 Hendrik Witbooi St.* ☎ *064/414–200* 🌐 *www.hansahotel.com.na* 🛏 *58 rooms* 🍴 *Breakfast.*

$ HOTEL **Hotel Zum Kaiser.** This new three-story boutique hotel by the beach—with its tones of silver, champagne and taupe, and modern art and orchid displays—is all contemporary elegance and comfort. **Pros:** many of the rooms have a partial sea view; amazing roof bar with great sunset views. **Cons:** Wi-Fi is spotty. [$] *Rooms from: US$102* ✉ *4 Sam Nujoma Ave.* ☎ *064/417–100* 🌐 *www.hotelzumkaiser.com* 🛏 *21 rooms* 🍴 *Breakfast.*

$$ HOTEL FAMILY **Swakopmund Hotel and Entertainment Centre.** At this hotel within the 1901 Old Station Building, the huge bustling lobby is a reminder of the building's previous incarnation as a railway station. **Pros:** conveniences of a large hotel with numerous facilities; lovely lobby architecture and pleasant (though unheated) pool. **Cons:** lack of real character or intimacy; often used as a business or conference center; nonsmoking rooms exist, but those sensitive to smoke may smell occasional smoke. [$] *Rooms from: US$220* ✉ *2 Theo-Ben Gurirab Ave.* ☎ *064/410–5200* 🌐 *www.legacyhotels.co.za* 🛏 *90 rooms* 🍴 *Breakfast.*

SPORTS AND THE OUTDOORS

Africa's second adventure-activity capital after Livingstone, Swakopmund is the departure point for all manner of tours that make use of its surreal location between the dunes and the sea. Daytime, moonlight, sunrise, and sunset horseback rides are possible with Okakambe Trails. Desert Explorers, Outback Orange, and the Swakopmund Skydiving Club can organize skydiving over the dunes, sandboarding, and quad-bike (ATV) trips. The Living Desert Tour is highly recommended, as is a 4x4 day trip to Sandwich Harbour, with its rich bird life and spectacular views. Numerous sea-based tours are also available but most depart from Walvis Bay. Finally, Namib Tracks & Trails can organize all manner of trips, including day trips a bit farther afield to sights like the amazing rock formations and bush paintings at Spitzkoppe or the seal colony at Cape Cross.

Tour Operators **Desert Explorers** ✉ *Nathaniel Maxuilili St.* ☎ *081/129–2380 (mobile), 081/124–1386 (mobile)* ✐ *info@namibiadesertexplorers.com* ⊕ *www. namibiadesertexplorers.com.* **Living Desert Tour** ☎ *064/405–070, 081/127– 5070* ⊕ *www.livingdesertnamibia.com.* **Namib Tracks & Trails** ✉ *14A Sam Nujoma Ave.* ☎ *064/416–820.* **Okakambe Trails** ✉ *11 km (7 miles) east of Swakopmund on the B2 to Windhoek, next to the camel farm, Erf 378 Swakopmund river plots* ☎ *064/402–799.* **Outback Orange** ✉ *44 Nathaniel Maxuilili St.* ☎ *064/406–096, 081/129–2380 (mobile)* ⊕ *www.outback-orange.com.* **Swakopmund Skydiving Club** ✉ *5 km east of Swakopmund on the B2, near the airport turn-off, Hanger 13B* ☎ *064/405–671* ⊕ *www.skydiveswakopmund. com.* **Tommy's Tours and Safaris** ☎ *081/128–1038* ⊕ *www.tommys.iway.na.*

WALVIS BAY

One of Southern Africa's most important harbor towns, the once industrial Walvis Bay has recently developed into a seaside holiday destination with a number of pleasant lagoonfront guesthouses and several good restaurants—including one of Namibia's best, Lyon des Sables. The majority of water activities advertised in Swakopmund actually depart from Walvis's small waterfront area, and there's an amazing flamingo colony residing in the Bay's 3,000-year-old lagoon.

WHEN TO GO
Like Swakopmund, Walvis Bay enjoys a mild climate. Although most of the local Christmas and Easter holidaymakers head to Swakops, the overflow can spill out here, so it can get crowded during these times.

GETTING HERE AND AROUND
About 15 km (9 miles) east of town, the Walvis Airport serves the region (including Swakopmund) and has direct flights to South Africa. The major car-rental companies are located at the airport. Thirty kilometers (18 miles) from Swakopmund, the drive takes about 40 minutes on the B2. The town itself lacks attractions, and most visitors will head straight to the Walvis Bay lagoon. Here you'll find the majority of accommodations; the waterfront, from where almost all activities (both sea- and land-based) depart; and a handful of restaurants. Most everything in the lagoon area is within walking distance.

SAFETY AND PRECAUTIONS
Be sure to turn your lights on when driving between Walvis and Swakops, even in the daytime. Locals say that the way light reflects between the dunes and the sea impairs depth perception.

TIMING
Most of Walvis's activities, including bird-watching, boat tours, and 4x4 day trips to Sandwich Harbour, depart relatively early. As such, spending the night before such an activity is certainly worthwhile. Given the new accommodations and restaurants in town, if time allows and you plan on participating in more than one activity, two nights wouldn't be wasted.

WHERE TO EAT

$ ✕**Anchors @ The Jetty.** This is the quintessential seaside restaurant to
SEAFOOD satisfy your appetite for seafood and a view. Sitting right on the water's
edge, Anchors is the perfect spot to sip a glass of wine, taste the freshest
west coast oysters or basic fish 'n' chips while mesmerized by the sparkling ocean. The service is prompt and friendly and while you sit and
watch the boats go to and fro, time will slowly slip by. Their grilled calamari is unrivaled. $ *Average main: US$8* ✉ *Waterfront* ☎ *064/205–762*
✎ *anchorsatthejetty@gmail.com.*

$$ ✕**Lyon des Sables.** Arguably Namibia's finest restaurant and a reason
FRENCH in itself to visit Walvis Bay, Lyon des Sables, at the seaside Walvis Bay
Fodor'sChoice Yacht Club, is owned and run by two Frenchmen who have found
★ their place under the African sun. Dishes present genius combinations
of texture and flavor, using the freshest ingredients. The seared tuna
starter with a pine nut pesto and balsamic reduction topped with hazel-
nut crumble, and the kingklip with marinated artichokes and oyster
cream sauce are highly recommended. Keep an eye out for theme nights,
like "sushi Wednesdays." The funky décor—purple walls and a sort
of retro-hip vibe—great cocktails and wine list, and friendly efficient
service complete the picture. Save room for dessert. $ *Average main:
US$13* ✉ *Walvis Bay Yacht Club., Atlantic St., Zone 55* ☎ *064/221–220*
✎ *lyondessables@gmail.com* ◷ *Closed Sun.*

WHERE TO STAY

*Hotel reviews have been shortened. For full information, visit Fodors.
com.*

$ ⌂**Egumbo Lodge.** This gorgeous guesthouse is located in a large thatch
B&B/INN roof, nine-room home. **Pros:** gorgeous decor; great location on the
lagoon; amazing wine and whiskey collection. **Cons:** only a few rooms
have lagoon views. $ *Rooms from: US$120* ✉ *42 Kovambo Nujoma
Dr., on the lagoon* ☎ *064/207–700* ⊕ *www.egumbolodge.com* ⇄ *9
rooms* ⦿| *Breakfast.*

$$ ⌂**Pelican Point Lodge.** Built from the old Lighthouse and Port Authority
HOTEL building, this completely unique and new lodge is as beautiful as it is
stark. **Pros:** unique and emotive lodge; incredible 360-degree view of
the ocean; personal service. **Cons:** no electricity after 10 pm; long and
very bumpy ride to get out there (it is remote after all). $ *Rooms from:
US$302* ✉ *Pelican Point* ☎ *061/239–199* ⊕ *www.pelicanpointlodge.
com* ⇄ *7 suites, 1 family suite* ⦿| *No meals.*

$ ⌂**Protea Hotel Pelican Bay.** This outlet of the Protea chain has a great
HOTEL location on the lagoon, and all 50 rooms enjoy lagoon views. **Pros:**
great location with amazing views of the lagoon; all the amenities of
a larger hotel, including free airport shuttle. **Cons:** rooms lack character and intimacy. $ *Rooms from: US$155* ✉ *The Esplanade on the
lagoon* ☎ *064/214–000* ⊕ *www.proteahotels.com/pelicanbay* ⇄ *50
rooms* ⦿| *Breakfast.*

SPORTS AND THE OUTDOORS

The most popular activities here are the seal and dolphin tours, fishing,
kayaking, and day trips to Sandwich Harbour.

VICTORIA FALLS

WELCOME TO VICTORIA FALLS

TOP REASONS TO GO

★ **A World-Class Phenomenon.** Not only can you experience Victoria Falls and the Batoka Gorge from every angle—the sheer size of this wonder fosters the delightful illusion of exclusivity.

★ **The Adrenaline Rush.** Looking for an adventure to get your heart pounding? From bungee jumping to elephant-back riding and skydiving, Victoria Falls truly has it all.

★ **Perfectly Indulgent Relaxation.** Massages are offered on the banks of the Zambezi River, sumptuous food is served wherever you turn, and there are few sights on earth that rival watching the spray of the Falls fade from rainbow to starlight while enjoying cocktails at the end of the day.

★ **Intact Africa.** The warm, rich heart of Africa is proudly showcased in a region governed by people who have lived here for centuries, adeptly utilizing the very latest in ecotourism and benefiting from environmentally conscious development.

1 Livingstone, Zambia. Named after the famous Dr. David Livingstone, the town was established in 1900, 10 km (6 miles) north of the Falls. Its main street, Mosi-oa-Tunya Road, still boasts examples of classic colonial buildings. The much-publicized political unrest in Zimbabwe has often caused tourists to choose Livingstone rather than Victoria Falls as a base for exploration of the area.

2 Victoria Falls, Zimbabwe. The town of Victoria Falls hugs the Falls on the Zambezi's southwestern bank. The view of the Falls and the gorge is spectacular from Zimbabwe. At one time, the town was the principal tourist destination for the area. The town of Victoria Falls continues to be perfectly safe and more relaxed than Livingstone, and the general atmosphere has greatly improved as tentative stability continues to return to the area.

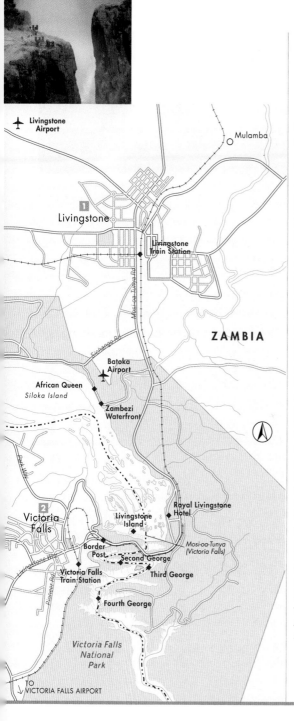

Livingstone
Airport

O Mulamba

1 Livingstone

Livingstone
Train Station

Mosi-oa-Tunya Rd

ZAMBIA

Sichanga Rd

Batoka
Airport

African Queen
Siloka Island

Zambezi
Waterfront

Park Way

2 Victoria
Falls

Livingstone
Island

Royal Livingstone
Hotel

Border
Post

Second George

*Mosi-oa-Tunya
(Victoria Falls)*

Victoria Falls
Train Station

Third George

Livingstone Way

Pioneer Rd

Fourth George

Victoria Falls
National
Park

TO
VICTORIA FALLS AIRPORT

GETTING
ORIENTED

Victoria Falls is in Southern Africa and physically provides a natural border between Zambia and Zimbabwe. Each country has a national park that surrounds the Falls (Mosi-oa-Tunya National Park in Zambia and Victoria Falls National Park in Zimbabwe), as well as a town (Livingstone in Zambia and Victoria Falls in Zimbabwe) that serves as the respective tourist center for each country. The fissure currently framing the Falls stretches over a mile, roughly from northwest to southeast. Livingstone lies to the north and the town of Victoria Falls immediately to the south of the Falls. The official border between the countries is within walking distance of the compact town of Victoria Falls but around 10 km (6 miles) from Livingstone. The stretch between the Falls border and town center on the Livingstone side should not be attempted on foot because of the dangers of wandering elephants, the African sun, and the occasional opportunistic thief.

10

Updated by
Christopher
Clark

Roughly 1,207 km (750 miles) from its humble origins as an insignificant spring in northern Zambia, the Zambezi River has grown more than a mile wide. Without much warning the river bends south, the current speeds up, and the entire mass of water disappears into a single fissure. More than 1 million gallons of water rush over a vertical, 328-foot-high drop in the time it takes an average reader to reach the end of this paragraph. The resulting spray is astounding, the brute force forming a cloud of mist visible 64 km (40 miles) away on a clear day.

The settlements of Livingstone in Zambia and Victoria Falls in Zimbabwe both owe their existence to the Zambezi and the Falls. Though they're located in different countries and intriguingly diverse in character, they function almost like two sides of one town. Crossing the border is a formality that generally happens with minimum fuss. Although the Zimbabwean town of Victoria Falls has escaped the political strife that has dogged the country in recent years, Livingstone on the Zambian side is determined to remain the favored destination. Zambia spoils guests with an overabundance of top-class safari lodges along the Zambezi, and this strong competition has resulted in an emphasis on personalized service, which enables you to tailor your visit.

On the other hand, Zimbabwe is slowly rebuilding itself and severe shortages of basic necessities are a thing of the past. The relative absence of large numbers of travelers is a luxury in itself, and this area currently provides good value for money.

The region as a whole deserves its reputation as an adventure center and offers adrenaline-inducing activities by the bucketful. The backdrop for any of these is stunning, and the safety record nothing less than spectacular.

WHEN TO GO

If you're at all sensitive to heat and humidity, visit May through August, when it's dry and cool, with pleasant days and cool to cold nights. The winter bush is dry, with most of the grass having died down, and the leaves fallen from the trees. The advantage is improved game-viewing, and most other adventure activities are more comfortable in the cooler weather. This is also the time when the mosquitoes are less active, although it remains a malaria area year-round, and precautions should always be taken.

The rainy season starts sometime around late October or early November and generally stretches well into April. As the heavens open up, the bug population explodes with mosquitoes, and the harmless but aptly named stink bug seemingly runs the show for brief periods of the day. Of course, the abundance of insect life also leads to great bird-watching. Although the rain showers tend to be of the short and spectacular kind, they can interfere with some activities, especially if your visit to the area is brief. Try to arrange excursions for the early hours of the day, as the rain generally falls in the late afternoon.

Peak flow for Victoria Falls occurs in late April and May, when rafting and visiting Livingstone Island might not be possible. If your visit coincides with school vacations in South Africa, the area can become quite crowded.

10

LIVINGSTONE, ZAMBIA

This marvelous old town, once the government capital of Northern Rhodesia (now Zambia), boasts a wealth of natural beauty and a surplus of activities. After a few decades of neglect it's recently recast itself as Zambia's tourism and adventure capital.

There's a tangible whiff of the past here: historic buildings outnumber new ones, and many local inhabitants live a life not that dissimilar to the one they would have experienced 50 years ago. Livingstone handles the surge of tourists with equal parts grace, confidence, banter, and nuisance.

Many visitors to this side of the Falls opt to stay in one of the secluded safari-style lodges on the Zambezi River. The Zambian experience sprawls out along the many bends of the large river and time ticks in a very deliberate African manner.

PLANNING

GETTING HERE AND AROUND

South African Airways and Comair/British Airways regularly fly from Johannesburg into Livingstone International Airport, 5 km (3 miles) out of town. The flight is a comfortable hop, less than two hours in duration, and the airport is small and friendly, with helpful staff to speed you on your way. ■TIP➜ If at all possible, don't check your luggage in Johannesburg and always lock suitcases securely, as luggage theft in South Africa is an everyday occurrence.

There's a perfectly reasonable traffic code in Zambia. Unfortunately, not many people have ever heard of it. You would do well to leave the driving to your local guides or negotiate an all-inclusive rate with a taxi driver recommended by your hotel or lodge for the duration of your stay. Note that taxis are generally not allowed to cross the border, so if you want to visit Zimbabwe, you'll have to book a tour that includes

FAST FACTS

Size 752,618 square km (290,587 square miles)

Number of National Parks 20. Kafue National Park, South Luangwa National Park, Lower Zambezi National Park, Mosi-oa-Tunya National Park (Victoria Falls National Park). There is also a growing number of private game reserves.

Population 15.2 million

Big Five The gang's all here.

Language Zambia has between 70 and 80 recorded languages, of which 42 are main dialects. Luckily English is the official language, and it's widely spoken, read, and understood.

Time Zambia is on CAST (Central African Standard Time), which is two hours ahead of Greenwich Mean Time and seven hours ahead of North American Eastern Standard Time. It's the same as South Africa.

transfers. Once at the border, it's feasible to walk into and around Victoria Falls town or rent a bicycle.

If you insist on renting a car, you should know that some of the roads have more potholes than tar. You don't necessarily need a 4x4, but it's not a bad idea, especially if you want to go off-road at all. Voyagers has two offices in Livingstone: Mosi-oa-Tunya Road (opposite Ngolide Lodge) and Livingstone Airport. Hemingway's rents out Toyota Hilux Double Cabs (similar to the Toyota Tacoma), fully equipped with tents and other camping equipment—you can even hire a driver! Costs start from US$220 per day for an unequipped vehicle.

■ TIP→ If you plan to add the popular Kafue and Lower Zambezi camps to your trip, you should book your transfers together with your accommodation through a travel agent or with your camp reservations, as air-transfer companies change hands and/or minds quite often in Zambia. A travel agent or camp will also assure that connection times work to your best advantage if they're responsible for the transfers.

ESSENTIALS
MONEY MATTERS

The Zambian government is curbing the use of U.S. dollars, and increasingly, places accept only Zambian *kwacha* (ZMW). The kwacha comes in denominations of ZMW2, ZMW5, ZMW10, ZMW20, ZMW50, and ZMW100 bills. Coins start at 5 *ngwee* (the local equivalent of cents) and work up to ZMW1. At the time of this writing, the conversion rate was about ZMW5.2 to US$1.

■ TIP→ Tipping is less common in Zambia because service charges are included, but it's appreciated. Small notes or 10% is appropriate. Gas-station attendants can be tipped, but tip a taxi driver only on the last day if you've used the same driver for a number of days.

Zambia has a 17.5% V.A.T. and a 10% service charge, which is included in the cost or itemized on your bill. International banks along Mosi-oa-Tunya Road in Livingstone have ATMs and exchange services. Banking hours are generally weekdays 8–2 (although some do open the last Saturday of the month). Many bank ATMs accept only Visa. It's also worth noting that queues for ATMs can get very long during working hours.

⚠ **You may be invited to do a little informal foreign exchange by persuasive street financiers. Resist the temptation—it's not worth the risk of being ripped off or arrested.** There are many reputable exchange bureaus throughout town, though they're sometimes flooded with dollars and low on kwacha, generally toward the end of the month. MasterCard and Visa are preferred by business owners and banks to American Express or Diners Club. Business owners always prefer cash to credit cards, and some smaller hotels levy fees up to 10% to use a credit card.

PASSPORTS AND VISAS

You'll need a valid passport and visa to enter Zambia. Nationals of any country not on the Zambian Immigration Referred Visa list can simply purchase a visa on entering the country. At this writing a standard U.S. single-entry visa costs US$50, and a single-entry and transit visa cost the same. Day-trip visas cost US$20 (often included in the cost of prebooked activities, so check with your booking agent). If you plan to return to Zambia in the near future, you'll need a multiple-entry visa, or you'll have to buy another visa on your return. Multiple-entry visas and visas for nationals from countries on the referred visa list (⊕ *www.zambiaimmigration.gov.zm*) can be purchased only at Zambian Missions abroad and not on arrival.

SAFETY AND PRECAUTIONS

For minor injuries, a test for malaria, or the treatment of non-life-threatening ailments, you can go to the Rainbow Trust Mwenda Medical Centre, Southern Medical Centre, or Dr. Shafik Hospital. For serious emergencies, contact SES (Specialty Emergency Services). There are a number of pharmacies in town including Health and Glow Pharmacy, Link Pharmacy, and HK Pharmacy. Pharmacies are generally open weekdays 8–8, Saturday 8–6, and Sunday 8–1.

It's always a good idea to leave ample space in your luggage for common sense when traveling to Victoria Falls. Wild animals abound throughout this area (even in the center of town from time to time) and must be given a lot of physical space and respect. You must also remember that Zambia is relatively poor. There are tourism police, but opportunistic thieving still happens occasionally. Although crime in this area is generally nonviolent, losing your money, belongings, or passport will result in spending the remainder of your trip with various officials in stuffy, badly decorated offices instead of sitting back on the deck of your sunset cruise with drink in hand.

As for the water, it's always advisable to drink bottled water, although the tap water in Zambia is generally considered safe. Should you develop any stomach upset, be sure to contact a physician, especially if you're running a fever, in order to rule out malaria or a communicable disease. Do remember to mention your visit to a malaria area to your doctor in the event of illness within a year of leaving Africa.

TELEPHONES

Telephone rates in Zambia are much cheaper and more stable than those in Zimbabwe. Check numbers very carefully, as some are Zimbabwean mobile phones. Zambia and Zimbabwe now both have cell coverage, and there are certain areas where the networks overlap and mobile telephones work in both countries. If you have any trouble dialing a number, check with a hotel or restaurant owner, who should be able to advise you of the best and cheapest alternative. International roaming on your standard mobile phone is also an option, as coverage is quite

> ### CHOBE: A GREAT DAY TRIP
>
> If it's serious game-viewing you desire, join a one-day excursion to Chobe National Park in Botswana. A trip will cost you about US$200 and usually includes transfers from Livingstone, a morning boat cruise, lunch with a drink, and an afternoon game drive. Reservations must be in writing and prepaid for both. ⇨ *To make reservations, see Bushtracks, in Sports and the Outdoors, for more information.*

extensive. Alternatively, you could purchase a local SIM card with pay-as-you-go fill-ups—this is probably your cheapest option. Pay phones aren't an option, and the costs of all telephone calls out of the country can be exorbitant.

The country code for Zambia is 260. When dialing from abroad, drop the initial 0 from local area codes and cell-phone numbers. Note that all telephone numbers are listed as they're dialed from the country that they're in. Although the number for operator assistance is 100, you'll be much better off asking your local lodge or restaurant manager for help.

ABOUT THE RESTAURANTS

In Zimbabwe, game meat can be found on almost any menu, but it's something of a delicacy in Zambia; superior free-range beef and chicken are available everywhere. The local bream, filleted or whole, is excellent, and the staple starch, a thick porridge similar to polenta—*sadza* in Zimbabwe and *nsima* in Zambia—is worth a try; use your fingers to eat it (you'll be given a bowl for washing afterward). Adventurous? Try *macimbi* or *vinkuvala* (sundried mopane worms) or *inswa* (flash-fried flying ants) during the flood season.

Meals are taken at regular hours, but during the week, restaurants close around 10. Dress is generally casual, but this part of Africa easily lends itself to a little bling, so you'll never be out of place in something more glamorous.

ABOUT THE LODGES

It's advisable to make both flight and lodge reservations ahead of time. Lodges tend to have all-inclusive packages; hotels generally include breakfast only. All hotels and lodges quote in U.S. dollars but accept payment in other major currencies at unfriendly exchange rates. It might be best to take an all-inclusive package tour because meals can be exorbitantly expensive. A 10% service charge is either included or added to the bill (as is the value-added tax) in both countries, which frees you to include an extra tip only for exceptional service. Although

air-conditioning can be expected in the hotels, lodges tend to have fans.
■TIP→ Travel with a sarong (locally available as a chitenge), which you can wet and wrap around your body, guaranteeing a cooler siesta.

WHAT IT COSTS IN U.S. DOLLARS				
	$	$$	$$$	$$$$
Restaurants	under $12	$12–$20	$21–$30	over $30
Hotels	under $250	$251–$450	$451–$600	over $600

Prices in the restaurant reviews are the average cost of a main course at dinner or, if dinner isn't served, at lunch; taxes and service charges are generally included. Prices in the lodging reviews are the lowest cost of a standard double room in high season.

VISITOR INFORMATION

Although the Zambia National Tourist Board (next to the museum; open weekdays 8–1 and 2–5, Saturday 8–noon) is very helpful and friendly, you might be better off visiting Jollyboys (behind the Livingstone Museum; open daily 7 am–10 pm) for comprehensive and unbiased advice.

CONTACTS

Airlines Comair/British Airways ☏ 213/32–2827 ✎ contactba.kenya@ba.com ⊕ www.britishairways.com. **South African Airways** ☏ 0213/32–3031 ⊕ www.flysaa.com.

Car Rental Companies Hemingway's ☏ 0213/32–3097, 0977/86–6492 ⊕ www.hemingwayszambia.com. **Voyagers** ☏ 0213/32–2753, 0213/32–3259 ✎ carrrental@voyagerszambia.com ⊕ www.voyagerszambia.com.

Embassies U.S. Embassy ⊠ Ibex Hill (eastern end of Kabulonga Rd.), Lusaka ☏ 0211/35–7000 ⊕ zambia.usembassy.gov.

Emergency Services Fire ☏ 993. **General emergencies** ☏ 999, 112 from mobile phones. **Police** ☏ 991. **SES** ☏ 213/32–2330 from landline, 0977/74–0308 from mobile ⊕ www.ses-zambia.com.

Hospitals Rainbow Trust Mwenda Medical Centre ⊠ Lusaka Rd., about 1 mile from center of Livingstone ☏ 213/32–3519. **Dr. Shafik Hospital** ⊠ Katete Rd. ☏ 213/32–1130. **Southern Medical Centre** ⊠ House 9, 1967 Mokambo Rd. ☏ 213/32–3547.

Visitor Information Jollyboys ⊠ 34 Kanyanta Rd. ☏ 213/32–4229 ⊕ www.backpackzambia.com. **Zambia National Tourist Board** ⊠ Tourist Centre, Mosi-oa-Tunya Rd. ☏ 0213/321–487 ⊕ www.zambiatourism.com.

EXPLORING

FAMILY **Batoka Gorge.** Just below the Falls, the gorge forms an abyss between the countries with edges that drop away from the cliffs of both Zambia and Zimbabwe. Each successive sandstone gorge is numbered in sequence starting from the youngest (First Gorge to Fifth Gorge), followed by Songwe Gorge and finally the official Batoka Gorge; it is common for all these gorges to be referred to collectively as "The Gorge" or as "Batoka

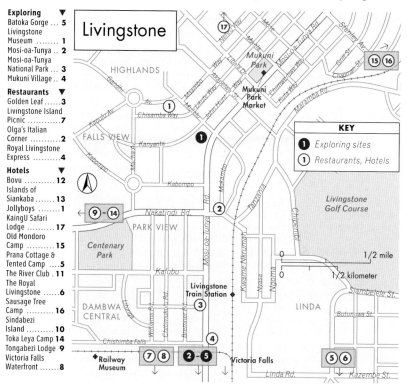

Gorge." Batoka Gorge is more than 120 km (75 miles) long with vertical walls that are an average of 400 feet high (the Zambezi river water levels fluctuates up to 65 feet between the wet and dry season). Batoka lies mostly within the Hwange Communal Land and is covered with mopane and riparian forests that are interspersed with grassland. On the Zambian side, the gorge is surrounded by the Mosi-oa-Tunya National Park, which contains a tropical rain forest that thrives on the eternal rainfall from the Falls. Victoria Falls National Park in Zimbabwe surrounds the other side of the gorge. Operators from both countries offer excursions to what is reputed to be the world's best one-day white-water rafting, with rapids rated between Class I and Class VI (amateurs can do only Class V and down commercially) that have been given evocative nicknames like "The Ugly Sisters" and "Oblivion." If you're "lucky" enough to experience what locals call a "long swim" (falling out of the raft at the start of a rapid and body surfing through), your definition of the word "scary" will surely be redefined. The walk in and out of the gorge is quite strenuous on the Zimbabwe side, but as long as you are reasonably fit and looking for adventure, you need no experience. On the Zambian side though, operators use a cable car to transport you from the bottom of the gorge to your waiting transportation (and beverage) at the top. Also on the Zambian side, travelers can walk down into the Boiling Pot (the first bend of the river after the

Falls) in the First Gorge. It's an easy walk down and slightly more challenging walk out of the gorge (lots of steps), but even young children enjoy it—be sure to carry extra sun protection and water.

FAMILY   **Livingstone Museum.** The country's oldest and largest museum contains history, ethnography, natural history, archaeology sections, and materials ranging from newspaper clippings to photographs of Queen Elizabeth II dancing with Kenneth Kaunda (Zambia's first president) to historical information dating back to 1500. Among the priceless David Livingstone memorabilia is a model of the mangled arm bone used to identify his body and various journals and maps from the period when he explored the area and claimed the Falls for the English queen. ⊠ *Mosi-oa-Tunya Rd., between civic center and post office* ☎ *213/32–0495* ▣ *USD$5* ☉ *Daily 9–4:30.*

FAMILY   **Mosi-oa-Tunya (The Victoria Falls).** Literally translated as "the Smoke that
Fodor's Choice   Thunders," the Falls more than lives up to its reputation as one of the
★   world's greatest natural wonders. Words can never do these incredible falls justice, and it's a difficult attraction to fully appreciate in a single visit, as it's constantly changing. The Zimbabwean side offers famously panoramic views, while the Zambian side of the Falls features the Knife Edge bridge, which allows guests to stand virtually suspended over the Boiling Pot (the first bend of the river after the Falls), with the deafening water crashing everywhere around you. From around May through August the Falls are a multisensory experience, and there may be too much spray to see the bottom of the gorge. In high season the entire experience can be summed up in two words: power shower! Prepare to get soaked. If you stand with your back to the sun, you'll be surrounded by a symphony of rainbows. A network of paths leads to the main viewing points; some are not well protected, so watch your step and wear sensible shoes, especially at high water, when you are likely to get dripping wet. You will have dramatic views of the full 1½ km (1 mile) of the ironstone face of the Falls, the Boiling Pot directly below, the railway bridge, and Batoka Gorge. During low water levels, it's possible to take a guided walk to Livingstone Island and swim in the **Devils Pool,** a natural pond right on the lip of the abyss. ⊠ *Mosi-oa-Tunya Rd., just before border post* ▣ *USD$10* ☉ *Daily 6–6, later during full moon.*

FAMILY   **Mosi-oa-Tunya National Park.** This park is a quick and easy option for viewing plains game. In fact, you are almost guaranteed to spy white rhinos. You can also visit the Old Drift graveyard, as the park marks the location of the original settlement of Livingstone. The park's guides are very knowledgeable, and while you're free to explore on your own, the roads do get seriously muddy in the rainy season, and a guide who knows where to drive becomes a near-necessity. ⊠ *Sichanga Rd., off Mosi-oa-Tunya Rd., 3.5 km (2 miles) from Livingstone* ▣ *$10 per person per day and $16 per vehicle per day* ☉ *Daily 6–6.*

FAMILY   **Mukuni Village.** Fascinated by the history, customs, and traditions of the area? Local guides can escort you on an intimate visit inside a house and explain the customs of the village. This is not a stage set but a very real village, so your tour will be different depending on the time of day. It is customary to sign in the visitors book and to pay a small fee to your guide. ⇨ *See Bushtracks, in Sport and the Outdoors, for information on booking a trip.* ⏲ *Daily 8–5.*

WHERE TO EAT

$$ INDIAN

🍴 **Golden Leaf.** The Moghuls themselves might declare a meal here a feast. Spicy but not hot, the curries are lovingly prepared from ingredients imported from India. The chicken tikka masala is a house specialty, and the handmade saffron *kulfi* is an inspired dessert at the end of another hot day in Africa. You'll do well to find better curry anywhere in Zambia, and portions and prices are reasonable. [$] *Average main: $18* ✉ *110 Mosi-oa-Tunya Rd., opposite Ngolide Lodge* ☎ *213/32–1266* ⏲ *No dinner Mon.*

A THREE-HOUR TOUR

Livingstone Walking Safaris. Many park guides are well informed, but the ultimate Mosi-oa-Tunya National Park experience is this three-hour guided walking safari. Not only can you see the endangered white rhino and other plains game, but your professional guide and park scout will impart detailed information on birding, flora, and the modern use of plants by local people. Walks are conducted early in the morning and late in the afternoon and cost US$75, including transfers within Livingstone, park fees and refreshments. ☎ *213/32–2267* ✉ *gecko@zamnet.zm* 🌐 *www.livingstonerhinosafaris.com.*

$$$$ ECLECTIC FAMILY Fodor's Choice ★

🍴 **Livingstone Island Picnic.** Available throughout the year whenever the water levels are low enough, this is a spectacular dining option. Livingstone Island is perched right on the edge of the void, where you'll dine at a table dressed with linen and gleaming silver on a delicious organic lunch (with salads) served by attentive waiters. You get there by boat (two engines, just in case). Brunch and afternoon tea are US$90 and US$120, respectively, and lunch is US$150, including transfers and a dip in Devil's Pool. The trips are run by Tongabezi Lodge, and there is a maximum of 16 guests. [$] *Average main: $120* ✉ *Livingstone Island* ☎ *213/32–7450* ✍ *Reservations essential* ⏲ *Closed a couple of months Feb.–June, depending on water levels. No dinner.*

$ ITALIAN FAMILY

🍴 **Olga's Italian Corner.** This restaurant delivers a double whammy. Not only does it serve genuine homemade Italian food prepared from fresh local ingredients, it's also part of an NGO project that trains and benefits the local youth. Open six days a week, Olga's features homemade croissants and muffins with Italian espresso for breakfast and seasonal delights for lunch and dinner. All the Italian pastas and pizzas are prepared on the premises and served with flavorful sauces made to order. [$] *Average main: $9* ✉ *20 Mokambo Rd.* ☎ *213/32–4160* 🌐 *www.olgasproject.com* 💳 *No credit cards.*

$$$$ SOUTH AFRICAN Fodor's Choice ★

🍴 **Royal Livingstone Express.** Walking the long stretch of red carpet alongside Locomotive 156 while it blows steam and rumbles in preparation for the journey is undeniably exciting and romantic. Dinner guests are seated in either the Wembley or Chesterfield dining carriage (both exquisitely restored) while the historic steam train pulls you through a bustling, charming shanty town, over the Sinde River Bridge, and then back through Mosi-oa-Tunya National Park at sunset. (On Wednesday and Saturday the train stops to watch the sunset on the magnificent Victoria Falls Bridge.) The gourmet dinner is beautifully presented and meticulously prepared, offering guests no fewer than five set courses (special dietary requests can be accommodated with advance notice). And yes, the train gives right-of-way to giraffes, elephants, and any other plains game who might decide to cross the tracks during dinner! **■TIP→ Dress code is "smart casual." No shorts are allowed.** [$] *Average main: $165* ✉ *Km 0 of the Mulobezi line on Mosi-oa-Tunya Rd.* ☎ *27/11–469–9300* 🌐 *www.royal-livingstone-express.com* ✍ *Reservations essential* ⏰ *Closed Mon. and Tues.*

WHERE TO STAY

CLOSE TO VICTORIA FALLS

$ B&B/INN FAMILY

🏨 **Bovu.** The vibe of California and Marrakesh in the '60s and '70s is alive and well at this collection of thatch huts and campsites along the banks of the Zambezi, 52 km (32 miles) upstream of the Falls. Take a good book or an excellent companion. Accommodations are basic but somehow quite perfect, each with gorgeous river views, and there are hot showers and flush toilets. The kitchen is the heart of the island, and the emphasis is on wholesome organic food ($–$$). Vegetarian diners are always catered to, and coffee is taken fabulously seriously. Whether you are taken for a swim in a shallow section of small rapids naturally protected from crocodiles or hippos (this is the theory) or on a sunrise canoe trip, every day will hold natural wonder. Warning: "island time" operates here and anything goes, so the staid or conservative are likely to find it unsuitable. Bovu does pickups from Livingstone Airport and lodges on a daily basis. Don't forget to check out the hat collection behind the bar in the main camp and add your own to the mix. **Pros:** Bovu is *the* Zambian chill-out zone; a great way to combine an educational canoe trip with a basic overnight camp; the perfect balance between comfort and a real commune with nature. **Cons:** this might be too basic for travelers who like their little luxuries; meals, fishing, and transfers are charged separately; guests have to bring their own towels. [$] *Rooms from: $50* ✉ *On Zambezi River, 52 km (32 miles) upstream from Victoria Falls* ☎ *097/872–5282* 🌐 *www.junglejunction.info* 🛏 *8 huts* 💳 *No credit cards* 🍴 *No meals.*

$$$$ ALL-INCLUSIVE Fodor's Choice ★

🏨 **Islands of Siankaba.** The lodge, located on two beautiful forested islands in the Zambezi River about 48 km (30 miles) upstream from Victoria Falls, was awarded the Environmental Certificate by the Environmental Council of Zambia in 2002. A suspension bridge links the two islands and leads to an overhead walkway in the tree canopy that connects the elevated chalets to the lodge's restaurant. The walkway protects the islands' delicate riverine environment. The lodge was constructed using mainly commercially grown, nonindigenous pine. Where local wood was used, the lodge planted hardwood saplings to replace them. Electricity is drawn from the Victoria Falls hydroelectric plant, and river water is recycled and treated on-site for use in the camp. Local tribes are employed by the lodge, where sunset cruises, mokoro rides, guided nature walks, white-water rafting, and bungee jumping are all on the menu. Guests can also opt to fly over Victoria Falls in a microlight plane. **Pros:** beautifully secluded location; innovative design; easy access to Chobe National Park just across the border into Botswana. **Cons:** 40-minute transfer from Livingstone might be daunting for visitors planning to partake in many of the activities based in town and around the Falls. $ *Rooms from: $1070* ✉ *On Zambezi River, 40 km (25 miles) from Livingstone along Nakatindi rd.* ☎ *097–772–0530 cell* ⊕ *www.siankaba.net* ⤳ *7 tented chalets* ⦿ *All-inclusive.*

$ ⌂ **Jollyboys.** The entire design of this small establishment is user-friendly,
B&B/INN   inviting, and certainly aimed at both private relaxation and easy interaction with other travelers. Superbly maintained and professionally run, the lodge offers a variety of room types to suit every budget and need. There are eight unisex dorms varying from 3 to 16 beds, 10 private rooms with shared bathrooms, five private en-suite rooms, and one executive suite with a private kitchen. The suite, five en-suite rooms, and two eight-bed dorms also have air-conditioning. The restaurant ($) serves the usual hamburger but also has a number of surprises on the menu, including a full roast on Sunday and exotic vegetarian soups made from local sweet potatoes and Indian spices. A kilometer away from the backpackers, just behind the Royal Livingstone Golf Course, is the new Jollyboys Camp, which is slightly more relaxed and family-friendly. It has a family room, two dormitories, seven private rooms with shared bathrooms and seven en-suite rooms. **Pros:** very central location; free daily transfers to the Falls. **Cons:** the lodge and camp are for backpackers, so are pretty basic; the location of the lodge right in the middle of town might not be exactly where you'd like to spend your holiday. $ *Rooms from: $45* ✉ *Kanyanta Rd.* ☎ *213/324–229, 213/324–756* ⊕ *www.backpackzambia.com* ⤳ *24 rooms* ▭ *No credit cards* ⦿ *No meals.*

$ ⌂ **Prana Cottage & Tented Camp.** Taking its name from the Sanskrit for
B&B/INN   breathing, this exclusive camp offers the perfect opportunity for taking
FAMILY   just that, a breather. Guests have their choice: stay in the main house or in one of the nine well-appointed, en-suite tented chalets. Spread out along one of the highest points in the region, the camp overlooks the surrounding bush. Plenty of staff are on hand to look after you and take care of the cooking, cleaning, and booking all of the area's adventure activities or safaris further afield for you. If you're on a self-drive safari, book the tents with the tented kitchen and braai area. Prana also hosts yoga retreats and individual yoga classes on the property. The lovely big house is rented exclusively for US$580 per night and sleeps eight adults plus children. ⚠ **There are no credit card facilities on the property, but you can pay via PayPal. Pros:** this is the best value for an exclusive stay in the area; you are assured of personal attention and being completely off the beaten track yet only 10 minutes from Livingstone and 10 minutes from the entry to Mosi-oa-Tunya Park at the Falls. **Cons:** if you don't have a car, you can feel a little isolated. $ *Rooms from: $116* ✉ *Off Mosi-oa-Tunya Rd.* ☎ *213/32–7120* ⊕ *www.pranazambia.com* ⤳ *1 house, 9 tented chalets* ▭ *No credit cards* ⦿ *Breakfast.*

$$$$ ⌂ **The River Club.** With split-level rooms that cling to the edge of the great
HOTEL   Zambezi, the River Club puts a modern spin on a Victorian house party.

10

Naming the Falls

Dr. David Livingstone, a Scottish medical doctor and missionary, visited Victoria Falls in 1855 and is widely credited with being the first European to document the existence of this natural wonder. He named it Victoria Falls in honor of his queen, although the Makololo name, Mosi-oa-Tunya (literally, "the Smoke that Thunders"), remains popular. Livingstone fell madly in love with the Falls, describing them in poignant prose. Other explorers had slightly different opinions. E. Holub could not contain his excitement and spoke effusively of "a thrilling throb of nature," A. A. de Serpa Pinto called them "sublimely horrible" in 1881, and L. Decle (1898) declared ominously that he expected "to see some repulsive monster rising in anger" at any moment. The modern traveler has the luxury of exploring every one (or all) of these perspectives. There's so much to do around the Falls that the only limitations will be your budget and sense of adventure or your lack thereof.

The view from the infinity pool seems unbeatable, until you watch the sun set from your claw-foot tub. Clever cooling mists of water draw flocks of birds to the gazebo, and the library begs for a glass of port and a serious book. History clings to the structure, built to the plans of the original house, but decorations have been lovingly collected from past and present. You could spend an entire day reading interesting anecdotes, old maps, *Punch* cartoons, and updates about the River Club's support of the local village. A candlelight dinner is followed by a game of tennis, or croquet on the floodlighted lawn before you retire to your partially starlit room. You approach the lodge from the river—purely for the spectacular effect—but it necessitates negotiating some steep stairs. If you think you'll struggle, ask to be transferred by vehicle. **Pros:** beautiful location with stunning views of the Zambezi; a/c and enclosed rooms are pluses for those who don't want to give up too many modern conveniences. **Cons:** colonial décor may not be Zambian enough for some travelers; 20-minute drive from town for any activities that are not in-house. $ *Rooms from: $780* ✉ *On Zambezi River, about 18 km (11 miles) upstream from Victoria Falls town, down same road as Tongabezi* ☎ *213/32–7457* ⊕ *www.theriverclubafrica.com* ⟳ *7 rooms, 4 suites* ❖ *Multiple meal plans.*

$$$$ **The Royal Livingstone.** This high-volume, high-end hotel has an incred-
HOTEL ibly gorgeous sundowner deck, arguably the best spot on the river, just upstream from the Falls. The attractive colonial safari-style buildings recall a bygone era of elegance and splendor. Set amid sweeping green lawns and big trees, the Royal boasts some fantastic views, although passing guest traffic makes for a lack of real privacy. The décor of the 17 residences, each with approximately 10 guest rooms, as well as the public rooms is deliberately colonial and ostentatious. Food is beautifully prepared ($$$–$$$$) from a blend of fresh local and exotic imported ingredients. The Royal contributes to a truly noteworthy number of local charities and environmental efforts. This resort is tremendously popular and can be extremely busy, especially during

peak times, but the staff are always friendly and helpful. Each room has a dedicated butler to take care of the individual needs of every guest. ■ TIP➜ **Vervet monkeys are an entertaining nuisance, so hang on to your expensive cocktail. Pros:** location, location, location; the level of service here is definitely that of a five-star international hotel; there is direct access to the Falls via a resort gate that opens onto the eastern cataract. **Cons:** volume of people can lead to occasional problems, omissions, and errors; it can feel a little impersonal; stay clear if colonial nostalgia isn't your thing. $ *Rooms from: $827* ⊠ *Livingstone Way* ☎ *27/11–780–7810* ✎ *zambia.reservations@zm.suninternational.com* ⊕ *www.suninternational.com* ⇴ *173 rooms* ℟ *Breakfast.*

$$$$
ALL-INCLUSIVE
Fodor's Choice
★

🏠 **Sindabezi Island.** This is the most environmentally friendly property on the Zambezi. The island makes use of solar power for heating, all the gray water is recycled, and the chalets are constructed mainly from sustainable forests. The island has a strict 10-guest maximum and is separated only by a stretch of river from the Zambezi National Park. Each of the island's chalets is raised on a wooden deck built artistically around the existing trees, and they are all completely open to the river with spectacular private views (curtains drop down at night). Each guest can plan a completely private itinerary, and every need is anticipated. Two honeymoon chalets also have bathtubs. There's absolutely no electricity on the island, but it's barely noticeable. If your party takes Sindabezi exclusively, the guide, boat, and land vehicle are at your disposal. Dinner is served by lantern and candlelight on a sandbank or wooden deck under the stars. **Pros:** lovely views of the national park on the Zimbabwean side from parts of the island; if you're lucky, elephants might swim across the Zambezi and graze a few meters from your bed; service is top-notch. **Cons:** it's very open, so if you are a bit nervous in the African bush, this might not suit you; there's no pool; it's difficult to get to. $ *Rooms from: $1190* ⊠ *On Zambezi River, about 19 km (12 miles) upstream from Victoria Falls* ☎ *213/32–7450, 213/32–7468* ⊕ *www.tongabezi.com* ⇴ *5 chalets* ℟ *All-inclusive.*

$$$$
ALL-INCLUSIVE

🏠 **Toka Leya Camp.** Spread out along the banks of the Zambezi River, the tents are set up on stilts, surrounded by a wooden deck that you can sit on and watch the world and the Zambezi River go by. The word "tent" is used liberally as the accommodation at Toka Leya resembles anything but camping. The 12 well-appointed, safari-style en-suite tents (three of which are family units that can sleep four) are remarkably spacious and join up to the main dining, bar, and pool area via a raised gangway, keeping guests out of the way of visiting hippos and elephants. Toka Leya is in the Mosi-oa-Tunya National Park, where a handful of Zambia's remaining white rhinos live. A game drive through the national park is a must. Priding itself on its greenness, the camp has gained a reputation for having incorporated several environmentally friendly systems, including the replanting of indigenous trees, a grey-water set-up, and a thriving worm farm for composting. There's great fishing on the river and you can arrange for a guide to take you out on a fully equipped boat so you can try your luck at landing a tiger fish. **Pros:** the camp is close to Livingstone and all of the activities offered in the area; there's a small spa on the banks of the river; almost all your activities

10

in included in the rates. **Cons:** décor makes it feel a bit like a hotel as opposed to a camp in the middle of the bush. [$] *Rooms from: $1408* ✉ *On Zambezi River, 12 km (7½ miles) upstream from Victoria Falls* ☎ *0027–11/807–1800 in South Africa, 0027–21/702–7500 in South Africa* 🌐 *www.wilderness-safaris.com* 🛏 *12 tent suites* 🍴 *All-inclusive.*

$$$$ ALL-INCLUSIVE Fodor's Choice ★ 🏨 **Tongabezi Lodge.** If you're looking for a truly African experience, this owner-run open-front lodge on the Zambezi River was designed to complement the Africa you have come to see, without trying to upstage it—but you'll still find indulgent offerings and personalized service at every turn. Standard cottages are spacious, cream-and-ocher rondavels featuring private verandas that can be enclosed in a billowing mosquito net. Three houses are built into a low cliff and incorporate the original riverine forest canopy; one house hugs the water with a private deck extending over the river; and the Nuthouse breaks with Tongabezi tradition, as it's entirely enclosed and also has an exclusive plunge pool. King-size beds set into tree trunks and covered by curtains of linen netting, oversize sofas in the sitting areas, and large claw-foot bathtubs on the private decks are all unashamedly indulgent. Every room has a local guide who acts as a personal valet and caters to your every whim. Room service is ordered via two-way radios, and the lodge has two masseuses. Tongabezi offers various meal options, including a romantic candlelit *san pan* (pontoon boat) floating on the Zambezi (with waiters delivering each course by canoe), as well as a number of private decks and the eclectic Lookout. **Pros:** the original open-front lodge; owner offers personal service and thoughtful touches; management is environmentally focused and community-aware. **Cons:** the use of local materials for building and decoration might not meet luxury standards for some; interaction with others is limited (though some might count this as a pro); a bit of a distance from town and most activities. [$] *Rooms from: $1190* ✉ *On Zambezi River, about 19 km (12 miles) upstream from Victoria Falls* ☎ *213/32–7468* 🌐 *www.tongabezi.com* 🛏 *6 houses, 5 cottages* 🍴 *All-inclusive.*

$ RESORT 🏨 **Victoria Falls Waterfront.** There's a hive of happy activity here ranging from opportunistic monkeys relieving unsuspecting tourists of their lunch to serious late-night boozing. Curiously, the spacious rooms where families can stay are reached only via a steep exterior wooden staircase, but this is also a popular spot for camping—there are campsites accommodating 86 campers. The recent addition of a professional chef tasked with updating the general pub fare to a standard that will match the fabulous location is promising. **Pros:** great location right on the river with beautiful sunsets; many of the adventure activities in the area are managed from the Waterfront, so this is an excellent choice for travelers who like socializing and one-stop convenience. **Cons:** can be very noisy as it caters to campers and backpackers; food can still be inconsistent. [$] *Rooms from: $200* ✉ *Sichango Rd., just off Mosi-oa-Tunya Rd.* ☎ *260/96–832–0606* 🌐 *www.safpar.net* 🛏 *23 chalets, 24 tents* 🍴 *Breakfast.*

ZAMBIAN SAFARI CIRCUIT

If you are eager to see more of Zambia than just Livingstone and the Victoria Falls area, Lower Zambezi National Park and Kafue National Park (the fifth biggest park in Africa) are spectacular destinations teeming with big game and first-class luxury lodges. Both are within a few hundred kilometers (62 miles) of Livingstone. Most lodges and hotels in and around Livingstone can arrange transfers either by road or by air.

EXPLORING

Kafue National Park. Kafue is Zambia's oldest and largest national park, covering a massive 2,240,000 hectares (about the size of Wales in the United Kingdom), which also makes it one of the largest parks in Africa and, for that matter, the world. Thanks to its size, variety of ecosystems, and the sustenance provided by the beautiful Kafue River, this park is absolutely teeming with game, from the popular heavyweights like lions, elephants, and leopards to one of Africa's largest wild dog populations—right through to rare species such as lechwes and yellow-backed duikers and more than 400 types of bird. The park is an easy two-hour drive from Livingstone. Despite all its highlights, the park remains largely wild and unexplored, particularly the northern reaches. But this may be the park's number-one draw. There are a handful of first-rate campsites and luxury lodges dotted in and around the edges of the park, almost all of which offer typically Zambian attention to detail in terms of service and providing the real bush experience. ✉ *About 175 km (110 miles) from Livingstone via the T1* ☎ *27/21–712–9875* ⊕ *www.zambiatourism.com.*

Lower Zambezi National Park. Lower Zambezi National Park may not be Zambia's biggest or best-known national park, but these are two of the main reasons it's worth a visit. The whole park retains a unique feeling of untouched African wilderness, and you certainly wouldn't think you were just a few hours from the urban hubs of Livingstone and Lusaka. When on game drives or guided bush walks through the park, you can go for hours without seeing another car, but the density of big game is astonishing. The vegetation and landscapes are spectacularly diverse, too, ranging from rugged, forested mountain escarpments to wide-open plains punctuated only by the occasional lonely baobab or palm tree. All six of the park's luxury and secluded camps are along the lush banks of the mighty Zambezi river, which serves as the natural southern border to the park as well as between Zambia and Zimbabwe's Mana Pools on the other side of the river. Lower Zambezi is a particularly special place for canoeing safaris and boat cruises, and is also a favorite with fishing aficionados. The quickest and easiest way to get to the park is to fly from Livingstone to Lusaka and then take a short chartered flight to Royal Airstrip within the park. ✉ *Lusaka* ☎ *27/21–712–9875* ⊕ *www.zambiatourism.com.*

WHERE TO STAY

$$$$
ALL-INCLUSIVE
FAMILY

⛺ **KaingU Safari Lodge.** KaingU Safari Lodge is a small camp comprised of a family house with two bedrooms and six classic en-suite safari tents. The tents are raised on rosewood decks to provide ideal views over the myriad channels and islands formed by the Kafue River. It's also very

10

remote—situated in the southern reaches of the Kafue National Park. This combination of intimacy and seclusion lends an undeniable flavor of mystery and discovery to your stay. The thatch main building has a lounge, bar, and dining room, where the hosted dinner conversations cover all topics. The lodge's guiding team is particularly fine-tuned to the many different wildlife stories constantly unfolding in the bush. Two activities are included every day, and the selection ranges from chilled-out river safaris to serious birding excursions. The natural splendor of deepest Zambia takes precedence—at this camp even the swimming pool is a wholly natural Jacuzzi in the rapids of the Kafue! From each nightly rate, $10 is paid into a registered Community and Conservation Trust. **Pros:** Africa untouched in all its glory; the owners have a true commitment to environmental and community development. **Cons:** road transfers from Lusaka take 5–6 hours but a charter flight to the nearby airstrip is a worthwhile alternative; the area has less big game than some other areas of the park. [$] *Rooms from: $750* ✉ *South Kafue, 400 km (250 miles) north of Victoria Falls* ☎ *097/784–1653* 🌐 *www.kaingu-lodge.com* 🛏 *1 family house, 6 luxury tents* 💳 *No credit cards* 🍴 *All-inclusive.*

$$$$ ALL-INCLUSIVE Fodor's Choice ★ 🏨 **Old Mondoro Camp.** The legend of a great white-maned lion that used to call this area its home lives on in the name of this camp, which is Shona for the "king of cats." If you're looking for an African adventure of the original epic variety and love the opportunity to take lots of pictures, then you need to stay at Old Mondoro. The gin-and-tonics are cold, and the game-viewing sizzles with close-up sightings of elephants, and leopard in trees. Old Mondoro is decorated in old-school safari style with showers and baths, all lit by romantic lanterns. There are camera charging and lighting facilities in each room, though. Tents with wide timber verandas are open (with canvas flaps at night) to maximize views of the surrounding floodplains, woodlands, and complex maze of waterways and hippo paths. The smell of fresh homemade bread introduces a back-to-basics bushveld kitchen repertoire that includes generous portions of hearty, flavorful meals. The entire experience manages to be marvelously satisfying without any fuss or complication. This is deliberately not a supercharged, over-the-top new safari palace where the design of the establishment completely usurps the natural environment and all local flavors are lost. **Pros:** great game drives led by top-notch wildlife guides; one of the best places to see leopards; best walking area in the Lower Zambezi. **Cons:** the open rooms have only canvas flaps to ward off the wild at night, and this might be too daring for some. [$] *Rooms from: $1782* ✉ *Lower Zambezi National Park, 142 km (88 miles) from Lusaka* ✣ *Old Mondoro is a 1-hr motorboat ride or a 2-hr game drive from its sister camp, Chiawa. Jeki Airstrip is only a 30-min game-drive away from Old Mondoro and can be reached via 2-hr flight from Livingstone or a 40-min flight from Lusaka* ☎ *211/261–588* 🌐 *www.oldmondoro.com* 🛏 *4 tents* ⏲ *Closed Nov.–May 1* 🍴 *All-inclusive.*

$$$$ ALL-INCLUSIVE 🏨 **Sausage Tree Camp.** There is no formal dress code, but this camp offers the perfect backdrop for throwing practicality to the wind and dressing up for dinner. All the hallmarks of the genuine safari experience

Continued on page 589

The first European to set eyes on the Falls was the explorer and missionary Dr. David Livingstone in the mid-1850s. Overcome by the experience he named them after the English queen, Victoria.

VICTORIA FALLS

Expect to be humbled by the sheer power and majesty. Expect to be deafened by the thunderous noise, drenched by spray, and overwhelmed at the sight. Expect the mighty swath of roaring, foaming Victoria Falls—spanning the entire 1-mile width of the Zambezi River—to leave you speechless.

On a clear day the spray generated by the Falls is visible from 31 miles (50 km) away—the swirling mist rising above the woodland savanna looks like smoke from a bush fire inspiring their local name, Mosi-Oa-Tunya, or the "Smoke that Thunders." The rim of the Falls is broken into separate smaller falls with names like the Devil's Cataract, Rainbow Falls, Horseshoe Falls, and Armchair Falls.

The Falls, which are more than 300 feet high, are one of the world's seven natural wonders and were named a UNESCO World Heritage Site in 1989. Upon seeing Victoria Falls for the first time Dr. David Livingstone proclaimed, "Scenes so lovely must have been gazed upon by angels in their flight." Truer words were never spoken.

updated by
Sanja Cloete-Jones

FALLS FACTS

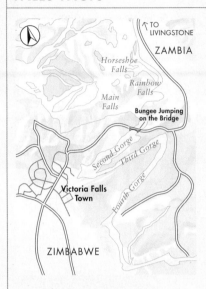

FORMATION OF THE FALLS

A basaltic plateau once stood where the Falls are today. The whole area was once completely submerged, but fast-forward to the Jurassic Age and the water eventually dried up. Only the Zambezi River remained flowing down into the gaping 1-mile-long continuous gorge that was formed by the uneven cracking of the drying plateau. The river charges through the ancient gorges creating some of the world's best commercial white water rapids.

WHEN TO GO

The Falls are spectacular at any time, but if you want to see them full, visit during the high water season (April–June) when more than 2 million gallons hurtle over the edge every second. The resulting spray is so dense that, at times, the view can be obscured. Don't worry though, the frequent gusts of wind will soon come to your aid and your view will be restored. If you're lucky to be there during a full moon, you might be able to catch a moonbow or lunar rainbow (a nighttime version of a rainbow) in the spray. The rest of the year offers its own charms with dry season–only activities like visiting Livingstone's Island, swimming in the Devil's Pool, and walking along the bottom of the Falls.

TO ZIM OR TO ZAM

Honestly? *Both* sides are great, but if you have to choose one, take the following into consideration: The Zambian side has more than four times the physical Falls frontage of Zimbabwe, but you're mostly looking across the gorge which means that Zimbabwe offers four times the visual display. Zimbabwe definitely has the most spray, the most rainbows, the best flat stone pathways for easy access, and the only views of the incredible Devil's Cataract. Rain forests with exotic flowers can be enjoyed on the Zimbabwe side year round and on the Zambian side during high water. Adventure seekers will love the Zam side's steep steps, the trail into the Boiling Pot, the slick Knife Edge bridge, and, during low water season visits to Livingstone Island, swimming in the Devil's Pool.

CROSSING THE FALLS

Built in 1905, Victoria Falls Bridge is one of the few useful remnants of the Colonial era. An important link in former South African Prime Minister Cecil John Rhodes's dream of creating the Cape-to-Cairo railway—it was never finished—the bridge continues to provide a convenient link between Zimbabwe and Zambia. It also offers a knockout view of the Falls and the Zambezi River raging through the Gorge, plus the added bonus of watching adrenaline junkies taking the 364-foot bungee plunge.

including beautiful bush views, great creature sightings and dining alfresco by lamplight are perfectly balanced by a splendidly chic minimalist design that focuses on space and pure white fabrics. Sausage Tree Camp is a very satisfying and perfectly decadent bush retreat. Sumptuous fabrics by night and elephants from canoe by day—simply bliss! You can also try Potato Bush, which is walking distance from

> ### GOOD SOUVENIRS
>
> Shona stone carvings from Zimbabwe, woven baskets from Botswana and Zambia, and soapstone from Zambia and Zimbabwe make great souvenirs. Make sure you pack these things carefully, especially the soapstone, as it's extremely fragile.

Sausage Tree, equally spectacular and falls under the same ownership. ⚠ The closest airstrip is Jeki, and this is two hours from Livingstone and 40 minutes from Lusaka in a small aircraft. Sausage Tree Camp is a one-hour drive from Jeki. **Pros:** gorgeous food and the services of a private *muchinda* (butler) to attend to every detail of your stay; the complimentary Mohini body-care products are infused with perfectly balanced Ayurvedic herbs. **Cons:** its remote location makes it very expensive and time-consuming to reach; if you don't like small-aircraft transfers, avoid coming here. $ *Rooms from: $1240* ⊠ *Lower Zambezi National Park, 140 km (85 miles) from Lusaka* ☎ *211/84–5204* ⊕ *www.sausagetreecamp.com* ↪ *5 tents, 3 suites* ⊙ *Closed Nov. 20– Apr.* ⦅◯⦆ *All-inclusive.*

SPORTS AND THE OUTDOORS

Livingstone can compete with the best as far as indulging the wildest fantasies of adrenaline junkies and outdoor enthusiasts goes. You can reserve activities directly with the operators, let your hotel or lodge handle it, or book through a central booking agent.

Bushtracks. This operator runs one-day excursions to Botswana's Chobe National Park. The trip includes transfers from Livingstone, a morning boat cruise, lunch with a drink, and an afternoon game drive. Bushtracks is also your best bet for a visit to the Mukuni Village. Reservations must be prepaid for both. ☎ *213/32–3232, 27–11/469–0484 in Johannesburg* ⊕ *www.gotothevictoriafalls.com* ✉ *Chobe National Park US$189, Mukuni Village US$45.*

Safari Par Excellence. Safari Par Excellence offers elephant-back safaris, game drives, river cruises, canoeing, and rafting as well as trip combinations, which are a good option if your time is limited or you just want to go wild. Discounted prices for combinations are available. ☎ *213/32–0606* ⊕ *www.safpar.net.*

BOATING

African Queen. Truly the monarch of the river, the *African Queen*— no relation to the movie—is an elegant colonial-style riverboat. Their sunset cruises offer the maximum style and splendor. ☎ *213/323–589* ✍ *reservations@livingstonesadventure.com* ✉ *Two-hr sunset cruise with open bar and snacks from US$75.*

10

"At the end of our safari, we went to Victoria Falls. . . . The thundering roar of the falls and the many rainbows were like nothing I had ever seen." —Pam Record, Fodors.com member

CANOEING

A gentle canoeing trip on the upper Zambezi is a great opportunity to see birds and a variety of game. Many of the lodges upriver have canoeing as an inclusive activity, but trips are also run by a number of companies, which are all reputable.

Bundu Adventures. Bundu Adventures offers custom-made canoe trips that range from half-day outings to multiday excursions. ✉ *Office is at Maramba River Lodge* ☎ *213/32–4407* ⊕ *www.bunduadventures.com* 🖃 *From US$116 for a half-day cruise.*

FLYING

Batoka Sky. Batoka Sky offers weight-shift Aerotrike twin-axis micro-lighting (flying jargon for what resembles a motorized hang glider) and helicopter flights over the Falls and through the gorges. There's a minimum of two passengers for helicopters. You are issued a flight suit (padded in winter) and a helmet with a headset, before you board the microlight, but you may not bring a camera for safety reasons. Batoka Sky has been operating since 1992, and has a 100% microlighting safety record. Flights are booked for early morning and late afternoon and are dependent on the weather. Transfer and a day visa, if you are coming from Victoria Falls, are included. The Helicopter Gorge picnic includes lunch and drinks for a minimum of six people. ✉ *Riverside Dr. off Mosi-oa-Tunya Rd., toward the Waterfront and David Livingstone Safari Lodge* ☎ *213/32–0058* ⊕ *www.livingstonesadventure. com* 🖃 *US$150–US$300, depending on length of flight and aircraft; Helicopter Gorge US$400.*

HORSEBACK RIDING

Ride Zambezi Horse Trails. You can take a placid horseback ride through the bush along the banks of the Zambezi with Chundukwa Adventure Trails. If you are comfortable enough to keep your cool while riding through the African hinterland, you may want to book a horseback bush trail. Half-day trips include lunch and refreshments. Fully inclusive overnight camping options are also available. ✉ *Chundukwa Horse, 25 km (15 miles) from Livingstone along Nakatindi Rd.* ☎ *213/32–7064* ⊕ *www.ridezambezi.com* ✉ *From US$75.*

JETBOATING

FAMILY **Jet Extreme.** If you want some thrills and speed but rafting seems a bit daunting, or you can't face the walk in and out, you'll probably enjoy jetboating with Jet Extreme. A new cable-car ride, included in the cost of the jetboat ride, means no more strenuous walking out of the gorge. Jetboating can be combined with a rafting excursion, as the jetboat starts at the end of the rafting run, or with a helicopter trip out of the gorge. ■TIP→ **The rafting and helicopter must be booked separately, although big operators like Safari Par Excellence and Livingstone's Adventure offer combinations.** Children over seven can jetboat if they are accompanied by an adult. ✉ *Safpar at David Livingstone Safari Lodge, for bookings* ☎ *213/32–1375* ⊕ *www.livingstonesadventure. com* ✉ *US$125 for 30 mins.*

RAFTING AND RIVERBOARDING

Safari Par Excellence. Safari Par Excellence offers half- and full-day rafting excursions to Batoka Gorge. The cable car transports rafters out of the gorge, so you only have to climb down. You can also do a combination helicopter-and-rafting trip. Bring secure shoes, dry clothes for the long drive home, a baseball cap to wear under your helmet, and plenty of sunscreen. You can also try river-boarding in which you hop off the raft onto a body board and surf suitable rapids. ✉ *Booking office, Safpar at David Livingstone Safari Lodge* ☎ *213/32–0606* ⊕ *www. safpar.net* ✉ *Half-day rafting US$150, full-day rafting US$175; riverboarding from US$185.*

SHOPPING

10

Kubu Crafts. This stylish home-décor shop features locally made furniture in hardwood and wrought iron. There's also a selection of West African masks and weavings and the work of numerous local artists. Local curios are attractively displayed and screened for quality. Kubu Crafts also provides both fair employment and training opportunities for the community. ✉ *Mosi-oa-Tunya Sq, 133 Mosi-oa-Tunya Rd.* ☎ *213/32–0230* ⊕ *www.kubucrafts.com.*

Mukuni Park Market. Although the park at the entrance to the Falls has stalls where you can find stone and wood carvings and simple bead and semiprecious-stone jewelry, the real gem of an African bazaar lies in the center of town, at Mukuni Park Market. ■TIP→ **This is the place to try your hand at bargaining.** ✉ *Mosi-oa-Tunya Rd. and Libala Dr..*

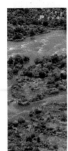

VICTORIA FALLS, ZIMBABWE

Victoria Falls started with a little curio shop and slowly expanded until the 1970s, when it became the mecca around which the tourist phenomenon of Victoria Falls pivoted. The political problems following independence have been well documented in the press worldwide and have certainly taken their toll, as has poaching in Zambezi National Park to the northwest (if you really want to have the African game experience, take a day trip to Chobe National Park, only 70 km [44 miles] away in Botswana).

However, the country is currently regaining political stability, and the town of Victoria Falls enjoys the happy coincidence of being a curio shopper's paradise inside a national park. This means you can literally buy an elephant carving while watching the real McCoy march past the shop window. The town has an easygoing feel and is extremely compact. Almost all the hotels are within walking distance, and the Falls are only 10 minutes away on foot. The main road that runs through town and goes to the Falls in one direction and to the airport in the other is called Livingstone Way. Park Way is perpendicular. Most of the shops, banks, and booking agents can be found on these two streets, and this part of town is also where most of the hawkers operate. ■TIP→ Give these vendors a clear berth, as their wares are cheap for a reason (the boat cruise is substandard, it's illegal to change money, etc.).

PLANNING

GETTING HERE AND AROUND

Tourists are slowly returning to Victoria Falls. If you choose to fly in and out of Victoria Falls Airport, most hotels will provide free shuttle service; book in advance.

FAST FACTS

Size 390,757 square km (150,872 square miles)

Number of National Parks 10. Hwange National Park; Victoria Falls National Park; Mana Pools National Park and Gonarezhou National Park are the most visited. Zimbabwe also has a small handful of exclusive private concessions and private game reserves, mostly concentrated around Victoria Falls.

Population 14.2 million

Big Five The gang's all here.

Language Zimbabwe has three official languages: English, Shona, and Ndebele. Although the number of native English speakers is small, English is widely understood and used.

Time Zimbabwe is on CAST (Central African Standard Time), which is two hours ahead of Greenwich Mean Time and seven hours ahead of North American Eastern Standard Time. It's the same as South Africa.

Hotels can summon reputable taxis quickly and advise you on the cost. Tipping isn't mandatory, but change is always appreciated.

Airlines Air Zimbabwe ☎ 263/457–5021 ⊕ www.airzimbabwe.aero. **Comair/ British Airways** ☎ 013/4–2053, 013/4–2388 ⊕ www.british-airways.com. **South African Airways** ☎ 27–11/978–5313 ⊕ www.flysaa.com.

Airport Victoria Falls Airport ✉ Livingstone Way ☎ 013/4–4428.

ESSENTIALS

MONEY MATTERS

Zimbabwe's currency used to be the Zimbabwe dollar, but now foreign currency is the only acceptable method of payment. Carry U.S. dollars in small denominations and stick to U.S. dollars for all activity payments to Zimbabwe-based operators (all activities are quoted in U.S. dollars). Credit card facilities aren't always readily available and MasterCard can only be used across the border in Zambia. (You'll also find Western Union banks in Victoria Falls and Livingstone, should you need to do cash transfers.)

PASSPORTS AND VISAS

It's possible to buy point-of-entry visas for Zimbabwe for US$60 for a single entry. If you leave Zimbabwe for more than 24 hours, you'll need to buy another to re-enter (unless you bought a double-entry visa for US$75). Visas can be purchased from a Zimbabwean embassy before departure (application for multiple-entry visas can only be lodged here), but it'll almost certainly be more trouble and generally cost more than buying them at the border.

SAFETY AND PRECAUTIONS

The political situation in Zimbabwe is currently fairly stable, but the damage from the lengthy dictatorship and internal strife is still very apparent. Prices have stabilized and basic goods have reappeared on the shelves, but the tourist capital of Victoria Falls has not yet regained its status as a prime international destination. All the activities, shopping, and dining options on offer on the Zimbabwean side can also be

10

enjoyed across the border in Zambia—without any of the uncertainty and potential for sudden political and economic upheavals that could result in cancellations or threats to visitors' safety. ■ TIP→ **The Victoria Falls town and tourism industry has managed to build itself up in a remarkably short time. The political situation is still not 100% resolved, but for now, Zimbabwean lodges offer good value and service.**

MARS (Medical Air Rescue Services) is on standby for all emergencies. Dr. Nyoni is a trauma specialist and operates a hospital opposite the Shoestring Lodge. Go to Victoria Falls Pharmacy for prescriptions.

Male homosexuality is illegal in Zimbabwe—female homosexuality isn't mentioned in law—and same-sex relationships receive no recognition. Attitudes are improving, but it's advisable to be extremely circumspect.

It's always a good idea to leave ample space in your luggage for common sense when traveling to Victoria Falls. Wild animals abound throughout this area (even in the center of town) and must be given a lot of physical space and respect. You must also remember that Zimbabwe is relatively poor. There are tourism police, but opportunistic thieving still happens very occasionally. Although crime in this area is generally nonviolent, losing your money, belongings, or passport will result in spending the remainder of your trip with various officials in stuffy, badly decorated offices instead of sitting back on the deck of your sunset cruise with drink in hand.

As for the water, it's always advisable to drink bottled water. Should you develop an upset stomach, be sure to contact a physician, especially if you're running a fever, in order to rule out malaria or a communicable disease. Do remember to mention your visit to a malaria area to your doctor in the event of illness within a year of leaving Africa.

Embassies U.S. Embassy ✉ *172 Herbert Chitepo Ave., Box 4010, Harare* ☎ *04/25–0593* ⊕ *harare.usembassy.gov.*

Emergency Services MARS ✉ *West Dr., opposite Shoestring* ☎ *013/4–4646* ⊕ *www.mars.co.zw.*

TELEPHONE
The country code for Zimbabwe is 263. When dialing from abroad, drop the initial 0 from local area codes. Ask a hotel or restaurant manager for exact telephone numbers and costs, should you wish to make any telephone calls from within Zimbabwe.

ABOUT THE RESTAURANTS
In Zimbabwe, game meat can be found on almost any menu, but it's something of a delicacy in Zambia; superior free-range beef and chicken are available everywhere. The local bream, filleted or whole, is excellent, and the staple starch, a thick porridge similar to polenta—*sadza* in Zimbabwe and *nsima* in Zambia—is worth a try; use your fingers to eat it (you'll be given a bowl for washing afterward). Adventurous? Try *macimbi* or *vinkuvala* (sundried mopane worms) or *inswa* (flash-fried flying ants) during the flood season.

Meals are taken at regular hours, but during the week restaurants close around 10. Dress is casual, but this part of Africa easily lends itself to a little bling, and you'll never be out of place in something more glamorous.

ABOUT THE LODGINGS

It's advisable to make both flight and lodge reservations ahead of time. Lodges tend to have all-inclusive packages; hotels generally include breakfast only. All hotels and lodges quote in U.S. dollars but accept payment in other major currencies at unfriendly exchange rates. It might be best to take an all-inclusive package tour because meals can be exorbitantly expensive. A 10% service charge is either included or added to the bill (as is the V.A.T.) in both countries, which frees you to include an extra tip only for exceptional service. Although air-conditioning can be expected in the hotels, lodges tend to have fans. ■**TIP→ Travel with a sarong (locally available as a chitenge), which you can wet and wrap around your body, guaranteeing a cooler siesta.**

WHAT IT COSTS IN U.S. DOLLARS				
	$	$$	$$$	$$$$
Restaurants	under $12	$12–$20	$21–$30	over $30
Hotels	under $250	$251–$450	$451–$600	over $600

Prices in the restaurant reviews are the average cost of a main course at dinner or, if dinner isn't served, at lunch; taxes and service charges are generally included. Prices in the lodging reviews are the lowest cost of a standard double room in high season.

VISITOR INFORMATION

The Victoria Falls Publicity Association is fairly well stocked with brochures. It's open weekdays 8–1 and 2–4 and Saturday 8–1. You could also choose to seek advice from one of the many safari companies in town.

Visitor Information Victoria Falls Publicity Association ⊠ *412 Park Way* ☎ *013/4-4202* ✐ *vfpa@mweb.co.zw.*

EXPLORING

10

FAMILY **Victoria Falls Bridge.** A veritable monument to Cecil Rhodes's dream of completing a Cape-to-Cairo rail line, this graceful structure spans the gorge formed by the Zambezi River. It would have been far easier and less expensive to build the bridge upstream from the Falls, but Rhodes was captivated by the romance of a railway bridge passing over this natural wonder. A net was stretched across the gorge under the construction site, which curiously prompted the construction workers to go on strike for a couple of days. They resumed work only when it was explained that they would not be expected to leap into it at the end of every workday. Although the workers did not share the current adrenaline-fueled obsession with jumping into the abyss, the net probably had a lot to do with the miraculous fact that only two people were killed during construction. The bridge was completed in only 14 months, and the last two cross-girders were defiantly joined on April 1, 1905.

To get onto the bridge, you first have to pass through Zimbabwean immigration and customs controls, so bring your passport. Unless you decide to cross into Zambia, no visa is necessary, though you will need a gate pass.

Depending on crowds, the simple procedure can take from five minutes to a half hour. The border posts are open daily from 6 am to 10 pm, after which the bridge is closed to all traffic. From the bridge you are treated to a fabulous view of the river raging through Batoka Gorge, as well as a section of the Falls on the Zambian side. An added bonus is watching the bungee jumpers disappear over the edge. ⊠ *Livingstone Way* ⊕ *www.victoriafallsbridge.com.*

FAMILY
Fodor's Choice
★

Victoria Falls National Park. Plan to spend at least two hours soaking in the splendors of this park. Avoid the crowds and the heat by getting there as early as possible. Bring snacks and water, and supervise children extremely well, as the barriers are by no means safe. Babies and toddlers can be pushed in a stroller. If you visit the Falls during the high-water peak, between April and June, you'd do well to carry a raincoat or umbrella (you can rent them at the entrance) and to bring along a waterproof, disposable camera because you *will* be drenched in the spray from the Falls, which creates a permanent downpour. Be prepared for limited photo opportunities due to the mist. ■ TIP➜ Leave expensive cameras, cell phones, and wristwatches in your hotel or lodge safe.

The constant drizzle has created a small rain forest that extends in a narrow band along the edge of the Falls. A trail running through this dripping green world is overgrown with African ebony, Cape fig, Natal mahogany, wild date palms, ferns, and deep-red flame lilies. A fence has been erected to keep non-fee-paying visitors at bay. Clearly signposted side trails lead to viewpoints overlooking the Falls. The most spectacular is **Danger Point,** a perilous rock outcropping that overlooks the narrow gorge through which the Zambezi River funnels out of the **Boiling Pot,** but be careful, as this viewpoint is hazardously wet and precarious. In low-water months (September–November) most of the water goes over the Falls through the **Devil's Cataract,** a narrow and mesmerizingly powerful section of the Falls visible from **Livingstone's statue.** Around the full moon the park stays open late so you can see the lunar rainbow formed by the spray—a hauntingly beautiful sight. Early morning and late afternoon are the best times to see the daylight rainbows most vividly. A booklet explaining the formation and layout of the Falls is available from the Victoria Falls Publicity Association for a small fee. ⊠ *Off Livingstone Way* ☎ *263/470–6077* 🖃 *US$30* ☉ *Daily 6–6, later during full moon.*

WHERE TO EAT

At the peak of Zimbabwe's political problems, shortages of even the most basic foods, like vegetables, were an everyday occurrence. Since the adoption of the USD as the official currency, however, hotels and restaurants have been able to restore some sanity, and in a short time, have been able to reestablish their unique flair for first-rate hospitality while maintaining a healthy dose of local flavor.

Exploring ▼

The Elephant Camp 4

Victoria Falls Bridge 3

Victoria Falls National Park ... 2

Victoria Falls Safari Lodge 1

Hotels ▼

Ilala Lodge 1

Victoria Falls Hotel 2

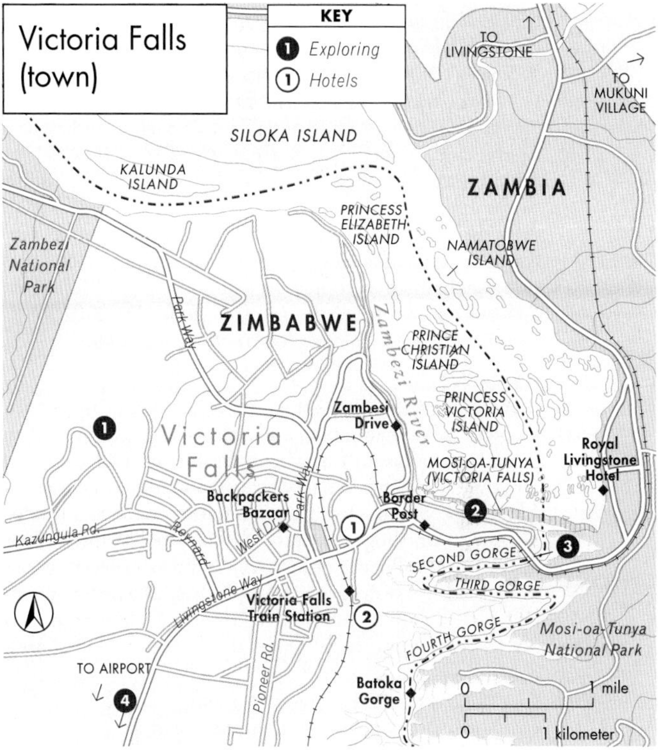

IN THE SAFARI CAMPS

$$ AFRICAN

🍴 **MaKuwa Kuwa.** Perched above a game-rich water hole at the Victoria Falls Safari Lodge, a spectacular view awaits diners at this memorable dining spot. On offer at breakfast is a combination of both cold and hot dishes; lunch ranges from great salads to huge gourmet burgers; dinnertime guests are treated to local a cappella performers. The à la carte supper menu has quality local and international fare with dishes such as grilled fresh bream (recommended) and, if you aren't too squeamish, crocodile simmered in red curry. Service can be a bit brisk, but it's friendly and the bar is well stocked. Though it's a bit of a drive from the town center, you would do well to find a better location anywhere on this side of the Falls. [$] *Average main: $18* ✉ *Victoria Falls Safari Lodge, 471 Squire Cummings Rd.* ☎ *013/432–1120* 🌐 *www.africaalbidatourism.com* ✍ *Reservations essential* 👔 *Jacket required.*

$$ AFRICAN

🍴 **The Palm Restaurant.** With tables flowing out onto the deep veranda of Ilala Lodge, the Palm has old-world grandeur with delicious modern cuisine. Lunches are light, including daring crocodile kebabs and the more familiar toasted panini with french fries. Dinner is a more formal affair with familiar and exotic dishes. ■ **TIP→ Reservations aren't necessary, but advisable for dinner.** From the outside tables you can see and hear the tumbling waters of the Falls. [$] *Average main:*

10

$20 ✉ *Ilala Lodge, 411 Livingstone Way* ☎ *013/4–4737, 013/4–4739* 🌐 *www.ilalalodge.com.*

$$$$ MODERN BRITISH Fodor's Choice ★ 🍴 **Stanley's Terrace.** A trip to Victoria Falls isn't complete without high tea (3–6 pm) on the Victoria Falls Hotel's terrace. A multilayer cake stand filled with an array of delicious treats, including cakes, tarts, and sandwiches, is served with a pot of tea or coffee. **TIP→ Don't have a big lunch beforehand!** The hotel is very grand, and although some of the furnishings are a little tired, the view out over the gorge and onto the bridge and falls is unforgettable. Also at the hotel is the more formal Livingstone Room Restaurant where you can make a reservation for their seven-course degustation meal ($$$$). [$] *Average main: $38* ✉ *The Victoria Falls Hotel, 2 Mallet Dr.* ☎ *013/4–4751* 🌐 *www.victoria-falls-hotels.net* ✍ *Reservations essential.*

IN TOWN

$ CAFÉ 🍴 **The Africa Cafe.** Find refuge on a hot day at the Africa Cafe in the Elephant's Walk Shopping and Artist's Village. The chef creates simple, delicious food, using ingredients freshly picked from the Happy Hippo Organic Herb and Veggie Garden, found just behind the restaurant. Dishes are varied—from crisp organic salads to buffalo or crocodile burgers to warthog ciabattas—and inspired by the fresh produce of the day with the influence of local Zimbabwean specialties. The Elephant's Walk is set in a lush garden shopping center where you'll find local craft and design, with artists working in situ. At dinnertime group bookings are by reservation only. There are plenty of shaded areas and comfy couches around, too, making it a good spot to escape the midday heat. [$] *Average main: $10* ✉ *Adam Stander Rd.* ☎ *771/402–081* 🌐 *www.elephantswalk.com* ✍ *Reservations essential.*

$$ TAPAS 🍴 **Lola's Tapas and Bar.** One of the town's newer restaurants, Lola's offers authentic Spanish flair in its cuisine and décor and is popular with the younger backpacker crowd. It's cool and open with tables and chairs spilling out onto a shaded courtyard. Choose from the reasonably priced tapas menu, or dine à la carte. The restaurant offers an array of dishes, from salad to steak and plenty of local game options. Try the crocodile meat if you feel like something different, or if you are really adventurous give the local "delicacy" of fried mopane worms a go. If you can't get enough, it's open for breakfast, lunch, and dinner. The coffee is probably the best in town. **TIP→ Bookings aren't essential but advisable for larger groups, especially for dinner during the busy season.** Lola's is open until the last drum beat from the group of musicians who provide entertainment on occasion. The food is tasty and reasonably priced. [$] *Average main: $18* ✉ *8 Landela Complex, Livingstone Way, in the tourist center* ☎ *013/4–2994.*

$$ AFRICAN 🍴 **Mama Africa Eating House.** This a good local food experience as the menu offers typical Zimbabwean dishes along with other African food and the atmosphere is colorful and celebratory. Tuesday and Friday nights are "Africa Nights" with a buffet dinner and live music from the local jazz band. There's usually some kind of live music every night of the week except Monday. There's a good selection of vegetarian and meat dishes, too; the Mama Africa Hot Pots are especially popular. There's a biltong and peanut butter stew, chicken with peanut butter

(*huku nedove*), and the Hunter's Hot Pot, which is the "catch of the day" game dish. All dishes are accompanied by either *sadza* (cooked cornmeal, a Zimbabwean staple) or rice. ⚠ **The chef prepares several dishes with peanuts, so if you have a severe allergy, it might be best to just enjoy the music and the atmosphere! ■ TIP→ It's advisable to make a reservation, especially for large groups and on Africa Nights.** [$] *Average main: $15* ✉ *Landela Complex, Matcalfe Rd.* ☎ *013/4–1725* 🌐 *www.mamaafricaeatinghouse.com* ✍ *Reservations essential* 🕒 *Daily 10 am–11 pm.*

WHERE TO STAY

With the introduction of the U.S. dollar as the official currency, there's no longer the rocketing inflation. However, an all-inclusive package tour is still a good bet in this area. Electricity and voltage are the same in Zimbabwe and South Africa.

$$$$ ALL-INCLUSIVE Fodor's Choice ★

🏨 **The Elephant Camp.** From the deck of your luxurious tented suite, you gaze out across the bush and down to the Batoka Gorge and the "smoke" rising up from the Victoria Falls, just 10 km (6 miles) away. Each suite has an indoor and outdoor shower, a big bath, and an intimate lounge with a minibar so you can enjoy a drink while you admire the view from your deck. Dinner is in the main lodge's dining room with the other guests; it's a fairly relaxed affair with delicious food. Don't be surprised if you're asked to be the guinea pigs for a new mouth-watering dish the chef is trying out. Breakfast and lunch are taken out on the deck that overlooks a water hole popular with buck and elephants. Three minutes' drive from the lodge is where the elephant ride begins. Even if you don't feel like hopping onboard one of these magnificent animals, guests of the camp can pop down and interact with them once they're back from their outing. The beauty of Elephant Camp is its simplicity, the wonderful attention to detail, and the staff who work there. This is the perfect place to relax, socialize, and take in Victoria Falls in its entirety. **Pros:** every suite has a plunge pool that's most welcoming in the summer months, although if you're feeling more social, the main lodge has a big pool, too. **Cons:** even though it's in the middle of a national game park, you'll be disappointed if you're there to see a variety of game. [$] *Rooms from: $880* ✉ *On Livingstone Way (road to the airport), 10 km (6 miles) outside of Victoria Falls* ☎ *013/4–4571* 🌐 *www.wildhorizons.co.za* 🛏 *12 tented suites* 🍴 *All-inclusive.*

$$ HOTEL FAMILY

🏨 **Ilala Lodge.** The lodge's elegant interior design is tempered with thatch roofs, giving it a graceful African look. Dining outside under the night sky at the award-winning Palm Restaurant ($$$), with the Falls thundering 300 feet away, is a particularly enticing way to while away a Zimbabwean evening. The Palm also serves a great terrace lunch overlooking the bush. Guest rooms are hung with African paintings and tapestries and filled with delicately caned chairs and tables and with dressers made from old railroad sleepers. French doors open onto a narrow strip of lawn backed by thick bush. Unlike most hotels in town, Ilala Lodge has no fence around it, so at night it's not uncommon to find elephants browsing outside your window or buffalo grazing on the lawn or at the pool. **Pros:** great central location; family-friendly;

10

only 10 minutes from the Falls by foot. **Cons:** the location in town can ruin expectations if you are keen on the peace of the African bush; the noise from the helicopters can be disturbing. [$] *Rooms from: $426* ✉ *411 Livingstone Way* ☎ *013/4–47379* 🌐 *www.ilalalodge.com* 🛏 *32 rooms, 2 suites* 🍴 *Breakfast.*

$$$$ ALL-INCLUSIVE 🏨 **Imbabala Zambezi Safari Lodge.** Imbabala is a charming lodge an hour's drive from Victoria Falls Airport, set about a hundred meters from the river's edge, close to where Zimbabwe, Namibia, Botswana, and Zambia converge. It's comfortable and laid-back and is one of the few "original" Zambezi River lodges that hasn't lost its authenticity. At the center of the lodge is a magnificent teak tree under which, weather permitting, all meals are served. (There's a thatch-roof dining and bar area that comes in handy in the rainy season.) Fanning out above that are the eight comfortably appointed en-suite rondavels. It's a good place to bring children over seven, as there's space to roam and the staff organize fun activities for them (on request). Bear in mind that the lodge is unfenced and in a park where animals are free to roam—a resident herd of impalas sleeps just in front of the rondavels. Game drives, fishing expeditions, guided walks (you'll need to arrange this in advance), and boat cruises are all part and parcel of the Imbabala package. Birders will revel in the birdlife on this part of the river, which is spectacular. **Pros:** authentic Zambezi River and bush experience. **Cons:** the chalets all look out onto the main lawn, so other guests walk past the front of them; the lodge isn't far from Kazungula and the noise from the late-night revelers on the Zambian side can detract a little from the experience—unless it's your kind of music. [$] *Rooms from: $600* ✉ *Kazungula Rd., 70 km (43 miles) from Victoria Falls* ☎ *013/4–4571* 🌐 *www.imbabalazambezisafarilodge.com* 🛏 *9 Chalets* 🍴 *All-inclusive.*

$$ HOTEL 🏨 **Victoria Falls Hotel.** Hotels come and go, but this landmark built in 1904 has retained its former glory as a distant, stylish outpost in empire days, while pandering to today's modern tastes, needs and wants. Such grandeur can be a little overwhelming, and especially surprising if you've just been on safari. The hotel's manicured lawns have sweeping views of the bridge and gorge, and soothing sounds permeate the gardens (and the rooms if you leave the windows open). Cool cream walls form the backdrop for elegant mahogany and wicker furniture. In the bathroom an old-fashioned drench shower will wash away the most stubborn African dust. Halls are filled with sepia-tone photos from throughout the hotel's history and animal trophies so old they are going bald. After checking your e-mail in the E-Lounge and visiting the salon, you can dine and dance at the elegant Livingstone Room ($$$$). Two far less formal restaurants include the Terrace ($–$$), with an à la carte menu, daily high tea and a beautiful view of the bridge, and Jungle Junction (US$35), which has a huge barbecue buffet and traditional dancers. **Pros:** one of the very best views of the Falls—it does not come closer than this! **Cons:** hotel is slightly run-down following the Zimbabwean political crises. [$] *Rooms from: $350* ✉ *2 Mallet Dr.* ☎ *013/4–4751* 🌐 *www.africansunhotels.com* 🛏 *161 rooms* 🍴 *Breakfast.*

$$ 🏨 **Victoria Falls Safari Lodge.** The lodge's location is atop a natural plateau
HOTEL   that perfectly frames the African sunset against a private water hole fre-
FAMILY   quented by various game throughout the entire year. It features elegant
Fodor's Choice   luxury, award-winning architecture, and every imaginable convenience
★   while succeeding in instilling a sense of respect and care for wildlife and
the environment in every guest. This hotel has been winning awards for
environmental consciousness and social responsibility since its inception
in 1993. The lodge maintains a strict natural vegetation policy—95%
of all plants are indigenous species and new trees are planted annu-
ally—and electricity and water are conserved aggressively through use
of grey water for plants. The lodge also takes responsibility for keep-
ing Victoria Falls clean and helped set up the Vic Falls Anti-Poaching
Unit, which it continues to support administratively and financially. The
Boma (part of the complex) is one of the premier ethnic restaurants in
Africa. **Pros:** fabulous architecture; beautiful location; great African
sunsets are guaranteed. **Cons:** can get quite busy; a little bit of a dis-
tance from the town's amenities. $ *Rooms from: $398* ⊠ *471 Squire
Cummings Rd.* ☎ *013/4–3211* ⊕ *www.victoria-falls-safari-lodge.com*
🛏 *72 rooms* ⬤| *Breakfast.*

SPORTS AND THE OUTDOORS

The town of Victoria Falls was the epicenter of extreme adventures
for many years. But at the peak of Zimbabwe's civil unrest, many of
the adventure operators either closed down or moved to the Zambian
side. Livingstone took over as the gateway to the Victoria Falls, the
Zambezi River, and all the activities associated with them. Over the
last few years, however, the Zimbabwean side has made a remarkable
comeback, with companies such as Adventure Zone, Wild Horizons,
and the original Shearwater offering all manner of thrills.

Adventure Zone. This is a one-stop booking agent for bungee jump-
ing, upper Zambezi River canoeing, white-water rafting, Victoria
Falls Bridge tours, transfers, and many other activities Victoria Falls
has to offer. ⊠ *Shop No.4, Phumula Centre* ☎ *013/4–4424* ⊕ *www.
adventurezonevicfalls.com.*

Shearwater. One of the oldest operating companies in Victoria Falls
(thrill-seeking since 1982) and unique in that it owns and operates the
majority of activities available in Victoria Falls, Shearwater can put
you in a helicopter or raft, or on an elephant or boat cruise. ⊠ *Park
Way and West Dr.* ☎ *013/4–4471* ⊕ *www.shearwatervictoriafalls.com.*

Wild Horizons. Need to get around? Wild Horizons runs transfers in and
around Victoria Falls, Livingstone, and Chobe, including airport pick-
ups and drop-offs as well as multiday tours and cross-border transfers
between Zambia, Zimbabwe, and Botswana. They also operate a range
of adrenaline activities in and around the falls. ⊠ *Livingstone Way*
☎ *013/4–4571* ⊕ *www.wildhorizons.co.za.*

10

THE SEYCHELLES

WELCOME TO THE SEYCHELLES

TOP REASONS TO GO

★ **Splashing in Solitude:** Home to the world's most beautiful (and empty) beaches, Seychelles' tropical waters are one big playground for snorkeling, diving, fishing, and kayaking.

★ **Unspoiled Nature:** Jungle-clad granite islands, where you can look a giant tortoise in the eye, have also become seabird sanctuaries, where the abundance of winged creatures will blow your mind.

★ **Island Hopping:** From "busy" Mahé to the empty beaches of coralline Denis to the überluxury of private-island resorts to the entirely undeveloped nature sanctuary of Aldabra—every island offers something different and unforgettable.

★ **Creole Culture:** Old French Victorian mansions, colorful gardens, a cuisine that blends Indian, French, and Southeast Asian influences—the friendly Seychellois culture is a lovely and unique melting pot.

North I.

Labriz
Silhouette

INNER ISLANDS

Ste. Anne

Round I.

VICTORIA ⊕

Cerf

1

Mahé

Seychelles
Bank

2 **Praslin.** Seychelles' second largest island, Praslin is much quieter than Mahé, with accommodations tending toward smaller and often homier resorts and guesthouses. Home to the Vallée de Mai, the UNESCO World Heritage Site protecting the famous Coco de Mer palm, Praslin also is a stepping-off point for numerous day trips to other smaller islands.

1 **Mahé.** Home to the International Airport, the capital of Victoria, and by far the largest (in population and size) and most developed island, "busy" Mahé is still slow-paced and charming by almost any definition. Mahé's size means dramatic views of forest-cloaked granite cliffs, and numerous empty bays and beaches. Many fine restaurants have emerged, mostly along popular Beau Vallon, which is the only place in Seychelles where motorized water sports are allowed.

Aride

Curieuse

Cousin

Cousine

Praslin

Round I.

La Digue

Frégate

GETTING ORIENTED

The three most popular islands in the Seychelles archipelago are Mahé, Praslin, and La Digue. Home to 98% of the Seychelles' population, these three are clustered in the archipelago's northeast area known as the Inner Island group. Mahé and Praslin are Seychelles' largest islands (nearby Silhouette Island is larger than La Digue, but less populated), and all three are granitic (versus coral). The Inner Islands also include other popular islands to visit, such as Denis, Bird, Silhouette, and North. Southwest of the Inner Islands lie the other island groups: Amirantes, Alphonse, Farquhar, and Aldabra. Barring a handful of private-island resorts, these islands are mostly uninhabited and accessible only by boat.

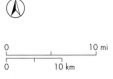

3 La Digue. This tiny charmer takes one back in time. With little motor traffic, most everyone on La Digue gets around on foot or bicycle, which is the perfect way to take in the lovely old Creole-French homes and gorgeous wild beaches, including the famous Anse Source d'Argent. For those seeking an unpretentious, laid-back beach lifestyle, this is your island.

0		10 mi
0	10 km	

By Lee
Middleton

One hundred fifteen coral and granite islands rising from the Indian Ocean make up the Seychelles, a pristine hide-away of white-sand beaches, majestic granite cliffs, palm-fringed jungles, and astonishing azure waters. Trading in exclusivity, luxury, and undeveloped natural environments, the Seychelles is an ideal beach escape for those who can afford all that gorgeous privacy.

With its countless perfect beaches and secluded coves fringed by sea-sculpted granite boulders, the Seychelles is a favored backdrop for fashion shoots and once-in-a-lifetime dream vacations. It has earned its reputation as an exclusive and costly destination, but in recent years, numerous self-catering options, locally owned guesthouses and two- and three-star hotels have opened their doors, making these islands more accessible. However, if ultraluxurious pampering, breathtaking style, and total privacy on some of the world's most stunning beaches are what you seek, Seychelles has them in spades, but not on a budget.

Beyond the luxury resorts—and really the basis for their existence—the Seychelles claim some of the world's best-preserved tropical habitats. Originally a huge granite shard attached to India's west coast, some event—probably a volcanic eruption or meteor impact—caused what would become the Seychelles to break free and begin its northward drift. Over time, that single mass became a shimmering line of islands, transformed by their isolation, 1,600 km (994 miles) from mainland Africa in the middle of the Indian Ocean.

Known as the Galápagos of the Indian Ocean, most of the islands were never settled by people (though many served as notorious pirate hideouts), and thus still harbor important populations of rare plants, birds, and animals, including the heartbreakingly beautiful ferry tern, the gentle giant tortoise, and the Coco de Mer—once thought to be the fruit of the Tree of Knowledge. On the islands where human-introduced predators like cats and rats have been removed, astonishing populations of seabirds thrive, allowing visitors a glimpse of what the first explorers might have seen.

Those first explorers were probably seafarers hailing from Austronesia, followed in turn by Arab traders. The first European to pass through was Portuguese Admiral Vasco da Gama in 1502, followed by the English in 1609. A transit point for trade between Africa and Asia, the islands were used by pirates until 1756, when the French took control, laying down their "Stone of Possession" (visible today at the museum in Mahé) and naming the islands after Jean Moreau de Séchelles. Britain and France fought over the islands from the late 18th to early 19th century, with Britain finally gaining control in 1814. Achieving independence from Britain in 1976, the Seychelles today is a true success story of people who claim origins from all over the world and live together with an unusual and inspiring degree of harmony in diversity.

PLANNING

WHEN TO GO

The Seychelles has two seasons: the cool southeast monsoon (May–September), and the hot northwest monsoon (October–April). During the cool season, breezes prevail, skies can be partly cloudy, temperatures are lower, and the sea less than perfect for diving and snorkeling. The hot northwest monsoon brings crystalline waters, incredible heat, and occasional but serious rainstorms, interspersed with perfect blue skies. The cusp months of November and April are optimal, with the best of both on offer. The super busy (and far more expensive) high seasons fall in August, and Christmas to New Year's.

GETTING HERE AND AROUND

AIR TRAVEL

The International Airport is on Mahé, 8 km (5 miles) south of Victoria. If you're coming from safari, you can catch flights departing from both Nairobi and Johannesburg twice a week (Kenya Airways and Air Seychelles). If you're coming directly to the Seychelles from the United States, it's often cheapest (and necessary) to route through the Middle East; look for cheaper airfares direct from Abu Dhabi and Dubai. Airlines with international routes include Air Seychelles, Emirates, Condor, Etihad, Air Austral, Mihin Lanka, and Ethiopian Airlines. Many cheaper fares route through Dubai or Abu Dabi.

The domestic terminal at Mahé will handle departures for all flights within the Seychelles—that is, the almost hourly 15-minute flight (US$144–US$225 one-way) to Praslin—and any of the other private islands (there's no airport on La Digue). Domestic flights are handled by Air Seychelles and the Island Development Company (the latter handles the outer islands and Desroches Island). Luggage limits are 20 kg (44 pounds). You can also charter a private helicopter to many private islands through Zil Air.

Contacts Air Austral ☎ *248/428–8909* ⊕ *www.air-austral.com.* **Air Seychelles** ☎ *439–1000* ⊕ *www.airseychelles.com.* **Condor** ☎ *49–6171/698– 8920 in Germany, 866/960–7915 in the U.S.* ⊕ *www.condor.com.* **Emirates** ☎ *429–2700, 800/777–3999 in the U.S.* ⊕ *www.emirates.com.* **Ethiopian Airlines** ☎ *27 21/819–7028 in South Africa, 800/445–2733 in the U.S.* ⊕ *www.ethiopianairlines.com.* **Etihad** ☎ *27–11/343–9140 in South Africa, 888/838–4423 in the U.S.* ⊕ *www.etihad.com.* **Island Development Company** ☎ *438–4640* ✎ *ceo@idc.sc.* **Kenya Airways** ☎ *866/536–9224 in the U.S.* ⊕ *www.kenya-airways.com.* **Mihin Lanka** ✉ *Ebrahim Building, Francis Rachel St., Victoria, Mahé* ☎ *432–3110, 422–4516* ⊕ *www.mihinlanka.com.* **Zil Air** ☎ *437–5100* ⊕ *www.zilair.com.*

BOAT AND FERRY TRAVEL

Travel by boat between Mahé, Praslin, and La Digue is easy and relatively cheap. The Cat Coco ferry connects Mahé and Praslin, and takes about the same time as the flight (factoring in the need to arrive 45 minutes before a flight). About one hour one-way, the ferry runs three times a day, for about US$65 one-way (about $83 in the upper air-conditioned lounge). Children under 12 pay half. Book through the ferry or a travel agent at least a day in advance during high season. Free shuttles to and from the airport are sometimes available.

To get to La Digue, Cat Coco runs one ferry a day from Mahé (via Praslin) and twice on Sunday (about 90 minutes, about US$80 one-way). You can also take a Cat Coco ferry to La Digue from Praslin, which runs about seven departures daily in each direction from about 7 to 5 (US$17 one-way, about 20 minutes). The ride can be a bit bumpy during the southeast monsoon. Book ahead through your hotel or tour operator.

Contacts Cat Cocos Catamaran ☎ *432–4843, 432–4844* ⊕ *www.catcocos. com.* **Inter-Island Ferry Co** ☎ *423–2394, 423–2329* ⊕ *www.seychelles.net.*

BUS TRAVEL

The bus system in Mahé and Praslin is surprisingly good and cheap, saving you from needing to rent a car if you don't mind the usual vagaries of public transport. Destinations and routes are usually marked on the front of the bus (always double check with the driver). There's a flat fee of 5 Seychelles rupees (Rs5; ⇨ *See Money Matters*) for any ride, or Rs10 on air-conditioned buses. Bus stops are painted on the road in places with no shoulder, or indicated by signs and small shelters. You can call the Seychelles Public Transport Corporation (SPTC) to get the Mahé route and schedule information weekdays from 8 to 4, or pick one up at the terminal for free.

Contacts Seychelles Public Transport Corporation ☎ *428–0280* ⊕ *www. sptc.sc.* **Seychelles Taxi Operators Association** ☎ *251–9355* ⊕ *www. seychelles.net.*

CAR TRAVEL

Having your own car is the only way to fully explore all of Mahé's charms. At least a day exploring this beautiful island—particularly the far southern reaches—is highly worthwhile. Though the paved roads are good, the combination of left-hand driving, numerous tourists in rental cars, and Mahé's frequently steep roads with hairpin bends and no shoulders (the roads literally drop off into ditches) can be nerve-wracking. The main rule of the road: drive slowly. On Praslin a car could also be handy, though the frequent shuttle services offered by many resorts to the islands' other "main" beaches and a decent public bus service (also present on Mahé) render the need for your own wheels less keen. None of the other islands offers car rentals. Numerous car rental agencies arc at the international terminal of the airport, as well as at points around the island. Most agencies can arrange delivery/drop-off at your hotel or the jetties for a small fee. Prices are fairly standard: the cheapest you're likely to find is about US$60 a day for an economy hatchback. If you take a car for more than three days, the price can be reduced to about $45 You can book at the airport, through a tour operator, or from your hotel. Most companies will accept your national license.

Contacts Aventure ✉ Amitié, Praslin ☎ 423–3805, 252–7291, 252–6805 ⊕ aventure@seychelles.net. **Avis** ✉ Seychelles International Airport, Victoria, Mahé ☎ 422–4511, 251–4512 ⊕ www.avis.com.sc. **Capricorn Car Rental** ✉ Bay St. Anne, Praslin ☎ 258–1110, 251–0446 ⊕ capcorn@seychelles.net. **Hertz** ✉ Seychelles International Airport, Victoria, Mahé ☎ 432–2447, 432–2669 ⊕ www.seychelles.net/hertz. **Omega Cars** ✉ Seychelles International Airport, Victoria, Mahé ☎ 437–6932, 251–1562 ⊕ www.omegacarhire.com. **Palm Cars** ✉ Anse a la Mouche, Mahé ☎ 436–1221, 271–2106, 271–2102 ⊕ carhire@hibiscus.sc.

TAXI TRAVEL

Independently owned taxis operate on Mahé and Praslin (as do a handful on La Digue) and can (sometimes) be hailed from the street, at designated taxi stands, or by phoning (most reliable). They're expensive, however, and it's advised to request a metered ride. The first kilometer is Rs50, after that Rs35. There's no night or weekend charge, and each piece of luggage is an additional Rs10. Following are sample approximate fares from the airport to: Victoria, Rs300; Beau Vallon, Rs500; Anse Soleil, Rs600. If there's no meter, agree on a price before getting in. You can also organize a half-day fixed rate "tour" with a taxi driver. A normal rate would be about Rs1,600 for a half day. All hotels have numbers of reliable drivers.

ESSENTIALS

HEALTH AND SAFETY

Free of malaria, venomous snakes and spiders, and other nasties, the worst you're likely to deal with in Seychelles is a sunburn. The public health system in Seychelles is good by African standards, and small clinics with nurses available are dotted around Mahé. Tourists are advised to go to the hospital in Victoria for anything serious. The hospital's pharmacy can also dispense prescriptions, though it's best to bring any needed prescription medications with you. Praslin also has a small hospital at Bay St. Anne, and a clinic at Grand Anse. There's a small hospital on La Digue. There are only two decompression chambers in Seychelles, one at the Mahé hospital, and the other on Silhouette

Island. Other than Silhouette, the outlying islands have little in the way of medical resources. Tap water on the main islands is safe to drink, but most people stick to bottled water or water treated by the resort. Food is well prepared and clean, though sometimes the Creole spices can affect sensitive stomachs. Most important for those traveling from a yellow-fever country—that is, much of Africa—you absolutely must have proof of vaccination before entering Seychelles. Health insurance with an evacuation policy is advised, as should anything serious happen, you'd want to be evacuated to South Africa or beyond.

Generally speaking, Seychelles is a safe place. However, most hotels provide a safe in your room or at reception, and it's wise to use it. When out and about, use common sense: don't leave valuables visible in a car in remote or quiet places, and if you go hiking alone or in just a pair, be alert to strangers. That said, violent crime is practically unheard of.

Emergency Contacts Emergency, Fire, Police, Ambulance ☎ *999.*

MONEY MATTERS

The currency in use is the Seychelles rupee (Rs). The exchange rate was US$1 to Rs12.99 at the time of writing. Although tourist prices are often quoted in euros, you can always pay in rupees at the current exchange rate, and increasingly in U.S. dollars. ATMs (which accept foreign cards) are available at the airports, in Victoria, and scattered around the larger towns on all three main islands. The most reliable bank for foreign cards is MCB (Barclays also has ATMs, but some don't accept foreign cards). Foreign exchange offices are fairly plentiful on Mahé, and exist on Praslin and La Digue in the touristy areas. Almost all hotels, restaurants, shops, and even small curio stalls take major credit cards, with a preference for Visa and MasterCard. Banks are open weekdays 8:30–2 and Saturday 9–11; they don't close for lunch.

ABOUT THE RESTAURANTS

The international dining scene in Seychelles has undergone a massive transformation in the last few years, and complaints of paying top dollar for subpar food should be a thing of the past. That said, prices are on the high side, but bear in mind that everything but seafood and some produce is imported. A cheaper option favored by many Seychellois is to get takeout for about Rs50, available in areas large enough to have shops or gas stations. Most hotels have their own restaurant (to which nonguests are usually welcome), often serving buffet meals of both international and Creole cuisine; a few of the finest à la carte restaurants are in hotels. Mixing Indian, Southeast Asian, and French influences and using the copious fresh seafood, fruits, and spices of Seychelles, Creole food is a real treat for those who enjoy spices. Octopus is used abundantly and is extremely good in all forms (salads and coconut curries); red snapper is a favorite grilled fish; and the adventurous could try a fruit–bat curry. A number of good restaurants—mostly Italian, French, and seafood or Creole—have emerged in the tourist areas around Mahé and Praslin, and serve as a welcome alternative to the hotel buffets. Most breakfast buffets start at 7 (until 10:30), but early departures can usually be accommodated. Lunch is typically served between noon and

3, and dinner from 7 to 10. The private islands and some upscale resorts will sometimes offer a more flexible dining schedule.

ABOUT THE HOTELS

The variety of hotels has exploded in the past few years. From ultraluxurious private island resorts to five-star global hotel brands to numerous three-star hotels, and an increasing number of guest houses, B&Bs, and self-catering units, there are plenty of choices. Almost all hotel rates include breakfast; many are on a half-board system, and a few (mostly the private islands) operate on a full-board system (i.e., all-inclusive). Most half- and full-board plans include a buffet dinner (versus the à la carte menu, if there's one at your hotel). If staying near a tourist destination where there are plenty of restaurant choices (such as Beau Vallon or Anse Royale in Mahé, or Côte d'Or in Praslin), it may be a better value (and more interesting) to take only the B&B option. All hotels accept credit cards. The star rating system that you'll find on the island is determined by the Seychelles Tourism Board.

WHAT IT COSTS IN DOLLARS			
	$	$$	$$$	$$$$
Hotels	under $200	$201–$400	$401–$600	over $600
Restaurants	under $18	$18–$27	$28–$37	over $37

Restaurant prices are the average cost of a main course at dinner or, if dinner is not served, at lunch. Hotel prices are the lowest cost of a standard double room in high season.

Our hotel reviews have been shortened. For full information, visit Fodors.com

VISITOR INFORMATION

The only tourist information body in the Seychelles is the generally very good Seychelles Tourism Board (STB). The head office is near the Inter Island-Quay, with smaller offices at the airports in Mahé and Praslin, and the jetties in Praslin and La Digue. The website is also tremendously helpful when planning a trip, and includes copious and regularly updated information from logistics to accommodation to activities. Maps of the main islands and consumer brochures are available for free. The largest tour operator in Seychelles is Mason's Travel. You can book any kind of tour imaginable with their helpful staff; note that their hotel rates can be more competitive than booking directly with the hotel. Walking trail maps can be purchased at the Botanical Garden and Antigone Bookshop for Rs25.

Contacts Mason's Travel ✉ *Michel Building, Revolution Ave., Victoria, Mahé* ☎ *428–8888* ⊕ *www.masonstravel.com.* **Seychelles Tourism Board** ✉ *Independence House, Victoria, Mahé* ☎ *461–0800 in Mahé, 423–3346 in Praslin, 423–4393 in La Digue* ⊕ *www.seychelles.travel.*

MAHÉ

Mahé is the archipelago's largest island at 27 km by 8 km (17 miles by 5 miles). Home to 90% of the country's population of 90,000, it displays an amazing ethnic diversity, with descendants of European colonists and African slaves living harmoniously with later settlers from Arabia, India, and China.

Mahé also displays the magnificent geology and verdant landscapes of the whole country with its own 3,200-foot granite peaks, virgin mist forests, and more than 65 exceptional beaches, making it the perfect one-stop island for a short visit. Mahé is the main transport hub for transfers to other islands in the archipelago, many of which can be visited on a long day trip. Tours of the capital Victoria or the whole island are enjoyable and educational, but many visitors may prefer to spend their time simply soaking in the tropical ambience on the sugarwhite beaches. North Mahé, home to famous Beau Vallon Beach, is more populous than other parts of the island, though its wide range of hotels and restaurants remains discreet and tasteful. In contrast, the farther south you go, the quieter it gets, with some of the most beautiful beaches and Creole villages found around Anse Intendance and Anse Forbans.

GETTING HERE AND AROUND

The domestic terminal at Mahé handles all flights anywhere else in Seychelles. Zil Air's helipad is adjacent to the International Airport runway. The Cat Coco ferry goes to Praslin three times a day (twice on Sunday). The 55-minute trip costs US$65 for adults. The Cat Coco also runs one trip a day to LaDigue, via Praslin (twice on Sunday). Having your own car is the best way to explore all of Mahé's nooks and crannies *(⇨ See Car Travel, above, for car rental info)*. But if the narrow roads and left hand driving put you off, have your hotel call you a taxi. Or take the public bus—a flat fee of Rs5 will get you anywhere on the island.

Timetables and maps are available at the terminus in Victoria, or call the SPTC line. Buses ply each route once an hour from 6 am until 7 pm.

SAFETY AND PRECAUTIONS

Generally speaking, Mahé is a very safe destination, and violent crime is practically unheard of. Still, it's best to avoid tempting petty theft: resist leaving cameras in open view in cars, or purses and cell phones unattended on beaches while swimming. If hiking in Morne Seychellois Park, don't leave valuables in sight in your car; better yet, leave them at the hotel.

TIMING

Many visitors base themselves on Mahé for the duration of their visit to the Seychelles, merely taking day trips to the other islands. If you plan to spend much time on other islands, bear in mind that Mahé is one of the most interesting islands, and excluding time to laze on the beach or go diving and snorkeling, three days could easily be filled with exploring Victoria, hiking one of the numerous inland or coastal trails, visiting the cluster of art galleries and Creole villages around Anse Soleil, and discovering your own empty beach.

ESSENTIALS

Banks and Currency Exchange Barclays Bank ⊠ *Independence Ave., Victoria* ☎ *438–3838* ⊕ *www.barclays.com.* **Mauritius Commercial Bank (MCB)** ⊠ *Manglier St., Victoria* ☎ *428–4555* ⊕ *www.mcbseychelles.com.* **Nouvobanq** ⊠ *Victoria House, State House Ave., Victoria* ☎ *429–3000* ⊕ *www.nouvobanq.sc.*

Emergency Contacts Mahé Police ⊠ *Revolution Ave., Victoria* ☎ *428–8000.*

Hospitals Victoria Hospital ⊠ *Mont Fleuri, Mahé* ☎ *438–8000.*

EXPLORING MAHÉ

VICTORIA

Seychelles' tiny capital, Victoria, is a bustling town and the nerve center of the Seychelles. Sheltered under the granite massifs on Mahé's northeast side, this town whose streets are lined with endemic palms is a hodgepodge of Creole-style houses, Indian shops, and British relics. The streets are clean and new buildings are going up all the time, though the variety of items for sale can be somewhat limited. This is the commercial center of Seychelles, all the banks have branches here, and if you need to buy anything (souvenirs or otherwise), this is your best bet. The nearby harbor is where boats of all types dock for travel to many other islands at the inter-island quay (aka wharf), and at the deep-water quay you'll find large cruise ships and cargo vessels. The funny smell in the air may be from the tuna-processing plant, also quayside.

TOP ATTRACTIONS

Seychelles National Botanical Gardens. Victoria's botanical gardens at Mont Fleuri on the outskirts of town were planted more than a century ago, and the comprehensive collection of native Mascarene plants and exotic imports stretches over five acres. The abundant palms—including the rare Coco de Mer—are the most important local species, and there is a fine spice garden. Watch out for the native Aldabra tortoises

Mahé

↖ Shark Bank

North Pt.

Mt. Howard ▲

Glacis
Sunset
Beau Vallon Bay
De Quincy Village
Aurore
Sainte Anne Marine National Park
Perseverance
Victoria see detail map
Saint Anne
Beacon I.

❶
②
Beau Vallon
Port I.
Round I.
Moyenne
Long I.
Cerf I.

Bel Ombre
❷
①
Danzil
Pascal Village
❸
❹
VICTORIA
Inter-Island Quay
Romainville
Baie Ternay Marine National Park
Mt. Le Niol ▲
Seychelles National Botanical Gardens
Victoria Hospital
Cerf Passage

Pt. Matoopa
Morne Seychellois National Park
Port Launay
Morne Seychellois ▲
Eden

Conception
Port Launay Marine National Park
Port Glaud
Grande Anse
La Misère
Cascade
Anonyme
Seychelles International Airport
Suète I.

Thérèse I.
Soleil I.
Anse aux Pins

INDIAN OCEAN
La Marine
▲ Brulée

Boileau Bay
Anse Boileau

0 ___ 4 mi
0 ___ 4 km

Michael Adams Studio
Anse à la Mouche
❻
Anse Forbans
Anse Royale
Anse Royale Bay

Anse Soleil
❺
①**⑤**
❼

Petite Anse
③①**⑨**
Nautica
Baie Lazare

④①**⑧**

Takamaka
Anse Intendance
Quatre Bornes

KEY
❶ *Restaurants*
① *Hotels*
⏊ *Beaches*
◣ *Dive sites*

Lighthouse ◆

Restaurants ▼

Anse Soleil Café **5**
Boat House **1**
Jardin du Roi **8**
Kannel Restaurant **3**
La Scala **2**

Les Dauphins Heureux
Cafe Restaurant **6**
Pink Salt **4**
Saffron Restaurant **7**
Leź **9**

Hotels ▼

Anse Soleil
Beachcomber **5**
Augerine Guesthouse **1**
Banyan Tree Seychelles **4**
Four Seasons **3**
Hanneman Holiday **2**

(some over 150 years old) and the flying foxes (large fruit-eating bats), which roost in the palm fronds. ⊠ *Mont Fleuri* ☎ *467–0558* ⌑ *USD$10* ⊙ *Daily 8–5.*

Sir Selwyn Selwyn-Clarke Market. Built in the 1840s in glorious early-Victorian style (and renovated in 1999), this national landmark, which is also Victoria's main market, is the place to buy the freshest fruit and fish and the most pungent spices. The market is a colorful place to browse for souvenirs and is particularly lively on Saturday morning (closed Sunday). ⊠ *Market St., Victoria* ⊙ *Weekdays early morning–4:30 pm, Sat. early morning–1 pm.*

WORTH NOTING

Bicentennial Monument. Erected in 1978, the monument commemorated the 200th anniversary of the founding of Victoria. This simple white structure, depicting three pairs of extended wings, was designed by artist Lorenzo Appiani, an Italian who made his home in Seychelles. ⊠ *Independence Ave.*

National Museum of History. Established in 1964, the national museum houses artifacts relating to traditional lifestyles of the pre-colonial peoples, plus items such as the oldest known map of the islands, drawn in 1517. On the frumpy side, the museum is nonetheless worth visiting for its informative displays, such as an extremely interesting section on the slave trade and its influences on Seychelles. ⊠ *Francis Rachel St., Victoria* ☎ *432–1333* ⌑ *Rs15* ⊙ *Mon., Tues., Thurs., and Fri. 8:30–4:30, Wed. 8:30–noon, Sat. 9–1. Closed Sun. and public holidays.*

Victoria Clock. The clock tower, known to the locals as Lorloz, is the symbolic heart of the city. Now surrounded by the high-rise signs of modern Mahé, this diminutive Big Ben replica was erected in 1903 to memorialize Queen Victoria; locals have been using it to set their own watches ever since. ⊠ *Corner of Albert St. and Independence Ave..*

ELSEWHERE ON THE ISLAND

Le Jardin Du Roi Spice Garden. From its elevated position above Anse Royale, the spice garden is a renovated plantation where vanilla, citronella, cinnamon, nutmeg, and other endemic plants are grown. Its Spice Shop trades in (surprise!) spices and crafts, and other buildings, such as a very small museum, can be visited. It's wise to book ahead at the popular open-air restaurant, which offers great Creole food and lovely views. ⊠ *Domaine de L'Enfoncement, Anse Royale* ☎ *437–1313* ⌑ *Rs120 (free Sun.)* ⊙ *Daily 10–5.*

Mission Lodge. An amazing viewpoint of Mahé's west coast from below the summit of Mt. Sans Souci. The site of a boarding school for liberated slave children in the late 1800s, the site only has a few stones left over along an avenue leading to a viewing platform. Here you can enjoy amazing views of verdant mountainsides. ⊠ *Mt. Sans Souci* ☎ *422–5240, 422–4542.*

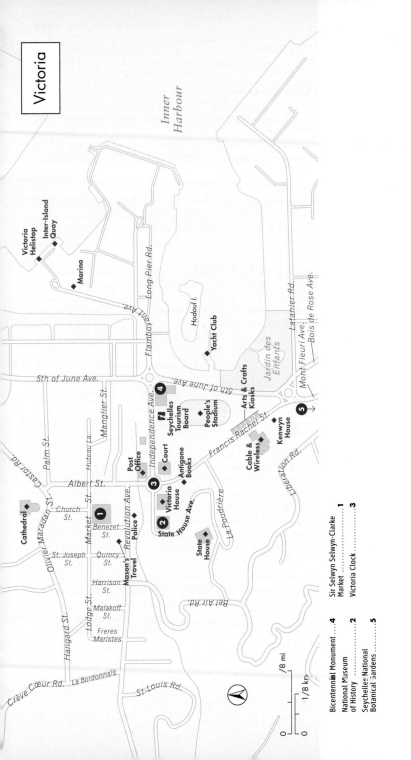

Victoria

Inner Harbour

Victoria Helistop
Inter-Island Quay
Marina

Long Pier Rd.

Flamboyant Ave.

Hodoul I.

Yacht Club

Jardin des Enfants

Latanier Rd.
Bois de Rose Ave.
Mont Fleuri Ave.

5th of June Ave.

Mangilier St.

Huteau La.

Palm St.

Castor Rd.

Independence Ave.

Post Office
Court
Antigone Books

3

Albert St.

Cathedral

Olivier Maradan St.

Church St.

Market St.

Benezet St.

1

Revolution Ave.

Police

Victoria House

State House Ave.

2

State House

La Poudrière

4 Seychelles Tourism Board
People's Stadium

5th of June Ave.

Arts & Crafts Kiosks

Francis Rachel St.

Cable & Wireless
Kenwyn House

Liberation Rd.

5

St. Joseph St.
Quincy St.

Mason's Travel

Harrison St.

Malakoff St.

Freres Maristes

Lodge St.

Hangard St.

Crève Cœur Rd. La Bordonnais

St-Louis Rd.

Bel Air Rd.

Bicentennial Monument **4**
National Museum of History **2**
Seychelles National Botanical Gardens **5**

Sir Selwyn Selwyn-Clarke Market **1**
Victoria Clock **3**

0   1/8 mi
0   1/8 km

BEACHES

11

Luxuriating on a magnificent beach under the shade of a swaying palm isn't self-indulgence—it's what you come to the Seychelles for. With more than 65 beaches to choose from, there's something for everyone. Even the busiest beaches won't be packed, and if you have a car, pack a picnic and find your own perfect spot. Beaches with rough currents will be signposted, so watch for and heed the warnings.

Anse à la Mouche. If you want a calmer experience, head for Anse à la Mouche, a crystal clear bay on the southwest coast of the island, where shallow, calm water reigns year-round. Good for kids. **Amenities:** food. **Best for:** swimming. ⊹ *From Les Canelles Rd., continue over hill, left at junction, and beachfront is in front of you.*

Anse Forbans. To get away from it all, head to this beach in the southeast. The sea, as you approach Anse Marie Louise (just past the Anse Forbans Chalets), can be rough—it's a favorite spot for surfers—but you may have the whole thing to yourself. The nearby Surfer's Café is a nice place for a snack or a drink. **Amenities:** none. **Best for:** solitude; surfing; swimming. ⊠ *Past the petrol station at Anse Royale.*

Anse Intendance. A half mile of powder-white sand, this is one of Mahé's most picturesque beaches. It's also one of the wildest, with the lack of a reef creating a large swell that makes it a favorite for surfers; swimming can be rough. It's also a favorite spot for sunbathing. The Banyan Tree Seychelles dominates the northern side of this beach, but it is open to nonguests. If you are organized, you could make a reservation at one of their excellent restaurants for lunch or dinner. Anse Intendance is one of the few places on Mahé where turtles still nest. **Amenities:** parking; toilets (only for hotel guests). **Best for:** surfing. ⊹ *Pass the Banyan Tree Resort (on your right). Beach is at end of road.*

Anse Royale. A large and beautiful white-sand beach fronting one of the larger "towns" in Mahé's south, Anse Royale hosts calm waters, plenty of shady palms, and a few restaurants, hotels, and shops supplying amenities just a few feet away. During the northwest monsoon this stretch of coast is calm and tranquil, making the stretch of small rock-fringed coves near the Anglican church great for swimming and snorkeling. Swim out from the rocks at "Fairyland" and up to the small island just off the coast. This area is enclosed by a reef and fairly shallow. Beware of currents, however. Les Dauphins Heureux restaurant is a great option when all the swimming and sunning have made you ravenous. **Amenities:** food and drink (at nearby restaurants and take-aways); toilets (at restaurants). **Best for:** snorkeling; swimming.

Anse Soleil. A calm, jade-blue bay fringed with granite boulders borders this great swimming beach. Its golden sands are a popular and photogenic spot, made more so by the Anse Soleil Café, —the only public property on the beach, where you can enjoy a fantastic seafood meal. Just offshore, massive underwater boulders make for good snorkeling, and onshore, large trees create good shade for committed beach lovers. Getting here is something of an off-the-beaten-track journey, but well worth the extra effort. **Amenities:** food; parking; toilets (at the restaurant). **Best for:** snorkeling; swimming. ⊹ *From Anse Soleil Rd., look* *for signpost for Anse Soleil Café, turn right on this track and continue downhill to café. Beach is past the café.*

Beau Vallon. Mahé's most popular beach, this 3-km (2-mile) crescent on the northwest coast enjoys surf from September to April, safe swimming year-round, and many hotel and dining facilities. The only beach where motorized water sports (Jet Skis, waterskiing) are allowed, there are also numerous recreation and water-sport operators to choose from. With a lifegurad on duty, and no strong currents, rocks, or corals, it's safe for children. It's also a popular beach for an evening run. On Wednesday evening a food market is held along a promenade between the Coral Strand and Savoy hotels: come join locals who buy delicious takeaway curries and treats to enjoy on the beach at sunset. **Amenities:** food and drink; lifeguards; parking; toilets (at hotels). **Best for:** swimming; walking; partiers. ⊠ *Beau Vallon Beach Rd..*

Sunset Beach. For great swimming and snorkeling, head to this small beach in the northwest, where turtle sightings are common and sunsets are breathtaking. Enjoy a sundowner at the Sunset Beach Hotel bar, where drinks come with mouthwatering baked coconut and plantain chips, as well as a perfect sea view. A good fringe of palms and trees makes this a lovely place to spend a day. **Amenities:** food and drink. **Best for:** swimming; snorkeling; sunsets. ⊹ *Pass Hilton Northolme Resort, Sunset Beach on the left.*

WHERE TO EAT

In Mahé you can indulge in the luxury of an ever-growing stable of true restaurants (not associated with a hotel), many of which are clustered in the Beau Vallon area, with a few also found around Anse Royale in the south. A few hotel restaurants are included here because of their exceptional food and willingness to accommodate outside guests; however, always call ahead to dine at hotel restaurants.

$$$ ✕ **Anse Soleil Café.** A popular toes-in-the-sand, small, family-run, open-
CREOLE   air restaurant on one of Mahé's most beautiful beaches, the café serves delicious Creole dishes with an emphasis on seafood, and some meat-and-fries options. The café does a hopping lunch business and can remain busy through dinner (last order at 7:30 pm). Meals are served family-style (big platters of whatever you've ordered to suit your numbers), and casual is king. Service is known to be erratic, so order ahead of your hunger if you've built up an appetite swimming and sunning all day long. $ *Average main: US$34* ⊠ *Anse Soleil* ☎ *436–1700, 436–1085, 251–1212* ⌛ *Reservations not accepted* ☉ *Closed June.*

$$$ ✕ **Boat House Restaurant.** This large and lively open-air institution across
CREOLE   the street from popular Beau Vallon beach serves a tasty Creole buffet
FAMILY   with more than 20 dishes every night, casual lunches, and breakfasts daily. The choice of salads is great, with flavorful renditions of the mango, papaya, and starfruit dishes that you may have become familiar with from other buffets. A chef grills fresh fish and chicken to order, and the curries are also delicious. It's an all-you-can-eat prix fixe, so come hungry. Plans of adding a sushi bar to this casual beach eatery are in the works. $ *Average main: US$31* ⊠ *Beau Vallon* ☎ *424–7898.*

$ ✕ **Jardin du Roi.** With soaring views through steep forested hills down to
CREOLE   a turquoise slice of Anse Royale, this quaint, open-air restaurant serves
very good Creole fare. Delicious salads of papaya, golden apple, and
mango accompany perfectly grilled fish, subtly spiced curries, and fragrant basmati rice. Crêpes, sandwiches, a few vegetarian options, and
the homemade ice creams are also great. Come on Sunday from noon
to 3 for the Lunch Planteur, a Creole feast that includes all the salads,
chutneys, and extras you might expect at a huge family potluck with the
home-style cooking to match for Rs325. ■ TIP→ Reservations essential in season. $ *Average main: US$17* ⊠ *Domaine de l'Enforcement,
Anse Royale* ☎ *437–1313* ⊘ *Closed Christmas, New Year's, and Easter.*

$$$$ ✕ **Kannel Restaurant.** Gleaming warm wooden tones and screens of metal
INTERNATIONAL   cutout flowers adorn this elegant yet casual poolside restaurant, which
serves lunch and dinner daily. Lunch menus focus on lighter international fare, like excellent salads, pastas, seafood dishes, and wood-oven baked pizzas. Dinners flaunt the chef's Creole and international
skills, with exquisite renditions of dishes such as a grilled octopus salad,
Singapore-style noodles, and heavenly curries served with local chutneys, such as the Creole fish curry. Nonhotel guests should be sure to
book ahead. $ *Average main: US$42* ⊠ *Four Seasons Resort, Petite
Anse, Baie Lazare* ☎ *439–3000* ⊕ *www.fourseasons.com* ⊜ *Reservations essential.*

$$ ✕ **La Scala.** Serving classically simple Italian fare in a beautiful white
ITALIAN   house atop granite rocks, this is one of Mahé's oldest and beloved
restaurants. The Italian chef-owner is also a fisherman, and in season
his catch of the day is the freshest you'll find. Pastas are largely homemade, and dishes like the tagliatelle with smoked sailfish or ravioli
with fish are recommended. The front of the house is managed by the
chef's wife, a charming lady who runs a tight ship. With sea breezes
wafting through from the tranquil Bel Ombre, the mood is romantic
and old world, making this a place to linger. $ *Average main: US$25*
⊠ *Bel Ombre* ☎ *424–7535* ⊕ *www.lascala.sc* ⊜ *Reservations essential*
⊘ *Closed Sun., and June. No lunch.*

$$ ✕ **Les Dauphins Heureux Cafe Restaurant.** Sitting on the beachfront facing
CREOLE   beautiful Anse Royale, this casual yet elegant restaurant serves excellent Creole and international fare, as well as a locally popular Sunday
lunch buffet. The smoked fish and mango salad is the perfect balance
of tart, sweet, and smoky, and the ginger crab curry is amazingly fragrant. Attentive owner-managed service makes this a romantic dinner
option, but with the beautiful beach view and shady outdoor seating
option, it's also a winner in the day. Cocktails are tasty and potent,
and there's a great wine list. Don't miss the incredible homemade ice
cream. And there's free Wi-Fi! $ *Average main: US$19* ⊠ *Anse Royale
Village, 5 June Ave., Anse Royale* ☎ *443–0100* ⊕ *www.piedansleau.sc*
⊘ *No dinner Sun.*

$$ ✕ **Maria's Rock.** Not only is Maria's Rock built in, among, and from
BARBECUE   the huge granite boulders that define Mahé, but this themed restaurant
FAMILY   also lets you cook your meal on that very same granite. With only one
culinary option—seafood or meat grilled on a hot rock at your table,
and served with rice and salad—this place isn't for everyone. But if you

like some DIY in your food experience (reminiscent of Korean BBQ) and don't mind the sweat that it may inspire, the place is charming, and the grill items, from fish fillets to prawns to beef, delicious and fresh. Kids will love the Fred Flinstone–meets–Pirate of the Caribbean Disney-ride atmosphere, heightened by the pirate ship and other structures they can play on. [$] *Average main: US$19* ✉ *Anse Gouvernement, Baie Lazare* ☎ *436–1812, 257–5544* ✍ *soubanamaria@hotmail.com* ⏲ *Closed Tues., and July.*

$$ CREOLE 🍴 **Marie Antoinette.** Housed in a charming old Creole-style wooden abode on a hill overlooking Victoria, Marie Antoinette has been serving the same "traditional" Creole set menu for over 30 years. You'll find fish prepared in four different styles, chicken curry, aubergine fritters, rice, and delicious assorted Creole "salads" (also referred to as chutneys) on the menu. A few simple local desserts sweeten the end. A pen of giant tortoises, a wall of business cards from patrons hailing worldwide, and rustic, homey décor add to the restaurant's charm. **TIP→ Reservations are essential during high season and on weekends.** [$] *Average main: US$21* ✉ *Serret Rd., St. Louis, Victoria* ☎ *426–6222* 🌐 *www.marieantoinette.sc* ✍ *Reservations essential* ⏲ *Closed Sun. and public holidays.*

$ CAFÉ FAMILY 🍴 **Pink Salt.** Set in a lovely old wooden house just on the edge of Victoria, this charming café serves a refreshingly simple menu of gourmet sandwiches, wraps, and salads. The panko-crumb chicken wrap with coriander and mango is both light and tasty, and the niçoise salad is a favorite. For the very hungry, the Aussie cheeseburger will hit the spot. Homemade desserts, including several cheesecakes that are becoming deservedly legendary, are also a draw. A lush garden setting and friendly staff further enhance the oasis atmosphere of this little gem. There's also a kid's menu. [$] *Average main: US$17* ✉ *Revolution Ave., Victoria* ☎ *432–4150* ⏲ *Closed Sun. No dinner.*

$$$ THAI Fodor's Choice ★ 🍴 **Saffron Restaurant.** If you're craving something different, this Thai restaurant at the Banyan Tree Hotel is a treat. In a simply elegant dining room of crimson hues and graced with sea views to gorgeous Anse Intendance, Saffron serves up delicious and authentic Thai food, including a seafood glass-noodle salad, a fabulous red curry duck with lychees, and delicately steamed red snapper in a chili lime sauce. The Thai chef and availability of locally grown Thai produce are no doubt behind the authentic flavors. [$] *Average main: US$34* ✉ *Banyan Tree Hotel, Anse Intendance* ☎ *438–3500* 🌐 *www.banyantree.com* ✍ *Reservations essential.*

$$$$ INTERNATIONAL Fodor's Choice ★ 🍴 **Zez.** Enjoying spectacular ocean and sunset views from its hillside perch above Petite Anse beach, the Four Season's fine-dining venue Zez is a romantic dinner venue serving perfectly executed international cuisine. Set the tone for a gorgeous meal with starters like the warm lobster and artichoke salad tossed in a sherry vinaigrette, or foie gras with apple tarte tatin. The chef's skills come out in dishes like the crab fettuccine, a perfectly balanced dish of homemade pasta, crispy soft-shell crab, fresh chilli, parsley, and lemon. If you're after something more substantial, the lobster risotto or lamb filet will satisfy. An excellent if pricey wine list, and great service accompany the meal. Elegant dark-wood

interiors and romantic lighting allow the stunning view to take center stage. $ *Average main: US$37* ✉ *Four Seasons Resort, Petite Anse, Baie Lazare* ☎ *439–3000* 🌐 *www.fourseasons.com/seychelles/dining/restaurants/zez* ✍ *Reservations essential.*

WHERE TO STAY

In recent years, accommodation in the Seychelles has expanded tremendously, with the majority of development on Mahé. Everything from superluxurious five-star resorts to self-catering bungalows can now be found. The Seychelles Tourism Board website *(⇨ See Essentials, above, for contact info)* is a great resource for reviewing the multitude of options.

$ B&B/INN Fodor's Choice ★ **Anse Soleil Beachcomber.** Set on a charming little bay on the island's southwest coast, all the rooms at this gem of a guest house are perched right on the beach among granite boulders with great sea views. **Pros:** great value for money; local place with a friendly philosophy; smack-dab on one of Mahé's nicest beaches; free kayaks, snorkeling gear, and Wi-Fi. **Cons:** rooms share walls; terraces are visible from the beach and some from the restaurant; Wi–Fi doesn't reach most of the rooms. $ *Rooms from: US$132* ✉ *Anse Soleil* ☎ *436–1461* 🌐 *www.ansesoleilbeachcomber.sc* *14 rooms, 4 apartments* ⏲ *Closed June* 🍽 *Multiple meal plans.*

$$ B&B/INN FAMILY **Augerine Guesthouse.** A family-run place on Beau Vallon beach, all of its pleasant, clean, and comfortable rooms have air-conditioning, standing fans, balconies, and sea views. **Pros:** good value for great beachfront location where all rooms have sea views; friendly service; close to all the Beau Vallon restaurants. **Cons:** rooms are a bit stark; no free Wi-Fi; next door to a large resort that can be noisy. $ *Rooms from: US$230* ✉ *Beau Vallon* ☎ *424–7257* 🌐 *www.augerinehotel.com* *12 rooms, 3 junior suites* 🍽 *Breakfast.*

$$$$ RESORT Fodor's Choice ★ **Banyan Tree Seychelles.** The only property on Anse Intendance—one of Seychelles' most beautiful beaches—the Banyan Tree Seychelles is an ideal honeymoon location with its large, quasi-French colonial villas that ooze luxury and privacy. **Pros:** beautiful beach location; idyllic for honeymooners and romance-seekers; great Thai restaurant. **Cons:** not great for children; the free equipment at the activities center could use an upgrade; sea here can be a bit rough from May to October. $ *Rooms from: US$1442* ✉ *Anse Intendance* ☎ *438–3500* 🌐 *www.banyantree.com* *60 pool villas* 🍽 *Multiple meal plans.*

$$$$ RESORT FAMILY Fodor's Choice ★ **Four Seasons.** Arguably Mahé's best resort, this stunning property provides exquisite service, fine dining, great activities, and a perfect beach surrounded by a forested natural amphitheater. **Pros:** spectacular villas with private plunge pools; fantastic beach with excellent snorkeling year-round; great activities center, and kids' program. **Cons:** because of hillside arrangement, some villas above yours can see into your outside private areas; garden villas closest to beach lack a sea view; steep hillsides discourage walking, making you reliant on buggy service. $ *Rooms from: US$1729* ✉ *Petite Anse, Baie Lazare* ☎ *439–3000*

Banyan Tree Seychelles

Four Seasons

🌐 *www.fourseasons.com* 🛏 *62 villas, 5 suites, 6 residences* 🍴 *Multiple meal plans.*

$$ RENTAL 🏠 **Hanneman Holiday Residence.** A four-minute walk to popular Beau Vallon beach, these sleek apartments provide independent travelers with modern lodgings complete with many conveniences. **Pros:** environmentally friendly measures have earned it the "Seychelles sustainability" certification; convenient location walking distance from Beau Vallon attractions, bus stop, and shops; helpful, friendly staff. **Cons:** décor might be a bit cold for some tastes; big resort across the way blocks sea view. [$] *Rooms from: US$260* ✉ *Beau vallon* ☎ *442–5000* 🌐 *www.hanneman-seychelles.com* 🛏 *8 apartments* 🍴 *Multiple meal plans.*

SHOPPING

Shops in Seychelles' resorts tend to stock imported crafts and clothing, plus high-value items like designer watches and diamond jewelry; however, there's a small and interesting selection of locally produced souvenirs for every budget. Black pearls are a specialty and make exquisite rings or necklaces. Look also for the fiery local rum. There are many tourist shops in Mahé's downtown, including a row of kiosks selling sarongs, hats, bags, and certified Coco de Mer seeds on Francis Rachel Street. The larger hotels usually have small souvenir shops.

Chanterelle. Probably the best bookstore for reads on the Seychelles, this shop—a sister to the older Antigone Books nearby—stocks everything from field guides to cookbooks, travel guides to coffee-table books. They also sell novels in English and a small stock of imported newspapers and magazines. There is a branch at the International Airport. ✉ *Quincy St., Victoria* ☎ *432–5424* 🕒 *Weekdays 9–4:30, Sat. 9–12:30.*

Kenwyn House. One of Seychelles' best examples of a 19th-century French colonial home, Kenwyn House is a historic monument as well as a duty-free shop and gallery. Built entirely from wood in 1855, this elegant home now houses a jewelry shop featuring South African diamonds and tanzanite, an art gallery, high-end souvenirs from the Indian Ocean region, and a charming, if only sometimes functioning, coffee shop. ✉ *Francis Rachel St., Victoria* ☎ *422–4440* 🌐 *www.kenwynhouse.com* 🕒 *Weekdays 9–5, Sat. 9–1.*

Fodor's Choice ★ **Michael Adams Studio.** Seychelles' best-known artist, Malaysian-born Michael Adams has studied the Seychelles' otherworldly jungle- and seascapes through dreamlike watercolors and silk screens for more than 30 years now. Visit his studio in Anse Poules Bleues to view (and purchase) his unique work, as well as that of his extremely talented children, Alyssa and Tristan, both of whom are also painters. ✉ *Anse Aux Poules Bleues* ☎ *436–1006* 🌐 *www.michaeladamsart.com* 🕒 *Weekdays 10–4, Sat. 10–noon.*

SPORTS AND THE OUTDOORS

DIVING AND SNORKELING

Qualified divers can book tanks and a guide to explore rich underwater worlds of coral reefs and abundant sea life. But you don't need to be a certified diver to enjoy the marine life of Seychelles, where shallow reefs and lagoons offer perfect conditions for snorkeling. The best time of year for diving is the hot season (November–April), when the waters achieve that legendary crystal-clear visibility. Unfortunately, the coral bleaching that affected the entire Indian Ocean in 2002 damaged the majority of the Seychelles' reefs, so don't expect acres of colorful corals. The real thrill of diving in the Seychelles is the abundance of game fish and the rich, large marine life—turtles, rays, and huge shoals of fish—centered on Seychelles' unique underwater granite formations.

BEST DIVE SITES

Port Launay Marine National Park. Located on the northwest coast, the Port Launay marine park is famous for its beautiful beaches and whale-sharks, which in season can be seen feeding on plankton. The white sand beach here, which is accessible by the Constance Ephelia Resort, is large and wide with plenty of shady trees, making it popular with picnickers on the weekends. If you come by boat you'll need a ticket for the marine park, but those just enjoying the beach don't need to pay. ☒ *Rs200* ☺ *Daily 9–5.*

Shark Bank. Also on the northwest coast, about 9 km (5 miles) off of Beau Vallon, this dive around a 30-meter granite pillar is famous for—surprise!—shark sightings. Usually divers will encounter reef sharks, though in season whale sharks also abound. Huge brissant rays, barracuda, batfish, and yellow snapper are common. This site is for experienced divers only, as a strong current runs here.

BEST SNORKEL SITES

Bay Ternay Marine National Park. On the northwest coast around the point from Port Launay, this marine park boasts reefs that are excellent for snorkeling. There is no vehicle road to Bay Ternay, so you must go by boat, usually with an organized tour.

Ste. Anne Marine National Park. The first protected marine park in the Indian Ocean, Ste. Anne Marine National Park was established in 1973. Just offshore (a 20-minute boat ride) from Mahé, its boundaries incorporate six islands, one of Seychelles' most important Hawksbill turtle nesting sites, and large sea-grass meadows. The warm, clear, shallow lagoons are perfect for snorkeling and exploring the profusion of marine life from tropical fish to corals and swaying anemones. The best way to get here is on one of the half- or full-day boat trips offered by tour operators on Mahé, or to stay on one of the islands with accommodation.

RECOMMENDED OPERATORS

Big Blue Divers. Located in Beau Vallon, these friendly folks have 20 years of experience and more than 75 dive sights to show you. They offer PADI certification, and focus on smaller groups. ☒ *Next to Divers Lodge, Beau Vallon* ☎ *426–1106, 251–1103* ⊕ *www.bigbluedivers.net.*

Dive Resort Seychelles. Another five-star PADI dive resort, this one is based in the south. Also with more than 20 years of experience in Seychelles, they are well versed in dive sights both in the inner and outer islands. ✉ *Anse a la Mouche* ☎ *437–2057, 271–7272* ⊕ *www. scubadiveseychelles.com.*

HIKING

Morne Seychellois National Park. If you want to get off the beach and explore some of the enticing lush jungle clinging to the steep cliffs around Mahé, this is the place to come. Seychelles' largest park was created in 1979 and covers an area of about 30 square km (12 square miles), or more than 20% of Mahé, and encompasses its eponymous peak, the highest point in Seychelles at 910 meters (2,985 feet). About 10 km (6 miles) in length and 3 km (2 miles) in width, the park is equipped with 12 different trails that can be explored on half- or full-day excursions. Rare orchids, endemic palms, and carnivorous pitcher plants are among the botanical treats. The trails are currently being upgraded, but at the time of writing covered more than 14 km (9 miles) in the park. Maps should be available at the head office of the tourism board. Many of the trails are easy and well marked. For the more difficult routes (e.g., Mont Serbert, Congo Rouge, and Les Trois Frères), hikers should definitely enlist the help of a guide. 🎫 *Free.*

RECOMMENDED GUIDES

Basil Beaudouin. Mahé's most famous hiking guide, Beaudouin is the Seychelles' answer to Crocodile Dundee. His knowledge is extensive, and he takes good care of his clients, regardless of skill level. ☎ *251–4972.*

SAILING

What better way to enjoy an island nation than to hop from one island to the next on a sailboat? Offering visitors the ultimate way to experience the diversity and beauty of the archipelago, a trip on a chartered boat can last a day or a week. Most trips leaving from Mahé will sail around the island itself, anchoring at snorkel spots, and including a bit of actual sailing at some point in the journey (wind providing). Diving, kayaking, and waterskiing may also be offered on your cruise. A week-long live-aboard is a truly special experience—itineraries vary depending on the time of year and sea conditions.

Fodor's Choice
★

Silhouette Cruises. Offering fabulous day- or week-long excursions on a fleet of beautiful live-aboard vessels, a journey with Silhouette Cruises may just be the highlight of your time in the Seychelles. Itineraries vary according to season to avoid rough seas, but always include visits to all major islands, multiple small islands, and snorkeling and swimming in otherwise inaccessible marine parks. Scuba fanatics should check out the "dive safari" trips, which take place between October and November. If you have the fortune of traveling from late September to early October, the special whale shark expedition is a trip of a lifetime. Delicious, hearty meals, a friendly professional crew (always including a licensed dive instructor), and clean comfortable cabins make this hotel on the sea a wonderful and über-relaxed way to explore numerous islands and their marine life at a leisurely pace. ✉ *Victoria* ☎ *432–4026, 251–4051* ⊕ *www.seychelles-cruises.com.*

PRASLIN

Praslin, at 11 km (7 miles) long and 4 km (2½ miles) wide, is the second-largest island in the Seychelles. First settled as a hideaway by pirates and Arab merchants, the island's original name, Isle de Palmes, bears testament to its reputation as home of the Vallée de Mai UNESCO World Heritage Site: the only place in the world where the famous Coco de Mer, the world's heaviest nut, grows abundantly in the wild.

Praslin's endemic palm forests shelter many rare species, and the island is a major bird-watching destination. Surrounded by a coral reef, majestic bays, and gorgeous beaches, Praslin is much quieter and less developed than Mahé. With few real "sights," the pleasures of Praslin largely involve relaxing in or exploring its stunning beaches and fantastical forests.

WHEN TO GO

The main areas where accommodations are found are Grande Anse on the west side, and Côte d'Or (or Anse Volbert) on the east side. Due to the nature of Seychelles' wind and weather patterns, the west coast beaches tend to gather seaweed and sea grass from May to September, during which time the Côte d'Or beaches are clear and clean. When the season (and wind) changes from October to April, the west coast clears up while the east coast waters can be a bit rougher. It's wise to note these differences when deciding where you want to stay.

GETTING HERE AND AROUND

Forty kilometers (25 miles) northeast of Mahé, Praslin is just a 15-minute flight or one-hour ferry ride away. The Cat Coco ferry from Mahé Inter Island Quay (US$65 one-way; one hour) docks at Praslin's main jetty at Bay St. Anne, which is also the departure point for most day-trip boat excursions (though several other small jetties exist around the island). The Inter Island ferry (also referred to as the Cat Rose), which travels to and from La Digue, takes about 20 minutes each way

Praslin

11

(US$17 one-way) and also docks here. The Praslin airport (with flights
to Mahé only) is in the west at Amitié, and also houses a landing pad
for helicopter flights.

Rental-car agencies have kiosks at the airport. The local agencies have
offices in Bay St. Anne, Grand Anse, and Côte d'Or, but you can usually arrange to have them meet you at a jetty or your hotel. The local
bus runs two routes, departing about once an hour, one plying the east
coast, the other the west. Double-check with the driver which route
you're on, as they sometimes fail to change the destination sign. The
fare is Rs5. Taxis are available at the airport and Bay St. Anne, as well
as around Grand Anse and Côte d'Or. Luggage is charged at Rs10 per
piece. Sample fares from the airport are Côte d'Or, Rs400; Anse Lazio,
Rs700; Bay St. Anne jetty, Rs300.

TIMING

Tour operators in Mahé often run day trips to Praslin to visit the famous
Vallée de Mai, but beautiful Praslin deserves at least a few days of its
own. At least half a day is needed to properly appreciate the aforemen-
tioned World Heritage Site. Praslin is also a great spot from which to
explore the numerous tiny islands that surround it, including the spectacular bird sanctuaries of Cousin and Aride, and gorgeous La Digue
(if you're not planning to overnight there, which would be a shame if

you are interested in seeing what the slow island life is all about). With all of these attractions, Praslin merits a minimum of two nights, and if you want to take it easy and explore Praslin's beaches, at least four nights would be required.

ESSENTIALS

Emergency Contacts Praslin Police ⊠ *Grand Anse* ☎ *423–3251* ✉ *Bay St. Anne* ☎ *423–2332.*

Ferry Service Inter Island Ferry (to La Digue) ⊠ *Bay St. Anne* ☎ *423–2329 for jetty, 423–2394 for office.*

Medical Assistance Bay St. Anne Hospital ⊠ *Bay St. Anne* ☎ *423–2333 Bay St. Anne, 423–3414 Grand Anse clinic.*

Rental Cars Amitié Curieuse Car Hire ⊠ *Amitié* ☎ *423–3358, 258–0787, 271–5800* ✎ *yvonesther@hotmail.com.* **Aventure** ⊠ *Amitié* ☎ *423–3805* ⊕ *aventure@seychelles.net.* **Capricorn Car Rental** ⊠ *Bay St. Anne* ☎ *258–1110, 251–0446* ✎ *capcorn@seychelles.net.* **Prestige Car Hire** ⊠ *Grand Anse* ☎ *423–3226, 251–5226.*

Visitor and Tour Information Mason's Travel ⊠ *Bay St., Praslin Airport* ☎ *428–8750 Bay St Ann, 428–8760 Praslin Airport* ⊕ *www.masonstravel.com.* **Seychelles Tourism Board** ⊠ *Bay St., Praslin Airport* ☎ *423–2669 at Bay St. Ann, 423–3346 at Praslin Airport* ⊕ *www.seychelles.travel.*

EXPLORING PRASLIN

TOP ATTRACTIONS

Fodor's Choice
★
Cousin Island. Cousin lies just off the southwest coast of Praslin, about 30 to 45 minutes away by boat. A nature reserve since 1968, Cousin is home to some of Seychelles' rarest birds, including the Seychelles bush warbler and the Seychelles magpie robin, and also serves as the breeding ground for thousands of lesser noddies, ferry terns, and tropic birds. Arriving on this small island, you'll see a sky darkened with the diving silhouettes of thousands of birds, and a visit gives a glimmer of an idea of what the first explorers to Seychelles might have experienced when alighting on these islands. In addition to its magnificent bird populations, the island is home to giant Aldabra tortoises, as well as being a favorite nesting site for hawksbill turtles. Your hotel can organize a trip to the island with one of the many boat excursion operators, or check out one of Masons Travel's excursions. The stop at Cousin will usually be one of three your boat will make. Be sure to bring your camera (fantastic photo ops of ground-nesting birds), mosquito spray (the mozzies can be thick in the interior), and a hat (they say it's good luck to be pooped on by a bird, but let your hat take the hit). ⊠ *Cousin* ☎ *460–1100 for Mahé office, 271–8816 for Cousin Island* ⊕ *www.natureseychelles.org* 🎟 *Rs500* ⊗ *Weekdays 10–noon.*

Fodor's Choice
★
Vallée de Mai National Park. Located on Praslin's southeastern end, the Vallée de Mai National Park protects some of the last ancient virgin Mascarene forest in the world. This UNESCO World Heritage Site is also the only place on earth where the unique double coconut or Coco de Mer palms grow wild and abundantly. Some 6,000 specimens

bearing the largest nut in the plant kingdom flourish here. This idyllic paradise is also home to the other five species of Seychelles endemic palms, the rare black parrot, freshwater crabs, giant crayfish, and vanilla orchids. Visitors can take the tarmac road from Bay St. Anne toward Grand Anse for a drive through the park that will introduce them to its charms, but the only real way to experience it is to walk along the very well-maintained nature trails (sandals will suffice) that run through the valley. Allow at least three hours to really explore the park. A nice gift shop where you can buy certified Coco de Mer seeds, a café, and luggage lockers are on the premises. There is also a free one-hour guided tour daily at 10 and 2. ⊠ *Vallée de Mai* ☎ *432–1735* ⊕ *www.sif.sc* 🖃 *Rs345 (cash only)* ⊙ *Daily 8–5:30.*

WORTH NOTING

Aride. A 30- to 45-minute boat trip from Praslin, Aride is one of the most pristine of the Seychelles islands and is known as the "seabird citadel" of the Indian Ocean, with more than a million seabirds breeding here each year. Protected as a reserve since 1967, Aride hosts 18 species of native birds, including the world's only hilltop colony of sooty terns and the only granitic breeding sites for the world's largest colony of lesser noddies. The Seychelles warbler was introduced from Cousin in 1988, as were the Seychelles fody and magpie robin in 2002. Aride also boasts one of the densest populations of lizards on earth, as well as unique endemic plants. A beautiful reef surrounds the island, and in season it is common to see whale sharks and flying fish in the waters just offshore. Visitors to the island must land between 9:30 and 10, but then may spend the whole day on the island if desired. Numerous operators can take you to Aride, and usually include lunch in the trip; inquire at your hotel. Due to weather conditions, Aride closes to visitors from May to September, when strong winds can prevent boats from landing. ☎ *271–9778 for island manager* ✉ *aride@seychelles.net* ⊕ *www.arideisland.com* 🖃 *Rs650* ⊙ *Weekdays 10–3:30 (boat-landing hrs)* ⊙ *Closed May–Sept., and when weather does not permit landings.*

Curieuse. Once known as Île Rouge on account of its red earth, this rugged island was previously home to a leper colony situated at Anse St. Joseph. The resident doctor's house, which dates back to the 1870s, was converted into an eco-museum and visitor center, and Aldabra tortoises roam freely. Aside from Praslin, Curieuse is the only other island where the Coco de Mer grows naturally (though they have been planted and cultivated elsewhere in the Seychelles). Curieuse also offers eight different species of mangrove. It is reachable by boat from Praslin, and often serves as a lunch spot on the various boat excursions from Praslin and La Digue. ⊠ *Curieuse* ☎ *422–5115, 256–0388 for ranger on island* 🖃 *Rs200* ⊙ *Daily 9–5.*

BEACHES

Fodor's Choice
★

Anse Georgette. This small bay of white sand punctuated by granite boulders could certainly contend for Praslin's prettiest beach—a complete lack of development and difficult access keep it so. Unfortunately, road access passes through the Constance Lemuria Resort, and nonguests must get permission to enter, which is not always an easy task. Call or email the resort at least 24-hours in advance if you want to be sure to get in. Alternatively, there is now a forest path from Anse Lazio, but it takes about an hour to walk between the two beaches, and decent shoes are needed. **Amenities:** none. **Best for:** snorkeling; swimming. ☎ 428–1281 for Constance Lemuria.

Anse Lazio. Praslin's most famous beach is located on the island's northeastern tip. A long strip of golden sand with stunning granite boulders on either end and takamaka trees providing much coveted shade, this calm beach is known for excellent swimming and snorkeling opportunities. Unfortunately, this postcard perfect spot can get extremely crowded, diminishing the magic for some. ■ TIP➔ When you arrive, head left and look for a nook at the very end between the boulders. The bus doesn't reach here, so you'll have to drive or walk about 20 minutes from the closest bus stop. Two restaurants operate on either end of the beach, about a 10-minute walk away from one another. **Amenities:** food and drink; parking; toilets (at restaurants). **Best for:** snorkeling; swimming.

Côte d'Or Beach. Also known as Anse Volbert, Côte d'Or Beach is an extensive and stunning white-sand beach that frequently appears on best-beach lists. There are quite a few hotels and restaurants nearby. The only downside to this gorgeous strip of sand, probably Praslin's most popular, is that you won't be alone, and you may get hassled by beach boys selling boat trips and the like. **Amenities:** food and drink; toilets (at hotels). **Best for:** swimming; partiers; walking.

Grand Anse. Grand Anse on the southwest coast is another large stretch of sand with several hotels and restaurants. Lovely from October to March, it can be the recipient of a lot of mucky sea grass the rest of the year. Good for swimming and water sports when sea grass is absent, there are also plenty of places to rent equipment for the latter. **Amenities:** food and drink; toilets (at hotels). **Best for:** swimming; walking.

WHERE TO EAT

Almost all of Praslin's hotels have a restaurant. The best area for dining is Côte d'Or, which boasts some very good hotel restaurants and most of the island's true stand-alone dining establishments.

$$$$
CREOLE

✕ **Beach Bar & Grill.** Serving fabulous Creole-inspired food in a gorgeous setting atop a small rocky outcrop between Grande and Petite Anse Kerlan, Constance Lemuria's elegant beach restaurant is well worth a visit for lunch or dinner. Lunch is more Creole-influenced, as seen in dishes like the whitefish ceviche marinated with lemongrass oil and served on a bed of dried coconut, and the whole grilled reef fish in a piquant Creole sauce. Dinner options include more international favorites like grilled ribeye or pork ribs. Enjoy the sea breezes that cross from bay to bay, and bird's-eye views of the small reef sharks that sometimes ply the granite boulders below. Nonguests should call ahead to make a reservation. $ Average main: US$40 ⊠ Anse Kerlan ☎ 428–1091 ⊕ www. lemuriaresort.com ⌕ Reservations essential.

Cousin Island, a nature reserve since 1968, is home to some of the Seychelles' rarest birds.

$$$
SEAFOOD

✕ **Bonbon Plume.** Located on lovely Anse Lazio beach, this outdoor establishment is open for lunch only, but serves delicious grilled seafood and Creole specialties right on the water's edge. Order grilled lobster, fish, scallops, or mussels Seychellois from the à la carte menu (all served with rice, salad, and lentils). A large open-air structure of thatch and wood, the restaurant's best tables are in the sand under umbrellas. Outside of lunch hours, juices, milkshakes, beer, and ice cream are available. $ *Average main: US$28* ⊠ *Anse Lazio* ☎ *423–2136* ☉ *Closed June.*

$$$$
INTERNATIONAL
Fodor'sChoice
★

✕ **Café des Arts.** Probably Praslin's best restaurant, Café des Arts is a funky, salmon- and aqua-tone haven of divine cuisine, located right on Côte d'Or, one of Seychelles' most beautiful beaches. The food here has a great reputation, meeting the fussiest fine diner's expectations. The octopus gratin with lobster and the tuna carpaccio with a caper, garlic, and olive oil dip are highly recommended. Save room for the desserts, which are fabulously decadent. The cheesy music is forgiven by the excellent and incredibly friendly service. Lunch consists of a lighter menu, served on the wooden deck set right on the beach. A new rooftop deck area is also a lovely place for a cocktail. $ *Average main: US$42* ⊠ *Côte d'Or* ☎ *423–2252* ⊕ *www.cafe.sc* ⤴ *Reservations essential* ☉ *Closed Mon.*

$$$$
INTERNATIONAL

✕ **Seahorse Restaurant.** The Constance Lemuria's fine-dining restaurant focuses on a compact and extremely well-executed menu of Creole and international dishes, such as slow-cooked red snapper with a breadfruit puree and truffle oil, and braised New Zealand lamb shoulder. "Healthy" dishes, like scallop carpaccio with an almond crumble, are indicated on the menu and are fresh and delicious. Enjoying garden views over the 11th green of the resort's award-winning championship golf course, the ambience is warm romantic with its dark-wood tones, candlelight, and open-air breezes. Great service and an excellent sommelier complete the picture. $ *Average main: US$37* ⊠ *Anse Kerlan* ☎ *428–1281* ⊕ *www.lemuriaresort.constancehotels.com* ⚏ *Reservations essential* ⊘ *No lunch.*

WHERE TO STAY

Compared to Mahé, Praslin's hotels are generally much smaller and less swish: there are only a handful of resorts and large hotels, and many of the latter are locally owned and enjoy a casual, friendly atmosphere. Most of Praslin's accommodations are clustered either on Côte d'Or (also known as Anse Volbert) on the island's east side, or Grand Anse on the west coast.

$
B&B/INN
Britannia Hotel. Set back about 100 meters (328 feet) from the beach in a residential neighborhood of pretty gardens and a backdrop of forested mountain, Britannia offers prices that reflect its lack of killer sea views. **Pros:** great value for money; five minutes' walk from Grand Anse; free shuttle three times a week to other popular beaches and dive sites. **Cons:** not on the beach. $ *Rooms from: US$162* ⊠ *Grand Anse* ☎ *423–3215* ⊜ *britania@seychelles.net* ⊕ *www.britanniapraslin.com* ⇥ *12 rooms* ⦿ *Multiple meal plans.*

$
B&B/INN
Chalet Côte Mer. This small, homey, owner-managed hotel has fantastic sea-facing rooms. **Pros:** gorgeous views and convenient location; great value; good French Creole restaurant. **Cons:** no actual beach nearby (but you can swim and snorkel); standard rooms are a bit small. ■ TIP→ Book directly for the best price and a complimentary transfer from the jetty. $ *Rooms from: US$184* ⊠ *Bay St. Anne* ☎ *429–4200* ⊕ *www.chaletcotemer.com* ⇥ *7 rooms, 6 apartments* ⦿ *Multiple meal plans.*

$$
RESORT
FAMILY
Coco de Mer and Black Parrot Suites. Located on more than 200 acres of forest and 1 km of beachfront, this lovely jungle-themed hotel is the only property on Anse Bois de Rose, and every room has sea views. **Pros:** sea views from all rooms; Black Parrot suites wonderfully romantic; free Wi-Fi in public areas. **Cons:** located on the western side of Praslin, where beach is subject to seaweed May–October. $ *Rooms from: US$388* ⊠ *Anse Bois de Rose* ☎ *429–0555* ⊕ *www.cocodemer.com* ⇥ *40 rooms, 12 junior suites* ⦿ *Multiple meal plans.*

$$$$
RESORT
FAMILY
Constance Lemuria Resort. Set on 370 acres of scenic palm groves, the Lemuria was Praslin's first five-star resort and remains a favorite luxury destination. **Pros:** access to three of Praslin's nicest beaches, including the famous Anse Georgette; the only 18-hole golf course in Seychelles; excellent facilities and beautiful pools. **Cons:** one of Seychelles' oldest resorts, the rooms don't quite live up to current five-star expectations. $ *Rooms from: US$1417* ⊠ *Anse Kerlan* ☎ *428–1281* ⊕ *lemuriaresort.constancehotels.com* ⇥ *105 rooms* ⦿ *Multiple meal plans.*

$$
HOTEL
FAMILY
Indian Ocean Lodge. Set in a lovely palm- and takamaka-tree-filled garden right on Grand Anse beach, this hotel creole in friendly service and homey atmosphere. **Pros:** good-value hotel with all the amenities on the popular Grand Anse beach; free daily shuttle to Côte d'Or beach;

superfriendly staff and management. **Cons:** located on the western side of Praslin, Grand Anse is subject to seaweed accumulation May–October; Wi-Fi in public areas only. [$] *Rooms from: US$370* ✉ *Grand Anse* ☎ *428–3838* 🌐 *www.indianoceanlodge.com* 🛏 *32 rooms* 🍴 *Multiple meal plans.*

$$$$ RESORT Fodor's Choice ★ 🏨 **Raffles Praslin Seychelles.** Praslin's newest luxury resort, the Raffles is composed of 86 überluxurious sea- and mountain-view villas dotting the hillside over Anse Takamaka bay. **Pros:** beautifully designed and appointed rooms; excellent spa. **Cons:** the hillside layout means only the uppermost villas feel entirely private when on balconies; steep hillsides discourage walking; depending on tide and time of year, the beach can be very small. **TIP→ For the best rate, book through an operator or check online prices.** [$] *Rooms from: US$2040* ✉ *Anse Takamaka* ☎ *429–6000* 🌐 *www.raffles.com* 🛏 *86 villas* 🍴 *Multiple meal plans.*

SHOPPING

Praslin's shops mostly offer artisanal crafts and curios and are fairly limited. The unique double-nut Coco de Mer seeds are on sale in the Vallée de Mai Park, but they're part of a strictly controlled quota—if you buy one, make sure that it has a label that authenticates its origins. Most shops cluster around the Bay St. Anne jetty and the popular Côte d'Or beach.

Black Pearl Praslin Ocean Farm. Located just outside the airport, you'll find black pearls from the Seychelles' black-lip oyster, a specialty of the islands, at the source. ✉ *Amitié* ☎ *423–3150* 🌐 *www.blackpearlseychelles.com* 🎫 *Rs50* 🕒 *Weekdays 9–5.*

La Vallée de Mai Boutique. The souvenir shop at the Vallée de Mai Park sells certified Cocos de Mer (about Rs3,000), books about Seychelles natural history, and other souvenirs. ✉ *Vallée de Mai* ☎ *432–1735* 🕒 *Daily 8–4:30.*

SPORTS AND THE OUTDOORS

BOAT EXCURSIONS

Half- or full-day snorkeling, sailing, and deep-sea fishing excursions are all possibilities. Most tours leave from Bay St. Anne, Côte d'Or, or Grand Anse.

RECOMMENDED TOUR OPERATORS

Creole Charters. Offering fishing and private boat excursions on a 28-foot catamaran, this company's trips typically include visits to Cousin, Aride, and Curieuse islands, complete with snorkeling and a beach BBQ. Deep-sea fishing on a half- or full-day basis is also offered. ✉ *New Emerald Cove, Anse La Farine* ☎ *271–2977* ✉ *abseychelles@gmail.com* 🌐 *www.creolecharters.com.*

DIVING AND SNORKELING

Qualified divers can book tanks and a guide to explore the rich underwater environment of coral reefs and abundant sea life at **Côte d'Or** (Anse Volbert). But you don't need to be a certified diver to enjoy the marine life of Seychelles. The shallow reefs and languid lagoons, particularly at **Anse Lazio** and **Anse Possession,** offer perfect conditions for snorkeling. You can while hours away watching the antics of schools of elegant angelfish or bold sergeant majors with their distinctive stripes. Even better, the snorkeling around the small islands of **Curieuse, Île Cocos, St. Pierre, Sisters,** and **Marianne,** is excellent. Numerous boat excursions offer snorkeling day trips, usually visiting two to three islands.

RECOMMENDED DIVE OPERATORS

Octopus Diver. A five-star, PADI-certified dive resort, the staff organize scuba and snorkeling excursions around Praslin and the surrounding small islands. ⊠ *Berjaya Praslin Hotel, Côte d'Or* ☎ *423–2602* ⊕ *www. octopusdiver.com.*

Whitetip Divers. Based at the Paradise Sun Hotel on Côte d'Or, the professionals at Whitetip take guests on dives of up to 20 meters (65 feet) only. Many of the sites are around underwater granite formations. They also organize snorkeling trips by boat. ⊠ *Paradise Sun Hotel, Côte d'Or* ☎ *423–2282, 251–4282* ⊕ *www.whitetipdivers.com.*

GOLF

Lemuria Resort Golf Course. Praslin is home to the only 18-hole golf course in the Seychelles. Surrounded by lush forested hills, this is probably one of the world's most beautiful greens. Tee times must be prebooked through the resort, which also rents all necessary equipment and golf carts. ⊠ *Anse Kerlan* ☎ *428–1230* ⊕ *www.lemuriaresort. constancehotels.com.*

HIKING

With countless secluded bays and forested nooks and crannies, Praslin is ideal for exploration on foot. The island is covered in a network of paths, and due to its small size, any path will lead to the coast within an hour, so there's very little chance of getting lost.

Vallée de Mai. The hauntingly beautiful primeval forest of the Vallée de Mai is home to some 6,000 Coco de Mer palm trees and was once believed to be the original Garden of Eden. The well-maintained trails here allow hikers the flexibility of doubling back before completing an entire circuit, but for thorough exploration of the park, it's best to allow three to four hours. The Vallée boasts all six of Seychelles' endemic palm species and many other indigenous trees, and it is the last habitat of the endangered black parrot (the only parrot endemic to Seychelles). A path branching off from the main circular track leads up to a sheltered viewpoint that looks out across the valley. The trails are very well maintained, and sandals will suffice.

Glacis Noire Trail. The Glacis Noire Trail leads to a fire tower built on a hilltop overlooking Praslin's east coast, allowing a fine view of La Digue and the surrounding smaller islands. This is a moderately difficult trail due to its ascent, so even though it measures just 0.8 miles, two hours should be allotted for the hike.

LA DIGUE

La Digue is the fourth-largest inhabited island of the Seychelles (though only 5 km [3 miles] long and 3 km [2 miles] wide) and the real deal when it comes to a laid-back tropical paradise. Only 6.4 km (4 miles) from Praslin (about a 20-minute ferry ride) and 43 km (27 miles) from Mahé, little La Digue nonetheless feels a world away.

With no natural harbor, La Digue is protected by a coral reef, which, together with masses of colossal pink granite boulders, encircle and protect the island. Streets here hum the quiet rhythm of local life: a melody of ox-carts and bicycles, paths shaded by flowers and lush vegetation, and old colonial-style houses that speak of times past. Named in 1768 after a ship in the fleet of French explorer Marc-Joseph Marion du Fresne, La Digue's economic mainstays used to be vanilla and coconut oil. The island's lovely beaches, lush interior, and colonial charm have made tourism its number-one industry today. The island's population of about 2,000 mostly reside in the west coast villages of La Réunion and La Passe.

GETTING HERE AND AROUND
The island's jetty and the majority of hotels are in La Passe. Large boats (like cruise ships) usually anchor in Praslin's Bay St. Anne, then use smaller craft to tender passengers to the jetty in La Passe. The trip between the islands takes about 20 minutes. There's no airport on La Digue; the only air travel is by helicopter. The best way to get around the island is on foot or bicycle, as any part of the island can be reached in less than an hour. Bicycle rentals are about Rs150–Rs200 per day, with discounts sometimes available for longer rentals. A handful of taxis and even some ox-carts are available in La Passe. The La Digue Public Transport shuttle is a van that covers a set route between the La Passe jetty and Belle Vue, to correspond with the arrival and departure of the ferry (Rs8 one-way).

KEY
❶ *Exploring sites*
① *Restaurants, Hotels*

INDIAN
OCEAN

La Digue

SAFETY AND PRECAUTIONS

La Digue's east coast is wild, with remote and beautiful pink-granite sand beaches, but dangerous currents prevail, and care must be taken anytime you go into the water.

TIMING

Many tour operators offer day trips to La Digue from Praslin. But on an island ruled by a pace that encourages one to watch the orchids grow, you really shouldn't rush your visit, and a minimum of two nights is recommended.

ESSENTIALS

Bike Rentals J&P Bicycle ✉ *La Passe* ☎ 259–1027, 253–6761. **Michelin Bicycle Rental** ✉ *Pension Residence, La Passe* ☎ 423–4043.

Emergency Contacts La Digue Police ✉ *La Passe* ☎ 423–4251.

Hospitals La Digue Logan Hospital ✉ *La Passe* ☎ 423–4255.

Taxis Elias Radegonde taxi ✉ *La Passe* ☎ 251–3338. **Jamie Ernesta taxi** ✉ *La Passe* ☎ 251–1015. **La Digue Public Transport Shuttle** ✉ *La Passe* ☎ 256–5053.

Visitor and Tour Information Mason's Travel ✉ *La Passe* ☎ 423–4227. **STB** ✉ *La Passe* ☎ 423–4393.

EXPLORING LA DIGUE

11

⇨ *See Praslin for more information on excursions to neighboring islands.*

L'Union Estate. Visit a traditional copra mill (once used to produce coconut oil from the dried flesh of the nut) at this grand plantation house. Stroll around the outside of the majestic old buildings framed by giant granite boulders, or go horseback riding. The grounds also house a small shipyard where displays (intermittently) show how craftsmen used to build pirogues and fishing boats. The estate is also home to the cemetery of the original settlers of La Digue and provides access to one of the most pristine beaches in Seychelles—the legendary Source d'Argent—among the most photographed beaches on earth. ☎ 423–4240 ⌧ *Rs100 (cash only)* ⊘ *Daily 7–5.*

Plantation House. This architectural gem is among the plantation houses remaining in Seychelles. Said to be one of the oldest, it is the focal point of L'Union Estate. Unfortunately at the time of writing, admission into the house was prohibited. ⊠ *L'Union* ☎ 423–4240 ⌧ *Rs100* ⊘ *Daily 7:30–5.*

Veuve Nature Reserve. La Digue is the last refuge of the rare black paradise flycatcher, of which there are only about 100 still in existence. Once on the brink of extinction, these rare birds, which the locals call the "*veuve,*" or widow, are now protected in this reserve, which is also home to two extremely rare species of terrapin. The Veuve Information Centre is also La Digue's only environment office, managing the Reserve, and providing the majority of information on the island's unique flora and fauna. Staff there can take visitors on short, guided tours upon request, but arrangements must be made in advance. ⊠ *Anse Réunion* ☎ 278–3114 ⌧ *Free* ⊘ *Weekdays 8–4.*

BEACHES

Anse Source d'Argent, La Digue's most famous beach, isn't necessarily its best. All of the island's beaches are picturesque. Some will even be empty, but those will require a hike. However, if it's privacy you're after, then you'll be in heaven.

Anse Bonnet Carré. If you're near Anse Source d'Argent but want more privacy, the neighboring beach of Anse Bonnet Carré has the same white sand and shallow warm waters, but fewer rocks and people. It requires a short walk, and thus is often deserted, but it's great if you want a dip rather than a proper swim. **Amenities:** none. **Best for:** swimming; walking; solitude.

Anse Gaulettes. A bit longer than Anse Patates, which makes it perfect for walking, this beach on the island's northern end has soft, white sand and calm seas. However, dangerous currents make it unsuitable for swimming or snorkeling. **Amenities:** none. **Best for:** walking.

Anse La Réunion. Closer to La Passe, this long, beautiful beach has fine views of neighboring Praslin Island. La Digue's most built-up beach in terms of surrounding hotels and restaurants, it's also great for

La Digue's Grand Anse is a beautiful beach, but you have to watch out for the dangerous undertow.

snorkeling and swimming. **Amenities:** food and drink; toilet. **Best for:** snorkeling; swimming; walking.

Anse Patates. Next to the longer Anse Gaulettes, this smaller beach on the island's northernmost end has soft, white sand and calm seas, making it well-suited for swimming and snorkeling. **Amenities:** none. **Best for:** snorkeling; swimming.

Anse Pierrot. If you're near Anse Source d'Argent but want more privacy, the neighboring beach of Anse Pierrot has the same white sand and shallow warm waters, but fewer rocks and people. It requires a short walk, and thus is often deserted. It's great if you want some privacy and a dip rather than a proper swim. **Amenities:** none. **Best for:** solitude; swimming; walking. ⊠ *Anse Pierrot.*

Anse Songe. If you're feeling adventurous, hire a guide (you can ask at the Loutier Coco restaurant, or organize one in advance) to take you to the beautiful, wild beaches at the island's southern tip. About a 20- to 40-minute walk from Grand Anse, Anse Songe is lovely and surrounded by trees so you can enjoy some shade. Another 20 to 40 minutes along from Anse Songe, **Grand Marron's** empty beach is a stunning and worthy reward for the adventurous. ■ TIP→ The hike from Anse Songe to Grand Marron involves climbing over some seriously rocky outcrops and is only for the fit and well-prepared (good water shoes are advised).

FAMILY **Anse Source d'Argent.** La Digue is home to some of the world's best beaches, including one of the most photographed, Anse Source d'Argent (the film *Cast Away* was filmed here). With its soft, white sand, clear turquoise water, and huge granite boulders, it's easy to see why this would be the case. However, the crowds it attracts could outweigh the beach's stunning natural attributes. In either case, it's worth visiting and deciding for yourself. The beach is accessible only through L'Union Estate, for which you must pay the normal entry fee of Rs100. **Amenities:** food and drink; toilet. **Best for:** snorkeling; swimming; walking.

Grand Anse. On La Digue's eastern side, this picturesque beach is known for its huge waves. The sea may look inviting, but there is an extremely strong undertow, so beware. Strong surfers may find a ride, but picnics and sunbathing are the recommended activities here. Grand Anse is home to the Loutier Coco restaurant. **Petite Anse**, just across the rocks from Grand Anse, is more private and great for picnics, but shares the same rough conditions as its big sister. **Amenities:** food and drink; toilet (at restaurant). **Best for:** solitude; sunrise; surfing; walking.

WHERE TO EAT

In the spirit of this super-chilled-out island, most of La Digue's restaurants are casual. There are a few great beachside joints, as well as a couple notable hotel restaurants.

$$$ INTERNATIONAL 🍴 **Le Combava.** Located on a covered white-washed deck at the harbor's edge, casually sophisticated Le Combava is a beautifully designed oasis offering a classically international lunch and dinner menu. Lunch items include delicious and generous portions of salads, burgers, pizzas, and mains from spaghetti bolognaise to seared swordfish. In the evening the choices go more upmarket, with starters like a lobster medallion served with risotto and vanilla emulsion or foie gras mousse with figs, and mains such as grilled beef filet or duck confit. The beach-chic seaside setting makes it a romantic evening treat. [$] *Average main: US$33* ✉ *Anse Severe* ☎ *4299–999* 🌐 *www.orangeraie.sc/content/le-combava-restaurant* ✍ *Reservations essential* 🕒 *No dinner Wed.*

$$$ ITALIAN 🍴 **Le Repair.** A wonderful new addition to La Digue's dining options, this friendly Italian restaurant on Anse Reunion serves excellent food in a tranquil garden setting. Wood-fired pizzas will hit the spot, as do the delicious pastas and risottos. Fish lovers are in for a treat, as the chef makes a point of using local fish and octopus, and the fish of the day with lime and Cointreau or panfried with white wine and capers are recommended. Dinner guests should come early and enjoy a sunset looking out to neighboring Praslin Island. [$] *Average main: US$28* ✉ *Anse Réunion* ☎ *423–4332, 253–0594* 🌐 *www.lerepaireseychelles.com* ✍ *Reservations essential* 🕒 *No lunch Tues.*

$$ CREOLE 🍴 **Loutier Coco.** The only restaurant on the east side of the island, casual and friendly Loutier Coco serves an extremely tasty lunch buffet of the usual Creole favorites. Expect items like a beautifully spiced octopus curry in coconut milk, delicious grilled fish, roast pork, veggie curries, several piquant salads of mango or papaya, and dessert. Located just off Grande Anse beach, the sand floors, coconut-frond and hibiscus-flower décor, and brightly painted rustic murals invite dining in one's swimsuit. ■ **TIP→ Try to arrive early, as items like the grilled fish tend to dry out a bit towards the end.** If you call a day ahead, you can organize a lobster feast. [$] *Average main: US$23* ✉ *Grande Anse* ☎ *251–4762, 256–5436* 💳 *No credit cards.*

$$ CREOLE 🍴 **Veuve Restaurant.** This restaurant at La Digue Island Lodge enjoys a location on the edge of beautiful Anse Réunion. Tables are set up by the white sand beach and are surrounded by views of a lush garden filled with massive pandanus palms, frangipani, and Indian almond trees. Dinners are buffet style with a focus on the international, which means that on any given night there will be some degree of influence from Asian, Middle Eastern, European, and of course, Creole cuisine. Great grilled fish, fresh salads, and reasonable Asian fare can be expected (pastas are not a highlight), though check in advance if there is a theme on the night you intend to go (Saturday is typically all Creole). Non-hotel guests are welcome, but large groups must reserve in advance. When the weather is fine, the beachfront tables, lit by gleaming oil lamps, are extremely romantic and peaceful. [$] *Average main: US$27* ✉ *Anse Réunion* ☎ *429–2525* 🌐 *www.ladigue.sc* ✍ *Reservations essential.*

WHERE TO STAY

La Digue's accommodations are largely comprised of smaller hotels, guesthouses, and an increasing number of self-catering options. Check out the STB's website for updated listings.

$ RENTAL 🏨 **Cabane des Anges.** Five minutes from Anse Réunion beach, this small guesthouse includes self-catering apartments and rooms alike. **Pros:** 15-minute walk from La Passe jetty and shops; good value; close to good restaurants and take-aways. **Cons:** no real views; not on the beach; kitchen gear is very basic. [$] *Rooms from: US$189* ✉ *Anse Réunion* ☎ *423–4112* 📧 *cabanedesange@seychelles.net* 🛏 *6 apartments, 3 rooms* 🍽 *No meals.*

$$ HOTEL 🏨 **Chateau St. Cloud.** Part of a former vanilla plantation in La Digue's lush interior at the foot of the island's only mountain, this lovely old chateau is surrounded by a tranquil garden filled with orchids and exotic flowers. **Pros:** tranquil garden setting; spacious rooms. **Cons:** not on the beach. [$] *Rooms from: US$270* ✉ *Anse Réunion* ☎ *429–5400* 🌐 *www.chateaustcloud.sc* 🛏 *29 rooms* 🍽 *Multiple meal plans.*

$$ HOTEL 🏨 **La Digue Island Lodge.** The 44 A-frame villas of La Digue's oldest hotel that dot Anse Réunion beach are fully equipped with the amenities expected of a large hotel. **Pros:** convenient and well-equipped rooms; pleasant swimming beach with great sunset views; house options are great for bigger groups or families. **Cons:** rooms are on the small side; Wi-Fi in rooms is not free. [$] *Rooms from: US$371* ✉ *Anse Réunion* ☎ *429–2525* 🌐 *www.ladigue.sc* 🛏 *44 chalets, 17 rooms* 🍽 *Multiple meal plans.*

$$$ HOTEL 🏨 **Le Domaine L'Orangerie.** The place to stay for those who swoon over elegant zen style, the hotel's 55 villas are set in an old orange-tree grove (hence the name) and along its granite hills among enormous granite boulders. **Pros:** stunning style and elegance; free bicycles and snorkeling equipment; gorgeous restaurants and pool area. **Cons:** some rooms are a bit dark; free Wi-Fi in public areas and garden villas only. [$] *Rooms from: US$486* ✉ *Anse Severe* ☎ *423–4444* 🌐 *www.orangerie.sc* 🛏 *55 villas* 🍽 *Multiple meal plans.*

SPORTS AND THE OUTDOORS

11

BOAT EXCURSIONS

⇨ *See Praslin, above, for more info on excursions to neighboring islands.*

Boat trips around La Digue offer opportunities for bird-watching and snorkeling, as well as island-hopping and Creole barbecues. Deep-sea fishing can also be arranged. Half- and full-day boat trips can be booked in Anse Réunion and La Passe.

RECOMMENDED TOUR OPERATORS

Belle Petra. This catamaran operates from La Digue with half- and full-day trips to the neighboring islands of St. Pierre, Cousin, and Aride, among others. Activities include snorkeling and bird-watching. ⊠ *La Passe* ☎ *423–4302, 271–6220* ✐ *petra@seychelles.sc.*

Nevis Ernesta Zico 1 Boat Excursions. This 9-meter catamaran can take up to eight people on half- or full-day big-game or bottom-fishing excursions. ⊠ *Anse Réunion* ☎ *251–5557* ⊕ *www.excursionsladigue.com.*

DIVING AND SNORKELING

La Digue and its neighboring islands are excellent dive destinations. Certified PADI instructors at Anse Réunion are available to introduce divers to the wonderful marine environment that La Digue has to offer: enjoy breathtaking granitic slopes; experience the thrill of diving among a school of reef sharks; and discover the Seychelles' extraordinary underwater life. Not so keen on bottled air? Snorkeling at Anse Réunion, Anse Patates, and Anse Source d'Argent is a simpler way to experience the marvels of the island's underwater world.

RECOMMENDED DIVE OPERATORS

Azzura Pro-Dive Center. The oldest dive center on La Digue, Azzura is associated with the La Digue Island Lodge, and can organize dive trips and open water to divemaster certification, as well as other excursions like snorkeling and island visits. Popular trips include Marianne for sharks, Anse Marron for tuna and sting rays, and the huge underwater mountain at the north Sister Island. ⊠ *La Digue Island Lodge, Anse Réunion* ☎ *429–2525* ⊕ *www.ladigue.sc* ☉ *Daily 8:30–5.*

HIKING

The best way to explore tiny La Digue when not on a bicycle is on foot. Numerous trails wend their way through this island paradise, allowing visitors to absorb the atmosphere like locals. From La Passe, take the main track in a southerly direction past the hotels and church to L'Union Estate. Though you must pay the entrance fee, if you stay on the track you'll be rewarded with a beautiful walk through massive granite boulders, winding in and out of the forest and along white sand coves until the trail ends at **Anse Source à Jean,** a beautiful place to spend the day. If you're feeling adventurous, hire a guide (ask at your hotel or the STB office) to take you around the island's southern end to **Anse Marron** and then up to **Grand Anse**—a gorgeous though at times quite challenging walk. Amphibious shoes with good soles are recommended, as are a hat and plenty of sunscreen.

Eagle's Nest Mountain (Nid d'Aigle) is La Digue's tallest peak at more than 305 meters (1,000 feet) above sea level. It's a steep but rewarding climb of about an hour to the top. On the way up Belle Vue, look out for the rare endemic paradise flycatchers and an enormous fruit-bat colony. From Anse Réunion take the first left toward the island's interior. Pass an old house surrounded by high walls ("the chateau"), then turn left down a small pathway past a small group of houses. This track will head up the mountain toward the peak.

RECOMMENDED GUIDES

Robert Agnes. A local licensed guide who can take clients on all levels of hikes around La Digue or Praslin. ⊠ *La Passe* ☎ *252–5357* ⊕ *www. seychelles-tourguide.com.*

PRIVATE ISLAND RESORTS

Largely uninhabited, a handful of private islands—most with nothing on them other than a single resort—will blow your mind (and possibly your budget).

$$$$
RESORT
Cousine Island. With only four villas, this resort is a birder's and naturalist's paradise. **Pros:** great food; with only four villas on this private island, total privacy and pampering are the name of the game. **Cons:** the gym is in need of a makeover; a prefab look to some of the structures. $ *Rooms from: US$2328* ⊠ *Cousine Island* ☎ *432–1107, 271–3418* ⊕ *www.cousineisland.com* ⇨ *4 villas* ¶⊙¶ *All meals.*

$$$$
RESORT
FAMILY
Fodor's Choice
★
Denis Private Island Resort. A spectacularly elegant yet unpretentious setting for 30 deluxe cottages on the beach (staggered for privacy, some sit partially behind the true beachfront units) Denis Resort features private sea-facing salas with daybeds, gorgeous outdoor bathrooms, iPod docks, king-size beds, and a private beachfront. **Pros:** nature walks with conservationists and great bird-watching; one of the more reasonably priced luxury private islands; 80% of the food served is grown or raised on the island. **Cons:** deluxe beach cottages are set further back for privacy and lack direct sea views. $ *Rooms from: US$1603* ⊠ *Denis Island* ☎ *428–8963, 429–5999* ⊕ *www.denisisland.com* ⇨ *30 cottages* ¶⊙¶ *All meals.*

$$$$
ALL-INCLUSIVE
FAMILY
Desroches Island. The only resort on the Amirantes coral island group (and situated within an entire atoll), Desroches will fulfill all your coconut-fringed, white-sand-beach-paradise fantasies. **Pros:** absolute heaven for active water-sports lovers and fishermen, with an incredible activities center and stunning diving and fishing sites; four-bedroom villas are an opulent yet affordable option for a large group or family; all rooms are 25 meters (82 feet) from the beach. **Cons:** villas are spaced close enough that you wouldn't want to sunbathe nude; the vegetation and wildlife are yet to be rehabilitated, so naturalists won't find an abundance of endemics or seabirds. $ *Rooms from: US$1701* ⊠ *Desroches Island* ☎ *422–9400 for reservations, 27–82/496–4570 in South Africa, 422–9003 on Desroches Island* ⊕ *www.desroches-island.com* ⇨ *49 villas* ¶⊙¶ *All-inclusive.*

$$$$
ALL-INCLUSIVE
Fodor'sChoice
★

🖼 **North Island Resort.** Brought to the world's attention as the honeymoon destination of the likes of Prince William and Kate, this private island takes the wow effect to new levels. **Pros:** villas that take space, privacy, and comfort to a new level of barefoot luxury (your villa may well have once hosted Hollywood celebrities and heads of state); all activities are included except full-day deep-sea-fishing charters and spa treatments. **Cons:** you may have to mortgage your house to holiday here; the dining experience is not up to snuff given the cost. $ *Rooms from: US$7465* ✉ *North Island* ☎ *429–3100, 27–11/807–1800 in South Africa* ⊕ *www.north-island.com* ⇝ *11 villas* |◯| *All-inclusive.*

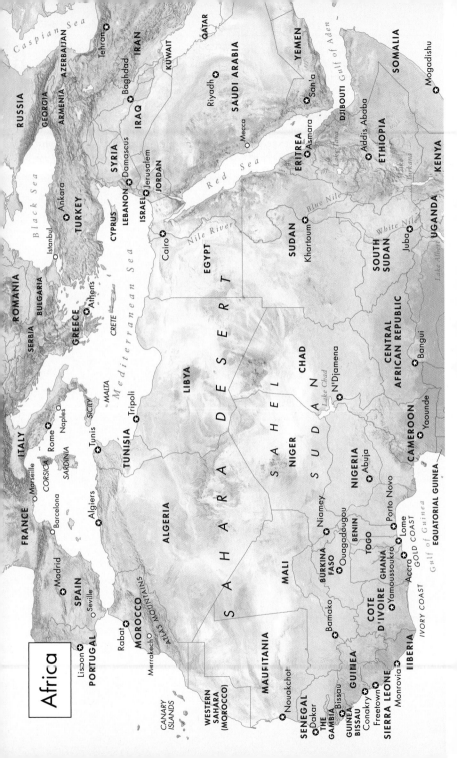

Africa

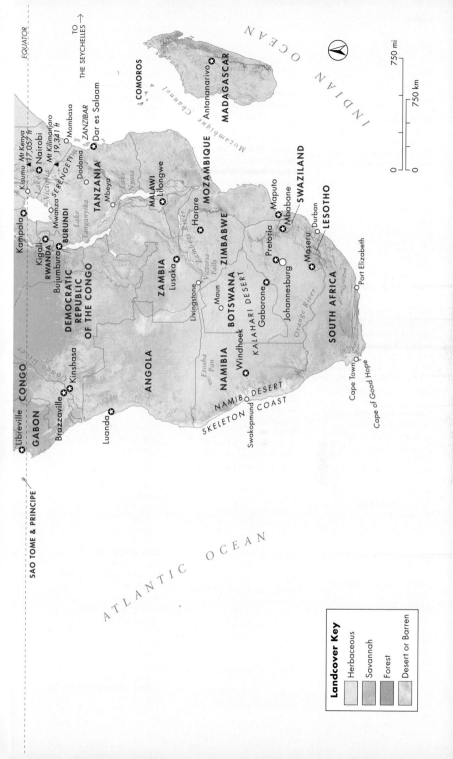

INDEX

PHOTO CREDITS

/ Alamy. 348 (top right), Reimar / Alamy. 349 (top left), Images of Africa Photobank / Alamy. 349 (bottom left), blickwinkel / Alamy. 349 (center right), Miguel Cuenca / Alamy. 349 (bottom right), Timothy Large/iStockphoto. 349 (top right), Perry Correll/Shutterstock. 350 (top left), Bernard O'Kane / Alamy. 350 (bottom left), Eric Miller / Picturedesk International/Newscom. 350 (right), ALEXANDER JOE/ AFP/Getty Images/Newscom. 351 (top), SIPHIWESIBEKO / Reuters. 351 (bottom), Adrian de Kock/ Pierre Tostee/ZUMA Press/Newscom. 356, Bruno Perousse/age fotostock. 365, larrya, Fodors.com member. 371, Stacy Freeman, Fodors.com member. 382, Nicholas Pitt / Alamy. 386, jspiegel, Fodors. com member. Chapter 7: Rwanda and Uganda: 390-391, Robert Haasmann/imageBROKER/age fotostock. 392, Shamwari Group. 393 (top), Lukas Maverick Greyson / Shutterstock. 393 (bottom), Vlad Karavaev / Shutterstock. 394, Przemyslaw Skibinski / Shutterstock. 398, Guenter Guni/iStockphoto. 400 and 403, Courtesy of Rwanda Development Board. 410, Pal Teravagimov /Shutterstock. 415, FLPA / Alamy. 419, Wildnerdpix / Shutterstock. Chapter 8: Botswana: 436-37, GlenRidgeDoug, Fodors.com member. 438, kolee5, Fodors.com member. 439, Beth Vorro, Fodors.com member. 440, scott bredbenner, Fodors.com member. 445, Des Curley / Alamy. 447, panecott, Fodors.com member. 451, hslogan, Fodors.com member. 452 (all), Wilderness Safaris. 459, Beth Vorro, Fodors.com member. 462, Kim Freedman, Fodors.com member. 463 (top and bottom right), Wilderness Safaris. 463 (bottom left), Julian Asher. 465, GlenRidgeDoug, Fodors.com member. 469, GlenRidgeDoug, Fodors.com member. 470 (all), Wilderness Safaris. 472, CJ Thurman, Fodors.com member. 474 (all), Kwando Safaris. 481, DAleffi, Fodors.com member. 483 (top), Sylvain Grandadam/age fotostock. 483 (bottom), Meredith Lamb/Shutterstock. 484 (left), Bill Bachmann /Alamy. 484 (bottom right), Tom Grundy/Shutterstock. 484 (top right), Meredith Lamb/Shutterstock. 485 (top left), J Marshall - Tribaleye Images / Alamy. 485 (bottom left), Rick Matthews/age fotostock. 485 (top right), Sylvain Grandadam/age fotostock. 485 (bottom right), Ulrich Doering /Alamy. 486, Neil Moultrie/South African Tourism. Chapter 9: Namibia: 492-93, Werner Bollmann/age fotostock. 494, Todd Cullen, Fodors.com member. 495, Heather Benfield, Fodors.com member. 496, Ashley Cullen, Fodors.com member. 501, jeep61, Fodors. com member. 504 and 509 (top and bottom left), Wilderness Safaris. 509 (bottom right), CCAfrica. 513, Gianluca Basso/age fotostock. 514 (top), Namibia Tourism Board. 514 (2nd from top), Dave Humphreys/Namibia Tourism Board. 514 (3rd from top), Dave Humphreys/Namibia Tourism Board. 514 (bottom), Namibia Tourism Board. 514-15, Images of Africa Photobank / Alamy. 516, Roine Magnusson/age fotostock. 517 (top), Charles Sturge / Alamy. 517 (bottom), Richard Wareham Fotografie / Alamy. 518, Karsten Wrobel / Alamy. 522 (top and bottom right), Wilderness Safaris. 522 (bottom left), Vingerklip Lodge. 525, Ashley Cullen, Fodors.com member. 533, Morales/age fotostock. 534 (top), Wilderness Safaris. 534 (bottom left and right), Namibia Wildlife Resorts. 543, Britton Upham, Fodors. com member. 554, World Travel / Alamy. Chapter 10: Victoria Falls: 564-565, David Wall / Alamy. 566 (bottom), Siankaba. 566 (top), globalvhc, Fodors.com member. 567, Lorrin, Fodors.com member. 568, TXJL, Fodors.com member. 570, James Mantock, Fodors.com member. 585, Patrick Ward / Alamy. 586-87, Exactostock/SuperStock. 590, Pam Record, Fodors.com member. 592, Pam Record, Fodors. com member. Chapter 11: The Seychelles: 602-03, Manfred Mehlig / age fotostock. 604 (top), victoria white2010/Flickr. 604 (bottom), Seycam, Wikimedia Commons. 605, The Leading Hotels of the World. 606, Fabio Calamosca/Flickr. 612, evhead/Flickr. 622 (top), The Leading Hotels of the World. 622 (bottom), Quentin Berryman/Four Seasons Resort Seychelles. 626, Sergey Khachatryan/Shutterstock. 631, fabio braibanti / age fotostock. 635, Tatiana Popova/Shutterstock. 638, Tobias/Wikimedia Commons. Back cover (from left to right): Pal Teravagimov / Shutterstock; Anna Omelchenko/Shutterstock; Worakit Sirijinda/Shutterstock. Spine: EcoPrint/Shutterstock.

About Our Writers: All photos are courtesy of the writers except for the following: Lauren Everitt, courtesy of Susan Everitt.

Writing development, environment, and humanitarian features in Africa since 2005, and based in Cape Town since 2006, American journalist and editor Lee Middleton has written for *Time Magazine, the Mail & Guardian, Africa Geographic Magazine,* and *Men's Health,* among others. Having also lived in Thailand, India, and Mexico as a wildlife researcher, Himalayan adventurer, and human rights worker, her penchant for exploration now manifests in food and travel writing from across the continent, with a focus on southern and eastern Africa and the Indian Ocean.

Anne-Marie Weeden first visited the African continent when she drove a pink Citroen van 4,000 miles from London to The Gambia. In 2008 she moved to Uganda, where she has lived ever since. She has written about wildlife tourism for *Africa Geographic* and African Wildlife Foundation among others, having worked across nearly every sector in the safari business—from running a backpackers' camp to designing once-in-a-lifetime helicopter tours for a luxury safari outfitter.

Cine Baranowski spent an idyllic childhood in a small town in Zimbabwe before moving to South Africa. Today she works in London as a travel writer and editor. Her favorite travels include backpacking in Laos and beach escapes in the Caribbean and Sri Lanka, but the most magical have been on safari in Africa.

Colleen Blaine is a travel writer based along South Africa's famous Garden Route. Her years living in and exploring all corners of Botswana, Zimbabwe, Mauritius, and South Africa have helped her share her knowledge and passion for southern Africa through writing. A regular contributor to a variety of local and international publications and blogs, she loves to travel like a local and is inspired by stories about people, conservation, and nature. She also writes at O'Live Travel focusing on exploring South Africa's olive and wine routes.

Christopher Clark is a freelance dreamer, writer, and wanderer based in Cape Town. Afflicted by itchy feet from a young age, he has traveled to and written from more than 50 countries across Africa and beyond. His work has been published by a number of regional and international publications including *Africa Geographic, News24, The Big Issue, Nkwazi Magazine, Contributoria,* and more. He has twice been named as one of South Africa's best writers by The Big Issue.

Lauren Everitt is a professional word wrangler with an affinity for East Africa. She has worked as a writer and editor in Rwanda, Kenya, and South Africa. Through travel, she's sipped lip-puckering banana beer in Rwanda, run alongside Kenyan marathoners (for a solid half second) in Nairobi, and witnessed a bull elephant charge in Zimbabwe. Her work has appeared in the *BBC, The Sunday Times Travel Magazine, allAfrica.com, and Thrillist Travel.*

Freelance travel journalists Narina Exelby and Mark Eveleigh have collectively written for more than 100 publications on 5 continents. They've travelled to almost every part of Kenya and stayed in everything from luxury lodges to a battered 1970's Land Cruiser. Living out of their kitbags, they're permanently on assignment . . . somewhere. Follow their journey at *kitbaggers.com.*

Brought up in the UK, James Gifford was lucky enough to be introduced to the wilds of Africa at an early age. After travelling to all seven continents, he finally settled in Botswana in 2006 where he now works as a freelance photographer and writer. Although assignments often drag him kicking and screaming to upmarket lodges, he is happiest camping solo in the bush, sleeping on top of his vehicle with just a mosquito net separating him from the ubiquitous stars.

Linda Markovina is a freelance photojournalist and travel writer based in South Africa. She considers herself to be the better-looking half of Moving Sushi Expeditions and is a blogger on its behalf for various online platforms. Having lived and travelled extensively through East and West Africa for the past 10 years, her main loves are writing about travel, the natural world around us, and how we as people interact with it, as long as it's not anything to do with snakes. Snakes give her the willies.